Intellectual Property and Development

Rami M. Olwan

Intellectual Property and Development

Theory and Practice

Springer

Rami M. Olwan
Faculty of Law
Queensland University of Technology (QUT)
Brisbane
Queensland
Australia

ISBN 978-3-642-27906-5 ISBN 978-3-642-27907-2 (eBook)
DOI 10.1007/978-3-642-27907-2
Springer Heidelberg New York Dordrecht London

Library of Congress Control Number: 2013930024

Printed on acid-free paper

Springer is part of Springer Science+Business Media (www.springer.com)

To my father and mother who taught me to love knowledge and not to be satisfied with what I have.

Foreword

When Dr Rami Olwan invited me to write a foreword for this book, I accepted his kind invitation without hesitation for a variety of reasons. The subject of the book, the relationship between intellectual property and development, is particularly dear to me and has been at the center of the international negotiations and debates in which I have had the privilege of being involved during the past decade. Throughout this time period, I never ceased to be surprised about the limited scholarship on the subject in many developing countries, and most particularly in the Arab world. Apart from a few noticeable exceptions, this scholarship tended to adopt a narrow technical view that did not apprehend intellectual property in the context of broader public policy and development objectives. In addition, it was often inclined to simply echo the prevailing affirmations about intellectual property and development that many developing countries were precisely contesting, at the international level, through initiatives, such as the *Development Agenda*, which they launched at the World Intellectual Property Organization (WIPO) in 2004.

Fortunately, the situation has been changing in recent years. A new generation of young scholars from developing countries is making valuable contributions to the scholarship on intellectual property and development, bringing a diversity of perspectives, as well as valuable empirical evidence and insightful case studies. This book is a much welcome contribution to this growing trend.

In this ambitious work, the author does not shy away from embracing the whole spectrum of the relationship between intellectual property and development, retracing its history, delineating the different views that have shaped the debate surrounding it, and presenting findings from recent economic research and empirical evidence that help to better understand its multiple facets and complexity. He then uses Jordan, his country, as a case study for a 'practical' approach to this relationship. In this context, he analyses Jordan's copyright law and makes several concrete suggestions of changes to make it more 'development oriented' and take full advantage of the possibilities offered by the digital environment. In this regard, he also elaborates on the contributions by the free and open source software, open access initiatives, and voluntary licensing schemes to access to knowledge. Finally, Dr Olwan proposes a 'policy road map' for intellectual property and development, where he puts forward a number of 'policies' that can help ensure that intellectual property regimes are supportive of social and economic development objectives. Some of the suggested policies are already being implemented by a growing number of developing countries such as those relating to the revision of intellectual property laws and the need to give greater consideration to limitations and exceptions. However, there are also some novel recommendations that merit closer consideration.

In this regard, one practical recommendation that I found of particular interest concerns the elaboration of an international course on intellectual property and development by the WIPO Academy. In effect, discussions about intellectual property and development tend to be confined to academic circles or to diplomatic deliberations in Geneva and, in both cases, are not easily accessible to a broader audience of researchers, students, and professionals, particularly from developing countries. A course on intellectual property and development could contribute towards a better understanding by a larger public of the nuances and diversity of views permeating this complex relationship. It would also represent a concrete contribution towards achieving the intended objective of the WIPO Development Agenda recommendations, adopted in 2007, of mainstreaming the 'development dimension' into all of the WIPO's activities.

Apart from the skillful manner in which the author has pulled together a vast array of material and presented it in a clear and articulate manner, he has also shown an acute awareness about the limitations of a purely 'legalistic' approach to many of the challenges that lie at the interface of the intellectual property and development nexus. In effect, for much too long, the attention of policymakers and scholars in developing countries was devoted to intellectual property legislations, and the extent to which such legislations were in conformity with international standards, rather than on the way and extent intellectual property regimes took into consideration specific socio-economic circumstances, related to other public policies, and effectively impacted on creativity and innovation. As put by the author, 'IP laws and systems will not help developing countries if they are introduced without proper consideration of the social and economic conditions for each country' and '...without having other policies in place that encourage development'. While there are encouraging signs that this may be changing as a growing number of developing countries adopt intellectual property policies and strategies, there is also risk that such policies and strategies continue to be based on a limited view, focusing on the 'use' and 'promotion' of the intellectual property system, rather than on a broader view, which acknowledges both the benefits and costs of intellectual property protection and seeks to ensure that the benefits outweigh the costs through a balanced and 'development-oriented' approach. Clearly, this will remain an ongoing challenge in the years to come.

Finally, this book comes at a very timely moment for the Arab world, the region from which the author originates. The Arab Spring, which has been sweeping the region for the past two years, provides a unique opportunity to reconsider many of the existing public policies. Citizens of the region have expressed with vigor aspirations and expectations for change and for reaping concrete benefits from such public policies. Intellectual property is one area where a reassessment is urgently needed. For a long time, the dominant discourse on intellectual property, in the region, has concentrated mainly on compliance and enforcement. For policymakers in the region seeking to move beyond this narrow focus, the 'policy road map' proposed in this book offers an alternative path that they can eagerly embrace.

Advancing the understanding of the relationship between intellectual property and development will remain a work in progress, in the coming years, as countries continue to put forward different interpretations about how this relationship should be operationalised in a concrete manner. Ongoing deliberations, in Geneva, concerning the implementation of the WIPO Development Agenda recommendations reflect these persistent differences. Academic scholarship can help achieve a better understanding and untangle the issues at stake through empirical evidence and 'outside-the-box' proposals. From this perspective, seeking to bridge the gap between 'theory' and 'practice' when it comes to intellectual property and development, as suggested in this book, is most pertinent and merits to be further pursued.

Ahmed Abdel Latif
Senior Program Manager
International Centre for Trade and Sustainable Development (ICTSD), Geneva
Former Egyptian IP Negotiator

Acknowledgments

I first became interested in intellectual property law in 1999, when I completed a Master of Laws in Commercial Law at Buckingham University in the United Kingdom. I subsequently practised intellectual property law from 2002 to 2004 at the law firm of Abu-Ghazaleh intellectual property in Amman, Jordan, as a member of its intellectual property legal department. At the same time, I worked as a project leader for Creative Commons-Jordan. Through this work, I became familiar with the various intellectual property laws applying across the Arab world. During this time, I discovered that many intellectual property laws in force in the Arab world failed to adequately address the issues arising from the use of digital technologies and the Internet.

I further pursued my interest in intellectual property when, in 2006, I obtained a scholarship from the Open Society Institute to complete a Master of Laws at Columbia University Law School in New York. At Columbia, I researched the importance of copyright for innovation and creativity and how intellectual property laws can have a significant impact upon the development of societies. In 2008, I was offered an Australian government scholarship to undertake a PhD in the Law Faculty at the Queensland University of Technology (QUT) in Brisbane, Australia. This allowed me to conduct research on intellectual property systems in developing countries and how these intellectual property systems need to be restructured to assist those countries in their path to social and economic development. This book is based on my PhD dissertation, which was completed in May 2011.

The completion of this project would not have been possible without the support and encouragement of many people to whom I owe thanks. Professor Brian Fitzgerald, my principal supervisor, has supported me with his valuable expertise and knowledge from the beginning of my doctoral program in 2008. He is a mentor and colleague from whom I have learned much. Professor Fitzgerald's office was always open, and he was always ready to engage in discussion with me about intellectual property and copyright law. Importantly, he encouraged me to pursue my research interests relating to intellectual property and development. I also would like to express my thanks to my associate supervisor, Professor Anne Fitzgerald, who shared with me her knowledge, experience, and insights.

I would like to express my gratitude to the Australian government, which, through the Department of Innovation, Industry, Science and Research, provided funding for my PhD scholarship and enabled this project to be undertaken. Many thanks are also owed to the ARC Centre of Excellence for Creative Industries and Innovation (CCi), which provided additional financial support. This work could never have been completed without the assistance of the staff of the QUT library, who provided me with all the research materials I requested; I am grateful for their help and support. I also wish to thank my friend and colleague, Anthony Austin, who spent many hours with me discussing the subject of intellectual property and development and assisted with editing. Valuable feedback, comments, and moral support were provided by the examiners and panellists who reviewed my thesis, faculty members, and colleagues, including Professor Peter Yu, Dr Jeremy Malcolm, Professor Rohan Kariyawasam, Neale Hooper, Benedict Atkinson, Dr Nicolas Suzor, Dr Sampsung Shi, Beryl Besse, and Dr Lucy Cradduck.

Finally, I wish to acknowledge the assistance of Anke Seyfried and Manuela Schwietzer of Springer, whose enthusiasm for, and encouragement of, this project has been greatly appreciated.

June 2012
Brisbane, Australia

Rami Olwan

Contents

List of Abbreviations

A2K	Access to knowledge
ACTA	Anti-counterfeiting trade agreement
Berne Convention	Berne convention for the protection of literary and artistic works of 1886
BIRPI	Bureaux internationaux réunis pour la protection de la propriété intellectuelle
CC	Creative commons
CDIP	Committee on development and IP (WIPO)
DMCA	Digital millennium copyright act of 1998
DRM	Digital right management
EC	European commission
EU	European Union
FDI	Foreign direct investment
FOSS	Free and open source software
FTAs	Free trade agreements
GATT	General agreement on tariffs and trade
GDP	Gross domestic product
ICT	Information communication technologies
IP	Intellectual property
IT	Information technology
JEUAA	Jordan EU association agreement
JUSFTA	Jordan United States free trade agreement
LDCs	Least developed countries
MNCs	Multinational corporations
NGOs	Non-profit organisations
Paris Convention	Paris convention for the protection of industrial property of 1883
PCT	Patent corporation treaty
R & D	Research and development
RMI	Rights management information
TK	Traditional knowledge

TPMs	Technological protection measures
TRIPS	Trade-related intellectual property aspects agreement
UCC	Universal Copyright Convention of 1952
UN	United Nations
UNCTAD	United Nations conference on trade and development
UNESCO	United Nations educational, scientific, and cultural organization
WCT	WIPO copyright treaty of 1996
WIPO	World intellectual property organization
WPPT	WIPO performers and phonograms treaty of 1996
WTO	World Trade Organization

Chapter 1
Intellectual Property and Development

> *[W]e are writing a bill of rights for the world, and one of the most important rights is the opportunity for development.*[1]
>
> *The challenge to development ... is to improve the quality of life. Especially in the World's poor countries, a better quality of life generally calls for higher incomes but involves much more. It encompasses, as ends in themselves, better education, higher standards of health and nutrition, less poverty, a cleaner environment, more equality of opportunity, greater individual freedom, and a richer cultural life.*[2]
>
> *When wisely applied, ICT offers enormous opportunities to narrow social and economic inequalities and support sustainable local wealth creation, and thus help to achieve the broader development goals that the international community has set. ICT cannot, of course, act as a panacea for all development problems, but by dramatically improving communication and exchange of information, it can create powerful social and economic networks, which in turn provide the basis for major advances in development.*[3]
>
> *Intellectual property is essential to development, not just in the narrow sense of efficiency, but in this broader view of expanding capability for central freedoms. Surely, copyright and patents determine our access to basic needs, from educational material to lifesaving medicines. . .Stated differently, the implications in intellectual property rights go well beyond incentives for innovation: these rights are related to questions of cultural relations, social development, and GDP growth.*[4]

---

[1] Eleanor Roosevelt, *My Day* (6 February 1947) The George Washington University <http://www.gwu.edu/~erpapers/myday/displaydoc.cfm?_y=1947&_f=md000567>.

[2] David A. Clark, *Visions of Development-A Study of Human Values* (Edward Elgar 2002) 20, citing World Bank (1991).

[3] Digital Opportunity Task Force, *Digital Opportunities for All: Meeting the Challenge* (11 May 2001) International Telecommunication Union (ITU) <http://www.itu.int/wsis/docs/background/general/reports/26092001_dotforce.htm>.

[4] Madhavi Sunder, 'Intellectual Property and Development As Freedom' in Neil Weinstock Netanel (ed), *The Development Agenda—Global Intellectual Property and Developing Countries* (Oxford, 2009) 453, 470.

R.M. Olwan, *Intellectual Property and Development*,
DOI 10.1007/978-3-642-27907-2_1, © Springer-Verlag Berlin Heidelberg 2013

1.1 Overview

What Is the Aim of This Book?

Intellectual property (IP) is important for the future of developing countries, but the implementation of IP systems in developing countries has been ungainly and, in many cases, ineffective. Some might go so far as to say that IP proponents who have attempted to uncritically push IP systems onto developing countries, without taking into account all the relevant considerations, have created an unworkable situation that does not benefit those countries.

The topic of IP and development has gained new momentum in recent years, as exemplified by the adoption of a development agenda at WIPO. However, the debate about IP and development has extended over many years and produced mixed results. If we are to move forward, we need to posit a framework for IP and development that is both acceptable and workable to people in developing countries.

This book aims to provide a framework for a better understanding of the role and impact of IP on development, with a view to producing worthwhile outcomes in the future. In doing so, it examines the history, economic impact, and cultural context of IP and development and then proposes the implementation of its findings through a series of practical measures that can be undertaken by developing countries. The important contribution that this book makes to the existing knowledge on this topic is twofold. Firstly, it provides a theoretical framework for IP and development. Secondly, it provides practical guidance to developing countries and WIPO as to how an effective program for IP and development might be implemented.

Why Is This Topic Important Today?

The long-term failure of the international community to produce an approach to IP laws that promotes development in developing countries has eroded the trust and confidence that such countries have in the international IP system. The adoption of the Development Agenda in 2007 at WIPO has provided new hope for developing countries. However, this program will amount to little more than mere words on paper if it cannot achieve real operational outcomes. This book aims to support and facilitate initiatives such as that taken by WIPO by providing theoretical and practical guidance on how to build successful outcomes. In a world where developing countries constitute the majority of members of WIPO and the WTO, it would be pointless to undertake yet another IP and development program that ignores the present-day realities. In fact, if the WIPO initiative does not address present realities in a practical manner, the danger is that it will only undermine the credibility and sustainability of the international IP system.

This book, which is built on the author's personal experience of living, studying, and working in developing countries, is designed to provide a practical pathway to progress for those countries. The significant shortcomings of various initiatives to date have been at the expense of those who lack the power to remedy the situation.

1.2 The Meaning of Development

At the outset, it is necessary to discuss the current thinking on the concept of 'development'.

1.2.1 The Meaning of Development Outside the Field of IP

1.2.1.1 Introduction

'Development' is one of the most important challenges facing the international community.[5] The importance of this challenge has been widely acknowledged in many international conventions and forums,[6] including the United Nations Declaration on the Right to Development (1986),[7] the United Nations Millennium Development Goals (2001),[8] the UNCTAD XI São Paulo Consensus (2004),[9] the Plan of Implementation agreed at the World Summit on Sustainable Development

---

[5] Valentina Vadi, 'Sapere Aude! Access to Knowledge as A Human Right and a Key Instrument of Development' (2008) 12 *International Journal of Communication Law and Policy* 345, 353.

[6] Ibid.

[7] The United Nations General Assembly adopted the Declaration on the Right to Development on 4 December 1986. The preamble recognised that:

> [D]evelopment is a comprehensive economic, social, cultural and political process, which aims at the constant improvement of the well-being of the entire population and all individuals on the basis of their active, free and meaningful participation in development and in the fair distribution of benefits resulting there from' Art 2(1) of the declaration also provides that: 'the human person is the central subject of development and should be the active participant and beneficiary of the right to development.

See United Nations High Commissioner for Human Rights (UNHCHR), Declaration on the Right to Development, Adopted by General Assembly Resolution 41/128 of 4 December 1986 <http://www.unhchr.ch/html/menu3/b/74.htm>; United Nations Development Programme (UNDP), *Measuring Human Development: A Primer-Guidelines and tools for Statistical Research, Analysis and Advocacy* (2 September 2007) <http://hdr.undp.org/en/media/Primer_complete.pdf>.

[8] The Millennium Development Goals (MDGs) are the eight goals set by the UN to be reached in 2015. These include the following: 1. eradicate extreme poverty and hunger; 2. achieve universal primary education; 3. promote gender quality and empower women; 4. reduce the mortality of children; 5. improve maternal health; 6. combat HIV/AIDS, malaria and other diseases; 7. ensure environment sustainability; and 8. develop a global partnership for development. See Interchurch Organisation for Development Cooperation (ICCO), *The Millennium Development Goals* <http://www.icco.nl/en/projects/millennium-goals>; Rohan Kariyawasam, *International Economic Law and the Digital Divide* (Edward Elgar, 2007) 278.

[9] United Nations Conference on Trade and Development (UNCTAD), *São Paulo Consensus* (25 June 2004) <http://www.unctad.org/en/docs/td410_en.pdf>.

(WSSD) (2002),[10] the Declaration of Principles of the first phase of the World Summit on the Information Society (WSIS) (2003),[11] the Doha Ministerial Declaration (2005),[12] the Brussels Declaration and the Programme of Action for the Least Developed Countries (LDCs) for the Decade 2001–2010 (2001),[13] the Monterey Consensus on Development and Assistance (2002),[14] and the Johannesburg Declaration on Sustainable Development (2002).[15]

The general long-term objective of 'developing countries' is to establish a sound economic base. This requires agricultural self-sufficiency and the stimulation and maintenance of commercial and industrial activities.[16] The United Nations recently undertook a firm commitment to address problems that particularly affect developing countries.[17] Innovation, development, and IP-related matters have been discussed and addressed by the UN since its foundation and long before the establishment of WIPO.[18]

1.2.1.2 The General Meaning of Development

Development studies are a multidisciplinary branch of social sciences, which seek to address issues of concern for 'developing countries'.[19] Historically, development studies have placed particular focus on issues relating to social and economic

[10] United Nations (UN), *Plan of Implementation of the World Summit on Sustainable Development* (Johannesburg, 2002) <http://www.un.org/esa/sustdev/documents/WSSD_POI_PD/English/WSSD_PlanImpl.pdf>.

[11] International Telecommunication Union (ITU), *Declaration of Principles of the World Summit of Information Society* (10-12 December 2003, Geneva) <http://www.itu.int/wsis/documents/doc_multi.asp?lang=en&id=1161|1160>.

[12] The Group of 77, *Doha Declaration* <http://www.g77.org/southsummit2/doc/Doha%20Declaration(English).pdf>.

[13] United Nations (UN), *Programme for Action for Least Developing Countries* for the *Decade 2000-2010 Implementation* <http://www.un.org/special-rep/ohrlls/ldc/Contributions/Matrix%202005-P2.pdf>.

[14] United Nations (UN), *Monterrey Consensus* <http://www.un.org/esa/ffd/monterrey/MonterreyConsensus.pdf>.

[15] European Commission (EC), Johannesburg Declaration on Sustainable Development <http://trade.ec.europa.eu/doclib/docs/2004/april/tradoc_116827.pdf>.

[16] World Intellectual Property Organization (WIPO), *The Role of Intellectual Property in Development and WIPO's Development Cooperation Program*, ch 3, 195 <http://www.wipo.int/about-ip/en/iprm/pdf/ch3.pdf>.

[17] Vadi, above n 5,353.

[18] Sisule F Musungu, *Rethinking Innovation, Development and Intellectual Property in the UN: WIPO and Beyond TRIPS*, Quaker International Affairs Programme, Issue Paper 5, (2005), The Quaker United Nations Office (QUNO), 11 <http://www.quno.org/geneva/pdf/economic/Issues/TRIPS53.pdf>.

[19] Wikipedia, *Development Studies* <http://en.wikipedia.org/wiki/Development_studies>.

development, the relevance of which may extend to communities and regions outside the developing world.[20]

'Development' is a contested term among scholars, international organisations, and development experts in developed and developing countries. It has several meanings and can be used in different contexts, including social development, economic development, sustainable development, human development, political development, micro-development, indigenous development, and basic needs development.[21] Generally, the concept of development encapsulates the improvement of the lives of individuals through improvements in education, skills, income, and employment.[22] It is a multi-dimensional process often involving major changes to the existing social structures and popular attitudes that transform a nation's overall standard of living from unsatisfactory to satisfactory.[23]

Development is regarded as the process of economic growth, with expanding output and employment, institutional transformation, and technological progress of a country that steadily improves the well-being of people.[24] Development can also be a 'process of expanding people's choices, enabling improvements in the collective and individual quality of life and the exercise of full freedom and rights'.[25]

According to the United Nations Declaration on the Right to Development (DRTD)[26] (adopted by the General Assembly in 1986 in its Resolution 41/128), development is 'an inalienable human right by virtue of which every human person

---

[20] Ibid.

[21] See for explanation of some of those terms, Kariyawasam, above n 8, 266-267. See also the fallowing approaches or (paradigms) to development: the classic; the neo-liberal; and the neo-populist paradigms. See Piers Blaikie et al., 'Knowledge in Action: Local Knowledge as a Development Resources and Barriers to its Incorporation in Natural Resource Research and Development', (1997) 55 (2) *Agricultural Systems* 217-237.

[22] Center to Bridge the Digital Divide (CBDD), *The Meaning of Development, Sustainable Development and Rural Development*, 59 <http://cbdd.wsu.edu/kewlcontent/cdoutput/TR501/page59.htm> (on file with author). See also Joseph Stiglitz, *Making Globalisation Work* (W.W. Norton & Co., 2006) 48-49.

[23] CBDD, above n 22.

[24] Kariyawasam, above n 8, 283; 291, citing *Consideration of the Sixth Report of the Independent Expert on the Right of Development*, EN/CN4/2004/ WG181 (2 February 2004), 4.

[25] Marie-Claire Segger, 'The Role of International Forums in the Advancement of Sustainable Development' (Fall 2009) *Sustainable Development Law and Policy*, 4 <http://www.wcl.american.edu/org/sustainabledevelopment/documents/SDLP_09Fall.pdf?rd=1>. See also Markus Gehring and Marie-Claire Segger, *Sustainable Development in World Trade Law* (Kluwer, 1992) 3; Subrata R Chowdhury, Erik M.G. Denters and Paul J.I.M. de Waart (eds), *The Right to Development in International Law* (Martinus Nijhoff Publishers, 1992).

[26] The DRTD is controversial and some countries, including the US, question whether it is legally binding. The DRTD has been subject to many interpretations. One commentator notes that: it 'is not legally binding under international law and that states other than parties to the Africa Charter to Human and People's Right cannot be held legally accountable for its implementation. This is not to deny the moral or political force'. See Laure-Hélène Piron, *The Right to Development, A Review of the Current State of the Debate for the Department for International Development* (April 2002) Overseas Development Institute (ODI) <http://www.odi.org.uk/resources/download/1562.pdf>.

and all peoples are entitled to participate in, and enjoy, economic, social, cultural and political development'.[27] Professor Amartya Sen, in *Development as Freedom*, defines development as 'the process of expanding the real personal freedoms that people might enjoy'.[28] Sen identifies five capabilities that need to be achieved to accomplish development: political freedom, economic facilities, social opportunities, transparency guarantees, and protective security.[29] Professor Martha Nussbaum explains that the concept of development is about achieving '[c]ertain basic functional capabilities which societies should obtain for their citizens, and by which their quality of life should be measured'.[30] These capabilities include the following:

(1) Being able to live a life of normal length;
(2) Being able to have good health, including reproductive health, and to receive adequate nourishment; and
(3) Being able to use one's senses and to imagine, think, and reason—and to do these things in a truly human way.[31]

According to the World Bank, development involves improvement in the quality of life in poor countries. It goes beyond merely raising income levels and encompasses better education, higher standards of health and nutrition, less poverty, clean environment, more equality of opportunities, greater individual freedoms, and richer cultural life.[32]

1.2.1.3 The Social and Economic Meaning of Development

The term 'social development' has been in use since the 1960s and 1970s. It became more prevalent during the 1980s and 1990s as the international community came to realise that not only that developing countries need financial support to develop but also that social empowerment is equally—if not more—important. In March 1995,

---

[27] Article 1 of the United Nations Declaration on the Right to Development (UNRD) (adopted by the General Assembly in 1986). See also Darell A. Posey and Graham Dutfield, *Indigenous Peoples and Sustainability - Cases and Actions* (IUCN Indigenous Peoples and Conservation Initiative, International Books,1997) 83.

[28] Amartya Sen, *Development as Freedom* (Oxford University,1999) 35. See also Julio Faundez, 'Rule of Law or Washington Consensus: the Evaluation of the World Bank's Approach to Legal and Judicial Reform' in Amanda Perry Kessaris (ed), *Law in the Pursuit of Development Principle into Practice?* (Routledge, 2010) 245; Faizel Ismail, 'A Development Perspective on the WTO July 2004 General Council Decision' (2005) *8 Journal of international Economic Law* 377; Gehring and Segger, above n 25, 4; Kariyawasam, above n 8, 266; 267; Sunder, above n 4, 453.

[29] Sen, above n 28, 38.

[30] Margaret Chon, 'Intellectual Property from Below: Copyright and Capability for Education' (2007) 40 *University California Davis Law Review, 803;* 818, citing Martha C. Nussbaum, 'Capabilities and Human Rights' (1997) 66 *Fordham Law Review* 273, 287.

[31] Ibid.

[32] Clark, above n 2, 20.

the World Summit for Social Development in Copenhagen identified three main objectives of social development: eradication of poverty, full employment, and social integration.[33]

Scholars have proposed various definitions for social development. One defines it as 'a reduction of absolute poverty, unemployment and income inequalities'. Another defines it as 'an improvement in social indicators including rates of life expectancy, adult literacy and infant mortality'.[34] It has been described as 'the process of planned change designed to bring about a better fit between human needs and social policies and programs',[35] which 'implies evolution and transformation through which people and societies maximize their opportunities, and become empowered to handle their affairs'.[36] Ultimately, social development 'is directed toward the release of human potential in order to eliminate social inequalities and problems'.[37]

'Economic development' simply means the ability of the economy to generate growth (i.e., an annual increase in gross national product (GNP)).[38] It has been defined as 'the process whereby the real per capita income of a country increases over a long period of time—subject to the stipulations that the number of people below an 'absolute poverty line' does not increase, and that the distribution of income does not become more unequal'.[39]

The implementation of the right of development requires developing countries to devise effective development policies at the national level, as well as to create an

[33] The United Nations (UN), Report of the World Summit noted:

> We gather here to commit ourselves, our Governments and our nations to enhancing social development through the world so that all men and women, especially those living in poverty, may exercise the rights, utilize the resources and share the responsibilities that enable them to lead satisfying lives and to contribute to the well-being of their families, their communities and human kind. To support and promote these efforts must be the overriding goals of the international community, especially with respect to people suffering from poverty, unemployment and social exclusion.

See United Nations (UN), *Report of the World Summit for Social Development* (1995), 3 <http://www.un.org/documents/ga/conf166/aconf166-9.htm at 1st October 2010>.

See also, Kumiko Sakamoto, *Social Development, Culture and Participation* (PhD thesis, Waseda University, 2002) <http://www.tzonline.org/pdf/socialdevelopment.pdf>.

[34] It can also be defined as 'increasing the awareness of citizens to lead better life that would help them to harness their social energies and skills'. See also Clark, above n 2, 23.

[35] Manohar S. Pawar and David R. Cox, *Social Development—Critical Themes and Perspectives* (Rutledge, 2010) 16, citing Hollister (1982) and Midgley (1993) 7.

[36] Ibid 16, citing Mohan and Sharma (1985) 12-23.

[37] Ibid 16, citing Meinert and Kho (1984) 10. See also Clark, above n 2, 20.

[38] Clark, above 2, 10.

[39] Gerald M. Meier and James E. Rauch (eds), *Leading* Issues in Economic Development (Oxford University, 6th ed 1995) 7. See also Stiglitz, above 22, 44-48.

equitable economic environment to attract international investment.[40] Economists typically measure the level of economic development based on economic growth or the average income per person. Critics of the use of this methodology in assessing economic development argue that it is too narrow and fails to recognise that development is 'a multi-faceted notion that should be conceived from the outset [and which is] considerably broader than income'[41] and other growth methods of assessment.

'Sustainable development' is a relatively new concept, which first emerged in the 1980s to emphasise the need to simultaneously address development and environmental goals.[42] The most generally accepted meaning of sustainable development is that set out in the 1987 Brundtland Report,[43] which defines it as 'development that meets the needs of the present without compromising the ability of the future generations to meet their own needs'.[44] It may also be defined as improving and maintaining the well-being of people and environmental ecosystems.[45]

1.2.2 The Meaning of Development Within the Field of IP

1.2.2.1 IP and Social and Economic Development

Scholars working in the field of IP have differing views on the relationship between IP and development. Some hold the view that development will be promoted through the introduction of IP systems in developing countries, whilst others are

---

[40] United Nations General Assembly (UNGA), *The Vienna Declaration and Program of Action* (25 June 1993), United Nations High Commissioner for Human Rights (UNHCHR) <http://www.unhchr.ch/huridocda/huridoca.nsf/(symbol)/a.conf.157.23.en>. See also Kariyawasam, above n 8, 287.

[41] James M. Cypher and James L. Dietz, *The Process of Economic Development* (Rotledge, 3rd ed 2009) 30. See also Clibert Rist, *The History of Development* (Academic Foundation, 2nd ed, 2002); Gerald M. Mier and Joseph E. Stiglitz (eds), *Frontiers of Development Economics* (Oxford University, 2001); George Mavrotas and Anthony Shorrocks, *Advancing Development—Global Themes in Global Economics* (Palgrave Macmillan, 2007).

[42] WA. Alan Strong and Lesley A. Hemphill, *Sustainable Development Policy Directory* (Blackwell Publishing, 2006) 1. See also Marie-Claire Cordonier Segger and Ashfaq Khalfan, *Sustainable Development Law: Principles, Practices and Prospects* (Oxford, 2005) 15-43.

[43] United Nations (UN), *Report of the World Commission on Environment and Development: Our Common Future*, ch 7 <http://www.un-documents.net/wced-ocf.htm>.

[44] Gehring and Segger, above n 25, 5. See also Strong and Lesley, above n 42, 1-3; Clark, above n 2, 19; Segger and Khalfan, above n 42, 1-5; Philippe Cullet, *Intellectual Property Protection and Sustainable Development* (Lexis-Nexis, 2005) 34-38; 43; Subhabrata Bobby Banerjee, 'Who Sustains Development? Sustainable Development and the Reinvention of Nature' (2003) 24 (1) *Organization* 143-180 <http://oss.sagepub.com/content/24/1/143.abstract>.

[45] Posey and Dutfield, above n 27, 33.

doubtful as to whether such systems are sufficient to support development. Theories on development originally formulated in the 1950s and 1960s suggest that a system of IP protection is a necessary part of the evolution of states from being 'underdeveloped' to becoming 'developed'.[46]

Generally, IP scholars provide several justifications for IP systems based on social, economic, and cultural theories.[47] Professor Julie Cohen[48] has recognised the increased interest of IP scholars in the 'capabilities approach to development' as suggested by Martha Nussbaum and Amartya Sen.[49] Professor Margaret Chon[50]

---

[46] Professor Ruth L. Gana (Okediji) notes:

> [T]he promise of development, for the most part, continues to form the basis of modern arguments insisting on particular forms and levels of intellectual property protection in developing countries. The lure of membership to international treaties was often made more appealing by the work of international institutions such as the World Intellectual Property Organization (WIPO) and UNESCO, which espoused the conventional wisdom of western intellectual property scholars that enactment of European-style intellectual property laws is necessary perquisite to economic progress and development.

See Ruth L. Gana (Okediji), 'The Myth of Development, the Progress of Rights: Human Rights to Intellectual Property and Development' (1996) 18 *Law and Policy Law Journal* 315, 331.

[47] There are four primary theories that justify IP. The utilitarian, labour, personality and social planning theories. The traditional justification for IP protection is that it promotes science and technology, and without its protection creators would not have any incentive to produce to the society valuable 'public goods'. See for a full explanation of those theories of IP, William Fisher, 'Theories of Intellectual Property' in Sephen Munzer (ed), *New Essays in Legal and Policitcal Theory of Property*, 168-199 (Cambridge University, 2001) Berkman Center for Internet and Society <http://cyber.law.harvard.edu/people/tfisher/iptheory.pdf>; Keith E. Maskus, *Intellectual Property and Economic Development*, a paper prepared for the series 'Beyond the Treaties: A Symposium on Compliance with International Intellectual Property Law', organized by Fredrick K. Cox International Law Center at Case Western Reserve University (6 February 2000) <http://www.colorado.edu/Economics/mcguire/workingpapers/cwrurev.doc>; Joseph Stiglitz, *Public Policy for a Knowledge Economy* (27 Janyary 1999) akgul.bilkent.edu.tr <http://akgul.bilkent.edu.tr/BT-BE/knowledge-economy.pdf>; Anselm Kamperman Sanders, 'Intellectual Property, Free Trade Agreements and Economic Development' (2007) 23 *Georgia State University Law Review* 893; Carlos M. Correa, *Bilateral Investment Agreements: Agents of New Global Standards for the Protection of Intellectual Property Rights?* (August 2004) International Center for Trade and Sustainable Development (ICTSD) <http://ictsd.net/i/ip/18366/>; Otunba Yinka Lawal-Solarin, 'Copyright and Education—A Publishers Perspective From A Developing World' (a paper presented at the Information meeting on Education and Copyright in the Digital Age, November 2005, at the Headquarters of the World Intellectual Property Organization (WIPO), Geneva, Switzerland)<http://www.wipo.int/edocs/mdocs/copyright/en/educ_cr_im_05/educ_cr_im_05_www_53637.pdf>; Craig Joyce 2, 'Articles in Honour of Professor L. Ray Patterson' (2003) 10 *Journal of Intellectual Property Law*, 239.

[48] George Town University.

[49] Julie Cohen, 'Creativity and Culture in Copyright Theory' (2007) 40 *University California Davis Law* 1151, 1159 <http://law.indiana.edu/students/centers/doc/Cohen2_000.pdf>. See also, Margret Chon, 'Copyright and Capability for Education: An Approach from Below' in Tzen Wong and Graham Dutfield, *Intellectual Property and Human Development* (Cambridge, 2011) 218.

[50] University of Seattle.

calls for the adoption of an 'IP-from-below' or a 'bottom-up rather than top-down' approach for IP and development, which she explains as follows:

> [IP] can no longer afford to be insular, as if it does not affect or is not affected by the provision of other global public goods. Explicit connections must be made between [IP] and other global public goods addressing basic development needs, including food, education as well as the already highly publicized health care sector. [IP], after all, cannot 'take root' absent a basic national capacity, which can only be developed with a population that has its essential needs met.[51]

Introducing IP systems into developing countries without fulfilling the basic needs of those countries will limit the effect of these laws and their contribution to society. It is not enough simply to enact IP laws in developing countries; rather, these laws must also be integrated into their national development strategies and policies. Professor Madhavi Sunder[52] argues that developing countries need to have IP systems that create 'cultural diversity'.[53] She explains the importance of 'culture' in the IP context:

> Cultural theory takes as a starting point that human beings are creative and cultural, continually seeking to make and remake our world, contributing to commerce and culture, science and spirituality. Individuals demand and deserve both recognition and remuneration for their intellectual production. But [IP] does not merely incentivizes and reward creators. [IP] structures social relations... A cultural approach to [IP] recognizes existing disparities in cultural capabilities resulting from economic, social, and cultural inequalities, and seeks IP laws that accommodate difference.[54]

Adopting a cultural approach towards IP would encourage learning and sharing of information within and amongst different cultures.[55] It may also increase the range of choices for people in developing countries and offer them sustainable development.[56]

The Publishers Association of South Africa believes that development requires a balance between the need to nurture and grow local authors, industries, and cultural

---

[51] See Margaret Chon, 'Intellectual Property and the Development Divide' (2006) 27 *Codozo Law Review* 2813, 2821; 2877 <http://papers.ssrn.com/sol3/papers.cfm?abstract_id=894162>.

[52] University of California.

[53] Madhavi Sunder, 'Cultural Dissent' (2001) 54 *Stanford Law Review, 495* <http://papers.ssrn.com/sol3/papers.cfm?abstract_id=304619>.

[54] See Madhavi Sunder, 'IP3' (2006) 59 (2) *Stanford Law Review* 257, 323; Sunder, above n 4, 453.

[55] Sunder, above n 54, 323.

[56] *Convention on the Protection and Promotion of the Diversity of Cultural Expressions* (DCE), open for signature on 20 October 2005, 2440 UNTS 311 (entered into force on 18 March 2007) <http://portal.unesco.org/en/ev.phpURL_ID=31038&URL_DO=DO_TOPIC&URL_SECTION=201.html>. See also Wong and Dutfield, above n 49.

production and the need for access to essential knowledge, information, and culture,[57] particularly in developing countries with extreme levels of poverty.[58]

Other scholars have similarly stressed the importance of an open, vibrant 'commons'[59] or 'public domain' for achieving development.[60] This virtual commons or public domain is vitally important for developing countries since it facilitates the utilisation of information and information-embedded goods and tools. It enables information outputs to be openly released and managed as a shared commons rather than as restricted property.[61]

The concept of the commons in fostering development in developing countries works hand in hand with 'voluntary mechanisms'[62] such as Creative Commons (CC), copyright licences, and free and open source software (FOSS).[63] Some scholars believe that development can only be attained through the application of

[57] See Publishers Association of South Africa, *PICC Report on Intellectual Property Rights in South Africa* (September 2004), 92 <http://www.publishsa.co.za/downloads/intellectual_property_report.pdf>. See also John Barton et al, Commission on Intellectual Property Rights (CIPR), *Integrating Intellectual Property Rights and Development Policy* (2002), <http://www.iprcommission.org/papers/pdfs/final_report/CIPRfullfinal.pdf>; James Boyle, 'A Manifesto on WIPO and the Future of Intellectual Property' (2004) 9 *Duke Law and Technology Review* 10 <http://scholarship.law.duke.edu/cgi/viewcontent.cgi?article=1113&context=dltr>; Lihong Li, 'Localizing WIPO's Legislative Assistance: Lessons from China's Experience with the TRIPs Agreement' in Jeremy de Beer, *Implementing the World Intellectual Property Organization's Development Agenda* (Wifrid Laurier, 2009) 123; 125.

[58] Publishers Association of South Africa, above n 57.

[59] The commons was traditionally defined as existing in forests, the atmosphere, fisheries and grazing lands, that were shared amongst all and no one owns. The same concept has been used to describe information accessible through the Internet. See James Arvanitakis, *Explaining the Common* (2010) <http://jamesarvanitakis.net/?page_id=247>.

[60] Anupam Chander and Madhavi Sunder, *The Romance of the Public Domain* (2004) 92 *California Law Review*, 1331, 1374 <http://papers.ssrn.com/sol3/papers.cfm?abstract_id=562301>.

[61] Yochai Benkler, *The Wealth of Networks* (Yale University, 2006) 320.

[62] Brian Fitzgerald and Rami Olwan, 'The Legality of Free and Open Source Software Licences: the Case of Jacobsen v. Katzer' in Mark Perry and Brian Fitzgerald (eds), *Knowledge Policy for the 21st Century* (Irwin Law, 2011); Brian Fitzgerald and Rami Olwan, 'Copyright Law in the United Arab Emirates (UAE) in the Digital Age (2010) 32 (11) *European Intellectual Property Law Review*, 565.

[63] 'From the 'digital divide', to biotechnology, to medical research, open source and open access have become key components in the strategy to boost the fortunes of developing countries.' See David W. Opderbeck, 'The Penguin's Paradox: The Political Economy of International Intellectual Property and the Paradox of Open Intellectual Property Models' (2007) 18 *Stanford Law and Policy Review* 102; Jennifer Papin-Ramcharan and Frank Soodeen, 'Open Source Software: A Developing Country View' in Kirk St. Amant and Brian Still (ed), *Handbook of Research on Open Source Software: Technological, Economic, and Social Perspectives* (Information Science Reference, 2007) 93-101; Alfreda Dudley-Sponaugle, Sungchul Hong and Yuanqiong Wang, 'The Social and Economic Impact of FOSS in Developing Countries' in Kirk Amant and Brian Still (ed), *Handbook of Research on Open Source Software: Technological, Economic, and Social Perspectives* (Information Science Reference, 2007) 102-115; Daniel F. Olejko, 'Charming a Snake: Open Source Strategies for Developing Countries Disillusioned with TRIPs' (2007) 25 *Penn State International Law Review*, 855.

a human rights-based approach to IP.[64] Such an approach requires the facilitation and promotion of scientific progress in a manner that benefits members of society on an individual level, as well as on a corporate level.[65] Implicit in such an approach is a right of access to the benefits of science and a right of protection from the potentially harmful effects of scientific and technological inventions.[66] Scholars and commentators are debating how this approach could be helpful to societies, including developing countries.[67]

Other scholars argue that IP by itself is not an answer to the problems of developing countries and that several other issues must be addressed if development is to be achieved.[68] WIPO has also noted that it is not enough to have IP laws

[64] Article 27(2) of the Universal Declaration of Human Rights (UDHR) provides that: '[e]veryone has the right to the protection of the moral and material interests resulting from any scientific, literary or artistic production of which he is the author'. See also Art 15 of the International Covenant on Economic, Social and Cultural Rights <http://www1.umn.edu/humanrts/instree/b1udhr.htm>; UN Committee on Economic, Social and Cultural Rights (CESCR), *General Comment No.* 17 (12 January 2006) United Nations High Commissioner for Refugees (UNHCR) <http://www.unhcr.org/refworld/category,LEGAL,CESCR,,,441543594,0.html>.

[65] Audrey R. Chapman, *A Human Rights Perspective on Intellectual Property, Scientific Progress, and Access to the Benefits of Science*, WIPO, 1, 38 <http://www.wipo.int/tk/en/hr/paneldiscussion/papers/pdf/chapman.pdf>.

[66] Ibid.

[67] See Laurence R. Helfer, 'Towards A Human Rights Approach Framework for Intellectual Property' (2007) 40 *University California Davis Law Review* 971; Orit Fischman Afori, 'Human Rights and Copyright: The Introduction of Natural Law Consideration to American Law' (2004) 14 *Fordham Intellectual Property, Media and Entertainment Law Journal* 497; Vadi above n 5, 345, Paul L.C. Torremans (ed), *Copyrights and Human Rights* (Kluwer, 2004); Michael Kirby, 'Forward' in Brian Fitzgerald and Benedict Atkinson (ed), *Copyright Future Copyright Freedom* (Sydney, 2011) 2, 8; Paul Goldstein and P. Bernt Hugenholtz, *International Copyright Principles, Law, and Practice* (Oxford University, 2010) 23-26.

[68] Professor Ruth L. Gana (Okediji) notes:

> What has become clear from the successful industrialization of countries in East Asia is that the process of development requires a careful mix of political reform, sound economic policies, and strategic exploitation of freely available technology, all of which must operates within a legitimate socio-cultural framework.

- Ruth L. Gana (Okediji), 'The Myth of Development, the Progress of Rights: Human Rights to Intellectual Property and Development' (1996) 18 *Law and Policy Journal* 315, 331, 332. See also Ruth L. Gana (Okediji), 'Has Creativity Died in the Third World? Some Implications of the Internationalisation Intellectual Property' (1995) 24 *Denver Journal of International Law and Policy*, 109.
- Professor Margaret Chon agrees that IP alone is not enough. She notes:

> In the current rule-generating and rule-interpreting environment of intellectual property globalisation, the presumption has been that intellectual property is good because it promotes economic growth. . .Intellectual property can no longer afford to be insular, as if it does not affect or is not affected by the provision of other global public goods. Explicit connections must be made between intellectual property and other global public goods addressing basic development needs, including food, education as well as the already highly publicized health care sector.

to achieve development, but there is a need to integrate these laws into the national policies of developing countries.[69]

Professor Ruth Okediji[70] states that IP protection has not enhanced the social welfare of developing countries, as it has done for developed countries, because developing countries do not share the same history, culture, political organisations, and legal institutions as that of developed countries.[71] Various scholars and commentators have noted that there are problematic aspects of the international IP system that have contributed to its ineffectiveness in fostering the development of developing countries.[72]

In contrast to the pro-IP views, Michele Boldrin and David Levine have doubted the importance of IP for development. They argue that IP is unnecessary and that

---

Chon, above n 51, 2877.

- Economist Keith Maskus also believes that many other 'variables' could affect the impact of IP protection. Such variable include macroeconomic stability, market openness, policies for improving an economy's technological infrastructure and the acquisition of human capital. Maskus, above n 47, 1. See also Hirouki Odagiri et al (eds), *Intellectual Property Rights, Development and Catch UP* (Oxford, 2010) 420; 427.

[69] Kamil Idris, former Director General of WIPO noted that:

> [A] national development strategy needs the strategic integration of intellectual property issues with other development policy issues, such as those in the economic, trade, financial, educational, social, cultural, environmental, and competition fields.

See Kamil Idris and Hisamitsu Arai, *The Intellectual Property-Conscious Nation: Mapping the Path from Developing to Developed*, WIPO Publication No. 988 (2006), 16. See also:

Denis Borges Barbosa, Margaret Chon and Andres Moncayo von Hase, 'Slouching Towards Development in International Intellectual Property' (2007) *Michigan State Law Review*, 71, 75 <http://papers.ssrn.com/sol3/papers.cfm?abstract_id=1081366>.

[70] University of Minnesota.

[71] Ruth Gana Okediji, 'Copyright and Public Welfare in Global Perspective' (1999-2000) 7 *Indiana Journal of Global Legal Studies* 122.

[72] Sisule F Musungu notes that:

> The principle of minimum intellectual property standards backed by trade retaliation; the loss of balance in intellectual property policy and rules; the incumbency problem; lack of economic analysis: fighting rather than embracing new technologies such as the internet; undemocratic and ideological international standard-setting processes; inconsistency and lack of coordination within and among developing countries; and glossing over historical evidence and lessons.

See Musungu, above n 18, 2; Ruth Okediji, 'Back to Bilateralism? Pendulum Swings in International Intellectual Property Protection' (2003) 1 *University of Ottawa Law & Technology Journal* 125 <http://papers.ssrn.com/sol3/papers.cfm?abstract_id=764725; Bilaterals.org, *Fighting FTAs an International Strategy Workshop* (July 2006) <http://www.bilaterals.org/IMG/pdf/Fighting-FTAs-summary-report.pdf>.

most innovations have taken place without its protection.[73] There is limited empirical evidence that tests the relevance of IP systems in promoting innovation and development within developing countries. The UNCTAD noted:

> Empirical evidence on the role of IP protection in promoting innovation and growth in general remains limited and inconclusive. Conflicting views also persist on the impacts of [IP] in the development prospects. Some point out that, in a modern economy, the minimum standards laid down in TRIPS will bring benefits to developing countries by creating the incentive structure necessary for knowledge generation and diffusion, technology transfer and private investment flows. Others stress that [IP], especially some of its elements, such as the patenting regime, will adversely affect the pursuit of sustainable development strategies by raising the prices of essential drugs to levels that are too high for the poor to afford; limiting the availability of educational materials for developing countries' school and university students; legitimising the piracy of traditional knowledge; and undermining the self-reliance of resource poor farmers.[74]

In summary, there is no agreement as to which kind of IP system can assist in the social and economic development of developing countries. Simply put, there are many views on the subject, and it is still a topic of active discussion among scholars.

Research on IP and development has recently gained renewed momentum.

Many scholars and international organisations are critical of the failure of the international IP system to assist developing countries and argue that it needs to be changed to meet the development ambitions and objectives of these countries. The issue of IP and development gained a new level of international prominence when, in September 2007, WIPO Member States adopted the WIPO Development Agenda.[75]

---

[73] See Michele Boldrin and David K. Levine, *Against Intellectual Property* (Cambridge University, 2008) <http://www.dklevine.com/general/intellectual/againstfinal.htm>; Brian Martin 'Against Intellectual Property, (1995) 21 *Philosophy and Social Action*, 7-22.

[74] ICTSD and UNCTAD, *Intellectual Property Rights: Implications for Development*, Policy Discussion Paper—UNCTAD—ICTSD Project on IPRs and Sustainable Development (August 2003) <http://www.iprsonline.org/unctadictsd/Policy%20Discussion%20Paper/PP_Introduction.pdf>.

Professor Alan Story has commented also that:

> Much less has been written about how the transplantation of what we might call a mature Western-style copyright regime and its infrastructure would generate significant economic growth in the South. Moreover, most of what has been written is neither convincing nor comprehensive and, to understate the point, contains gaping analytic holes.

Alan Story, 'Burn Berne: Why the Leading International Copyright Convention Must be Repealed' (2003) 40 3 *Houston Law Review* 763, 774. See also Ruth L. Okediji, 'Development in the Information Age', Issue Paper No. 9—UNCTAD—ICTSD Project on IPRs and Sustainable Development (May 2004), 6 <http://www.iprsonline.org/unctadictsd/docs/CS_Okediji.pdf>. See for a recent book that attempts to provide empirical evidence, Odagiri et al, above n 68.

[75] See ch 2 for a full explanation of the WIPO Development Agenda.

1.2.2.2 Copyright and Social and Economic Development

This book focuses on how a particular form of intellectual property, namely copyright, may contribute to social and economic development in developing countries. Copyright has had a special role in the context of development since the 1950s, when the political map of the world changed considerably. During this period, several states progressively became independent or were newly created. Since that time, developing countries have had to cope with the enormous problems of educating their populations.[76]

Copyright has shifted from being an esoteric and technical legal subject to one that affects musicians, designers, artists, students, authors, ordinary consumers, and more generally, anyone involved in any way in cultural production.[77] In that regard, it has enormous potential to generate positive growth and development and to create an impact on the progress of all countries, including developing countries.[78]

While the importance of copyright is mainly recognised by copyright scholars and lawyers, many others remain doubtful as to its effectiveness in the Internet age, especially with the increased use of technological protection measures (self-help) and contracts.[79]

There is now an international trend toward increasing the level of copyright protection not only in developed countries but also in developing countries.[80]

---

[76] WIPO, above n 16.

[77] See Lawrence Liang, *Guide to Open Content Licenses*, Piet Zwart Institute (2004) <http://www.theartgalleryofknoxville.com/ocl_v1.2.pdf>.

[78] Katie Lula, 'Neither Here Nor There But Fair: Finding an International Copyright Legal system Between East and West' (2003) 8 *Asian Pacific Law and Policy Journal* 18-19, citing WIPO Massage; Philip G. Altbach (ed), *Copyright and Development: Inequality in the Information Age* (Bellagio, 1995) 1-11.

[79] See Eben Moglen, 'Anarchism Triumphant: Free Software and the Death of Copyright' in Niva Elkin- Koren and Neil Weinstock Netanel (eds), *The Commodification of Information* (Kluwer International, 2002) 107; P. Bernt Hugenholtz, *Code as the Law or the End of Intellectual Property as we Know it*, University of Amsterdam, Institute for Information Law <http://www.ivir.nl/publications/hugenholtz/maastricht.doc>.

[80] Grain, *Freedom from IPR: A Convergence of Movements* (28 October 2004), 1 <http://www.grain.org/seedling/?id=301>; Lawrence Lessig, *Free Culture: How Big Media Uses Technology and the Law to Lock Down Culture* (Penguin, 2004); William Fisher, *Promises to Keep Technology, Law, and the Future of Entertainment* (Stanford University, 2004); Peter Biddle et al, *The Darkest and the Future of Content Distributions* (18 November 2002) Bearcave <http://www.bearcave.com/misl/misl_tech/msdrm/darknet.htm>; Koren and Netanel above n 79, 79-106; Jessica Litman, *Digital Copyright* (Kluwer Law International, 2001) 179; Urs Gasser and Silke Ernst, *From Shakespeare to Dj danger Mouse: A Quick Look at Copyright and User Creativity in the Digital Age* (2006) SSRN <http://papers.ssrn.com/sol3/papers.cfm?abstract_id=909223>; Pamela Samuelson, *Preliminary Thoughts in Copyright Reform* (2007) SSRN <http://papers.ssrn.com/sol3/papers.cfm?abstract_id=1002676>; Musungu above n 18, 11; Ahmed Abdel Latif, 'A Perspective on Reform in Arab Countries' in Ricardo Melendez-Ortiz and Pedro Roffe (ed), *Intellectual Property and Sustainable Development: Development Agenda in a Changing World* (Edward Elgar, 2010) 51, 59; James Bessen and Eric Maskin, *Intellectual Property on the Internet: What's Wrong with Conventional Wisdom?* (2004) Research on Innovation

Several scholars and international organisations have noted that stringent copyright laws are either of no or limited benefit to developing countries as they can decrease the incentives to innovate,[81] impede the sharing of information, and reduce licensing opportunities to those able to afford paying licensing fees.[82] Professor Joseph Stiglitz noted that 'strengthening [copyright] often means raising the price of a key ingredient into research—knowledge—and thus it is possible that an excessively 'strong' [copyright] regime may actually inhibit the pace of innovation'.[83] These practices could have particularly damaging consequences for the impoverished developing countries.[84]

Many scholars have stressed that a 'one-size-fits-all', Western-style copyright regime is not suited to developing countries as it has the potential to impede access to knowledge (A2K) and social advancement.[85] The 2006 Gower Review of IP in the UK noted:

> The economic evidence and, in particular, the history of currently developed countries suggests that a single one-size-fits-all approach is inappropriate. Stronger [copyright] protection can ultimately reap rewards in terms of greater domestic innovation in developing countries and in developing countries with sufficient capacity to innovate. However, it has little impact on innovation in developing countries without the capacity to innovate, and it may impose additional costs. Given that different [copyright] regimes are more appropriate at different stages of development, it would make sense to allow individual nations to choose when to strengthen their [copyright] regimes, rather than to seek to enforce a certain perspective.[86]

Increasingly, IP scholars are accepting that the 'one-size-fits-all' approach is inappropriate and this is particularly true for developing countries. At the present time, there is no clear guidance available to developing countries on how to design IP laws that are tailored to suit their social and economic development needs.

<http://www.researchoninnovation.org/iippap2.pdf>. See also Contra R. Polk Wagner 'Information Wants to be Free: Intellectual Property and the Methodologies of Control' (2003) 103 *Columbia Law Review* 995.

[81] Claudia Schmid, *Is Copyright Protection Necessary to Promote Innovation? An Evolutionary Economics Approach*, International Association for the Advancement of Teaching and Research in Intellectual Property (ATRIP), 12 <http://www.atrip.org/Content/Essays/Claudia%20Schmid.pdf>.

[82] Bessen and Maskin, above n 80.

[83] Stiglitz, above n 47.

[84] John Barton et al, above n 57, 101.

[85] Sunder, above n 54, 260.

The Commission of Intellectual Property Rights (CIPR) noted that:

> Indeed, it is arguably the case that many poor people in developing countries have only been able to access certain copyrighted works through using unauthorized copies available at a fraction of the price of the genuine original product. We are therefore concerned that an unintended impact of stronger protection and enforcement of international copyright rules as required, *inter alia*, by TRIPS will be simply to reduce access to knowledge products in developing countries, with damaging consequences for poor people.

John Barton et al, above n 57, ch 5. See also Bessen and Maskin, above n 80.

[86] The Gower Review of Intellectual Property (November 2006) UK Home Treasury <http://www.hm-treasury.gov.uk/d/pbr06_gowers_report_755.pdf>.

Education is at the heart of development.[87] A well-informed, educated, and skilled citizenry is indispensable to the development process[88] and fundamental to the capacity building upon which all further progress is made.[89] Dissemination of knowledge will act to further the educational, cultural, and technical development of the people of developing countries.[90] One of the most important development objectives affected by copyright is access to educational materials.[91] Copyright

---

[87] Article 26 of the Universal Declaration of Human Rights states that:

(1) Everyone has the right to education. Education shall be free, at least in the elementary and fundamental stages. Elementary education shall be compulsory. Technical and professional education shall be made generally available and higher education shall be equally accessible to all on the basis of merit.
(2) Education shall be directed to the full development of the human personality and to the strengthening of respect for human rights and fundamental freedoms. It shall promote understanding, tolerance and friendship among all nations, racial or religious groups, and shall further the activities of the United Nations for the maintenance of peace.
(3) Parents have a prior right to choose the kind of education that shall be given to their children.

See the Universal Declaration of Human Rights, adopted on 10 December 1948 by the United Nations General Assembly, GA Res 217A (1948), UN Online <http://www.un.org/Overview/rights.html>.

The International Bank for Reconstruction and Development (IBRD) and the World Bank note that:

> Knowledge is like light. Weightless and intangible, it can easily travel the world, enlightening the lives of people everywhere. Yet billions of people still live in the darkness of poverty unnecessarily.' 'Without having proper education, developing countries will inevitably fall behind developed countries and experience intellectual and economic marginalization and isolation. The result will be continued, if not rising, poverty.

IBRD and the World Bank, *Higher Education in Developing Countries Peril and Promise* (February 2000) The Task Force on Higher Education and Society, 223 <http://www.tfhe.net/report/downloads/report/whole.pdf>. See also Andrew Rens, *Implementing the WIPO Development Agenda - Treaty Provisions on Minimum Exceptions and Limitations for Education*, Shuttleworth Foundation Working Paper on Intellectual Property (2008) International Development Research Center <http://web.idrc.ca/openebooks/454-3/#page_158>; Ruth L Okediji, *The International Copyright System: Limitations, Exceptions and Public Interest Considerations for Developing Countries*, Issue Paper No. 15—UNCTAD—ICTSD Project on IPRs and Sustainable Development (2006), 32 <http://www.unctad.org/en/docs/iteipc200610_en.pdf>; Chon, above n 49, 218.

[88] Okediji, above n 87.

[89] Chon, above n 51, 2855; IBRD and the World Bank, above n 87, 223.

[90] Lauren Loew, 'Creative Industries in Developing Countries and Intellectual Property Protection', (2006) 9 1 *Vanderbilt Journal of Entertainment and Tech*, 171, 176 <law.vanderbilt.edu/publications/journal-entertainment-technology law/archive/download.aspx?id=1692>.

[91] Okediji, above n 74, 37. See also Chon, above 49.

may either facilitate or hinder access of developing countries to the free educational materials that are abundantly available through the Internet.[92]

Copyright laws have an important role to play in facilitating A2K and in bolstering a 'public domain'[93] that could be used to assist developing countries in their development. There is still no uniformly accepted view on what is meant by 'A2K'. Jeremy Malcolm, of Consumers International (CI), defines A2K as 'maintaining fair public access to the fruits of society's cultural and scientific output'.[94] It counterbalances the biases in copyright and increases developing countries' opportunities. Others view A2K as having a relevance that extends beyond access to education and opportunities for learning. Within this framework, the term 'knowledge' is understood broadly to refer to data, information, tools, inventions, literature, scholarship, art, popular media, and other expressions of human inquiry and understanding.[95]

Creativity has a profound effect on society and is associated with 'originality, imagination, inspiration, ingenuity and inventiveness'.[96] It refers to the formulation of new ideas and the application of these ideas to produce original works of artistic cultural products, functional creations, scientific inventions, and technological innovations.[97] Copyright is now widely acknowledged as an essential tool for development.[98] It rewards the expression of human creativity and provides individuals with

---

[92] Okediji above n 74, 38; Dalindyebo Shabalala, *Towards A Digital Agenda for Developing Countries*, Research *Papers 13* (August 2007) South Center, 21 <http://www.southcentre.org/index.php?option=com_content&task=view&id=65&Itemid=1>.

[93] Consumers International, *Copyright and Access to Knowledge, Policy Recommendations on Flexibilities in Copyright Laws* (2006) Soros Foundation <http://www.soros.org/initiatives/information/focus/access/articles_publications/publications/copyright_20060602>.

[94] Jeremy Malcolm, 'Intellectual Property as a Consumer Issue and Global Consumer Dialogue on A2K issues'(Presentation at the A2K Conference, Kuala Lumpur, Malaysia, 17 February 2009).

[95] See Lea Shaver (ed), *Access to Knowledge in Brazil* (Bloomsbury, 2010); Jack M. Balkin, 'What is Access to Knowledge?' (21 April 2006) <http://balkin.blogspot.com/2006/04/what-is-access-to-knowledge.html>.

[96] United Nations (UN), *Creative Economy Report* (2008) UNCTAD <http://www.unctad.org/en/docs/ditc20082cer_en.pdf>. Michael Kelly notes that 'Creativity and its cognates mean that ability to produce something original (in the sense of new rather than authentic) in the arts, in the sciences and other endeavour'. See Michael Kelly, *Encyclopaedia of Aesthetics* (Oxford University, 1998) 453, 456.

[97] It is also important to examine how IP laws can boost innovation in developing and emerging economies. See Luisa Massarani, *Brazil's Innovation Law: Lessons for Latin America* (3 August 2006) SciDev.net <http://www.scidev.net/en/editorials/brazils-innovation-law-lessons-for-latin-america.html>.

[98] Ibid. John Howkins notes that: '[c]reativity has a profound effect on society, and is considered as a 'critical component of success in the global knowledge-based economy… [it] is the origin of human and economic growth and of socio- cultural political development'. See also John Howkins, *Who Owns the Law? A New Approach to Intellectual Property*, based on a submission to the Gowers Review, UK, TM Treasury <http://www.hm-treasury.gov.uk/d/john_howkins_230_33kb.pdf>; UNCTAD, *World Investment Report Foreign Direct Investment and the Challenge of Development* (1999) <http://www.unctad.org/en/docs/wir1999_en.pdf>.

the incentives to engage in the creativity process and to receive an award through the grant of time-limited monopolies.[99] It plays an important role in determining how humans think about creativity.[100] Creativity is universally agreed to be a good that copyright law should seek to promote,[101] and IP scholars are debating what could be the best form of copyright protection suitable to promote it.[102]

1.2.2.3 Copyright and Social and Economic Development in the Internet Age

Much of the digital content that is distributed and made available for viewing or downloading through the Internet is protected by copyright.[103] Copyright has

---

[99] WIPO noted that:

> Copyright provides protection to original works of authorship, such as paintings, sculpture, music, novels, poems, plays, architecture, dance, instruction manuals, technical documentation and software. Copyright laws give statutory expression to the economic and moral rights of creators in their creations and the rights of the public in the access to those creations. They also aim to promote, as a deliberate act of government policy, creativity and the dissemination and application of its results and encourage fair-trading as a means by which to contribute to economic and social development.

See WIPO, *Intellectual Property on the Internet: A Survey of Issues* (December 2002) <http://www.wipo.int/export/sites/www/copyright/en/ecommerce/pdf/survey.pdf>; UN, above n 96, 144.

[100] Liang, above n 77.

[101] Professor Cohen argues that:

> Put differently, if copyright is not the most important factor in stimulating creativity; it still may be the most important factor within our control. If copyright serves other important functions, such as the organization of private cultural production and the distribution of artistic and intellectual goods, perhaps strong copyright is good policy. Here the decentred model of creativity makes its second contribution: it provides a firmer foundation for arguments about the systemic harms that a regime of copyright can produce. Critics of copyright maximalism have long argued that overly rigid control of access to and manipulation of cultural goods stifles artistic and cultural innovation, and a growing body of anecdotal evidence suggests that copyright's 'permission culture' does exert a substantial constraining influence on creative practice . . . . Copyright fulfils some important economic functions (of which more shortly), and therefore plays an important role in organizing cultural production, but it is hardly ever the direct cause of a representational shift in creative practice, nor does it appear to play a direct role in motivating much that is normal science. Scholars who ask how deploying copyright might stimulate creativity (as opposed to production) are asking the wrong question. Neither creative inspiration nor the creative outputs that follow from it are so easily engineered. Questions remain, however, about the extent to which the contextual factors that are more important in stimulating creativity are amenable to social engineering.

Cohen, above n 49, 1193; Dennis S. Karjala, *Creativity and Copyright* (February 2008) <http://works.bepress.com/cgi/viewcontent.cgi?article=1002&context=dennis_karjala>.

[102] Cohen, above n 49, 101.

[103] Brian Fitzgerald et al, *Internet and E-Commerce Law* (Thomson, Sydney, 2007) 154.

emerged as one of the most forceful means of regulating the flow of ideas and knowledge-based products in the twenty-first century.[104] It is at the centre of our society, government, social networking, and digital content production and consumption; education and research rely on copyright. Its ultimate goal is to encourage innovation and creativity.[105] Consumers in developing countries are using new types of media via the Internet such as YouTube,[106] MySpace,[107] Facebook,[108] Flickr,[109] Twitter,[110] and Wikipedia,[111] and these platforms continue to raise significant challenges for copyright. The important question is whether those copyright systems introduced as a result of globalisation and internalisation have led to social and economic development in developing countries.

The challenge for developing countries is to design copyright systems that will deal properly with the difficulties posed by the rise of the Internet and digital technologies. If developing countries want to develop their knowledge-based economy and to become a regional hub for information communication technologies, they need to critically examine their existing copyright systems.

1.2.3 Relevance of the Internet to Developing Countries

The Internet has emerged as one of the most profound social, technological, and business phenomena in the history of humankind. It is transforming businesses, altering the way people communicate, and providing humans with access to a

---

104 See Tana Pistorius, 'Developing Countries and Copyright in the Information Age—The Functional Equivalent Implementation of the WCT' (2006) 9 (2) Potchefstroom Electronic Law Journal/Potchefstroomse Elektroniese Regsblad <http://www.saflii.org/za/journals/PER/2006/11.html>, citing, Armstrong and Ford (2005); United Nations Educational, Scientific and Cultural Organization (UNESCO), *World Information Report* (1997/98) <http://unesdoc.unesco.org/images/0010/001062/106215e.pdf>.

105 Professor Neil Netanel notes that 'copyright should also encourage creative expression on a wide array of political, social and aesthetic issues as a vital component of a democratic civil society'. See Neil W Netanel 'Copyright and a Democratic Civil Society' (1996) 106 *Yale School Law Journal* 283.

See also Eddan Katz, Rudy Kleysteuber and Christen Linke Young, *Common Knowledge - How Access to Information and Ideas Can Drive Development* (2011) Panos London <http://panos.org.uk/wp-content/files/2011/03/common_knowledgeeI172y.pdf>. Altbach, above n 78; Okediji, above n 87.

106 YouTube <http://www.youtube.com>.

107 MySpace <http://www.myspace.com>.

108 Facebook <http://www.facebook.com>.

109 Flickr <http://www.flickr.com>.

110 Twitter <http://www.twitter.com>.

111 Wikipedia <http://www.wikipedia.org>.

wealth of easily accessible information.[112] Technological developments such as the printing press, telephones, nuclear technology, aerospace technology, environmental technology, and computing technology have fundamentally changed society. The most notable change in recent times that has transformed our daily lives in many respects has been the advancement of digital technologies.[113] Digital technologies and interconnected networks have an important role to play in developing countries in expanding and improving education, putting knowledge and research outputs into the public domain, and facilitating collaborations amongst tertiary and research bodies.[114]

The globalisation of information offers a vast array of opportunities for all persons. The Internet has the potential to neutralise inequities based on gender, race, creed, or nationality by making such factors irrelevant in providing opportunities for economic advantage.[115] Developing countries that traditionally have insufficient capacity to disseminate and effectively utilise educational information and knowledge may finally be in a position to accelerate their development through the use of Internet technologies.[116]

Internet applications offer an unprecedented possibility for access and delivery of important socio-economic inputs such as education, medical information, and, in a more limited fashion, health care and other associated services. They also offer new opportunities for domestic cultural industries to penetrate global markets.[117] The Internet has made it possible to access up-to-date information about any number of subjects and to improve the quality of educational materials, innovation, and research[118] that are currently available in developing countries.[119] The Internet can also have a hortatory effect on the quality of life in developing countries by improving the levels of general participation in civil society and, ultimately, improving democratic governance and delivery of government services.[120] It can also be used to address infrastructure barriers that have hindered traditional means of supply and distribution in developing countries.[121]

---

[112] International Telecommunication Union (ITU), *Internet for the Arab World* (2000) <http://www.itu.int/ITU-D/ict/papers/egypt2000/15-e.pdf>.

[113] Fitzgerald, above n 103,154.

[114] Pistorius, above n 104.

[115] Okediji, above n 71,181.

[116] Shabalala, above 92, 6-15.

[117] Okediji, above 74, 12-16 and 32.

[118] Professor James Boyle was optimistic about the Internet revolution. He notes:

> The Internet offers us remarkable opportunities to achieve the real goals that intellectual property policy *ought* to serve: encouraging innovation and facilitating the dissemination of cultural and educational materials.

Boyle, above 57.

[119] Benkler, above 61, 354.

[120] Ibid.

[121] Ibid.

The Internet is a 'democratising technology' that has tremendous potential to provide freedom of expression to persons who do not own a printing press or a television station.[122] Commercially, it also offers new opportunities to increase economic productivity in all countries, regardless of the level of their development.[123]

The Internet also gives citizens in developing countries the power to participate in the global phenomenon of 'remix culture',[124] which has been facilitated through the Internet. Remix culture is a growing movement to create new artistic and creative work by combining elements of existing work, which is substantially supported through Internet technologies. It is becoming more and more prevalent because digital technologies allow for the effortless modification of existing works, and the combination of existing works increases the possibility of creating new and improved works.[125] Remix is a key feature of the data-driven world we now inhabit. Remix culture is no longer seen as a fringe activity; rather, it is a methodology that underpins the construction of knowledge in the Internet age. Large corporations, governments, NGOs, individuals, and educational institutions are using the Internet to access public sector information (PSI) and data research materials as part of their everyday activities.

The Internet could also assist developing countries in producing cultural works because it allows them 'to think for themselves reflecting Kant's aspiration for humankind'.[126] The Internet and digital technologies also help music producers and artists to penetrate certain global markets[127] that they could not previously access.

It is, however, noted that the benefit that can be derived from the Internet cannot be realised without having trained persons who are fully capable of absorbing what technology has to offer and integrating it into their daily lives and work activities.[128] It is also important to design appropriate IP systems to ensure that the Internet is ultimately used to widen human choices and foster development in developing countries.[129]

As part of this subsection, the various meanings of 'developing countries' will be examined.

---

[122] Many scholars are hoping that the technological revolution would fuel a social one, ushering in a 'semiotic democracy' in which everyone would have the power to create and disseminate cultural knowledge. See Sunder, above 54, 279.

[123] Okediji, above 74,11.

[124] For an explanation of the 'remix culture', see Lawrence Lessig, *Remix: Making Art and Commerce Thrive in the Hybrid Economy* (Bloomsbury, 2008).

[125] Yuko Nouguchi, 'Toward a Better—Balance Copyright Regulations in the Digital and Network Era - Law, Technology, and the Market in the US and Japan' (unpublished SJD Thesis, Stanford University, 2006) 32.

[126] Sunder, above 54, 276.

[127] Okediji, above 74, 32.

[128] Kariyawasam, above n 8, 253.

[129] Wong and Dutfield, above 49, xvil.

1.2.4 The Meaning of 'Developing Countries'

There is no established convention for designating a country as 'developed' or 'developing',[130] and major international organisations apply different factors in classifying countries.[131] The International Monetary Fund (IMF) divides countries into two major groups: advanced economies or emerging economies and developing economies.[132] The United Nations categorises developing countries into several groups based on factors such as income, education, healthcare, and life expectancy.[133] The World Bank classifies countries, according to their gross national income (GNI) per capita,[134] into the following categories:

- Low income ($995 or less);
- Lower middle income ($996–$3,945);
- Upper middle income ($3,946–$12,195); and
- High income ($12,196 or more).[135]

The UNCTAD 'Trade and Development Report 2011' identifies Japan and Israel (in Asia), Canada and the United States (in North America), Australia and New Zealand (in Oceania), and the EU Member States as developed countries,[136] while others are either developing countries or least developing countries (LDCs).[137] Henrik Horn and Petros Mavroidis have proposed five criteria for assessing whether a country falls within the category of developing countries:

---

[130] Organisation for Economic Co-operation and Development (OECD), *Developed, Developing Countries* (4 January 2006) <http://stats.oecd.org/glossary/detail.asp?ID=6326>; World Trade Organization (WTO), *Who are the Developing Countries in the WTO?* <http://www.wto.org/english/tratop_e/devel_e/d1who_e.htm>

[131] By Tina Aridas and Alessandro Magno, *Countries Classified by Income Group*, Global Finance <http://www.gfmag.com/tools/global-database/economic-data/10298-countries-by-income-group.html#axzz1IitlGIPQ>.

[132] International Monetary Fund (IMF), *WEO Groups and Aggregates Information* (1 April 2010) <http://www.imf.org/external/pubs/ft/weo/2010/01/weodata/groups.htm#oem>.

[133] See also United Nations Statistics Division (UNSTATS), *Composition of Macro Geographical (continental) Regions, Geographical Sub-Regions, and Selected Economic and other Groupings* (17 February 2011) <http://unstats.un.org/unsd/methods/m49/m49regin.htm>.

[134] That is 'the dollar value of a country's final income in a year divided buy its population'. See Aridas and Magno, above n 131.

[135] World Bank, *How We Classify Countries* <http://data.worldbank.org/about/country-classifications>.

[136] United Nations Conference on Trade and Development (UNCTAD), *Trade and Development Report 2011* <http://www.unctad.org/en/docs/tdr2011_en.pdf>.

[137] The Organisation for Economic Co-operation and Development (OECD) has three members not considered as developed countries, but emerging economies and these are: Mexico, Turkey and the Russian Federation. See OECD, *Members and Partners* <http://www.oecd.org/pages/0,3417,en_36734052_36761800_1_1_1_1_1,00.html>.

i) Small GNP relative to the major players in the trade arena;
ii) Limited domestic resources;
iii) Exports concentrated in terms of products and trading partners;
iv) High average trade barriers; and
v) Economic and political dependence on industrial countries.[138]

Within the category of developing countries, it is also possible to distinguish between 'LDCs' and 'emerging economies' or 'newly industrialised countries'. The United Nations applies three criteria for identifying LDCs:

i) A low-income criterion based on a 3-year average estimate of the gross national income (GNI) per capita (under $905 for inclusion, above $1,086 for graduation);[139]
ii) A weak human capital status criterion, involving a composite of human assets index (HAI) based on (a) nutrition: percentage of population undernourished; (b) health: mortality rate for children aged 5 years or under; (c) education: gross secondary school enrolment ratio; and (d) adult literacy rate;[140] and
iii) An economic vulnerability criterion measured through a composite economic vulnerability index (EVI) based on indicators of (a) population size; (b) remoteness; (c) merchandise export concentration; (d) share of agriculture, forestry, and fisheries in gross domestic products; (e) homelessness owing to natural disasters; (f) instability of agricultural production; and (g) instability of exports of goods and services.[141]

Countries in the LDC category are the poorest in the world. While poverty exists in both developed and developing countries, it is most prevalent in LDCs.[142] The United Nations currently designates 48 countries as LDCs, 33 of which are in Africa, 14 in Asia, and one in Latin America and the Caribbean.[143]

[138] See Henrik Horn and Petros C. Mavroidis, *Remedies in the WTO Dispute Settlement System and Developing Countries Interests* (20 March 1999) Henrik Horn <http://www.econ-law.se/Papers/Remedies%20990611-1.pdf>.

[139] See Office of the High Representative for the Least Developed Countries, *Landlocked Developing Countries and Small Island Developing States (UN-OHRLLS)* <http://www.unohrlls.org/en/ldc/related/59/>.

[140] Ibid.

[141] Ibid.

[142] See Yong-Shik Lee, 'Theoretical Basis and Regulatory Framework for Microtrade: Combining Volunteerism with International Trade towards Poverty Elimination', (2009) 2 (1) *Law and Development Review* 367-399 <http://www.lawanddevelopment.net/yslee_microtrade_october2010.pdf>.

[143] See UN-OHRLLS, *LDCs* <http://www.unohrlls.org/en/ldc/related/62/>. See also One World Nations Online, *Countries of the Third World* <http://www.nationsonline.org/oneworld/third_world.htm>.

'Emerging economies' can be defined as 'countries that are restructuring their economies along market-oriented lines and [that] offer a wealth of opportunities in trade, technology transfers, and foreign direct investment'.[144] These countries are also known as 'newly industrialised countries' or NICs, defined as 'countries with economies more advanced and developed than those in developing countries, but not yet with the full signs of a developed country'.[145] According to the World Bank, the five biggest emerging markets are China, India, Indonesia, Brazil, and Russia.[146]

There is a lack of uniformity in the way the various terms and classifications are used. One categorisation distinguishes between industrialised countries, emerging economies, and developing countries. Another divides countries into two main groups, developed countries and LDCs, with the LDC category also encompassing developing countries. Others use the term 'less-developed countries' to describe the broad category that includes both developing countries and LDCs. Shamand Basheer and Annalisa Primi argue that there is a need to move away from an outdated developed-versus-developing-countries classification and to differentiate developing countries according to their technological and innovative proficiencies.[147] Such differentiation, in their opinion, would help calibrate IP norms according to the specific developmental needs of a country in question.[148] The problem with such a proposal is the difficulty in reaching an agreement on the criteria to be used in assessing and classifying countries according to their technological or innovative capabilities.

This book primarily focuses on developing countries, the term being used to refer to countries identified as such by applying the factors described by the United Nations[149] but excluding those countries that fall within the category of LDCs.[150] Use of the term 'developing countries' in this sense—that is, excluding LDCs—is generally accepted among experts and international organisations working in the field of development studies.

---

[144] John F. Robinson and Gary D. Mizel, The New Global Economy (Opportunities for M/WBEs In Emerging Markets Worldwide) (5 Janyary 2010) The National Minority Business Council <http://nmbcblog.wordpress.com/2010/01/05/the-new-global-economy-opportunities-for-mwbes-in-emerging-markets-worldwide/>, citing Chuan Li, *What are Emerging Markets?*

[145] Ibid.

[146] Ibid.

[147] Shamnad Basheer and Annalisa Primi, 'The WIPO Development Agenda: Factoring in the 'Technologically Proficient', Developing Countries' in Jeremy de Beer, *Implementing the World Intellectual Property Organization's Development Agenda* (Wifrid Laurier, 2009) 100, 102.

[148] Ibid.

[149] See UNSTATS, above n 133.

[150] See UN-OHRLLS, above n 139.

1.2.5 Concluding Remarks

'Development' is a contested term among scholars, organisations, and development experts in developed and developing countries. Nevertheless, it is one of the most important challenges facing the international community and has been widely acknowledged in many international conventions and forums (including the United Nations Millennium Summit in 2000). Generally, development encapsulates the improvement of the lives of individuals by providing better education, skills development, income, and employment. It can also mean the improvements of people lives either socially or economically. Sustainable development is a concept that was first developed in the 1980s and is mostly related to protecting the environment. 'Developing countries' are those countries with low levels of income and standards of living.

There are differing views on the interaction between IP systems and development. Theories originally formulated in the 1950s and 1960s suggest that a system of IP is a necessary part of the evolution of developing countries from being 'underdeveloped' to becoming 'developed.' These theories suggest that a strong IP system is needed in developing countries to achieve social and economic development. Many IP scholars are doubtful as to whether having these laws would be enough to assist developing countries. They believe that it is important to first build strong political and economic systems that will promote the development of developing countries.

IP forms the legal sinews of the information age; it affects everything from the patterns of international development to the communication architecture of the Internet.[151] IP is a means of promoting development (and, implicitly, a means of thwarting development)[152] since it calibrates the flow of innumerable goods and resources that are relevant to advancing capabilities in all developing countries, including medicine, books, computers, seeds, radios, and clean-energy turbines.[153] Copyright protects a wide range of tools that are vital to the education, health, technical literacy, and development of developing countries. Copyright laws have an important role to play in facilitating A2K and in bolstering a rich and open public domain that developing countries need in order to achieve human welfare and economic development. Appropriate copyright laws that reward creators in developing countries can also enrich creativity.

The Internet provides developing countries with many opportunities that they can utilise to further their development. For the citizens of those countries, it opens a world of information and knowledge that could be used to develop research and education and to increase economic returns. Furthermore, it allows people to express their opinions freely without being subjected to anyone's prior approval,

151 Boyle, above n 57.

152 Sunder, above 54, 314.

153 Wong and Dutfield, above n 49, xvxvii.

and this would result in technological independence.[154] It is important to structure appropriate IP laws that allow people in developing countries to use the Internet for their development advantage.

1.3 Scope and Structure of the Book

1.3.1 Scope

This book conceptualises the theory of IP and development and provides specific suggestions and recommendations for developing countries to assist them in their path towards social and economic development. It considers in a holistic way the historical, economic, cultural, and practical effects of introducing IP systems into developing countries[155] and suggests the adoption of a development-oriented approach.

---

[154] The potential for Internet usage could be limited by the digital divide and this need to be addressed. Developing countries have to: 1) raise the awareness of the general public and decision makers of the importance of the Internet for social and economic development; 2) formulate and develop policies related to Internet and its impact on citizens; 3) introduce new laws or amend old ones to guarantee the non interference with Internet usage of citizens for development purposes; and 4) support Internet usage and accessibility through public resources. See also Rami Olwan and Ghaith El Lawzi, *ICT and Digital Divide in the Arab World, Olwan.com* <http://www.olwan.com/newsDetails.asp?InfoID=947&CatID=&CatName=&PICNAME=Publications>.

[155] See generally the following research on IP and development:

Robert M. Sherwood, *Intellectual Property and Economic Development* (Westview, 1990); Philip G. Altbach (ed), *Copyright and Development: Inequality in the Information Age* (Bellagio, 1995); Yong Shik Lee, *Reclaiming Development in the World Trading System* (Cambridge, 2006); Keith Maskus, *Intellectual Property Rights in the Global Economy* (Institute for International Economics, 2000) <http://bookstore.piie.com/book-store//99.html>; Keith Maskus (ed), *Intellectual Property, Growth and Trade* (Elsevier, 2008); Jeremy de Beer, *Implementing the World Intellectual Property Organization's Development Agenda* (Wilfrid Laurier University, 2009); Carsten Fink and Keith Maskus (ed), *Intellectual Property and Economic Development Lessons from the Recent Economic Research* (The World Bank, 2005); Neil Weinstock Netanel (ed), *The Development Agenda- Global Intellectual Property and Developing Countries* (Oxford, 2009); Tzen Wong and Graham Dutfield, *Intellectual Property and Human Development* (Cambridge, 2011); Ricardo Melendez-Ortiz and Pedro Roffe (ed), *Intellectual Property and Sustainable Development: Development Agenda in a Changing World* (Edward Elgar, 2010); Hirouki Odagiri et al (eds), *Intellectual Property Rights, Development and Catch UP* (Oxford, 2010); Nagla Rizk and Lea Shaver (ed), *Access to Knowledge in Egypt* (Bloomsbury, 2010); Lea Shaver (ed), *Access to Knowledge in Brazil* (Bloomsbury, 2010) <http://www.law.yale.edu/documents/pdf/ISP/A2KBrazil_bkmk.pdf>; Margaret Chon, 'Intellectual Property and the Development Divide' (2006) 27 *Cardozo Law Review*, 2821, <http://www.abifina.org.br/arquivos/encontros/Margaret_Chon.pdf>; Denis Borges Barbosa, Margaret Chon and Andres Moncayo von, 'Slouching Towards Development in International Intellectual Property' (2007) *Michigan State Law Review*, 71 <http://papers.ssrn.com/sol3/papers.cfm?abstract_id=1081366>; Margaret Chon, *Intellectual Property from Below: Copyright and Capability for Education*, 818, <http://papers.ssrn.com/sol3/papers.cfm?abstract_id=971294>; Madhavi Sunder, 'IP3' (2006) 59 (2) *Stanford Law Review* <http://papers.ssrn.com/sol3/papers.cfm?abstract_id=897753>;

Social and economic development is a complicated process that involves government efficiency, coherent economic policies, political stability, educated human capital, technical infrastructure, availability of financial resources (loans), the rule of law, and an effective judiciary. There is no specific definition of 'development', and there are many definitions that could be used, depending on the outcome that the particular developing country wants to achieve (whether political, economic, or social). In examining the relationship between IP systems and development, this book focuses on social and economic development.

Jordan is selected as the subject for a case study for a number of reasons. Being a middle-income developing country, Jordan represents the category of developing

---

Ruth L. Okediji, *Development in the Information Age*, Issue Paper No. 9 - UNCTAD – ICTSD Project on IPRs and Sustainable Development (May 2004) <http://www.iprsonline.org/unctadictsd/docs/CS_Okediji.pdf>; Ruth L Gana (Okediji), 'The Myth of Development, the Progress of Rights: Human Rights to Intellectual Property and Development (1996) 18 *Law and Policy Law Journal*, 315; Ruth Gana Okediji, 'Copyright and Public Welfare in Global Perspective' (1999-2000) 7 *Indiana Journal of Global Legal Studies* 117,181; Lea Shaver, 'The Right to Science and Culture' (2010) *Wisconsin Law Review* 121, 160 <http://papers.ssrn.com/sol3/papers.cfm?abstract_id=1354788>; Rosemary J Coombe, *The Culture Life of Intellectual Properties* (Duke University, 1998); Nicole Aylwin, Rosemary J. Coombe and Anita Chan, *Intellectual Property, Cultural Heritage and Rights-Based Development: Geographical Indication as Vehicles for Sustainable Livelihoods*, York University <http://www.yorku.ca>; Emmanuel Hassan, Ohid Yaqub and Stephanie Diepeveen, *Intellectual Property and Developing Countries: A Review of the Literature*, a technical report prepared to the UK Intellectual Property Office and the UK Department for International Development, (2010) RAND Corporation (Europe) <http://www.rand.org/pubs/technical_reports/2010/RAND_TR804.pdf>; Jean Raymond Hormere, Intellectual Property Rights Can Help Stimulate the Economic Development of Least Developed Countries (2004) 27 (2) *Columbia Journal of Law and the Arts* 277-299; Assafa Endeshaw, *Intellectual Property in Asian Emerging Economies* (Ashgate, 2010), ch 12; Bryan Mercurio,'Intellectual Property Rights and Economic Development' in *Law and Development Perspective on International Trade Law*, edited by Y.S. Lee et al, (Cambridge University, 2011); Michael Blakeney and Getachew Mengistie, 'Intellectual Property and Economic Development in Sub-Saharan Africa' (2011) 14 *Journal of World Intellectual Property* 238; Jeremy de Beer and Chidi Oguamanam, Intellectual Property Training and Education, Issue Paper No. 31 - UNCTAD–ICTSD Project on IPRs and Sustainable Development (November 2010) <http://ictsd.org/downloads/2010/11/iptrainingandeducation.pdf>; Matthews Duncan, *Intellectual Property, Human Rights and Development The Role of NGOs and Social Movement* (Edward Elgar, 2011); Ramesh Subramanian and Lea Shaver (eds), *Access to Knowledge in India* (Bloomsbury Academic, 2011); Hiroko Yamane, Interpreting TRIPS (Hart, 2011) ch 2; Chidi Oguamanam, *Intellectual Property in Global Governance: A Development Question* (Routlege, 2012); Jonathan D. Putnam and Andrew B. Tepperman, 'Intellectual Property Rights and Economic Progress: A Review of the Literature' in Robert E. Litan, Handbook on Law, Innovation and Growth (Edward Elgar, 2011), 113; Margaret Chon, 'A Rough Guide to Global Intellectual Property Pluralism' in Rochelle C. Dreyfuss et al (ed), *Working with the Boundaries of Intellectual Property* (Oxford, 2010) 446, 458-463; Ida Madieha Abdul Ghani Azmi, Lim Heng Gee and Rokiah Alavi, *Intellectual Property System and Industrial Development in Malaysia* (International Islamic University Malaysia, 2009).

countries within the classification adopted by the World Bank.[156] It is a good example of a developing country that is using its limited resources to make necessary changes for social and economic development. Jordan considers its people to be at the heart of its development and future strength. Consequently, it has adopted a human-centred approach to development that enhances people's choices in every aspect of life, traversing the social, economic, and cultural spheres.[157] Like many other developing countries, Jordan perceives the importance of trade and investment to its economic future and has embarked upon major economic reforms to make it a more attractive environment for foreign direct investment. Jordan signed an association agreement with the European Union on 24 November 1997, became a member of the WTO on 11 April 2000, and, on 24 October 2000, became only the second Middle East country (after Israel) to sign a free trade agreement (FTA) with the US. It has also entered into FTAs with other countries, including Canada, Singapore, Malaysia, and Turkey.

Another important reason for selecting Jordan is that it has introduced a high level of IP protection similar to that found in the IP systems in force in developed countries. Upon accession to the WTO, it was necessary for Jordan to restructure its IP legal system to bring it into conformity with international standards. Jordan introduced many new IP laws and joined major IP treaties, including the WCT and WPPT, in the hope that this would boost innovation and development. Despite these major economic and legal changes, there are concerns that they have had limited impact on the country and its social and economic development. The purpose of the case study is to evaluate and examine how IP systems in a developing country such as Jordan may more effectively boost innovation and social and economic development.

1.3.2 Structure

This book is divided into two parts and is comprised of eight chapters. Part I examines the theory of IP and social and economic development (Chaps. 2–4). It discusses the views of IP scholars and economists on whether, and how, IP systems can contribute to the social and economic development of developing countries. Part II examines the practice of IP and social and economic development. It provides practical guidance on how IP systems, and particularly copyright, may serve the social and economic development objectives of developing countries (Chaps. 5–7).

---

[156] The World Bank lists 56 developing countries as lower middle income economies, 40 of those are classified as lower income economies and 48 are classified as upper middle income economies. See the World Bank, *Country and Lending Groups* <http://data.worldbank.org/about/country-classifications/country-and-lending-groups>.

[157] United Nations Development Program (UNDP), *Jordan Human Development Report Building a Sustainable Livelihood*, (2004) <http://hdr.undp.org/en/reports/national/arabstates/jordan/jordan_2004_en.pdf>.

Chapter 2 provides a historical introduction to the chapters that follow. It begins by examining how the term 'development' was considered when European countries initiated the international IP system in the nineteenth century. It shows that the discussions on IP and development commenced much earlier than has been generally recognised, when developing countries were obliged by their colonizers to join the international IP treaties. The chapter traces the fierce opposition of developing countries and their constant demands to change the international IP system to meet their developmental needs. Brazil and India led other developing countries in obtaining revisions to the Berne and Paris conventions and have made numerous revisions to their domestic IP laws to suit their local conditions. The chapter also considers the development of the international IP system through the linking of IP and trade as embodied in the *TRIPS Agreement* adopted at the conclusion of the Uruguay Round in 1994. Developments at the international level post-TRIPS, including the expansion in FTAs, the Doha Round of WTO negotiations, the WIPO Development Agenda, the A2K Treaty and ACTA, are also considered.

Chapter 3 examines the relationship between IP and economic development and assesses the extent to which the international IP system can assist developing countries in their economic development. Little is gained by repeating the traditional argument—constantly reiterated by scholars and international organisations—that having an IP system enables developing countries to develop economically. The chapter confirms the findings of other studies that the introduction of IP systems, without more, is not sufficient to assist developing countries in their economic development. The chapter examines the various issues that need to be carefully considered by any developing country that wishes to use the IP system to support its economic development. Empirical evidence is examined to evaluate the effect of IP on the economic performance of developing countries.

Chapter 4 serves as a transitional chapter between parts I and II. It considers the importance of localization of culture in the IP and development debate. It examines particularly the relationship between IP and social development and the relevance of culture in shaping IP laws in developing countries. It also considers the views of scholars on the importance of IP systems for ensuring the continuance of local cultures and concludes by proposing the adoption of a cultural policy for IP and social development in developing countries and the implementation of flexible copyright laws that preserve culture and promote development.

Chapter 5 deals with how, in practice, a development-oriented approach to IP and copyright can be implemented in the IP laws of developing countries. The chapter considers the Jordanian IP system as a case study, with a particular focus on copyright law. An overview of the copyright law in Jordan is provided, and historical influences on its development are described. In the Jordanian context, proposals are made for amendments to the copyright law to enable it to better serve the developmental needs of Jordan and its citizens. The chapter also provides practical suggestions and recommendations for improvements to the copyright laws in developing countries, to enable it to grasp the various opportunities that the Internet offers.

Chapter 6 discusses how voluntary mechanisms—in particular, FOSS and open content licences (such as CC licences)—can be used to manage IP rights in a manner consistent with development objectives. The licensing of copyright materials under CC licences is seen as a mechanism for fostering open access to knowledge-based content in developing countries. The chapter provides an overview of the development of the 'openness movement' in the IT industry, particularly in relation to open source software and its spread in popularity. The philosophy and basic principles of FOSS and CC copyright licensing are considered, as well as the legality and enforceability of open content licences. The chapter concludes by setting out practical recommendations as to how developing countries can make use of open copyright licensing models such as FOSS and CC to advance their social and economic development.

Chapter 7 provides policy recommendations for developing countries on how to utilise and implement IP laws to further social and economic development. Chapter 8 ties together the various themes explored throughout the book. It provides specific recommendations for developing countries on how to best structure their IP systems in a manner that will serve their social and economic development objectives.

Chapter 6 discusses how voluntary mechanisms [illegible] content [illegible] such as CC licences can be used [illegible]

Part I
The Theory of Intellectual Property and Social and Economic Development

Many studies consider only the economic benefits of IP systems for developing countries. However, there are many different perspectives on the relationship between IP and development. Part I analyses these different perspectives, going beyond the economic perspective to consider the history of the adoption of IP systems by developing countries. It calls for a broader theory of IP and development which extends to incorporate cultural perspectives on IP and social and economic development. This part is intended to contribute to the formulation of a new theory of IP and development, based on interrelations between history, economics, culture and other issues relevant to the interests of developing countries.

Chapter 2
The History of International Intellectual Property and Development

> *If it is a sin for the poor to steal from the rich, it must be a much bigger sin for the rich to steal from the poor. Don't rich countries pirate poor countries' best scientists, engineers, doctors, nurses and programmers? When global corporations come to operate... [D]on't they pirate the best people from local firms? If it is bad for poor countries like ours to pirate the IP of rich countries, isn't it a lot worse for rich countries like the US to pirate our intellectuals? In fact, we are benign enough to take only a copy, leaving the original behind; rich countries are so greedy that they take away the originals, leaving nothing behind.*[1]
>
> *Our missionaries live in Hollywood. Expecting the Berne Appendix to be of any serious value to the countries of the global South is simply another missionary fantasy story, whether it is made in Hollywood or Bollywood... or by an NGO.*[2]

Abstract Having examined the meaning of development, Part I considers the theories of IP as they relate to development. This chapter examines the history of the international IP system from the perspective of development, drawing conclusions and lessons for the future. It shows the divergent approaches of developed and developing countries towards IP and how developing countries consistently, but unsuccessfully, sought changes to the international IP system. The chapter demonstrates that there is no evidence to show that the development of developing countries has been promoted by the adoption of IP systems and that, to the contrary, many countries have developed even though they have no, or weak, IP systems. The chapter provides some suggestions for consideration by developing countries and serves as a foundation for subsequent chapters that require a degree of familiarity with the stages in the development of the international IP system.

---

[1] Roberto Verzola, 'Pegging the World's Biggest' (1997) 12 (2) *Earth Island Journal* 41.

[2] Irving Kristol, cited in Alan Story, 'A2K the Berne Appendix' on A2K (29 September 2009) <http://lists.essential.org/pipermail/a2k/2009-September/004954.html>.

R.M. Olwan, *Intellectual Property and Development*,
DOI 10.1007/978-3-642-27907-2_2, © Springer-Verlag Berlin Heidelberg 2013

2.1 Overview

The history of IP and development has passed through three distinctive phases.[3] In the first phase, which saw the emergence of IP systems in medieval Europe, developing countries played no part in shaping the international IP system. This phase witnessed the first formal encounter of developing countries with the international IP system in the colonial era. The second phase was the international period during which few developing countries joined the *Paris Convention* and the *Berne Convention* but repeatedly called for revision of these conventions. The third phase witnessed the successful lobbying of developed countries, particularly the US, which led to the linking of IP with trade, the establishment of the WTO, and the adoption of the *TRIPS Agreement* (Trade-Related Intellectual Property Aspects). This period witnessed an increase in the number of developing countries seeking to reform the international IP system, to take into account their needs and local conditions.

In this chapter, the history and development of the international IP system are examined. Studying the political influences that shaped the discussions about IP between developed and developing countries enables their divergent views on IP to be understood and reconciled and contributes to the rethinking of the international IP system. This chapter demonstrates that there is no established case to support assertions that adopting strong IP systems assisted developing countries in their development. It offers suggestions for developing countries that can be useful for the future development of the international IP system.

2.2 The Evolution of the International IP System in the Nineteenth Century

The desire of the international community to reach a consensus on international IP is not a new phenomenon.[4] The first contact between developing countries and the global IP system occurred at the end of the nineteenth century, when developed

---

[3] See Peter Drahos, *The Universality of Intellectual Property Rights: Origins and Development*, WIPO, 8 <http://www.wipo.int/tk/en/hr/paneldiscussion/papers/pdf/drahos.pdf>.

[4] On the historical development of the international IP system, see the following:

Silke V. Lewinski, *International Copyright Law and Policy* (Oxford University, 2008) 13-32; Paul Goldstein, *International Copyright Principles, Law and Practice* (Oxford University, 2001) 53; S. M. Stewart, *International Copyright and Neighbouring Rights* (Butterworths, 2nd, 1989); Zorina Khan, *Intellectual Property and Economic Development: Lessons from American and European History* (September 2002) Commission on Intellectual Property Rights <http://www.iprcommission.org/papers/pdfs/study_papers/sp1a_khan_study.pdf>; John Barton et al., *Integrating Intellectual Property Rights and Development Policy* (September 2002) Commission on Intellectual Property Rights (CIPR) <http://www.iprcommission.org/papers/pdfs/final_report/CIPRfullfinal.pdf>; Alan Story, 'Burn Burne, Why the Leading International Copyright Convention Must Be Repealed' (2003) 40 *Houston Law Review* 763, 792; Ruth L. Gana (Okediji), 'The Myth of Development, the Progress of Rights: Human Rights to Intellectual Property and Development' (1996) 18 *Law and Policy Journal* 315, 319-328; Christopher May and Susan K.

countries adopted the first multilateral agreements, although new developing countries were also signatories to these treaties. Developing countries began to question the suitability of the international IP system to meet their needs and to request specific adjustments[5] to the two main treaties, the *Paris Convention* and the *Berne Convention*.[6]

2.2.1 *The Paris Convention of 1883*

The preparatory work towards a multilateral treaty for international patent protection began with several conferences held in various European cities, but primarily in Vienna and Paris, between 1873 and 1882. These conferences led to the signing of the final text of the *Paris Convention* on 20 March 1883.[7]

The *Paris Convention*[8] is considered one of the oldest international treaties on the protection of industrial property.[9] It aims to prevent IP from posing barriers to

---

Sell, *Intellectual Property—A Critical History* (Lynne Rienner, 2006) chs 3-6; Peter Burger, 'The Berne Convention: Its History and Its Key Role in the Future'(1988) 3 *Journal of Law and Technology* 1; Roberto Garza Barbosa, 'Revisiting International Copyright Law' (2007) 8 *Barry Law Review* 43, 43-80; Susan K. Sell, *Power and Ideas—North South Politics of Intellectual Property and Antitrust* (New York University, 1998), ch 4; Christopher May, *The Global Political Economy of Intellectual Property Rights* (Routledge, 2nd ed, 2010) ch 2; Henry C. Mitchell, *The Intellectual Property Commons—Toward and Ecology of Intellectual Property* (Lexington Books, 2005), chs 5-6; Anne Fitzgerald and Brian Fitzgerald, *Intellectual Property in Principle* (LBC Thomson, 2004) 1-26, 82-84; Benjamin Kaplin, *An Unhurried View of Copyright* (Columbia University, 1967) ch 1; L Ray Patterson 'Free Speech, Copyright, and Fair Use' (1987) 40 (1) *Vanderbilt Law Review* 1; David Hindman, 'The Effect of Intellectual Property Regimes on Foreign Investments in Developing Economies' (2006) 23 (2) *Arizona Journal of International & Comparative Law* 467; David Saunders, *Authorship and Copyright* (Routledge, 1992), chs 2-6; Siva Vaidhyanathan, *Copyrights and Copywrongs, the Rise of Intellectual Property and How It Threatens Creativity* (New York University, 2001), chs 1-3; Layman Ray Patterson, *Copyright in Historical Perspective* (Vanderbilt University, 1968); Isabella Alexander, *Copyright Law and the Public Interest in the Nineteenth Century* (Hart Publishing, 2010); Benedict Atkinson, *The True History of Copyright—The Australian Experience* 1905-2005 (Sydney University, 2007), ch 14; Ronan Deazley, *Rethinking Copyright* (Edward Elgar, 2006), chs 1-3.

[5] Peter Drahos, 'Negotiating Intellectual Property Rights' in Peter Drahos and Ruth Mayne (eds), *Global Intellectual Property—Access to Knowledge and Development* (Palgrave Macmillan, 2002) 166.

[6] Ibid.

[7] Pedro Roffe and Gina Vea, 'The WIPO Development Agenda in an Historical and Political Context' in Neil Weinstock Netanel (ed), *The Development Agenda: Global Intellectual Property and Developing Countries* (Oxford University, 2008) 83.

[8] *Paris Convention for the Protection of Industrial Property*, as last revised at Stockholm, opened for signature on 14 July 1967, 828 UNTS 305 (entered into force 26 April or 19 May 1970) <http://www.wipo.int/treaties/en/ip/paris/trtdocs_wo020.html> (*Paris Convention*); WIPO, *WIPO Intellectual Property Handbook: Policy, Law and Use*, ch 5 <http://www.wipo.int/export/sites/www/about-ip/en/iprm/pdf/ch5.pdf#paris>.

[9] *Paris Convention*, above n 8, arts 4-11.

trade and serves as the foundation of international and regional trade treaties.[10] It protects patents,[11] trademarks,[12] industrial designs,[13] utility models,[14] trade names,[15] geographical indications (indications of source and appellations of origin),[16] and the repression of unfair competition.[17] Few developing countries were among the original signatories to the Convention, which included Brazil, Ecuador,[18] Guatemala,[19] El Salvador,[20] and Tunisia.[21]

The vast majority of developing countries have adopted the *Paris Convention* through colonisation and the transplanting of European IP laws to their domestic laws[22] as colonial powers imposed their IP laws on those countries.[23]

Property rights were considered as alien to many traditional and indigenous approaches to the stewardship of ideas, knowledge, and innovation that were available in many developing countries.[24] The transplanting of European IP laws to developing countries was considered a civilised act and a precondition for their progress from being 'underdeveloped' to becoming 'developed'.[25] Professor Ruth Okediji explains how European powers perceived IP:

> IP law was not merely an incidental part of the colonial legal apparatus, but a central technique in the commercial superiority sought by European powers in their interactions

---

[10] Ellen P. Winner and Arrow W. Denberg, *International Trademark Treaties* (Oceana Publications, 2004) 48; Jon O Nelson, *International Patent Treaties* (Oceana Publications, 2007) 16.

[11] *Paris Convention*, above n 8, arts 4, 4bis, 4ter, 4quarter, 5, 5bis, 5ter, 5quarter.

[12] Ibid, arts 6, 6ter, 6quater, 6quinquies, 6sexies, 6septies, 7, and 7bis.

[13] Ibid, art 5quinquies.

[14] Ibid, art 1.

[15] Ibid, art 8.

[16] Ibid, arts 1 (2), 10 and 10bis.

[17] Ibid, art 10bis.

[18] Withdrawn from the *Paris Convention* in 1886. See Roffe and Vea, above n 7, 83, citing Surendra J. Patel, 'The Patent System and the Third World' (1974) 2 (9) *World Development* (Special Issue on Patents), 4.

[19] Withdrawn from the *Paris Convention* in 1895. Ibid.

[20] Withdrawn from the *Paris Convention* in 1887. Ibid.

[21] The original countries from Europe that signed the *Paris Convention* were Belgium, France, Great Britain, Italy, the Netherlands, Portugal, Serbia, Spain, and Switzerland. Ibid.

[22] Peter K. Yu, 'The International Intellectual Property Regime Complex: International Enclosure, the Regime Complex, and Intellectual Property Schizophrenia' (2007) *Michigan State Law Review* 1, 4; Peter Drahos, *An Alternative for the Global Regulation of Intellectual Property Rights*, Working Paper October 2005, The Australian National University, Centre for Governance of Knowledge and Development, 9 <https://www.anu.edu.au/fellows/pdrahos/articles/pdfs/2005analternativeframework.pdf>.

[23] Carolyn Deere, *Developing Countries Perspectives on Intellectual Property in the WTO: Setting the Pre-TRIPS Context*, SSRN, 1-26 (1) <http://papers.ssrn.com/sol3/papers.cfm?abstract_id=1405430>; Drahos, above n 22, 9, 21.

[24] Deere, above n 23, 1.

[25] Ibid.

> with each other in regions beyond Europe. The early period of European contact through trade with non-European peoples thus was characterized predominantly by the extension of IP laws to the colonies for purposes associated generally with the overarching colonial strategies of assimilation, incorporation and control. It was also characterized by efforts to secure national economic interests against other European countries in colonial territories.[26]

Article 2 of the *Paris Convention* facilitated transplanting through what is called the 'colonial clause'.[27] It provides as follows:

> (1) Nationals of any country of the Union shall, as regards the protection of industrial property, enjoy in all the other countries of the Union the advantages that their respective laws now grant, or may hereafter grant, to nationals; all without prejudice to the rights specially provided for by this Convention. Consequently, they shall have the same protection as the latter, and the same legal remedy against any infringement of their rights, provided that the conditions and formalities imposed upon nationals are complied with.

One commentator criticised colonial powers for obligating developing countries to adopt the *Paris Convention* through colonisation. This process has resulted in ignorance of their local conditions and hampered their internal growth and development.[28] The ignorance of local conditions of developing countries in multilateral IP treaties would be also a feature of the bilateral treaties signed with those countries. Many IP scholars would later criticise the drafting of these international treaties and argue that the concerns of developing countries need to be taken into consideration when drafting any future agreement related to IP.

2.2.2 Revisions of the Paris Convention

The most important discussions between developed and developing countries in relation to how the international patent system should be structured to take into account their interests were made in the revision to the *Paris Convention*. Developing countries that were original or later signatories to the *Paris Convention*

---

[26] Ruth L. Okediji, 'The International Relations of Intellectual Property: Narratives of Developing Country Participation in the Global Intellectual Property System' (2003) 7 *Singapore Journal of International and Comparative Law* 315, 324-325, cited in Yu, above n 22, 1, 4-5.

[27] The 'colonial clause' is a particular clause in an international convention that extends the application of the convention to the dependent territories of contracting states. There are three forms of that clause: 1) an automatic application of the convention to the dependent territories, 2) optional application of the convention to the dependent territories, and 3) optional application of the convention to the dependent territories. The general rule is that the convention applies to all territories of contracting parties, including their dependent territories, unless there is an express or implied provision to the contrary that was agreed upon by the parties to the convention. See Yuen-Li Liang, 'Colonial Clauses and Federal Clauses in United Nations Multilateral Instruments' (1951) 45 (1) *The American Journal of International Law*, 108-128 (108).

[28] Peter K.Yu, 'Dean's Lecture Series: A Tale of Two Development Agendas' (2009) 35 *Ohio Northern University Law Review* 466, 470.

argued that the Convention constituted a barrier to their economic developmental objectives and requested that it be revised to meet their interests and local conditions.[29]

The government of Brazil,[30] an original signatory to the *Paris Convention*, raised the question, in 1961, of the effects of patents on the economies of developing countries. At the General Assembly of the UN, upon the call of Brazil,[31] Resolution No. 1713 (XVI) was issued on 19 December 1961, asking the Secretary-General of the UN,[32] in consultation with appropriate international and national institutions, to prepare a report on 'the effects of patents on the economy of

[29] Developing countries were particularly concerned that

> The international patent system was unbalanced in favour of developed countries and also questioned the purported links between stronger [IP] protection and increased domestic innovation, noting that even where patents were granted in their countries, 'a very small number were actually used in domestic production'. In addition, they contended that the monopoly IP rights frustrated competition and made many technologies unaffordable in their markets.

See Deere, above n 23, 7.

[30] On the Brazilian activist role on behalf of developing countries, see Cícero Gontijo, *Changing the Patent System from the Paris Convention to the TRIPs Agreement*, Global Issue Paper No 26 (December 2005) FDCL, 18 <http://www.fdcl-berlin.de/fileadmin/fdcl/Publikationen/GIP_Gontijo-Patente.pdf>; Andréa Koury Menescal, 'Changing WIPO's Ways? The 2004 Development Agenda in Historical Perspective' (2006) 8 (6) *Journal of World Intellectual Property* 761, 765; Mark A. Franz, 'A Message to Verity: Don't Let the U.N. Undermine Patents' (1988) 85 *Backgrounder Update*; Ruth L Okediji, 'History Lessons for the WIPO Development Agenda' in Neil Weinstock Netanel, *The Development Agenda: Global Intellectual Property and Developing Countries* (Oxford University, 2008) 143; Graham Dutfield and Uma Suthersanen, *Global Intellectual Property Law* (Edward Elgar, 2008) 274; Pedro Roffe and Gina Vea, 'The WIPO Development Agenda in an Historical and Political Context' in Neil Weinstock Netanel, *The Development Agenda: Global Intellectual Property and Developing Countries* (Oxford University, 2008) 95; Peter K. Yu, 'Dean's Lecture Series: A Tale of Two Development Agendas' (2009) 35 *Ohio Northern University Law Review* 465-573, 449; Carolyn Deere, *Developing Countries Perspectives on Intellectual Property in the WTO: Setting the Pre-TRIPs Context*, SSRN, 8 <http://papers.ssrn.com/sol3/papers.cfm?abstract_id=1405430>; Paul S. Haar, 'Revision of the Paris Convention: A Realignment of Private and Public Interests in the International Patent System' (1982) 8 *Brooklyn Journal of International Law* 84.

[31] BIRPI (later WIPO) reacted promptly to the Brazilian call when its Director 'immediately despatched a letter to the Secretary-General of the UN drawing his attention to the interest of the International Bureau in this Resolution and offering any needed help'. See (1962) *Industrial Property*, 40, cited in Menescal, above n 30, 768.

[32] UNCTAD, *The Role of the Patent System in the Transfer of Technology to Developing Countries*, UNCTAD/ TD/BC.11/19/Rev.1, UNCTAD, 1975, 35.

underdeveloped countries' and 'recommend on the advisability of holding an international conference in developing countries' in connection with that matter.[33]

The UN Department of Economic and Social Affairs (DESA) published the Report in 1964 under the title *The Role of Patents in the Transfer of Technology to Developing Countries*. It concluded that there was no urgent need to hold a conference to review the *Paris Convention* for the purpose of addressing the special needs of developing countries, as capacity-building effort at the domestic level was considered to be more important than the reform of the international IP system.[34] Brazil was not satisfied with the conclusion reached and took up the matter in several other forums and conferences.[35]

In 1970, developing countries achieved a UN General Assembly Resolution on an 'International Development Strategy for the Second UN Development Decade', which included a call for a program to promote technology transfers from industrialised countries to developing countries.[36] Developing countries also called for an International Code of Conduct on the Transfer of Technology because they felt that multinational corporations (MNCs) abused the power[37] given to them by

---

[33] In addition, the report should contain:

> ...b) A survey of patent legislation in selected developed and under developed countries, with primary emphasis on the treatment given to foreign patents; c) An analysis of the characteristics of the patent legislation of under-developed countries in the light of economic development objectives, taking into account the need for rapid absorption of new products and technology and the rise of the productivity level of their economies.

Ibid; Carolyn Deere, *the Implementation Game: The TRIPS Agreement and the Global Politics Intellectual Property* (Oxford University, 2008) 44.

[34] The main findings of the Report were the following:

> In fact, as pointed out in the report, the problems arising in connection with the transfer of technology to developing countries go much beyond the operation of the national patent system or the conduct of international patent relations, so that a conference such as that contemplated in the resolution could only deal with parts of the issues. More could be done through the combination of appropriate legislative and administrative measures at the national level with action to curb restrictive business practices in international licensing agreements, and the provision of technical and financial assistance to developing countries along the line discussed in the report.

UNCTAD, above n 32; Roffe and Vea, above n 7, 96.

[35] Including the Conference on Science and Technology, which was held in Brasilia, Brazil, in 1972. It was of the opinion that:

> IP regimes 'have become inadequate and have been exploited by technology exporters to impost consumption patterns and obtain production, distribution and trade privileges.' It proposed the revision of national regimes and inter-American treaties on patents and trademarks to assist in promoting social and economic development objectives.

See Roffe and Vea, above n 7, 97.

[36] Deere, above n 33, 44.

[37] 'Developing countries also called for a UN Code of Conduct on Transnational Corporation (TNCs) to better regulate the monopoly power of transnational corporations.' See Deere, above n 23, 45.

national patent laws, as they demanded high prices from recipients in developing countries and, as a result, constituted a barrier to their economic development.[38]

UNCTAD, DESA, and the International Bureau of WIPO updated the UN Report of 1964 and published it under the same title in 1975, in accordance with Resolution No. 39 (III) on the transfer of technology, adopted on 16 May 1972 at the third session of UNCTAD.[39] The Report was much more confronting than the earlier UN 1964 Report, recommending a careful revision of the complex international patent system.[40]

The *Paris Convention* has been revised in 1900 (Brussels), 1911 (Washington), 1925 (The Hague), 1934 (London), 1958 (Lisbon), 1967 (Stockholm) and has been amended in 1979.[41] Led by Latin American states (Brazil, Mexico, and the Andean Pact countries) and India, developing countries called for a revision of the *Paris Convention* to balance patent holders' rights with the public interest and the broader needs of economic development.[42] They sought to weaken the IP protection standards of the Convention by incorporating tough sanctions against patent holders who abused their monopoly privileges.[43]

One of the key revisions of the *Paris Convention* requested by developing countries related to art 5 (A, B, C, D)[44] and particularly art 5A.[45] Developing countries have asked for the exclusion of art 5 from the Convention because it does not regulate the question of protection of industrial property, only the protection of the imported goods, which is outside the Convention and under the jurisdiction of

---

[38] On the International Code of Conduct on the Transfer of Technology, see Sell, above n 4, 79-105; Yu, above n 28, 492-507.

[39] The resolution, in [10], called for:

> [A] study with a view to bringing up to date the report prepared by the Secretary-General of the United Nations on the role of patents in the transfer of technology to the developing countries and to devote special consideration in this study to the role of international patent systems in such transfers, with a view to providing a better understanding of this role in the context of a future revision of the system.

UNCTAD, above n 32, 35; Roffe and Vea, above n 7, 97.

[40] UNCTAD, above n 32, 64.

[41] See Guy Tritton (ed), *Intellectual Property in Europe* (Sweet & Maxwell, 3rd ed, 2008) 64; Drahos, above n 3, 8.

[42] Susan K. Sell, 'Intellectual Property as a Trade Issue: From the Paris Convention to GATT' (1989) 13 (4) *Legal Studies Forum* 407, 409-410.

[43] Ibid.

[44] Article 5 of the *Paris Convention* today relates to failure to work, insufficient working and compulsory licenses of patents. See art 5 of the *Paris Convention*, above n 8. On negotiating of art 5 of the *Paris Convention* between developing and developed countries, see Sell, above n 4, 119-130.

[45] Article 5A of the *Paris Convention* today relates to compulsory licenses. See art 5A of the *Paris Convention*, above n 8.

national legislation and international agreements.[46] Developing countries wanted also to revise, in particular, art 5A in relation to compulsory licensing, so that it should be applied only in their case and without any time limitation.[47] In short, developing countries wanted to 'reshape the notions of local-working, remedies to abuses and the relationship between compulsory forfeiture or revocation of patents'[48] in the *Paris Convention*. All the attempts by developing countries to revise the *Paris Convention* and change the international patent system in Geneva, Nairobi, and again at Geneva between 1980 and 1983[49] were unsuccessful because developed countries, particularly the US,[50] were against any undermining of the international patent system.

2.2.3 Berne Convention of 1886

The *Berne Convention* has witnessed the real confrontation between developed and developing countries in relation to how the international copyright system should be structured. In 1886, a diplomatic conference at the initiative of the Swiss federal government was convened at Berne to adopt the *Berne Convention*.[51] The Convention was signed by Belgium, France, Germany, Great Britain, Haiti, Italy, Liberia, Spain, Switzerland, and Tunisia on 9 September 1886[52] and became effective on 5 December 1887.[53] From its inception, the membership of the Convention has comprised countries that were at widely different stages in their economic development.[54] Only very few developing countries were among the original signatories of the *Berne Convention*, and these include Tunisia and Haiti.[55]

Developing countries that were not original signatories of the *Berne Convention* in Asia, America, and Africa were also subject to the Convention by virtue of the

---

46 Subrata Roy Chowdhury, Erik Denters, P.J. I.M. de Waart, *The Right of Development in International Law* (Martinus Nijhoff, 1992) 300.

47 Ibid.

48 Roffe and Vea, above n 7, 86-91; 101.

49 J.H. Reichman, 'Intellectual Property in International Trade: Opportunities and Risks of a GATT Connection' (1989) 22 *Vanderbilt Journal of Transnational Law* 750, 759.

50 United States General Accounting Office, *Strengthening Worldwide Protection of Intellectual Property* (April 1987), 267-277 <http://archive.gao.gov/d2t4/132699.pdf>.

51 Petya Totcharova, *UNESCO Copyright Activities*, Asia Pacific Cultural Centre for UNESCO <http://www.accu.or.jp/appreb/10copyr/pdf_ws0509/2_2_unesco.pdf>.

52 Lewinski, above n 4, 30.

53 Ibid.

54 Sam Ricketson, *The Berne Convention for the Protection of Literary and Artistic Works: 1886-1986* (Longman, 1987) 592. See also Sam Ricketson and Jane C. Ginsburg, *International Copyright and Neighbouring Rights—The Berne Convention and Beyond* (Oxford University, 2nd ed, 2006) vol 2, 879-963.

55 Deere, above n 23, 1.

'colonial clause'.[56] Article 19 of the *Berne Convention* allowed European powers to include their colonies[57] and protectorates under the Convention.[58] It provides that '[t]he provisions of this Convention shall not preclude the making of a claim to the benefit of any greater protection which may be granted by legislation in a country of the Union'. This means that if European power (France, Great Britain, Belgium, Italy, and Spain) has adopted a stronger copyright law, the citizens of the other country who are a party to the Convention could request protection under such law. Even without a formal provision allowing countries to ratify the *Berne Convention* on behalf of sovereigns, European powers could have independently extended the *Berne Convention* directly to their colonies in Asia, Africa, and South America.[59] The non-amendment of the 'colonial clause' in the *Berne Convention* is a major criticism of the international IP system and is described by one influential IP scholar as a form of European domination over that system.[60] The Berne Convention is one of the oldest international copyright treaties that were adopted when many developing countries were not recognised. Even later when these countries were established, it was difficult for these countries to understand its implications on their social development.

2.2.4 *Revisions of the Berne Convention*

The *Berne Convention* has been amended several times, in Berlin (1908), Berne (1914), Rome (1928), Brussels (1948), Stockholm (1967), and Paris (1948).[61] These revisions are particularly relevant to the discussions on IP and development.

2.2.4.1 The Stockholm Revision Conference of 1967

Developing countries were not satisfied with the international copyright system and therefore argued that the *Berne Convention* should be revised in order to take into

---

[56] See Ruth L Okediji, 'Africa and the Global Intellectual Property System: Beyond the Agency Model' in Abdulqawi A Yusuf, (2004) 12 *African Yearbook of International Law* (2004) 207, 217; Drahos, above n 22, 9; Ricketson, above n 54, 593.

[57] These colonies include India, Pakistan, Brazil, Kenya, Egypt, Ghana, and many others.

[58] Okediji, above n 56, 217.

[59] Ibid.

[60] Ibid 219.

[61] *Berne Convention for the Protection of Literary and Artistic Works* (as amended), opened for signature 9 September 1886, S. Treaty Document No. 99-27 (1986) (Berne Convention) <http://www.wipo.int/treaties/en/ip/berne/trtdocs_wo001.html>; Professor Peter Yu's website, House Report of the Berne Convention Implementation Act of 1988, H.R. Rep. No. 100-609 (1988) <http://www.peteryu.com/intip/bciahr.pdf>.

consideration their developmental interests and local conditions.[62] They proposed to include in the *Berne Convention* concessions for their benefit and a system of reservations that they could use when needed. On 14 November 1960, at the 11th General Conference of UNESCO, India emerged as a prominent advocate of the interests of developing countries in the context of copyright.[63] A series of conferences preparatory to the revisions of the *Berne Convention* were concluded in a number of developing countries to provide specific recommendations for the improvement of the *Berne Convention* and the international copyright system. Among these, the African Study Conference on copyright organised a conference held jointly by UNESCO and BIRPI (later WIPO) in Brazzaville (the capital of Congo) on August 1963. The purpose of the meeting was to assist the new African countries to formulate appropriate principles for drafting their own copyright laws.[64] The meeting called for a review of art 7 (reduced term of protection) and art 20 (enable making of bilateral agreements in promoting exchanges in derogation of the text) of the original *Berne Convention* to be more compatible with the interests of developing countries.[65]

It was proposed that a model copyright law that is suitable for African conditions and needs should be developed and that UNESCO and BIRPI should assist in this task.[66] The Brazzaville meeting described the international copyright conventions in their present form as biased toward the interests of exporters of intellectual works and requested their re-examination in the light of the specific needs of African countries and developing countries.[67] The recommendations of the Brazzaville meeting were met with significant opposition,[68] and the issues raised therein proved a discordant topic between developed and developing countries. In January 1967, and echoing the concerns of the Brazzaville meetings, a seminar was held in New Delhi, India, to discuss a potential draft model copyright law for developing countries, in addition to discussing proposals for the *Berne* revision.[69] The Indian

[62] Ricketson, above n 54, 594; Yu, above n 28, 470.

[63] India is an important 'developing country' that influenced the discussions of how the international copyright system should be structured, and it only joined the *Berne Convention* when the UK was admitted as a member. Professor Sam Ricketson noted that 'India expressed its concerns about 'the high prices and frequent unavailability of [copyright] works from the developed countries' and strongly advocated the need for special and differential treatment that would 'allow for the freer circulation of works in developing countries'. See Ricketson, above n 54, 596. Yu, above n 28, 477.

[64] Ricketson, above n 54, 596, 606.

[65] Ndene Ndiaye, 'The Berne Convention and Developing Countries' (1986-1987) 11 *Columbia Journal of Law and the Arts* 47; Ricketson, above n 54, 596.

[66] Ricketson, above n 54, 596.

[67] Irwin A. Olian, 'International Copyright and the Needs of Developing Countries: The Awakening at Stockholm and Paris' (1974) 7 (2) *Cornell International Law Journal* 98; Okediji, above n 56, 239-240.

[68] Okediji, above n 56, 239-240.

[69] Anne Mira Guha, *Charles F. Johnson's Timeline of the Origins of the 1967 Stockholm Protocol for Developing Countries* (18 October 2010) Knowledge Ecology International

delegation proposed the preparation of a study on the possibility of adopting compulsory licences into the Convention for the reproduction of protected works for educational purposes, as well as translation licences[70] similar to those available in the Universal Copyright Convention (UCC).[71]

A Swedish/BIRPI Study Group was established to study the recommendations received.[72] It proposed to include certain reservations to the right of translation, term of protection, and a specified limitation for educational purposes.[73] In 1968, the Berne Union members convened in Stockholm, once again with the intention of making substantive changes[74] that would be of special importance to developing countries and that would improve the Convention.[75] The Stockholm Protocol was adopted but later failed to gain the required number of ratifications for its approval and has never become part of the international copyright system[76] as it did not meet the needs of publishers and copyright owners[77] in developed countries.[78]

---

http://keionline.org/node/983>. India also discussed adding special provisions in the Draft Model Copyright Law concerning folklore. See Marc Perman, 'From 'Folklore' to 'Knowledge' in Global Governance in Mario Biagioli, Peter Jaszi, and Martha Woodmansee (eds), *Making and Unmaking of Intellectual Property* (University of Chicago, 2011) 115, 116-117.

[70] Ndiaye, above n 65, 48; Kelsey Martin Mott, 'The Relationship between the Berne Convention and the Universal Copyright Convention' (1966-1967) 11 *Patent Trademarks and Copyright Journal* 306.

[71] The Universal Copyright Convention (UCC) was created in Geneva in 1952 under the auspices of UNESCO to provide an alternative multilateral convention to Berne. It was later revised in Paris in 1971. See *Universal Copyright Convention* as revised in Paris, opened for signature 24 July 1971, 943 UNTS 178 (entered into force on 10 July 1974) <http://portal.unesco.org/en/ev.php-URL_ID=15241&URL_DO=DO_TOPIC&URL_SECTION=201.html>. See also Melville B. Nimmer and David Nimmer, *Nimmer on Copyright*, vol 17 (Matthew Bender, 1976) 10-11.

[72] Olian, above n 67, 97. See also, Rickeston, above n 54, 598; Okediji, above n 56, 240.

[73] Olian, above n 67, 97; J.A.L Sterling, *World Copyright Law* (Sweet and Maxwell, 2003) 21-22.

[74] Burger, above n 4, 38-39.

[75] The other purposes of the Stockholm Revision were to cope with the technological developments that were taking place and to introduce administrative amendments that would make the *Berne Convention* more effective in practice: WIPO, above n 8, ch 5.

[76] Okediji, above n 56, 239-240.

[77] Professor Sam Ricketson has identified four problems with the Protocol from the perspective of developed countries:

> [T]he Protocol embodied too many concessions in favour of the developing countries. Four particular areas of concern can be identified: the lack of any guarantee that authors would be paid in case of use for 'teaching, scholarship and research' and the problems that might arise with respect to transmittal of compensation in case of other reservations; the provisions allowing export of copies to other developing countries, the inadequate definition of a developing country, and the lack of any direct incentive to developing countries to improve the level of protection beyond that offered by the Protocol.

Ricketson, above n 54, 621-622. For a criticism of the Protocol, especially from developed countries, see Yu, above n 28, 478; Burger, above n 4, 38-39; Olian, above n 67, 104.

[78] These countries include Canada, Denmark, Finland, West Germany, Israel, Spain, Sweden, Switzerland, and the UK.

As a result of the failure of the Protocol, an 'international copyright crisis' occurred, and for the first time in history, the *Berne Convention* had become politicised, and its status as one of the pre-eminent international conventions dealing with private rights in a generally non-partisan manner had been severely weakened.[79] In June 1969, the International Copyright Study Group met in Washington and formulated a number of recommendations that would guide the proposed revision of both the *Berne Convention* and the UCC simultaneously.[80] These recommendations were accurately described as a 'package deal'[81] that formed the basis for the revisions of the *Berne Convention* during the summer of 1971.[82]

2.2.4.2 The Paris Revision Conference of 1971

The conferences for the revision of the *Berne Convention* and the UCC were held concurrently in Paris from 5 to 24 July 1971 to satisfy the needs of developing countries to access educational, scientific, and technical works without at the same time weakening the structure and scope of the international copyright protection.[83] After much discussion between developed and developing countries, the UCC gave the contracting developing countries, according to the requirement of art Vbis[84] in the Appendix Declaration Relating to art XVII,[85] the right to benefit in particular from the exceptions provided in arts Vter (translation of a work)[86] and Vquater (reproduction of a work).[87] The basic revision of the *Berne Convention* original text consisted of instituting a new, preferential system in favour of developing countries.[88] This was in the *Appendix on Special Provisions Regarding Developing Countries*,[89] which allows a developing country to 'grant non-exclusive,

[79] Ricketson, above n 54, 622; Yu, above n 28, 481-482.

[80] For a summary of the main recommendations that were agreed on in Washington, see Rickeston, above n 54, 629.

[81] Ibid 628-629.

[82] Olian, above n 67, 104.

[83] Ibid.

[84] See Appendix A.

[85] See Appendix A.

[86] See Appendix A.

[87] See Appendix A.

[88] See Appendix B.

[89] See Appendix B. See also Olian, above n 67, 103; Yu, above n 28, 478; WIPO, *Introduction to Intellectual Property, Theory and Practice* (Kluwer Law International, 1997) 385-394; James Love, *Berne Convention Appendix regarding Special Provisions regarding Developing Countries* (18 October 2010) Knowledge Ecology International <http://keionline.org/node/984>.

non-transferable licences to its nationals, for the translation[90] or reproduction[91] of foreign-owned, copyright works for educational or research purposes'.[92]

Compared with the Stockholm Protocol, the Berne Appendix represented a far more satisfactory balancing act of the interests of developed and developing countries in international copyright.[93] In practice, it was only used by fewer than 20 developing countries.[94] Several scholars and commentators have criticised it as being lengthy, complex, burdensome,[95] and costly for developing countries to make operational in practice.[96]

2.2.5 Concluding Remarks

The discussion leading to the revisions of the *Paris Convention* for industrial property and the *Berne Convention* for copyright witnessed the first clash between developing and developed countries in relation to how the IP system should be structured to take into consideration each others' needs. Developed countries requested a system that did not weaken the structure and scope of the international IP system that had evolved in Europe over a period of several hundred years, while

---

[90] See Appendix B.

[91] See Appendix B.

[92] Calestous Juma, *Intellectual Property Rights and Globalization: Implications for Developing Countries,* Center for International Development at Harvard University, 5 <http://www.cid.harvard.edu/archive/biotech/papers/discuss4.pdf>; Burger, above n 4, 40.

[93] Olian, above n 67, 107.

[94] These countries include the following: Republic of Yemen, Samoa, Democratic Socialist Republic of Sri Lanka, Syrian Arab Republic, Republic of Uzbekistan, Socialist Republic of Vietnam, Kingdom of Thailand, Republic of Cuba, Mongolia, United Arab Emirates (UAE), Republic of the Philippines, People's Republic of Bangladesh, Sultanate of Oman, Jordan, and Democratic People's Republic of Korea.

See WIPO, *Berne Members* <http://www.wipo.int/treaties/en/ShowResults.jsp?lang=en&treaty_id=15>; Manon Ress, *More on Countries That Have Availed Themselves of the Berne Appendix?* (28 September 2009) <http://lists.essential.org/pipermail/a2k/2009-September/004950.html>; Okediji, above n 56, 240.

[95] Any developing country that avails itself of the *Berne* Appendix must renew its declaration every ten years; otherwise, it will lose the benefits. See art 1 of Appendix B.

[96] Okediji, above n 56, 240; Rickeston, above n 54, 663-664; Story, above n 4, 792; Yu, above n 28, 481-482; James W. Peters, Toward Negotiating a Remedy to Copyright Piracy in Singapore (1986) 7 *Northwestern Journal of International Law & Business* 561, 585-589. Professor Margret Chon is of the opinion that there is a pressing need to reform the licensing provisions of the *Berne Appendix* in order to provide access to materials for developing countries; see Margret Chon, 'Intellectual Property and the Development Divide' (2006) 27 *Cardozo Law Review* 2821, 2835. See also, for a recent study on the subject, Alberto Cerda Silva, 'Beyond the Unrealistic Solution for Development Provided by the Appendix of the Berne Convention on Copyright' (2012) 4 (1) PIJIP Research Paper Series <http://digitalcommons.wcl.american.edu/research/30/>.

developing countries requested a more balanced IP system that would be responsive to their needs and developmental goals. The debates over copyright principles between developed and developed countries raged over issues relating to the appropriateness of control of knowledge and the responsibilities that developed countries had towards building the educational and scientific system of the newly developing countries. Developing countries have never argued for the abolition of the IP system but felt that developed countries have a moral responsibility, because of their colonial past, to give them concessions in the international IP system that would accommodate their economic, social, and cultural development needs.[97]

The revisions of the Paris and the Berne conventions have contributed substantially to the development of the international IP system and are considered as a first step toward resolving controversies between developed and developing countries.[98] History shows that developing countries were keenly interested, from the early development of the international IP system, to change the system to suit their developmental needs, but their demands were not listened to by developed countries, which insisted that the system should remain as it is.

2.3 The Establishment of WIPO as a Specialised UN Agency

Following the adoption of the Paris and Berne conventions, WIPO was established. One of the functions of WIPO was to administer both conventions. This subsection examines the historical establishment of WIPO and gives special attention to its role in shaping the international IP system, particularly in relation to developing countries.

2.3.1 Pre-establishment of WIPO and the Role of BIRPI

Before the establishment of WIPO, BIRPI was established in Berne, Switzerland, in 1883. In the world post-1945, the membership profile of BIRPI started to shift from being dominated by industrialised countries to newly independent, emerging states.[99] These developing countries wanted recognition of their interests within the new, global, democratic structures of the UN and its General Assembly.[100]

Arpad Bogsch, the Deputy Director-General of BIRPI, strove to establish a universal organisation for the protection of IP and saw the link with the UN as a

[97] Yu, above n 28, 477. See also, Philip G. Altbach, 'The Subtle Inequalities of Copyright' (1997) 31 (2), *Copyright Bulletin*, 9 <http://unesdoc.unesco.org/images/0011/001107/110771Eb.pdf>; Philip G. Albatch (ed), *Copyright and Development: Inequality in the Information Age* (Bellagio, 1995).

[98] Olian, above n 67, 110.

[99] Christopher May, 'The Pre-History and Establishment of the WIPO' (2009) (1) *The WIPO Journal* 20 <http://www.wipo.int/about-wipo/en/pdf/wipo_journal.pdf>.

[100] Ibid.

mechanism crucial to this end.[101] Bogsch was of the opinion that working inside the UN system would encourage developing countries to join and would enable the internal administration of the organisation to benefit from the economies of scale available inside the UN.[102]

BIRPI saw its duty to educate the public and the politicians in developing countries on the importance of IP for the development and progress of their national economies.[103] To encourage developing countries to join, and to convince them that BIRPI was interested in the IP issues of the south, in the 1950s and the 1960s, several conferences were organised by BIRPI to discuss how the international IP system should be more responsive to the needs of developing countries. BIRPI also drafted the *Model Law for Developing Countries on Inventions* in 1965 to meet the interests of developing countries as technology importers from industrialised countries[104]; unfortunately, the model law has not had wide acceptance and implementation by developing countries as it did not meet their expectations in relation to compulsory licensing and lapse or revocation of unexploited patens.

2.3.2 *The Establishment of WIPO*

The Convention Establishing WIPO was concluded in Stockholm on 14 July 1967[105] and entered into force in 1970.[106] On December 1974, the wishes of Arpad Bogsch (later a Deputy-General of WIPO) came true when WIPO was finally recognised as a UN specialised agency[107] primarily to cooperate with other UN

---

[101] Ibid 22.

[102] Arpad Bogsch, 'The First Twenty-Five Years of the World Intellectual Property Organization' (1992) 28, cited in May, above n 99, 23.

[103] Menescal, above n 30, 775.

[104] John Braithwaite and Peter Drahos, *Global Business Regulation* (Cambridge University, 2000) 81; Deere, above n 23, 1-26; Edith Penrose, 'International Patenting and the Less-Developed Countries' (1973) 83 (331) *The Economic Journal* 768,780 <http://www.jstor.org/stable/pdfplus/2230670.pdf >.

[105] WIPO, *Introduction to the Concept of Intellectual Property*, 3 <http://www.wipo.int/about-ip/en/iprm/pdf/ch1.pdf>.

[106] Ibid 4.

[107] Article 1 of the Agreement between the UN and WIPO provides that:

> The United Nations recognizes the World Intellectual Property Organization (hereinafter called the 'Organization') as a specialized agency and as being responsible for taking appropriate action in accordance with its basic instrument, treaties and agreements administered by it, *inter alia,* for promoting creative intellectual activity and for facilitating the transfer of technology related to industrial property to the developing countries in order to accelerate economic, social and cultural development, subject to the competence and responsibilities of the United Nations and its organs, particularly the United Nations Conference on Trade and Development, the United Nations Development Program and the

agencies[108] in its field of competence.[109] This recognition served to increase the number of developing countries that joined the organisation in the late 1960s and early 1970s[110] as they believed that joining would allow them to accelerate technology transfer to their economies.[111] Representatives of member states in WIPO were concerned that these new, developing country members might question and undermine the main mission of WIPO's activities[112] in spreading a wide adaptation of IP rules and protection. This proved to be a legitimate concern later, especially in 2004 when Brazil and Argentina submitted to the WIPO General Assembly, the WIPO Development Agenda, requesting an overhaul of the activities of WIPO for the benefit of developing countries.

WIPO is an intergovernmental organisation with headquarters in Geneva, Switzerland, established to promote 'the protection of IP throughout the world

---

> United Nations Industrial Development Organization, as well as of the United Nations Educational, Scientific and Cultural Organization and of other agencies within the United Nations system.

See *Agreement between the United Nations and the World Intellectual Property Organization* (entered into force on 17 December 1974) <http://www.wipo.int/treaties/en/agreement/> (Agreement between the UN and WIPO).

[108] WIPO agreed to co-operate with the United Nations Conference on Trade and Development, the United Nations Development Programme, and the United Nations Industrial Development Organization, as well as other agencies. For more details, see Yu, above n 28, 490.

[109] Article 10 of the Agreement between the UN and WIPO provides that:

> The Organization agrees to co-operate within the field of its competence with the United Nations and its organs, particularly the United Nations Conference on Trade and Development, the United Nations Development Programme and the United Nations Industrial Development Organization, as well as the agencies within the United Nations system, in promoting and facilitating the transfer of technology to developing countries in such a manner as to assist these countries in attaining their objectives in the fields of science and technology and trade and development.

See Agreement between the UN and WIPO, above, n 107.

[110] Arpad Bogsch, the former WIPO Director, mentioned the benefits of approving WIPO as a specialised UN agency as follows:

> (i) [T]he fact that dealing with intellectual property was the prerogative and the task of WIPO would receive worldwide recognition, (ii) WIPO would have more or less the same members as the United Nations, and in particular, many developing countries would join WIPO (only very few of them belonged to BIRPI), (iii) the governments of member States would be liberated from having to deal with the fixing of salaries, other working conditions and pensions of the staff, since salaries and pensions would automatically follow the so-called 'common system' of the United Nations and its specialized agencies.

Arpad Bosgsch, 'Brief History of the First Twenty Years of the Intellectual Property Organisation' (1992) 18-21, cited in Yu, above n 28, 458, 486.

[111] Debora Halbert, *What if WIPO Never Existed?* (9 July 2009) Copysouth <http://www.copysouth.org/portal/node/12>; Yu, above, n 28, 485.

[112] WIPO, 'Records of the Intellectual Property Conference of Stockholm' from 11 June to 14 July 1967' (Geneva: WIPO, 1967) 830, cited in May, above n 99, 23.

through cooperation among states'[113] and for the administration of various multilateral treaties dealing with the legal and administrative aspects of IP.[114] In its first report of 1975, WIPO recognised its obligation toward developing countries as follows:

> [O]ne of the main objectives of WIPO is to assist developing countries in their development. WIPO assists developing countries in promoting their industrialization, their commerce and their cultural, scientific and technological development through the modernization of their industrial property and copyright systems and in meeting some of their needs in scientific documentation and the transfer of technology and technical know-how.[115]

In 1977, WIPO's members adopted a Declaration of Objectives to set the framework for the subsequent Diplomatic Conference. The Declaration emphasised that industrial property systems should help advance the industrialisation in developing countries by improving access to technology, technology transfer, working of inventions in developing countries, and greater inventive activity within their borders.[116] As of June 2012, WIPO had 185 member countries,[117] including more than 150 developing countries and LCDs.[118]

2.3.3 *WIPO and Developing Countries*

WIPO distinguished itself in the mid-twentieth century as an institution that is crucial to the coordinated efforts, led by the UN, to address problems related to developing countries and to integrate them into the international economic system.[119] The WIPO Secretariat was active in promoting a pro-IP discourse through educating governments and stakeholders in developing countries on the nature and

---

[113] Article 3 of WIPO provides that its objectives are

> (i) [T]o promote the protection of intellectual property throughout the world through cooperation among States and, where appropriate, in collaboration with any other international organization; (ii) to ensure administrative cooperation among the Unions.

See Convention Establishing the World Intellectual Property Organization, opened for signature on 14 July 1967, 828 UNTS 3 (entered into force on 26 April 1970) <http://www.wipo.int/treaties/en/convention/trtdocs_wo029.html#P68_3059> (WIPO Convention); WIPO, above n 105, 5.

[114] WIPO Convention, above n 113, art 3.

[115] May, above n 99, 25; see also WIPO, *WIPO's Legal and Technical Assistance to Developing Countries for the Implications of the TRIPS Agreement* <http://www.wipo.int/edocs/mdocs/mdocs/en/pcipd_1/pcipd_1_3.pdf>.

[116] Deere, above n 23, 1.

[117] See WIPO's page <http://www.wipo.int/members/en/>.

[118] WIPO, Member States <http://www.wipo.int/members/en/>.

[119] Okediji, above n 30, 143.

importance of IP for development and creativity.[120] It emphasised the importance of stronger IP protection and promoted an IP culture for modernisation, innovation, and increase in FDI and technology transfer to developing countries.[121] The clear message provided to developing countries by WIPO was that participation in the international IP system would lead to development, while non-participation would place them at some developmental risk.[122]

To give a brief idea of the work that WIPO is conducting, WIPO has four regional bureaus for each region of developing countries (Africa, Arab, Asia and Pacific, Latin America, and Caribbean), as well as a WIPO Academy, an LDC unit, and a relatively recent initiative known as WIPONET.[123] All of these are involved in providing legal advice, technical assistance, and advice on IP legislation to developing countries and beyond. WIPO drafted a proposal called Transfer of Technology Patent, which is contained in the annex to the *WIPO Model Law on Inventions for Developing Countries*, promulgated in 1980.[124] WIPO is committed to supporting developing countries in their efforts to maximise their use of IP as a tool for social, economic, and cultural development.[125] For that purpose, WIPO has assisted developing countries in the preparation of their IP laws, regulations, and administrative mechanisms and trained government officials to manage and use IP systems in their countries.[126] It has also developed with the WTO a joint initiative to provide technical cooperation for developing countries that have newly joined

[120] Deere, above n 33, 170; Katie Lula, 'Neither Here nor There but Fair: Finding an International Copyright System between East and West' (1996) 8 *Asian-Pacific Law and Policy Journal* 96, 131; A. Samuel Oddi, 'The International Patent System and Third World Development: Reality or Myth?' (1987) 5 (5) *Duke University Law Journal* 831, 854.

[121] See Kamil Idris, *Intellectual Property—A Power Tool for Economic Growth*, WIPO Publication Number 888.1 (June 2003) WIPO <http://www.wipo.int/freepublications/en/intproperty/888/wipo_pub_888_1.pdf>; Kamil Idris and Hisamitsu Arai, *The Intellectual Property-Conscious Nation: Mapping the Path from Developing to Developed*, WIPO Publication No. 988 (2006); WIPO, *The Economics of Intellectual Property* (January 2009) <http://www.wipo.int/export/sites/www/ip-development/en/economics/pdf/wo_1012_e.pdf>.

[122] Oddi, above n 120.

[123] Paul Salmon, 'Globalisation's Impact on International Trade and Intellectual Property Law: Cooperation between the World Intellectual Property Organisation (WIPO) and the World Trade Organisation (WTO)' (2003) 17 *St John's Journal of Legal Commentary* 429, 437.

[124] WIPO, *First Session, Geneva, November 25-29/1974, Working Group on Model Law for Developing Countries on Inventions and Know-How*, WC/ML/INV/1/3 (10 September 1974) <http://www.wipo.int/mdocsarchives/WG_ML_INV_I_74/WG_ML_INV_I_3_E.pdf>; Suzanne F. Greenberg, 'The WIPO Model Laws for the Protection of Unpatented Know-How: A Comparative Analysis' (1985-1986) 3 *International Tax and Business Lawyer* 52.

[125] François Lefèbvre, *WIPO and the Developing World*, The Courier ACP-EU No (November-December 2003) European Commission <http://ec.europa.eu/development/body/publications/courier/courier201/pdf/en_024.pdf>.

[126] United States General Accounting Office, above n 50, 24.

the organisation to help those countries in complying with their treaty obligations under the *TRIPS Agreement*.[127]

WIPO also has special programs for indigenous and local communities in developing countries, which aim to strengthen the capacity of these communities so they can make their own choices concerning IP and derive benefits from it.[128] The WIPO Patent Information Services (WPIS) is a free service that allows developing countries to access and use technological information contained in patent documents in order to accelerate the social, economic, and cultural development of those countries.[129] WIPO also established various programs that provide developing countries with information, education, and skills training programs relating to electronic commerce, particularly under the auspices of the WIPO Worldwide Academy.[130] The WIPO Academy operates a distance-learning program, as well as local seminars and courses for training lawyers in developing countries on IP issues.[131]

Several scholars have noted that the advocacy of WIPO toward the interests of developing countries is compromised by its heavy reliance on the management of the Patent Cooperation Treaty (PCT), primarily by pharmaceutical, agricultural, and financial service industries, which constitute 85% of WIPO's budget.[132] The Knowledge Ecology International (formerly Consumer Project on Technology) criticised WIPO in the Geneva Declaration on the Future of WIPO for 'creating and expanding monopoly privileges in developing countries, often without regard to the consequences that may arise such as social and economic costs that hampered and threatened creativity and innovation' instead of nourishing it.[133] Several scholars are doubtful that issuing IP laws in developing countries and LDCs, based on WIPO's recommendations, has resulted in any kind of economic, social, cultural, or political development in these countries.[134]

---

[127] WTO, *WTO and WIPO Join Forces to Help Developing Countries* (Press Release, PRESS/108, 21 July 1998) <http://www.wto.org/english/news_e/pres98_e/pr108_e.htm>.

[128] Lefèbvre, above n 125.

[129] WIPO, *Patent Information Services for Developing Countries* <http://www.wipo.int/patentscope/en/data/developing_countries.html>.

[130] WIPO, *WIPO's Assistance to Developing Countries in the Field of Electronic Commerce: Progress Report*, prepared by the International Bureau (18 May 1999) <www.wipo.int/edocs/mdocs/mdocs/en/pcipd_1/pcipd_1_11.doc>.

[131] Ibid.

[132] See Susan K. Sell, *Private Power, Public Law: The Globalisation of Intellectual Property Rights* (Cambridge University, 2003) 175.

[133] Consumer Project on Technology (now Knowledge Ecology International), *The Geneva Declaration on the Future of the World Intellectual Property Organization* (October 2000) <http://www.cptech.org/ip/wipo/futureofwipodeclaration.pdf>. See also the *Geneva Declaration on the Future of WIPO* <http://www.futureofwipo.org/futureofwipodeclaration.pdf>; Michael Blakeney and Getachew Mengistie, 'Intellectual Property and Economic Development in Sub-Saharan Africa' (2011) 14 *Journal of World Intellectual Property* 238, 247.

[134] Debora Halbert investigated whether being a member of WIPO has helped LDCs (mainly Chad and Mali) to gain economic development and spur domestic innovation and foreign investment. She found that WIPO has neither been necessary nor sufficient for economic development and spurring foreign investment or domestic innovation in these countries. See Halbert, above n 111.

WIPO cannot be held responsible for the developmental failures of LDCs and other developing countries. Development cannot be achieved merely by joining an international organisation or by having strong IP laws in place. To achieve development, developing countries should give attention to other critical issues that are equally—if not more—important, including political stability, economic policies, and intellectual capital. These issues are further explained in Chap. 3.

2.3.4 Concluding Remarks

Although WIPO was primarily created to administer the Paris and Berne conventions, it was given many other responsibilities, especially with respect to developing countries that were yet to realise and act upon the importance of IP for their development. Both developed and developing countries were not completely satisfied with WIPO. While developed countries recognised its weak enforcement mechanism and dispute settlement procedure, developing countries realised that WIPO was practically controlled by MNCs that were funding its activities and influencing its decisions.

It is noted that developed countries wanted a new system to be applied to all countries that would not contain the flaws in WIPO's dispute settlement and minimum standards of protection. Developing countries tried to resist this move as it might require them to raise the level of IP protection. This is the reason they were much more comfortable with WIPO rather than with any future international trade agreement.

2.4 The Views of Developed and Developing Countries on IP and Development

Given these remarks on how developing countries wanted WIPO to consider their interests in IP, it is helpful to compare some of the views of developed and developing countries on appropriate IP systems.[135] While rapid advances in information and communication technologies have increased opportunities for international trade in knowledge-based goods, they also multiplied the possibilities for imitation, copying, and unauthorised use of technologies.[136] The flourishing of piracy industries in developing countries constitutes a serious problem, particularly for IP holders from developed countries[137] who are concerned about the lack of

---

[135] L. Danielle Tully, 'Prospects for Progress: The TRIPS Agreement and Developing Countries after the Doha Conference' (2003) 26 *Boston College International and Comparative Law Review* 137, 138.

[136] Deere, above n 33, 46.

[137] Bénédicte Callan, 'Pirates on the High Seas: The United States and Global Intellectual Property Rights' (1998) 52-63, cited in Marney L. Cheek, 'The Limits of Informal Regulatory Cooperation in International Affairs: A Review of the Global Intellectual Property Regime' (2001) 33 *George Washington International Law* Review 277, 290. See also Peter Drahos and John Braithwaite, *Information Feudalism—Who Owns the Knowledge Economy?* (Earthscan, 2002) 19-38.

enforcement mechanisms therein, which in turn undermines the IP system.[138] Developed countries are using a range of initiatives locally and internationally to reduce piracy in the foreign markets of developing countries.

The international movement of IP has been from developed to developing countries.[139] Developed and developing countries have different views in relation to the benefits or burdens of the IP system. The main contention between the two groups is whether the international IP system is biased toward the interests of industrialised, developed countries or whether it truly helps developing countries in achieving social and economic development.[140]

2.4.1 The Views of Developed Countries

The main pressure on developing countries to increase their protection and enforcement of IP came from the US, Europe, and Japan. It is important to examine how these countries have used IP systems to meet their interests, according to their different stages of development. From the start of the Industrial Revolution, every country that became economically great began by copying: the Germans copied the British, the Americans copied the British and the Germans, and the Japanese copied everybody.[141] This has now changed because developed countries are providing heightened levels of IP protection and taking tough measures against copying and imitation.

Developed countries now argue that having strong IP laws would encourage FDI[142] and the transfer of technology[143] from their countries to developing

[138] Braithwaite and Drahos, above n 104, 61.

[139] Margret Chon criticised this model of international IP system and argued that a new system should be put in place. The new system should take into consideration the interests of developing countries, particularly their education under a 'substantive equality principle'. See Chon, above n 96, 2821-2912; Drahos, above n 5, 164.

[140] Evelyn Su, 'The Winners and the Losers: The Agreement on Trade-Related Aspects of Intellectual Property Rights and Its Effects on Developing Countries' (2004) 23 (1) *Houston Journal of International Law* 170.

[141] Peter K. Yu, *TRIPS and Its Discontents* (2006) 10 *Marquette Intellectual Property Law Review* 369, 383 <http://law.marquette.edu/ip/Yu.pdf>.

[142] Robert Sherwood and Carlos Braga explain that this is essentially an empirical question, and empirical evidence has actually found that having strong IP protection has significant effect on the increase of private investment in developing countries. See also Robert M. Sherwood and Carlos A. Primo Braga, 'Intellectual Property, Trade, and Economic Development: A Road Map for the FTAA Negotiations' (1996) *The North-South Agenda Papers* 21, 2; Michael P. Ryan, *Intellectual Property, Trade and Foreign Direct Investment* (May 2004) <http://www.wipo.int/edocs/mdocs/arab/en/wipo_reg_ip_amm_04/wipo_reg_ip_amm_04_4.pdf>.

[143] Technology transfer from industrialised countries to developing countries will not materialise by merely having strong IP systems in place. Licensors in developed countries need to take into consideration several factors, including the following: the level of technology, know-how, and R&D available in the country; capital market size; business cultures; local personnel and skills; competition; export control labiality; and other legal and business factors. See for further explanation, Harry Rubin, *International Technology Transfer* (Kluwer Law International, 1995) 97-152.

countries,[144] increase growth and living standards,[145] and result in social[146] and economic development.[147] Furthermore, they stress that strong IP systems are much needed to encourage local innovators to remain in their countries and develop local research and domestic enterprises.[148]Although developed countries agree that strong IP is needed for the economic and social development of developing countries, they differ on which level is required and what measures they should take to push developing countries to respect and enforce IP. It is noted that the US has played the leading role in pushing developing countries to adopt the strictest IP systems (compared to other developed countries in Europe and Japan) despite the

[144] See, generally, Evelyn Su, 'The Winners and the Losers: The Agreement on Trade-Related Aspects of Intellectual Property Rights and Its Effects on Developing Countries' (2004) 23 (1) *Houston Journal of International Law* 199; Robert F. Dale and James K. Huntoon, 'A Cost-Benefit Study of the Domestic and International Patent Systems' (1967) 11 *The Patent, Trademark and Copyright Res and Edu* 351; Kunz-Hallstein and Hans Peter, 'The Revision of the International System of Patent Protection in the Interest of Developing Countries' (1979) 10 (6) *International Review of Industrial Property and Copyright* 649; S. Lall, 'The Patent System and the Transfer of Technology to Less-Developed Countries' (1976) 10 *Journal of World Trade Law* 1, 14; Ituku Elangi Botoy, 'From the Paris Convention to the TRIPS Agreement: A One Hundred and Twelve Year Transitional Period for the Industrialized Countries' (2005) 7 (1) *Journal of World Intellectual Property* 115, 125-126; Franz Mark, 'A Message to Verity: Don't Let the UN Undermine Patents'(1988) *Backgrounder Update* 85; The Federalists Society for Law and Society, 'Does IP Harm or Help Developing Countries?' (2007) *University of Illinois Journal of Law, Technology and Policy* 65, 87; Md Golam Robbani, 'Trade Related Aspects of Intellectual Property Rights and Least Developed Countries' (2005) 8 (4) *The Journal of World Intellectual Property* 565, 567; Susan Sell, *Private Power, Public Law, the Globalisation of Intellectual Property Rights* (Cambridge University, 2003) chs 4-5; Duncan Matthews, *Globalising Intellectual Property Rights—The TRIPS Agreement* (Routledge, 2002) 108-116; Alan S. Gutterman, 'The North-South Debate regarding the Protection of Intellectual Property Rights' (1993) 28 *Wake Forest Law Review*, 89-139, 118-119; Michael P. Ryan, Knowledge-Economy Elites, the International Law of Intellectual Property and Trade and Economic Development' (2002) 10 *Cardozo International and Comparative Law Journal*, 271-303; Robert M. Sherwood, *Intellectual Property and Economic Development* (Westview, 1990); Eric Garduño and Frank Pietrucha, 'Intellectual Property Rights in the Arab World' (Winter/ Spring, 2003) *Georgetown Journal of International Affairs* <http://www12.georgetown.edu/sfs/publications/journal/Issues/ws03/gardunolocked.pdf>; Jean Raymond Homere, 'Intellectual Property Rights Can Help Stimulate the Economic Development of Least Developed Countries' (2004) 27 (2) *Columbia Journal of Law and Arts* 277, 286-288.

[145] The Federal Reserve Bank of San Francisco (FRBSF) Economic Letter, *Can International Patent Protection Help a Developing Country Grow* (14 May 2004) <http://www.frbsf.org/publications/economics/letter/2004/el2004-11.pdf>.

[146] Professor Ruth L. Gana (Okediji) believes that it is unrealistic to think that technology transfer alone will salvage the process of development in developing countries. There is a wide range of changes that must be taken in developing countries to achieve development, including political, social, and economic changes. As for technology, Professor Okediji notes that it is not a panacea for underdevelopment. Like all other resources, its potential is dependent on the existence of a carefully planned and stable socio-economic environment. See Okediji, above n 4, 315, 335, 341.

[147] Edith Penrose argues that '[n]on-industrialized states do not derive any direct benefit from granting patents for inventions that have already been patented and exploited abroad'. See Edith Penrose, (1974), cited in Gontijo, above n 30, 1.

[148] Su, above n 140, 200.

fact that, once, the US was considered a pirate nation in relation to its dealing with IP.[149]

The subsection examines how developed countries historically perceived IP, especially in their early stage of development, and how they look at it now.

2.4.2 *The United States*

2.4.2.1 Historical Aspects of IP Protection in the US

In the nineteenth century, the US was considered a pirate nation, stealing the work of foreign authors of developed countries without providing any kind of compensation. This practice was not considered as immoral or wrong but, on the contrary, a legitimate and sensible way for an aspiring country to develop and catch up with developed countries in Europe.[150]

One of England's most popular authors, whose work was repeatedly pirated by American publishers,[151] was Charles Dickens, who was disappointed at the degree of piracy committed upon his work in the US.[152] Dickens visited the US to convince Americans of the importance of protecting international copyright, but his mission

---

[149] Cheek, above 137, 281; Lawrence Lessig, 'Keynote: The International Society Symposia' (2004) 24 (1) *Loyola Los Angeles Entertainment Law Review*; Sell, above n 132, 6, ch 3.

[150] See, generally, Lawrence Lessig, 'Keynote: The International Society Symposia' (2004) 24 (1) *Loyola Los Angeles Entertainment Law Review*; Susan Sell, *Private Power, Public Law, the Globalisation of Intellectual Property Rights* (2003) 6, ch 3; Lawrence Lessig, *A Taste of Our Own Poison: A Modest Proposal: Hold Hollywood Hostage Till We Kill Farm Subsidies*, (2004) Issue 12.01 *Tana Pistorius* <http://www.wired.com/wired/archive/12.01/view.html?pg=5>; *Wired* Pretorius, 'TRIPS and Developing Countries: How Level Is the Playing Field?' in Peter Drahos and Ruth Mayne, *Global Intellectual Property Rights: Knowledge, Access and Development* (Palgrave Macmillan, 2002) 188; Ruth L Gana (Okediji), 'The Myth of Development, the Progress of Rights: Human Rights to Intellectual Property and Development' (1996) 18 *Law and Policy Journal* 315; Melville B. Nimmer and David Nimmer, *Nimmer on Copyright*, vol 1 (Matthew Bender, 1976), 1-16; Siva Vaidhyanathan, *Copyright and Copywrongs —The Rise of Intellectual Property and How It Threatens Creativity* (New York University, 2001) ch 2, 35-80; Benedict Atkinson, *The True History of Copyright—The Australian Experience 1905-2005* (Sydney University, 2007), ch 14, 393 <http://www.austlii.edu.au/au/journals/SydUPLawBk/2007/19.html>; Yong-Shik Lee, *Reclaiming Development in the World Trading System* (Cambridge University, 2006) 124-125.

[151] The Director of DuPont's Chemical Department, Elmer Bolton, noted that '[b]efore the presence of the internet, American agents cabled from London to the US the entire contents of a book published by the Queen within 24 hours of its release'. Elmer Bolton, cited in Drahos and Braithwaite, above n 137, 33; Susan Sell, 'Intellectual Property and Antitrust in the Developing World: Crisis, Coercion, and Choice' in Peter Drahos, *Intellectual Property* (Ashgate Publishing Company, 1999) 433-467.

[152] Gerhard Joseph, 'Charles Dickens, International Copyright, and the Discretionary Silence of Martin Chuzzlewit' (1991-1992) *Cardozo Arts and Entertainment Law Journal* 523, 523-524.

was entirely and humiliatingly a failure.[153] Great Britain, the world leader in technology at that time, attacked the US for not providing strong IP protection, but its complaints had very little or no effect[154] because of the opposition of American publishers, who believed that there was no use protecting IP of foreign authors as it was considered an unfavourable tax on their account.

In 1891, under pressure from English publishers, the US Congress passed the *International Copyright Act of 1891*,[155] more commonly known as the *Chace Act*, providing for the first time some form of copyright protection for foreign authors,[156] provided that they complied with the requirements of the

---

[153] Ibid. See also William P. Alford, *To Steal a Book Is an Elegant Offense* (Stanford University, 1995) 5.

[154] Khan, above n 4, 24.

[155] For a complete historical overview of the development of American copyright law, see generally, Paul Goldstein, *International Copyright—Principles, Law and Practice* (2001) 18; Robert A. Gorman and Jane C. Ginsburg, *Copyright Cases and Materials* (Foundation, 7th ed, 2006) 1-12; John Barton et al., *Integrating Intellectual Property Rights and Development Policy* (September 2002) Commission on Intellectual Property Rights (CIPR), 18-19 <http://www.iprcommission.org/papers/pdfs/final_report/CIPRfullfinal.pdf>; Melville B. Nimmer and David Nimmer, *Nimmer on Copyright*, vol 1 (Matthew Bender, 1976), 1-16; Margreth Barrett, *Intellectual Property Cases and Materials* (West Group, 2nd ed, 1995); John W. Hazard, *Copyright Law in Business and Practice* (West Group, 1989) 3-4; Donald S. Ghisum and Michael A. Jacobs, *United States—World Intellectual Property Guide* (1992) 4-7 (on file with author); L Ray Patterson and Stanley W Lindberg, *The Nature of Copyright Law—A Law User's Rights* (University of Georgia, 1991) 74-102; Peter Drahos and John Braithwaite, *Information Feudalism—Who Owns the Knowledge Economy?* (Earthsacan Publications, 2002) 33; Zorina Khan, *Intellectual Property and Economic Development: Lessons from American and European History* (September 2002) Commission on Intellectual Property Rights (CIPR), 39-40 <http://www.iprcommission.org/papers/pdfs/study_papers/sp1a_khan_study.pdf>.

[156] Section 13 of *International Copyright Act of 1870 (Chace Act)* provides that:

> [T]his act shall only apply to a citizen or subject of a foreign state or nation when such foreign state or nation permits to citizens of the United States of America the benefit of copyright on substantially the same basis as [to] its own citizens; or when such foreign state or nation is a party to an international agreement which provides for reciprocity in the granting of copyright, by the terms of which agreement the United States of America may, at its pleasure, become a party to such agreement. The existence of either of the conditions aforesaid shall be determined by the President of the United States by proclamation made from time to time as the purposes of this act may require.

See *International Copyright Act of 1870 (Chace Act)*, enacted by the Fifty-First Congress on 3 March 1891 <http://www.ellenwhite.info/copyright_law_us_1891.htm>. For more information on the *Chace Act*, see Nimmer and Nimmer, above n 71, vol 4, 13; Barbosa, above n 4, 43-110; Goldstein, above n 4, 18,

Act.[157] Therefore, after a century of lobbying by interested parties on both sides of the Atlantic, and based on reasons that ranged from economic to moral, international copyright law was recognised in the US for the first time.[158] This only happened when American publishers became more competitive in the international market in their reproduction of literary and artistic works.[159]

In addition, American patent laws protected US citizens by providing incentive for domestic innovation,[160] but these laws were constantly amended to meet the demands of US industries.[161] Between 1790 and 1836, the US restricted the issue of patents to its own citizens and residents,[162] and in 1861, foreigners were treated on a non-discriminatory basis, along with American inventors, but they were required to pay patent fees ten times the rate of US citizens.[163] The drafting of appropriate IP laws allowed American citizens to imitate creative innovators in Europe and boosted the American economy in its early stages of development.[164] This obviously has changed over time as the US has amended its IP laws significantly to reflect its position as a leader of technological innovation and creativity and a champion of IP protection.

In the mid-1980s, high technology and entertainment goods became a significant portion of US exports.[165] The US industries were concerned about the free riding on their R&D investments that was taking place, particularly in developing countries. For that purpose, they called on the US government[166] to help halt imitation, copying and reverse engineering abroad.[167] The US government responded to this request and began to pursue a series of policies to secure protection of American IP

---

[157] Such as notice, registration, and deposit requirements. See Nimmer and Nimmer, above n 71, 13.

[158] One commentator believes that this simply was not the case. Although the law affected the worst case of piracy that was happening in the US, especially for major literary works like that of Charles Dickens, it did not stop piracy in the country. See James L. W. West III, 'The Chace Act and Anglo-American Literary Relations' (1992) 45 *Studies in Bibliography* <http://etext.virginia.edu/etcbin/browse-sb?id=sibv045&images=bsuva/sb/images&data=/texts/english/bibliog/SB&tag=public>.

[159] Khan, above n 4, 44.

[160] Susan Sell, 'Intellectual Property at a Cross Road: The Use of the Past in Intellectual Property Jurisprudence: Intellectual Property and Public Policy in Historical Perspective: Contestation and Settlement' (2004) 38 *Loyola of Los Angeles Law Entertainment Review* 267, 282-283.

[161] Khan, above n 4, 44.

[162] Barton et al., above n 4, 18-19.

[163] Ibid, Ghisum and Jacobs, above n 155, 2-14.

[164] In addition to having appropriate IP laws in place, the US had remarkable judges and legal practitioners who adopted an instrumentalist approach that interpreted the law in ways that favoured economic development. See Khan, above n 4, 24, 54.

[165] Braithwaite and Drahos, above n 104, 61.

[166] In the US, four agencies the share primary responsibilities for international IP rights policy: the State Department (executive branch), the Office of the US Trade Representative (USTR) (executive branch), the Patent and Trademark Office (USPTO) of the Department of Commerce (executive branch), and the Copyright Office of the Library of Congress (legislative branch). See also Cheek, above n 137, 277, 304.

[167] Ibid 303-304.

around the world.[168] Amongst the most effective policies is the unilateral trade sanctions imposed by the US against developing countries under Section 301 of the *US Trade Act*.[169]

2.4.2.2 Special 301 Threats of the US

The US Trade Representative (the USTR) has repeatedly used actions under Section 301[170] of the *Trade Act of 1974*, as amended, to challenge developing countries' IP systems,[171] combined with threats to withdraw the Generalized System of Preferences (GSP) program[172] that was given to these countries.[173] Section 301 is part of the US *Trade Act*, which is used by the USTR[174] to address

---

[168] Ibid.

[169] Ibid 300.

[170] The regular users of the US 301 Section include a list of organisations that aim to lobby for the highest IP protection in developing countries. These include the International Intellectual Property Association (IIPA), American Film Marketing Association, Association of American Publishers, Information Technology Association of America, Motion Picture Association of America, National Music Publishers Association, and Recording Industry of America. See Braithwaite and Drahos, above n 104, 71; Deere, above n 23, 11-12; Sell, above n 151, 439-450; Sell, above n 132, chs 4-5; Susan K. Sell, 'Intellectual Property as a Trade Issue: From the Paris Convention to GATT', (1989) 13 (4) *Legal Studies Forum* 411, 419.

[171] Jerome H. Reichman, 'Intellectual Property in the Twenty-First Century: Will the Developing Countries Lead or Follow?' (2009) 46 *Houston Law Review* 1115, 1177.

[172] This program allows exporters from certain developing countries such as Brazil, Turkey, Thailand, Egypt, the Philippines, and others to enter their goods (wood, stone, agricultural products, etc) to the US market without any tariffs. See Abigail L. Ho, 'Government Seeks Renewal of U.S. GSP Privileges', Philippine Daily Inquirer (online), 13 January 2011 <http://business.inquirer.net/money/topstories/view/20110113-314274/Govt-seeks-renewal-of-US-GSP-privileges>.

[173] Reichman, above n 171, 159.

[174] The USTR investigations under Special 301 process can result in one of four outcomes:

> First, the USTR may be satisfied with the progress being made in the country under investigation and take no action. Second, a country may be placed on the USTR's 'watch list' which is used 'as a means of monitoring progress in implementing commitments with regard to the protection of intellectual property rights.' Third, a country may be placed on the USTR's 'priority watch list' which is comprised of countries in which 'the lack of adequate and effective intellectual property protection or market access is especially significant for US interests.' Fourth, the USTR may designate a country as a Priority Foreign Country. It is only this final designation that is mandated by statute.

See Cheek, above n 137, 277, 292, 301-302; Braithwaite and Drahos, above n 104, 62; Drahos, above n 3, 9; Peter Drahos, 'Bits and BIPs—Bilateralism in Intellectual Property' (2001) 4 (6) *Journal of World Intellectual Property*, 791, 793; Peter Drahos, 'Global Property Rights in Information: The Story of TRIPs at the GATT' in Peter Drahos, *Intellectual Property* (Ashgate Publishing Company, 1999) 419-431; Reichman, above n 49, 761; Sell, above n 132, chs 4-5; Sell, above n 4, 130-139.

what is considered as unfair trading practices by any foreign government that burdens or restricts US commerce,[175] and that includes infringements of American IP rights.[176] Its main effect was to bring developing countries to the bilateral negotiating table and improve US protection of IP abroad.[177]

Crucial to the evolution of the US trade-based strategy for IP was the work of the Advisory Committee for Trade Negotiating (ACTN).[178] This Committee was designed to provide direct input by the US business sector into US trade policy.[179] The task force recommended the US government to develop IP policies to deal with infringements of American IP rights overseas.[180] In 1984, the IIPA was also founded to promote US copyright interests. It emerged quickly as a powerful and effective lobbying arm, representing over 1,500 corporations[181] interested in protecting and enforcing their IP rights overseas. Section 301 was used against several developing countries, including India and Brazil, that were not protecting American IP interests as they need to be.

In summary, the US pressured developing countries to respect IP by using the old 'stick-and-carrot' method of negotiating.[182] The stick was the threat of trade sanctions if they did not comply, and the carrot was 'favourable consideration' in relation to aid and preferential trade benefits in future bilateral trade agreements.[183] However, the coercive strategy in Section 301 that the US has used against developing countries to offer stronger protection of IP achieved limited results[184] as most countries resisted implementing and enforcing these policies.[185]

---

[175] *Trade Act of 1974*, 19 USC ch 12 sub 3 § 2415<http://www.law.cornell.edu/uscode/text/19/2415>.

[176] Braithwaite and Drahos, above n 104, 792.

[177] Ibid. The Special 301 process has induced numerous developing countries to change their national laws and policies in relation to IP. Among these countries are Brazil, China, Thailand, Singapore, Korea, Taiwan, and many others. See Myles Geltan, 'TRIPS and the Future of Section 301: A Comparative Study in Trade Dispute Resolution' (1996) 34 *Columbia Journal of Transitional Law* 174; James W. Peters, 'Toward Negotiating a Remedy to Copyright Piracy in Singapore' (1986) 7 *Northwestern Journal of International Law & Business*, 561, 580; Peters, above n 96, 576-580; Alford, above n 153, Taiwan (95-111) and China (112, 123).

[178] Drahos (1999), above n 174, 421-422.

[179] Ibid.

[180] Ibid.

[181] Sell, above n 132, 84.

[182] Pretorius, above n 150, 184.

[183] Ibid.

[184] Sell, above n 151, 436.

[185] Ibid 441; Deere, above n 33, 160.

2.4.3 Europe

2.4.3.1 Historical Aspects of IP Protection in Europe

In the second half of the nineteenth century, some European countries (e.g., Holland and England) resisted providing patent protection and only decided to do so when their industries had reached a certain degree of development.[186] Copyright was also not protected in some European countries such as Belgium because publishers wanted to use creative works of foreign publishers and did not want to pay any remuneration.[187]

Today, very few developed countries would seriously consider eliminating statutory protection for IP, but in the second half of the nineteenth century, this was a much discussed topic in Europe between the advocates of IP rights and the abolitionists.[188] It was only in response to international pressures from major European countries such as England and Germany that other European countries began to respect and protect international IP.

2.4.3.2 E.C Regulation 2641/84

After European countries colonised many parts of the world in Africa, Asia, and Latin America, they wanted their colonies and protectorates to provide laws that were based entirely on their models of IP protection. The existence of IP laws in their colonies and protectorates was considered as a necessary prerequisite for civilisation and as evidence of progress towards 'Western-style development'.[189]

For a long time after gaining independence, many developing countries either did not have appropriate IP laws in place or did not enforce these laws, as expected by European countries. This has led the European Commission (EC) to follow the American route of developing tools that link IP with trade benefits.[190]

The EC trade laws were revised to accommodate the rise in the level of piracy in developing countries.[191] On 23 September 1984, a Council Regulation empowered

[186] Pretorius, above n 150, 184; Sell, above n 160, 282-283; Botoy, above n 144, 115, 125; Khan, above n 4, 12. See also Barton et al., above n 4, 18-20.

[187] For a historical introduction of the law of copyright in Europe, see Khan, above n 4, 31-35; John S. McKeown, *Fox Canadian Law of Copyright* (Carswell, 3rd ed, 2000) 13-32; Sam Ricketson, *The Law of Intellectual Property* (Sydney Law Book, 1984) 57-77; J.A.L. Sterling, *World Copyright Law* (Sweet and Maxwell, 2003) 5-24; Kevin Garnett, Jonathan Rayner James, and Gillian Davies, *Copinger and Skone James on Copyright* (Sweet and Maxwell, 14th ed, 1999) 31-50.

[188] Khan, above n 4, 29.

[189] Gana (Okediji), above n 4, 332; Deere, above n 33, 36.

[190] Deere, above n 23, 12.

[191] Drahos, above n 5, 178.

the EC to engage in trade retaliation against 'illicit commercial practices' (defined as violations of 'international law or generally accepted rules') by non-EU countries that affect EU economic interests.[192] This Regulation was drafted (a) to defend vigorously the legitimate trade interests of Europeans in bilateral and multilateral organisations, particularly in the General Agreement on Tariffs and Trade (GATT), and (b) to ensure that the EC acts with as much speed and efficiency as its trading partners.[193] Possible forms of retaliation for EC members in the Regulation include the (a) suspension or withdrawal of any concession resulting from commercial policy negotiations, (b) raising of existing customs duties or introduction of any other charge on imports, and (c) introduction of quantitative restrictions or any other measures modifying import or export conditions or otherwise affecting trade with the third country concerned.[194] The EC version of Section 301 was used against certain developing countries that were considered to be failing to provide satisfactory protection of IP for European inventors and authors. Among the developing countries that were targets of the EC trade laws were Indonesia and Thailand.[195]

Professor Ruth Okediji criticised how some industrialised European countries turned a blind eye to their early history of IP protection when they did not protect it and then required developing countries and LDCs to adopt IP systems that were alien to, and in sharp contrast with, their native conceptions and domestic conditions.[196] She suggested giving developing countries some period of time before it becomes viable (if ever) for them to join the international IP system.[197] Actually, this has been recognised in the *TRIPS Agreement*, where least developing countries have until 1 July 2013 to make their laws and practice of IP (except for pharmaceutical patents, which have been extended until 1 January 2016) fully compliant with their obligations under the WTO.

2.4.4 *Japan*

2.4.4.1 Historical Aspects of IP Protection in Japan

Japan is an ambitious proponent of heightened standards of IP protection and supports fully the efforts taken by the US and other developed countries to raise

[192] Ibid; Michael Buton Devine, 'The Adoption of ECC Regulation 2641/84 on Illicit Commercial Practices with Special Reference to the U.S.A' (1988) 22 *The International Lawyer* 1091.

[193] Ibid 1091. See also James R. Atwood, 'The European Community's New Measures against Unfair Practices in International Trade: Implications for United States Exporters' (1985) 19 *International Law* 361, 361.

[194] Atwood, above 193, 366-367.

[195] Sell, above n 151, 448, and 450.

[196] Gana (Okediji), above n 4, 327.

[197] Ibid.

internationally the level of protection. This attitude toward IP protection changed sharply over the years when Japan was considered a developing country.[198]

Japan is known to have greatly benefited from IP generated in other developed countries in its early stage of development,[199] primarily the US and German patent systems.[200] After World War II (1939–1945), the Japanese government's policy was quite aggressive and biased toward the interests of foreign investors,[201] who were required to make their technologies available to domestic industries. For example, in the context of the IT sector, in the late 1950s, a vice-minister at the Japanese Ministry of International Trade and Industry (MITI) allegedly warned IBM that '[w]e will take every measure possible to obstruct the success of your business unless you license IBM patents to Japanese firms and charge them no more than a 5% royalty'. IBM had little choice but to comply.[202]

---

[198] Hisamitsu Arai, former Vice-Minister for International Affairs, Ministry of International Trade and Industry (MITI) in Japan noted that:

> [T]he first JPO Commissioner was Korekiyo Takahashi, who had served as interpreter to Dr Morley, who had come from the United States to help Japan formulate its educational system. Even 120 years ago, Takahashi reports that Morley complained that Japan was a nation of copiers and asserted that patents, trademarks, and copyrights were very important assets in the US.

See Hisamitsu Arai, *Intellectual Property Policies for the Twenty-First Century: The Japanese Experience in Wealth Creation* (WIPO Publication 2006), 86 <http://www.wipo.int/export/sites/www/freepublications/en/intproperty/834/wipo_pub_834.pdf>.

[199] Christopher Heath (ed), *Intellectual Property Law in Asia* (Kluwer Law International, 2003) 173; Khan, above n 4, 28.

[200] Hiroyuki Odagiri, A. Gotto, and A. Sunami, 'IPR and Catch UP Process in Japan' in Hirouki Odagiri et al. (eds), *Intellectual Property Rights, Development and Catch UP* (Oxford, 2010) 125.

[201] Graham Dutfield and Uma Suthersanen noted the following example:

> [I]n 1960, Texas Instruments filed a patent in Japan on the integrated circuit, arguably one of the most important inventions of the second half of the twentieth century. The Japan Patent Office allowed itself 29 years to grant the patent. By that time Japanese companies, free to read the patent specification 18 months after filing, acquired the technology, improved upon it, and controlled 80% of the U.S. market for computer semiconductor.

See Chalmers A. Johnson, *Japan: Who Governs? The Rise of the Developmental State* (W.W. Norton & Company, 1995) 74–5, cited in Graham Dutfield and Uma Suthersanen, 'Harmonisation or Differentiation in Intellectual Property Protection? The Lesson of History' (2005) 2 (23) *Prometheus: Critical Studies in Innovation* 131, 136.

[202] See M. Fisher 'Growth of the Japanese Patent System: A Lesson for Us All?' (2004) 22 (1) *Intellectual Property Quarterly* 85, 113, cited in Dutfield and Suthersanen, above n 201, 131, 142.

2.4.4.2 Current Japanese Attitude Toward IP Protection

The first IP law in Japan was the *Trademark Act* in 1884. One year later, the first Japanese *Patent Monopoly Act* was enacted in 1885[203] despite argument, even within the government, that such law would deprive the Japanese of the ability to imitate advanced products, thereby hindering Japan's catching up.[204] In 1888, the patent law was passed,[205] and it was later amended in 1899, 1921, and 1959, in conformity with Japan's dynamic industrial development.[206] The ultimate objective of this law was to contribute to the development of Japanese industry and not to be an end in itself.[207] These IP laws have helped the country to develop its own technology and gradually grow to stand shoulder-to-shoulder with other developed countries.[208] One recent empirical study attributed to Japan's success is not only having IP laws in place but also making modifications to these laws to suit the changing economic needs of the country.[209] In essence, Japan regularly changed its IP systems to encourage the development of new inventions.[210]

Japan has supported developing countries in training officials in Asian developing countries to be more efficient in patent administration. This program has been very well received in developing countries, with a total of 1,000 officers trained.[211] The country is also cooperating with patent and trademark offices in Asian countries to computerise their national offices.[212]

After examining these aspects of the development of the IP system in certain developed countries, it is important to now examine the views of developing countries.

2.4.5 *The Views of Developing Countries*

The views of developing countries are contrary to that of developed countries in relation to the importance of IP to their national interests and economic

[203] Arai, above n 198.

[204] Odagiri et al., above n 200, 98.

[205] Ibid 99.

[206] Heath, above n 199, 175.

[207] Masaaki Kotabe, 'A Comparative Study of U.S. and Japanese Patent Systems' (1992) 23(1) *Journal of International Business Studies* 147-168. 1992, cited in Nagesh Kumar, *Intellectual Property Rights, Technology and Economic Development: Experiences of Asian Countries* (September 2002) Commission on Intellectual Property Rights <http://www.iprcommission.org/papers/pdfs/study_papers/sp1b_kumar_study.pdf>.

[208] Arai, above n 198, 64.

[209] Odagiri et al., above n 200, 122.

[210] Ibid.

[211] Arai, above n 198, 64.

[212] Ibid.

development. Some commentators argue that strong IP would hamper the free flow of information and A2K that they need to advance their societies. Others see that there is no benefit deriving from strengthening IP laws in developing countries as this will block technology transfers from industrialised developed countries to their countries.[213] Few developing countries have rejected the notion of IP or argued that creators should not be compensated in return for their effort as it is a 'common heritage of mankind'.[214] Developing countries see that strict protection for IP may impede their technological development; a 'western-style IP system' may hinder their innovation and creativity. Moreover, they argue that stronger protection and enforcement of IP will increase holders' control over technology, resulting in anti-competitive practices and prohibitive high prices.[215]

[213] Ruth L. Okediji, 'Africa and the Global Intellectual Property System: Beyond the Agency Model' in Abdulqawi A. Yusuf *African Yearbook of International Law* (2004) 207, 236. See also Evelyn Su, 'The Winners and the Losers: The Agreement on Trade-Related Aspects of Intellectual Property Rights and Its Effects on Developing Countries' (2004) 23 (1) *Houston Journal of International Law* 200; Douglas F. Greer, 'The Case against Patent Systems in Less-Developed Countries' (1973) 8 *Journal of International Law and Economics* 223; Helge E. Grundmann, 'Foreign Patent Monopolies in Developing Countries: An Empirical Analysis' (1976) 12 *Journal of Development Studies* 186; H. Kornstein and I. Till, 'A Re-evaluation of the International Patent Convention' (1947) 12 *Law and Contemporary Problems* 765, 766; Constantine Vaitsos, 'Patents Revisited: Their Function in Developing Countries' (1972) 9 *Journal of Development Studies* 71, 89-90; A. Samuel Oddi, 'The International Patent System and Third World Development: Reality or Myth?' (1987) 5 *Duke University Law Journal* 831,854; John Barton et al., *Integrating Intellectual Property Rights and Development Policy* (September 2002) Commission on Intellectual Property Rights (CIPR) <http://www.iprcommission.org/papers/pdfs/final_report/CIPRfullfinal.pdf>; Margret Chon, 'Intellectual Property and the Development Divide' (2006) 27 *Cardozo Law Review*, 2821, 2861; Md. Golam Robbani, 'Trade Related Aspects of Intellectual Property Rights and Least Developed Countries' (2005) 8 (4) *The Journal of World Intellectual Property* 565, 568-569; J. H. Reichman, 'Intellectual Property in International Trade: Opportunities and Risk of GATT Connection' (1989) 22 (4) *Vanderbilt Journal of Transnational Law* 747, 761-763; Carlos M. Correa, *Trade Related Aspects of Intellectual Property Rights—A Commentary on the TRIPS Agreement* (2007), ch 4; Suerie Moon, *Does TRIPS Art 66.2 Encourage Technology Transfer to LDCs? An Analysis of the Country Submissions to the TRIPS Council*, Brief Number 2 (December 2008) UNCTAD-ICTSD Project on IPRs and Sustainable Development Policy <http://www.iprsonline.org/New%202009/Policy%20Briefs/policy-brief-2.pdf>; Wolfgang E. Siebeck et al. (eds), *Strengthening Protection of Intellectual Property in Developing Countries—A Survey of Literature* (The World Bank, 1990); Charles E. Walker and Mark A. Bloomfield, *Intellectual Property Rights and Capital Formation in the Next Decade* (University Press of America, 1988) 57-106; Alan S. Gutterman, 'The North-South Debate Regarding the Protection of Intellectual Property Rights' (1993) 28 *Wake Forest Law Review*, 89-139, (121-125). R. A. Mashelkar, 'Intellectual Property Rights and the Third World' (2005) 81 (1) *Current Science* 955; Jean Raymond Homere, Intellectual Property Rights Can Help Stimulate the Economic Development of Least Developed Countries, (2004) 27 (2) *Columbia Journal of Law and Arts* 277, 285.

[214] Sell, above n 151, 436.

[215] Maria Julia Olivia, 'Intellectual Property in the FTAA: Little Opportunity and Much Risk' (2003) (19) *American University International Law Review* 45, 53.

Among the most important developing countries[216] that have shaped the international debate over IP and development are India and Brazil. China is also a potential rising actor in the debate around IP and development.

2.4.6 *India*

India has played a critical role in the shaping of the international IP system. In the revision of the *Paris Convention*, India pushed for provisions that would give developing countries more access to technologies that had been locked up by the international patent system.[217] During the 1967 Stockholm Revision Conference of the *Berne Convention*, India demanded special concessions in the international copyright system that would take into consideration the economic, social, cultural, and technological conditions of developing countries.[218] It argued specifically that the ability of developing countries to educate their people was limited by publication cartels and the high royalties and licensing fees demanded by copyright holders in developed countries.[219]

On the national level, Indian chemical and pharmaceutical corporations tried to develop their own technology in the 1960s but ran into trouble with foreign patent owners in developed countries. This situation has led to increasing public pressure to amend the *Patent and Design Act of 1911*, which was inherited from Great Britain.[220] Two Indian expert committees, The Tek Chand Committee (1948) and the Ayyangar Committee (1959),[221] were created to review the patent law in India,

---

[216] In this section, India, Brazil, and China are discussed in terms of developing countries. While their status has changed over the last 10-15 years, at this point of time, they are in their early stages of development. Today, they are acknowledged as leading emerging market economies.

[217] Braithwaite and Drahos, above n 104, 61.

[218] Yu, above n 22, 1, 5.

[219] Deere, above n 33, 42.

[220] Kumar, above n 207.

[221] The Supreme Court Justice of India, Rajagopala Ayyangar, was asked after a lengthy discussion of the costs and benefits of having a patent system for a developing country such as India. He answered:

> With all the handicaps which the system involves in its application to under-developed countries, there are no alternatives methods for achieving better results. At the best there is no country in the world that does not adopt the patent system of rewarding investors, whatever differences in detail there might be in the laws of the various countries due to local conditions or historical reasons.

He further noted that:

> [T]he precise provisions of the patent law have to be designed with specific reference to the economic conditions of the country, the state of its scientific and technical advance its future needs and other relevant factors so as to minimise if not eliminate the abuses to which a system of patent monopoly is capable of being put.

in order to make it more suitable for the country.[222] After careful consideration by the two committees and an elaborate discussion in Parliament, it was decided that the Indian patent system had failed to 'stimulate inventions among Indians and to encourage the development and exploitation of new inventions'.[223]

Based on this finding, India decided that instead of abandoning its patent law, it would redesign it to suit its national circumstances.[224] In 1970, the *Indian Patent Act* was enacted[225] to strike a balance between the interests of investors and consumers and ensure that the benefits of new technological developments reached the Indian people without any monopoly control.[226] The enactment of the *Indian Patent Act* proved to be a boost to Indian technological capabilities, particularly in the chemical and pharmaceutical industries.[227] Because of this law, India did not join the *Paris Convention* until 7 December 1989, when it later modified[228] it to be fully compatible with the international patent system.[229]

India is a truly great example for other developing countries that want to develop their own IP system to suit their needs and local conditions. It showed how,

---

See Ayyangar, 1959, 18-19, cited in Bhaven N. Sampat, 'Indian Pharmaceutical and Software' in Odagiri et al., above, 200, 365.

[222] Roffe and Vea, above n 7, 92.

[223] N Mehrota noted that:

> Both the commissions found ample evidence of misuse of patent protection by foreign companies (who owned more than 90% patents in India) and it was clear that many patents were taken by MNCs basically to ensure protected exported markets... [I]t was observed that the country was denied by its own national law the right of getting in many cases, goods even though they were essential for industrial production, or for the health and safety of the community, at cheaper prices available from alternative sources because of patent protections.

N.N. Mehrota, '*Indian Patent Act, Paris Convention* and Self-Reliance' (1987) *Economic and Political Weekly* 1461. See also Svedaraman, 'The New Indian Patent Law' (1972) 3 *The International Review of Industrial Property and Copyright Law* 39; Drahos, above n 5, 165.

[224] Drahos, above n 5, 165; Sampat, above n 221, 365.

[225] See the *Indian Patent Act of 1970*, arts 47, 66, 89, 100, 101, and 102 (related to the protection of public interests). See the website of the Indian Office of the Controller General of Patents, Designs and Trademarks, *Indian Patent Act of 1970* <http://ipindia.nic.in/ipr/patent/patact1970-3-99.html>; UNCTAD, above n 32, 56-61.

[226] Mehrota, above n 223, 1461.

[227] The Indian Patent Law, has been hailed by the UN agencies as a model law for other developing countries that want to design specific laws that meet their local conditions. See Drahos above n 5, 165; Mehrota, above n 223, 1461; Kumar, above n 207; World Health Organization (WHO), *Public Health, Innovation and Intellectual Property Rights* (2006), 83-84 <http://www.who.int/intellectualproperty/documents/thereport/ENPublicHealthReport.pdf>; Kevin Donovan, *A Brief History of Intellectual Property in China and India* <http://www.techdirt.com/articles/20090530/1620345062.shtml>; Dutfield and Suthersanen, above n 201, 140-141.

[228] Mehrota, above n 223, 1461-1464

[229] For a review of the *Indian Patent Act* and its amendments, see Alan S Gutterman and Bentley J Anderson, *Intellectual Property in Global Markets: A Guide for Foreign Lawyers and Managers* (Kluwer Law International, 1997) 379-384; Indian Patent Office, *History of Indian Patent System* <http://ipindia.nic.in/ipr/PatentHistory.htm>.

in practice, a country could benefit a great deal from a carefully revised patent law that could facilitate the faster accumulation of innovative capabilities.[230] It also showed the unsuitability of a 'one-size-fits-all' approach to IP, which is constantly suggested by developed countries to be applied in the context of developing countries.

2.4.7 *Brazil*

The Brazilian government was convinced that it must play a central role in advancing national development. For that purpose, it deployed several policies, including import controls to protect domestic markets, subsidies to channel investment into new sectors, foreign investment regulation to spur backwards linkages and technology transfer,[231] and IP law reforms to suit its local interests.[232] The government has also included restrictions on foreign holders of patent rights and provided licensing practices that were favourable to local producers.[233]

On the international scene, Brazil played an important role in the early nineteenth century in defending the interests of developing countries in relation to how the IP system should be structured, bringing forward development issues and public interest concerns[234] to the *Paris Convention* and the *Berne Convention*. Brazil and India were also important in preventing the US and Japan from signing an international treaty for the protection of layout designs of integrated circuits.

As a thorn on the part of American MNCs that want to globalise IP standards, the US has made a variety of threats against Brazil. In 1987, the US Pharmaceutical Manufacturers Association initiated a 301 action against Brazil for failing to protect pharmaceutical products and processes.[235] The action ultimately resulted in former President Ronald Reagan authorising the imposition of trade duties in the amount of US$39 million on Brazilian products imported into the US.[236] On 8 January 2001, twelve days before President Clinton left office, the USTR filed a complaint with

[230] Sampat, above n 221, 372.

[231] Deere, above n 23, 4. See also, Roberto Mazzoleni and Luciano Martins Costa Povoa, 'Accumulation of Technological Capabilities and Economic Development: Did Brazil's IPR Regime Matter?' in Odagiri et al., above n 200, 280–311.

[232] Brazil was the fourth country after England, the US, and France to issue an industrial property law. It has drafted its first patent law since 1809 to correspond with its developmental needs and local conditions. See Gontijo, above n 30, 13; Pedro Nicleti Mizukami and Ronaldo Lemos, 'Limitations and Exceptions to Copyright in the Brazilian Law: A Need for Reform' in Lea Shaver (ed), *Access to Knowledge in Brazil* (Bloomsbury, 2009) 67, 70-76 <http://www.law.yale.edu/documents/pdf/ISP/A2KBrazil_bkmk.pdf>. See also Mazzoleni and Povoa, above n 231, 280-311.

[233] Deere, above n 23, 4

[234] Menescal, above n 30,761

[235] Braithwaite and Drahos, above n 104, 79.

[236] Ibid.

the WTO over the Brazil compulsory licensing law.[237] At issue was art 68 of Brazil's patent law, which allows a compulsory licence to be issued in the situation where the patent holder does not locally manufacture the patent product.[238] In June 2001, in the face of enormous negative publicity from NGOs, the Brazilian government, and the media, the Bush administration withdrew the complaint.[239]

Brazil is an interesting example of what the US will do to protect the IP rights of Americans abroad. The US decided to suspend any action against the infringement of its IP in Brazil only when it determined that such a manoeuvre would inflict harm upon the subsidies of the American MNCs working in Brazil. Brazil also learned the hard way that the high costs of sanctions on American-Brazilian subsidies would make the US rethink of any such action.

2.4.8 China

The history of IP in China dates back to the beginning of the twentieth century, when its first laws were introduced (copyright law 1910 and patent law 1912).[240] In reality, effective IP systems were introduced in China much later, in the 1980s and the 1990s, prior to China's accession to the WTO and after joining the major international IP treaties. The main purpose of introducing IP laws in China was to attract foreign capital, acquire know-how and technology from developed countries, and protect local indigenous technology.[241]

In general, while China's IP systems have played a role in stimulating innovation by both multinational and domestic firms, its net impact on the economic development of the country is not totally established.[242] There were several complementary factors that helped China in its economic development, such as market-oriented reforms of the economic system, the recognition of private property rights, the transition and optimisation of the National Innovation System (NIS), and persistent and comprehensive policies opening it up to the world.[243] The US has exercised

[237] Deere, above n 33, 166.

[238] Ibid.

[239] Ibid.

[240] Deli Yang, 'The Development of Intellectual Property in China' (2003) 25 *World Patent Information* 131; Lan Xue and Zheng Liang, 'Relationship between IPR and Technology Catch-UP: Some Evidence in China' in Odagiri et al., above n 200, 319. See also Alford, above n 153, 41-42.

[241] Yang, above n 240, 136.

[242] Xue and Liang, above 240, 356.

[243] Ibid 355. Professor Peter Yu adds that 'the drastically lower production costs, the country's enormous market, its efficient economic system, and the preferential treatment of foreign investors have all helped to attract FDI in China'. See Peter K. Yu, 'Intellectual Property, Economic Development, and the China Puzzle' in Daniel Gervais (ed), *Intellectual Property, Trade and Development-Strategies to Optimize Economic Development in a TRIPS-Plus Era* (Oxford University, 2007) 182.

tremendous pressures on China to change its IP systems and provide strong protection for American corporations working in the country. The US used various measures (Section 301) against China in the late 1980s and early 1990s to provide strong protection for IP and to bring its laws into accordance with international standards in IP treaties.[244]

China is an interesting case for study by IP scholars in developing countries because although IP may not be a prerequisite for economic development, it is an integral and essential part of the country's innovation system, which is important for progress.[245] The Chinese experience illustrates that to understand the full effect of IP systems on the economic development of the country, one needs to take into considerations not only the law but also the political, economic, and judicial influences that shape the society and economy.[246] China is important for understanding how IP systems affect economic development and will play an important role in the future in shaping the debate around IP and development.

2.5 The General Agreement on Tariffs and Trade

Before examining the *TRIPS Agreement* in relation to developing countries, it is necessary to briefly look at General Agreement on Tariffs and Trade (GATT), which linked IP with trade.

GATT and the *Charter of the International Trade Organisation* (ITO) were drafted in the negotiating sessions in 1946–1947.[247] GATT was an agreement between states aiming to eliminate discrimination and reducing tariffs and other trade barriers with respect to trade in goods.[248] All WTO contracting parties are obliged to abide by the provisions of GATT, the legal instruments concluded under it, the understandings concluded during the Uruguay Round on the interpretation of GATT, and the Marrakesh Protocol on Tariffs and Concessions.[249] GATT consists of 38 provisions divided into four parts; Part IV aims to increase trade opportunities for developing countries.[250]

---

[244] Yang, above n 240, 138, Yu, above n 243, 186.

[245] Yu, above n 243, 220

[246] Ibid 213.

[247] Raj Bahala, *Trade, Development and Social Justice* (Carolina Academic, 2003) 14; Christopher Arup, *The World Organisation Knowledge Agreements* (Cambridge University, 2nd ed, 2008) 165-179.

[248] UNCTAD, *Dispute Settlement World Trade Organisation* (2003) <http://www.unctad.org/en/docs/edmmisc232add33_en.pdf>.

[249] Ibid.

[250] See *General Agreement on Tariffs and Trade*, opened for signature on 30 October 1947, 55 UNTS 187 (entered into force on 1 January 1948) <http://www.wto.org/english/docs_e/legal_e/gatt47.pdf> (GATT); Robert Read, *A Summary of the GATT Articles* (Lancastor University) <http://www.lancs.ac.uk/staff/ecarar/gatt%20articles.doc>; UNCTAD, above n 248.

The continuation of WIPO as the main multilateral forum for negotiations on IP posed a dilemma for developed countries, which realised that it only offered minimal standards of protection and lacked effective enforcement mechanisms.[251] Such important considerations made developed countries move the international negotiation of IP to a new forum.[252] This strategy is called 'regime shifting' or 'forum shifting'.[253] It is defined as 'an attempt to alter the status quo by moving treaty negotiation, lawmaking initiatives, or standard setting activities from one international venue to another'.[254]

In February 1982, just over 2 years after the conclusion of the Tokyo Round, the US proposed holding a new round to examine various trade issues (including commercial counterfeiting) that were left unresolved in the Tokyo Round.[255] The inclusion of IP in a new round was a novel topic of discussion with GATT and proved to be a source of great discord between developing and developed countries.[256] At the Ministerial Meeting at Punta del Este in September 1986, the US succeeded, with the support of Europe, Canada, and Japan, in linking IP with trade[257] in the Uruguay Round between 1986 and 1994.[258]

A small and loosely coordinated grouping of ten developing countries (namely Argentina, Brazil, Cuba, Egypt, India, Nicaragua, Nigeria, Peru, Tanzania, and Yugoslavia) engaged in IP discussions in GATT in the early days of the Uruguay

---

[251] Viviana Munoz Tellez, 'The Changing Global Governance of Intellectual Property Enforcement: New Challenges for Developing Countries' in Xuan Li and Carlos M. Correa (eds), *Intellectual Property and Enforcement* (Edward Elgar, 2009) 6.

[252] Ibid.

[253] Forum shifting encompasses three kinds of strategies as follows: moving an agenda from one organisation to another, abandoning an organisation, and pursuing the same agenda in more than one organisation. See Braithwaite and Drahos, above n 104, 564; Denis Borges Barbosa, Margaret Chon, and Andres Moncayo von Hase, 'Slouching Towards Development in International Intellectual Property' (2007) 71 *Michigan State Law Review* 85.

[254] Professor Peter Yu noted the difference between the following:

> An 'intra-regime shift' reflects a move from one venue to another venue situated within the same regime—for example, from bilateral intellectual property agreements to a multilateral intellectual property convention. By contrast, an 'inter-regime shift' reflects a move from one venue to another venue located in an entirely different regime—for example, from the intellectual property regime to the public health or human rights regime.

Yu, above n 22.

[255] Goldstein, above n 4, 53.

[256] Dennis DeConcini 'Patent Protection Abroad for U.S. Pharmaceuticals' (1991) 5 *World Intellectual Property Report* 336, 338, cited in Alan S. Gutterman and Bentley Anderson, 'Review of Intellectual Property in Global Markets' (November 1998) *European Intellectual Property Law Review* 17.

[257] One scholar argues that the linkage between IP and trade did not start in *TRIPS Agreement* but earlier in the *Paris Convention* and GATT in 1947. See, Botoy, above n 144, 122. On the linkage of trade and IP, see Barbosa, Chon, and Hase, above n 253, 81-83.

[258] Braithwaite and Drahos, above n 104, 63.

Round[259] but resisted the inclusion of the so-called 'trade-related IP' in the trade negotiations.[260] Their line of argument was that GATT was primarily concerned with trade in goods and not IP rights, and such rights fell within WIPO's work.[261] In the end, developing countries accepted the idea and became members of the WTO and agreed to abide by the *TRIPS Agreement*. Why have they agreed on such terms? Did they have any other option?

There are several reasons developing countries agreed to join the WTO and abide by the *TRIPS Agreement*. Developing countries had limited expertise in IP issues and trade, and they did not work effectively with each other in that regard.[262] They believed that their acceptance of the *TRIPS Agreement* would stop the US from threatening them with unilateral trade sanctions[263] and mandating high standards of IP protection.[264] More importantly, developing countries acquiesced because of expected gains in other areas[265] such as textiles and agriculture.[266] Furthermore, the onset of the debt crisis and the influence of World Bank and International Monetary Fund (IMF) conditions attached to bail-out loans had induced many developing countries to undertake unilateral liberalisation, and they wanted to extract reciprocal concessions from other countries in recompense.[267] Finally, it is noted that European countries could not support the position of the developing countries as the US threatened them with a full-scale trade war in

---

[259] Deere, above n 33, 52.

[260] Tellez, above n 251, 7; Goldstein, above n 4, 53; Drahos (2001), above n 174, 793.

[261] Drahos, above n 5, 166; Pretorius, n 150, 184; Peggy E. Chaudhry and Michael Walsh, 'Intellectual Property Rights: Changing Levels of Protection under GATT NAFTA and the EU' (1995) 30 (2) *The Columbia Journal of World Business* 80, 82. See also Rorden Wilkinson and James Scott, 'Developing Country Participation in the GATT: A Reassessment' (2008) 7 (3) *World Trade Review* 473, 502.

[262] Wilkinson and Scott, above n 261.

[263] Ibid 473-475; Carlos Correa, *Review of the TRIPS Agreement Fostering the Transfer of Technology to Developing Countries,* Third World Network <http://www.twnside.org.sg/title/foster.htm>; Sell, above n 132, 9.

[264] Professor Ruth L. Gana (Okediji) adds also:

> [B]ecause they [developing countries] did not have the political or economic wherewithal to negotiate better terms of the accession to turn the direction of the treaties to reflect their interests. In addition, these concepts were new to most developing countries and their relative lack of experience with these norms would have constituted a major handicap to effectively challenging the premises of the international system.

See Gana (Okediji), above n 4, 333; Deere, above n 33, 52; Drahos (1999), above n 174, 424; Goldstein, above n 4, 53; Drahos (2001), above n 174, 793.

[265] Matthew Turk, 'The Bargaining and Intellectual Property Treaties: The Case for a Pro-Development International TRIPS but Not TRIPS Plus' (2010) 42 *New York University Journal of International Law and Policies* 981.

[266] Jayashree Watal, 'Developing Countries and the Protection of Intellectual Property Right' in George A. Bermann and Petros C. Mavroidis, *WTO Law and Developing Countries* (Cambridge University, 2007) 129, 130-131.

[267] Wilkinson and Scott, above n 261, 503

agriculture, backed up by export subsidies if they did not agree on holding a new round of talks.[268]

As discussed below, developing countries thought that the *TRIPS Agreement* would be the ceiling for the international protection of IP, but this was not the case as the US later treated TRIPS as a floor[269] and a beginning for demanding higher protection of IP in the post-TRIPS era.

2.6 The Trade-Related Intellectual Property Aspects Agreement (TRIPS)

On 15 April 1994, as part of the negotiation of the Uruguay Round of GATT, the *TRIPS Agreement* was adopted in Marrakesh, Morocco. The Agreement did not actually become effective until 1 January 1995.[270] Any country that wishes to join the WTO must also agree to abide by the *TRIPS Agreement*.[271]

The purpose of the *TRIPS Agreement* is to provide adequate and effective protection for IP in order to reduce impediments to international trade and promote global competition.[272] The *TRIPS Agreement* imposes three main obligations on member countries. Firstly, it requires WTO members to provide minimum IP rights protection in their national laws, in accordance with several multilateral treaties, in particular, the *Berne Convention* and the *Paris Convention*.[273] Secondly, it requires them to provide effective enforcement mechanisms for these rights. Thirdly, it obliges WTO member states to agree to submit to a new dispute settlement system.[274]

2.6.1 Origin and Negotiations of the TRIPS Agreement

Developed countries participated in the negotiation of the *TRIPS Agreement*, hoping that an expanded and strengthened protection of IP would increase flows

---

[268] Ibid. See also, for explanation of the GATT and its history, Lynden Griggs et al., *Managers and The Law* (Lawbook, 3rd ed, 1999) ch 14.

[269] Sell, above n 132, 175.

[270] Su, above n 140, 183.

[271] Ibid.

[272] Marrakesh Agreement Establishing the World Trade Organization, opened for signature 15 April 1994, 1867 (entered into force 1 January 1995, Annex 1C Trade-Related Aspects of Intellectual Property Rights (*TRIPS*), arts 9-40; Su, above n 140, 184.

[273] *TRIPS*, above n 272, arts 9-40. See Carlos M Correa, *Trade Related Aspects of Intellectual Property Rights—A Commentary on the TRIPS Agreement* (Oxford, 2007), chs 5-12; Sol Picciotto, 'Defending the Public Interest in TRIPS and the WTO' in Peter Drahos and Ruth Mayne, *Global Intellectual Property Rights: Knowledge, Access and Development* (Palgrave Macmillan, 2002) 235.

[274] *TRIPS*, above n 272, arts 63-64; Tully, above n 135, 134.

of FDI, technology transfers to their countries and stimulate local innovation.[275] The main concern of developed countries was to offer the utmost protection to their IP right holders in the national laws of developing countries and to enforce these rights easily. Not all developing countries participated in the TRIPS negotiations, but the key developing countries, most notably India and Brazil, did send negotiators.[276]

2.6.2 *The TRIPS Agreement and Development*

Developing countries accepted the *TRIPS Agreem*ent, although they were not sure whether the new international IP system would assist them in achieving development. Some of them feared that the enhanced protection given to IP would not effectively promote their development process but instead limit their access to technology.[277]

TRIPS includes several provisions that could be used for the benefit of developing countries.[278] Part I of the General Provisions and Basic Principles of the Agreement provides certain flexibilities to WTO country members in art 7 (objectives)[279] and art 8 (principles).[280] Article 27 of the *TRIPS Agreement*

---

[275] Correa, above n 263.

[276] Drahos, above n 5, 166; Matthews, above n 144, 29-45.

[277] Correa, above n 263.

[278] Mitsuo Matsushita and Thomas Schoenbaum note that WTO has two kinds of provisions beneficial for developing countries and these are: 1) preferential treatment for developing countries based on the concept of non-reciprocity; and 2) special and differential treatment for developing countries. See Mitsuo Matsushita, Thomas J. Schoenbaum, and Petros C. Mavroidis, *The World Trade Organization Law Practice and Policy* (Oxford University, 2003) 390.

[279] Article 7 of the *TRIPS Agreement* provides as follows:

> The protection and enforcement of intellectual property rights should contribute to the promotion of technological innovation and to the transfer and dissemination of technology, to the mutual advantage of producers and users of technological knowledge and in a manner conducive to social and economic welfare, and to a balance of rights and obligations.

TRIPS, above n 272, art 7. See also Daniel Gervais, *The TRIPs Agreement—Drafting History and Analysis* (Sweet and Maxwell, 2nd ed, 2003) 115-120; Correa, above n 273, 287-294; UNCTAD-ICTSD, *Resource Book on TRIPS and Development* (Cambridge University, 2005) 118-133.

[280] Article 8 of the *TRIPS Agreement* provides as follows:

> 1. Subject to the provisions of paragraphs 2, 3 and 4, no Member shall be obliged to apply the provisions of this Agreement before the expiry of a general period of one year following the date of entry into force of the WTO Agreement.
>
> 2. A developing country Member is entitled to delay for a further period of four years the date of application, as defined in paragraph 1, of the provisions of this Agreement other than Articles 3, 4 and 5.

also gives developing countries some kind of flexibility in the exclusion of patentable subject matter.[281] Transitional arrangements in art 65[282] and

---

3. Any other Member which is in the process of transformation from a centrally-planned into a market, free-enterprise economy and which is undertaking structural reform of its intellectual property system and facing special problems in the preparation and implementation of intellectual property laws and regulations, may also benefit from a period of delay as foreseen in paragraph 2.
4. To the extent that a developing country Member is obliged by this Agreement to extend product patent protection to areas of technology not so protectable in its territory on the general date of application of this Agreement for that Member, as defined in paragraph 2, it may delay the application of the provisions on product patents of Section 5 of Part II to such areas of technology for an additional period of 5 years.
5. A Member availing itself of a transitional period under paragraphs 1, 2, 3 or 4 shall ensure that any changes in its laws, regulations and practice made during that period do not result in a lesser degree of consistency with the provisions of this Agreement.

TRIPS, above n 272, art 8. See Gervais, above n 279, 120-122; UNCTAD-ICTSD, above n 279, 118-133.

[281] Article 27/A of the *TRIPS Agreement* provides as follows:

1. Subject to the provisions of paragraphs 2 and 3, patents shall be available for any inventions, whether products or processes, in all fields of technology, provided that they are new, involve an inventive step and are capable of industrial application.(5) Subject to paragraph 4 of Article 65, paragraph 8 of Article 70 and paragraph 3 of this Article, patents shall be available and patent rights enjoyable without discrimination as to the place of invention, the field of technology and whether products are imported or locally produced.

2. Members may exclude from patentability inventions, the prevention within their territory of the commercial exploitation of which is necessary to protect *order public* or morality, including to protect human, animal or plant life or health or to avoid serious US. prejudice to the environment, provided that such exclusion is not made merely because the exploitation is prohibited by their law.

TRIPS, above n 272, art 24/A. See Gervais, above n 279, 217-234; Correa, above n 273, 287-294; UNCTAD-ICTSD, above n 279, 351-383.

[282] Article 65 of the *TRIPS Agreements* provides as follows:

1. Subject to the provisions of paragraphs 2, 3 and 4, no Member shall be obliged to apply the provisions of this Agreement before the expiry of a general period of one year following the date of entry into force of the WTO Agreement.

2. A developing country Member is entitled to delay for a further period of four years the date of application, as defined in paragraph1, of the provisions of this Agreement other than Articles 3, 4 and 5.
3. Any other Member which is in the process of transformation from a centrally-planned into a market, free-enterprise economy and which is undertaking structural reform of its intellectual property system and facing special problems in the preparation and implementation of intellectual property laws and regulations, may also benefit from a period of delay as foreseen in paragraph 2.
4. To the extent that a developing country Member is obliged by this Agreement to extend product patent protection to areas of technology not so protectable in its territory on the general date of application of this Agreement for that Member, as defined in paragraph 2,

art 66[283] could also be used by developing countries and LDCs to delay the application of the *TRIPS Agreements* to further their development.[284] Article 67[285] of the *TRIPS Agreement* imposes an obligation on developed countries to assist LCDs to reform their IP laws[286] to satisfy their treaty obligations.[287] There are also many other important provisions in the *TRIPS Agreement* that developing countries could use to their development advantage.[288]

---

it may delay the application of the provisions on product patents of Section 5 of Part II to such areas of technology for an additional period of 5 years.

5. A Member availing itself of a transitional period under paragraphs 1, 2, 3 or 4 shall ensure that any changes in its laws, regulations and practice made during that period do not result in a lesser degree of consistency with the provisions of this Agreement.

TRIPS, above n 272, art 65.

[283] Article 66 of the *TRIPS Agreement* provides as follows:

1. In view of the special needs and requirements of least-developed country Members, their economic, financial and administrative constraints, and their need for flexibility to create a viable technological base, such Members shall not be required to apply the provisions of this Agreement, other than Articles 3, 4 and 5, for a period of 10 years from the date of application as defined under paragraph 1 of Article 65. The Council for TRIPS shall, upon duly motivated request by a least-developed country Member, accord extensions of this period.

2. Developed country Members shall provide incentives to enterprises and institutions in their territories for the purpose of promoting and encouraging technology transfer to least-developed country Members in order to enable them to create a sound and viable technological base.

TRIPS, above n 272, art 66.

[284] See Gervais, above n 279, 346-353; UNCTAD-ICTSD, above n 279, 705-724.

[285] Article 67 of the *TRIPS Agreements* provides as follows:

In order to facilitate the implementation of this Agreement, developed country Members shall provide, on request and on mutually agreed terms and conditions, technical and financial cooperation in favour of developing and least-developed country Members. Such cooperation shall include assistance in the preparation of laws and regulations on the protection and enforcement of intellectual property rights as well as on the prevention of their abuse, and shall include support regarding the establishment or reinforcement of domestic offices and agencies relevant to these matters, including the training of personnel.

TRIPS, above n 272, art 67. See also Gervais, above n 279, 705-724.

[286] Suerie Moon came to the conclusion that there is concrete evidence to support the compliance of developed countries with their obligations. He provided several recommendations to improve the current reporting system. See Moon, above n 213. See also Gervais, above n 279, 730-738.

[287] Cheek, above n 137, 277, 306; Gervais, above n 279, 353-355; UNCTAD-ICTSD, above n 279, 730-738.

[288] See *TRIPS*, above n 272, arts 1.1, 4, 6, 27 (2), 27 (3a), 27 (3b), 30, 31, 31 bis (1), 37, 65 (1), 65 (2) 65 (3), 65 (4), and 66 (1). See also Alhaj Tejan-Cole, *Flexibilities in the TRIPS Agreement and Its Impact on National Intellectual Property Policy* (2011) Belize Intellectual Property Office <http://www.belipo.bz/wp-content/uploads/2011/12/TRIPS-FLEXIBILITIES.pdf>. For an explanation of the provisions of the *TRIPS Agreement* that developing countries could use, see Gervais, above n 279; Chon, above n 96, 2835-2844; Barbosa, Chon, and Hase, above n 253, 92-95; UNCTAD-ICTSD, above n 279.

2.6.3 Impact of the TRIPS Agreement on Developing Countries

The impact of the *TRIPS Agreement* on developing countries[289] differs from one country to another. The prior existence of IP protection and a country's technological and economic development also play a substantial role in determining its impact.[290]

The *TRIPS Agreement* is based on the so-called development theory, according to which developing countries should import the normative, judicial, and administrative infrastructure of industrialised, developed countries to achieve economic development.[291] This is the theory. However, does the *TRIPS Agreement* help member developing countries? To what extent are the flexibilities contained in the Agreement implemented in practice in developing countries? Did developed countries fulfil their obligations under the provisions of the Agreement, as specified under art 67 and art 66.2?

Answering these questions is difficult as it requires conducting empirical research to determine to what extent developing countries benefited from joining the Agreement, but the various views expressed by the commentators on the *TRIPS Agreement* might give some indications that help our appreciation of the issue.

Several commentators have argued that the *TRIPS Agreement* simultaneously narrows developing countries' access to technology[292] and use of technological knowledge to promote public interest goals[293] such as health, nutrition, and envi-

289 Matthews, above n 144, 108-122.

290 Tully, above n 135, 137-138.

291 Daniel Gervais, *TRIPS and Development in Intellectual Property, Trade and Development* (Oxford University, 2007) 3-59.

292 Evelyn Su, 'The Winners and the Losers: The Agreement on Trade-Related Aspects of Intellectual Property Rights and Its Effects on Developing Countries' (2004) 23 (1) *Houston Journal of International Law* 184; Carlos Correa, *Review of the TRIPS Agreement Fostering the Transfer of Technology to Developing Countries*, Third World Network <http://www.twnside.org.sg/title/foster.htm>; Philip G. Altbach, 'The Subtle Inequalities of Copyright' (1997) 23 (2) *Copyright Bulletin*, 7-14 <http://unesdoc.unesco.org/images/0011/001107/110771Eb.pdf>; Calestous Juma, *Intellectual Property Rights and Globalization: Implications for Developing Countries*, Center for International Development at Harvard University, 2 <http://www.cid.harvard.edu/archive/biotech/papers/discuss4.pdf>; Carlos Correa, 'Intellectual Property Rights, the WTO and Developing Countries' (2000) 18-19, cited in Martin Khor, 'Rethinking Intellectual Property Rights and TRIPS' in Peter Drahos and Ruth Mayne, *Global Intellectual Property Rights*: Knowledge Access and Development (Palgrave Macmillan, 2002) 172; Susan Sell, 'Intellectual Property at a Cross Road: The Use of the Past in Intellectual Property Jurisprudence: Intellectual Property and Public Policy in Historical Perspective: Contestation and Settlement' (2004) 38 *Loyola of Los Angeles Entertainment Law Review* 267, 316.

293 In August 2000, The UN Commission on Human Rights approved a resolution affirming that the implementation of the *TRIPS Agreement* does not adequately reflect the fundamental nature and indivisibility of all human rights, including the right of everyone to enjoy the benefits of scientific progress and its application, the right to health, the right to food, and the right of self determination. See Picciotto, above n 273, 233.

ronmental conservation.[294] Influential scholars also criticised the *TRIPS Agreement* and questioned how its basic structure affected developing countries. Professor Jeffrey Sachs[295] in 1999 called for a new international IP system that is equitable and fair to developing countries.[296] Professor John Barton,[297] who has noted that the international IP system must consider one common standard for developed countries and another one for developing countries, expressed a similar view.[298] Professor Joseph Stiglitz[299] has argued that TRIPS is a failure when it comes to assisting developing countries in achieving development. He questioned and criticised its underlying philosophy that does not differentiate between developing and developed countries.[300] Other commentators are also doubtful about the *TRIPS Agreement* and how it might be used by developing countries to achieve development.[301]

To be fair, the failure of developing countries and LDCs to achieve economic development after the adoption of the *TRIPS Agreement* cannot be blamed on the Agreement itself or the international economic system. Governments in developing countries must share the responsibility for their failure to achieve economic development. Most developing countries have not designed appropriate IP policies that take into account their different industrial structures, modes of agricultural production, cultural values, development needs, and availability of natural and human resources.[302]

Professor Daniel J Gervais[303] noted the importance of embracing the *TRIPS Agreement* not in isolation but within broader, comprehensive, domestic innovation and knowledge optimisation strategies that take into consideration the local

---

[294] Juma, above n 92, 2. See also Peter Drahos, 'Thinking Strategically about Intellectual Property Rights' (1997) 21 (3) *Telecommunications Policy*, 201-211 <http://www.anu.edu.au/fellows/pdrahos/articles/pdfs/1997thinkingstratippolicy.pdf>.

[295] From Columbia University, Director of the health institute.

[296] Jeffrey Sachs, *Helping the World's Poorest* (14 August 1999) Center for International Development at Harvard University <http://www.cid.harvard.edu/cidinthenews/articles/sf9108.html>.

[297] From Stanford University.

[298] John Barton, 'Intellectual Property, Biotechnology, and International Trade: Two Examples', cited in Correa, above n 263.

[299] From Columbia University.

[300] Joseph Stiglitz, 'Intellectual Property Rights and Wrongs' Daily Times (LahorePakistan) 16 August 2005 <http://www.dailytimes.com.pk/default.asp?page=story_16-8-2005_pg5_12>.

[301] Khor, above n 292, 203; Correa, above n 263; Botoy, above n 144, 129; Sell, above n 132, 13; Lee, above 150, 123-132.

[302] Carlos Correa, 'Formulating Effective Pro-Development National Intellectual Property Policies' in Christopher Bellmann and Graham Dutfield, *Trading in Knowledge-Development Perspective in TRIPS, Trade and Sustainability* (Earthscan Publications, 2003) 209, 211; John Barton, 'Integrating IPR Policies in Development Strategies' in Christopher Bellmann, Graham Dutfield, and Ricardo Melendez-Ortiz, *Trading in Knowledge-Development Perspective in TRIPS, Trade and Sustainability* (2003) 57-64.

[303] From Vanderbilt University.

conditions and needs of each developing country.[304] Emerging economies such as South Korea, China, Brazil, and India are successful examples of how effectively the *TRIPS Agreement* may be used to boost innovation and raise developmental levels.[305] Professor Peter Yu[306] also puts the blame on developing countries as they have drafted 'western-style IP laws' and have not interpreted the *TRIPS Agreement* through a 'pro-development lens'.[307] He goes further in blaming them for not understanding the consequences of the Agreement and how the required protection would impact on their countries in other areas such as agriculture, health, environment, education, and culture, during the TRIPS negotiations.[308]

Experts with considerable knowledge of IP were very scarce in developing countries during the TRIPS negotiations, and even they did not comprehend the broad implications of the *TRIPS Agreement.* This was the case not only for developing countries but also for representatives of many developed countries who did not understand the extent of the linkages between the protection of IP and critical issues such as trade, education, health, and food. If these important matters had been clarified from the beginning, then the destiny of the *TRIPS Agreement* may have been different.

Many developing countries have emphasised the difficulties that they have confronted in putting into practice the massive legislative changes required by the *TRIPS Agreement* and the developed countries' non-fulfilment of their obligations to assist LDCs under art 67 of the *TRIPS Agreement.*[309] They argue that developed countries have done little to satisfy their treaty obligations and effectively facilitate and promote technology transfer from their countries to developing countries.[310]

---

[304] Gervais, above n 291, 3, 47, 52. The Commission on Intellectual Property Rights (CIPR) argues that the interests of developing countries are best served 'by tailoring their intellectual property regimes to their particular economic and social circumstances'; Barton et al., above n 4; Maria Julia Olivia, 'Intellectual Property in the FTAA: Little Opportunity and Much Risk' (2003) 19 *American University International Law Review* 45, 53; Drahos, above n 22, 15; Susan K. Sell, 'What Role for Humanitarian Intellectual Property? The Globalisation of Intellectual Property Rights' (2004) 6 *Minnesota Journal of Law* 191, 210.

[305] Gervais, above n 291, 48.

[306] From Drake University.

[307] Yu, above n 141, 387.

[308] Ibid 375.

[309] Correa, above n 263.

[310] Professor Susan Sell noted that:

> [A]lthough the provisions of the TRIPS Agreement is quite promising to developing and LDCs in terms of technology transfer and other issues important to developing countries, there is little practical evidence that developed countries are fulfilling their obligation under the Agreement toward developing countries. There is also little evidence to support that TRIPS would assist developing countries in achieving socio-economic and technological development and furthermore there is no evidence that developing countries are making good on their commitment to open their markets more widely to developing countries.

See, for a full critique of TRIPS, Sell, above n 132, 13, 137.

To overcome these problems, Professor Carlos Correa believes that a solution would be to build procedures for the effective transfer of technology, at fair and reasonable costs, to developing countries so as to harmonise the objectives of the *TRIPS Agreement*.[311] Internationally, India has suggested that, in particular, art 31 (compulsory licensing) and art 33 (term of patent protection) of the *TRIPS Agreement* be reviewed to make the transfer of technology provisions operational in practice.[312] Professor Martin Khor also suggested that developed countries and their enterprises should be obliged to put into effect the transfer and dissemination of technology to developing countries.[313]

It is important to examine how the *TRIPS Agreement* is being used by developing countries to further their developmental interests.[314] This will be seen more clearly by examining briefly some of the important cases that discuss the provisions of the *TRIPS Agreement* and how they can be used by developing countries.

2.6.4 Flexible Implementation of the TRIPS Agreement at WTO

Several cases brought before The WTO's Dispute Settlement Body (DSB) suggest that the *TRIPS Agreement* should be implemented loosely for the benefit of member states.[315] Two important cases worthy of examination were filed by the US under

---

[311] Professor Carlos Correa also mentioned, rightly, that:

> Any future action concerning technology transfer within WTO should recognize the strong linkages existing between the transfer and local technological capacity building, which remains a main responsibility of host countries. The improvement of the conditions for access to and effective use of foreign technologies will require a broad approach beyond the TRIPs Agreement.

Correa, above n 263.

[312] Ibid.

[313] Khor, above n 292, 211.

[314] See, for more radical practical approaches, Professor Lawrence Lessig, who suggested that:

> A block of powerful developing nations should first take a page from the U.S. *Copyright Act of 1790* and enact national laws that explicitly protect their own rights only. It would not protect foreigners. Second, these nations should add a provision that would relax this exemption to the extent that developed nations really opened their borders. If we reduce, for example, the subsidy to agribusiness by 10%, then they would permit 10% of our copyrights to be enforced (say, copyrights from the period 1923 to 1931). Reduce the subsidy by another 10%, then another 10% could be enforced. And so on.

See Lawrence Lessig, *A Taste of Our Own Poison: A Modest Proposal: Hold Hollywood Hostage Till We Kill Farm Subsidies*, (2004) Issue 12.01 *Wired* <http://www.wired.com/wired/archive/12.01/view.html?pg=5>.

[315] Matthew Turk argues that WTO jurisprudence is unsettled with respect to whether or not it adopts a pro-development interpretation of the *TRIPS Agreement*. See Matthew Turk, 'The

the WTO Dispute Settlement System (DSS). These cases illustrate the importance of flexible implementation of the *TRIPS Agreement* in the local IP laws of member states. The cases involve India and China.[316]

2.6.4.1 India Mail Box Case: Patent Protection for Pharmaceutical and Agricultural Chemical Products—1997 (US v India)

This was one of the first cases filed by the US against India. The US filed a case against India claiming that its patent law did not protect pharmaceutical and agricultural chemical products in accordance with art 27 of the *TRIPS Agreement* and that it failed to provide means for the filing of patent applications pursuant to art 70.8 of the *TRIPS Agreement.*[317] In particular, India was criticised for failing to establish the so-called 'mail box' to receive and preserve patent applications and to adopt legislation authorising the grant of exclusive marketing rights (EMRs).[318]

The Panel reached the conclusion that India should adapt its patent protection of pharmaceutical and agricultural chemical products in conformity with its obligations under the *TRIPS Agreement.*[319] India appealed against some aspects of the Panel decision, but the WTO Appellate Body upheld the findings of the Panel.[320] The Appellate Body noted that:

> But what constitutes such a sound legal basis in Indian law? To answer this question, we must recall first an important general rule in the *TRIPS Agreement*. Article 1.1 of the *TRIPS Agreement* states, in pertinent part: Members shall be free to determine the appropriate method of implementing the provisions of this Agreement within their own legal system and practice. Members, therefore, are free to determine how best to meet their obligations

---

Bargaining and Intellectual Property Treaties: The Case for a Pro-Development International TRIPS but Not TRIPS Plus' (2010) 42 *New York University Journal of International Law and Policies* 989.

[316] WTO, United States-Subsidies on Upland Cotton—2002 (*Brazil v US*) <http://www.wto.org/english/tratop_E/dispu_e/cases_e/ds267_e.htm>.

[317] Appellate Body Report, India—Patent Protection for Pharmaceutical and Agricultural Chemical Products, WT/DS50/AB/R, 19 December 1997, 1 See also UNCTAD, above n 248.

[318] UNCTAD, above n 248.

[319] The Panel specifically found that:

> [On] the basis of the findings set out above, the Panel concludes that India has not complied with its obligations under... the TRIPS Agreement, because it has failed to establish a mechanism that adequately preserves novelty and priority in respect of applications for product patents in respect of pharmaceutical and agricultural chemical inventions during the transitional period to which it is entitled under the Agreement, and to publish and notify adequately information about such a mechanism; and that India has not complied with its obligations [under] the TRIPS Agreement, because it has failed to establish a system for the grant of exclusive marketing rights.

Appellate Body Report, above n 317, 2. See also J. H. Reichman, 'Securing Compliance with the TRIPS Agreement after U.S. v India' (1998) *Journal of International and Economic Law* 595.

[320] Ibid.

> under the *TRIPS Agreement* within the context of their own legal systems. And, as a Member, India is 'free to determine the appropriate method of implementing' its obligations under the *TRIPS Agreement* within the context of its own legal system.[321]

Professor J. H Reichman explains the importance of that decision for developing countries:

> As the appellate Body makes clear, position papers deposited in the courts of the negotiations do not constitute controlling sources of law because only the black letter rules apply; and the means of implemen[ting] them are expressly reserved to local law in Article 1 of the TRIPS Agreement. The developing countries remain free, therefore, to adopt a more [pro-competitive] approach to implementing the TRIPS Agreement, as I have recommended, provided that such implementation remains consisted with a good faith application of the relevant international standards of intellectual property protection. Phrased differently, the decision in U.S v India confirms that the developing countries are free to adopt their own laws and policies with respect to all the intellectual property issues that were not expressly unharmonized intellectual property law survived the TRIPS Agreement, the developing countries necessarily retain a high degree of discretion with which to reconcile the burdens that the TRIPS Agreement did impose with needs of their own national systems of innovation.[322]

The decision confirms that developing countries are free to implement their own IP laws and policies in accordance with their legal systems and local conditions,[323] provided they comply with their minimum obligations under the *TRIPS Agreement.*

2.6.4.2 China: Measures Affecting the Protection and Enforcement of IP–2007 (US v China)

A proceeding was brought on 10 April 2007 by the US against China in relation to its enforcement of IP.[324] The US pleaded that China had not fulfilled its obligations under art 61 and art 41.1 of the *TRIPS Agreement* (primarily China's copyright law and customs measures). The Panel concluded that pursuant to art 19.1 of the Dispute Settlement Understanding (DSU) of the WTO, China should bring its copyright law and customs measures into conformity with its obligations under the *TRIPS Agreement.*[325] Although the Panel ruled in favour of the US, it gave China 'extensive leeway to determine how to dispose of infringing goods and where to set the threshold for criminal enforcement'.[326] It emphasised that the wording of

---

[321] Appellate Body Report, above n 317, 58

[322] See also Reichman, above n 319, 596-597.

[323] Ibid 597.

[324] WTO, China: Measures Affecting the Protection and Enforcement of Intellectual Property Rights (United States vs China) <http://www.wto.org/english/tratop_e/dispu_e/cases_e/ds362_e.htm>.

[325] Panel Report, *China Measures Affecting the Protection and Enforcement of Intellectual Property Rights*, WTDS362/R (26 January 2009), 8.3-8.5.

[326] Panel Report, *China Measures Affecting the Protection and Enforcement of Intellectual Property Rights*, WTDS362/R (26 January 2009), 761-762. See also Rochelle C. Dreyfuss, *The*

the enforcement provisions requires members to give judicial authorities the power to order particular remedies but does not require specific results.[327] In particular, the Panel noted that:

> The Panel recalls that the third sentence of Article 1.1 of the TRIPS Agreement, quoted and discussed at paragraphs, provides as follows:
>
> Members shall be free to determine the appropriate method of implementing the provisions of this Agreement within their own legal system and practice.
>
> This provision confirms that the TRIPS Agreement does not mandate specific forms of legislation. The Panel may not simply assume that a Member must give its authorities wide discretion to determine what is on a commercial scale in any given case, and may not simply assume that thresholds, including numerical tests, are inconsistent with the relative benchmark in the first sentence of Article 61 of the TRIPS Agreement. As long as a Member in fact provides for criminal procedures and penalties to be applied in cases of wilful trademark counterfeiting or copyright piracy on a commercial scale, it will comply with this obligation.[328]

This decision also gives developing countries some degree of flexibility in implementing their IP obligations under the *TRIPS Agreement*. It is noted that developing countries should be regular users of the WTO adjudication process as this pushes both panels and the Appellate Body to scrutinise more carefully the balancing factors favouring developing countries' interests that are already built into the *TRIPS Agreement*.[329]

2.7 Post-TRIPS

In the post-TRIPS era, many developed countries were not completely satisfied with the level of international IP protection that had been achieved so far, either in the international IP treaties or with the adoption of the *TRIPS Agreement*. The US,

---

Role of India, China and Brazil and Other Emerging Economies in Establishing Access Norms for Intellectual Property and Intellectual Property Law Making, IILJ (Institute for International Law and Justice) Working Paper 2009/5; NYU School of Law, Public Law Research Paper No. 09-53 <http://papers.ssrn.com/sol3/papers.cfm?abstract_id=1442785>.

[327] Dreyfuss, above n 326.

[328] The Panel Report also noted that:

> The first sentence of Article 1.1 sets out the basic obligation that Members 'shall give effect' to the provisions of this Agreement. This means that the provisions of the Agreement are obligations where stated, and the first sentence of Article 61 so states. The second sentence of Article 1.1 clarifies that the provisions of the Agreement are minimum standards only, in that it gives Members the freedom to implement a higher standard, subject to a condition. The third sentence of Article 1.1 does not grant Members freedom to implement a lower standard, but rather grants freedom to determine the appropriate method of implementation of the provisions to which they are required to give effect under the first sentence.

See Panel Report, above n 325, 513, 761-762.

[329] Reichman, above n 171, 1115, 1180; Reichman, above n 319, 587-588.

leading this approach with the help of its MNCs, continued to push for a higher set of standards in IP protection in the post-TRIPS era. While these post-TRIPS tactics are varied and numerous,[330] this subsection will examine the most important developments in the post-TRIPS era, to see their relevance to IP and development debate. It is important to note that these alternatives to TRIPS are pursued not only by developed countries but also by developing countries.[331]

2.7.1 New Treaties

In 1993, a working group was established as part of the US National Information Infrastructure Initiatives (NIII) to examine the threats that the Internet poses to authors in cyberspace. The working group was of the opinion in its 1995 Report that distribution of copyright materials must be within the reproduction right and that the circumvention of technological protection measures that aim to prevent copyright infringement must be prohibited by criminal sanctions.[332]

Based on this study, the US and other developed countries pushed the international community, through WIPO, to negotiate and adopt new multilateral treaties

---

[330] They include the following:

> (i) extending patents and copyright to new kinds of subject matter; (ii) eliminating or narrowing permitted exceptions, including those still provided in U.S. and European IP laws; (iii) extending protection terms; (iv) introducing new TRIPS-mandated IP rules earlier than the transition periods allowed by TRIPS; and (v) ratifying new WIPO treaties containing TRIPS-plus measures.

See Dutfield and Suthersanen, above n 201, 133.

A bilateral agreement that:

> Requires a Member to implement a more extensive standard; or which eliminates an option for a Member under a TRIPS standard, is for the purpose of this article, a TRIP-plus standard. Bilateral treaties also set standards on issues that TRIPs does not deal with—e.g. whether reproduction in copyright law includes temporary copies—and which are therefore not strictly TRIPs-Plus.

See Drahos (2001), above n 174, 792.

[331] For example, several developing countries and emerging economies (India, Egypt, and Turkey) have also requested TRIPS-plus protection in the field of geographical indications. They were particularly concerned with the lack of IP protection offered under the *TRIPS Agreement* to basmati rice, tea, beer, handicrafts products, and other specified products. They argued that the protection regime of geographical indications under the *TRIPS Agreement* for spirits and wines (art 23.1) should be extended to other products, particularly those of interest to these countries. See, Correa, above n 263; Michael Blakeney, 'TRIPS after the Doha Ministerial Declaration' in Christopher Antons, Michael Blakeney, and Christopher Health (eds), *Intellectual Property Harmonisation within the ASEAN and APEC* (Kluwer Law International, 2004) 12-18.

[332] Braithwaite and Drahos, above n 104, 64.

that would protect IP in the digital age. This later resulted in the adoption of the 1996 'Internet treaties', that is, the WCT and the WPPT.[333]

2.7.2 Free Trade Agreements (FTAs)

Perhaps the most significant new development in the field of IP is the proliferation of bilateral and regional negotiations on trade and investments that have led to many developing countries adopting heightened standards of IP protection.[334] The US and EU were not satisfied with the level attained in multilateral treaties, particularly in relation to the minimum IP standards that developing countries were required to adopt under the TRIPS. That is why they pushed for higher levels of IP protection through FTAs. These bilateral trade agreements extend patents' protection to new subject matters, eliminate certain exceptions, increase copyright requirements, and require developing countries to accede to particular international conventions,[335] which they are not required to do under the *TRIPS Agreement*.

The US has entered into FTAs with many developing countries, including Chile, Colombia, Panama, Bahrain, Peru, Jordan, Morocco, the Dominican Republic, and others. The EU also followed the US in signing bilateral trade agreements with a number of emerging economies and developing countries such as India, South Africa,[336] and a series of Mediterranean countries.[337]

The US approach of raising the level of IP protection after the *TRIPS Agreement* was heavily criticised by many commentators and scholars. Professor Lawrence Lessig has criticised the US for using its power in trading to change the *TRIPS Agreement*, forcing developing countries to adopt absolute IP protection that, in effect, will undermine the balance that should be preserved in the system.[338] Professor Peter Drahos also criticised FTAs that erode the ability of developing countries to set domestic standards, and he also recognised that this is the price that these countries have to pay to gain entry into the lucrative markets of the EU and the

---

[333] For a good interpretation of the WIPO Internet treaties, see, generally Mihály Ficsor, *The Law of Copyright and the Internet 1996 WIPO Treaties, Their Interpretation and Implementation* (Oxford University, 2002); Julie Cohen et al. (eds), *Copyright in a Global Information Economy* (Aspen Law and Business, 2002); Christopher May, *The Global Economy of Intellectual Property Rights: The New Enclosure* (Edward Elgar, 2nd ed, 2010) ch 4; Roberto Garza Barbosa, 'Revisiting International Copyright Law' (2007) 8 *Barry Law Review* 43, 59-60; Jessica Litman, *Digital Copyright* (Prometheus Books, 2001).

[334] Dutfield and Suthersanen, above n 30, 40.

[335] Deere, above n 33, 152.

[336] The EU utilised the bilateral trade negotiations with South Africa to gain additional IP protection (geographical indications) for various grape varieties and sherries for which it wanted special protection. See Pretorius, above n 150, 194.

[337] Deere, above n 33, 153; Pretorius, above n 150, 194.

[338] Lessig, above n 150, 34.

US.[339] Finally, it is noted that developing countries have signed these FTAs without being able to negotiate its IP provisions and without having the required IP expertise in understating the implication it may have not only on the economy but also on the society in general. This has resulted in finding these countries locked in unfavourable bilateral treaties that are not suitable to their circumstances and conditions.

2.7.3 The WTO Doha Fourth Ministerial Conference (The Development Round)

Developing countries continued to express their concerns that the *TRIPS Agreement* raises the prices of obtaining drugs and education materials, legitimises the 'biopiracy' of genetic resources and traditional knowledge, and blocks the transfer of technologies greatly needed for their development.[340]

On 14 November 2001, at the Doha Ministerial Conference, members of the WTO agreed on three texts in relation to IP and developing countries: (i) the Ministerial Declaration[341] (Ministerial Declaration), (ii) the Declaration on the TRIPS Agreement on Public Health[342] (Doha Declaration), and (iii) the Decision on Implementation-Related Issues and Concerns.[343] Article 17 of the Ministerial Declaration recognised the importance of supporting public health in developing countries.[344] It provides as follows:

> We stress the importance we attach to [the] implementation and interpretation of the Agreement on Trade-Related Aspects of IP Rights (TRIPS Agreement) in a manner supportive of public health, by promoting both access to existing medicines and research and development into new medicines and, in this connection, are adopting a separate declaration.[345]

---

[339] Drahos (2001), above n 174, 803-805.

[340] Dutfield and Suthersanen, above n 30, 37.

[341] *Doha Ministerial Declaration* (14 November 2001) WTO <http://www.wto.org/english/thewto_e/minist_e/min01_e/mindecl_e.htm>.

[342] *Doha Declaration on the TRIPS Agreement on Public Health* (14 November 2001) WTO <http://www.wto.org/english/thewto_e/minist_e/min01_e/mindecl_trips_e.htm>

[343] *Doha Decision on Implementation-Related Issues and Concern* (14 November 2001) WTO <http://www.wto.org/english/thewto_e/minist_e/min01_e/mindecl_implementation_e.htm>.

[344] Blakeney, above n 331, 11-28.

[345] Paragraphs 4 and 5 of the Doha Declaration states:

4. We agree that the TRIPS Agreement does not and should not prevent members from taking measures to protect public health. Accordingly, while reiterating our commitment to the TRIPS Agreement, we affirm that the Agreement can and should be interpreted and implemented in a manner supportive of WTO members' right to protect public health and, in particular, to promote access to medicines for all.

The Doha Declaration recognised the right of countries under TRIPS to use, to the maximum degree possible, the flexibilities contained under the Agreement to protect public health and promote access to medicines for all.[346] It clarifies the right of governments to use compulsory licensing as a means of resolving tensions that may arise between IP and public health.[347]

The Doha Development Round was described by Michael Moore, the previous Director of WTO (from 1999 to 2002), as a 'turning-point in the history of the WTO and the trading system and the relationship between developed and developing countries'.[348] Developing countries showed how they could be fierce negotiators when they resisted the US and EU attempts to 'divide and conquer'[349] but worked effectively together to bring issues dear to them to the negotiating table and succeeded partially in the inclusion of favourable provisions that correspond to their developmental objectives, particularly in relation to health.[350]

2.7.4 The WIPO Development Agenda

In the context of the overall efforts that have been made by developing countries to integrate development with global trade and IP systems, fourteen developing

---

5. Accordingly and in the light of paragraph 4 above, while maintaining our commitments in the TRIPS Agreement, we recognize that these flexibilities include:
   a) In applying the customary rules of interpretation of public international law, each provision of the TRIPS Agreement shall be read in the light of the object and purpose of the Agreement as expressed, in particular, in its objectives and principles.
   b) Each member has the right to grant compulsory licences and the freedom to determine the grounds upon which such licences are granted.
   c) Each member has the right to determine what constitutes a national emergency or other circumstances of extreme urgency, it being understood that public health crises, including those relating to HIV/AIDS, tuberculosis, malaria and other epidemics, can represent a national emergency or other circumstances of extreme urgency.
   d) The effect of the provisions in the TRIPS Agreement that are relevant to the exhaustion of intellectual property rights is to leave each member free to establish its own regime for such exhaustion without challenge, subject to the MFN and national treatment provisions of Articles 3 and 4.

Doha Declaration, above n 342.

[346] WTO, *The Doha Declaration Explained* <http://www.wto.org/english/tratop_e/dda_e/dohaexplained_e.htm>; WHO Commission, above n 227, 117.

[347] WTO, above 346; WHO, above n 227, 120.

[348] Michael Moore, 'WTO and the New Round of Trade Talks' (A speech delivered at the 14th General Meeting of the Pacific Economic Cooperation Council, Hong Kong, 28 November 2001).

[349] Yu, above n 141, 403.

[350] Susan K. Sell, 'Intellectual Property and the Doha Development Agend' (2006) 6 (2) *Global Social Policy* 147-150 <http://gsp.sagepub.com/cgi/reprint/6/2/147>.

countries (known as 'the Friends of Development')[351]presented a comprehensive proposal to establish a Development Agenda for WIPO during the organisation's General Assembly, which was held from 27 September to 5 October 2004.[352] The proposal was submitted on 26 August 2004 by the delegates from Brazil[353] and Argentina[354] to the WIPO General Assembly,[355] asking WIPO to adopt a development-oriented approach to IP and to rethink its work in relation to developing countries.

In 2007, WIPO member states adopted a historic decision for the benefit of developing countries to establish a WIPO Development Agenda[356] to ensure that IP rights are not considered in isolation but within a broader picture of economic, social, and public interests. The WIPO General Assembly established a Committee on Development and IP (CDIP) to:

---

[351] Those countries are Brazil, Argentina, Bolivia, Cuba, Dominican Republic, Ecuador, South Africa, Egypt, Kenya, Iran, Peru, Sierra Leone, Tanzania, and Venezuela.

[352] Ahmed Abdel Latif, 'The Evolution of the A2K Movement' in Hala Essalmawi *Bibliotheca Alexandria Access to Knowledge Toolkit I, (A2K)*, Alexandria, Egypt: Bibliotheca Alexandria (2009), 9-38 <http://www.bibalex.org/a2k/attachments/references/reffileh150fxqxns2lld55djrkderc.pdf>; WIPO, *The Proposal by Argentina and Brazil for the Establishment of a Development Agenda for WIPO* <http://www.wipo.int/edocs/mdocs/govbody/en/wo_ga_31/wo_ga_31_11_add.pdf>.

[353] Cícero Gontijo explains why Brazil had the authority to make such a proposal on behalf of developing countries, due to its history of participation in and contributions to the forums on intellectual rights' protection, including the *Paris Convention*, and its role in recommending the preparation of a study on the role of patents in developing countries. See Gontijo, above n 30, 19.

[354] The proposal noted:

> [T]he need to integrate the 'development dimension' into the policy-making on intellectual property protection and called for, among other things, the establishment of a new subsidiary body within WIPO to examine technology transfer; a new treaty to promote access to the results of publicly-funded research in developing countries; fair enforcement of IP rights; and more development-oriented technical cooperation and assistance. The proposal concludes by saying that 'a vision that promotes the absolute benefits of intellectual property protection without acknowledging public policy concerns undermines the very credibility of the IP system. Integrating the development dimension into the IP system and WIPO's activities, on the other hand, will strengthen the credibility of the IP system and encourage its wider acceptance as an important tool for the promotion of innovation, creativity and development.'

WIPO, above n 352. See also Jack Lerner, 'Intellectual Property and Development at WHO and WIPO' (2008) 34 *American Journal of Law and Medicine* 296.

- Professor Peter Yu also noted that 'the Development Agenda decisively rejects the intellectual property-centric view. It posits that strong intellectual property protection does not consistently promote creative activity, facilitate technology transfer, or accelerate development'. See Yu, above n 28, 519.

[355] WIPO, above n 352.

[356] The World Health Organization (WHO) has also launched its own development agenda with the intergovernmental Working Group on Public Health, Innovation and IP (IGWG), which is tasked with preparing a 'global strategy and plan of action', aimed at '[s]ecuring an enhanced and sustainable basis for needs-driven, essential health research and development relevant to diseases that disproportionately affect developing countries'. See Lerner, above n 354, 296.

(a) Develop a work program for the implementation of the adopted recommendations of the Provisional Committee on WIPO and Development Agenda (PCDA)[357];
(b) Monitor, assess, discuss, and report on the implementation of all recommendations adopted, and for that purpose it shall coordinate with relevant WIPO bodies; and
(c) Discuss IP and development-related issues as agreed by the Committee, as well as those decided by the General Assembly.[358]

The first session of the CDIP was held in Geneva, Switzerland, from 3 to 7 March 2008, and the second was from 7 to 11 July 2008. In the first session, member states approved the rules of procedure of the Committee and started discussions on its work.[359] The CDIP, in the second session, discussed a revised text of proposed activities for the implementation of particular recommendations for the Committee.[360] The third session was held from 27 April to 1 May 2009. It approved the Report of the second session and discussed IP and development-related issues, as agreed by the Committee.[361] The fourth session was held from 16 to 20 November 2009. It adopted the revised draft Report of the third session of the CDIP, accredited the observers, and continued the discussion on coordination mechanisms and monitoring, assessing, and reporting of the Committee.[362]

The fifth session, held from 26 to 30 April 2010,[363] was attended by 107 member states and 44 observers who discussed and approved various documents

---

[357] The PCDA adopted 45 recommendations (of the 111 original proposals) covering six clusters of activities. These are (a) technical assistance and capacity building; (b) norm setting, flexibilities, public policy, and public knowledge; (c) technology transfer, information and communication technology (ICT), and access to knowledge; (d) assessments, evaluation, and impact studies; (e) institutional matters, including mandate and governance; and (f) other issues.

See WIPO, *Member States Adopt a Development Agenda for* (2007) <www.wipo.int/pressroom/en/articles/2007/article_0071.html>.

[358] WIPO, *Summary by the Chair* <http://www.wipo.int/meetings/en/doc_details.jsp?doc_id=104452>.

[359] WIPO, *Committee on Development and Intellectual Property (CDIP) First Session* <http://www.wipo.int/ip-development/en/agenda/cdip/>.

[360] WIPO, *Committee on Development and Intellectual Property (CDIP) Second Session* <http://www.wipo.int/ip-development/en/agenda/cdip/cdip_2.html>.

[361] WIPO, *Committee on Development and Intellectual Property (CDIP) Third Session* <http://www.wipo.int/meetings/en/details.jsp?meeting_id=17382>.

[362] WIPO, *Committee on Development and Intellectual Property (CDIP) Fourth Session* <http://www.wipo.int/meetings/en/details.jsp?meeting_id=17460>.

[363] WIPO, *Committee on Development and Intellectual Property (CDIP) Fifth Session* <http://www.wipo.int/meetings/en/details.jsp?meeting_id=19686>.

prepared by the Committee.[364] At the sixth session, held from 22 to 26 November 2010,[365] the Director-General announced that the Development Agenda projects would be included for the first time in the budgetary process cycle of WIPO.[366] At the seventh session, held from 2 to 6 May 2011,[367] the CDIP postponed the organisation of an international conference on IP and development and agreed to allocate the funds required for that event in the budget for 2012–2013.[368] During the eighth session, held from 14 to 18 November 2011,[369] the CDIP agreed to establish an ad hoc working group on the External Review of Technical Assistance.[370] The ninth session, held from 7 to 11 May 2012, considered project evaluations related to the CDIP and discussed a work program on flexibilities in the IP system (patent and copyright).[371] The tenth session is scheduled for 12 to 16 November 2012.

Several commentators have noted the similarities between the new WIPO Development Agenda and the old agenda demanded in the 1960s and 1970s by developing countries, particularly Brazil and India.[372] If we compare the two agendas, we can find that the WIPO Agenda covers not only IP issues but also a wide variety of other topics relevant to development and developing countries, including information and communication technologies (ICT), technology transfer, A2K, technical assistance, capacity building, and others.

---

[364] These include the Director General's Report on Implementation of the Development Agenda, IP and the public domain, WIPO's contribution to the UN Millennium Development Goals (MDGs), patent-related flexibilities in the multilateral legal framework, and others. See WIPO, CDIP/5/10, Report of the Fifth Session of the Committee on Development and Intellectual Property (CDIP) <http://www.wipo.int/edocs/mdocs/mdocs/en/cdip_5/cdip_5_ref_summary_ revised.pdf>.

[365] *WIPO, Committee on Development and Intellectual Property (CDIP) Sixth Session* <http://www.wipo.int/meetings/en/details.jsp?meeting_id=19688>.

[366] WIPO, Document CDIP/5/10 Report of the Sixth Session of the Committee on Development and Intellectual Property (CDIP) <http://www.wipo.int/edocs/mdocs/mdocs/en/cdip_6/cdip_6_ref_summary.pdf>.

[367] *WIPO, Committee on Development and Intellectual Property (CDIP) Seventh Session* <http://www.wipo.int/meetings/en/details.jsp?meeting_id=22102>.

[368] WIPO, CDIP/6/13—Report <http://www.wipo.int/edocs/mdocs/mdocs/en/cdip_6/cdip_6_13.pdf>.

[369] WIPO, *Committee on Development and Intellectual Property (CDIP) Eight Session* <http://www.wipo.int/meetings/en/details.jsp?meeting_id=22206>.

[370] WIPO, *Summary of the Chair* <http://www.wipo.int/edocs/mdocs/mdocs/en/cdip_8/cdip_8_summary.pdf>.

[371] *WIPO, Committee on Development and Intellectual Property (CDIP) Ninth Session* <http://www.wipo.int/meetings/en/details.jsp?meeting_id=25013>; WIPO, *Summary of the Chair* <http://www.wipo.int/edocs/mdocs/mdocs/en/cdip_9/cdip_9_summary.pdf>.

[372] Yu, above n 28, 469-573; Sisule F Musungu, *Rethinking Innovation, Development and Intellectual Property in the UN: WIPO and Beyond* TRIPS, Quaker International Affairs Programme, Issue Paper 5 (2005), The Quaker United Nations Office (QUNO) <http://www.quno.org/geneva/pdf/economic/Issues/TRIPS53.pd*f*>.

Andréa Koury Menescal has noted that one of the most important differences between the old agenda and the WIPO Development Agenda is that the latter proved that public interest IP concerns are no longer an issue for developing countries alone but are of equal importance to NGOs, academics, researchers, consumers, and a large number of individuals as well.[373] The same commentator heavily criticised WIPO for imposing treaties and agreements on developing countries based on the assumption that more is better, ignoring the public interest concerns within IP and failing to act as a body responsible 'for promoting creative intellectual activity and for facilitating the transfer of technology related to industrial property to the developing countries in order to accelerate economic, social and cultural development'.[374]

It is noted that many IP scholars and international organisations involved in IP issues understand the concerns of developing countries and are sympathetic to some of their demands to change the international IP system to one that is more favourable to their needs. Developing countries have to work together to request WIPO to take appropriate action. Chapter 7 of the book explains how developing countries can utilise the WIPO Development Agenda to their advantage.

2.7.5 The Access to Knowledge Treaty (ATKT)

Certain non-governmental and consumer organisations such as the Trans-Atlantic Consumer Dialogue (TACD),[375] the Consumer Project on Technology,[376] in cooperation with a number of experts, put forward a proposal on 9 May 2005 for an A2K Treaty.[377]

The incomplete A2K Treaty has many 'pro-development' IP provisions that developing countries can utilise when they are drafting their IP laws. Article 3-1(d) requires parties to the Treaty to implement general copyright exceptions applicable in special cases for social, cultural, educational, and developmental benefits.[378] It also requires its members to give persons with disabilities the right of access to copyrighted materials[379] and implement measures that ensure access to orphans' works.[380] The A2K Treaty considers the *Berne Appendix* to be ineffective for

[373] Menescal, above n 30, 793. On the role of civil society, see Deere, above n 33, 168; Laurence R. Helfer, *Nesting and Complexity in the International Intellectual Property Regime*, Princeton University <http://www.princeton.edu/~smeunier/Helfer%20memo.pdf>.

[374] Menescal, above n 30, 786.

[375] *The Trans Atlantic Consumer Dialogue* <http://www.tacd.org/>.

[376] *The Consumer Project on Technology* <http://www.cptech.org/>.

[377] Abdel Latif, above n 352, 15; the Access to Knowledge Treaty <http://www.cptech.org/a2k/a2k_treaty_may9.pdf> (A2K Treaty).

[378] A2K Treaty, above n 377, arts 3-1.

[379] Ibid, arts 3-3.

[380] Ibid, arts 3-8.

developing countries, and therefore it recommends the development of a new protocol for access to copyrighted works.[381] It also contains other provisions that facilitate access to publicly funded research[382] and promote the free movement of researchers.[383] The Treaty also favours open standards,[384] establishment of knowledge commons databases,[385] and access to open journals.[386]

Two central themes on which the A2K Treaty concentrates are, firstly, the need for strong and explicit limitations and exceptions in copyright and patent laws and, secondly, the promotion of access to publicly funded research.[387] The goal of the draft treaty is to contribute towards enhanced access to knowledge through a number of provisions that aim at enhancing the social, economic, and development benefits of A2K.[388] Amy Kapaczynski from the Yale Law School Information Society Project[389] has summarised the parameters of the A2K Treaty as follows:

> The current draft of the A2K Treaty bears the telltale fingerprints of multiple authors with diverse (if not divergent) interests. It includes a dozen articles on limitations and exceptions to copyright and related rights, provisions on patent protection aimed at 'expanding and enhancing the knowledge commons,' measures to promote open standards and control anticompetitive practices, and a hodge podge of miscellaneous and unfinished clauses on technology transfer, copyright collecting societies, and financial obligations. Several common threads connect these varied provisions. First, according to observers at the Geneva meeting, the treaty's proponents strongly support the view that 'access to knowledge' is a basic human right, and that [restrictions] on access ought to be the exception, not the other way around.[390]

---

[381] Ibid, arts 3-12.

[382] Ibid, arts 5-2.

[383] Ibid, arts 10-1.

[384] Ibid, arts 6-1, 6-2, 6-3, 6-4.

[385] Ibid, arts 5-6.

[386] Ibid, arts 5-1, 5-2.

[387] Karsten Gerloff, '*Access to Knowledge in a Network Society*' (an L.L.M thesis, Universität Lüneburg, 2006) <http://nearlyfreespeech.org/downloads/a2k.netsoc.pdf>.

[388] Abdel Latif, above n 352, 15.

[389] The Yale Law School Information Society Program (ISP) has organised two major international conferences on A2K since 2006. These conferences have contributed to the momentum experienced by A2K while also strengthening the links of the A2K movement with academia and researchers. See, for more information, Abdel Latif, above n 352, 21.

[390] Laurence R. Helfer, 'Toward a Human Rights Approach Framework for Intellectual Property' (2007) 40 *University of California Davis Law Review* 971.

Valantina Vadi highlights that:

> Access to Knowledge Treaty is an ambitious initiative whose major merit rests on the fact of being elaborated by a group of technical experts from different disciplines and background. This various composition enables the synopsis of a wide range of different perspective on the topic. Further, the document at least provides a starting point for further discussion, crystallising a series of different approaches and demands. Crucially, the treaty's proponents strongly support the view that 'access to knowledge is a basic human right, and that restrictions on access ought to be the exception, not the other way round.

One commentator doubts the effectiveness of the A2K Treaty in the context of WIPO alone and recommends that the role of other UN institutions, starting with the UN General Assembly, needs to be reconsidered and that their mandates and activities should be reformed where appropriate.[391] Although the A2K Treaty was never completed and did not attract the sponsorship of developing countries, it is a useful source for policymakers in those countries to study it if they decide to draft IP laws that are development friendly.

2.7.6 The Anti-Counterfeiting Trade Agreement (ACTA)

In October 2007, the US, the EU, Switzerland, and Japan announced that they would negotiate a new multilateral treaty on enforcement, called the Anti-Counterfeiting Trade Agreement (ACTA).[392] A number of developing countries have also participated in the negotiation of the ACTA, which include Mexico and Morocco.[393] The main purpose behind the Agreement is to raise internationally the level of IP enforcement above the *TRIPS Agreement* and increase the sharing of information between signatory countries for better international enforcement of IP.

At the beginning of the negotiations, very little information was made available to the public on the content of this Agreement. This led a number of civil groups to request their governments to provide more information on the content and the future implications of the ACTA.[394] James Love, Director of Knowledge Ecology International, requested the Office of the USTR to provide him with copies of the ACTA text,[395] but the request was denied on the ground that the text is confidential and to divulge it would jeopardise national security.[396]

Valantina Vadi, 'Sapere Aude! Access to Knowledge as a Human Right and a Key Instrument of Development' (2008) 12 *International Journal of Communication Law and Policy* 345, 350.

391 Musungu, above n 372, 18.

392 Electronic Frontier Foundation (EFF), *Anti-Counterfeiting Trade Agreement* <http://www.eff.org/issues/acta>; Robin Gross, *White Paper on the Proposed Anti-Counterfeiting Trade Agreement (ACTA)* (25 March 2008) IP Justice <http://ipjustice.org/wp/2008/03/25/ipj-white-paper-acta-2008/>.

Principles for ACTA Negotiations Australian Digital Alliance <http://www.digital.org.au/our-work/publication/principles-acta-negotiations>; KEI, *ACTA* <http://www.keionline.org/acta>.

393 EC, 'EU, U.S. and Others Hold Geneva Talks on Anti-Counterfeiting Trade Agreement' (5 June 2008) European Commission Trade Website <http://trade.ec.europa.eu/doclib/docs/2008/june/tradoc_139086.pdf>.

394 James Love, 'Obama Administration Rules Texts of New IPR Agreement Are State Secrets' The Haffingotn Post (online), 12 March 2009 <http://www.huffingtonpost.com/james-love/obama-administration-rule_b_174450.html>.

395 Ibid.

396 Letter from the Office of the US Trade Representative to James Love, 10 March 2009 <http://www.keionline.org/misc-docs/3/ustr_foia_denial.pdf>.

Following a series of leaks of the draft text on the Internet in 2009 and 2010, the negotiating parties decided to publish an official version of the first draft on 20 April 2010.[397] A subsequent draft was published, in English, French, and Spanish language versions, on 15 April 2011.[398] The Treaty is open to those countries that participated in its negotiation,[399] as well as to other WTO members who agree to join, up until 1 May 2013. ACTA entered into force when Japan, the US, Australia, Canada, Morocco, New Zealand, Singapore, and South Korea signed it in Tokyo on 1 October 2011.[400] The Treaty consists of the following 6 chapters with 45 articles:

- Chapter 1: Initial Provisions and General Definitions (5 arts);
- Chapter 2: Legal Framework for Enforcement of Intellectual Property Rights (22 arts);
- Chapter 3: Enforcement Practices (5 arts);
- Chapter 4: International Cooperation (3 arts);
- Chapter 5: Institutional Arrangements (3 arts); and
- Chapter 6: Final provisions (7 arts).[401]

ACTA contains extensive provisions that could have significant implications for the practice of IP enforcement in developing countries. Developing countries that choose to be members of the Treaty will be required to make extensive revisions to their IP laws, offer cross-border protection measures, and cooperate with other

---

[397] See Anti-Counterfeiting Trade Agreement (ACTA) (12 April 2010 draft) <http://trade.ec.europa.eu/doclib/docs/2010/april/tradoc_146029.pdf>

[398] See *Anti-Counterfeiting Trade Agreement (ACTA)* (15 November 2010 draft) <http://keionline.org/sites/default/files/acta_15nov2010.pdf>.

[399] These include Australia, the Republic of Austria, the Kingdom of Belgium, the Republic of Bulgaria, Canada, the Republic of Cyprus, the Czech Republic, the Kingdom of Denmark, the Republic of Estonia, the European Union, the Republic of Finland, the French Republic, the Federal Republic of Germany, the Hellenic Republic, the Republic of Hungary, Ireland, the Italian Republic, Japan, the Republic of Korea, the Republic of Latvia, the Republic of Lithuania, the Grand Duchy of Luxembourg, the Republic of Malta, the United Mexican States, the Kingdom of Morocco, the Kingdom of the Netherlands, New Zealand, the Republic of Poland, the Portuguese Republic, Romania, the Republic of Singapore, the Slovak Republic, the Republic of Slovenia, the Kingdom of Spain, the Kingdom of Sweden, the Swiss Confederation, the United Kingdom of Great Britain and Northern Ireland, and the United States of America.

[400] The Office of the United States Trade Representative, Joint Press Statement of the Anti-Counterfeiting Trade Agreement Negotiating Parties (press release October 2011) <http://www.ustr.gov/about-us/press-office/press-releases/2011/october/joint-press-statement-anti-counterfeiting-trade-ag>.

[401] See Anti-Counterfeiting Trade Agreement (ACTA), opened for signature on 1 May 2011 (entered into force on 1 October 2011) <http://www.international.gc.ca/trade-agreements-accords-commerciaux/assets/pdfs/acta-crc_apr15-2011_eng.pdf>.

member countries in that regard. Professor Michael Geist noted that ACTA capacity building and technical assistance provisions[402] confirm that developing countries will ultimately be pressured to join it,[403] and this will be contrary to their efforts in WIPO to have a 'pro-development' approach to IP that takes into consideration their interests and particular needs.[404]

2.8 Conclusion

It is critical to study the history and the development of IP, especially from the perspective of developing countries. This will be important for the future progress of a more international IP system that takes into consideration the particular needs and developmental objectives of these countries. Developing countries should learn from their past failures in attempting to revise the international IP system in the *Paris Convention* and the *Berne Convention* and develop new negotiating tactics to be more successful in any future multilateral treaty on IP.

It is noted that WIPO has not played an important role, as it should have, in shaping a balanced system of international IP that caters to the interests of developing countries. Although WIPO has assisted developing countries a great deal in drafting their national IP laws, has provided technical assistance, and sponsored major conferences to discuss the importance of IP, it has failed to influence the

---

[402] Article 35 of ACTA provides that:

1. Each Party shall endeavour to provide, upon request and on mutually agreed terms and conditions, assistance in capacity building and technical assistance in improving the enforcement of intellectual property rights to other Parties to this Agreement and, where appropriate, to prospective Parties. The capacity building and technical assistance may cover such areas as:

   (a) Enhancement of public awareness on intellectual property rights; (b) development and implementation of national legislation related to the enforcement of intellectual property rights; (c) training of officials on the enforcement of intellectual property rights; and (d) coordinated operations conducted at the regional and multilateral levels.

2. Each Party shall endeavour to work closely with other Parties and, where appropriate, non-Parties to this Agreement for the purpose of implementing the provisions of paragraph 1.
3. A Party may undertake the activities described in this Article in conjunction with relevant private sector or international organizations. Each Party shall strive to avoid unnecessary duplication between the activities described in this Article and other international cooperation activities.

Ibid 401.

[403] Michael Geist, *New ACTA Leaks: Criminal Enforcement, Institutional Issues, and International Cooperation* (19 March 2010) Boingboing <http://boingboing.net/2010/03/19/new-acta-leak-its-a.html>; Cory Doctorow, *New ACTA Leak: It's a Screw Job for the World's Poor Countries* (19 March 2010) Boingboing <http://boingboing.net/2010/03/19/new-acta-leak-its-a.html>

[404] Geist, above n 403.

debate over IP and development. It will be difficult to change the status quo of the global IP system in relation to developing countries, even when WIPO is more willing to rethink how it should approach IP and development.

History has shown how developed countries such as the US, Europe, and Japan did not respect IP protection when they were weak and still developing. They argued that there was no use for IP protection as they needed to imitate other countries to advance their economies. These countries have only respected IP when they found themselves in a good position to do so. It is submitted that it is unfair to ask developing countries to apply a 'western-style IP system' that does not suit their interests and local conditions. It took developed countries more than 200 years to reach the level they are at now in terms of technological development and IP protection. The major lesson that one derives from studying the history of IP protection in the US, the EU, and Japan is that IP is best reached when it evolves in tandem with other institutions and in accordance with the needs and interests of the social and economic development of each country.[405]

The US has been the most aggressive advocate of IP protection, compared to other developed countries in Europe and Japan. It uses multiple techniques and tactics against developing countries in the form of bilateral and multilateral treaties to make them protect IP. Brazil and India were the most important actors in shaping the debate about international IP between developed and developing countries, especially in the 1960s and the 1970s. These developing countries are still important, but recent developments have witnessed the rise of China, which is also fuelling the debate on IP and challenging common understandings of the relationship between IP and development.

The history of the international IP system showed from the beginning that it was put in place to promote the creators of IP, who most came from developed countries. Although developing countries fought hard in the 1960s and the 1970s to revise the system to create a more balanced one, their efforts were not successful and were met with scepticism from developed countries. The next few years in WIPO, especially after its agreement to consider the WIPO Development Agenda, are critical for developing countries in knowing whether they can ever reap their countless efforts to achieve a balanced international IP system that caters to their needs and interests.

[405] Khan, above n 4, 58.

Chapter 3
Intellectual Property and Economic Development

The historical record in industrialized countries, which began as developing countries, demonstrates that IP protection has been one of the most powerful instruments for economic development, export growth, and the diffusion of new technologies.[1]

There are multiple relationships between IP protection and economic development, most of them complex and difficult to measure. Despite extensive literature on the subject, much of the available evidence is anecdotal and may be interpreted in various ways.[2]

We have followed a path that will allow the technological revolution to harness our available talent into productive sectors that can fuel and sustain economic growth.[3]

Abstract Developed countries often argue that the introduction of IP systems will bring economic development to developing countries. This raises the question of whether IP systems do in fact have the effect of generating economic development in developing countries. This chapter considers the accuracy of claims that IP systems assist developing countries in their economic development and the extent to which they find support in the literature and empirical evidence. It investigates the correlation between IP and economic development in developing countries and argues that IP is not an important factor for their economic development. Further, IP is ineffective in promoting development in developing countries in the absence of other important factors that should be given priority by those countries. The chapter applies the literature on IP and economic development and uses Jordan as a case study. It

[1] National Law Centre for Inter-American Free Trade, *Strong Intellectual Property Benefits for Developing Countries* (1997) <http://www.natlaw.com/interam/mx/ip/sp/spmxip11.htm>.

[2] Keith Maskus, 'Incorporating a Globalized Intellectual Property Rights Regime into an Economic Development Strategy' in Keith Maskus (ed), *Intellectual Property, Growth and Trade* (Elsevier, 2008) 497, 500.

[3] His Majesty King Abdullah II, 'Making a Difference: A View from the Developing World' (A speech delivered at the World Economic Forum, Davos, Switzerland, 30 January 2000) <http://www.kingabdullah.jo/index.php/en_US/speeches/view/id/137/videoDisplay/0.html>.

R.M. Olwan, *Intellectual Property and Development*,
DOI 10.1007/978-3-642-27907-2_3,

investigates whether introducing strong IP systems in Jordan has had a major effect on its economic development, particularly in the pharmaceutical and IT sectors.

3.1 Overview

The role of IP in assisting developing countries to achieve economic development has always been controversial.[4] Many scholars and government officials, especially in developed countries, support the view that developing countries need to adopt strong IP laws to advance their economic development. Despite the abundance of support for this view, there are many government officials, economists, development theorists, and IP scholars who believe that introducing strong IP laws will not lead to economic development in developing countries.

Research that examines the relationship between IP and economic development is scant and non-conclusive.[5] This is because many economists who write about these matters do not possess the necessary specialised knowledge about IP that allows them to produce properly researched work. By the same token, many IP scholars who want to address the economic aspects of IP are not trained to produce empirical studies (the use of statistics and data to support an argument) as they do not possess the economic scientific knowledge that is critical for conducting such studies. It is imperative for someone who wants to examine the importance of IP to economic development to be familiar with the economic aspects of IP and the studies that have been written on the subject.[6]

This chapter will examine the correlation between IP and economic development. It will assess the influence of IP systems in developing countries on their economic development. The main argument of this chapter is that IP is not an important factor for the economic development of developing countries and that it is completely ineffective in the absence of other factors that should be considered carefully by those countries. Three sections in the chapter support this argument.

In Sect. 3.2, the available theoretical literature about IP and economic development will be examined. The benefits and disadvantages of having IP laws in developing countries and their effect on the economic development of these countries will also be explored. It will discuss mainly how economists and IP scholars value the relevance of IP systems in assisting developing countries in their economic development. Section 3.6 will examine the empirical evidence on the subject and will focus particularly on the literature that discusses the effect of introducing IP laws in developing countries on domestic innovation, FDI, economic growth, and R&D. Finally, Sect. 3.7 will evaluate the situation of Jordan in relation to IP and economic development. It will examine to what extent the country has benefited from introducing strong IP systems based on the available academic and empirical literature.

---

[4] See HA-Joon Chang, 'Intellectual Property Rights and Economic Development: Historical Lessons and Emerging Issues' (2001) 2 (2) *Journal of Human Development and Capabilities* 287.

[5] See Robert M. Sherwood, *Intellectual Property and Economic Development* (Westview, 1990) ch 1.

[6] Keith Maskus, 'Teaching the Economics of Intellectual Rights in the Global Economy' in Yo Takagi, Larry Allman, and Mapazi A. Sinjela (eds), *Teaching of Intellectual Property* (Cambridge University, 2008) 166-185.

3.2 Examination of Theoretical Literature on IP and Economic Development

3.2.1 *Introduction*

The following questions have been asked by IP scholars and economists about IP and economic development:

- What is the exact correlation between IP and economic development?
- Does having a system of IP law bring economic development to developing countries?

Before answering these questions and for the purpose of clarifying the discussions that follow in this chapter, it is necessary to explain how economists perceive IP. Economists have many different views on IP that do not correspond with the views of lawyers and scholars working in the field of IP. Developed and developing countries have divergent views on the importance of economic development and the role of states in boosting the national economy, welfare, and prosperity of their citizens. It has been stated that 'developed countries are interested in strengthening the national economy to be able to compete more effectively internationally, while developing countries are eager to establish an efficient economy that will be able to provide prosperity and stability to their citizens'.[7]

Although it is beyond the scope of this chapter to delve into pure economists' views of how to achieve economic development in developing countries, nevertheless it proves useful to provide some preliminary thoughts on the matter. Developing countries are often reminded from time to time that they need to adopt a set of 'good policies' and to establish 'good institutions' that would help them to achieve economic development.[8] The 'good policies'[9] that developing countries should adopt include 'trade liberalization, domestic regulation, privatisation,[10] and a

[7] Sameh Y. El-Torgoman, *The Egyptian Capital Market and Economic Development* (SJD Thesis, Stanford University, 1997) 1.

[8] In a very influential work, Professor Ha-Joon Chang, in *Kicking Away the Ladder - Development Strategy in Historical Perspective*, reviews the situation of developed countries. He found that developing countries have not applied the policies that they believe should be practised by developing countries to achieve economic development. Instead, he argues that developed countries have used 'bad trade' and industrial policies that are not acceptable these days and that developed countries are actually making it difficult for developing countries to achieve economic development. See Ha-Joon Chang, *Kicking Away the Ladder - Development Strategy in Historical Perspective* (Anthem, 2003) 2, 3.

[9] Ibid 1.

[10] There are also alternative theories that do not place the same confidence in markets, especially those in developing countries. See Joseph E. Stiglitz and Andrew Charlton, *Fair Trade for All - How Trade Can Promote Development* (Oxford University, 2005) 89.

strong competition policy'.[11] On the other hand, the 'good institutions' that developing countries should establish include democracy, 'good bureaucracy', an independent judiciary, transparent and market-oriented corporate governance, financial institutions, and a strong private property rights system (including IP).[12] Developing countries often hope that being members of the WTO and introducing a set of appropriate IP laws will aid them to be part of the international trade regime[13] and will ultimately boost their economic growth and hasten their development. However, will the introduction of these 'good policies' to developing countries by itself be enough to achieve economic development?

Unfortunately, economic development is more complicated than theorists would suggest. Many developing countries are now part of the international trade regime but are still struggling to achieve economic development. As one influential World Bank General Counsel from Egypt noted:

> Economic development is a long-term process that takes years to be implemented and achieve its results. It is not considered in isolation to other aspects and includes a well developed legal framework, an efficient administration system, and well functioning judicial institutions.[14]

[11] Peter Drahos and Imelda Maher, 'Innovation, Competition, Standards and Intellectual Property: Policy Perspectives from Economics and Law' (2004) 16 *Information Economics Policy*, Australian National University <http://www.anu.edu.au/fellows/pdrahos/articles/pdfs/2004innovation competitionIP.pdf>. The Washington Consensus (upon which most WTO rules are based) has adopted many of those policies. See Stiglitz and Charlton, above n 10, 89.

[12] On the rule of law for achieving economic development, see Chang, above n 8, 1; Daron Acemoglu, *Root Causes - A Historical Approach to Assessing the Role of Institutions in Economic Development* (2003) International Monetary Fund <http://www.imf.org/external/pubs/ft/fandd/2003/06/pdf/acemoglu.pdf>; Peter Drahos, 'Intellectual Property Rights in the Knowledge Economy' in David Rooney, Greg Hearn and Abraham Ninan (eds), *Handbook on the Knowledge Economy* (Edward Elgar, 2005) 139.

[13] Some scholars would argue that the way forward for developing countries to achieve economic development through international trade is to sign FTAs with major economic powers. Developing countries hope that by signing FTAs, they will be able to increase their international trade through expanding their exports to international markets. See Dennis Arnold, 'Free Trade Agreements and Southeast Asia' 36 (2) *Journal of Contemporary Asia* 205-206, 214; Linda Y. Yueh, 'Global Intellectual Property Rights and Economic Growth' (2007) 5 (3) *Northwestern Journal of Technology and Intellectual Property* 448; Danielle Gervais, 'Policy-Calibration and Innovation Displacement' in Neil Weinstock Netanel (ed), *The Development Agenda: Global Intellectual Property and Developing Countries* (Oxford University, 2008) 51, 58; Marwa Al Nasa'a et al., *The Jordan-U.S. Free Trade Agreement: Eight Years Later* (21 March 2008) University of Michigan, Gerald R. Ford School of Public Policy, International Economic Development Program, 2-3 <http://www.umich.edu/~ipolicy/Policy%20Papers/jordanusfta.pdf>.

[14] Ibrahim F. Shihata. *The World Bank in Challenging World* (World Bank,1995), vol 2, 127-145, cited in Torgoman, above n 7, 2.

3.2.2 The Meaning of IP from an Economic Perspective

Instead of defining IP from a purely legal viewpoint, it is more relevant to concentrate on its economic perspective. It is important to explain the views of economists on IP to understand its relationship with economic development. IP has been regarded as the natural field for studying the economic aspects of law.[15] Most economists are not interested in IP per se but rather are interested in studying how best it could promote economic efficiency and a systematic allocation of meaningful resources.[16]

3.2.2.1 The Economics of IP

To understand the law of IP and its relationship with economics, there is a need for a preliminary understanding of the basic economic terms that are used by economists.[17] Economists perceive IP differently from IP lawyers and consider it as 'public goods'[18] and 'knowledge products'.[19] Public goods include policies and infrastructure that are systemically provided by private market forces and have an

[15] William M. Landes and Richard A. Posner, 'An Economic Analysis of Copyright Law' (1989) 18 *Journal of Legal Studies*, Berkman Center for Internet and Society at Harvard Law School, 325 <http://cyber.law.harvard.edu/IPCoop/89land1.html>.

[16] Ibid.

[17] It is also important to be familier with the basic concepts of property rights before indulging in the discussion of IP. As one scholar explained that:

> Property rights in tangibles are a response to scarcity. Scarcity is opposed to abundance and arises where different individuals want to use a single object in ways which cannot all simultaneously be indulged in. It is hardly worth establishing property rights on abundant commodities: all can use them to their heart's content without exhausting the supply.

See Ejan Mackaay, *The Economics of Intellectual Property Rights in Civil Law Systems* (2007) University of Montreal, 2 <https://papyrus.bib.umontreal.ca/jspui/handle/1866/722>; Richard A. Posner, 'The Law and Economics of Intellectual Property' (2002) 131 *Daedalus* 2; Joseph Stiglitz, *Making Globalisation Work* (W.W. Norton, 2006) 107.

[18] Landes and Posner, above n 15; Joseph E. Stiglitz, *Public Policy for a Knowledge Economy* (27 January 1999) Akgul.Bilkent <http://akgul.bilkent.edu.tr/BT-BE/knowledge-economy.pdf>; Joseph E. Stiglitz, 'Toward a Pro-Development and Balanced Intellectual Property Regime' (a speech delivered at the Ministerial Conference on Intellectual Property for Least Developed Countries, Seoul, Korea, 25 October, 2004) Columbia Business School <http://www2.gsb.columbia.edu/faculty/jstiglitz/download/2004_TOWARDS_A_PRO_DEVELOPMENT.htm>; Stiglitz, above n 17, 111.

[19] Carlos Alberto Primo Braga, 'The Economics of Intellectual Property Rights and the GATT: A View from the South' (1989) 22 *Vanderbilt Journal of Transnational Law* 244; Suzanne Scotchmer, *Innovation and Incentives* (MIT, 2004) ch 2; Dominique Foray, *Economics of Knowledge* (MIT, 2000) 113-129; Stiglitz and Charlton, above n 10; 142.

important international externality effect.[20] It has been stated that '[a] public good is a good whose consumption is considered as non-rivalrous'.[21] It is important to explain the non-rival nature of public goods and their effect on the market. One scholar explains that '[a]non-rival good is one that can be used simultaneously by many people; its use by one person does not make it harder for other people to use the same non-rival good'.[22] Acquiring IP for a good that is created from knowledge is an example of making a non-rival good excluded from being used simultaneously by other people.[23] Economists are particularly interested in this particular feature of the IP system.[24] For example, the use of someone else's private car would mean that the owner would not be able to drive and enjoy his ownership, while if someone has read a book of another, he would not diminish the IP right of the author. It may be also possible to increase the value of the book if it is discussed or evaluated in an online review forum.

In the case of absence of protection or weak protection of IP, the 'market efficiency' would be affected as a result.[25] To overcome this, some economists would recommend government intervention through an IP system to support the market and the creative process.[26] Others reject the IP system as a whole[27] and simply suggest a new system that allows new technologies and products to be widely accessed once a marginal cost is paid to the owner.[28] In the mind of an economist, IP has two objectives. Professor Keith Maskus summarises them as follows:

[20] Keith E. Maskus and Jerome H. Reichman, 'The Globalisation of Private Knowledge Goods and the Privatization of Global Public Goods' in Keith E. Maskus and Jerome H. Reichman, *International Public Goods and Transfer of Technology Under Globalized Intellectual Property Regime* (Cambridge University, 2005) 8.

[21] Joseph E. Stiglitz, 'Economic Foundations of Intellectual Property Rights' (2008) 57 *Duke Law Journal*, 1693, 1700; Mackaay, above n 17, 8.

[22] Christine Greenhalgh and Padraig Dixon, *The Economics of Intellectual Property: A Review to Identify Themes for Future Research*, University of Oxford, Department of Economics, Economics Series Working Papers No. 135 (2002) IDEAS, 4 <http://ideas.repec.org/p/oxf/wpaper/135.html>.

[23] Ibid.

[24] Ibid.

[25] See, for the negative effects on the market, Stiglitz, above n 21; Keith E Maskus, *Intellectual Property Rights and Economic Development*, prepared for the series 'Beyond the Treaties: A Symposium on Compliance with International Intellectual Property Law', organised by Fredrick K. Cox International Law Center at Case Western Reserve University (University of Colorado Boulder), 2 <www.colorado.edu/Economics/mcguire/workingpapers/cwrurev.doc>; Posner, above n 17, 9; Drahos, above n 12, 146.

[26] Stanley M. Besen and Leo J. Raskind, 'An Introduction to the Law and Economics of Intellectual Property' (1991) 5 (1) *Journal of Economic Perspectives* 3-4; Mackaay, above n 17, 8.

[27] Michele Boldrin and David K. Levine, *Against Intellectual Property Monopoly* (Cambridge University, 2008).

[28] Maskus, above n 25, 2; Mackaay, above n 17, 5.

> The first is to promote investments in knowledge creation and business innovation by establishing exclusive rights to use and sell newly developed technologies, goods, and services. The second is to promote widespread dissemination of new knowledge by encouraging (or requiring) rights' holders to place their inventions and ideas on the market.[29]

Economic agents[30] are described as rational profit maximisers[31] who will aspire to place their IP on the market to reap the maximum pecuniary rewards for their inventions.[32] In summary, economists have described IP as 'policy instruments designed, in principle, to resolve market failures and address externalities that arise in the development and exchange of knowledge, technology, and cultural goods'.[33]

3.2.2.2 Forms of IP

It is important to distinguish between the different forms of IP and to explain how economists perceive each of them. Basically, there are two distinct branches of IP rights, industrial property and copyright. Industrial property includes patents, trademarks, design, trade secrets, integrated circuits, commercial names, geographical indications, and protection against unfair competition.[34] Copyright protects works of authors, which include maps, charts, prints, musical compositions, dramatic works, photographs, paintings, drawings, and many others. Related rights (neighbouring rights) protect creators who contribute to the producing and dissemination of work, and they include performers, phonogram producers, and broadcasters. The patent system is a system of incentives and rewards.[35] The government offers the inventor, in return for making their invention known to the public, a reward in the form of a monopoly for a limited period of time.[36] This encourages inventors to produce new inventions that are useful to society.[37]

---

[29] Maskus, above n 25, 2; Mackaay, above n 17, 1.

[30] An economic agent is 'a person or firm with the power to make decisions about output, investment and prices'. See the definition of economic agent, Donald Rutherford, *Routledge Dictionary of Economics* (Taylor and Francis, 2nd ed, 2002).

[31] Drahos, above n 12, 143.

[32] Steve P. Calandrillo, 'An Economic Analysis of Property Rights in Information: Justifications and Problems of Exclusive Rights, Incentives to Generate Information, and the Alternative of a Government-Run Reward System' (1998) 9 *Fordham Intellectual Property, Media and Entertainment Law Journal* 301, 355.

[33] Maskus, above n 2, 500. See also Robert P. Merges, 'Of property Rules, Coase, and Intellectual Property' (1994) 94 *Columbia Law Review*, 2655, 2661; Stiglitz, above n 21,1695; Calandrillo, above n 32, 355; Besen and Raskind, above n 26, 5.

[34] WIPO, *Understanding Industrial Property, WIPO Publication No. 895(E)* <http://www.wipo.int/freepublications/en/intproperty/895/wipo_pub_895.pdf>.

[35] Besen and Raskind, above n 26, 8.

[36] See, for more economic explanation, on patents, Michael P. Ryan, 'Knowledge-Economy Elites, the International Law of Intellectual Property and Trade and Economic Development' (2002) 10 *Cardozo International and Comparative Law Journal* 271, 284-286.

[37] For a criticism of the patent system and for alternatives, see Stiglitz, above n 21, 1702-1723.

The patent holders can either license their rights for the payment of a royalty or retain its exploitation for their own benefits.[38]

Trademark law is essential to the proper functioning of a market economy.[39] It provides incentives to producers to establish goodwill in the marketplace.[40] A trademark can be a word or words, a number or character, a picture or symbol or graphic design, or sound or some combination of these that an enterprise uses to identify its goods or services and to distinguish them from those of others.[41] Trademarks can serve consumers by not allowing them to fell prey to deceptive practices in trade and business.[42] They also protect commercial goodwill, to ensure that people's business reputations are not exploited unfairly, without proper compensation.[43] Trade secret law (unfair competition law) protects the unauthorised use of confidential proprietary business information by others.

Governments protect copyrighted works from infringement to encourage them to communicate their informational and cultural products to the world. Protecting knowledge without a proper compensation system would result in not using it in the market. In essence, copyright provides owners with a fair opportunity to recoup their investment by licensing it commercially to potential buyers. This sort of business might be a risky one, especially with the rise of digital copying technologies and the immense power of the distribution capabilities of the Internet.[44]

3.3 The Views of Developed and Developing Countries on IP and Economic Development

Can IP increase economic development for a developing country? How can IP assist a developing country to increase its economic returns? What is the economic situation of a developing country that has introduced a strong IP system and that has joined the international trade system? Did this help, by any means, to increase its economic development?

A debate exists today between those who believe that IP could accelerate economic development and those who are doubtful whether the introduction of IP can cause any economic development to developing countries.[45]

---

[38] Besen and Raskind, above n 26, 3, 8.

[39] Rayan, above n 36, 279.

[40] Ibid.

[41] Ibid.

[42] Mahesh Bissau, *Economic Dimension in Trademark Law: Evolution Trough Judicial Pronouncements*, Legal Services India <http://www.legalserviceindia.com/articles/tm_d.htm>.

[43] Ibid.

[44] Ryan, above n 36, 288.

[45] Peter M. Beattie, 'The (Intellectual Property Law &) Economics of Innocent Fraud: The IP & Development Debate' (2007) 38 (1) *International Review of Intellectual Property and Competition*, 6, 10.

3.3.1 *Positive Effects of IP on Economic Development: The Views of Developed Countries*

Developed countries argue that the level of economic development of developing countries is closely correlated with the availability and enforcement of IP laws in those countries.[46] Developing countries that have no or weak IP protection will ultimately experience a low level of economic development.[47]

IP can accelerate economic development in a developing country by significantly reducing 'the transaction costs involved in licensing technologies and supporting growth in technological trade'.[48] IP can also help in disseminating knowledge, particularly when patent applications are published and competitors are allowed to use such information to develop further inventions.[49] The IP systems are seen to accelerate economic development in developing countries in several ways. It can promote domestic innovations and increase investments and revenues in developing countries that provide for its proper protection and enforcement.

Some believe that IP can increase economic development indirectly in three ways. Firstly, an IP system may affect innovative activity that, in turn, is the source

---

[46] The commentator Robert Sherwood supports such view. Sherwood argues that IP is to be considered as infrastructure for the economic development of developing countries. He notes that:

> [T]he infrastructural context places attention on assessing the contribution to economic growth and development arising from the presence, in a developing country, of reliable safeguards for new technology and creative expression.

He explains further his concept of IP as being infrastructure for economic development:

> The concept of *infrastructure* has proven useful in examining economic development. Roads, irrigation, sewers, schools, water supply, health care and electrical systems are among the preconditions thought beneficial for development. Creation of infrastructure is accorded priority because of this. Although largely invisible, an IP system which protects innovation and creative expression may be viewed as a helpful precondition to creating and using new technology which boosts economic growth and aids development.

See Sherwood, above n 5, ch 1.

Economics Professor Michael Ryan supports the importance of IP for economic development of developing countries, defending the arguments of developed countries (what he calls elite countries). He criticised scholars who support what he called the 'conventional wisdom', which fails to realise the importance of IP in accelerating development in developing countries by facilitating trade and the flow of investment to developing countries and enabling the acquisition of technology and knowledge. See Ryan, above n 36, 274; Jean Raymond Homere, 'Intellectual Property Rights Can Help Stimulate the Economic Development of Least Developed Countries' (2004) 27 (2) *Columbia Journal of Law and Arts* 277, 286-288.

[47] Professor Michael P. Ryan believes that weak IP could actually impede the economic development of certain developing countries, as the result of conferring *hazards* that negatively influence firms that want to gain access to markets of those countries. Managers of these firms are only interested in entering countries where the risk of infringement of IP is at the lowest. See Ryan, above n 36, 301.

[48] Maskus, above n 2, 501.

[49] Ibid 506.

of total factor productivity.[50] Secondly, it could affect the inflows of FDI and technology transfers that could impinge upon economic growth.[51] Thirdly, an IP system could lead to some redistribution of income between countries and between communities within developing countries.[52] IP can promote domestic innovations through protecting nascent technology and preventing the loss of human resources, ensuring that local innovators are rewarded properly for their efforts.[53] They could also increase government tax revenues from registration fees and create new jobs.[54] Strong IP protection attracts capital and technology transfers that are essential for encouraging R&D investments in developing countries.[55]

Innovation can flourish in developing countries that support strong IP since MNCs are willing to provide novel marketing approaches and new products only into those markets that they believe would support their activities. Developing countries that have appropriate investment and IP laws provide a strong signal to potential inventors in developed countries that there is no risk of them losing revenues through the absence of strong IP laws and enforcement. This encourages potential investors to go to those developing countries and conduct business there.

Patents, in particular, provide a legal basis for trading[56] and could stimulate acquisition and dissemination of new information.[57] Copyright protection can induce investments and stimulate innovation in creative activities such as advertising, film,

---

[50] John Black, Nigar Hashimzade, and Gareth Myles note that:

> Factor Productivity is the output of a plant, a firm, or an industry per unit of factor input... Total factor productivity relates the value of output to total factor inputs, aggregated at some set of relative prices. This can change through changes in effort, managerial efficiency, or available techniques, or through scale effects when the output level varies.

See John Black, Nigar Hashimzade, and Gareth Myles, *A Dictionary of Economics* (Oxford University, 3rd, 2009). See also Nagesh Kumar, *Intellectual Property Rights, Technology and Economic Development: Experiences of Asian Countries* (September 2002) Commission on Intellectual Property Rights <http://www.iprcommission.org/papers/pdfs/study_papers/sp1b_kumar_study.pdf>.

[51] Kumar, above n 50, 13.

[52] Ibid.

[53] David Hindman, 'The Effect of Intellectual Property Regimes on Foreign Investments in Developing Economies' (2003) 23 *Arizona Journal of International and Comparative Law* 467-474.

[54] Ibid; Mikhaelle Schiappacasse, 'Intellectual Property Rights in China: Technology Transfers and Economic Development', (2003-2004) 3 *Buffalo Intellectual Property Law Journal* 164, 168.

[55] Hindman, above n 53.

[56] Keith E. Maskus, Sean M. Dougherty, and Andrew Mertha, 'Intellectual Property Rights and Economic Development in China' in Carsten Fink and Keith E. Maskus (eds), *Intellectual Property and Development: Lessons from Recent Economic Research* (World Bank and Oxford University, 2005) World Bank, 295-331 <http://siteresources.worldbank.org/INTRANETTRADE/Resources/Pubs/IPRs-book.pdf>

[57] The World Bank, *Global Economic Prospects and the Developing Countries* (the International Bank for Reconstruction and Development/ the World Bank, 2002) 135 <http://siteresources.worldbank.org/INTGEP/Resources/335315-1257200370513/gep2002complete.pdf>.

publications, and software and video games.[58] In the field of trademarks, they allow new firms to enter into the market, and as a result, this diminishes the possibility of exploiting[59] scale economies.[60]

If IP is not protected in developing countries, economic development will suffer as a result of either non-existent or insufficient protection. Consumers will run the risk of using poor quality goods and accepting sub-standard services.[61] As a result, investment of MNCs will stay away from developing countries that do not respect and enforce IP.[62] This may also result in forcing large corporations to either shut down operations[63] or abandon their expansion investment strategies in those countries. In addition, local innovators, upcoming local artists, and entrepreneurs will suffer as a result, as the non-protection of IP will impede the creative and cultural development of those countries.[64]

Developing countries with weak IP will also experience a degree of isolation from modern technologies as MNCs will refuse to transfer them to those countries.[65] Subsequently, developing countries will have to develop their own technologies, which could be expensive and time-consuming. Such countries experience fewer 'spillover' benefits,[66] less production techniques and know-how.[67] In addition, they will not be exposed to technological changes that are important for stimulating domestic innovation and will be subject to a limited inward flow of technology.[68]

[58] Ibid; Landes and Posner, above n 15; Maskus, Dougherty, and Mertha, above n 56, 5, 9.

[59] Maskus, Dougherty and Mertha, above n 56, 9.

[60] John Black, Nigar Hashimzade, and Gareth Myles note that 'scale of economies is the reduction in cost per unit resulting from increased production'. See Black, Hashimzade and Myles, above n 50.

[61] Hindman, above n 53.

[62] Ibid; Michael P. Ryan, 'Intellectual Property, Trade and Foreign Direct Investment' (a paper presented at the WIPO Arab Regional Meeting on Intellectual Property as a Power Tool for Economic Growth, Amman, Jordan, 1-3 June 2004) <http://www.wipo.int/edocs/mdocs/arab/en/wipo_reg_ip_amm_04/wipo_reg_ip_amm_04_4.pdf>.

[63] Hindman, above n 53.

[64] Maskus, above n 2, 506.

[65] Eric Garduño and Frank J. Pietrucha, 'Intellectual Property Rights in the Arab World' (Winter/Spring 2003) *Georgetown Journal of International Affairs,* 57-63 <http://www12.georgetown.edu/sfs/publications/journal/Issues/ws03/gardunolocked.pdf>.

[66] 'Spillover' is defined as the 'effects of economic activity or process upon those who are not directly involved in it'. See Jack P. Friedman, *Dictionary of Business Terms* (Barron's Educational Series, 4th ed, 2007).

[67] Ryan, above n 62; Maskus, Dougherty, and Mertha, above n 56, 9.

[68] Maskus, Dougherty, and Mertha, above n 56.

3.3.2 The Negative Effects of IP on Economic Development: The Views of Developing Countries

Developing countries have argued that the reasons put forward by developed countries to support claims that the adoption of IP would accelerate economic development in developing countries are not economically sound.[69] On the contrary, they argue that adopting IP can result in heavy financial burdens that could impede their economic development. Although many developing countries have agreed to introduce IP and have joined the WTO, it is useful to examine their main concerns regarding how IP could limit their economic development.

3.3.3 Rent Transfer

One of the main points that developing countries bring to this issue is that providing IP to MNCs will lead to 'rent transfer'[70] from technology importers to technology developers.[71] Professor Keith Maskus described how IP could cause 'rent transfer' and damage to the economies of developing countries. This could be as follows:

> The most frequently expressed fear about IP is that they create strong market positions, from which firms can raise prices to monopolistic levels. The concern is strongest in developing countries, because applications for IP come overwhelmingly from foreign firms, meaning that the associated profits are transferred abroad. This represents a loss in the technology-importing countries' terms of trade, ultimately slowing growth.[72]

Another commentator described it as follows:

> Developing countries fear that patent protection for new products and technologies will merely enable large multinational corporations to secure global monopolies, and thereby charge exorbitant prices for their goods. As a result patents may be used as a means of preventing others from making or selling the product in the market. This will lead to the under-utilization[73] of inventions in developing countries.[74]

---

[69] Braga, above n 19, 254.

[70] Rent is 'a general term for payment in excess of opportunity cost. It can be created by monopoly power, by legislation, or by network externalities'. An example is as follows: If a patent holder is willing to license his invention for the amount of $20 000 to a local corporation in a developing country and instead obtained $30 000 a year, the economic rent would be $10 000 a year. See Black, Hashimzade, and Myles, above n 50; Lee G. Branstetter, 'Do Stronger Patents Induce Mode Local Innovation?' in Keith E. Maskus and Jerome H. Reichman, *International Public Goods and Transfer of Technology Under Globalized Intellectual Property Regime* (Cambridge University, 2005) 309-321 (310).

[71] World Bank, above n 57, 136.

[72] Maskus, Dougherty, and Martha, above n 56, 13.

[73] The term 'under-utilization' means too little or inefficiently.

[74] Alan S. Gutterman, 'The North-South Debate Regarding the Protection of Intellectual Property Rights', (1993) 28 *Wake Forest Law Review*, 89, 121-124; Chang, above n 4, 302.

In the context of patents in developing countries, they are usually owned by MNCs located in industrialised countries. These MNCs could gain monopolistic power in a global market, simply through the ownership of IP. As a result, they could set higher prices for the licensing of their products that developing countries may critically need, and the revenues received from such licensing goes straight to the MNC, instead of being reinvested in the developing country.[75] The consequences that could result from 'rent transfer' of IP are not the same in all developing countries. It could be adjusted in countries that develop inventions and have inventive enterprises, but this will not be the case for technology-importing countries.[76]

3.3.4 *High Administrative Costs*

Another argument for not adopting IP as advanced by developing countries, particularly LDCs, is that introducing IP laws and a system of enforcement would impose a heavy financial burden upon them that they would not be able to afford.[77] Costs for establishing and updating IP systems include 'upgrading offices for registering and examining patents and trademarks; accepting deposits of plant materials; training examiners, judges, and lawyers; improving courts[78] to manage IP litigation; and training customs officers and undertaking border and domestic enforcement actions'.[79]

---

[75] The World Bank conducted a study in 1995 after the conclusion of the *TRIPS Agreement* to assess the patent rents associated with stronger IP protection in 28 countries. It found that:

> Overwhelmingly the United States would gain the most income in terms of static rent transfers, with a net inflow of some $19.1 billion per year . . . and Germany would earn an additional net income of $6.7 billion on its patent portfolio. The study showed that 'many countries would experience a rising net outflow of patent rents because they tend to be net technology importers. Korea in the amount of $15.3 billion each year and China of around $5.1 billion per year.

See World Bank, above n 57, 137; Stiglitz (2004), above n 18.

[76] World Bank, above 57, 136.

[77] UNCTAD provided some estimates of the administrative costs of complying with *TRIPS Agreement* in various developing countries and LDCs. It noted that:

> In Chile, additional fixed costs from this upgrade were estimated at $718 000 and annual recurrent costs at $837 000. Egyptian fixed costs would be perhaps $800 000, with additional annual training costs of around $1 million. Bangladesh anticipated one-time costs of administrative TRIPS compliance (drafting legislation) amounting to $250 000, and over $1.1 million in annual costs for judicial works, equipment, and enforcement efforts.

Ibid. See also James W. Peters, 'Toward Negotiating a Remedy to Copyright Piracy in Singapore' (1986) 7 *Northwestern Journal of International Law & Business* 561, 563-569; Homere, above 46, 285-286.

[78] For quite useful suggestions for developing countries in that regard, see Sherwood, above 5, ch 8.

[79] World Bank, above 57, 136; Chang, above n 4, 299.

The commentator Robert M. Sherwood compared each IP system in relation to its costs. He noted that:

> The patent regime is the highest cost form of protection in terms of system expense, followed by the trademark system. Both involve registries. The layout-design system also involves registration, but involves a much smaller volume of items. The copyright system is more nearly self-executing, although a registry plays a part. The trade secret, which involves no bureaucracy, is the lowest cost form. Enforcement is a critical aspect of the system for each of the forms of protection.[80]

It is questionable whether developing countries and LDCs would be willing to incur these costs[81] or whether they would achieve more social benefits as a result of their investments.[82] Furthermore, it is more beneficial to developing countries to invest in other critical matters such as health and education, rather than in IP, as both are of crucial importance to the survival, well-being, and future development of the citizens of these countries.[83] Some counter the developing countries' argument by noting that they can easily offset the administrative fees either by charging fees for IP registration or by requesting financial assistance from international organisations involved in the protection of international IP such as WIPO.[84]

While charging fees for registration could help in offsetting some of the financial burden, it is doubtful whether registration fees alone would provide the funding necessary to establish and maintain these services. In addition, requesting international organisations for financial assistance may not be a wise decision as these countries will have to think carefully of long-term strategies that would maintain these IP services after such financial assistance has been exhausted. Other costs that developing countries will need to consider include 'the cost of additional domestic R&D and the eventual loss of consumer surplus brought by higher prices that could result from the 'monopolization' that could happen as a result of MNCs refuse to license their IP rights'.[85]

[80] Sherwood, above n 5, ch 8.

[81] World Bank, above n 57, 136.

[82] Ibid.

[83] See also, Stiglitz, above n 17, 118.

[84] World Bank, above n 57, 136. For an elaborative discussion on how to offset these administrative costs by developing countries, see Sherwood, above n 5, ch 8.

[85] Braga, above n 19, 256.

3.3.5 Other Concerns of Developing Countries

Other economic burdens that developing countries feel would impede their economic development as a result of introducing and enforcing IP include raising prices for medicinal drugs, agricultural products, and technology acquisition.[86] Developing countries often resist patent protection for pharmaceutical products, simply because they have many people who cannot afford to pay high prices that MNCs want to charge for genuine medications, especially for epidemic diseases such as AIDS and others.[87] They also stress the importance of making necessary medicines affordable to their citizens as a matter of national sovereignty[88] since their governments need to act appropriately in case of epidemic diseases targeting the health of their nationals. As for educational materials, developing countries that introduce copyright laws will have to pay huge amounts to publishers to educate their citizens.[89]

Many developing countries rely on industrialised countries to provide them with heavy machinery and other necessary technological products. As a result of MNCs obtaining monopolistic power and dominant position in the markets of developing countries, they would have to pay higher acquisition costs to acquire the necessary technological products that they critically need for development.

3.4 The Views of Prominent Economists on IP and Economic Development

Some commentators argue that IP could reduce the supply of public goods that developing countries need in order to accelerate their economic development. These public goods include scientific research, educational materials, health care, biodiversity, and environmental protection,[90] all of which would, in one way or another, suffer as a result of introducing IP systems. This section will explain the views of prominent economists on IP and economic development.

---

[86] See also the effect of IP on the economic development of developing countries, John Barton et al., Commission on Intellectual Property Rights (CIPR), *Integrating Intellectual Property Rights and Development Policy* (September 2002), <http://www.iprcommission.org/papers/pdfs/final_report/CIPRfullfinal.pdf>.

[87] Professor Jagdish Bhagwati differentiates between two types of diseases, the likes of Malaria, which are primarily present in developing countries and LDCs, and AIDS; he notes that the argument perceived by pharmaceutical companies that they suffer as a result of not having IP in developing countries is flawed. See for further explanation, Jagdish Bhagwati, *In Defence of Globalisation* (Oxford University, 2004) 184-185.

[88] Gutterman, above n 74, 121-125.

[89] See also Kim, cited in Maskus, above n 2, 498-499.

[90] Maskus and Reichman, above n 20, 6.

3.4.1 Joseph Schumpeter

Joseph Schumpeter, regarded as the father of modern evolutionary economists,[91] is well known for his explanation of business cycles and for his appraisal of the mutual evolution of socialism and capitalism.[92] His theories were set out in the *Theory of Economic Development* (1912 [1934]) and *Business Cycles* (1939). Although he did not address the position of developing countries, his views are relevant to explaining economic development. Schumpeter suggests that innovation and technology diffusion are driving forces behind industrial advances and global development.[93] Entrepreneurial activity is central in Schumpeter's scholarship. It is the introduction of novel ways of conducting economic activity that is important.[94] Innovation is considered as 'the novelties, the impossibilities rendered actual, and the sources of economic variety on which the competitive process operates to evaluate the new and adapt according to the relative advantages that the new possess over the old ways'.[95] Schumpeter's identification of the role of capital and credit in the funding and filtering of emergent novelty is one of his major contributions to the understanding of innovation.[96] He describes entrepreneurs not as those people who present the obvious but as those who carry out the innovative act.

One of the most important contributions of Schumpeter's theory of innovative development is the identification, in an original and independent way (using, particularly, Darwinian analogies), of the *crucial ingredients* of an evolutionary theory in economics.[97] Schumpeter wrote in 1912 that small firms provide the most significant stimulus to innovation but reversed this position later in 1942, when he argued instead that large firms, operating in concentrated industries, drive innovative development.

[91] Geoffrey M. Hogson noted in 1993 that:

> Evolutionary Economics is part of mainstream economics as well as heterodox school of economic thought that is inspired by evolutionary biology. Much like mainstream economics, it stresses complex interdependencies, competition, growth, structural change, and resource constraints but differs in the approaches which are used to analyse these phenomena.

See Geoffrey M. Hodgson, *Economics and Evolution: Bringing Life Back Into Economics* (Cambridge and University of Michigan, 1993); J.S. Metcalfe, 'The Broken Thread: Marshall, Schumpeter and Hayek on the Evaluation of Capitalism' in Yuichi Shionoya and Tamotsu Nishizawa, *Marshall and Schumpeter on Evolution: Economic Society of Capitalist Development* (Edward Elgar Publishing, 2008) 117.

[92] Sherwood, above n 5.

[93] Sherwood, above n 5.

[94] Metcalfe, above n 92, 118.

[95] Ibid.

[96] Ibid 220.

[97] Ulrich Witt, 'How Evolutionary Is Schumpeter's Theory of Economic Development' (2002) 9 (1/2) *Industry and Innovation, 7-22* <http://www.econ.mpg.de/files/2004/staff/witt_HowEvolutionaryIsSchumpertersTheory.pdf>.

Schumpeter defined economic development as 'such things in economic life as are not forced upon it from without but arise by its own initiative, from within'. In his view, it is accompanied by growth that depends primarily upon productivity increases based on innovation.[98] Schumpeter's work comprises one of the few systematic bodies of thought that clearly present how economic development occurs.[99] To Schumpeter, economic development begins when an entrepreneur introduces an innovation that enables the enterprise to earn an extra (monopolistic) profit and stimulates the demand for credit to finance new investments and that will result in the 'the swarming of entrepreneurs'.[100] This can take place not only in developed countries but also in developing countries, contrary to the views of some who contend that Schumpeter's theory is inapplicable in developing countries since they live in a 'non-Schumpeterian world' and their goal of development is neither private enrichment nor the 'the establishment of a position of wealth and power for the entrepreneur'.[101] Schumpeter's physiological trait of entrepreneurial action consists of 'the dream and the will to found a private kingdom'; 'the will to conquer: the impulse to fight, to prove oneself superior to others, to succeed for the sake, not of the fruits of success, but of success itself'; and 'the joy of creating, of getting things done, or simply of exercising one's energy and ingenuity'.[102] Schumpeter himself acknowledges that increases in population and wealth are 'frequently a condition of development', but they do not by themselves embody 'qualitatively new phenomena', such as innovation and entrepreneurship.[103]

Schumpeter's work on innovation, technological progress, and entrepreneurship has been taken up by others[104] and influenced an emerging appreciation of the role of IP[105] in economic development.[106] It can be interpreted to suggest that IP plays an important role in entrepreneurship.[107] His work adds much to understanding how innovation and technical change can occur in all countries, including developing countries. Schumpeter's legacy is of relevance to developing countries and

[98] Panayotis G. Michaelides et al., 'Emil Leader and Joseph Schumpeter on Economic Growth', Technology and Business Cycles' (2010) 39 *For Social Economics* 171, 175.

[99] Douglas Rimmer, 'Schumpeter and the Underdeveloped Countries' (1961) 75 (3) *The Quarterly Journal of Economics* 422-423.

[100] Michaelides et al., above n 98, 181-182.

[101] Rimmer, above n 99, 428-429.

[102] The Theory of Economic Development (Harvard University Press, 1934), 74-94, cited in Rimmer, above n 99, 430.

[103] Ibid, 444.

[104] Sherwood, above n 5.

[105] Schumpeter has never discussed IP in his scholarship because, in 1942, it did not make any sense to anyone to write about it during that time. See Mark Blaug, 'Why Did Schumpeter Neglect Intellectual Property Rights' (2005) 2 (1) *Review of Economic Research* 69-74 <http://papers.ssrn.com/sol3/papers.cfm?abstract_id=1144888>.

[106] Ibid.

[107] Greenhalg and Dixon, above n 22, 6.

emerging economies as they strive to understand the complex relationship between innovation, entrepreneurship, and economic development.

3.4.2 Jagdish Bhagwati

Jagdish Bhagwati has not written much about IP, but he writes frequently about developing countries, as he is a native of India. He is considered the most creative international trade theorist of his generation and a leader in the fight for free trade.[108] Globalisation can bring economic development to developing countries[109] and is about the free flow not only of labour and capital but also of ideas, and that is relevant to the discussion of this chapter.[110] Bhagwati's thoughts are laid down in his highly acclaimed book, *In Defence of Globalization* published by Oxford University in 2004.[111]

Bhagwati is critical of the IP system and believes that it should not be included in the first place in the trade agreements (such as the Uruguay Round).[112] Developing countries were, in his opinion, 'bamboozled into accepting IP even though it was clearly not a trade issue'.[113] In his opinion, pharmaceutical and software companies muscled their way into the WTO, and turned it into a royalty agency, as it can apply trade sanctions.[114] He criticised the argument of the pharmaceutical companies that they are seriously handicapped in their R&D by the lack of IP in developing countries and believes that it is particularly flawed because these companies will earn little money to cover their costs in the markets of poor countries.[115]

He proposes that access to the generic drugs produced in emerging economies such as India and Brazil should be freely available for poor countries that have medical emergencies such as AIDS.[116] Bhagwati has many brilliant ideas to offer

---

[108] Mark Horowitz, *Keep Free Trade Free* (22 September 2008) Wired <http://www.wired.com/politics/law/magazine/16-10/sl_bhagwati>.

[109] Foreign Affairs and International Trade Canada, *Interview with Jagdish Bhagwati* <http://www.international.gc.ca>; Jagdish Bhagwati and T.N.Srinivasan, *Trade and Poverty in the Poor Countries*, Yale Department of Economics <http://www.econ.yale.edu/~srinivas/trade_poverty.pdf>; Jagdish Bhagwati, 'The East Asian Model of Economic Development and Developing Countries' (2002) 18 *Journal of Developing Societies* 331-353.

[110] Horowitz, above n 108.

[111] Bhagwati, above n 87.

[112] See also, for similar views, Yong-Shik Lee, *Reclaiming Development in the World Trading System* (Cambridge, 2006) 124-125.

[113] Jagdish Bhagwati, *What Really Happened in Seattle* <http://time.dufe.edu.cn/wencong/bhagwati/really.pdf>.

[114] Bhagwati, above n 87, 182.

[115] Ibid 184.

[116] Ibid.

developing countries that want to use the global trade system to accelerate their economic development. Developing countries can better understand IP systems and critique it more effectively if they understand the international trading system and how it should be changed to meet the interests of all countries.

3.4.3 *Joseph Stiglitz*

Joseph Stiglitz, like Schumpeter, recognises the importance of innovation as a transformative engine of the life of many people, including those living in developing countries.[117] For Stiglitz, IP plays an important role in stimulating innovation.[118] Stiglitz believes that the current IP system goes too far in terms of protection because it can impede knowledge creation and production. To him, IP should not be perceived as an end in itself to achieve economic development but rather as one of the means, among others, that countries should give particular attention to in order to promote societal well-being.[119]

In the book *Fair Trade for All - How Trade Can Promote Development*, Stiglitz and co-author Andrew Charlton present a new economic model designed to open up markets in developing countries to enable them to flourish. In their opinion, international trade can have a significant and positive effect on the economic development of developing countries.[120] They argue that the current structure of the international trade system is faulty and not based on fairness for developing countries that guarantee its stability. An overhaul of the current global trade system is needed[121] to further the interests of developing countries.[122] This new trade system should give developing countries the freedom to develop their own policies that are tailored to meet their own idiosyncratic circumstances[123]; it also needs to be fair and limited to trade-related and development issues.[124]

The question arises whether we can apply some of the proposed features of this trade system in the context of IP. The answer to this is yes. Any IP law in any developing country should be assessed in terms of its impact on the development of its citizens. If the law does not promote development, then it is suggested that it

[117] Stiglitz, above n 17, 106.

[118] Ibid.

[119] Stiglitz (1999), above n 18, 9.

[120] Stiglitz and Charlton, above n 10, vi and 11.

[121] According to the World Bank, economic development in developing countries will not happen unless the global trade regime is reshaped to take into account their interests. Only a reshaped, global architecture international trade system will have a dramatic and positive effect on the lives of the poor. See World Bank, above 57, 153.

[122] Stiglitz and Charlton, above n 10, ch 7-12.

[123] Ibid 17.

[124] Ibid 68.

should be reconsidered. IP laws should be fair and take account of the interests of the society as a whole and not only the interests of copyright owners or right holders. This perspective is currently missing from the IP laws of many developing countries.

3.4.4 Ha Joon Chang

Professor Ha Joon Chang showed that there is no sound theoretical and empirical support for the argument that strong protection of IP is necessary for the economic development of developing countries.[125] He notes that developing countries have not been able to generate the promised economic growth during the last two decades, but on the contrary, their economic growth has collapsed.[126]

In *Kicking Away the Ladder - Development Strategy in Historical Perspective* (2003), Chang argues eloquently that developed countries are making it harder for developing countries to achieve economic development when they insist they should follow 'good policies' and establish 'good institutions' (including IP).[127] These suggested policies and good institutions had not been implemented by developed countries themselves when they were considered as developing countries. By asking developing countries to adopt these policies, developed countries are simply 'kicking away the ladder' for developing countries to become economically developed. This is because they are not allowing them to go through the stages of development that they need to go through before being economically developed. Chang proposes that developing countries rethink their approach to international economic development and reassess some of what he calls 'myths of economic development', as frequently suggested by developed countries and international monetary organisations such as the International Monetary Fund (IMF) and the World Bank.[128]

Are the suggestions of Professor Chang of any relevance to the discussion of IP and economic development in developing countries?

---

[125] Chang, above n 4, 301.

[126] Chang, above n 8, 140.

[127] Professor Chang argues that:

> TRIPS will reduce the ability of developing countries to catch up through imitation and adaptation of advanced technologies through informal channels (e.g. reverse engineering involving minor modifications, developing an alternative process for a patented chemical substance) ... Indeed, it may be argued that, for the developing countries, 'informal' knowledge transfer may be more important than 'formal' transfer. Therefore, the TRIPS may reduce the effectiveness of technology transfer from the developing country point of view, especially if we consider both formal and informal channels of such transfer.

See Chang, above n 4, 301.

[128] Chang, above n 8, 140. See also other interesting proposals, Chang, above n 4, 304-305.

There is much to learn from the scholarship of Professor Chang. Developing countries should learn from the history of IP in developed countries and should reassess what are considered as 'bad policies' or 'good policies' in economic development generally and particularly IP. IP should not be applied across the board for all countries since it could be useful for some, but it could also be harmful for others.

3.4.5 Summary of Views

Based on these views, the adoption of policies and institutions by developing countries that are more suitable to their stage of economic development and to other conditions they experience will definitely enable them to accelerate their economic development.[129]

Economists who examined the correlation between IP and economic development in developing countries believe that IP alone cannot result in the economic development of developing countries. These scholars are critical of the IP system and the trading system and believe that the latter has many problems as it does not take into consideration the full concerns of developing countries.

3.5 Overall Assessment of Academic Literature

Before proceeding with the assessment of IP and economic development in academic literature,[130] it would be useful to provide some preliminary comments.

The relationship between IP and economic development has been studied by various scholars who bring different perspective to the topic and who apply different methods of research. It is noted that while some IP scholars might prefer

---

[129] Chang, above n 8, 141.

[130] Among the research that discusses the academic literature, see the following: Carlos A. Primo Braga and Carsten Fink, 'The Relationship between Intellectual Property Rights and Foreign Direct Investment' (1998) 9 *Duke Journal of International and Comparative Law* 163, 182; Anselm Kamperman Sandres, 'Intellectual Property Treaties and Development' in Daniel Gervais (ed), *Intellectual Property, Trade and Development, Strategies to Optimize Economic Development in A TRIPS Plus Era* (Kluwer Law International, 2004) 157, 163, 170; Wolfgang E. Siebeck et al. (eds), *Strengthening Protection of Intellectual Property Protection of Intellectual Property in Developing Countries - A Survey of Literature* (Word Bank, 1990), chs 2-3; Emmanuel Hassan, Ohid Yaqub, and Stephanie Diepeveen, *Intellectual Property and Developing Countries: A Review of the Literature*, a technical report prepared for the UK Intellectual Property Office and the UK Department for International Development (2010) RAND Corporation (Europe) <http://www.rand.org/pubs/technical_reports/2010/RAND_TR804.pdf>; Ida Madieha Abdul Ghani Azmi, Lim Heng Geee, and Rokiah Alavi, *Intellectual Property System and Industrial Development in Malaysia* (International Islamic University Malaysia, 2009) 161-167.

to examine the relationship from an entirely academic perspective, others would prefer to base their studies solely on empirical evidence. Applying and comparing the various methods of research may result in conflicting, and sometimes contradictory, results.

Notwithstanding the great deal of literature that examines the correlation between IP and economic development, we still know alarmingly little about the actual effects of IP on the activity patterns of developing countries.[131] This is because this sort of relationship is complex and based on multiple variables that are sometimes difficult to determine and specify.[132] Some studies have acknowledged the fact that it is not correct to assume that causation between IP and economic development works in one direction. Instead, it is more appropriate to think that economic development can also influence IP. This has been proven in a number of developed countries that only found it appropriate to strengthen their IP when they became wealthier and more technologically sophisticated.[133]

It is also noted that some academic studies make certain assumptions upon which their results are based despite the fact that those assumptions are yet to be established. For example, some scholars have assumed that both developed and developing countries have innovative capabilities, whilst other scholars made the assumption that innovation is only prevalent in developed countries and not in developing countries. Based on these two assumptions, IP can be read as having either a positive or a negative effect on economic development.[134]

It is also important not to consider developing countries as a homogeneous group.[135] This has been found in a number of studies that speak of developing countries as if they are all the same and that suggest that they all should adopt a certain level of IP. It is unlikely that LDCs will benefit from an IP system that is designed to advance their economic development when there is an absence of infrastructure and a viable domestic market.[136] It is noted that having an IP system in developing countries would not result in the economic development of those countries, and other complementary factors play a much more important role in that regard.[137]

---

[131] Robert Sherwood, 'Global Prospects for the Role of Intellectual Property in Technology Transfer' (2002) 42 *IDEA Journal of Law and Technology* 27.

[132] Maskus, above n 25, 1.

[133] Ibid 4.

[134] Sourav Chatterjee et al., *Intellectual Property Rights in Developing Nations* (4 March 2008) Nera Publications <http://www.mondaq.com/unitedstates/article.asp?articleid=57856>.

[135] Barton et al., above n 86, 14; Daniel Gervais, 'Intellectual Property, Trade and Development: The State of Play' (2005) 74 *Fordham Law Review*, 505, 519 <http://works.bepress.com/cgi/viewcontent.cgi?article=1003&context=daniel_gervais>.

[136] Ibid.

[137] Professor Keith Maskus prefers to give particular attention to what he calls 'variable effects' that could dominate over IP and that could influence economic development. Such variable effects include macroeconomic stability, market openness, policies for improving the economy's technological infrastructure, and the acquisition of human capital. The significance of these elements would differ from one developing country to another, but in a broad setting of appropriate

3.6 Examination of the Empirical Evidence on IP and Economic Development

After examining the positive and negative theoretical literature on IP and economic development, it is necessary to look at empirical evidence that supports those views.

---

complementary policies and transparent regulation, IP could play a relatively positive role in promoting economic development. See Maskus, above n 2, 504; Maskus and Reichman, above n 20, 16. See also Professor Yong Shik Lee for his suggestion in relation to 'microtrade' and developing countries. Yong-Shik Lee, 'Theoretical Basis and Regulatory Framework for Microtrade: Combining Volunteerism with International Trade Towards Poverty Elimination' (2009) 2 (1) *Law and Development Review*, 367-399 <http://www.lawanddevelopment.net/yslee_microtrade_october2010.pdf>.

- Professor Peter Yu argues that the effectiveness of IP in promoting economic development depends not only on the economic circumstances of each country but also on complementary factors, including structural reforms to increase entrepreneurship and the flexibility of enterprises, expanded liberalisation of restrictions on trade, the level of investment, technology agreements, and additional steps to ensure competition in domestic markets amongst firms and across regions. See Peter K. Yu, 'Intellectual Property, Economic Development, and the China Puzzle' in Daniel Gervais, *Intellectual Property, Trade and Development - Strategies to Optimize Economic Development in a TRIPS Plus Era* (Oxford University, 2007) 214.
- Professor Yong Shik Lee adds other important factors that are necessary to achieve economic development in developing countries, including a good education system; consistent and coherent economic policies; access to capital; an efficient, reliable, and non-corrupted government; social peace; political stability; entrepreneurship; and sound work ethics. See Lee, above n 112, 160.
- Professor Ruth L Gana (Okediji) believes that there is a wide range of changes that must be taken in developing countries to achieve development, including political, social, and economic changes. As for technology, Professor Okediji notes that it is not a panacea for underdevelopment. Like all other resources, its potential is dependent on the existence of a carefully planned and stable socio-economic environment. See Ruth L Gana (Okediji), 'The Myth of Development, the Progress of Rights: Human Rights to Intellectual Property and Development' (1996) 18 *Law and Policy Journal* 315, 335, 341.
- According to Mikhaelle Schiappacasse, the economic development of developing countries does not happen in isolation and is affected by other important factors that should work in close proximity. These include human capital (particularly in technical skills), technical infrastructure, efficient managerial techniques, and the active cultivation of international trade and investment from developed to developing countries. See Schiappacasse, above n 54, 166.
- The commentator Peter Beattie believes that robust and dynamic competition policies are important for making the market of developing countries work effectively. See Beattie, above n 45, 28.
- The commentator Robert M. Sherwood argues that developing countries cannot rely on IP alone to achieve economic development, but they also have to establish and structure a judicial system that can implement those laws. This could happen either by having specialised courts for IP disputes or by having qualified judges who are familiar with IP and its importance to the economic development of developing countries. See Sherwood, above n 5.
- The commentator Carlos Alberto Primo Braga argues that IP is only one of the relevant variables that could be attributed to the increase in R&D and that it could be completely ineffective in the absence of additional conditions (such as a larger stock of human capital). See Braga, above n 19, 259.

Globalisation has been the transcendent commercial and political force[138] of the twenty-first century. It is the process by which national and regional markets are more tightly integrated through the reduction of governmental and natural barriers to trade and the flow of technology.[139] To be integrated into the global trade system and to be a member of the WTO, developing countries need to update their IP laws and provide strong enforcement mechanisms.[140]

There are now a substantial number of empirical studies that examine the relationship between IP and economic development. Among the subjects that these studies examine to determine the effect of IP on economic development are FDI, technology transfer, economic growth, R&D, domestic innovation, and others.

3.6.1 IP and FDI

FDI is considered by developed countries as an important force behind economic development.[141] It can be in the form of 'establishing or acquiring a foreign subsidiary over which the investing firm has substantial management control'.[142] To attract the widest range of possible investors and MNCs, many developing countries have embarked upon economic reform measures to create the best environment for attracting investors and for doing business.[143] It is hoped that

---

[138] Keith Maskus, 'The Role of Intellectual Property Rights in Encouraging Foreign Direct Investment and Technology Transfer' (a paper presented at the conference Public-Private Initiatives after TRIPS: Designing a Global Agenda, Brussels, Belguim, 16-19 July 1997), 1 <http://siteresources.worldbank.org/INTRANETTRADE/Resources/maskus2.pdf>.

[139] Ibid.

[140] It took developed countries long time to agree on the liberal, open-economy ideas that developing countries have strongly been advised to follow. For a brief overview of the history in the twentieth century, see Ryan, above n 36, 271, 293.

[141] Hindman, above n 53, 467; Ansem Kmperman Sanders, 'Intellectual Property, Free Trade Agreements and Economic Development' (2007) 23 *Georgia State University Law Review* 893, 896; Arnold, above n 13, 195; Peter Magic, *International Technology Transfer and Intellectual Property Rights* (30 November 2003) Department of Computer Science at University of Texas at Austin, 5 <http://www.cs.utexas.edu/~fussell/courses/econtech/public-final papers/Peter_ Magic_International_IP_Rights.pdf>; Maskus, above n 25, 18-19; Ryan, above n 62.

[142] Schiappacasse, above n 54, 173. Keith Maskus provides similar definition to FDI. He defined it as 'the act of establishing or acquiring a foreign subsidiary over which the investing firm has substantial management control'. See Maskus, above n 138, 7.

[143] Among the measures that these countries have taken to create a favourable environment for investors are 'tax incentives, upgraded infrastructures, streamlined bureaucracies to handle investment regulations, access to specific natural resources, a beneficial labour situation, and reduced costs of capital'. See Hindman, above n 53, 467. See other important factors that MNCs take into account before transferring investments to developing countries, Schiappacasse, above n 54, 172; Yu, above 137, 177.

these advances will lead to increased exports and a more significant role for developing countries in the global trade economy.[144]

If investors and MNCs found that there are good opportunities for doing business in one particular developing country and a high prospect of success, they would agree to transfer FDI to that country. They would do so through various means, including 'the purchase of capital assets (mergers and acquisitions), joint ventures, buying property, investing in plants and equipment, and transferring managerial expertise and technological skills to those countries'.[145] MNCs, through their local subsidiaries in developing countries, can practise either horizontal or vertical FDI. In the first kind, they would produce mainly for local market consumption, while in the second, they would be producing for export purposes.[146] FDI may assist developing countries in many ways, including creating new jobs, facilitating access to new technologies, increasing productivity, transferring of new technologies, advancing management strategies, and creating a base for a strong economy that drives long-term economic growth.[147]

3.6.2 IP, FDI, and Developing Countries

One of the studies that examined the relationship between FDI and patents came to the conclusion that American firms limit their investments in countries with weak patent rights.[148] Moreover, their decisions to increase FDI to those countries depend, to a large extent, on the ability to maintain control over their rights through defence of IP.[149] This is usually done in the local courts of developing countries,

[144] Hindman, above n 53, 467.

[145] Ibid; Maskus, above n 138, 3; Schiappacasse, above n 54; Yu above n 137, 178; Keith E. Maskus, Kamal Saggi, and Thitima Puttitanun, 'Patent Rights and International Technology Transfer Trough Direct Investment and Licensing', in Keith Maskus and Jerome Reichman, *International Public Goods and Transfer of Technology under a Globalised Intellectual Property Regime* (Cambridge, 2005) 267.

[146] Schiappacasse, above n 54, 173-174; Yu, above 137, 182.

[147] Hindman, above 53, 475, 492. See also the views of developing countries and emerging economies such as India, Pakistan, and Egypt that are not totally in concurrence with the views that FDI liberalisation would cause technology transfer and, therefore, economic development to those countries. See Yong Jian Wang, 'Further Protection of Intellectual Property Rights in the WTO Linking Transfer of Technology with Foreign Direct Investment' (2006) 8 (6) *Journal of World Intellectual Property* 798, 803; Azmi, Geee and Alavi, above n 130, 156-166.

[148] Maskus, Dougherty and Mertha, above n 56, 9.

[149] Ibid.

which must have the capability to handle these disputes, which need the special technical knowledge of both judges and lawyers working in the field.

The World Bank, in its study, recognised open trade economies in developing countries and found that having strengthened IP systems in those countries would allow them to experience more economic growth than others. Moreover, IP is one factor that encourages inward FDI, provided that other appropriate conditions are fulfilled, including the consideration of competitive rules, the availability of programs that promote national technical change, and the allocation of sufficient budgetary resources.[150] A study supported by the Organisation for Economic Co-operation and Development (OECD) found also that the strength of patent protection is positively associated with inward FDI, merchandise imports, and service imports. This relationship is applicable to all groups of countries either developed, developing, or LDCs. The study also found quantitatively that the above association is considered to be strongest in developed countries.[151]

One economist found that 'the effect of IP strength on FDI is not straight forward' but realised that poor IP regimes tend to adversely affect the investment climate and the probability of FDI occurring. He noted that the strength of IP promotes arm's-length licensing but that they generally have no significant effect on international technology transfers.[152] The economist Keith Maskus found that the mere availability of IP laws does not mean that a particular country would witness an increase in FDI over another. It is the entire 'pro-competitive business' environment that matters most for FDI.[153] This has been proven in a number of countries in Eastern Europe that have strong IP but have had difficulties in attracting high levels of FDI,[154] compared to other emerging economies such as China and Brazil, which have witnessed an increase in FDI although they do not have strong IP systems.

There are few dependable empirical studies that provide a clear perspective on the situation of a developing country when it adopts strong IP systems and the effect of that on the amount of FDI to that country. Among the few studies in that regard are two attentive studies done by Professor Mansfield for the World Bank in 1995.[155]

---

[150] World Bank, above 57, 144-145.

[151] Walter G. Park and Douglas C. Lippoldt, *Technology Transfer and the Economic Implications of the Strengthening of Intellectual Property Rights in Developing Countries, OECD Trade Policy Working Papers* No. 62, (25 June 2008) OECD Publishing <http://www.american.edu/cas/faculty/wgpark/upload/Tech-Transfer-w-Doug-Lippoldt.pdf>.

[152] Kumar, above n 50, 4.

[153] Maskus, above n 138, 13.

[154] See for an explanation of the situation in Eastern Europe, Chatterjee et al., above n 134, 20.

[155] Edwin Mansfield, *Intellectual Property Protection, Direct Investment, and Technology Transfer: Germany, Japan, and the United States*, International Discussion Paper, Discussion Paper 27 (September 1995) Bibliotheca Virtual <http://www.bvindecopi.gob.pe/colec/emansfield.pdf>. See also Robert M. Sherwood, 'Human Creativity for Economic Development: Patent Propel Technology' (2000) 33 (3) *Akron Law Review* <http://www.uakron.edu/law/lawreview/v33/docs/sherwoodgood333.pdf>.

Professor Mansfield conducted a survey of developing countries to discover whether a correlation exists between the strength of IP and the level of FDI. He found that enhanced protection of IP (patents and trade secrets) would attract more FDI in the areas of industrial chemicals, pharmaceuticals, and electrical equipment, including computer technology.[156] Two other empirical studies did not find a positive relationship between IP and the international distribution of FDI by US multinational enterprises.[157]

Another empirical study, in 1996 by Lee and Mansfield, asked 94 firms on their views on IP laws in 14 developing countries and how these laws had affected their investment strategies in those countries. They analysed the collected data and found that patent protection made it more likely that firms would increase their investments to those countries.[158] Walter Park and Douglas Lippoldt noted that the evidence on the effects of IP (patents, trademarks, and copyright) on FDI is mixed, and studies in the field that use sectorial and industrial data seem to find that technology-sensitive FDI does respond to IP in developing countries.[159] Professor Joseph Stiglitz also criticised the empirical studies that suggest that developing countries will not be able to attract investments if they do not have strong IP systems,[160] arguing that the results of these studies are ambiguous and that many of their assumptions are difficult to ascertain.[161]

A study of the World Bank found that it is not correct to suggest that IP is important for FDI across all sectors and industries, but instead it is only relevant for firms that would suffer heavily, financially, from infringements in areas such as pharmaceuticals and the software industries and not for those firms that are producing low-technology goods and services.[162] These findings weigh against the assumption that FDI goes up uniformly as IP is strengthened in developing countries.[163] The true relationship is much more complex than conventional wisdom would claim.[164]

---

[156] Magic, above n 141, 5.

[157] Keith E. Maskus, 'Intellectual Property Challenges for Developing Countries: An Economic Perspective' (2001) *University of Illinois Law Review* 457, 466; Chatterjee et al., above n 134, 17.

[158] Chatterjee et al., above n 134, 14.

[159] Park and Lippoldt, above n 151, 11.

[160] Chang, above n 4, 287-308; Professor Peter Yu argues that strong IP is not always needed for attracting FDI. On the contrary, it can encourage investors to conduct arm's-length transactions and would drain a developing country's scarce governmental resources, render cutting-edge foreign technologies inaccessible, and stifle the development of local industries. See Yu, above n 137, 183.

- The UK-based Commission on IP rights agrees with that and notes that IP could only be important for economic development when a certain developing country changes its position to that of an upper middle income country. See Barton et al., above n 86.

[161] Stiglitz (2004), above n 18; Maskus, above n 138, 22.

[162] World Bank, above 57, 133-134; Beattie, above n 45, 17; Maskus, above n 138, 15; Ryan, above n 36, 301.

[163] Beattie, above n 45, 17.

[164] Ibid.

Carsten Fink, Keith Maskus, and Carlos Primo Braga have confirmed the importance of the market size in attracting foreign FDI but added also that for firms in developing countries to capture 'economies of scale', they must have markets that are sufficiently large to do so.[165]

It is noted, after examining some of the academic and empirical literature on the relationship between FDI and IP, that the latter is not enough for, and could be irrelevant to, the acceleration of economic development in developing countries without other appropriate conditions that must also be met to conduct business in those countries. IP is mostly important for firms of creative activities that invest in IP and want certain guarantees that they will not suffer economic losses if they decided to conduct business in developing countries.

3.6.3 IP and Technology Transfer

Some developing and emerging economies have witnessed more of an increase in technology transfer from industrialised countries than others, as the result of adopting open trade regimes. Some scholars would argue that strong IP systems have greatly contributed to this increase and that without such systems, technology transfer simply would not happen or, at most, would be marginal.[166] 'Technology' can be defined as 'the systematic knowledge for the manufacture of a product, for the application of a process, or for the rendering of a service, including any integrally associated managerial and marketing techniques'.[167] A technology transfer is a 'process by which science and technology are diffused throughout human activity'.[168]

Technology transfer is one of the primary mechanisms for stimulating economic development in developing countries.[169] It is critical for those countries 'that do not possess a large amount of protected technology upon which they can build new technology and research'. It is also critical for developing countries that have insufficient resources in technical experts and trained personnel to perform research and development in new technologies.[170] Transfer of technology (including know-how) may take place in a number of ways, including 'trade in goods, trade in

[165] Yu, above n 137, 177. It is noted that most of the studies that assess the relationship between IP and economic development agree that the size of a potential market is the major factor that attracts FDI to a particular developing country. The larger is the market, the greatest is the incentive to enter it through FDI, in order to take advantage of scale economies. This fact is consistent with the concentration of FDI going to emerging economies in East Asia and Latin America in the last ten years because of the large size of potential markets in these regions. See Maskus, above n 138, 20.

[166] See Schiappacasse, above 54, 172.

[167] Ibid.

[168] Ibid.

[169] Ibid.

[170] Magic, above n 141, 172.

services, technology licensing, technical assistance, government procurement, and trade-related FDI'.[171] MNCs transfer technologies either 'through internal channels by internalising the technologies to affiliates under their ownership and control in the host countries or through external channels by externalising the technologies to other firms in the form of franchising, licensing, technical service or subcontracting'.[172]

One of the central concerns among policymakers in developing countries is to understand the relationship between IP and technology transfer, to assist those countries to acquire the necessary technology and expertise that they particularly need to stimulate their economic development.[173] One economist has argued that there is no convincing empirical evidence that stronger patents in poor and small countries lead to an increase in inward technology transfer and accelerate economic development. He adds that many developing countries have inadequate investment environments, poor infrastructure, and limited skills, which would hinder the advantage gained by any IP system.[174]

One of the studies examines the factors that enhance the prospects of the success of technology transfer in developing countries, such as the 'ability of firms to engage in a continuous process of learning by evaluating the acquirement of foreign technologies'.[175] Another study by the World Bank analysed the process by which industrialisation moves forward in developing countries.[176] Other studies also examined technology-sharing alliances, new patterns of international competition in selected areas, and the role of institutions in dynamic comparative advantage.[177]

Another study used German patent data and concluded that there is a weak relationship between technology transfer and the availability of patent rights systems.[178] Another study concluded that patents are positive contributors to technology transfer as they 'directly facilitate additional information transfer (if not know-how diffusion) by disclosing the details of inventions'.[179] Branstetter, Fisman, and Foley found a positive and significant relationship between IP and US multinational firms transferring technology to developing countries.[180] However,

---

[171] Wang, above n 147, 799. See, for similar views, Maskus and Reichman, above n 20, 11; World Bank, above n 57, 144; Maskus, above n 157, 462-466.

[172] Wang, above 147, 799.

[173] See also Maskus, Saggi, and Puttitanun, above n 145, 265.

[174] Maskus, above n 2, 508.

[175] Sherwood, above n 5.

[176] Ibid.

[177] Ibid.

[178] Ahisha Arora, Andrea Fosfuri, and Alfonso Gambardella, 'Markets for Technology, Intellectual Property Rights, and Development' in Keith E. Maskus and Jerome H. Reichman, *International Public Goods and Transfer of Technology under Globalized Intellectual Property Regime* (Cambridge University, 2005) 321, 328.

[179] Maskus, above n 138, 17.

[180] Chatterjee et al., above n 134, 21.

their results have been criticised for not being sufficient to demonstrate that there is a positive relationship between IP and technology transfer.[181]

Keith Maskus, Kamal Sagi, and Thitima Puttitanun gave particular attention to labour skills and argued that these are a central element in attracting technology transfer to developing countries. MNCs generally would seek to transfer technology to locations with an abundance of skilled and semi-skilled workers.[182] Political and economic stability, appropriate policies regarding education, capital accumulation, R&D incentives, and the integration of research conducted in universities and public laboratories with private sector commercialisation were also considered as important factors for those MNCs.[183] It was also noted that it is unlikely that the strengthening or weakening of IP by developing countries will have a noticeable effect on the global markets for technology transfer.[184] However, since stronger IP can also improve the efficiency of technology transactions, it is also likely that stronger IP will improve the ability of developing countries to benefit from technologies generated elsewhere,[185] but the available evidence to support this proposition is mixed.[186] Finally, it is noted that there are various views on the effect of IP on technology transfer and economic development in developing countries. Most of these views cannot prove that there is a positive correlation between IP and technology transfer.

3.6.4 IP and Economic Growth

Economic growth is the increase of per capita gross domestic product (GDP) per year or any other measure of aggregate income, such as national income per capita and consumption per capita.[187] Economic growth is described as positive when a nation's wealth increases over time and negative when the opposite is actually happening.[188] Natural and human resources, capital, and technological development in the economy, along with institutional structure and stability, influence the

---

[181] Ibid.

[182] Maskus, Saggi, and Puttitanun, above n 145, 269

[183] Ibid.

[184] Arora, Fosfuri, and Gambardella, above n 178, 335.

[185] Ibid.

[186] Others doubt the importance of IP alone to economic development in the context of technology transfer and argue that other factors play a much more important role for developing countries in that regard, including the establishment and maintenance of an open economy and transparent markets.

See Schiappacasse, above n 54, 167; Maskus, Saggi, and Puttitanun, above n 145, 266.

[187] World Bank, *Beyond Economic Growth* Student Book (2004) <http://www.worldbank.org/depweb/english/beyond/global/glossary.html>.

[188] Encyclopaedia Britannica, Inc., *Britannica Concise Encyclopaedia*, Encyclopaedia Britannica, Inc, 2006) 594.

rate of economic growth.[189] Theories of economic development associate economic development with economic growth. In that sense, economic development simply means the 'process whereby simple, low-income national economies are transformed into modern industrial economies'.[190]

One of the frequently cited arguments advanced by proponents of stronger IP systems is that they accelerate economic growth in developing countries. Developing countries are advised to adopt the technology of developed countries to 'catch up' and achieve economic growth and technology diffusion in their countries.[191] It is important in this regard to examine fully the statistics issued by the various international economic organisations that determine the level of economic growth in developing countries and emerging economies, especially in the last 10–15 years.[192]

The commentator Peter Beattie reviewed the varied empirical evidence available on the positive relationship between IP and economic growth. He noted that '[t]he weakest support comes in the form of armchair theorising and anecdotal evidence and the stronger support comes in the form of modelling and comparison of statistical samples'.[193] Thompson and Rushing found, in 1996, a non-linear and positive relationship between IP (patents) and economic growth in countries with per capita GDP above US$3,400 but no relationship for countries with lower income levels.[194] Falvey, Foster, and Greenaway conducted a study in 2006 to assess the effect of IP protection (patents) on economic growth. They noted theoretically that the strength of IP protection had an ambiguous effect on economic growth.[195] Gould and Gruben confirmed such findings and came to the conclusion that the effects of IP (patents) may be tempered in less competitive, closed markets and not applicable for all markets.[196] Their findings give a clear message that before having appropriate IP laws (patent laws) in place, developing countries need to pursue market and trade liberalisation to achieve economic growth.[197]

---

[189] Ibid.

[190] Ibid.

[191] Yueh, above n 13, 442.

[192] The World Bank indicated in its report of 2009 that developing countries and emerging economies such as Brazil, China, India, Egypt, South Africa, and the Russian Federation have been affected differently by the 2008 global financial crisis. Despite that, the GDP growth remains positive in all six countries. See World Bank, *World Development Indicators 2009* (World Bank, 2009) 196-262.

[193] Beattie, above n 45, 15.

[194] Chatterjee et al., above n 134, 22.

[195] Ibid 21.

[196] Robert L. Ostergard, 'Economic Growth and Intellectual Property Rights Protection: A Reassessment of the Conventional Wisdom' in Daniel Gervais, *Intellectual Property, Trade and Development* (Kluwer Law International, 2004) 115, 128; Chatterjee et al., above n 134, 16.

[197] Maskus, above 25, 18-19; The World Bank, above n 57, 135; Beattie, above n 45, 21; Maskus, above n 157, 457-471.

Park and Ginarte, in 1997, studied how IP affects growth and investment[198] and found that IP protection (patents) did not contribute positively to economic growth but concluded at the same time that they could affect economic growth through the encouragement of capital accumulation, both tangible and intangible.[199] The World Bank criticises empirical studies that find a positive correlation between IP and economic growth and argues that history does not support the conclusion that IP can boost economic growth in developing countries.[200] Professor Daniel Gervais recognises the importance of IP to economic growth but adds that IP is insufficient by itself. He acknowledges that each developing country needs a comprehensive 'knowledge optimisation strategy' to successfully exploit IP to maximise its economic growth.[201] Professor Keith Maskus also agrees with Professor Gervais and advises developing countries to embody IP into a broader development policy that encourages innovation, human capital, and dynamic competition.[202]

Robert Sherwood gathered most of the economic empirical evidence that examines the relationship between IP and economic development and found that there is a positive relationship between IP and economic development.[203] It is noted that his particular research is quite outdated now as it was conducted before the 1990s. Also, it is criticised for arguing that IP has a positive relationship with economic growth based on what has been achieved in developed countries (primarily the US), without consideration of the real economic and social conditions in developing countries that are very different from that of an economic power such as the US.[204]

The question of the effects of IP on economic growth and development in developing countries remains difficult to answer. What has been discussed here is minimal, and there remain many studies that needed to be explored. It is hoped that more collaboration occurs between international economic institutions and IP

[198] Maskus, above n 25, 18-19.

[199] Chatterjee et al., above n 134, 14; World Bank, above n 57, 135.

[200] World Bank, above n 57, 200.

[201] The knowledge strategy that a particular developing country should take into account includes education, institutional capacity building, regulatory adaptation, FDI marketing, and patent mining. (linking technology development to business strategies). See Daniel Gervais, *Intellectual Property, Trade and Development - Strategies to Optimize Economic Development in a TRIPS Plus Era* (Oxford University, 2007) 524, 535.

[202] Maskus, above n 2, 512.

[203] Robert Sherwood notes that:

> [I]t is now well understood that the introduction of new technology into an economy accounts for a great portion of the economic growth of that economy and produces a very high social rate of return. It can also be noted that in countries without effective IP protection, that high social rate of return is sacrificed in favour of a high private rate of return for a few.

Sherwood, above n 5. See also Azmi, Geee and Alavi, above n 130, 163.

[204] Ibid.

organisations to produce better supported results in the field. It is noted that empirical evidence does not establish that having an IP system in developing countries results in their economic development.

3.6.5 IP and R&D

Between 2002 and 2007, the number of researchers in developing countries increased from 1.8 to 2.7 million, according to the third survey on statistics of science and technology (S&T) of the UNESCO Institute for Statistics (UIS).[205] Developing countries accounted for 24% of the total gross domestic expenditure on R&D in 2007, which is an increase from 17% of the global share seen in 2002.[206]

According to UNCTAD, R&D consists of four types of activities: basic research, applied research, product development, and process development.[207] Basic research consists of original experimental work without a specific commercial aim and is frequently undertaken by universities.[208] Applied research consists of original experimental work with a specific aim.[209] Product development is the improvement and extension of existing products, and process development is the creation of new or improved processes.[210] Question relating to R&D in developing countries include the following: Does the adoption of stronger IP in developing countries, as a consequence of joining the global trade regime (WTO), result in any increase in R&D in these countries? To what extent is it important for developing countries to create appropriate IP laws that would accelerate R&D in these countries? What is the exact relationship between IP and R&D? Furthermore, what does the academic and empirical evidence tell us in that regard?

Professor Amy Jocelyn Glass recognised the importance of IP for R&D. She noted that even weak IP protection keeps the costs of R&D low, which avoids wasting scarce resources.[211] Professor Nagesh Kumar from the Research and Information System for Developing Countries (RIS) agrees partially with such findings and, based on his empirical research, argues that weaker IP can stimulate domestic innovative activities in developing countries and result in the absorption

---

205 UNESCO in the Spot Light: Science and Communication (18 October 2009) <http://unescoscience.blogspot.com.au/2009/10/developing-countries-boost-their-r.html>, citing UNESCO Institute for Statistics, *Developing Countries Boost Their R&D Efforts* <http://unescoscience.blogspot.com.au/2009/10/developing-countries-boost-their-r.html>.

206 Ibid.

207 UNCTAD, *Globalization of R&D and Developing Countries*, Proceedings of the Expert Meeting Geneva, 24-26 January 2005 <http://www.unctad.org/en/docs/iteiia20056_en.pdf>.

208 Ibid.

209 Ibid.

210 Ibid.

211 Amy Jocelyn Glass, *Costly R&D and Intellectual Property Rights Protection*, Texas A&M University, Department of Economics <http://econweb.tamu.edu/aglass/cos.pdf>.

of 'spillovers'[212] of foreign firms conducting R&D in developing countries.[213] Schneider disagreed with both of these arguments and believes that even weak protection of IP is not needed for R&D conducted in developing countries, as it is mostly imitative and not innovative.[214]

An empirical study conducted in the 1980s confirmed the non-importance of IP for R&D. Lee Branstetter and Mariko Sakakibara studied the effects of patent reforms in developed countries on R&D input and output.[215] They concluded that there is no evidence of an increase in either R&D input or output that could plausibly be ascribed to patent law reforms.[216] Commentator Carlos A. Primo Braga, who is quite sympathetic to IP and *TRIPS Agreement*, admits that there is very little evidence to support the statement that stronger IP encourages greater R&D in developing countries.[217] Indeed, the recent research on technology issues in developing countries shows that the most important forms of new or novel knowledge such as tacit and localised knowledge, which is necessary to assimilate advanced technologies for developing countries, does not depend on IP systems, including patents.[218]

Professor Keith Maskus noted that even in the US where the highest expenditure on R&D is being spent, research managers in US-based corporations find that patents are rarely viewed as important incentives for undertaking R&D investments, except in pharmaceuticals and selected chemicals and biotechnology industries.[219] The question is whether these results regarding IP and R&D generated in developed countries can be applied to developing countries. Robert M. Sherwood answers this question in the affirmative, as he believes that the results could be easily applied to developing countries.[220] However, it is unclear if the same results could be transferred to developing countries as it is difficult to carry

---

[212] John Black, Nigar Hashimzade, and Gareth Myles notes that:

> A connection between different parts of the economy. Spillovers may be pecuniary or non-pecuniary. A pecuniary spill-over occurs, for example, when changes in one industry affect factor supplies to another: if a new factory bids up the wages of unskilled labour so that local people find cleaners or gardeners more expensive, this is a pecuniary spill-over. Pecuniary spillovers produce their effects through markets. A non-pecuniary spillover occurs when one industry inflicts a negative externality on another: there is usually no market through which they can be paid not to do so. Non-pecuniary spillovers provide a prima facie case for government intervention, by regulation or taxation, whereas pecuniary spillovers do not, except on grounds of income distribution.

See Black, Hashimzade, and Myles, above n 50.

[213] Kumar, above n 50, 16.

[214] Chatterjee et al., above n 134, 21.

[215] Branstetter, above n 70, 313.

[216] Ibid.

[217] Chang, above n 4, 298-299.

[218] Ibid.

[219] Levin (1987) and Cohen (2000), cited in Keith Maskus, above n 2, 514.

[220] Sherwood, above n 5.

and apply them across the board. Developed countries spend a huge amount of money on R&D, while developing countries spend much less.[221] In addition, the type of R&D done in developed countries is sophisticated when compared to that conducted in developing countries, which can be described as imitative and preliminary.

Firms from developed countries involved in R&D are changing their perspectives on where and how to conduct R&D. Many of these firms have chosen their R&D to take place in emerging economies such as China, India, and Brazil. Providing R&D producers from developed countries with free entry to these markets and having minimum standards of IP protection in place would protect their ideas and inventions and would allow them to conduct business in those countries, but this alone would not result in economic development of developing countries, which cannot rely on IP systems alone to achieve such end.

3.6.6 IP and Domestic Innovation

'Innovation' is closely related to invention, which is defined as the 'creation of new knowledge'. On the other hand, innovation (or 'commercialisation') refers to the development of marketable products from that knowledge.[222] Developing local expertise and innovation is important for the economic development of developing countries. These countries often lose some of their finest brains through immigration to the west as a result of poor local environments that do not support their creativity and development. Some believe that the only way for developing countries to keep their local expertise is by providing strong IP systems that reward creators and condemn free riders.[223] There are various empirical studies that examine the relationship between IP and local innovation, particularly in the context of patents. These studies either examine a particular policy change in great depth or attempt to examine the average impact of a number of reform policies on patents.[224]

One of those studies that examined the importance of the use of trademarks to domestic innovation in one developing country (Lebanon) found that innovation through product development and the entry of new firms into the local market are

---

[221] For example, in 1992, developed countries spent $372 billion on R&D (2% GDP), while developing countries spent only 57 billion on R&D (less than 1% of GDP in almost all developing countries). See Carlos A. Primo Braga, Carsten Fink, and Caludia Paz Sepulveda, *Intellectual Property Rights and Economic Development* (World Bank, 2000) 12.

[222] Maskus, Dougherty, and Mertha, above n 56, 5.

[223] See, in support of this view, Robert M. Sherwood. 'The TRIPS Agreement: Benefit and Costs for Developing Countries' (2000) 19 (1/2) *International Journal of Technology Management* 57, 63.

[224] Branstetter, above n 70, 361.

motivated in part by trademark protection.[225] The study noted that firms in Lebanon that were capable of designing high quality clothes were frustrated by the number of infringements that occurred locally on their designs. This has restrained their efforts to build a strong market in Lebanon in the fashion and design industry.[226] Another study examined IP systems in Jamaica and Senegal. It found that while there is a thriving musical business in those countries, weak protection of copyright and absence of supporting institutions such as professional collecting societies inhibited investment and domestic innovation in the music industry.[227]

There are few empirical studies that discuss the situation of developing countries and present a challenging laboratory environment to test the conclusions reached in these studies. This is because some developing countries still only offer weak protection for IP, whilst others provide stronger protection, and there is value in examining the effect of both weak and strong systems on innovation. It is also not possible to gain an impression from these studies as to how the different forms of IP such as trademarks, copyright, and design laws interact with each other to produce innovation, something not shown by solely studying a particular form of IP rights.[228]

Professor Lee Branstetter criticised these studies and believes that they fail to show evidence of a strong positive response by domestic innovators that could be reasonably ascribed to the effect of a stronger IP system (patents). He believes that '[t]he benefits of stronger [IP] to the extent that [it] exist at all- are more likely to come instead from acceleration in the domestic deployment of advanced technology by the affiliates of foreign firms'.[229]

The problem with most of these studies is that they fail to prove a strong positive relationship between IP and increases in levels of domestic innovation.[230] Having said that, it is important to note that a number of studies support the opposite view and argue that IP could actually reduce domestic innovation.[231]

A final word on this matter is that while IP has a positive influence on domestic innovation in some developing countries, it would be difficult to argue that IP alone results in innovation in all countries. Many of the studies that examined the situation of developing countries were broad and applied in the context of specific industries (fashion and entertainment) that cannot ultimately function effectively without a proper system of IP in place.

---

[225] Keith Maskus, 'Strengthening Intellectual Property Rights in Lebanon' in Carsten Fink and Keith Maskus (ed), *Intellectual Property and Development: Lessons from Recent Economic Research* (World Bank and Oxford University, 2005) 259-295.

[226] World Bank, above n 57, 135.

[227] Ibid.

[228] Sherwood, above n 5.

[229] Branstetter, above n 70, 336.

[230] Ibid 360.

[231] See, for a full explanation of how the different forms of IP induce innovation and economic development of developing countries, World Bank, above n 57, 144.

3.6.7 Overall Assessment of Empirical Evidence

To this day, there are still few empirical studies that help us understand what will happen when a developing country adopt IP systems and the effect of that on its FDI, technology transfer, local innovation, R&D, economic growth, and development.[232] Among the few important studies that have been written in the field are the studies prepared by Professor Mansfield for the World Bank in 1994 and 1995.[233]

It is important to mention that developing countries differ in terms of their scientific and technical capacities and inequalities of income and wealth.[234] This means that even the results obtained from one single developing country could not be applied to another without studying the situation and conditions of that country. Empirical evidence provides some insights on the relationship between IP and economic development, but because much of it exists at the aggregate level and relies on survey evidence, it should be treated with caution.[235]

The commentator Robert Sherwood conducted a comprehensive overview of the empirical studies that have been written on the subject and outlined the difficulties that researchers might encounter if they want to conduct such a study.[236] The empirical literature confirms the complexity of the issues found in the theoretical literature. There is some disagreement about whether the correlation between IP protection and economic development in developing countries is negative or zero. This is important as it addresses the question of whether these countries should adopt stronger IP protection or whether they need to provide additional incentives to compensate for the adverse effects of stronger IP protection.[237]

---

[232] See also Gervais, above n 135, 517.

[233] Mansfield, above n 155; Sherwood, above n 155.

[234] Barton et al., above n 86.

[235] Maskus, Saggi, and Puttitanun, above n 145, 271.

[236] Robert Sherwood explains these as follows:

> First, until 1987 there were few changes in the protective regimes of developing countries which would provide an opportunity to study 'before and after' situations. The recent changes may not have been in place long enough yet to show much contrast in behaviour, although some evidence is accumulating. Second, public statistics in the developing countries are of generally poor quality, if kept at all. Third, businessmen in developing countries typically do not respond to questionnaires. The business community tends to be adverse to information gathering, especially by governments, on the supposition that the gathered information is unlikely to advance business interests. Fourth, protection of new technology involves more than patents. Trade secrets and industrial copyright play a synergistic role and the trade secret is hard to trace since no public registry is utilized. Fifth, in many developing countries a good deal of incremental technological activity appears to be taking place in the 'informal sector', sometimes also known as the underground economy. Here again, activity is hard to measure.

Sherwood, above n 5. See also Park and Lippoldt, above 151, 12; Siebeck et al., above n 130.

[237] Chatterjee et al., above n 134, 24.

It is noted that it is one thing to examine the statistics and relationships in developing countries that have positive IP systems (meaning strong IP systems, with proper enforcement measures) but quite another to do so against the background of negative or weak systems that are available in other developing countries.[238] If there is an intention to transfer some of the findings of these studies to developing countries, it should be done with utmost care.[239]

One problem in conducting empirical research is to measure the level of IP protection in developed and developing countries. Different measures have been employed to determine the level of IP in developing countries. Some scholars measured only patent laws as a reflection of a country's level of IP.[240] Others have used surveys or combined personal knowledge and experience with professional interviews to assess the level of IP protection.[241] It important to scrutinise those measures as employing and favouring a single measure over another measure could severely affect results reached in the empirical studies.

Many of the empirical studies have also been criticised for measuring the number of IP laws that a developing country had and for not measuring the extent to which those statutes and laws are enforced.[242] It is noted that it is not enough to have IP laws in place, but what is of equally critical importance is the ability to enforce these laws.[243] Measuring both laws and the enforcement of these laws will produce better empirical results. Most studies that confirm that there is a positive link between IP and FDI or innovation or economic growth do not tell how important are other factors for economic development, such as tax incentives, quality of infrastructure, cultural ties, skills availability and input prices.[244]

3.6.8 Concluding Remarks

As shown in Sects. 3.5 and 3.6, there are two types of studies that examine the relationship between IP and economic development, either theoretical or empirical. The theoretical literature considers the costs and benefits of introducing or increasing IP protection.[245] On the other hand, the empirical evidence tries to establish the actual

[238] Sherwood, above n 5.

[239] Ibid.

[240] Most of the empirical evidence that has been conducted in essence measures the impact of IP, mostly in patents; see Robert P. Merges, 'The Economic Impact of Intellectual Property Rights: An Overview and Guide' (1995) 19 *Journal of Cultural Economic* 109-117.

[241] Robert L. Ostergard, 'The Measurement of Intellectual Property Rights Protection' 2000 (31) (2) *Journal of International Business Studies* 349, 351; Braga, Fink, and Sepulveda, above n 221, 182.

[242] Ostergard, above n 241, 353.

[243] Ibid.

[244] Braga, Fink and, Spulveda, above n 221, 180-181.

[245] Chatterjee, et al., above n 134, 3.

loss or gain as a result of implementing IP.[246] Empirical evidence can come either from surveys of foreign investors in industrial countries or from econometric studies[247] evaluating the impact of different IP systems on a cross-section of countries, including developing countries.[248]

These studies also fall into two further camps, either general or particular studies. General studies are not concerned with a particular form of IP but rather try to examine the effect of IP generally on economic development.[249] On the other hand, particular studies (also called narrow approach studies) try to answer specific questions as to how IP can accelerate or impede economic development. For example, such a study may assess the effect of a patent on a particular industry or analyse specific doctrines such as fair use (fair dealing, in some jurisdictions) in copyright law or non-obviousness in patent law from a pure economic perspective.[250]

The adoption of stronger IP in developing countries is often supported by studies claiming that these reforms will increase FDI, encourage local innovation and R&D, and as a result, accelerate economic development.[251] However, many of the studies that have been reviewed, whether academic or empirical, show that this is not simply the case. It is submitted that IP alone cannot accelerate the economic development of developing countries. Instead, it should be regarded as just one policy, among others, that governments in developing countries should give particular attention to.[252]

---

246 Developed countries that have developed sophisticated technologies are sometimes described as the 'north', while developing countries that often have imitated and copied developing technologies are sometimes described as the 'south'. See Maskus, Saggi, and Puttitanun, above n 145, 270; Chatterjee et al., above n 134, 3.

247 John Black, Nigar Hashimzade, and Gareth Myles note that:

> Econometrics is a discipline that develops mathematical and statistical methods, applies them to the estimation of economic models, and conducts quantitative analysis of the behaviour of economic data. Econometric theory mainly deals with establishing the statistical properties of estimators and the development of tests, while applied econometrics uses statistical methods to test and evaluate economic theories, and to forecast future values of economic variables.

See 'econometrics', Black, Hashimzade, and Myles, above n 50.

248 Braga, Fink, and Spulveda, above n 221,175.

249 See, for more information, Chatterjee et al., above 134, 3.

250 Merges, above n 240, 109; Maskus, above n 138, 18.

251 Maskus, above n 25, 19.

252 This has been shown in a number of emerging economies such as India, China, and Brazil, which have managed to use IP as leverage for achieving economic development. See Beattie, above n 45, 22; Joseph Strauss, 'The Impact of the New Order on Economic Development: The Role of the Intellectual Property Rights Systems' (2007) 15 *European Review* 47, 51; Kumar, above n 50, 2.

3.7 Intellectual Property Laws and Economic Development in Jordan

The case study of Jordan demonstrates some lessons on the theory of IP and economic development and whether the introduction of strong IP systems will accelerate the economic development of developing countries. This section will give an overview of the economic and legal contexts of Jordan; then it will assess to what extent the enhanced protection of IP has accelerated economic development in Jordan in two important sectors of the economy: the pharmaceutical sector and the information technology (IT) sector. The reason for choosing these two sectors and not others is that IP is central to their operation and the Jordanian economy witnessed a boost as a result of their heightened performance in recent years.

3.7.1 History and Demographics of Jordan

Although Jordan, or what is termed officially as the 'Hashemite Kingdom of Jordan' (Jordan), was formally established in 1921, it is quite rich in history as several civilisations have inhabited it, including the Persians, Greeks, Romans, Arab Muslims, and others. Throughout history, Jordan has been at the crossroads connecting the continents of Asia, Africa, and Europe. This mid-field position has benefited Jordan as a conduit for trade and communication, but at the same time it has had its downside, especially in turbulent times.[253] Jordan borders Syria to the north, Iraq to the north-east, Israel and Palestine to the west, and Saudi Arabia to the east and south. It has a land mass of 89,778 sq kms[254] and a total population estimated in 2010 to be 6.32 million.[255]

3.7.2 The Economic Environment in Jordan

Jordan's geo-political position has had major effects on its economic development.[256] This is because the Jordanian economy has been influenced by the migration of people flooding to the country as a result of wars and the instability

[253] Atef Abu Hamid, *An Analysis of ICT Integration within the Jordanian Education System* (A PhD thesis, University of Technology Sydney, 2008) 12.

[254] With only 26 km of coastline on the Gulf of Aqaba on the Red Sea.

[255] The vast majority of Jordanians are Arabs, with other minorities living in the country, such as Circassians, Kurds, Chechens, and Armenians. Many of the ruling class (the military and the police) in Jordan are Bedouins, who mostly came to the country from the Arabic Peninsula, which is located in Southwest Asia.

[256] Paul Rivlin, *Arab Economies in the Twenty-First Century* (Cambridge University, 2009) 160.

of the region. Jordan's major natural resources are phosphate, limestone, and marble. Minimal oil resources are available in the country, but have been mostly left untouched, as there are no huge commercial benefits in drilling, compared to other surrounding countries such as Iraq and Saudi Arabia. Jordan has limited agricultural land (12%) as most of the land is desert (75%), and the country suffers from a scarcity of water resources. Because of its poor natural resources, Jordan has relied heavily, and continues to rely heavily, on its human resources, who are highly educated and skilled, compared to other human resources in its neighbouring countries.[257] Jordan is classified by the World Bank as a 'lower income country'.[258] Despite some economic growth since the latter part of the 1990s, and with more than 4% growth in 2000 and 2002 compared to 1% between 1996 and 1998, the country's capacity for economic growth remains fragile.[259]

After Jordan supported the Iraqi Saddam Hussein regime in its invasion of Kuwait, Jordan lost the support of the US and oil-rich countries, including Kuwait, which expelled thousands of Jordanians working there, who then did not have any alternative but to return to Jordan. This had a major effect on the economy and the limited resources of the poor country. To break out of this situation, Jordan embarked on economic reforms that started with the late King Hussein signing a peace treaty with Israel in 1995 and improving relationships with the US and other major powers.[260] His son, King Abdullah II, continued the economic reforms and the development process that his father started.[261] These economic

---

[257] Many of Jordan's workforces are employed in the Gulf oil-rich countries and have remitted much foreign exchange to the country since the 1980s, contributing to the boosting of the Jordanian economy. See Nesreen Barakat and Ibrahim Saif, 'Exit-Dynamics: Case of Manufacturing Sector in Jordan' in Khalid Sekkat (ed), *Market Dynamics and Productivity in Developing Countries: Economic Reforms in the Middle East and North Africa* (Springer, 2010); Emaduldeen (2007), cited in Abu Hamid, above n 253, 12.

[258] See also Travel Document Systems Inc., *Jordan* <http://www.traveldocs.com/index.php?page=about-jordan-2>.

[259] This is because limited resources characterise the Jordanian economy, reliance on the service sector, continuous budget deficits, dependence on foreign aid, excessive foreign debt, a high unemployment rate (about 14%), and low labour productivity and labour market imbalances. It is also criticised for having limited sources of funding, an unfavourable taxation structure (among the highest within Arab countries), and costly transport infrastructure and utilities, all of which have affected the development of private companies. See Abu Hamid, above n 253, 13; Bashar Malkawi, *Jordan and the World Trading System–A Case Study Submitted for Arab Countries* (a PhD thesis, American University, 2005) 135; Government of Jordan, *2006-2015 National Agenda the Jordan We Strive* <http://www.carim.org/public/polsoctexts/PS2JOR027_EN.pdf>.

[260] Rivlin, above 256, 160.

[261] The purpose of these reforms is twofold. The first was to strengthen the economy, increase employment, and reduce poverty, all of which threatened social and political stability. The second aim was political, to position Jordan closer to the US and the global economy. See Rivlin, above n 256, 169; Al-Abdulrazag Bashier and Bataineh Talal, 'Forecasting Foreign Direct Investment Inflow in Jordan: Univariate ARIMA Model' (2007) 3 (1) *Journal of Social Sciences* 1.

Table 3.1 The growth of the GDP in the Jordanian Economy since 2000 until 2010

Year	2000	2002	2004	2006	2008	2010
GDP at Market Prices (in Million US$)	8,463	9,584	11,411	15,645	22,696	27,573
Real GDP Growth Rate (%)	4.2	5.8	8.6	7.9	7.6	3.1
GDP per Capital Current Prices (US$)	1,764	1,902	2,157	2,826	3,922	4,560

reforms[262] resulted in real GDP growth and relatively low inflation of 3.1% on average per year from 2000 to 2007. The reforms also contributed to a reduction in public debt, from 98.4% of GDP in 2002 to 60.3% by March 2008.[263] Table 3.1 shows the GDP growth in the Jordanian economy from 2000 to 2010.[264]

Jordan has an economy dominated by services (around two thirds of its GDP). Manufacturing is the second most important sector (about one fifth of GDP); agriculture's contribution to GDP is quite low at 3%.[265] The industrial sector in Jordan is divided into the manufacturing sector (pharmaceuticals, phosphates, and textiles) and the mining and quarrying sectors.[266] Jordan's imports have increased in line with its significant economic growth in 2003–2007. Total merchandise imports more than tripled from US$4,013 million in 2000 to US$13,531 million

[262] These reforms included privatisation projects, integrating Jordan into the world economy through accession to the WTO; trade liberalization; introducing major changes to the legal environment; signing a series of FTAs and partnerships with the US (2000), the EU (1997), and other countries; and the establishment of the Aqaba Special Economic Zone (ASEZ). See Nerin Abu-Keer, Mera Al-Horani, Aroob Tamimi, *The Economic Impact of Free Trade on Jordan's Balance of Payments* University of Jordan, Department of Business (January 2009) <http://www.scribd.com/doc/14853171/The-effect-of-FTA-on-Jordans-Balance-of-Payment?secret_password=&autodown=doc>; Ministry of Trade and Economy, *Jordan and the World Trade Organization* <http://www.mit.gov.jo/Default.aspx?tabid=810>; *Jordan's Foreign Trade Policy* <http://www.mit.gov.jo/tabid/475/Jordan%20Foreign%20Trade%20Policy.aspx>; Travel Document System, above n 258; Embassy of Jordan in Washington, D.C., *Political and Socio-Economic Model* – Building a New Model <http://www.jordanembassyus.org/new/aboutjordan/er2.shtml>; Jordan Economic and Commerce Bureau, *About Jordan* <http://www.jordanecb.org/public/English.aspx?Lang=1&Page_Id=1287&Menu_ID=31>; Michael T. Dabit, 'The Investment Environment in Jordan' (2004) 20 (5) *Journal of International Business Law Review* 240.

[263] WTO, Trade Policy Review Report by the Secretariat, Jordan, WT/TPR/S/206 (6 October 2008) <www.wto.org/english/tratop_e/tpr_e/s206-00_e.doc>. See also Barakat and Saif, above n 257, 15; Rivlin, above n 256, 159.

[264] World Bank, *Current GDP (US)* <http://data.worldbank.org/indicator/NY.GDP.MKTP.CD/countries>. See also Jordan's Economic and Commerce Bureau, Department of Statistics <http://www.jordanecb.org/Public/Main_English.aspx?site_id=1&Page_ID=308>.

[265] WTO, above n 263. See also Rivlin, above 256, 159, Barakat and Saif, above n 257, 13; The World Bank, *Jordan Country Brief* <http://web.worldbank.org>.

[266] Barakat and Saif, above n 257, 15; Yusuf Mansur, *Overcoming Barriers to Foreign Direct Investment in Jordan*, International Research Foundation of Oman and the Fraser Institute of Canada (June 2008), Freetheworld.org, 14 <http://www.freetheworld.com/arab/Overcoming-Barriers_Foreign-Direct-Investment.pdf>, Oxford Business Group, *Business Jordan Country Report* <http://www.oxfordbusinessgroup.com>.

in 2007.[267] The US is by far Jordan's biggest market, accounting for almost a third of the country's total exports.[268] It is noted that the development of the Jordanian economy and the economic growth that Jordan has witnessed in recent years can be attributed to various factors, including the economic reforms, the high influx of immigrants from oil-rich surrounding countries who have transferred foreign currency into the country, and finally, the increased US financial assistance to the Jordanian economy, which is considered amongst the largest aid programmes in the world.[269]

3.7.3 The Legal Environment in Jordan

As a result of joining the WTO, Jordan had to amend many of its laws, especially those of a commercial nature,[270] to be compatible with international standards. The country was particularly interested in the development of its investment laws and wanted to make sure that these laws operated in such a way as to attract the widest possible number of investors to Jordan.

The *Investment Law Promotion Law No. 16 of 1995*, as amended, regulates FDI[271] in Jordan. The law offers non-discriminatory treatment and incentives in certain sectors of the Jordanian economy service industries such as IT, hospitals, and others. Moreover, it designates certain locations in Jordan for investment promotion (industrial estates, development areas, free zones, and the Aqaba Special Economic Zone (ASEZ)), each of which has its own investment incentive

[267] Government of Jordan, above n 259.

[268] Ame Info, *Jordan Looks Near and Far for Economic Growth* (14 February 2007) <www.ameinfo.com/110694.html>.

[269] According to the US Embassy in Jordan, the American financial assistance to Jordan has exceeded $2.3 billion over the last decade, while in 2002 and 2003, it exceeded $1 billion. See, Issam Qadamani, 'US Provides $200m to Jordan in Economic Aid', Jordan Times (online), 12 July 2004 <http://www.jordanembassyus.org/07122004001.htm>.

[270] The foundation for all private and commercial laws in the country is the Jordanian *Civil Code No. 43 of 1976* (Civil Code). It forms the legal basis for all contracts that any investor is willing to conclude in Jordan (arts 87-248), including partnerships and joint ventures (arts 582-610), leases (arts 658-710), contracts for independent work (arts 780-804), work contracts in general (arts 780-804), contract of employment (arts 805-832), and contracts of agency (arts 833-867). The *Civil Code* is derived from Islamic fiqh (jurisprudence). See, for more information about civil legal systems in the Arab World, Nabil A. Saleh, 'The Law Governing Contracts in Arabia', *The International and Comparative Law Quarterly* (1989) 38 (4), 761-787.

[271] Jordan's average annual inflow of FDI jumped from an average of US$155 million during 1990s (37.1% of GDP in 2000) to US$3121 million in 2006 (114.2% of GDP). In 2008, FDI has accumulated close to JD 1.376 billion in 2008. See Ministry of Trade and Economy, above n 262. See also Barakat and Saif, above n 257, 15; WTO, above n 263; Bashier and Talal, above n 261, 2. See also the American Chamber of Commerce in Jordan, *Jordan-Foreign Direct Investment*, Fact Sheet, (June 2009) <http://www.amchammena.org/Jordan/Foreign%20Direct%20Investment.pdf>.

scheme.[272] The Jordan Investment Board (JIB),[273] an independent body, supervises the smooth implementation of this law and manages investment procedures for exemptions and benefits of inventors whenever applicable.[274]

In summary, Jordan has an impressive number of IP and investment laws[275] that can, if properly implemented, guarantee that investors are truly protected in Jordan. Nonetheless, to what extent have these laws boosted the Jordanian economy? This will be treated under a separate section.

3.7.4 The Role of IP in Accelerating Economic Development of the Pharmaceutical and IT Sectors in Jordan

The pharmaceutical and IT sectors in Jordan have contributed significantly to the growth of the Jordanian economy. The pharmaceutical industry in Jordan is regarded by the Jordanian government as one of the most important foreign exchange-earning industries of the economy.[276] By the end of 2002, pharmaceutical industry exports outnumbered those of other manufacturing industries (cement, phosphate, and potash)[277] by approximately US$202 million in 2002, compared to only US$49 million in 1991.[278] The early beginning of the Jordanian pharmaceutical industry was very modest, with the first local manufacturer starting production in 1966.[279] At present, there are 18 registered Jordanian pharmaceutical companies.[280] The working capital of these pharmaceutical companies is worth

[272] WTO, above n 263.

[273] Jordan Investment Board <http://www.jordaninvestment.com/>.

[274] The American Chamber of Commerce in Jordan, above n 271; Dabit, above n 262.

[275] These investment laws are the *Trademarks Law No. 34 of 1999*; the *Patent Law No. 32 of 1999*; the *Industry and Trade Law No. 18 of 1998*; the *Law of Free Zones Corporation No. 32 of 1984*, as amended; the *Custom Law No. 20 of 1998*, as amended by the *Law No. 16 of 2000;* the *Companies Law No. 22 of 1997*, as amended; the *Commercial Agents and Mediators Law No. 28 of 2001*; the *Banking Law No. 31 of 2001*; the *Investment Promotion Law No. 16 of 1995*, as amended by the *Law No. 16 of 2002*; the *Company Law No. 22 of 1997*; the *Labour Law No. 8 of 1996*, as amended; the *Arbitration Law No. 31 of 2001*; the *Insurance Law No. 33 of 1999*; the *Competition Law No. 33 of 2004*; the *Aqaba Special Economic Zone Law No. 32 of 2000*; the *Sales Tax Law of No. 29 of 2009*, as amended; the *Income Tax Law No. 57 of 1985*, as amended; and other laws.

[276] M. Javedanfar, *Analysis of Health and Pharmaceuticals Sectors* (20 July 2005) Meepas <http://www.meepas.com/jordan_health_Pharm_sector.htm>.

[277] Philip Dew and Jonathan Wallace (eds), *Doing Business in Jordan* (Kogan Page, 2004) 175.

[278] Ibid.

[279] United Nations Industrial Development Organisation (UNIDO), *Pharmaceutical Sector* <http://exchange.unido.org/upload/3423_Pharmaceutical20sector.pdf>.

[280] Five of those companies dominate the local market and account for more than 90% of the country's total production. Those are Hikma Pharmaceuticals, Arab Pharmaceuticals Industries (APHA), Dar Al Dawa (DADI), Jordanian Pharmaceutical Manufacturing (JPM), and United Pharmaceuticals (UPM). The Jordanian Association of Manufacturers of Pharmaceuticals and

approximately US$600 million.[281] Internationally, the Jordanian pharmaceuticals industry has earned a reputation in the region as a pioneer in the production of high-quality products.[282] After joining the WTO, Jordan had to introduce to its laws major changes that regulate the pharmaceutical industry. Among the important legislative changes that were introduced in the field of patent law is the *Patent Invention Law No. 32 of 1999*, as amended.[283]

Jordan's IT sector is thriving and has become a major contributor to Jordan's economy.[284] IT Jordanian companies work in all sorts of information and communication technologies (ICT) activities, including consulting, software development, communication and Internet service, hardware sales and technology provision, and licensing.[285] Among the fastest growing industries of the Jordanian IT sector is software development.[286] Jordan is now regarded as a leader in developing software tailored to the needs of the Arabic-speaking world.[287]

IT is one of the largest contributors to the Jordanian economy.[288] In 2004 alone, the IT sector posted a turnover of US$440 million, which was an increase of 160% since 2001.[289] The sector as a whole registered by far the most rapid growth of any sector for FDI with more than US$1.5 billion invested since 2000.[290] Annual

Medical Appliances (JAPM) was established in 1996 to oversee the development of the pharmaceutical sector in Jordan. See Dew and Wallace, above n 277, 179; The Jordanian Association for Physicists in Medicine (JAPM), *How Did We Start* <http://www.japm.com/Public/English.aspx?Lang=2&Page_Id=141&Menu_Parent_ID=2&type=R>; UNIDO, above n 279.

281 JAPM, above 280.

282 Dew and Wallace above 277, 175.

283 For further explanation of the law that governs IP generally and the pharmaceutical industry specially, see Dew and Wallace, above n 277, 286-292.

284 Ministry of Information Communication and Technology (MICT), *R&D Strategy for ICT in Jordan* 2007-2010 (3 April 2007) <http://www.thieswittig.eu/docs/MPC_Strategies/Jordan/JORDAN_ICT_Strategy_Volume_1-Final_May_20007.pdf>.

285 Mediterranean Exchange, *Overview of the Information Technology Sector* <http://mediterranea-nexchange.unido.org/upload/1726_1144770426_ICT.pdf>; Dew and Wallace, above n 277, 213.

286 Dew and Wallace, above 277, 213.

287 Phillip Kurata, *Harnessing Creativity Vital to Economic Growth* (21 August 2008) American.gov Archive <http://www.america.gov/st/econ-english/2008/August/20080821162947cpataruk9.969729e-02.html>.

288 David Morgan, *IT a Vital Component of Jordan's New Economy* (3 December 2009) Global Arab Network <http://www.english.globalarabnetwork.com/200912033875/Technology/it-a-vital-component-of-jordans-new-economy.html>.

289 Mediterranean Exchange, above n 285. See also, AME info, *Microsoft Deal Boosts Jordan's ICT Ambitions* (29 August 2007) Ameinfo <http://www.ameinfo.com/130311.html>; MICT, *Invest in ICT in Jordan* <http://www.moict.gov.jo>; Morgan, above n 288; Jordan Investment Board, *ICT Sector* <http://www.jordaninvestment.com>; Ameinfo, *Jordan ICT Sector Achieves 30 per cent Growth in Revenues* (13 September 2004) <http://www.ameinfo.com/45170.html>.

290 MICT, *Jordan's Growing and Competitive ICT Landscape Offers Attractive Investment Opportunities* <http://www.moict.gov.jo>.

growth for the IT sector has risen to an estimated 50% from 2006 until 2009.[291] The expansion of the ICT industry also resulted in some 80,000 new jobs being created between 1999 and 2008.[292]

The accelerated economic growth of the Jordanian IT sector would not have been possible without having appropriate policies to develop this sector.[293] As a result of joining the WTO, Jordan has given particular attention to the laws that are of importance to the ICT sector, particularly software development. This is mainly the *Copyright Law No. 22 of 1992* that has been amended several times more than any other IP law in the country.[294]

3.7.5 Assessment of the Effect of IP on Economic Development of the Pharmaceutical Sector

How has joining the WTO helped Jordanian pharmaceutical companies to penetrate international markets and raise their revenues? There are two responses to this question, one that argues that IP has accelerated the economic development of the Jordanian pharmaceutical sector and the other that, on the contrary, believes that it has inhibited its economic development.

The International IP Institute (IIPI), based in Washington, DC, supports the first opinion. It argues that the Jordanian pharmaceutical sector has capitalised on the trade benefits that the WTO and the JUSFTA have provided as the Jordanian international exporting is more diversified and international than it was before.[295] As a result of introducing IP, Jordanian companies have become attractive business partners and have concluded licensing agreements and joint ventures with

291 Morgan, above n 288.

292 Mohammad Ghazal, *ICT Sector Created 80,000 Jobs over Past Decade* <http://www.zawya.com/story.cfm/sidZAWYA20091223064113/ICT_sector_created_80000_jobs_over_past_decade>.

293 Among these polices is the REACH initiative, which was started by the Information Technology Association Jordan (INTAJ) in 1999 as a national policy for the development of the IT sector. See Morgan, above n 288.

294 The enforcement of the copyright law is given to the National Library of Jordan (NLJ). The NLJ has taken comprehensive measures against infringement and infringers. See AGIP, *Jordan National Library Deals with 2347 Copyright Infringements*, AGIP Bulletin (February 2009) <http://demo5.agip.com/bulletin_news.aspx?id=1625&month=2&year=2009&lang=en>; *Jordan*, International Intellectual Property Alliance (IIPA), *Special 301 Report on Jordan* (2009) 385–88 <http://www.iipa.com/rbc/2009/2009SPEC301JORDAN.pdf>; Saleh Al Sharari, 'Intellectual Property Rights Legislation and Computer Software Piracy in Jordan' (2006) 2 (1) *Journal of Social Sciences*, 7, 9; Garduño and Pietrucha, above n 65.

295 International Intellectual Property Institute (IIPI), *The Role of Intellectual Property in the Jordanian Industry* <http://www.iipi.org>.

international pharmaceutical companies.[296] Furthermore, this has helped the Jordanian pharmaceutical companies to increase their local innovation and establish new clinical research organisations (CROs) that are much needed for the future development of the industry.[297]

The Capital Bank of Jordan[298] agrees that Jordan's smooth accession to the WTO in April 2000 has opened the doors for Jordanian pharmaceuticals companies to penetrate foreign markets, which they could not have done without respecting international standards and protecting IP.[299] The approvals that some Jordanian corporations have obtained from health authorities in Europe and the US demonstrate that they are, in fact, manufacturing high-quality products.[300] As a result, the Jordanian pharmaceutical sector has become a significant source of income for the Jordanian economy.[301]

Professor Michael Ryan of Georgetown University (a former advisor to the Jordanian government) and Jillian Shanebrook conducted a study on the development of the Jordanian pharmaceutical industry. They attributed the development of the pharmaceutical sector to changing IP laws in Jordan. They explained that:

> Jordan's economy has expanded significantly since Jordan implemented better IP laws between 1998 and 2001, particularly in contrast to other Middle East neighbours in the post-9/11 context. Growth has been robust in Jordan's pharmaceutical and bio-medical technology industries. Much of this success can be attributed to the improved protections for IP rights (e.g., patents and trademarks)...The improved IP regime paved the way for a broad range of benefits in the Jordanian health care sector and has fuelled the growth of Jordan's knowledge economy. This has been reflected in the growth of health-service contributions to the Jordanian GDP, which increased from 2.8 per cent in 1997 to 3.5 per cent in 2001. Health-services employment has grown 52 per cent since 1997. The increase in employment opportunities reflects, in part, the contribution of clinical research and trials. Health care sector growth has included the development of new sub-sectors, like contract clinical research organizations, and the integration of Jordan's scientific community into international clinical research.[302]

All these are obviously good for the development of the pharmaceutical industry and health sector in Jordan. However, this study can be criticised for failing to

---

[296] Such as Organon, Novartis and Aventis, Fujisawa, Roche, Takeda, and others located in the US, Japan, Korea, Italy, Switzerland, and the UK. See IIPA, above n 295; Dew and Wallace above 277, 179.

[297] IIPI, above n 295.

[298] See the Capital Bank (formerly known as the Export and Finance Bank of Jordan) <http://www.capitalbank.jo/node/17>.

[299] Dew and Wallace above n, 277, 181.

[300] Ibid.

[301] Ibid 181-182.

[302] Michael Ryan and Jillian Shanebrook, *Establishing Globally Competitive Pharmaceutical and Bio-Medical Technology Industries in Jordan: Assessment of Business Strategies and the Enabling Environment*, 2 <http://www.iipi.org/>; IIPI, *Jordan Pharmaceutical Report Released* <http://iipi.org/2004/10/jordan-pharmaceutical-industry-report-released/>; IIPI, above n 295; Kurata, above n 287.

provide sufficient supporting economic evidence to explain how the introduction of patent laws has helped the growth of the Jordanian pharmaceutical sector. It also did not mention or assess the role of other regional factors that have contributed to the growth of the Jordanian economy.

In 2009, Rohit Maplpani, from Oxfam's International's Access to Medicine campaign, conducted a study examining the costs and benefits of signing the JUSFTA in relation to the pharmaceutical industry in Jordan. The study found that there were no FDI inflows to Jordan between 2002 and mid-2006 to develop local medicine companies.[303] Furthermore, the JUSFTA has not encouraged Jordanian companies to engage in R&D, and it contributed to a 20% increase in medicine prices in the country during the same period.[304]

Another study was conducted by the Gerald R. Ford School of Public Policy at the University of Michigan to assess the impacts of the JUSFTA on Jordan's pharmaceutical industry. The study found that:

> Supporters who argue that the JUSFTA provides incentives for U.S. firms to contract research and development activities to Jordan face a similar challenge when trying to prove economic relevance. U.S. pharmaceutical imports from Jordan totaled only $7 million in 2006; a significant increase over 2001 numbers, but still less than one-half of one percent of Jordan's total exports to the United States . . . . Jordan's TRIPS Plus status is unlikely to have a significant impact on its pharmaceutical trade with other MENA countries. In addition, even with TRIPS Plus and duty-free status, Jordanian pharmaceutical firms face substantial non-tariff barriers when attempting to penetrate developed markets. Pharmaceutical regulations in the United States, the European Union, and Japan are forbiddingly strict. Jordanian producers, for example, are unlikely to meet the U.S. Federal Drug Administration's —Good manufacturing practices for pharmaceuticals and will therefore be unable to provide contract manufacturing to U.S. firms. Due to all these factors, the impact of the JUSFTA on Jordan's pharmaceutical industry is likely to remain small.[305]

---

[303] Rohit Malpani, 'All Costs, No Benefits: How the US-Jordan Free Trade Agreement Affects Access to Medicine' (2009) 6 (3) *Journal of Generic Medicine* 213, 214.

[304] The study also found the following negative impacts on access to medicine in Jordan:

- TRIPS-plus rules, particularly data exclusivity, independently prevent generic competition for 79% of medicines launched by 21 multinational pharmaceutical companies since 2001.
- Additional expenditures for medicines with no generic competitor, as a result of enforcement of data exclusivity, were between $6.3 and $22.04 m.
- New product launches in Jordan are only a fraction of total product launches in the USA and the EU. Many new medicines launched in Jordan are exorbitantly priced and unaffordable for ordinary people. Few or no units of these recently launched medicines have actually been purchased on the local market.

See Oxfam International, 'All Costs, No Benefits: How TRIPS-Plus Intellectual Property Rules in the US-Jordan FTA Affect Access to Medicines', Oxfam Briefing Paper 102 (March 2007), 20 <http://www.oxfam.org/sites/www.oxfam.org/files/all%20costs,%20no%20benefits.pdf>.

[305] Nasa'a et al., above n 13, 13-14. Another study that was prepared by a Jordanian lawyer also supported the same conclusion. It found that:

> It seems that, with the Jordanian pharmaceutical industry's lack of a research and development base, the interest of major foreign pharmaceutical companies in the sector is mainly driven by the desire to benefit from its well-developed regional distribution networks and not necessarily the sector's products or patents. Given the sector's dependence on generics

Two Jordanian scholars named Hamed El Said and Mohammed El Said, one of whom is an economist and the other an IP lawyer, have produced an empirical study that refutes the claims of Professor Michael Ryan and his co-author Jillian Sharebrook. They found that, contrary to the above views, the Jordanian economy and, particularly, the pharmaceutical sector, have not witnessed economic growth as a result of Jordan's joining the WTO and the introduction of new patent laws. There were much more important factors that contributed to economic growth in Jordan, including the arrival of more than 80,000 wealthy Iraqis following the 2003 US-led war against Iraq, who invested huge sums of money into the Jordanian market; the large increase in the US aid to Jordan in the post-1999 period; and the establishment of the quantifying industrial zones (QIZ) in the late 1990s.[306]

Some observations can be made. It is rare to find empirical research studies in Jordan that assess the importance of IP to the Jordanian economy. More studies assessing the situation in Jordan and the Arab world are required. The empirical study based its results on interviews conducted over a short period of time (3 weeks), which can be regarded as insufficient to reach sound, accurate conclusions about a sector that has been evolving for almost 40 years. Although the purpose of the questionnaire was to 'generate both qualitative and quantitative data on the impact of the JUSFTA on the local pharmaceutical sector',[307] most of the data generated was qualitative rather than quantitative.[308]

Another study prepared by two economists, Jane Harrigan and Hamed El Said, also argued that the economic growth that Jordan had witnessed after joining the WTO has been exaggerated.[309] It is hard to determine the specific reasons Jordan witnessed a high economic growth after joining the WTO. It is noted that having IP and other investment laws has assisted this increase, but they are not to be considered as a major factor for contributing to Jordan's economic growth.

---

production and the limited technology transfer occurring under technology transfer contracts, one finds little evidence pointing to well defined benefits that would not have materialized for the sector had Jordan not acceded to the WTO or signed the JUSFTA.

See Ferris K. Nesheiwat, 'The Adoption of Intellectual Property Standards beyond TRIPS - Is It a Misguided Legal and Economic Obession by Developing Countries' (2010) 32 *Loyala of Los Angeles International and Comparative Law Review* 361, 381.

306 Hamed El-Said and Mohammed El Said, 'TRIPS-Plus Implications for Access to Medicines in Developing Countries: Lesson from Jordan-United States Free Trade Agreement' (2007)10 (6) *The Journal of World Intellectual Property* 438, 453.

307 Ibid 439.

308 Miranda Forsyth explains that '[q]ualitative method is primarily concerned with collecting empirical data in a numerical way while qualitative data involve the direct observation, in-depth interviews, group discussion narratives and the analysis of documentary evidence'. See Miranda Forsyth, 'Second Annual Conference on Empirical Legal Studies' (2007) 11 (2) *Journal of South Pacific Law* 204 <http://www.paclii.org/journals/fJSPL/vol11no2/pdf/forsyth2.pdf>.

309 Jane Harrigan and Hamed El-Said, *Aid and Power in the Arab World* (Palgrave Macmillan, 2009) 75; Jane Harrigan, Hamed El-Said and Chengang Wang, 'The IMF and the World Bank in Jordan: A Case of over Optimism and Elusive Growth' (2006) 1 (3) *The Review of International Organizations* 263-292.

This is supported by reading the empirical literature conducted by the various Jordanian economists.

A study conducted by Professor Yusuf Mansour on FDI flows to Jordan found that the Jordanian economy has done well in recent years because of the 'regional factors and not local factors'.[310] Mansour investigated the history of FDI flows into Jordan since 2000 and came to the conclusion that the rise in economic growth was the result of investors considering Jordan as a safer and more secure country when compared to other countries in the region.[311] In 2004–2005, the same author noted that regional events, particularly the war in Iraq, made Jordan the only viable refuge for more than 80,000 displaced Iraqis, increasing FDI in Jordan.[312]

Professors Manhal Shotar and Basher Abdulrazaq conducted an empirical study examining the impact of FDI on the economic growth of the Jordanian economy. While recognising the importance of FDI to the economic growth of the country, they empirically established that FDI is thought to be the last resort for the economic advancement of the Jordanian economy.[313] This is because Jordan is a small country with limited resources, and the private sector is unable to contribute much to trade and economic development.[314] Professors Aktham Maghyereh and Ghassan Said Omet also conducted an empirical study on the economic growth of the Jordanian economy and found that foreign debt has reached an excessive level in Jordan, amounting to 53% of GDP. This has impacted heavily on the economic growth of the Jordanian economy and its development.[315]

In light of these views, it is noted that IP has played a minor role in the development of the Jordanian pharmaceutical sector and, accordingly, the growth of the Jordanian economy.

3.7.6 Assessment of the Effect of IP on the Economic Development of the Information Technology Sector

The question is this: To what extent has possessing a wholly revised copyright law in Jordan since 1992 assisted the IT sector to develop economically? It is difficult to

[310] Mansur, above n 266, 21.

[311] Ibid.

[312] Ibid.

[313] Manhal M Shotar and Basher A Abdulrazag, 'The Impact of Foreign Direct Investment on Economic Growth in Jordan' (2003) 1 (1) *Journal of International Business and Entrepreneurship Development* 20.

[314] Ibid 14.

[315] Aktham Issa Maghyereh and Ghassan Said Omet, *External Debt and Economic Growth in Jordan: The Threshold Effect* (2002) SSRN <http://papers.ssrn.com/sol3/papers.cfm?abstract_id=317541>.

obtain proper statistics in Jordan that can give an exact estimate of the contribution of the IT sector to the Jordanian economy.

Similar claims have been put forward by various commentators who argue that introducing copyright law has helped the economic development of the IT sector and increased the flow of FDI to the country.[316] The American commentators Eric Garduño and Frank Pietrucha wrote a short article appraising Jordan's IP system, noting that without amending the Jordanian copyright law, the IT sector would not witness economic growth.[317] One study found that introducing a new copyright system in Jordan has given Jordanian IT firms the 'legal grounding' that they need to conduct business.[318] It has also caused the return of business that had left Jordan due to the high volumes of software piracy that were taking place in the country.[319] It added that Jordan witnessed an accelerated economic development in the IT sector because the IT exporting of Jordanian firms had reached a growth rate of more than 100%.[320]

A 2003 study prepared by the United States Agency for International Development (USAID) found that, contrary to the high hopes held for Jordan's ICT sector, it could not be considered as a major source of FDI but only as an important source for the development of the local Jordanian IT skills.[321] The study also recognised that the rise in exports of IT services from Jordan to neighbouring markets was attributed to the significant increase in hardware and technology provision services in those neighbouring Arab markets.[322] This proved to be an external factor related to the needs of the ICT market in the region rather than to the availability of a copyright system in Jordan.

A study conducted by a Jordanian lawyer also found that:

> [It] is reasonable to assume that the FDI neither had an intellectual property component nor was influenced by intellectual property standards in Jordan. Indeed, the 2006 data shows that 80 percent of the FDI went to the industrial sector, with 14 per cent earmarked for the country's growing tourism industry. Those numbers shed light on the dismal role intellectual property played in attracting FDI into Jordan.[323]

Another study also doubts whether the JUSFTA will attract foreign ICT investment to Jordan and contribute to the economic development of the country.[324]

[316] It is also important to discuss the impact of having a newly copyright regime on the Jordanian publication sector, see Raid al Khouri, *Report on Copyright Industries in Jordan* (October 2002) WIPO <http://www.wipo.int/about-ip/en/studies/pdf/study_r_khouri.pdf>.

[317] Garduño and Pietrucha, above n 65.

[318] IIPI, above n 295.

[319] Ibid.

[320] Ibid.

[321] USAID, *ICT Sector Baseline Industry Survey*, AMIR II Achievement of Market-Friendly Initiatives and Results (January 2005) <http://pdf.usaid.gov/pdf_docs/PNADH816.pdf>.

[322] IIPI, above n 295.

[323] Nesheiwat, above n 305, 388.

[324] Nasa'a et al., above n 13, 13-14.

This is because there remain significant challenges that the Jordanian ICT sector has to overcome.[325] These include a high cost of local phone calls that limits Internet diffusion, a high cost of computers that prevents significant public adoption of ICT, a deficiency of diversified ICT demand as the Jordanian government is the principal buyer of ICT services, and a lack of IT soft skills by Jordanian IT graduates.[326]

Finally, it is noted that many of the views expressed in the economic studies that appraise the economic development of the IT sector in Jordan are not supported by empirical evidence. They are of a general nature that only supports one point of view, without the proper consideration of other views that doubt the importance of IP to the economic development of Jordan.

3.7.7 Jordanian Case Study Concluding Remarks

The section has examined the effect of IP (patent and copyright) on the most important sectors of the Jordanian economy, including the pharmaceutical and IT sectors. Both of the two views in Sect. 3.7.5 have some value. However, it is not clear whether IP systems were important to the economic development of the pharmaceutical and IT sectors in Jordan. This is because of the external factors that influenced the growth of the Jordanian economy. These factors are hard to predict and can change from one year to another because of the instability of the region.

It is hoped that more comprehensive empirical studies on the importance of IP to economic development are conducted in the future, which would give a better idea of the exact importance and effect of IP on the economic development of developing countries. A good approach would be to examine the sectors in developing countries that are most affected by IP and see how they helped the country improve its economic situation.

This can only be done by economists, IP scholars, and government institutions working together to produce specialised technical studies. The Jordanian case study has tried to show the importance of being specific as far as possible when studying a particular developing country rather than just giving generalised results about the importance of IP to economic development.

[325] Jordan is ranked 50th overall in the World Economic forum's 2010-2011 Global Information Technology Report's Networked Readiness Index. See Soumitra Dutta and Irene Mia, *Global Information Technology Report 2010-2011* (2011) World Economic Forum <http://www3.weforum.org/docs/WEF_GITR_Report_2011.pdf>.

[326] Nasa'a et al., above n 13, 19.

3.8 Conclusion

The relationship between IP and economic development is best understood by studying to what extent having IP laws would assist any country to increase its local innovation, FDI, domestic innovation, economic growth, and R&D.

It is fair to say that theoretical and empirical studies reach conflicting views about the importance of IP to economic development. Such a result is considered unsatisfactory for any scholar who wants to prove or disprove the argument constantly put forward by developed countries that developing countries can only develop economically if they adopt IP systems similar to those available in developed countries. This sort of result is predictable and not very surprising. This is because IP scholars and economists, who wrote these studies, have various backgrounds and use divergent methodologies. Despite this, it is hoped that there would be, in the future, specific studies with supportive results that will give clearer answers to the relationship between IP and economic development and to what extent introducing IP would accelerate economic development in developing countries.

IP is not important for the economic development of developing countries, and there are more important factors that should be given more precedence. These include market openness; an efficient, reliable government; coherent economic policies; political stability; talented human capital; technical infrastructure; the rule of law; and a qualified judicial system.

Jordan is an interesting country for a case study as it has since 2000 introduced major economic reforms, joined the WTO, and completely restructured its IP systems to be compatible with international standards. However, did this ultimately help the Jordanian economy?

From the statistics mentioned in the study, the contributions of the pharmaceutical and IT sectors to the Jordanian economy have risen since Jordan introduced its major economic reforms. It is submitted that the economic boost that the Jordanian economy has witnessed cannot be attributed to having an IP system but is due to other external factors, including the influx of rich immigrants to Jordan due to the instability of the region, the financial assistance that Jordan has obtained, and the major economic reforms that the country has introduced. Nonetheless, there is no doubt that having a favourable legal environment for investment in Jordan and introducing IP laws assisted many investors, especially those working in creative activities, to make sensible decisions on whether to conduct business and transfer their FDI to Jordan.

It is hoped that this sort of study would encourage IP scholars and economists from developing countries to publish more often in this field, so that the correlation between IP and economic development can be better understood.

Chapter 4
Intellectual Property, Culture, and Development

Culture is the beginning and the end of development.[1]

If one assumes that enacted laws, ideally and magically, ought to work exactly as planned, then culture is indeed an obstacle, since it is the culture which determines the amount of deviance from the norm. But the assumption is, of course, absurd. One might just as easily assume that no law printed on paper ever came to life without some cultural input, in which case, it is the culture which is the sole source of effectiveness of law.[2]

Abstract The previous chapter examined the correlation between IP and the economic development of developing countries. However, it is not sufficient to examine IP and development merely from an economic perspective. It is important to go beyond the economic theory of IP and consider IP from the perspective of culture and social development. While other perspectives may also be relevant, adopting a cultural perspective is an important step towards formulating a broader theory of IP and development. Understanding culture is important in structuring an IP system that takes into consideration local conditions and the interests of developing countries. This chapter examines the relevance of culture and local contexts to the IP debate. Taking the Islamic and Arab world as a case study, it examines the relevance of culture in shaping people's attitudes toward IP, particularly copyright. Culture plays an important role in influencing how people perceive and enforce IP. The chapter calls for adoption of a cultural policy of IP by developing countries to better serve their social and economic development needs and objectives.

[1] Léopold Sédar Senghor (Senegalese poet), *Culture Auction Floor A Match for Development* (2010) European Union <http://ec.europa.eu/europeaid/infopoint/publications/europeaid/documents/177a_culture_auction_floor_booklet_en.pdf>.

[2] Lawrence M. Friedman, 'Legal Culture and Social Development' (1969) 4 (1) *Law and Society Law Review* 29, 41.

R.M. Olwan, *Intellectual Property and Development*,
DOI 10.1007/978-3-642-27907-2_4, © Springer-Verlag Berlin Heidelberg 2013

4.1 Overview

In the foreword to Dr Mohammed El Said's book, *The Development of Intellectual Property Law in the Arab Countries*,[3] Professor Drahos noted that 'the Quran and Islamic teaching more widely offer a differential philosophical resource to construct a culture approach to [IP]'.[4] He suggested that '... [I]ntellectual leaders in those countries would be better to look toward Islamic teachings in order to construct a theory of justice of knowledge that entrenches access rights'.[5]

The basic intention of this chapter is not to 'construct a theory of knowledge based on Islamic teachings' but, rather, to give attention to an important area of research that has, to date, not been accorded much attention by IP scholars studying IP not only from an economic perspective but also, more broadly, from a cultural perspective consistent with the interests of developing countries.[6]

Among the relatively few scholars who have studied the relationship between IP and 'culture' are Professor Madahvi Sunder and Rosemary Coombe. Professor Madahvi argues that "[r]ather than narrowly viewing intellectual property as *incentives-for-creation*, we must understand intellectual property as *social and cultural relations*".[7] Professor Coombe studies IP from an anthropological lens, calling for cultural studies of IP.[8] Several IP scholars have noted that people in developing

---

[3] Mohammed El Said, *The Development of Intellectual Property Law in the Arab Countries* (Edwin Mellen, 2008).

[4] Ibid.

[5] Ibid.

[6] See also, generally, the following research that studies IP beyond an economic perspective:

Ruth L Gana (Okediji), 'The Myth of Development, the Progress of Rights: Human Rights to Intellectual Property and Development' (1996) 18 *Law and Policy Law Journal* 315; Denis Borges Barbosa, Margaret Chon, and Andres Moncayo von Hase, 'Slouching Towards Development in International Intellectual Property' (2007) 1 *Michigan State Law Review* 71, 75 <http://papers.ssrn.com/sol3/papers.cfm?abstract_id=1081366>; Ruth Gana Okediji, 'Copyright and Public Welfare in Global Perspective' (1999-2000) 7 *Indiana Journal of Global Legal Studies* 117, 181; Peter Drahos, *An Alternative Framework for the Global Regulation of Intellectual Property Rights* Centre for Governance of Knowledge and Development Working Paper (October 2005) <https://www.anu.edu.au/fellows/pdrahos/articles/pdfs/2005analternativeframework.pdf>; Margaret Chon, 'Intellectual Property and the Development Divide' (2006) 27 *Cardozo Law Review* 2821, 2835 <http://papers.ssrn.com/sol3/papers.cfm?abstract_id=894162>; Margaret Chon, 'Intellectual Property 'From Below': Copyright and Capability for Education' (2007) 40 *University California Davis Law Review* 803 <http://papers.ssrn.com/sol3/papers.cfm?abstract_id=971294>; Lea Shaver, 'The Right to Science and Culture' (2010) *Wisconsin Law Review* 121, 160 <http://papers.ssrn.com/sol3/papers.cfm?abstract_id=1354788>.

[7] Madhavi Sunder, 'IP3' (2006) 59 *Stanford Law Review* 257, 285; Michael F. Brown, 'Can Culture Be Copyrighted' (1998) 39 (2) *Current Anthropology* 193-222.

[8] Rosemary J. Coombe, *The Culture Life of Intellectual Properties* (Duke University, 1998). See also Peter Krapp, 'The Cultural Life of Intellectual Properties: Authorship, Appropriation, and the Law' (2004) 58 *Cultural Critique*, 198-201 <http://muse.jhu.edu/journals/cultural_critique/v058/58.1krapp.pdf>; Rosemary J. Coombe, 'Legal Claims to Culture in and against the Market: Neoliberalism and the Global Proliferation of Meaningful Different' (2005) *Law, Culture and*

countries do not take IP seriously and are not willing to enforce it because of the cultural differences that exist between them and those in developed countries.[9] Further, they note that IP systems in the West are based on ideologies (individualism, commodification, reward, and consumerism)[10] that do not align with the beliefs of indigenous and local communities in developing countries (collectivism, universal access, and community).[11]

This chapter examines the accuracy of such claims and explores the relationship between IP (copyright) and culture from the perspective of developing countries. It examines how culture interacts with IP and how its protection may assist the social and economic development of these countries.

It is submitted that IP (copyright) laws should not be imposed on developing countries without a proper understanding of their local context and culture. Having IP laws that are inconsistent with the local culture renders them irrational, unfair, and difficult to be understood and enforced. This does not mean that we should always have laws that are in alignment with culture, but the local context needs to be taken into consideration when drafting them. This chapter proposes a bottom-up approach to IP that is more aligned to the interests of developing countries. It shows the importance of understanding cultural and social contexts by scholars studying

---

the Humanities 1, 35-52; Rosemary J. Coombe, 'Tenth Anniversary Symposium: New Direction: Critical Cultural Studies' (1998) 10 *Yale Journal of Law and Humanities* 463; Nicole Aylwin, Rosemary J. Coombe and Anita Chan, *Intellectual Property, Cultural Heritage and Rights-Based Development: Geographical Indication as Vehicles for Sustainable Livelihoods*, York University <http://www.yorku.ca>; Rosemary Coombe, 'Is There a Cultural Studies of Law' in Toby Miller (ed), *A Companion to Cultural Studies* (Blackwell, 2006) <http://www.yorku.ca/rcoombe/publications/Coombe_Cultural_Studies_of_Law.pdf>. See also Susan S Silbey, 'Making a Place for Cultural Analysis of Law' (1992) 17 (1) *Law and Social Inquiry* 39-48 <http://web.mit.edu/anthropology/faculty_staff/silbey/pdf/25cultural.pdf>; Lawrence Liang, 'Piracy, Creativity and Infrastructure', in Ramesh Subramanian and Eddan Katz (eds), *The Global Flow of Information (*New York University, 2011) 54-89; Mario Biagioli, Peter Jaszi and Martha Woodmansee, *Making and Unmaking of Intellectual Property* (ed), (University of Chicago, 2011) 80-132.

[9] Alan Story, Colin Darch and Debora Halbert, *The Copy/South Dossier-Issues in the Economics, Politics, and Ideology of Copyright in the Global South* (2006) The Copy/South Research Group, 61 <http://www.copysouth.org/en/documents/csdossier.pdf>; Daniel Burkitt, 'Copyrighting Culture—the History and Cultural Specificity of the Western Model of Copyright' (2001) 2 (2) *Intellectual Property Quarterly* 146; William P. Alford, *To Steal a Book is an Elegant Offense* (Stanford University, 1995) 9-29.

[10] See for explanation of those terms, Dzenan Sahovic, 'Accessing the Socio-Cultural Viability of Rule of Law Policies in Post-Conflict Societies' in Amanda Perry Kessaris (ed), *Law in the Pursuit of Development: Principle into Practice?* (Routledge-Cavendish, 2010), 245; Patrick H. Hu, 'Mickey Mouse in China: Legal and Cultural Implications in Protecting U.S. Copyrights' (1996) 14 (81) *Boston University International Law Journal* 1196; Nelson C. Lu, 'To Steal a Book Is No Longer Such an Elegant Offence: The Impact of Recent Changes in Taiwanese Copyright Law' (1998) *5 Asian Law Journal* 289; Sanqiang Qu, 'A Dilemma for Feudal China to Launch a Copyright in the Late 19th Century' (2010) 5 (3) *Frontiers of Law in China*, 319, 322.

[11] See explanations of the ideologies of the South, Story, Darch and Halbert, above n 9, 71; Hu, above n 10; Lu, above n 10; Qu, above n 10; Burkitt, above n 9; Brown, above n 7; Alford, above n 9, ch 2.

IP. Furthermore, it calls for proper treatment for traditional knowledge (TK) and traditional cultural expressions (TCEs) in the IP laws of developing countries.

The chapter is divided into four sections. Section 4.2 defines 'culture' and examines its relationship to social development. Section 4.3 looks at the theory of IP (copyright) and culture and examines how prominent IP scholars perceive culture and the need to develop a cultural theory of IP. Section 4.4 examines the influences of culture and legal culture on the protection of IP in developing countries, particularly Arab countries. Finally, Sect. 4.5 discusses the development of a cultural policy in Arab countries.

4.2 Definitions of Culture and Its Relationship with Social and Economic Development

4.2.1 The Meanings of 'Culture'

We live in a globalised world that facilitates the flow of people, information, and ideas across countries.[12] As a result of trade liberalisation, culture barriers are collapsing as people are allowed to share their practices and experiences easily with each other.[13] This section will examine the effect of law on culture[14] and the effect of culture on IP laws and enforcement.

The definition of the term culture is highly controversial among scholars involved in social sciences. Academics give divergent views on its meaning, depending on their field of social science and the methodology of research that they follow.[15] It is fair to say that it is difficult to agree on a specific definition of culture as the term is inherently fluid in its content, evaluation, and delimitation.[16] The Oxford Concise English Dictionary[17] defines culture to mean 'the customs, civilization and achievement of a particular time or people'.[18] The Macquarie

---

[12] Madhavi Sunder, 'Cultural Dissent' (2001) 54 *Stanford Law Review* 495, 498 <http://papers.ssrn.com/sol3/papers.cfm?abstract_id=304619>.

[13] Tormer Broude, *Conflicts and Complementarity in Trade, Cultural Diversity and Intellectual Property Rights* 12 (July 2007) WorldTradeLaw.net <http://www.worldtradelaw.net/articles/broudecomplementarity.pdf>.

[14] World Bank, *Legal Culture and Judicial Reform* <http://siteresources.worldbank.org/INTLAWJUSTINST/Resources/LegalCultureBrief.pdf>.

[15] Ali Acar, *The Concept of Legal Culture with Particular Attention to the Turkish Case* (2 February 2010) Civil Law Network <http://civillawnetwork.wordpress.com/2010/02/02/the-concept-of-legal-culture-with-particular-attention-to-the-turkish-case/>.

[16] Broude, above n 13, 11.

[17] See also Bruce Moore, *The Australian Oxford Dictionary* (Oxford University, 2nd, 2004).

[18] Catherine Soanes and Angus Stevenson (eds), *The Oxford Concise English Dictionary* (Oxford University, 11th ed, 2009). See also Michael King, 'Comparing Legal Cultures in the Quest for Law's Identity' in David Nelken (ed), *Comparing Legal Cultures* (Dartmouth, 1997) 119,121.

Dictionary defines it as 'the sum total of ways of living built up a by a human being, which is transformed from one generation to another'.[19] The Merriam Webster Dictionary defines culture as 'the integrated pattern of human knowledge, belief, and behaviour that depends upon man's capacity for learning and transmitting knowledge to succeeding generations'.[20]

One scholar defines it as 'a set of shared understandings or the complex of beliefs, attitudes, cognitive ideas, values and modes of reasoning and perception which are typical of particular society'.[21] Others define it as 'the set of attitudes, values, beliefs, and behaviours shared by a group of people, communicated from one generation to the next'.[22] It comprises 'artefacts, goods, technical processes, ideas, habits, and values'.[23] Sociologists define culture as 'ideas and values that change relatively quickly and that may vary widely within a single society, neighbourhood, or even family'.[24] According to English anthropologist Edward Tylor, culture is the 'complex whole which includes knowledge, belief, art, law, morals, custom, and any other capabilities and habits acquired by man as a member of society'.[25]

Roger Sutton defines culture as 'the creation and creators of elites'.[26] According to the American anthropologist Clifford Geertz, it is 'the numerous different systems of shared practices and understandings which are inherited and adapted by each generation, and which allow for the communication of meaning within the system'.[27] The UNESCO *Universal Declaration on Cultural Diversity* (2001) defines it as 'the set of distinctive spiritual, material, intellectual and emotional features of society or a social group, which encompasses, in addition to art and literature, lifestyles, ways of living together, value systems, traditions and beliefs'.[28]

---

[19] A. Delbridge et al. (eds), *The Macquarie Dictionary* (Macquarie Library, 5th ed 2009).

[20] The Merriam Webster Dictionary <http://www.merriam-webster.com/dictionary/culture>.

[21] King, above n 18. See also, for the definition of culture, Acar, above n 15.

[22] Kenneth H. Rubin and Melissa Menzer, *Culture and Social Development* (6 January 2010) <http://www.enfant-encyclopedie.com/pages/PDF/Rubin-MenzerANGxp.pdf>.

[23] Ruth Benedict, *Race, Science and Politics* (New York: University, 1959) 13, cited in Sunder, above n 12, 512.

[24] Jay Gabler, *Sociology for Dummies* (John Wiley & Sons 2010) 82. See also Charlene M. Solomon, *Managing Across Culture* (McGraw Hill, 2009) ch 3.

[25] Dennis O'Neil, *Human Culture: What is Culture* (26 May 2006) <http://anthro.palomar.edu/culture/culture_1.htm>.

[26] Roger Scruton, *Culture Counts—Faith and Feeling in a World Besieged* (Encounter Books, 2007) 2.

[27] Clifford Geertz (1973), *The Interpretation of Cultures* (New York: Basic Books), cited in Christopher Ray, 'Culture, Intellectual Property and Territorial Rural Development' (1998) 38 (1) *Sociologia Ruralis* <http://onlinelibrary.wiley.com/doi/10.1111/1467-9523.00060/pdf>.

[28] UNESCO, *Ten Keys to the Convention on the Protection and Promotion of the Diversity of Cultural Expressions* <http://unesdoc.unesco.org/images/0014/001495/149502e.pdf>.

It can also mean the 'totality of the mental and physical reactions and activities that characterize the behaviour of the individuals composing a social group collectively and individually in relation to their natural environment, to other groups, to members of the group itself and of each individual to himself'.[29] It is also 'the whole complex of traditional behaviour which has been developed by the human race and is successively learned by each generation'.[30] The term 'culture' is broad and is often used to mean different things, depending on the context in which it is used. One simple definition of culture refers to 'the total way of life of people'[31] or the social assemblage of practices and beliefs'[32] that humans inherit from their ancestors.

4.2.2 *The Meaning of 'Legal Culture'*

It is important to consider the term 'legal culture' because it is relevant to the discussions that follow. The term legal culture has a specific meaning to legal scholars and lawyers that is not shared by other scholars.

According to Professor Lawrence Freedman,[33] legal culture means 'the ideas, values, attitudes and opinions people in some societies hold with regard to law and the legal system'.[34] Freedman explains the term in a series of questions as follows:

> These are the values and attitudes which bind the system together, and which determine the place of the legal system in the culture of the society as a whole. What kind of training and habits do the lawyers and judges have? What do people think of law? Do groups or individuals willingly go to court? For what purposes do people turn to lawyers; for what purposes do they make use of other officials and intermediaries? Is there respect for law, government tradition? What is the relationship between class structure and the use or non-use of legal institutions? What informal social controls exist in addition to or in place of formal ones? Who prefers which kind of controls, and why? These aspects of law -the legal culture- influence all of the legal system. But they are particularly important as the source of demands made on the system. It is the legal culture, that is, the network of values and

---

[29] Franz Boas, 'The Mind of Primitive Man', (1938), 159, cited in Sunder, above n 12, 512. See also Clifford Geertz, 'Thick Description: Toward an Interpretative Theory of Culture' in *Anthropology in Theory* (Basic Blackwell Publishing Books, 2006) 236.

[30] Margaret Mead, *Cooperation and Competition among Primitive Peoples* (1937), 17, cited in Sunder, above n 12.

[31] Clyde Kluckhohn, 'Mirror for Man', cited in Geertz, above n 29, 236. See also Jane E. Anderson, *Law, Knowledge, Culture–The Production of Indigenous Knowledge in Intellectual Property Law* (Edward Elgar, 2009) 190.

[32] Edward Sapir, 'Language' (1921), 221, cited in Sunder, above n 12, 512; Anderson, above n 31.

[33] Professor Lawrence M. Friedman is founder of the law and society movement in North America; see Lawrence M Friedman <http://www.law.stanford.edu/directory/profile/23/>.

[34] Lawrence M. Friedman, 'Is there a Modern Legal Culture' (1994) 7 (2) *Ratio Juris* 118. See also Lawrence M Friedman, above n 2, 29; Roger Cotterrell, 'The Concept of Legal Culture' in David Nelken (ed), *Comparing Legal Cultures* (Dartmouth, 1997) 15, 34, 35; Acar, above n 15.

> attitudes relating to law, which determines when and why and where people turn to law or government, or turn away.[35]

According to Friedman, there are two kinds of legal culture:[36] the first is internal and 'refers to the attitudes and behaviours of legal professionals' and the second is external and 'refers to those of lay people'.[37] Legal culture can also mean 'those historically conditioned, deeply rooted attitudes about the nature of law and the proper structure and operation of a legal system that are at large in the society'.[38]

Professor Roger Cotterrell criticised the term legal culture proposed by Professor Friedman, arguing that it is 'vague, open-ended',[39] 'lacks rigour',[40] and is without theoretical foundation.[41] Professor Michael King, another legal scholar, has also criticised the term, arguing that:

> If a legal culture can be said to exist, then why not a political culture, a scientific culture, a religious culture and so on? If all of these 'cultures' can be seen to coexist, how are their boundaries defined and what kinds of relationship may they have with one another? The reason that it is impossible to answer these questions in a satisfactory manner and why divisions of the world into different cultures cannot be taken seriously can be found in the inherent indeterminacy of the notion of 'culture'. This, unlike the anti-poetic concept of 'communication system', is simply impossible to define in a manner which would justify the demands of rigorous sociological observation or empirical research.[42]

Legal scholars are not the only scholars who criticise the term legal culture as there are also many other scholars from outside the legal field who oppose it and share similar concerns.[43] It is important to examine whether the law needs to be sensitive to local culture and how law and culture affect and influence each other.

---

[35] Friedman, above n 2, 34.

[36] There are various other types of 'legal culture', including 'modern legal culture', 'Western legal culture', 'emergent legal culture', and 'array of cultures'. See Cotterrell, above n 34, 16.

[37] Acar, above n 15.

[38] J. H. Merryman and D.S. Clark, *Comparative Law: Western European and Latin American Legal Systems* (Bobbs Merrill, 1978) 29, cited in Anthony Ogus, *The Importance of Legal Infrastructure for Regulation (and Deregulation) in Developing Countries*, Centre on Regulation and Competition Working Paper Series No. 65 (June 2004), Centre on Regulation and Competition <http://www.competition-regulation.org.uk/publications/working_papers/WP65.pdf>.

[39] Cotterrell, above n 34, 26.

[40] Ibid 14; Roger Cotterrell, *Law, Culture and Society* (Ashgate Publishing, 2006) 81.

[41] Cotterrell, above n 34.

[42] King, above n 18, 126-127.

[43] Even outside the legal arena, social science scholars have also criticised the concept as follows:

> The concepts of culture and legal culture are of limited explanatory value for sociological studies. As many anthropologists and sociologists have noted, culture is an amorphous term, covering an indeterminate range of phenomena: it is a kind of aggregate, useful to refer in general terms to a broad swath of experiences of impressions of a place or time. But it does not indicate precise variables.

See Cotterrell, above n 40, 8.

Professor Lawrence Friedman argues that it is important to consider culture when considering any particular law. He notes:

> [L]egal systems are not collections of brittle little sticks to be picked up and discarded at the command of the rulers. Some parts of the living law are deeply imbedded in national culture; and to replace major parts of it either means to uproot something quite fundamental, at considerable cost in disruption, or face the possibility that new law will lapse into ineffective life.[44]

Ugo Matteti, a prominent comparative law professor, claimed in his research that Euro–American scholarship was 'lacking in cultural content'.[45] Writers from developing countries have been quick to criticise the imposition of European law on Asian and African peoples. The international law scholar, Professor R. P. Anand from India, argues that:

> '.... [L]aw can win the respect of the new states only if it reflects the attitudes toward law and justice that correspond with the attitudes held by these countries in their own cultural backgrounds'. ... [T]he creation of an effective world law requires a new conceptual synthesis grounded on the basic fact of ideological and cultural pluralism. "No nation will ever accept, nor should it ever accept, any positive legal decision by any legal body that violates its own indigenous living law norms.". ... [L]aw must contain not merely the legal thinking of the west, but also living law norms of Confucian, Buddhist, Hindu, and Muslim countries of Asia and Africa.[46]

Professor Roger Cotterrell encourages legal scholars to study the links between culture and law,[47] but he expresses reservations about the appropriate method to be used to measure how they affect each other.[48] The law must always adapt and change accordingly to developments occurring in the society. Despite the criticism of the term 'legal culture', it is still useful for any legal scholar to know not only what the law is but also how people will perceive and enforce it. Culture is a 'broad, catch-all term'[49] that needs to be defined as concisely as possible to examine how it can influence people's perception and enforcement of the law.

---

[44] Friedman, above n 2, 38.

[45] Ugo Matteti, 'Three Patterns of Law: Taxonomy and Change in the World's Legal Systems' (1997) 45(1) *The American Journal of Comparative Law* 5, 11 <http://www.jstor.org/stable/840958>. See also Benny Simon Tabalujan, *Legal Development in Developing Countries—The Role of Legal Culture,* (2001) SSRN <http://papers.ssrn.com/sol3/papers.cfm?abstract_id=268564>.

[46] See Richard E. Vaughan, 'Defining Terms in the Intellectual Property Protection Debate: Are the North and South Arguing Past Each Other When We Say 'Property'? A Lockean, Confucian, and Islamic Comparison' (1996) 2 *Journal of International and Comparative Law* 307, 335; James W. Peters, 'Toward Negotiating a Remedy to Copyright Piracy in Singapore' (1986) 7 *Northwestern Journal of International Law & Business*, 561, 587; R.P. Anand, *New States and International Law* (Hope India, 2 ed, 2008) 49.

[47] Cotterrell, above n 40, 102, 105.

[48] Cotterrell, above n 34, 25.

[49] World Bank, above n 14.

4.2.3 Culture and Social and Economic Development

Several scholars and commentators have recognised the importance of protecting cultural works in developing countries. As Professor Amartya Sen argues, culture can be a very positive and constructive part in understanding human behaviour.[50] To him, culture counts as it has a major influence on work ethics, responsible conduct, spirited motivation, dynamic management, entrepreneurial initiatives, and willingness to take risks.[51] All these can have implications on social development.

Professor Madhavi Sunder notes that culture plays an important role 'in meeting the UN Millennium Development Goals, which include the eradication of extreme poverty, universal education, gender equality, child and maternal health, combating HIV/AIDS, and achieving environmental sustainability'.[52] To Sarah Radcliffe, it indexes concerns about maintaining cultural diversity,[53] respecting local values, and ending discrimination against the socially marginalised people.[54] Professor Rosemary Coombe notes that culture can also promote social cohesion, prevent rural-to-urban migration, and offer new livelihood opportunities.[55] Furthermore, it can reduce social conflict, spur economic and sustainable development,[56] and preserve biodiversity.[57]

It is noted that culture can play an important role at the individual and the collective levels. For individuals, it contributes to personal fulfilment and promotes freedom in the social, political, and economic spheres of life.[58] On the collective level, it reinforces the 'feeling of belonging and identifying oneself to common

---

[50] Amartya Sen, *How Does Culture Matter*? (March 2002) <http://www.cscs.res.in/dataarchive/textfiles/textfile.2009-08-24.9377468545/file>.

[51] Ibid 4.

[52] Madhavi Sunder, *Beyond Economic Analysis of Intellectual Property: The Need for Social and Cultural Theory* (9 March 2009) University of Chicago Law School <http://uchicagolaw.typepad.com/faculty/2009/03/beyond-economic-analysis-of-intellectual-property-the-need-for-social-and-cultural-theory-madhavi-su.html> ; see also UNESCO, above n 28.

[53] See for explanation of 'culture diversity' and IP, Broude, above n 13, 15.

[54] Sarah Radcliffe, 'Culture in Development Thinking: Geographies, Actors, and Paradigms', 1-8, cited in Rosemary J. Coombe, 'The Expanding Purview of Cultural Properties and their Politics' (2009) 5 *Annual Review of Law and Social Science* 393, 395.

[55] Coombe, above n 54.

[56] Rosemary Coombe, *Cultural Rights and Intellectual Property Debates* (22 Spril 2005) Carnegie Council <http://www.carnegiecouncil.org/resources/publications/dialogue/2_12/section_3/5152.html>.

[57] Rosemary J. Coombe, 'Legal Claims to Culture in and against the Market: Neo-liberalism and the Global Proliferation of Meaningful Difference' (2005) *Law Culture and the Humanities* 35 <http://www.yorku.ca/robarts/projects/global/papers/gcf_legalclaims.pdf>.

[58] Sunder, above n 52; European Commission (EC), *Culture and Social and Human Development* <http://capacity4dev.ec.europa.eu/system/files/briefing_note_cult_en.pdf>; Justin VanFleet, 'Protecting Knowledge' (19 June 2003) Carnegie Council <http://www.carnegiecouncil.org/resources/publications/dialogue/2_09/articles/942.html>.

values'.[59] Culture can also impact on the gross domestic product (GDP) of the country. Several studies support the finding that cultural sectors can have a direct impact on the economic performance of developed and developing countries alike.[60]

4.3 The Theory of IP and Culture

The section will firstly consider how prominent IP scholars use and perceive culture in their scholarship. Its main inquiry will be to what extent IP scholars have developed a theory of IP and culture.

4.3.1 Culture in IP Scholarship

4.3.1.1 The Use of Culture Generally

Professor James Boyle uses the term culture to denote different meanings. It is used generally to mean works that the public can benefit from and build upon. He also uses the term 'maximalist rights culture' to refer to people who believe that more IP would serve and promote better innovation, education, and trade.[61] The term 'cultural environmentalism'[62] is also used and borrowed from the environmental movement[63] to offer a theoretical framework for the 'free culture' movement. The 'free culture' movement is a social movement that promotes the freedom to distribute and modify creative works by using the Internet as an empowering tool. It objects to overly restrictive IP laws (copyright) that hinder creativity and innovation on the Internet. The agenda of the free software movement is overly

[59] European Commission, above n 58.

[60] Ibid.

[61] James Boyle, 'A Manifesto on WIPO and the Future of Intellectual Property' (2004) 9 *Duke Law and Technology Review* 10 <http://scholarship.law.duke.edu/cgi/viewcontent.cgi?article=1113&context=dltr>.

[62] See, for criticism of the concept, David W. Opderbeck, 'Deconstructing Jefferson's Candle: Towards a Critical Realist Approach to Culture Environmentalism and Information Policy' *Seton Hal Public Research Paper* (2008) SSRN, 18-19 <http://papers.ssrn.com/sol3/papers.cfm?abstract_id=1091024>.

[63] James Boyle, 'Cultural Environmentalism?', Columnists (online), 20 February 2006 <http://www.ft.com/cms/s/2/cc8e24ce-a242-11da-9096-0000779e2340.html>; James Boyle, 'A Politics of Intellectual Property: Environmentalism for the Net?' (2007) 47 *Duke Law Journal* 87 <http://www.law.duke.edu/shell/cite.pl?47+Duke+L.+J.+87>. See also Stanford Internet and Society Law Center, *Cultural Environmentalism* <http://cyberlaw.stanford.edu/conferences/cultural/>.

ambitious. This does not come as a surprise as the 'culture manifesto' was drafted by young enthusiasts and supporters who were born in the Internet age.[64]

Professor Lawrence Lessig uses the term 'free culture' to mean granting limited IP to creators and innovators, to allow innovation and creativity to flourish.[65] Professor Yochai Benkler devotes a whole chapter in his book, The Wealth of Networks: How Social Production Transforms Market and Freedom,[66] to 'cultural freedom'. He notes that '[i]nformation, knowledge, and culture are central to human freedom and human development'.[67] Professor Peter K. Yu argues that it is a common misconception to think that copyright piracy is considered as a culture problem.[68] The commentator John Caroll argues that there is no complete understanding of IP in developing countries (Middle East) without an understanding of the cultural and religious forces.[69] Professor Molly Land notes that IP rights are critically important as they can affect both the ability to participate in cultural life, as well as the very essence of people's culture.[70] Professor Rosemary Coombe argues that the international IP system cannot achieve global legitimacy without balancing the rights of people with respect to their culture and heritage.[71] Professor Jack Balkan argues that IP should achieve 'cultural democracy'. Balkan notes that:

> [C]ultural democracy is [mimetic] democracy, the continuous distribution, circulation, and exchange of bits of culture from mind to mind. This vision of culture is not democratic because people are voting on what is in their culture. It is democratic because they get to participate in the meaning-making processes that form and reproduce culture. Moreover, democratic culture is not democratic because people are participating in processes of deliberation about governance, or even public issues. Rather, it is democratic because it

---

[64] The 'free culture' movement is explained further in the 'culture manifesto' that recognises that:

> The mission of the Free Culture movement is to build a bottom-up, participatory structure to society and culture, rather than a top-down, closed, proprietary structure. Through the democratizing power of digital technology and the internet, we can place the tools of creation and distribution, communication and collaboration, teaching and learning into the hands of the common person – and with a truly active, connected, informed citizenry, injustice and oppression will slowly but surely vanish from the earth.

See Freeculture.org, *Free Culture Manifesto* <http://wiki.freeculture.org/Free_Culture_Manifesto>.

[65] Lawrence Lessig, *Free Culture, The Nature and Future of Creativity* (Penguin, 2004).

[66] See Yochai Benkler, *The Wealth of Networks*: How Social Production Transforms Market and Freedom (Yale University, 2006).

[67] Ibid.

[68] Peter K. Yu, 'Four Commons Misconceptions about Copyright Piracy' (2003) 25 *Loyola of Los Angeles International and Comparative Law Review* 127, 131.

[69] John Carroll, 'Intellectual Property Rights in the Middle East: A Cultural Perspective' (2001) 11 (3) *Fordham Intellectual Property and Entertainment Law Journal* 555, 557.

[70] Molly Beutz Land, *Intellectual Property Rights and the Right to Participate in Cultural Life* (November 2008) SSRN <http://papers.ssrn.com/sol3/papers.cfm?abstract_id=1475430>.

[71] Coombe, above n 56.

is participation in the creation and shaping of culture, which is, at the same time, participation in the growth and development of the self.[72]

Based on the above views, IP scholars use the term culture in different contexts to mean different things. The nature of culture is undefined in IP scholarship, and there is 'an apparent assumption that culture is socially construed all the way'.[73] Many scholars believe that culture should be freed from restrictive IP regimes (copyright) that need to be flexible as much as possible. These views will become even clearer in the next section.

4.3.1.2 The Use of Culture in the Context of the Internet

IP scholars have used the term culture more often in the Internet context. There are basically two views in relation to the importance of IP to the development of culture on the Internet. The first view comes from supporters of restrictive laws, which protect creators of IP. Without such laws, culture would suffer on the Internet and creators would refuse to produce cultural works.[74] The second view argues that the way forward for the development of culture on the Internet is not to have restrictive laws as they can hurt and impede producing new cultural works. It comes mostly from academics who are worried about the current development of IP laws on the Internet as they believe that it is restricting freedom and innovation and inhibiting the ability of Internet citizens to be creative.[75] Rick Carnes, a successful American musician, supports the first view, arguing that more IP laws are indeed important for culture to develop over the Internet. He notes that restrictive IP laws 'have resulted in tremendous access to culture and economic growth'.[76] Professor Benkler believes that the Internet empowers and offers unprecedented opportunities for

[72] Jack M. Balkin, 'Digital Speech and Democratic Culture: A Theory of Freedom of Expression for the Information Society' (2004) 79 *New York Law Review* 1, 37 <http://www.yale.edu/lawweb/jbalkin/telecom/digitalspeechanddemocraticculture.pdf>.

[73] Opderbeck, above n 62.

[74] See Rick Carnes, *Copyright is Crucial for Culture: Strong Intellectual-Property Rights Have Helped the Arts and the Economy* Allbusiness <http://www.allbusiness.com>.

[75] Lawrence Lessig, *Free Culture: How Big Media Uses Technology and the Law to Lock Down Culture* (The Penguin, 2004); William W. Fisher, *Promises to Keep Technology, Law, and the Future of Entertainment* (Stanford University, 2004); Peter Biddle et al., *The Darkest and the Future of Content Distributions* (18 November 2002) Bearcave <http://www.bearcave.com/misl/misl_tech/msdrm/darknet.htm>. See also, Niva Elkin-Koren and Neil Weinstock Netanel (eds), (Kluwer, 2002) 79-106; Jessica Litman, *Digital Copyright* (Prometheus Books, 2001) 179. Urs Gasser and Silke Ernst, *From Shakespeare to Dj danger Mouse: A Quick Look at Copyright User Creativity in the Digital Age* (2006), Berkman Center for Internet and Society; Pamela Samuelson, *Preliminary Thoughts in Copyright Reform*, (2007) SSRN, <http://papers.ssrn.com/sol3/papers.cfm?abstract_id=1002676>.

[76] Carnes, above n 74.

the development of culture. Benkler uses the term quite extensively in Internet contexts.[77] He notes:

> The networked information economy.. affects the ability of individuals and groups to participate in the production of the cultural tools and frameworks of human understanding and discourse. It affects the way we, as individuals and members of social and political clusters, interact with culture, and through it with each other. It makes culture more transparent to its inhabitants. It makes the process of cultural production participatory in nature as it allows those who live together within a culture to actively participate in its creation.[78]

Professor Benkler warns that the current copyright regime does not optimise creativity or welfare of the networked information economy but rather extracts unnecessary 'rents'.[79] Professor Madhavi Sunder agrees with Benkler and adds that the Internet is changing the way we look at culture. She believes that culture denotes a non-traditional meaning on the Internet (participatory community)[80] that allows individuals to participate democratically in making culture and reforming social relations.[81] Professor Molly Beutz Land notes that overly restrictive copyright laws and enforcement would undermine the dissemination of cultural goods over digital technologies.[82] Professor Niva Koren argues that copyright law should be adjusted to provide an adequate basis for cultural reaction and social dialogue.[83] Professor Brian Fitzgerald agrees and notes that we need 'to reconsider the fundamentals of copyright law and how it serves the need of life, liberty and economy of the 21st century'.[84] Professor Jessica Litman notes that the Internet has given much more importance to IP laws. She argues that we need to reform these laws because they need to be sensible and fair.[85] The commentator Jessica Reyman notes that copyright law can only change 'when social groups have come to consensus about the role of digital technology in cultural production'.[86] Professor Peter K. Yu recognises that the solution to the problem of copyright law in the

---

77 Professor Yochai Benkler uses the term 'legal culture' and defines it as 'the beliefs of judges, the practices of lawyers'. See Benkler, above n 66, 116.

78 Ibid 275.

79 Ibid 439.

80 Sunder, above n 52.

81 Sunder, above n 7, 257, 312.

82 Land, above n 70.

83 Ibid.

84 Brian Fitzgerald, 'Copyright 2010: The Future of Copyright Law' in Brian Fitzgerald (ed) et al., *Copyright Law, Digital Content and the Internet in the Asia–Pacific* (Sydney University, 2008) 173.

85 Jessica Litman, 'Copyright Noncompliance' (or Why We Can't 'Just Say Yes' to Licensing) (1997) 29 *New York University Journal of International Law and Policy* 237 <http://www-personal.umich.edu/~jdlitman/papers/no.htm>. See also Fisher, above n 75, 199-256; Boyle, above n 61, 10.

86 Jessica Lee Rayman, *The Rhetoric of Intellectual Property: Copyright Law and Regulation of Digital Culture* (Routledge, 2009) 142.

digital era does not rest solely with copyright reform, but there are many other effective, alternative, non-legislative proposals that need to be addressed as well, and they include licensing, technological protection measures (TPMs) and compensation systems.[87]

When reading the scholarship on Internet and culture, it is noted that determining the nature of culture in the network environment becomes a more important matter, which will help in structuring an appropriate IP model that could expand and preserve culture. It is noted that despite all of the research work that has been done in that area, IP scholars have not developed a comprehensive theory of IP and culture in the Internet era.

4.3.1.3 The Need to Develop a Cultural Theory of IP in Developing Countries

In her research 'IP3', Professor Madhavi Sunder argues that we should look at IP not only from an economic perspective but also from a cultural one.[88] She criticises the approach that is currently taken by IP scholars (mostly Americans) who study IP from a purely economic perspective and not from a social and cultural one. According to Professor Sunder, developing a cultural theory of IP can improve our descriptive account of how culture is created,[89] recognise the independence of cultures, and foster opportunities for learning and sharing within and among cultures.[90] The commentator Nicole Aylwin agrees on the importance of developing such a theory, arguing that IP rights historically were committed to balancing the rights of artists, owners, and users of culture rather than focusing on sorting out ownership and property claims.[91] To her, this would give a new life to IP rights and make them attend to the social functions that culture and cultural goods should achieve.[92]

It is noted that Professor Madhavi Sunder has given us a good starting point on the importance of looking to IP beyond an economic point of view, but she has not offered specific solutions on how we could develop a cultural theory of IP and what this theory should include. How can we change traditional mindsets of IP scholars towards embracing a cultural theory of IP? How can international organisations, including WIPO, take into consideration a cultural approach to IP? How can cultural and local contexts be taken into consideration when drafting IP laws? All

---

[87] Yu, above n 68.

[88] Sunder, above n 7, 257, 260. See also Alford, above n 9.

[89] Sunder, above n 52.

[90] Sunder, above n 7, 324, 325.

[91] Nicole Aylwin, *Moving from Property towards Policy: Intellectual Property as Cultural Policy* (16 February 2009) IP Osgoode <http://www.iposgoode.ca/2009/02/moving-from-property-towards-policy/>.

[92] Ibid.

these questions remain to be answered by scholars interested in the culture studies of IP.

It is noted that scholars who are interested in studying IP and development have not given enough attention to culture and how it can influence social and economic development.[93] There should more interest in this particular area of research.[94] This would provide us with a full understanding of the role that IP should have in promoting social and economic development.

4.3.2 *The Role of IP and International Conventions in the Protection of Culture*

Globalisation has had an effect on the commercialisation of culture.[95] Most developing countries do not produce a large number of protected works by their authors and inventors compared to the amount produced in the West, but they have native culture that they can use for their benefit.[96] Businesses turn to culture to 'commodify' it and sell it across international borders. This means that culture and the heritage of developing countries would collide with the global consumer culture.[97] This is, of course, facilitated by the huge demands on culture from all over the world, including from ecotourism, cultural tours, and souvenir artefacts.[98]

IP scholarship is divided on the best way to protect cultural works and whether IP could be used in the first place 'to help indigenous peoples to protect their

[93] Margret Chon, 'Intellectual Property and the Development Divide' (2006) 27 *Cardozo Law Review* 2821, 2835; Margaret Chon 'Intellectual Property 'From Below': Copyright and Capability for Education', (2007) 40 *University California Davis Law Review* 803 <http://papers.ssrn.com/sol3/papers.cfm?abstract_id=971294>. See generally also, Friedman, above n 2, 30.

[94] Professor Roger Cotterrell noted that:

> There is an increased interest by various legal scholars in studying legal rules from broader perspectives including sociological and cultural. As one scholar has noted, 'an adequate understanding of legal ideas - for lawyers, no less than for other citizens - is impossible without adopting a sociological perspective, a perspective informed by social theory.

Cotterrell, above n 40, 3.

[95] See Erica-Irene A. Daes, *The Impact of Globalization on Indigenous Intellectual Property and Cultures* (25 May 2004) Museum of Sydney, Australia <http://www.hreoc.gov.au/about/media/speeches/social_justice/indigenous_ip.html>.

[96] Doris Estelle Long, 'The Impact of Foreign Investment on Indigenous Culture: An Intellectual Property Perspective' (1998) 23 *North Carolina Journal of International Law & Commercial Regulation* 229, 245.

[97] Ibid 279. Marilyn Strathern, 'Social Inventions' in Mario Biagioli, Peter Jaszi and Martha Woodmansee, *Making and Unmaking of Intellectual Property* (ed), (University of Chicago, 2011) 99, 100.

[98] Ibid 230.

cultural innovations'.[99] One group of scholars argue that international IP systems (patent, copyright, trademarks, geographical indications, copyright, and unfair competition) can provide a sufficient protection for it,[100] while others are doubtful of such protection.[101]

The advocates of the 'pure market' solution who argue that IP creates the necessary environment for sufficient cultural production and product variety support the first view.[102] WIPO also supports this view, arguing that the current international IP system is effective enough to protect the culture of developing countries. For that purpose, it has provided extensive consultation assistance to those countries on how best to protect their culture based on international IP systems (mainly copyright, trademarks, and patent laws).

Professor Rosemary Coombe believes that it is important for indigenous people to claim that their culture is protected under IP as this is 'just one part of a larger set of claims relating to self determination'.[103] Professor Doris Estelle Long argues that protecting culture is a matter of survival for developing countries.[104] She adds that having inappropriate IP regimes 'can prevent local indigenous communities from using their knowledge for medical care, agricultural production, or sacred purposes, thus undermining their social, economic, and cultural rights'.[105] It can also serve to countervail oppression and as a source of empowerment.[106]

---

[99] Rosemary Coombe, *In Conversation with Lawrence Liang*, York University <http://www.yorku.ca/rcoombe/publications/interview.pdf>.

[100] See for support, Madhavi Sunder, 'Intellectual Property and Identity Politics: Playing with Fire' (2000) 4 *The Journal of Gender, Race and Justice* 69, 74 <http://papers.ssrn.com/sol3/papers.cfm?abstract_id=279318>; Rosemary J. Coombe, 'Cultural Agencies' in Biagioli, Jaszi and Woodmansee, above n 97, 81, 93.

[101] See, for explanation of those views, especially in relation to copyright, Rosemary J. Coombe, 'Fear, Hope, and Longing for the Future of Authorship and a Revitalized Public Domain in Global Regimes of Intellectual Property' (2003) 52 *DePaul Law Review* 1171 <http://www.yorku.ca/rcoombe/publications/Fear_Hope_and_Longing.pdf>; Sunder, above n 100; J. Janewa OseiTutu, 'A Sui Generis Regime for Traditional Knowledge: The Cultural Divide in Intellectual Property Law', (2010) 12 *Marquette Intellectual Property Law Review*, 145, 184 <http://papers.ssrn.com/sol3/papers.cfm?abstract_id=1574996>; Djims Milius, 'Justifying Intellectual Property in Traditional Knowledge' (2009) 2 *Intellectual Property Quarterly* 185, 200; Marc Perlman, "From 'Folklore' to 'Knowledge' in Global Governance" in Biagioli, Jaszi and Woodmansee, above n 97, 101, 121; Marilyn Strathern, 'Social Inventions' in Biagioli, Jaszi and Woodmansee, above n 97, 97, 102.

[102] Branislav Hazucha, *Intellectual Property and Cultural Diversity: Two Views on the Relationship between Market and Culture*, SSRN 8 <http://papers.ssrn.com/sol3/papers.cfm?abstract_id=1470103>; Coombe, above n 57, 35-52.

[103] Coombe, above n 99.

[104] Long, above n 96, 280.

[105] VanFleet, above n 58.

[106] Sunder, above n 100, 74.

Many indigenous people around the world oppose Western-style IP as a method of protecting their TK and intangible cultural heritage.[107] They point out that there is a danger in making culture property as it 'will affect how culture can be understood and be produced'.[108] It can also limit the right to take part in the cultural life of indigenous people.[109] It is noted that not all aspects of culture (such as, but not limited to, fables, stories, myths, rituals, costumes, folk medicine) can fit with an international IP model[110] since they lack identifiable creators or holders of rights and they are currently considered as part of the public domain.[111] The commentator Daniel Burkitt notes that IP is not appropriate in that regard. According to him:

> Attempts to map Western legal constructs onto indigenous systems of regulation can ignore the ideological and cultural imperatives of non-Western societies. In this part, discussion of copyright and its uneasy induction into Aboriginal culture once again draws attention to the failure of the Western model to recognise authorial creation as a process of transmission and its inability to incorporate (related) notions of collective ownership of intellectual works.[112]

Professor Erica-Irene Daes noted that many developing countries are not happy with the international treaties that protect national folklore (e.g., the *Berne Convention*) because it is nearly impossible for them to enforce such international laws in industrialised countries.[113] Various commentators noted that it would be much more beneficial for developing countries to develop a new model of protection that emphasises mutual aid and cultural sharing over commodification.[114] Although this model could offer many benefits to developing countries, there still exist many

---

[107] Rosemary J. Coombe, *First National Intangible Cultural Heritage Concerns: Prospects for Protection of Traditional Knowledge and Traditional Cultural Expression in International Law* 255 York Univesity <http://www.yorku.ca/rcoombe/publications/RCoombe-BellChapter8.pdf>.

[108] Anderson, above n 31, 188.

[109] Land, above n 70.

[110] In relation to TCEs, it is not clear who is the author of TCEs and whether the protection period in most copyright laws (50 years after the author's death) would be enough to protect TCEs. This question and others might be better addressed under a *sui generis* regime. See also Wend B. Wendland, 'Intellectual Property, Traditional Knowledge and Folklore: WIPO's Exploratory Program' (2002) 33 (4) *International Review of Intellectual Property and Competition Law* 485-504.

[111] Long, above n 96, 269-270. See also Teshager *Worku* Dagne, *Law and Policy of Intellectual Property, Traditional Knowledge and Development: Legally Protecting Creativity and Collective Rights in Traditional Knowledge-Based Agricultural Products through Geographical Indication* (2010) (11) (1) *Estey Centre Journal of International Law and Trade Policy*, SSRN <http://papers.ssrn.com/sol3/papers.cfm?abstract_id=1600293>; Coombe, above n 107.

[112] Burkitt, above n 9, 181.

[113] Erica-Irene A. Daes notes that:

> The real issue is not the problem of defining Indigenous cultural and intellectual property, nor of agreeing that the heritage of Indigenous peoples, should in principle, be protected by law, like other property. The real issue is *enforcement,* where disputes routinely cross international frontiers, and generally involve parties with vastly different levels of power, information and financial resources.

Daes, above n 95.

[114] Story, Darch and Halbert, above n 9, 71.

questions about its characteristics and how it could, if ever, replace the current international IP model.

TK refers to 'knowledge systems, creations, innovations and cultural expressions which: have generally been transmitted from generation to generation that are pertaining to a particular people or its territory'.[115] TCEs or expressions of folklore refer to traditional forms of artistic expression of a people, group, or community.[116] These include music, art, designs, names, signs and symbols, performances, architectural forms, handicrafts, and narratives. The protection of TK and TCEs promotes creativity, enhances cultural diversity, and preserves cultural heritage.[117] It aims to recognise the value of indigenous knowledge and promote respect for such knowledge. In addition, it aims to repress unfair and inequitable uses, safeguard the knowledge, and promote community development.[118]

There are two broad approaches to protecting TK. These are the defensive protection of TK and the positive protection of TK.[119] The first pertains to measures that developing countries can utilise to make sure that their TK is not misappropriated by others without their authorisation. These include, for example, establishing TK digital libraries in developing countries that can be used when their TK has been misappropriated and to take appropriate legal action. The second form of protection is a positive one that empowers TK holders to protect and promote TK, including sui generis systems of protection.[120] WIPO has established, on October 2000, the Intergovernmental Committee on Intellectual Property and Genetic Resources, Traditional Knowledge and Folklore (IGC) to reach an agreement on a text of an international legal instrument (or instruments) that will ensure the effective protection of TK, TCEs, and genetic resources.[121]

---

[115] WIPO, *Traditional Knowledge–Operational Terms and Definitions*, WIPO/GRTKF/IC/3/9 (20 May 2002) <http://www.wipo.int/edocs/mdocs/tk/en/wipo_grtkf_ic_3/wipo_grtkf_ic_3_9.pdf>; WIPO, *Traditional Knowledge, Genetic Resources and Traditional Cultural Expressions/Folklore* <http://www.wipo.int/tk/en/>. See also Ataur Rahman, *Development of an Integrated Traditional Scientific Knowledge Base: A Mechanism for Accessing, Benefit Sharing and Documenting Traditional Knowledge for Sustainable Soci—Economic Development and Poverty Alleviation–* Prepared for Expert Meeting on Systems and National Experiences for Protecting Traditional Knowledge, Innovation and Practices Geneva, Switzerland, 30 October–1 November 2000 (UNCTAD) <http://www.unctad.org/trade_env/docs/rahman.pdf>.

[116] See the definition of Canadaian government, *Copyright Reform Process* <http://www.ic.gc.ca/eic/site/crp-prda.nsf/eng/rp01101.html>.

[117] WIPO, *Traditional Cultural Expressions (folklore)* <http://www.wipo.int/tk/en/folklore/>; Zhiwen Liang, 'Traditional Cultural Expression and the Public Domain under Chinese Copyright Law and Practice' (2010) 4 (6) *European Intellectual Property Law Review* 632, 641; OseiTutu, above n 101, 180.

[118] OseiTutu, above n 101, 183. See also Liang, above n 117, 636.

[119] WIPO, above n 115. See also Rahman, above n 115.

[120] Ibid.

[121] WIPO, *Intergovernmental Committee* <http://www.wipo.int/tk/en/igc/index.html>.

On the international level, there is now an increased interest in global policymaking for cultural works.[122] The *TRIPS Agreement*,[123] the *Convention on Biological Diversity* 1992 (CBD),[124] the *Convention for the Safeguarding of the Intangible Cultural Heritage 2003* (ICH),[125] and the UNESCO Convention on the *Protection and Promotion of the Diversity of Cultural Expressions* 2005 (DCE)[126] are among several international conventions that recognise cultural works[127] of indigenous people and local communities. The CBD is the first convention that recognises TK and encourages member countries to provide some protection to it. There are now 193 countries that have joined the Convention, and the majority of those countries are developing countries and emerging economies.[128] The ICH requires state parties to take appropriate practical measures to safeguard their intangible cultural heritage[129] within their territories[130] and to cooperate with other state members to safeguard the international intangible cultural heritage.[131] The DCE recognises cultural diversity as a rich asset for individuals and societies.[132] It acknowledges the sovereignty of the states to maintain, adopt, and implement policies and measures that they deem appropriate for the protection and promotion of the diversity of cultural expressions on their territory. These three international conventions that recognise the cultural works of indigenous communities do not establish specific enforcement mechanisms that can be used

[122] Coombe, above n 54.

[123] TRIPS do not have specific provisions that deal with 'cultural works' or traditional knowledge (TK), but they are protected under various forms of IP. See Marrakesh Agreement Establishing the World Trade Organization, opened for signature 15 April 1994, 1867 (entered into force 1 January 1995), Annex 1C Trade-Related Aspects of Intellectual Property Rights (*TRIPS*), part 2. See for explanation of TRIPS, Coombe, above n 107.

[124] *Convention on Biological Diversity* (CBD), open for signature 5 June 1992, 1760 UNTS 143 (entered into force on 29 December 1993) <http://www.cbd.int/convention/convention.shtml>; <http://www.cbd.int/>. See for explanation of CBD, Coombe, above n 107.

[125] *Convention on the Safeguarding of Intangible Cultural Heritage* (ICH), open for signature on 17 October 2003, 2368 UNTS 1 (entered into force on April 2006) <http://www.unesco.org/culture/ich/index.php?lg=EN&pg=00022>.

[126] *Convention on the Protection and Promotion of the Diversity of Cultural Expressions* (DCE), open for signature on 20 October 2005, 2440 UNTS 311 (entered into force on 18 March 2007) <http://portal.unesco.org/en/ev.phpURL_ID=31038&URL_DO=DO_TOPIC&URL_SECTION=201.html>.

[127] WIPO, *Intellectual Property and Traditional Cultural Expression/ Folklore* <http://www.wipo.int/freepublications/en/tk/913/wipo_pub_913.pdf>.

[128] See the lists of countries signatory to the *Convention on Biological Diversity* 1992 (CBD) available here <http://www.cbd.int/information/parties.shtml>.

[129] Intangible cultural heritage can include (a) oral traditions and expressions (language); (b) performing arts; (c) social practices, rituals, and festive events; (d) knowledge and practices concerning nature and the universe; (e) traditional craftsmanship. See (ICH), above n 125, art 2 (2).

[130] Ibid art 11.

[131] Ibid art 16.

[132] The DCE, above n 126, preamble.

by developing countries in the event that their TK and TCEs would be imitated and misappropriated by others.

Finally, it is noted that IP can have various effects on culture, either facilitating or hampering it. In the first instance, it can simplify channels of communication by protecting inventions, creative content, brands, titles, etc.[133] In the second instance, it may increase the costs of obtaining knowledge or permit it to be obtained in certain situations or by certain groups.[134]

4.3.3 The Role of Social Norms in the IP Debate

Human behaviours are shaped not by laws alone but by various factors as well, including informal rules, implicit understandings, and social norms.[135] According to Professor Lawrence Lessig, there are four modalities or constraints that regulate behaviour: laws, social norms, market forces, and architecture. These operate together and constitute a sum of forces that guide an individual to behave, or act, in a given way.[136]

It is important to define the meaning of 'social norms' and examine why they are particularly important in the IP context. Social norms are defined as 'the informal social and moral standards of a particular group which regulate the behaviour of individuals within that group'.[137] They are also 'informal social regularities that individuals feel obligated to follow because of an internalized sense of duty or fear of external non-legal sanctions, or both'.[138] They can also refer to the 'patterns of conduct explained by non-legal motivations, including habit, values, culture, and non-legal sanctions such as shaming'.[139]

Social norms can be classified into injunctive and descriptive norms. The first arise from a person's perception of how others (family, peers, voluntary

---

[133] Broude, above n 13, 12.

[134] Ibid.

[135] Mark F. Schultz, *Copynorms: Copyright Law and Social Norms*, Escholarship <http://escholarship.org/uc/item/7c94551s>.

[136] Lawrence Lessig, 'The New Chicago School, Social Norms, Social Meaning, and the Economic Analysis of Law' (1998) 27 (2) *The Journal of Legal Studies* 661, 663.

[137] Geoffrey Neri, 'Sticky Fingers or Sticky Norms? Unauthorized Music Downloading and Unsettled Social Norms' (2005) 93 *Georgetown Law Journal* 733, 746. See also Emmanuelle Fauchart and Eric Von Hippel, *Norms-based Intellectual Property Systems: The Case of French Chefs*, 5 <http://www2.druid.dk/conferences/viewpaper.php?id=242&cf=8>; Robert B. Cialdini et al., 'A Focus Theory of Normative Conduct: A Theoretical Refinement and Revaluation of the Role of Norms in Human Behaviour' (1991) 24 *Advances in Experimental Social Psychology* 201, cited in Schultz, above n 135, 11, 12.

[138] Richard H. McAdams, 'The Origin, Development, and Regulation of Norms' (1997) 96 (2) *Michigan Law Review* 338, 340.

[139] Tai-Heng Cheng, 'Power, Norms, and International Intellectual Property Law' (2006) 28 *Michigan Journal of International Law* 109, 123, 124.

associations, authority figures) believe they should behave.[140] Descriptive norms, however, arise from a person's own perception of how they need to behave.[141] The sources of norms are many, including religion, philosophy, culture, ideology, education, commercial practice, and the consciously and unconsciously imparted values of social, professional, and political groups.[142] IP social norms specify the nature and extent of rights that a group of individuals asserts over IP.[143] This includes their views on IP laws and to what extent they believe that they should be observed and enforced. IP users do not behave identically; some choose to respect the law, while many others prefer not to, depending on their beliefs and opinions about the subject.[144]

IP norms can be various, and they can include, in the context of copyright for example, copying a CD for a friend, selling copied materials, and file sharing through peer-to-peer (P2P) networks such as Gnutella, Kazaa, BitTorrent, and Direct Connect.[145] There are also social norms such as those advocated by Creative Commons, open source community, and norms of librarians.[146] Several scholars have emphasised the importance of respecting laws from within. This means that people should not be pushed to respect IP laws but rather should be encouraged to do so.[147] This obviously can happen in ideal situations but may not be applicable in many countries, including developing countries.[148] Professor Mark Schultz noted that:

---

[140] Cialdini, cited in Schultz, above n 135, 11-12.

[141] Ibid.

[142] Schultz, above n 135, 11.

[143] Fauchart and Hippel, above n 137. See also Matt Haughey, *Lawrence Solum on Copynorms* (15 August 2003) Creative Commons <https://creativecommons.org/weblog/entry/3805>.

[144] Neri, above n 137, 748. See also Yuval Feldman and Janice Nadeler, 'The Law and Norms of File Sharing' (2006) 43 *San Diego Law Review* 577, 591 <http://papers.ssrn.com/sol3/papers.cfm?abstract_id=799364>.

[145] See, for further explanation of social norms, Tim Wu, 'When Code isn't Law' (2003) 89 (4) *Virginia Law Review* 679, 723-726; Jessica Litman, 'Sharing and Stealing' (2004) 27 (1) *Hasting Communication and Entertainment Law Journal*, 1; Cheng, above n 139.

[146] Schultz, above n 135, 38.

[147] As L. Ray Petterson and Stanley W Lindberg noted:

> Most [people] think of law as consisting of written rules in the form of legislative statute or court decisions. But law also grows out of what people actually do, that is, out of custom. Even the most comprehensive legal statute is skeletal in content, while court decisions tend to be fact-intensive (resolving disputes between litigants over specific, concrete issues). Between these two poles, therefore, there is an enormous amount of room for private action, and consistent private action can essentially "make" law by reshaping existing customs (or even creating new ones) that may subsequently be honoured by the courts.

L. Ray Petterson and Stanley W. Lindberg, *The Nature of Copyright* (University Of Georgia, 1991) 9, 10.

[148] Mark F. Schultz, 'Fear and Norms and Rock and Roll: What Jambrands Can Teach US About Persuading People to Obey Copyright Law' (2006) 21 *Berkeley Technological Law Journal* 651, 694.

> The problem of non-compliance with copyright would be so much easier to solve if only people could be convinced to comply voluntarily with copyright law, because they think it is the right thing to do.... People do indeed obey the law because they believe that it is the right thing to do. In fact, numerous studies show that people are more likely to comply with law for normative reasons rather than because of fear of legal consequences. When surveyed, people were most likely to claim they obeyed the law for moral reasons.[149]

The following section will explain the importance of social norms in relation to IP in developing countries, taking the Islamic Arab World as a case study.

4.4 The Cultural Architecture of IP in Developing Countries: A Case Study of the Islamic Arab World

To understand the cultural architecture of IP in a society, it is necessary to understand the legal and non-legal factors that influence people's behaviours in relation to IP. This section examines the influence of culture and legal culture on how people perceive IP, particularly, copyright in the Islamic Arab world.

4.4.1 The Influence of Islam on IP Protection

There have been a number of studies that discuss Islam's views on IP. Most of these studies argue that Islam is not against the protection of IP but, on the contrary, supports it in various ways.[150] It is noted that many scholars and commentators writing about Islam's position on IP do not have a solid understanding of Islamic rules and jurisprudence. Furthermore, they are mostly familiar with the Western

---

[149] Schultz, above n 135, 38.

[150] Heba A. Raslan, 'Shari'a and the Protection of Intellectual Property Rights, the Example of Egypt' (2007) 47 *IDEA: Intellectual Property Law Review* 497; Muhammad Amanullah, 'Author's Copyright: An Islamic Perspective' (2006) *Journal of World Intellectual Property* 301; Amir H. Khoury, 'Ancient and Islamic Sources of Intellectual Property Protection in the Middle East: a Focus on Trademarks' (2003) 43 *IDEA: Intellectual Property Law Review* 151; Ida Madieha bt. Abdul Ghani Azmi, 'The Philosophy of Intellectual Property Rights over Ideas in Cyberspace: a Comparative Analysis between the Western Jurisprudence and the Sharai'ah' (2004) 19 *Arab Law Quarterly* 191; Jonathan A. Claypod, 'Islamic Law and Modern Patent Law' (2007) 14 CASRIP's Newsletter<http://www.law.washington.edu/Casrip/Newsletter/default.aspx?year=2007&article=newsv14i2Claypool>; Silvia Beltrameti, 'The Legality of Intellectual Property Rights under Islamic Law' in Mach, T. et al. (eds), *The Prague Yearbook of Comparative Law* (Prague, 2010) 55-94. <http://www.digitalislam.eu/article.do?articleId=2729>; Qais Ali Mahafzah, Bassem Melhem and Histham A Haloosh, 'The Perspective of Moral and Financial Rights of Intellectual Property in Islam'(2009) 23 *Arab Law Quarterly* 457, 461; Sajjad Chowdhry, *Intellectual Property in Islam* (6 March 2006) Dinar Standard <http://dinarstandard.com/leadership/intellectual-property-rights-in-islam/#>; Mustafa Salman Habib, *Copyrights Under Islamic Law* <http://mshabib.tripod.com/page6.html>.

property models that protect cultural production and not the local systems of protection.[151] This can have an implication on analysing the rules of Sharia and its position on IP protection.

4.4.2 Some Basics about Islam and Culture

Islam is the act of submission to the will of God (Allah).[152] It prescribes a complete lifestyle that a human being should follow in life to receive the blessing of God. This is in accordance with the Quran that says: 'we have not left out anything informative but included it in this Book'[153] and 'we have sent down the Book to thee as exposition of everything and a guidance and a mercy, and glad tidings for those who render perfect obedience'.[154]

There are five necessary interests needed to be fulfilled under Islam. These comprise the deen (religion), nafs (life or self), nasl (family or progeny), mal (property), and aql (intellect or reason).[155] Sharia is the 'path' or 'way' in English. It is basically the law that Muslims should follow in life. As Ibn Al-Qayyim says, '[t]he [Sharia] is founded and based on wisdom and the benefit of people in this life and in the eternal life'.[156] Sharia recognises three different types of rights, the rights reserved to God (worship and prayer), the rights of the society, and the rights of the individual to himself.[157] Sharia requires Muslims to be moral and ethical in their daily activities. This is in accordance with the Quran, which says that '[s]urely

---

[151] Ugo Mattei, 'Three Patterns of Law: Taxonomy and Change in the World's Legal Systems' (1997) 45 *American Journal of Comparative Law*, 39. Anthony Ogus also notes that:

> The main characteristics of the indigenous law are: a strong foundation in a particular, often hierarchical, social structure; family or kinship groups, then individuals as the principle legal "units"; and a high level of discretion in decision markets

See Read, J.S. 'Law in Africa: Back to the Future' in I. Edge (ed), *Comparative Law in Global Perspective*, (Ardsley, N.Y: Transnational, 2000) ch 7, cited in Anthony Ogus, *The Importance of Legal Infrastructure for Regulation (and Deregulation) in Developing Countries* <http://www.competition-regulation.org.uk/publications/working_papers/WP65.pdf>.
above n 2.

[152] Carroll, above n 69, 583.

[153] Quran, Surah al-An'am, (the cattle) 6:38.

[154] Quran, Surah al-Nahal, (the bee) 16:89.

[155] Abdel Hameed M. Bashir, 'Property Rights, Institutions and Economic Development: An Islamic Perspective' (2002) 18 (3) *Hummonics* 75, 82.

[156] Muzammil H. Siddiqi, *Ethics of Shari'ah and Our Responsibility* (28 July 2005) Islamic Champer <http://islamicchamper.wordpress.com/2012/04/30/ethics-of-shariah-and-our-responsibility/>.

[157] Habib, above n 150.

Allah enjoins justice, kindness and doing of good to kith and kin, and forbids all that is shameful, evil, and oppressive. He exhorts you so that you may be mindful'.[158]

The two primarily sources of Sharia are the Quran and Suuna. The Quran is the unalterable word of God that constitutes the final divine revelation to humanity.[159] The Sunna is the pronouncements and deeds of the Prophet Muhammad (PBUH), which are known connectively as Hadith.[160] There are also two secondary sources of Sharia, namely Ijima and Quas: Ijma is the third source and refers to the unanimous agreement or consensus of Islamic scholars[161] on an issue that is not mentioned in the Quran and the Sunna. Qiyas is the last source and is the technique that an Islamic scholar may use to compare two issues where one of them is not mentioned in the primary source.

Under Sharia, Muslims' behaviours can be halal, makrouh, or haram. Halal is allowed under Islamic rules, and haram is forbidden. Muslims will be condemned if they do haram. Muslims have the option of doing makrouh or not doing it. An example of the first one is property obtained properly under Sharia rules. Haram is riba (interest) and adultery. An example of makrouh is smoking. Muslims can smoke, but they will be more blessed by God if they do not.[162] There are four Sunni schools of jurisprudence, and each contributes to a different interpretation of Sharia. These include the Hanafi (Turkey and Pakistan), the Shafi (mainly in Malaysia and Indonesia), the Maliki (North and West Africa), and the Hanbali school (mainly Saudi Arabia).[163]

4.4.3 Perspectives from Pre-Islam and Islam Periods

Before the arrival of Islam (570 A.D.), the Arabic language was mainly a spoken language with an oral literature of elaborate poetry and, to a lesser extent, prose.[164] Writing was not common at this time and memorisation was the most common means of preserving the Arabic literature.[165] Arabs regarded highly poetry and

---

[158] Quran, Surah al-Nahal, (the bee) 16:90.

[159] James J. Heckman, Robert L. Nelson and Lee Cabatingan, *Global Perspective on the Rule of Law* (Routledge, 2009) 89.

[160] Carroll, above n 69, 586.

[161] Beltrameti, above n 150.

[162] Some Muslims believe that smoking is not considered as haram based on the recent Fatwas that regard it as such.

[163] Ibid.

[164] Elsayed M.H Omran, *Islam,* 'The Qur'an and the Arabic Literature' (1988) 14 (1) *Al Serat,* <http://www.al-islam.org/al-serat/arabic.htm>.

[165] Ibid; Akiko Motoyoshi Sumi, *Description in Classical Arabic Poetry: Wasf, Ekphrasis, and Interarts Theory* (Brill Academic, 2003).

poets who were given a role of social prominence in the society.[166] As Ibn Qutayba noted:

> Poetry is the mine of knowledge of the Arabs and the book of their wisdom, the archive of their history and the reservoir of their epic days, the wall that defends their exploits, the impassable trench that preserves their glories, the impartial witness for the day of judgement.[167]

'Intellectual theft' (plagiarism) was common, even before the arrival of Islam. Some poets were copying intentionally and unintentionally from each other without proper attribution. This sort of behaviour was condemned by Arabs as it is considered unethical and against the moral equalities of the poet. There were also prominent poets who were mentioning in their poetry how others had copied them. To make sure that poetry was authentic, Arabs developed seasonal competitions and duels that were held in public (in the market place),[168] without any financial incentive available.[169] The arrival of Islam did not stop 'intellectual theft', and there were few poets who were not called 'thieves'. Muslims have adopted various ways for authentication. The science of the Hadith was introduced to ascertain the correctness of every single statement attributed to the Prophet Muhammad (PBUH).[170] It requires the authentication and verification[171] not only of the content (matn)[172] but also of the people who narrated the hadith (alsnad).[173] Muslim poets travelled across the Islamic empire, reaching Spain to find caliphs, kings, and sultans who valued poetry and gave wealth and high esteem to talented poets.[174] It was a common practice in the Islamic state to pay writers and scholars to write on various topics that were of relevance to the state.[175]

In the Bbasiyah monarchy around the nineth century, Muslims knew a profession known as 'warraq',[176] similar to a publisher nowadays. The author used to

---

[166] See 'Arabic literature.' Encyclopædia Britannica, *Encyclopædia Britannica Online Academic Edition* (Encyclopædia Britannica Inc, 2012) <http://www.britannica.com/EBchecked/topic/31722/Arabic-literature>.

[167] Omran, above n 164. See also Khoury, above n 150, 151.

[168] Khoury, above n 150, 155.

[169] Story, Darch and Halbert, above n 9, 63.

[170] Azami, (1977), cited in Yunus Yusoff, Roslan Ismail and Zainuddin Hassan, 'Adopting Hadith Verification into Digital Evidence Authorisation' (2010) 6 (5) *Journal of Computer Science* 484, 485.

[171] Chowdhry, above n 150; Beltrameti, above n 150.

[172] Yusoff, Ismail and Hassan, above n 170. See also G.H. A. Juynboll, *Encyclopaedia of Canonical Hadith* (Brill, 2007) ch 1.

[173] Yusoff, Ismail and Hassan, above n 170.

[174] See Ammer al-Kaswani, 'Intellectual Property 32' (El Warrak Institute, 1998) 36, cited in Khoury, above n 150, 183.

[175] Khoury, above n 150, 185.

[176] Qaiser Iqbal, *Intellectual Property Rights and Islam*, A Research Paper submitted to the International Management Sciences, International Islamic University (2009), 76 <http://www.iefpedia.com/english/wp-content/uploads/2009/10/Intellectual-Property-Rights-and-Islam.pdf>.

collaborate with warraq to publish his books. Warraq was responsible for selling the books and obtaining royalties for the author.[177] Muhammad Ibn Salam (765–845) was among the first Arabs who wrote a book about 'intellectual theft' in Arabic literature. The book was a first attempt to outline the problem. Jalal al-Din al-Suyuti (1445–1505) also wrote another one entitled *Al-Fariq bayn al-Musannif Wa Al-Sariq*,[178] which explored the difference between the writer and the thief.[179] It is noted that Arabs used various terms in Arabic to refer to 'intellectual theft' or plagiarism, which they divided into various classes.[180]

4.4.4 Current Perspectives on the Protection of IP in Islam

This section examines the views that support the protection of IP under Islam and the views that do not support it. However, a proper examination of such views would not be adequate without a basic understanding of how Islam perceives property and ownership. It is important to note that even within the Islamic perspective of property, there are those scholars who believe that Islam should not support the protection of IP because it is not considered as a real property and, hence, it should not be protected. These views will be explained in Sect. 4.4.4.2.

4.4.4.1 Property and Ownership in Islam

Islam acknowledges the rights of human beings to enjoy their property[181] and, at the same time, clearly and explicitly states that God is the owner of all property. According to Islam, people are merely trustees or custodians of the property (land) for the will of God[182] and they need to follow his orders in that regard. Sharia clearly and explicitly specifies the rights to own, use, and dispose of property.[183] It requires the individual to respect the property of others and the state to establish institutions to protect and enforce those rights for the benefit of the society.

Private property and ownership are such important concepts in the Quran and Hadith.[184] The Quran states, 'and do not eat up your property among yourselves for

---

[177] Ibid.

[178] Amanullah, above n 150, 302.

[179] See also Gustave E. von Grunebaum, 'The Concept of Plagiarism in Arabic Theory' (1994) 3 (4) *Chicago Journals of Near Eastern Studies* 234.

[180] Ibid.

[181] Iqbal, above n 176, 77.

[182] Heckman, Nelson and Cabatingan, above n 159.

[183] Bashir, above n 155, 78.

[184] See Mahafzah, Melhem and Haloosh, above n 150; Chowdhry, above n 150; Beltrameti, above n 150.

vanities',[185] and orders Muslims not to 'knowingly devour a portion of the property of others wrongfully'.[186] The Prophet Muhmmad (PBUH) acknowledged the importance of property in his Farewell Sermon, saying that '[v]erily your blood, your property are as sacred and inviolable as the sacredness of this day of yours, in this month of yours, in this town of yours'.[187] He also said that 'whoever is killed while protecting his property then he is a martyr'[188] and 'whoever is the first to acquire a thing is more entitled to keep it'.[189]

According to Islam, property or 'mal' means 'all that has commercial value, or [t]hose corporeal, usufructuaries and other rights of any kind the exchange of which is customary'.[190] The right of ownership in Islam is not absolute but is limited by certain considerations that a Muslim should observe. These include the prohibition of riba (usury) and giving zakat (sweetening),[191] in accordance with the rules of Sharia.[192] It is also forbidden in Islam to obtain property through improper means such as gharar (speculation), maysar (gambling), bribing, stealing, cheating, or any other means that Islam considers to be haram or forbidden.[193]

Property in Islam is essentially ruled by the concept of 'amar ma'ruf nahi munkar' (do good deeds and prevent ill deeds).[194] This means that property in Islam serves a social function[195] and not an economic one. This perspective is different from the property system in the West and has various implications on how property should be controlled and used in accordance with the Sharia rules of Islam.

4.4.4.2 The Views Supporting the Non-protection of IP in Islam

Islamic scholars who do not support the notion that Islam should protect IP argue that this is because there is no single verse (Aya) in the Quran and Hadith that

---

[185] Quran, Surah al-Baqarah, (the cow) 2:188. See also Muhammad Muhsin Khar and Taqi-id Bin al Hilalti, *Interpretation of the Meanings of the Noble Quran* (2nd ed, Darussalam, 2007).

[186] Ibid.

[187] Hadith, Farwell Sermon of the Prophet, Hadith Library <http://ahadith.co.uk/>.

[188] Hadith, Hadith Library <http://ahadith.co.uk/>.

[189] Hadith, Hadith Library <http://ahadith.co.uk/>; cited in Chowdhry, above n 150.

[190] Ida Madieha bt. Abdul Ghani Azmi, *Intellectual Property Laws and Islam in Malaysia* (PhD Thesis, Queen Mary & Westfield College, London, 2005) 61. See also the definition of Mal in various schools of Islamic jurisprudence, Iqbal, above n 176, 72-73.

[191] Bashir, above n 155, 77.

[192] Every Muslim should give zakat of 2.5% of the wealth in his position for every lunar year. If the wealth amounts to less than the nisab (threshold figure,), then no zakat is payable. This threshold limit is 87.48g (3oz) of gold or its equivalent in cash. See islamic-relief, *Zakat Questions and Answers* <http://www.islamic-relief.com/zakat/zakintro1.htm>.

[193] Bashir, above n 155, 81.

[194] Iqbal, above n 176, 65.

[195] Ibid.

mention it.[196] In addition, they note that according to Islam, knowledge should be disseminated rather than monopolised[197] and controlled by certain people. To those scholars, knowledge is considered to be acts of proximity to, and obedience to God, not acts of business and trade.[198] Muzammil H. Siddiqi, the former President of the Islamic Society of North America replied to their argument as follows:

> It is correct that the knowledge is a common property. But it does not mean that people cannot sell books or own books. It does not mean that people can go and steal books or take over other people's labs and libraries. It means that all people should be free to learn. No one group should have a monopoly on knowledge.[199]

The Quran contains numerous injunctions against the concealment of knowledge (ilm).[200] The Prophet Muhammad (PBUH) said that 'seeking knowledge is obligatory on all Muslims';[201] 'there is no other form of sadaqah that equals knowledge which is being disseminated'[202] and 'the one who conceals knowledge would appear on the Day of Resurrection as reined in a bridle of fire'.[203]

Al-Afghani is one of those scholars who oppose the protection of IP in Islam. He believes that IP will not bring any benefits to society as it involves 'importing a cabalistic legal concept and stamping God's word on it'.[204] Several other prohibitions could also arise if we allow the protection of IP that would conflict with established Islamic rules and doctrines. These include the mashala (interest doctrine), prohibiting myser (gambling), and usury or interest. The latter happens when someone is profiting from IP more than the effort he invested in it; this is considered as a sin and haram in Islam.[205]

The argument forwarded by Islamic scholars who oppose the protection of IP is quite weak. This is because most of the sources that they rely upon to support their views are taken out of their context and are not particularly related to IP.

---

[196] Mahafzah, Melhem and Haloosh, above n 150, 457, 459.

[197] Ibid 463. See also Story, Darch and Halbert, above n 9, 61, 136.

[198] Amanullah, above n 150, 303.

[199] Iqbal, above 176, 54.

[200] Ida Madieha Azmi, 'Basis for the Recognition of Intellectual Property in Light of the Shari'ah' (1996) 27(5) *International Review of Intellectual Property and Competition Law* 649, 652.

[201] Hadith, Ibn 'Adiyy, Al-Bayhaqi & Al-Tabarani, Hadith Library <http://ahadith.co.uk/>.

[202] Hadith, Hadith Library <http://ahadith.co.uk/>.

[203] See the source of the Hadith, Wahbah al-Zuhayli, *Al-Mu'amalat al-Maliyyah al-Mu'asirah*, (Dar al-Fikr al-Mu'asir, 2002) 590, 570, cited in Amanullah, above n 150, 301.

[204] Mahafzah, Melhem and Haloosh, above n 150, 464.

[205] Raslan, above n 150, 528-529.

4.4.4.3 The Views Supporting the Protection of IP in Islam

Islamic scholars supporting the protection of IP in Islam give several justifications to support their views based on primary and secondary resources of Sharia.[206]

The protection of IP can be justified on the basis of work or the doctrine of economic gain through labour (amal).[207] The Quran and the Sunna have mentioned the importance of working on numerous occasions. They also recognise the right of the individual to accumulate wealth in accordance with the Sharia. The Quran says that 'Allah does not allow to be lost the reward of the doers of the good'[208] and 'whoever does a good deed it is for himself, and whoever does evil, it is against the self',[209] and 'wealth ..[is] an ornament of life of the world. But good deeds which endure are better in the Lord's sight for reward and better in respect of hope'.[210] The Prophet Muhammad (PBUH) said that 'every work is rewarded according to the intention behind it'[211] and 'the best work is that which is consistent and continuous'.[212]

The other justification is to consider IP as property. There are many Hadith that order Muslims to respect the property of others. The Prophet Muhammad (PBUH) said that 'a Muslim's property is not permitted (to be taken by others) without his consent'[213] and that 'whoever precedes others in gaining a Halal thing, will be more entitled to own it',[214] and 'a Muslim's wealth is forbidden for others to use without his permission'.[215] The Prophet Muhammad (PBUH) also said that 'whoever is the first to acquire a thing is more entitled to keep it'.[216] Based on that, most Islamic scholars would argue that receiving compensation for writing books is allowed.[217] Professor Mahmoud Akam noted that:

> Copyright is like money, which no one is permitted to take except through [Sharia] based contracts. This is the case whether the owner of these programs is a Muslim or non-Muslim individual, or a Muslim or non-Muslim state....[218]

The Committee of Al-Azhar issued a Fatwa in 2000 and 2001:

---

[206] Beltrameti, above n 150.

[207] Azmi, above n 200, 671.

[208] Quran, Surah Hud, 11: 15. See also, Khar and al Hilalti, above n 185.

[209] Quran, Surah Al-Jathiyah, 45: 15. See also Khar and al Hilalti, above n 185.

[210] Quran, Surah Al-Khaf (the cave), 18: 46. See also, Khar and al Hilalti, above n 185.

[211] Hadith, Hadith Library <http://ahadith.co.uk/>.

[212] Hadith, Hadith Library <http://ahadith.co.uk/>.

[213] Hadith, Hadith Library <http://ahadith.co.uk/>.

[214] Hadith, Hadith Library <http://ahadith.co.uk/>.

[215] Hadith, Hadith Library <http://ahadith.co.uk/>.

[216] Hadith, Hadith Library <http://ahadith.co.uk/>; cited in Chowdhry, above n 150.

[217] Amanullah, above n 150, 304.

[218] Iqbal, above n 176, 57.

> Islam gives the owner the freedom to dispense of the property owned thereby as he wishes; no other person may dispose of, copy, enjoy, use, or attribute such property thereto without the prior consent of the owner, whether for a compensation or not.[219]

The Fiqh Council passed a resolution in the 2001 session, which was held in Kuwait. The resolution was as follows:

> A. Commercial names and addresses are the particular rights of their owners. These rights have monetary value; the Islamic Shariah respects such value, so violating them is forbidden.
>
> B. The copyright, inventions and research work are respected in Sharia.[220]

Religion and Fatwas play an important role in the Arab world.[221] Few governments in the Arab world, such as the Egyptian government, have resorted to religious condemnation of copyright and IP piracy to promote compliance with the law, without dedicating significant financial resources to enforcement.[222]

Another justification for IP protection in Islam is that a Muslim (or a Muslim state) should respect the contract that he concludes with others and honour his agreement. The Quran says 'freedom from obligation from Allah and his messenger toward those of the idolaters with whom ye made a treaty'.[223] 'Allah loveth those who keep their duty',[224] and 'o you who believe, fulfil the contracts'.[225] The Prophet Muhammad (PBUH) said that 'Muslims are bound by their stipulations'[226] and that 'Muslims must abide by their agreements, except an agreement that make haram what is halal or make halal what was haram'.[227] The Prophet Muhammad (PBUH) also said 'keep and pay back the trusts of those who entrust you'.[228]

Using Qayas (analogy), Al-Darini, an Islamic scholar, argues that IP rights are protected in Islam based on public interests or manfa'ah.[229] Manafah are all sorts of things that can bring interests to the people.[230] If there is a particular custom that gives IP creators monetary compensation, then Muslims should follow it,[231]

---

[219] Raslan, above n 150, 501; Iqbal, above n 176, 52.

[220] The Islamic Workplace, *Islam Forbids the Violation of Copyrights and Laws Regarding Intellectual Property* (3 September 2008) <http://makkah.wordpress.com/2008/09/03/islam-forbids-the-violation-copyright-laws-and-laws-regarding-intellectual-property/>.

[221] Raslan, above n 150, 503.

[222] Nagla Rizk and Lea Shaver, *Access to Knowledge in Egypt* (Bloomsbury Academic, 2010) 125.

[223] Quran, Surah Al-Taubah, 9:1. See also Khar and al Hilalti, above n 185.

[224] Quran, Surah Al-Taubah, 9:7. See also Khar and al Hilalti, above n 185.

[225] Quran, Surah Al-Maidah, 5. See also Khar and al Hilalti, above n 185.

[226] Hadith, Hadith Library <http://ahadith.co.uk/>.

[227] Hadith, Hadith Library <http://ahadith.co.uk/>.

[228] Hadith, Hadith Library <http://ahadith.co.uk/>.

[229] Azmi, above n 190, 61.

[230] Azmi, above n 200, 649, 662.

[231] Amanullah, above n 150, 301, 304; Mohammad Al Shalash, 'Rights of Intellectual Property from Legal and Jurisprudence Perspective' (2007) 21 (3) *Al Najah Journal for Research (in Arabic)* 768,795.

provided that it does not contradict Sharia. As Sheikh Muhammad bin Salih Al-Uthanimeen has noted that 'whatever is customary among people should rule'.[232] Other Islamic scholars believe that that reasonableness and Mawat[233] (land) theories give the necessary justifications for the protection of IP under Sharia rules. However, what happens when a Muslim infringes an IP right of another? What sort of punishment should be inflicted on him?

The Quran and the Hadith prohibit dishonesty and unfair trade practices.[234] Some Islamic scholars argue that such violation constitutes a sin (haram) for which one must repent and provide restitution.[235] Others note that this would entail a disciplinary punishment that should be prescribed in accordance with the law.[236] Professor Fadel Al-Milani of the Council of Imam Al-Khaw'i's institution in London answered:

> In spite of the fact that the description of theft in [Sharia] does not apply to the question in hand, yet one's copying others' thoughts and attributing them to oneself is a clear dishonesty, and flagrant breaching of others' rights to their intellectual properties... Hence, I believe that if the plagiarizer benefits from stealing others' thoughts and attributing them to himself, he is to compensate the original authors for his wronging them in this respect.[237]

Sheikh Muhammad Hussein Fadl Allah, Shiite jurist,[238] went further in clearly saying that plagiarising is a crime.[239] Professor Shaykh Muhammad Bazmul suggests that blessings of God do not flow from such action of theft.[240] It is noted that proponents of Islamic protection of IP have the stronger arguments to support their views. The many Fatwas issued that do not allow Muslims to violate IP rights and consider such behaviour as haram or constituting a sin further support their views.

---

[232] See *Islam Awakening* <http://forums.islamicawakening.com/f16/pirated-software-7965/>.

[233] Raslan, above n 150.

[234] The Quran says:

> Woe to those who use measure and measure, who when receiving take for themselves a full measure, but when measuring or weighting for others give less' and 'Plead to those on behalf of those that are unfaithful to themselves. Surely Allah loves not those who are perfidious and persistent sinners.
>
> (Quran, 83:1) See also Khar and al Hilalti, above n 185.

The prophet also said that:

> When you come to a land where they give full measure and full weight, stay there. When you come to a land where they shorten the measure and weight, then do not stay there very long.

Hadith, Hadith Library <http://ahadith.co.uk/>.

[235] Mahafzah, Melhem and Haloosh, above n 150, 461.

[236] Iqbal, above n 176, 52.

[237] Iqbal, above n 176, 54.

[238] Ibid 52.

[239] Ibid.

[240] Mahafzah, Melhem and Haloosh, above n 150, 462.

4.4.4.4 Concluding Remarks on Islamic Influence on IP and Issues for Future Research

Islamic Sharia was aware of the importance of scientific honesty but did not indulge in codifying any rules[241] that require Muslims to respect IP. The Islamic notion of IP is different from the Western notion. Islam does not recognise IP as an individual right but, more importantly, as a public interest one. Islamic authorship is not about pure commercial reward to the person who is responsible for the realisation or development of useful ideas but responsibility to the community and society.[242] It allows the financial compensation of the creator only equal to his efforts but gives much more importance to the community and the society rather than the individual. As Ida Madieha Azmi rightly noted:

> [I]t would seem that the notion of authorship cannot be divorced from its function as an institution of culture. Islam, as advanced earlier, necessitates that copyright should not be seen *purely* as a market mechanism, free from any ethical aspect. The notion provides many challenges to some of the fundamental presuppositions underlying copyright as understood in modern perceptions and more importantly to the way information is viewed as a mere 'commodity'.[243]

It is noted that there is a need to do further research on how Arabs perceive 'intellectual thefts' or plagiarism before and after the arrival of Islam. Arabic heritage is full of literature that shows that Arabs developed various systems to authenticate and protect their creative works.[244] This kind research would be of interest to international IP scholars since it would offer a non-Western perspective on IP protection. It is clear that religion (Islam) can affect the way people perceive and act within an IP system. The question still remains whether IP laws should be mindful of the cultural context in which they sit.

4.5 The Influence of Culture on IP Protection in the Islamic Arab World

This section examines how culture shapes Arabs' attitudes toward IP, particularly copyright. Many Arab countries now have IP laws that protect authors and creators of creative works. These laws were introduced recently as developed countries

[241] Siddiqi, above n 156.

[242] Azmi, above n 190, 131.

[243] Ida Madieha Azmi, 'Authorship and Islam in Malaysia: Issues in Perspective' (1997) 28 (5) *International Review of Intellectual Property and Competition Law* 671, 677.

[244] Grunebaum, above n 179, 234.

pressurised those countries to join the WTO and to be part of the international trading system. Despite introducing such laws, many commentators are sceptical that they will be effective[245] in practice. This is because Western ideals of free market, individual rights, and economic gains[246] are not rooted in Arabic culture.

4.5.1 Some Basics about Arabs and Culture

It is useful in this context to identify the most basic beliefs and values of Arabs. It is these beliefs and values[247] that shape the behaviour of the people. 'The Arab region comprises a unique socio-cultural heritage that is the outcome of a long and rich tribal history.'[248] The Arab society is conservative and has a high regard for traditions and customs.[249] It is generally influenced by the rules of Sharia as Islam is the predominant religion of the Arab world.

Arabs give a high importance to family and friendship. For an Arab, good manners require that one never openly refuses a request from a friend.[250] Generally, people in the Arab world are very close and they grow up helping each other.[251] They live in a society that demands they share things with each other.

4.5.2 The Influence of Arabic Culture and Social Norms on IP Protection

History, economic situations and social factors can influence the protection of IP in a certain society. Historian Peter Mansfield has suggested that Arabs nowadays are experiencing an 'immobilism' that has followed a loss of cultural vitality,[252] which

---

[245] Vaughan, above n 46, 335.

[246] Ibid. See also Joost Smiers, *Why Impose Copyright on Non-Western Countries?* (9 October 2009) The Copysouth Research Group <http://www.copysouth.org/portal/node/37>; Danny Lam, Jeremy T. Paltiel and John H. Shannon, 'The Confucian Entrepreneur? Chinese Culture, Industrial Organization and Intellectual Property Piracy in Taiwan' (1994) 20 (4) *Asian Affairs* 205.

[247] Margaret K. Nydell, *Understanding Arabs* (Intercultural, 2006) ch 1.

[248] Nagla Rizk, 'Arab Musiconomics, Culture, Copyright, and the Commons' in Neil Weinstock Netanel, *The Development Agenda: Global Intellectual Property and Developing Countries* (Oxford University, 2009) 341, 349.

[249] Nydell, above n 247.

[250] Ibid ch 2.

[251] Al Jaimat, *Plagiarism from a Cross-Cultural Perspective* (4 June 2009) <http://www.al-jamiat.com/college-lifestyle/plagiarism-crosscultural-perspective/>.

[252] Peter Mansfield, *The Arabs* (Penguin, 3rd, 1992) 532 (quoting Howard M. Sachar, 1936-1954, 608-09 (1974)); Carroll, above n 69, 589.

is combined with a historically imbued resistance to external influences and, particularly, Westerners.[253] Mansfield argued that:

> The impact of the Western invasion and colonization of the Arab world was far-reaching. It stirred the Arabs profoundly after a long period of political and social stagnation and created many external changes. But the dynamic for progress or modernization had to come from within Arab society, and this is as true today as it ever was.[254]

In the eyes of many Arabs, the West is perceived to have emasculated the Arab world since the times of the Crusades through colonialism, contributing to the decline of Muslims.[255] Muslims are no longer following what their religion says but doing what the West wants them to do.

In relation to IP, some Arabs may consider it to be 'a new tool of the West to monopolise the economic system of predominantly Muslim countries'. Arabs consider IP piracy and counterfeiting as good things as they would allow 'extracting revenge from the West's relentless commercial conquest' of the Arab World.[256] As the commentator John Carroll has explained that:

> However, Western intellectual property rights are, to a great extent, presently unrecognized in the Middle East. The reluctance to enforce intellectual property law stems from at least two interconnected frames of reference. First, the West is perceived to have emasculated the Middle East since the times of the crusades through colonialism until now, contributing to the decline of Islam at each turn. Second, Western culture is generally thought to be immoral and corrupt; so, if Middle Eastern governments were to acknowledge that Westerners were entitled to enforceable intellectual property rights, they would be giving governmental, and thus religious, sanction to sacrilege. Islam strongly animates political and commercial life throughout the Middle East to a degree that Westerners have difficulty appreciating.[257]

Economic situations can also influence people's behaviours toward the protection of IP. IP pirates in the Arab world argue that they are benefiting their society since they often need products for a suitable price, while consumers believe that it is legitimate to pirate copyrighted materials since most people cannot afford paying high prices to obtain those works.[258] Many Muslims are reluctant to enforce IP rights simply because they think that the concept of IP stems from the West and not from their religious sources.[259]

Social norms are particularly important in understanding why people enforce or fail to enforce IP rights[260] in the Arab world. There are very limited legal studies that discuss social norms and custom (urf) in the Arab world, and this is certainly

[253] Carroll, above n 69, 589-590.

[254] Mansfield, above n 252, 532.

[255] Carroll, above n 69, 596.

[256] Beltrameti, above n 150.

[257] Carroll, above n 69, 596.

[258] Raslan, above n 150, 503-504.

[259] Beltrameti, above n 150.

[260] Litman, above n 85.

applicable to IP research. Students studying law in the Arab world have to take introductory courses on custom (urf)[261] and its relationship to the law. Unfortunately, legal scholars in the Arab world do not teach social norms in IP courses in law schools. It is critically important to develop comprehensive IP courses in the Arab world that not only teach the law but also examine the relevance of social norms to the IP debate. This would give students a better understanding of how people perceive and comply with IP.

There are various customs and practices in the Arab world that might influence people's attitudes toward IP. For example, the 'gift culture' in the Arab world would mean that it is not socially acceptable to refuse to lend your friend a CD or a DVD. It is also unacceptable to say 'no' to a family member or a friend who wants to copy a book that is bought.[262]

4.5.3 A Case Study of the Music Industry in the Arab World

What is special about Arabic music? Why is studying it important when examining the influence of culture on IP, particularly copyright, in the Arab world? The music industry works differently in the Arab world to other parts of the world, and many forms of Arabic music cannot fit with the Western notion of copyright.

Raï music is a popular kind of music in the Arab world that sometimes does not have any true 'author' in the Western, copyright sense of the term. This is because singers borrow songs or choruses from each other.[263] Even if one Rai singer believes that the other singer has copied parts of his songs, he would not take any action against him. It is further noted that many Rai singers produce music at their own expense and on their own initiative.[264]

Arabs are proud of their music and consider many of the Arabic songs to be 'common heritage', even if the copyright term of the work has not expired. That would justify why many Arabs are against IP as they would restrict their freedom to

---

[261] Compare social norms with custom or urf in (Arabic), which is defined as 'recurring practices, which are acceptable to people of sound nature'. There are two main types of urfs, general or public and private. The first is prevalent everywhere, and the second is prevalent in a particular locality, profession, or trade. Two conditions must be met to qualify as an urf, and these include the following: i) it must represent a common and recurrent phenomenon; and ii) it must also be in existence at the time a transaction is concluded. See Kamali, Muhammad Hashim, *Principles of Islamic Jurisprudence* (Islamic Texts Society, 1991) 286, cited in Azmi, above n 190, 68.

[262] Rizk and Shaver, above n 222, 122; Anas Tawileh, *A Study of the Music Industry in the Arab World* (5 April 2008) Creative Commons <http://archive.icommons.org/articles/a-study-of-the-music-industry-in-the-arab-world>.

[263] Bouziane Daoudi and Hadj Miliani, *L'Aventure du Raï: Musique et Société* (Paris: Éditions du Seuil, 1996), 126-29 cited in Story, Darch and Halbert, above n 9, 59.

[264] Story, Darch and Halbert, above n 9, 63.

listen to and share with each other the music they love.[265] For example, the songs of Marcel Khalifah and Oum Khaltoum are considered as a 'common heritage' as they are sung by nearly everybody.[266] To be popular in the Arab world is more important than money for the artist and could provide the necessary stimulation to keep him producing creative work.[267]

Professor Nagla Rizk from American University in Cairo conducted an excellent study on the Arabic music industry. The research has revealed interesting insights that explain the co-existence of a strong 'gift culture' in the Arab world.[268] Many Arab artists would tolerate the downloading of their music freely on the Internet. This would serve as an excellent marketing tool and increase the popularity of the artist.[269] The artist would capitalise on his popularity by conducting live performances and wedding parties that can generate high revenues (up to $37,000 for a single performance or a party).[270] Professor Rizik explains that:

> Artists' main earnings come from the live scene. Under the prevailing differentials in artists' earnings between the live performance and the copyrighted recording, and in light of a weak enforcement of the copyright law and the weak institutional structures, artists use the copyrighted item as a reputation device, while the main benefit is achieved through the live performance. Music lovers are also comfortable with accessing music through this group experience within social gatherings and irrespective of copyright.[271]

As for collective societies, they are not present in the Arab world, as they are known in Europe and Western countries. Arab countries do not have collecting societies that collect royalties on behalf of artists. Lebanon is one of the few countries that have a collecting society called the Societe des Auteurs, Compositeurs et Editeurs (SACEM).[272] SACEM found that it was impossible to collect royalties every time music was played in Lebanon and instead decided to charge television, radio stations, and restaurants a fixed amount of money each year for the right to broadcast and play recorded music.[273]

---

265 Azmi, above n 200, 651.

266 Story, Darch and Halbert, above n 9, 62, 63.

267 Ibid.

268 Tawileh, above n 262.

269 Rizk, above n 248, 356.

270 Tawileh, above n 262; Rizk, above n 248, 352, 365.

271 Rizk and Shaver, above n 222, 110.

272 Story, Darch and Halbert, above n 9, 63.

273 Ibid.

4.5.4 The Influence of Legal Culture on IP Protection in the Arab World

This subsection examines the influence of legal culture on people's attitudes toward IP in the Arab world and particularly how lawyers and the judicial system in the Arab world deal with IP.

Although Arab countries have amended many of their old IP laws or introduced new ones, most fail to enforce them, and therefore they largely remain ineffective in practice. Many believe that these laws have been introduced just for the purpose of making the American government, foreign corporations, and investors happy that there is a sort of IP protection in the Arab world. This obviously was not enough for the US which developed the Special 301 Watch List (many Arab countries were on the priority watch list) and has signed with other developed countries (Japan, Australia, and Canada) an international enforcement agreement entitled the *Anti-Counterfeiting Trade Agreement* (ACTA).[274]

There are limited numbers of lawyers specialising in IP in the Arab world, but the number of those lawyers is increasing. This is because many Arab students are taking postgraduate degrees overseas, specialising in IP and Internet law. It is important to note that these students who take IP programs overseas are influenced by the Western IP methods of thinking that generally does not give proper attention to the problems of IP in relation to developing countries and how these countries need to be revised and adapted to favour their particular needs and interests. Local firms, which specialise in IP in the Arab world, are limited, and most of them would prefer to work in a variety of other areas of law in order to be successful in business. Generally speaking, many Arabs are not used to consulting lawyers and paying them money. This is certainly applicable in poor countries in the Arab world but not fully true in the Gulf countries (Kuwait, Oman, Bahrain, Saudi Arabia, Qatar, and the United Arab Emirates), where there exist many international organisations that constantly request legal advice from international and local law firms.

The Arabic judicial system is still underdeveloped as it suffers from poorly trained judges and staff, overcrowded dockets, antiquated facilities, and inadequate technology.[275] As explained by two prominent Arab lawyers:

> One of the central reasons for the failure of Arab economies to properly integrate into this new economic climate is the primitiveness of the legal system and weakness of judicial process in many parts of the Arab world. In many parts of the Arab world, outdated state economic institutions, overstaffed and meddlesome government bureaucracies, antiquated legal processes and a slow, underpaid, overworked and uninformed judiciary all stifle and

---

[274] See ch 2.

[275] Sharif Al Zu'bi and Zeid D. Hanania, *Legal and Judicial Reform in the Arab World* Arab, World Economic Forum United Nations Development Programme (UNDP), Regional Bureau for Arab States (RBAS) <http://www.pogar.org/publications/other/gen/04e-abc-legal-reform.pdf>.

stunt economic development and contribute to keeping Arab countries at the bottom of the global economic cellar.[276]

They further note that:

The central problem in many Arab societies is that the legal process is overshadowed by a parochial system of patronage whereby unofficial relationships such as family connections, personal ties with the state or elites replace the formal authority of the law in commercial relationships.[277]

In terms of IP cases, there are few judges who are knowledgeable in IP, and unfortunately, there are no specialised IP courts. There were various initiatives taken in a few Arab countries to develop specialised IP courts, but this proved to be difficult and costly. Many of the judgements that were issued in the Arab world in copyright dealt with publications' contracts, authors' remunerations, and other basic matters. All these peculiarities that characterise the judicial system in Arab countries ultimately influence, in one way or another, the protection of IP in the Arab world.

4.6 Developing a Cultural IP Policy in Arab Countries

A cultural policy for IP should be discussed on two levels, the national level and the international level. The question is what should be included in that policy if a developing country or an Arab country decides to develop one?

The national cultural IP policy should give proper attention to the laws that protect TK and TCEs of indigenous communities in Arab countries.[278] Having appropriate IP and sui generis systems is important for the social and economic development of the countries that have natural TK resources.[279]

IP laws and sui generis systems should be flexible enough to aid development, promote local creativity and innovation, and preserve the local culture of indigenous communities. They also need to include appropriate limitations and exceptions[280] that guarantee the existence of a 'vibrant and diverse public domain'[281] that allows indigenous communities to flourish and continue to develop. IP laws should be sensitive to the social and cultural contexts.

For Arabic countries that have strong Islam influences, the scope of IP laws should be determined in accordance with Sharia's public policy rules and

[276] Ibid.

[277] Ibid.

[278] Coombe, above n 56.

[279] Feifei Jiang, 'The Problems with Patents' (2005) *Harvard Internationl Review* 30, 33.

[280] Land, above n 70; Coombe, above n 56.

[281] Land, above n 70.

morality.[282] This would make IP laws more appealing to the citizens and better enforced in Arab and Islamic countries. This can be done by including appropriate limitations and exceptions for social and cultural purposes in the copyright laws of Arab countries. An example of such law is art 52 (1) (i and za) of the Indian *Copyright Law Act, 1957, as amended.*[283] Article 52 provides that:

> (1) The following acts shall not constitute an infringement of copyright, namely:
>
> (I) the performance of a literary, dramatic or musical work by an amateur club or society, if the performance is given to a non-paying audience, or for the benefit of a religious institution;
>
> (za) the performance of a literary, dramatic or musical work or the communication to the public of such work or of a sound recording in the course of any *bona fide* religious ceremony or an official ceremony held by the Central Government or the State Government or any local authority.

Unfortunately, in many Arab countries, TCEs and TK are not given the importance they deserve compared to other countries in the world.[284] Jordan is an Arab country that does not give proper IP protection to TK and TCEs. Article 7 of the *Copyright Law No 22 for 1999* (the *Copyright Law*), as amended, in Jordan[285] provides as follows:

> The protection stipulated in this law shall not encompass the following works unless the collections of these works were distinguished by a personal effort involving innovation or arrangement.
>
> C. The works that reverted to the public domain. For the purpose of this article folklore shall be considered in the public domain with the Minister exercising the copyrights of these works against distortion, misrepresentation or damage to cultural interests.

---

[282] Azmi, above n 243, 687-698; Raslan, above n 150, 559; Beltrameti, above n 150.

[283] *The Copyright Act of 1957 (Law* No. 14 (No. 49)), as amended. See India, WIPO, <http://www.wipo.int/wipolex/en/text.jsp?file_id=128098>.

[284] There are some developing countries that have given a particular attention to these laws. These laws include the following: *Provisional Measure No 2. 186-16 on Access to Genetics Recourses and Traditional Knowledge* 2001 (Brazil); *The Law of Kyrgyz Republic on the Protection of Traditional Knowledge No 116, 2007* (The Kyrgyz Republic), *The Protection and Promotion of Traditional Thai Medicine Act B.E 2542* (1999) (Thailand); *Indigenous Peoples Rights Act 1997* (Philippines); *Law Introducing a Protection Regime for the Collective Knowledge of Indigenous People Derived from Biological Resource, N 27811, 2002* (Peru); The African Model Legislation for the Protection of Rights of Local Communities, Framers and Breeders, and for the Regulation of Access to Biological Recourses 2000 (Organisation of African Unity). See also WIPO, *Comparative Summary of Existing National Sui Generis Measures and Laws for the Protection of Traditional Knowledge* <http://www.wipo.int/export/sites/www/tk/en/laws/pdf/grtkf_ic_5_inf_4_annex.pdf>.

[285] *The Copyright Law No. 22 of 1992*, Official Gazette No. 3821, 16 April 1992 (*Copyright Law*) <http://www.lob.gov.jo/ui/laws/search_no.jsp?no=22&year=1992>. See also Office of the High Commisioner for Human Rights (OHCHR), *Review of Developments Pertaining to the Promotion and Protection of the Rights of Indigenous Peoplesnnnnnnnnnnnn Including their Human Rights and Fundamental Freedoms*, <HTTP://WWW2.OHCHR.ORG/ENGLISH/ISSUES/INDIGENOUS/DOCS/WGIP23/CRP3.DOC>.

Article 60 of the same law provides:

The Council of Ministers shall issue the regulations necessary to implement the law.

Unfortunately, The Jordanian Minister of Culture has not issued any regulation that explains art 7 of the *Copyright Law*. Article 7 of the *Copyright Law* in Jordan is the only provision that mentions TCEs and folklore.[286] It is criticised for the following reasons.

Firstly, it is submitted that it is unsatisfactory to include only one provision in the *Copyright Law* in Jordan that deals with folklore and TCEs because they are considered as national cultural heritage that should be given much more importance by any legislator in developing countries. Secondly, the *Copyright Law* in Jordan is criticised for not providing a definition of folklore or at least proving a non-exhaustive definition of the term folklore. Does folklore include only verbal expressions and musical expressions? What about physical expressions and tangible expressions? Copyright systems that are based on the continental European system do not tend to give definitions. The definition of the term folklore is important for having a clear effective law that can protect the rights of indigenous communities. Thirdly, the Jordanian legislator took an unusual approach to the protection of folklore and TCEs when it considered that they are in the public domain. It is not clear why the Jordanian legislator has protected folklore under copyright law when it determined that it is in the public domain. This is surprising as there is no protection offered for works that are available in the public domain. The Jordanian approach is criticised as it turns folklore into a freely available resource for commercial utilisation by foreign corporations located either in Jordan or overseas. Fourthly, the law does not recognise the importance of moral rights (right of integrity and attribution) in relation to TCEs.[287] It is critically important for local communities to be given moral rights in relation to their TCEs to prevent unauthorised and derogatory treatment of their works.[288] This would allow these communities to take legal action when necessary.[289] While the law recognised that the Minister of Culture in Jordan can protect what some might see as the substance of moral rights. It is hard to imagine how art 7(C) could be implemented once the folklore has become public domain. Finally, it is noted that Jordan has not issued

[286] See also USAID, *Update on Compliance with Intellectual Property Rights in Jordan* (2007) <http://pdf.usaid.gov/pdf_docs/PNADM871.pdf>.

[287] There are countries such as Australia that have developed proposals on indigenous communal moral rights (ICMR). See New South Wales Government, *Indigenous Communal Moral Rights* (ICMR) <http://ab-ed.boardofstudies.nsw.edu.au/go/aboriginal-art/protecting-australian-indigenous-art/background-information/proposals-for-change/indigenous-communal-moral-rights-icmr>.

[288] Ibid. See also Jean Raymond Homere, 'Intellectual Property Rights Can Help Stimulate the Economic Development of Least Developed Countries' (2004) 27 (2) *Columbia Jounral of Law and Arts* 277, 297.

[289] Ibid.

any other law that deals with TK and TCEs.[290] This approach is unsatisfactory because it does not give the required protection to Jordanian local industries such as Jordanian crafts and arts (hand-made traditional women dresses). Having specific law that protect these local industries does not only preserve and protect indigenous knowledge but also supports their innovation and future development.[291]

In addition to having appropriate laws that protect TK and TCEs, it is also important for IP offices in Arab countries to help local communities by giving them proper legal advice on the best way to protect their rights from being misappropriated and imitated by others. They also need to establish TK knowledge Digital Libraries (such as those available in emerging economies in China and India)[292] to help determine whether TK can be protected through the patent system. These digital libraries could also be valuable resources for researchers and anthologists contributing to the development of indigenous communities and the economy.

The national cultural policy could not work without being combined with other related policies and measures that are implemented in the country. As Professor Branislav Hazucha explains:

> [I]t is essential that the institutions responsible for cultural affairs and intellectual property policies understand that the only way to achieve efficient protection and promotion of cultural diversity is to strike an appropriate and adequate balance between individual cultural policies i.e. intellectual property, and other cultural policies.[293]

The governments of Arab countries should, in addition to having properly structured IP laws, employ other measures outside the legal arena, such as grants,[294] subsidies, taxes, or screen quotas[295] to support indigenous people and the development of their local communities. There is also a need to strengthen the communication between TK holders, the private sector, governments, NGOs, and other stakeholders to better serve the interests of their local communities.[296] Having all these groups work together would provide better support for indigenous people and their communities contributing to their social development.

On the international level, Arab countries that wish to develop an international cultural policy should consider acceding to the international conventions that promote the culture of indigenous people, such as the CBD. This should be done only after a careful consideration of the costs and benefits of joining these international conventions. Arab countries must also be active participants in international

---

290 Jordan has only issued the *Urban Heritage Law No 5 of 2005*. See the *Urban Heritage Law No 5 of 2005*, Official Gazette No. 4702, 31 March 2005 <http://www.lob.gov.jo/ui/laws/search_no.jsp?no=5&year=2005>.

291 Milius, above n 101, 187.

292 OseiTutu, above n 101, 206.

293 Hazucha, above n 102, 29.

294 Ibid 18.

295 Ibid 18.

296 Wendland, above n 110, 504.

meetings around culture and support the work of international organisations, including the WIPO Intergovernmental Committee on IP and Generic Resources, Traditional, Knowledge and Folklore. They also need to closely monitor the proposals submitted by WIPO on genetic resources, TCEs, folklore,[297] and TK and to try to benefit from those proposals at the national and international levels.[298]

4.7 Conclusion

The studying of culture in IP scholarship has developed from the time when few scholars mentioned the subject. We are beginning to witness the increased interest of IP scholars in the cultural studies of IP that should be given much more importance. IP scholars like Rosemary Coombe and Madhavi Sunder are constantly requesting the study of IP not only from an economic perspective but also from a cultural one. This would be particularly helpful for developing countries, which have many indigenous populations and local communities.

Unfortunately, despite recognising the need to structure appropriate IP systems sensitive to culture, there is little research that provides developing countries with a clear cultural theory of IP; furthermore, it does not tell us how IP laws should be reformed to take into consideration cultural and local contexts. The chapter examined the influence of culture and legal culture on the protection of the IP systems. It found that culture could indeed influence people's attitudes toward the protection of IP.

Before and after the arrival of Islam, Arabs condemned 'intellectual theft' or plagiarism and developed their own systems of protection to authenticate and protect authorship. Islam supports the protection of IP. This is based on primary and secondary sources of Sharia. Arabic culture and social norms are non-legal factors that influence the attitude of Arabs toward IP. Legal culture in the Arab world can play an important role, as well as influence the enforcement of IP laws.

---

[297] WIPO, *Draft Provision on Traditional Cultural Expression* <http://www.wipo.int/tk/en/consultations/draft_provisions/draft_provisions.html>.

[298] Olufunmilayo B. Arewa argues that:

> The Copyright law should be to a greater extent allow for more flexibility for local communities. In cases of local knowledge, this means that local communities should have some ability to participate in decisions regarding uses of local knowledge as well as the development of intellectual property frameworks that influence the treatment of such knowledge. Such steps may help encourage the development of technological, scientific, and institutional capacity that could help local communities realize more broadly the benefits of free trade.

See Olufunmilayo B. Arewa, 'TRIPS and Traditional Knowledge: Local Communities, Local Knowledge, and Global Intellectual Property Framework' (2006) 10 (2) *Marquette Intellectual Property Law Review* 169-170 <http://works.bepress.com/cgi/viewcontent.cgi?article=1006&context=o_arewa>.

There is a need to develop a cultural theory of IP that would help developing countries to understand the relationship between culture and social and economic development. It is important, in order to make sure that IP laws are respected, to take into consideration the social contexts and culture. This will correspond with the wishes of the indigenous people in developing countries and may also assist in their path to social and economic development.

Arab countries in particular are advised to develop IP cultural policies that give proper protection to TK and TCEs. This can be done by adjusting their current IP systems and issuing separate *sui generis* laws that provide proper protection to the cultural works of their indigenous and local communities.

IP scholars interested in development issues should give more importance in their research to the role of IP in promoting culture and social and economic development. They should also assist developing countries in formulating national and international cultural policies.

Part II
The Practice of Intellectual Property and Social and Economic Development

Part I examined the different theories for IP and development and suggested that the time has come for a new theory of IP and development to be formulated, taking into account the historical, economic, cultural and other issues relevant to the advancement of developing countries.

The problem with much of the scholarship on IP and development is that it does not provide practical guidance for developing countries on how to apply those theories in a practical way for their benefit. Developing countries require more than theories; they need practical and specific measures to assist in their social and economic development.

Part II sets out to provide developing countries with some practical measures for adoption. It includes a case study highlighting the consequences that flow when a developing country adopts a copyright law without fully considering its effect on local industries, local conditions and social and economic development. The lessons from the case study can be used as a guide by other developing countries to ensure that their copyright laws allow their citizens to access knowledge and to benefit fully from opportunities for learning and education provided by the Internet. Part II also considers the use of voluntary mechanisms such as free and open source software (FOSS) and creative commons licences (CC) by developing countries in their path to social and economic development. Finally, it proposes that developing countries should formulate and implement their own policies which integrate IP laws with social and economic development.

Chapter 5
Rethinking the Jordanian Copyright Law in the Internet Age: A Developmental Perspective

For too long IPRs have been regarded as food for the rich countries and poison for poor countries .... [I]t is not as simple as that. Poor countries may find them useful provided they are accommodated to suit local palates.[1]

Abstract This chapter analyses copyright law in Jordan from a developmental perspective. It shows how, in practical terms, a development-oriented approach may be implemented in the copyright laws of developing countries. While a case study is made of Jordan, similar considerations could apply to other jurisdictions that are in the process of updating their copyright laws. There should be a careful consideration of the local situation of each developing country and full compliance with obligations under international copyright treaties to which they are signatories. This chapter examines the provisions of Jordanian copyright law, especially those related to the Internet and provides specific recommendations for policymakers and legislators when copyright laws are being updated. This pro-development approach would serve better the social and economic developmental needs of Jordan and its citizens.

5.1 Overview

Jordan has been a WTO member[2] since 11 April 2000 and, as a condition of its accession, was required to amend many laws to bring them into conformity with its international obligations. Jordan was the first Arab state from the Middle

[1] John Barton et al., Commission on Intellectual Property Rights (CIPR), *Integrating Intellectual Property Rights and Development Policy* (September 2002), <http://www.iprcommission.org/papers/pdfs/final_report/CIPRfullfinal.pdf>.

[2] Jordan is the 136th member of the WTO, see WTO, *Jordan and WTO* <http://www.wto.org/english/thewto_e/countries_e/jordan_e.htm>; Ghadeer Taher, 'Jordan's WTO Accession Bid

DOI 10.1007/978-3-642-27907-2_5,

East[3] to sign the JUSFTA, which entered into force on 17 December 2001, and required the Jordanian legislature to enact further amendments to adequately protect IP. Jordan joined the *Paris Convention* on 17 July 1972, *Berne Convention* on 28 July 1999, the *WCT* on 27 April 2004, and the WPPT on 24 May 2004.[4] As a result, it introduced new amendments to its IP system, including the *Copyright Law No. 22 for 1999* as amended (*Copyright Law*). The latest amendments made to the *Copyright Law* took place on 2005, when protection of Rights Management Information (RMI) and Technological Protection Measures (TPMs) were introduced for the first time.[5]

This chapter has two aims: firstly, to examine to what extent the *Copyright Law* serves the developmental needs of Jordan and its citizens and, secondly, to critique the *Copyright Law* and offer specific recommendations to improve it. The 2002–2005 amendments to the *Copyright Law* are overly restrictive as they do not serve the development needs of the country. The *Copyright Law* should not only foster foreign investments in Jordan but also boost innovation and promote creativity. An urgent revision needs to be made to the *Copyright Law* in Jordan, taking into account the social and economic developmental needs of the country and the future welfare and prosperity of its citizens.

This chapter is divided into four sections. Section 5.2 provides an overview of IP systems in the Middle East, focusing on copyright laws in force in Jordan and the Arab world. Section 5.3 examines the fundamentals of copyright law in Jordan, giving particular attention to the Internet and digital issues. As it will be discussed later, most of the recent amendments made to Jordanian copyright law relate to digital issues. It is important to consider how the law needs to be structured in the digital age to meet the development interests of the country. Section 5.4 analyses and critiques the copyright law, and Sect. 5.5 provides proposals for reform.

5.2 The Jordanian IP System

On 11 April 2000, after 2 years of negotiations, Jordan became the 136th member of WTO. The Jordanian parliament ratified the WTO treaty on 24 February 2000.[6] Achieving ratification in a limited period of time was difficult because major

Held up by Needed Reforms, Business Opposition', Jordan Times (online), 14 April 1999 <http://www.jordanembassyus.org/041499005.htm>.

[3] The other three Arab countries that singed FTAs with the US are Bahrain (2004), Morocco (2004), and Oman (2006). The US is also pursuing an FTA with the United Arab Emirates (UAE), Qatar, and Kuwait.

[4] See WIPO, *Summary Table of Membership of the WIPO and the Treaties Administered by WIPO, plus UPOV, WTO and UN* <http://www.wipo.int/treaties/en/summary.jsp>.

[5] *Copyright Law No. 22 of 1992*, as amended *(Copyright Law*), Official Gazette No. 3821, 16 April 1992 (Jordan) , arts 45-55.

[6] The *Law of the Accession of Jordan to the WTO*, 24 February 2000, Official Gazette of Jordan No. 4415/2000.

economic and legislative reforms were made in order to bring the Jordanian foreign trade regime into conformity with the WTO requirements.[7]

Many important amendments and laws were introduced, particularly in the field of IP.[8] These laws include *Patent Law No. 32 of 1999*,[9] *Trademark Law No. 34 of 1999*,[10] *Industrial Design and Model Law No. 14 of 2000*,[11] *Plant Varieties Law No. 24 of 2000*,[12] *Geographical Indication Law No. 8* of *2000*,[13] *Unfair Competition and Trade Secret Law No. 15 of 2000*,[14] and the *Protection of Layout-Designs of Integrated Circuit Law No. 10 of 2000*.[15] Other amendments were also made to many other laws,[16] but a discussion of those laws is beyond the scope of this chapter.

5.2.1 The United States–Jordan Free Trade Agreement (USJFTA)

Jordan was the first Arab state from the Middle East to sign a US FTA. The JUSFTA, which entered into force on 17 December 2001, required the Jordanian legislature to enact further amendments to its laws to adequately protect IP. Several economic and political reasons led the US to negotiate this agreement with Jordan.[17]

---

[7] Ministry of Industry and Trade (MIT) <http://www.mit.gov.jo>.

[8] Ibid.

[9] *Patent Law No. 32 of 1999* (Patent Law), Official Gazette No. 4389, 1 November 1999.

[10] *Trademark Law No. 34 of 1999*, Official Gazette No. 4389, 1 November 1999.

[11] *Industrial Design and Model Law No. 14 of 2000*, Official Gazette No. 4423, 2 April 2000.

[12] *Plant Varieties Law No. 24 of 2000*, Official Gazette No. 4443, 2 July 2000.

[13] *Geographical Indication Law No. 8 of 2000*, Official Gazette No. 4423, 2 April 2000.

[14] *Unfair Competition and Trade Secret Law No. 15 of 2000* (Unfair Competition and Trade Secret Law), Official Gazette No. 4423, 2 April 2000.

[15] The *Protection of Layout-Designs of Integrated Circuit Law No. 10 of 2000*,Official Gazette No. 4423, 2 April 2000.

[16] Some 160 laws have been promulgated in Jordan. See Nail-Biting, Jordan's Fairly Election, *Economist*, 21 June 2003. One commentator noted that having these laws is good for economic linearisation in the country in the absence of Parliament. See Bashar Malkawi, *Jordan and the World Trading System–A case Study Submitted for Arab Countries* (PhD thesis, American University, 2005) 232.

[17] For more information, see Bashar Malkawi, 'The Intellectual Property Provision of the United States- Jordan Free Trade Agreement: Template or not Template' (2006) 2 *Journal of World Intellectual Property* 213-229; Marwa Al Nasa'a et al., *The Jordan-U.S. Free Trade Agreement: Eight Years Later* (21 March 2008) University of Michigan, 3-4 <http://www.umich.edu/~ipolicy/Policy%20Papers/jordanusfta.pdf>; James Cassing and Anna Maria Salameh, *Jordan-United States Free Trade Agreement Economic Impact Study: Searching for Effects of the FTA on Exports, Imports and Trade Related Investments, Achievement of Market-Friendly Initiatives and Results Program*, (June 2006) University of Pittsburgh <http://www.econ.pitt.edu/papers/James_10.JUSFTA__Economic_Impact_Study_2006.pdf>.

The US has markedly increased aid to Jordan since the mid-1990s to help strengthen the economy, maintain domestic stability, and improve its relations with Israel.[18] Jordan seeks to benefit as much as possible from joining the JUSFTA as it wants to obtain preferable treatment on goods exported to the US market. The JUSFTA contains extensive post-TRIPS (TRIPS-plus) IP law provisions[19] that require Jordan to undertake and commit to regulatory changes that go beyond what Jordan had agreed in its accession to the WTO, WPPT, and WCT.

Article 4 of the JUSFTA, which deals with IP, is considered the largest of all the provisions of the FTA. It contains certain provisions that protect trademarks and geographical indications,[20] copyright and related rights,[21] and patents.[22] The JUSFTA concentrates on enforcement of IP, including the availability of injunctions, damages, and other remedial measures.[23] The JUSFTA also contains a Memorandum of Understanding on Issues Related to the Protection of Intellectual Property Rights (MOU), particularly in connection with patent and copyright, which Jordan is also required to meet.[24] There are various TRIPS-plus provisions that are included in the JUSFTA. Article 4(1) of the JUSFTA requires Jordan to accede to IP treaties that are not part of the *TRIPS Agreement*.[25] It provides that:

[18] Since 2003, Jordan's total assistance package has averaged over $762 million per fiscal year. See Jeremy M. Sharp, *The US Foreign Assistance to the Middle East: Historical Background, Recent Trends and the FY 2008 Request* (2010) Federation of American Scientists <http://fas.org/sgp/crs/mideast/RL32260.pdf>; Paul Rivlin, *Arab Economics in the Twenty First Century* (Cambridge University, 2009) 155-73; Al Nasa'a et al., above n 17, 2-6.

[19] For further explanation of the TRIPS model in Jordan and the Arab World, see Hamed EL Said and Mohammed El Said, 'TRIPS-Plus Implication for Access to Medicine in Developing Countries: Lessons from Jordan–United States Free Trade Agreement' (2007) 10 (6) *Journal of World Intellectual Property Review* 438-475; Mohammed El Said, *The Development of Intellectual Property Protection in the Arab World* (The Edwin Mellen, 2008) ch 4-6; David Price, *The Development of Intellectual Property Regimes in the Arabian Gulf States* (Routledge, 2009) ch 4-6.

[20] Jordan United States Free Trade Agreement (JUSFTA), art 4, 10-16, signed on 24 October 2000 (entered into force 17 December 2001) <http://www.mfa.gov.jo/uploads/textagrusjofta.pdf>.

[21] JUSFTA, above n 20, art 4, 6-9.

[22] JUSFTA, art 4, above n 20, arts 17-20.

[23] JUSFTA, art 4, above n 20, arts 24-28.

[24] JUSFTA, The Memorandum of Understanding on Issues Related to the Protection of Intellectual Property Rights (MOU) The Jordan–US Free Trade Agreement <http://www.jordanusfta.com/documents/memo_property.pdf>.

[25] Agreement on Trade-Related Aspects of Intellectual Property Rights, 15 April 1994, Marrakesh Agreement Establishing the World Trade Organization, opened for signature 15 April 1994, 1867 (entered into force 1 January 1995, Annex 1C Trade-Related Aspects of Intellectual Property Rights (TRIPS).

1. Each Party shall, at a minimum, give effect to this Article, including the following provisions:

   (b) Articles 1–22 of the International Convention for the Protection of New Varieties of Plants (1991) ('UPOV Convention');
   (c) Articles 1–14 of the WIPO Copyright Treaty (1996) ('WCT'); and
   (d) Articles 1–23 of the WIPO Performances and Phonograms Treaty (1996) ('WPPT').

2. Each Party shall make best efforts to ratify or accede to the Patent Cooperation Treaty (1984) and the Protocol Relating to the Madrid Agreement Concerning the International Registration of Marks (1989).[26]

Article 4(20) also provides a TRIPS-plus provision in relation to compulsory licensing in a health crisis.[27] It provides as follows:

> Neither Party shall permit the use of the subject matter of a patent without the authorization of the right holder except in the following circumstances:
>
> (a) To remedy a practice determined after judicial or administrative process to be anti-competitive;
> (b) In cases of public non-commercial use or in the case of a national emergency or other circumstances of extreme urgency, provided that such use is limited to use by government entities or legal entities acting under the authority of a government; or
> (c) On the ground of failure to meet working requirements, provided that importation shall constitute working.[28]

One Jordanian legal scholar has described the IP provisions in the JUSFTA as follows:

> The intellectual property provisions of the US–JO FTA are one-sided. They were drafted to protect US intellectual property rights. In great parts, the intellectual property part of the US–JO FTA reflects the laws and views of the USA...[29]

While the Jordanian scholar is correct in that the agreement is one sided, it is important to examine the real motivations that led Jordan to draft such restrictive

---

[26] JUSFTA, above n 20, art 4, 1.

[27] Rohhit Malpani from Oxfam International's access to medicine campaign argues that USJFTA has created a public health crisis in Jordan. He notes that there were no benefits from signing the USJFTA as claimed by US officials in relation to the development of the pharmaceutical industry in Jordan. He explains:

> [S]ince the FTA was signed, FDI, in the words of most generics manufacturers and government officials, has been a 'disappointment'. From 1995 to 2000, there was hardly any investment in Jordanian pharmaceutical manufacturing, and following the passage of the FTA, despite claims by United States Trade Representative (USTR) that FDI would flow to Jordan, it never materialised. Furthermore, local generics companies complained that multinational pharmaceutical companies neither signed more licensing agreements nor transferred technology to local manufacturers. Thus, most new medicines are imported rather than produced locally. According to the Jordanian Association of Pharmaceutical Manufacturers, most licensing agreements that are in effect today were signed before 1999.

Rohhit Malpani, 'All Costs, No Benefits: How The US–Jordan Free Trade Agreement Affects Access to Medicine' (2009) 6 (3) *Journal of Genetic Medicines* 206, 213.

[28] JUSFTA, above n 20, art 4,1.

[29] Malkawi, above n 17, 221.

provisions.[30] One important question that arises is whether this is a general pattern with all other FTAs signed between the US and other Arab countries.

It is noted that other FTAs signed between the US and other Arab countries contain extensive provisions that deal with all forms of IP that are not much different from the Jordanian FTA.[31] Furthermore, many go even further than the JUSFTA, demanding a higher level of IP protection, particularly in connection with extending the copyright term to be 70 years (instead of 50) after the author's death.[32]

---

[30] Ahmed Abdel Latif noted that:

> It is not always clear if these TRIPS-Plus obligations in national laws are the result of a conscious and deliberate choice by legislators and policy-makers, or are more the result of inadequate legislative advice given to these Arab countries in the process of modernization of their IP laws by certain bilateral donors and international organizations with a vested interest in promoting higher IP standards.

See Ahmed Abdel Latif, 'A Perspective on Reform in Arab Countries' in Ricardo Melendez-Ortiz and Pedro Roffe (ed), *Intellectual Property and Sustainable Development: Development Agenda in a Changing World* (Edward Elgar, 2010) 51, 56.

[31] The Bahrain United States Free Trade Agreement (BUSFTA), art 14, signed on 14 September, 2004 (entered into force 1 August 2006) <http://www.ustr.gov/trade-agreements/free-trade-agreements/bahrain-fta/final-text>. The Morocco United States Free Trade Agreement (MUSFTA), art 15, signed on 15 June 2004 (entered into force 1 January 2006) <http://www.ustr.gov/trade-agreements/free-trade-agreements/morocco-fta/final-text>. The Oman United States FTA (OUSFTA), art 15, signed on 19 January 2006 (entered into force 1 January 2009) <http://www.ustr.gov/trade-agreements/free-trade-agreements/oman-fta/final-text>.

[32] Article 14.4.4 of the BUSFTA provides that:

> Each Party shall provide that, where the term of protection of a work (including a photographic work), performance, or phonogram is to be calculated: (a) on the basis of the life of a natural person, the term shall be not less than the life of the author and 70 years after the author's death; and (b) on a basis other than the life of a natural person, the term shall be (i) not less than 70 years from the end of the calendar year of the first authorized publication of the work, performance, or phonogram, or failing such authorized publication within 50 years from the creation of the work, performance or phonogram, not less than 70 years from the end of the calendar year of the creation of the work, performance, or phonogram

BUSFTA, above n 31, art 14.4, 4.
Article 15.5.5 of the MUSFTA provides that:

> Each Party shall provide that, where the term of protection of a work (including a photographic work), performance, or phonogram is to be calculated: (a) on the basis of the life of a natural person, the term shall be not less than the life of the author and 70 years after the author's death; and (b) on a basis other than the life of a natural person, the term shall be (i) not less than 70 years from the end of the calendar year of the first authorized publication of the work, performance, or phonogram, or (ii) failing such authorized publication within 50 years from the creation of the work, performance, or phonogram, not less than 70 years from the end of the calendar year of the creation of the work, performance, or phonogram.

MUSFTA, above n 31, art 15.5.5
Article 15.4.4 of the OUSFTA provides that:

> 4. Each Party shall provide that, where the term of protection of a work (including a photographic work), performance, or phonogram is to be calculated:(a) on the basis of the life of a natural person, the term shall be not less than the life of the author and 70 years after the author's death; and (b) on a basis other than the life of a natural person, the term

Jordan was fortunate enough to sign the FTA with the US in 2001 before many other Arab countries were obliged to sign onto tougher IP systems.[33]

The JUSFTA resembles the language of the DMCA of 1998[34] but goes even further in demanding a higher level of copyright protection.[35] The DMCA-style

---

> shall be (i) not less than 95 years from the end of the calendar year of the first authorized publication of the work, performance, or phonogram, or (ii) failing such authorized publication within 25 years from the creation of the work, performance, or phonogram, not less than 120 years from the end of the calendar year of the creation of the work, performance, or phonogram.

OUSFTA, above n 31, art 15.4.4.

[33] See, for TRIPS plus provisions, art 14.3 of the BUSFTA provides that:

> 1. Each Party shall require that the management of its country-code top-level domain (ccTLD) provide an appropriate procedure for the settlement of disputes, based on the principles established in the Uniform Domain-Name Dispute-Resolution Policy (UDRP), in order to address the problem of trademark cyber-piracy.
> 2. Each Party shall require that the management of its ccTLD provide online public access to a reliable and accurate database of contact information for domain-name registrants.

BUSFTA, above n 31, art 14.3.
Article 15.4 of the MUSFTA provides that:

> 1. In order to address the problem of trademark cyber-piracy, each Party shall require that the management of its country-code top-level domain ("ccTLD") provide an appropriate procedure for the settlement of disputes, based on the principles established in the Uniform Domain-Name Dispute-Resolution Policy.
> 2. Each Party shall require that the management of its ccTLD provide online public access to a reliable and accurate database of contact information for domain name registrants.

MUSFTA, above n 31, art 15.4.
Article 15.3 of the OUSFTA also provides that:

> 1. In order to address the problem of trademark cyber-piracy, each Party shall require that the management of its country-code top-level domain ("ccTLD") provide an appropriate procedure for the settlement of disputes, based on the principles established in the Uniform Domain-Name Dispute-Resolution Policy.
> 2. Each Party shall require that the management of its ccTLD provide online public access to a reliable and accurate database of contact information for domain-name registrants.

OUSTA, above n 31, art 15.3.

For TRIPS plus provisions, see also art 15.5.8 of the MUSFTA and art 14.4.7 of the BUSFTA that do not require knowledge in relation to the act of circumvention. See Gwen Hinze, *Seven Lessons from a Comparison of the Technological Protection Measures Provisions*, Electronic Frontier Foundation <http://www.eff.org/pages/seven-lessons-comparison-technological-protection-measure-provisions>.

[34] Digital Millennium Copyright Act of 1998, Pub. L. No. 105-304, 112 Stat. 2860 (1998) (codified in scattered sections of, *inter alia*, 17 U.S.C. §§ 1201–05 (2006).

[35] Professor Peter Yu explains:

> The DMCA was designed specifically to deal with the threat created by digital technologies under conditions specific to the United States, including the stage of its economic development, the structure of its content and communications industries, the state of available

provisions have been heavily criticised by American and international IP scholars and various commentators.[36] The *Copyright Law* in Jordan has adopted certain provisions from the DMCA verbatim, without assessing their appropriateness to the social and economic development of the country. This approach of legal transplanting is heavily criticised as it is not based on a deep understanding of domestic needs or a correct assessment of the cost and benefits of transplanting.[37]

Jordan and the US have also signed a Joint Statement on Electronic Commerce; the statement discusses many issues related to electronic commerce, including electronic authentication, electronic signatures, electronic payment, and privacy and consumer protection.[38]

The position of the Obama government in relation to protecting American IP interests may not be totally clear. It is hoped that the American government will be

---

> technology, the overall market conditions, and the average living standards of local consumers. Because these conditions are unlikely to be present in less developed countries, the DMCA serves as an inappropriate model for the implementation of the WIPO Internet Treaties.

Peter K. Yu, 'Working Together in a Digital World: An Introduction: Article: Anticircumvention and Anti-anticircumvention' (2006) 84 *Denver University Law Review* 13, 42.

[36] For critiques of DMCA, see the following: Fred Von Lohman and Wendy Seltzer, *Death by the DMCA* (June 2006) Ieee Spectrum <http://www.spectrum.ieee.org/computing/software/death-by-dmca>; Pamela Samuelson, 'Intellectual Property and The Digital Economy- Why the Anti Circumvention Regulation Needs to be Revised' (1999) 14 *Berkeley Technology Law Journal* 519; Anne Hiaring, 'What's New in the Neighbourhood the Export of the DMCA in Post- TRIPS FTAs' (2005) 11 (1) *Annual Survey of International & Comparative Law* 171; Dan L. Burk, 'Anticircumvention Misuse' (2003) 50 *University of California Los Anglos Law Review* 1095.

On appraisal of the DMCA, one Jordanian legal scholar noted that the DMCA is a model law for implementing the anti-circumvention provisions of the WCT and WPPT treaties; he further argued that it is a good example in achieving an appropriate balance between the legal rights of authors and users; see Fayad Al Qudah, 'Legal Protection of Databases; a Study of Jordanian Law' (2008) 22 *Arab Law Quarterly* 360,378, 381.

[37] This has also occurred in other countries such as China, which based part of its copyright law on the DMCA model. Professor Hong Yue notes:

> A successful legal transplant should be based on the comprehensive study of the legal context of the transplanted law, deep understanding of the domestic need and correct assessment of the cost and benefit of the transplanting. Most importantly, transplanting the norms from the foreign law should be strategic rather than expedient, thoughtful rather than unperceptive, creative rather than plagiaristic. Only through the careful cultivation can the healthy, valuable and adaptive flowers bloom in the new legal system.

Hong Xue, 'Les Fleurs Du Mal A Critique of the Legal Transplants Chinese Internet Copyright Protection' (2007) 34 *Rutger Computer and Technology Law Journal* 168-210.

[38] See The *US-Jordan Joint Statement on Electronic Commerce*, The Jordan–US Free Trade Agreement <http://www.jordanusfta.com/documents/joint_statement_on_e-commerce.pdf>. The Statement particularly requests Jordan to provide high protection for e-commerce, including business-method patents to which the *Patent Law* in Jordan does not currently give protection. Ibid.

more willing to listen to a diversity of voices on IP matters, especially those of developing countries such as Jordan.[39]

5.2.2 *Jordan–EU Association Agreement (JEUAA)*

The JEUAA[40] was signed on 24 November 1997 and entered into force on 1 May 2002 to develop close political relations and a free trade area for 12 years[41] between Jordan and the EU. Jordan was the third Arab state from the Middle East to sign a JEUAA with the EU.[42] The JEUAA was preceded by several protocols signed over the past 20 years between Jordan and the European Communities (EC).[43]

---

[39] The Obama administration is not totally clear in its position in relation to IP policies in developing countries. One commentator was optimistic as he notes: '[w]ith the Obama administration being possibly more willing to listen to a diversity of voices on matters such as open source—as are many other governments throughout the world.' Another commentator has also mentioned that:

> [H]opefully we will find a broader vision that goes from President Obama down to USTR [the US Trade Representative's Office] and USPTO [US Patent and Trademark Office] negotiators that would allow us to see the US showing real engagement in WTO and WIPO negotiations and regaining a leadership already lost.

Professor Lawrence Lessig also was of the opinion the following opinion: 'I don't expect there will be a fundamental change in IP policy, unfortunately, but of course I believe there will be a strong press to realize change'. See Liza Porteus Viana, *Obama Victory Draws Quick Reactions From IP Tech Communities*, (2 November 2008) IP Watch <http://www.ip-watch.org/2008/11/05/obama-victory-draws-quick-reactions-from-ip-tech-communities/>; Liza Porteus and William New, *Who Will Advise Obama on IP? Let The Name Games Begin,* (6 November 2008) IP Watch <http://www.ip-watch.org/2008/11/06/who-will-advise-obama-let-the-names-begin/>.

[40] Jordan has also signed an FTA with Canada. See *Jordan Canada Free Trade Agreement*, signed on 28 June 2009, (entered into force 24 March 2010), SICE the OAS Foreign Trade Information System (SICE) <http://www.sice.oas.org/TPD/CAN_JOR/Text_CAN_JOR_e/index_e.asp>.

[41] The first two Arab countries that signed an AA agreement with the EU were Tunsia (Decision 98/238/EC, entered into force on 1 March 1998) and Morocco (Decision 2000/204/EC entered into force on 1 March 2000). See Europa, *Euro-Mediterranean Association Agreement* <http://europa.eu/legislation_summaries/external_relations/relations_with_third_countries/mediterranean_partner_countries/r14104_en.htm>.

[42] The other three Arab countries that singed an AA with the EU after Jordan were Egypt (Decision 2004/635/EC, entered into force on 1 June 2004), Algeria (Decision 2005, 690/EC, entered into force on 1 September 2005), and Lebanon (2006/356/E.C, entered into force on 1 April 2006). Ibid.

[43] The first co-operation Agreement between Jordan and the EC was signed on 18 August 1977. See the Jordanian Ministry of Industry and Trade, *Summary of the Provisions of the Jordan–EU Association Agreement* <http://www.mit.gov.jo/portals/0/JORDAN%20AND%20THE.pdf>; Marwan A. Kardoosh, Jordan–*EU Association Agreement: Passport to Export Prosperity or Open Cheque Book,* Jordan Centre for Public Policy Research and Dalogue <http://www.jcpprd.org/Files/ResearchDatabase/Jordan-EU%20Association%20Agreement_1.pdf>.

The EU is Jordan's main source of imports, ahead of the neighbouring Kingdom of Saudi Arabia and China. EU imports to Jordan in 2008 totalled €2.6 billion. At the same time, the EU is only Jordan's 7th main export destination.[44] In 2008, the EU assisted Jordan with a total amount of €65 million under the European Neighbourhood Policy Instrument (ENPI), targeted at priority areas such as support for trade and investment development through the allocation of €48 million; support for reformation of the criminal justice system, anti-corruption, and the fight against radicalisation through a €7 million program; and support for the building of government and social institutions through the allocation of €10 million.[45]

The JEUAA is made up of 107 provisions and 7 annexes, supplemented with 4 protocols.[46] Article 56 of the JEUAA provides that:

> 1. Pursuant to the provisions of this Article and of particularly Annex VII, the Parties shall grant and ensure adequate and effective protection of intellectual, industrial and commercial property rights in accordance with the highest international standards, including effective means of enforcing such rights.

The JEUAA requires Jordan to provide adequate and effective protection and enforcement of IP and to grant most-favoured-nation treatment, subject to the limitation under the *TRIPS Agreement*. Annex VII of the JEUAA requires Jordan to join a number of international treaties related to copyright, and these include the *Berne Convention* and the *Rome Convention*.[47] Annex VII of the EU AA with Jordan provides that:

> 1. By the end of the fifth year after the entry into force of the Agreement, Jordan shall accede to the following multilateral conventions on property rights:
>
> — Berne Convention for the protection of literary and artistic works (Paris Act 1971),
> — The Convention for the Protection of Performers, Producers of Phonograms and Broadcasting Organisations (Rome, 1961)
> — Nice Agreement concerning the International Classification of Goods and Services for the Purposes of the Registration of Marks (Geneva Act 1977 and amended in 1979),
> — Madrid Agreement concerning the International Registration of Marks (Stockholm Act 1967 and amended in 1979),
> — Protocol relating to the Madrid Agreement concerning the International Registration of Marks (Madrid 1989),
> — Budapest Treaty on the International Recognition of the Deposit of Micro-organisms for the Purposes of Patent Procedure (1977, modified in 1980),
> — The International Convention for Protection of New Varieties of Plants (UPOV) (Geneva Act 1991).

[44] Europa, *Jordan*, <http://ec.europa.eu/trade/issues/bilateral/countries/jordan/index_en.htm>.

[45] The European Neighbourhood Policy (Press Release, RAPID 09/186, 23 April 2009) <http://europa.eu/rapid/pressReleasesAction.do?reference=MEMO/09/186&format=HTML&aged=0&language=EN&guiLanguage=en>.

[46] Jordan–EU Association Agreement (JEUAA), signed on November 1997 (entered into force on May 2002) EUR-Lex <http://eur-lex.europa.eu/LexUriServ/LexUriServ.do?uri=OJ:L:2002:129:0003:0165:EN:PDF>.

[47] Jordan has not been a signatory to the Rome Convention of 1961.

2. Not later than the seventh year after the entry into force of the Agreement, Jordan shall accede to the following multilateral conventions:
   — Patent Cooperation Treaty (Washington 1970, amended in 1979 and modified in 1984).
3. . . .[48]

The JEUAA imposes general obligations on Jordan in connection with the protection and enforcement of IP and softer obligations regarding copyright and related rights when compared to the FTA that Jordan has signed with the US.[49] The European Neighbourhood Policy (ENP) also requires Jordan to protect and enforce IP similar to a level of protection applicable in the EU.[50]

5.2.3 *Overview of Internet Use in the Arab World*

Many governments are beginning to realise the benefits of the Internet and are eager to transform their countries into e-societies. Countries within the Arab world are no exception.[51] The Arab world is currently pursuing a series of important initiatives to take advantage of the digital revolution. In Dubai, an Internet city[52] and a media city[53] were built to attract global investors and a highly qualified labour force. In Jordan, an ICT-based national development strategy[54] is being designed and implemented to establish IT industries and services.[55] In Tunisia, the Five Year Development Plan (Plan) emphasises the necessity of developing 'knowledge economy' as a key dimension.[56] The Plan was developed through a large consultation process and prescribes policy measures in multiple domains such as education, research, trade, industry, agriculture, and regional policies with the planned creation of ten technological policies in the coming decade.[57]

[48] JEUAA, Annex VII, above n 46.

[49] Compare art 4 of the JUSFTA with art 56 of the AA. See JEUAA, above n 46.

[50] EU/Jordan Action Plan, European Commission <http://trade.ec.europa.eu/doclib/docs/2006/march/tradoc_127735.pdf>. See also Abdel Latif, above n 30.

[51] ITU, *Internet for the Arab World* <http://www.itu.int/ITU-D/ict/papers/egypt2000/15-e.pdf>.

[52] Dubai Internet City <http://www.dubaiinternetcity.com/>.

[53] Dubai Media City <http://www.dubaimediacity.com/>.

[54] Jordan Ministry of Information and Communication Technologies (MICT) <http://www.moict.gov.jo/moict/en_index.aspx>.

[55] Jean-Eric Aubert, *Promoting Innovation in Developing Countries, a Conceptual Framework* (2004) World Bank Institute <http://info.worldbank.org/etools/docs/library/137729/0-3097 AubertPaper%5B1%5D.pdf>.

[56] Triki Abdelhamid, *Knowledge Based Economy in Tunisia* Investment Tunisia <http://www.investintunisia.tn/document/295.pdf>.

[57] Aubert, above n 55.

It is estimated as of 31 December 2011 that there were over 77 million Internet users in the Middle East,[58] accounting for 3.1% of the world's Internet population. Moreover, the rate of Internet usage grew 185.3% between 2000 and 2010.[59] Interestingly, the number of broadband subscribers in the Arab world grew by 38% in 2006, while the number of those subscribers using DSL access technology grew by 81.9% to 4.3 million.[60] The Initiative for Open Arab Internet (IOAI) stated, in a study concluded in 2007, that there were (at that time) around 40,000 Arabic blogs in the Arab world, most of which had been created since 2006. The Egyptian bloggers have guided other Arab bloggers.[61] Despite the novelty of blogging in the Arab world, it has become an effective tool for Arab populations to express themselves and to reveal both public and personal grievances.[62]

Most of the countries in the Arab world introduced the Internet to promote economic development and competitiveness; however, they soon realised that the Internet made it more difficult for them to control the flow of information both within the country and across international borders. The availability and accessibility of information, as well as the ability to create and disseminate information anonymously, has led to a sense of freedom among many Arab Internet users.[63] Internet users in the Arab World are using new types of media via the Internet like YouTube,[64] MySpace,[65] Facebook,[66] Flickr,[67] Twitter,[68] and Wikipedia,[69] and

---

[58] The list of countries include, in addition to the Arab countries, Israel and Iran; see Internet World States, *Internet Usage Statistics* <http://www.internetworldstats.com/stats.htm>.

[59] Ibid.

[60] AME Info, *DSL Forum Acclaim Middle East and Africa Broadband Growing Faster than any Region in the World* <http://www.ameinfo.com/116548.html>. It is interesting to note that Facebook is among the most visited websites in the Middle East and North Africa, with nearly 2.5 million users (2009). See Wael Gouneim, Google Middle East, 'Internet Use in the Middle East and North Africa' (A presentation to Open Content Arabic Workshop, Abdul-Aziz City for Science & Technology (KACST), Riyadh (17-18 January, 2009).

[61] The Initiative for an Open Arab Internet (IOAI), *Implacable Adversaries: Arab Government and the Internet* (2006) <http://old.openarab.net/en/node/346>; Marc Lynch, *Blogging the New Arab Public*, IOAI (2007) Arab Media Society <http://www.arabmediasociety.org/articles/downloads/20070312155027_AMS1_Marc_Lynch.pdf>; Bruce Etling et al., *Mapping the Arabic Blogosphere: Politics, Culture, and Dissent*, (2009) Berkman Centre for Internet and Society <http://cyber.law.harvard.edu/sites/cyber.law.harvard.edu/files/Mapping_the_Arabic_Blogosphere_0.pdf>.

[62] IOAI, above n 61.

[63] Open Net Initiative, *Middle East and North Africa Regions* (2006-2007) Open Net <http://opennet.net/research/regions/mena>; Rasha A. Abdullah, *The Internet in the Arab world- Egypt and Beyond* (Peter Lang, 2007) 33-39.

[64] Youtube <http://www.youtube.com>.

[65] Myspace <http://www.myspace.com>.

[66] Facebook <http://www.facebook.com>.

[67] Flickr <http://www.flickr.com>.

[68] Twitter <http://www.twitter.com>.

[69] Wikipedia <http://www.wiipedia.org>.

these platforms continue to raise significant challenges for copyright policies. The important question is whether copyright laws and policies in Arab countries have led to creativity, innovation, and development. The challenge for these countries is to adopt a mix of legal and non-legal copyright policies to design an appropriate model to deal with the rise of digital technologies and the Internet. If Arab countries want to develop the knowledge-based economy and become a regional hub for ICT, they need to critically examine their existing IP systems. However, the pertinent questions are what kind of IP systems are required and on what basis are they required.

5.2.4 The Copyright Laws of Arab Countries

The first Jordanian copyright law (The Ottoman Copyright Law of 1910) dates back to the beginning of the nineteenth century, when most Arab countries[70] were under the governance of the Ottoman Empire.[71] The first *Egyptian Copyright Law No. 354 for 1954*, as amended, formed the basis upon which most Arab countries drafted their own copyright laws.[72] Copyright laws in Arab countries differ to a large extent, but they can be categorised under three distinct groups. Firstly, there are countries with a no or low level of implementation, including Palestine,[73] Somalia,[74] Comoros,[75] Iraq,[76] and Libya.[77] The second group is characterised by middle-level implementation and includes those countries that made amendments

[70] The 22 Arab countries are Algeria, Bahrain, Comoros, Djibouti, Egypt, Iraq, Jordan, Kuwait, Lebanon, Libya, Mauritania, Morocco, Oman, Palestine, Qatar, Saudi Arabia, Somalia, Sudan, Syria, Tunisia, United Arab Emirates (UAE), and Yemen.

[71] Morocco remained largely independent of the Othman Turkish Empire; see Anahita Bint Abd Al-Karim Al-Hakim Al-Fassi, *A Taste of Maghribi History,* Dar Anahita <http://home.earthlink.net/~lilinah/Library/HistoryMaroc.html#osman>.

[72] See Nowaf Kanan, *Jordanian Copyright Law* 44-45 (4th ed, Dar Althaqafa, 2004) (2000) 44-45.

[73] Palestinian copyright laws go back to the Othman Empire (1299–1923) and the British mandate for Palestine (1920–1946). The laws that are applicable are *the Law of Copyright and Authorship No. 46 of 1911* (Palestine) and the *Law of Copyright and Authorship No. 16 of 1924* (Palestine). *See* Ihab G. Samaan, A Historical View of Intellectual Property Rights in the Palestinian Territories (1 December 2003) (unpublished L.L.M. thesis, University of Georgia) <http://digitalcommons.law.uga.edu/cgi/viewcontent.cgi?article=1049&context=stu_llm>.

[74] Somalia does not currently have an IP system. It has been a member of WIPO since 1982 and the African Regional Intellectual Property Organization (ARIPO). *See* Somalia, WIPO <http://www.wipo.int>.

[75] *Copyright Law of March 11, 1957 on Literary and Artistic Property* (Comoros). *See Comoros,* WIPO <http://www.wipo.int/wipolex/en/details.jsp?id=8839>.

[76] *The Coalition Provisional Authority has amended the Copyright Law No. 3 of 1971 for the Protection of Copyright* (Iraq). *See* Abu Ghazaleh Intellectual Property <http://www.agip.com>.

[77] Protection of Copyright (*Law No. 9/1968*) (Libya). See Libya, WIPO, <http://www.wipo.int/wipolex/en/details.jsp?id=10149>.

to their copyright laws in the 1990s and after; this group consists of Lebanon,[78] Syria,[79] Tunisia,[80] Qatar,[81] Saudi Arabia,[82] Algeria,[83] Egypt,[84] Djibouti,[85] Mauritania,[86] Kuwait,[87] Sudan,[88] Yemen,[89] and the United Arab Emirates (UAE).[90] The last group comprises those countries with a high level of implementation, particularly those countries that entered into FTAs with the US. As a result, those countries updated, or are soon to update, their copyright laws significantly in

[78] Protection of Literary and Artistic Property (*Law No. 75/1999*) (Lebnon). See Lebanon, WIPO, <http://www.wipo.int/wipolex/en/details.jsp?id=2786>.

[79] *Copyright Law of Syria* (Law No. 12/2001) (Syria). See Syrian Arab Republic, WIPO, <http://www.wipo.int/wipolex/en/details.jsp?id=6648>.

[80] Literary and Artistic Property (*Law No. 94-36/1994*) (Tunis.). See Tunisia, WIPO, <http://www.wipo.int/wipolex/en/details.jsp?id=3840>.

[81] *Protection of Copyright and Neighbouring Rights* (*Law No. 7/2002*) (Qatar). See Qatar, WIPO, <http://www.wipo.int/wipolex/en/details.jsp?id=3567>.

[82] Copyright Law issued by Royal Decree No. M/41, 2 Rajab, 1424 (30.08.2003) (Saudi Arabia). See Saudi Arabia, WIPO, <http://www.wipo.int/wipolex/en/text.jsp?file_id=129516>.

[83] *Copyright and Neighbouring Rights* (*Order Act No. 03-05/2003*) (Algeria). See Algeria, WIPO, <http://www.wipo.int/wipolex/en/details.jsp?id=1194>.

[84] *Law No. 82 of 2002* (Law on the Protection of Intellectual Property Rights), *Al-Jarida Al-Rasmiyya*, 3 June 2002, (Egypt) <http://www.wipo.int/wipolex/en/text.jsp?file_id=126540>. See Egypt, WIPO, <http://www.wipo.int/wipolex/en/details.jsp?id=7296>. It is a comprehensive IP law that deals with patents, utility models, integrated circuits, confidential information, trademarks, geographical indications, and copyright. *See* Bassem Awad, Moatasem El-Gheriani and Perihan Abou Zeid, *Egypt Country Report on A2K* (Country Report: Egypt) <http://www.aca2k.org/attachments/154_ACA2K%20EGYPT%202009%20CR%20WEB-011209.pdf>. The law repealed the *Copyright Law No. 354 of 1954*, as amended, and introduced new sections on copyright and neighbouring rights. Book 3 of the law consists of 50 articles that deal with copyright (articles 138–88). The Egyptian Prime Minster issued later an implementation Decree No. 497 of 2005 for the law that was effective on 29 March 2005. Egypt has been a member of the WIPO since 21 April 1975, the Berne Convention since 7 June 1977, the WTO since 30 June 1995, but it is not yet a member of the WCT and WPPT. *See Egypt*, WIPO, <http://www.wipo.int/wipolex/en/profile.jsp?code=EG#a6>.

[85] A new IP Law was passed in Djibouti, which was adopted by the Council of Ministers on 27 January 27 2009. It repealed the *Law No. 114/AN/96/36 for the Protection of Author's Rights. See New IP Law in Djibouti*, AFRO-IP, (4 February 2009) <http://afro-ip.blogspot.com/2009/02/new-ip-law-in-djibouti.html>.

[86] *Code of Commerce* (Law No. 2000/05) (Mauritania). *See* Mauritania, WIPO, <http://www.wipo.int/wipolex/en/details.jsp?id=7477>.

[87] *Concerning Intellectual Property Rights* (Decree No. 64/1999) (Kuwait). *See* Kuwait, WIPO, <http://www.wipo.int/wipolex/en/details.jsp?id=2784>.

[88] *Copyright Law and Neighbouring Rights Protection Act* (No. 54/1996) (Sudan). See Sudan, WIPO, <http://www.wipo.int/wipolex/en/details.jsp?id=3605>.

[89] *The Unified Intellectual Property Rights Law No. 19 of 1994* (Yemen) was waiting an implementing regulation to be issued, but this did not happen.

[90] *Copyright and Neighbouring Rights* (*Federal Law No. 7/2002*) (UAE). See UAE, WIPO <http://www.wipo.int/wipolex/en/details.jsp?id=7>.

order to ensure conformity with their treaty obligations. Those countries are Jordan,[91] Bahrain,[92] Morocco,[93] and Oman.[94]

Of the 22 Arab countries, only 12 have joined the WTO[95]; only 17 have joined the *Berne Convention*[96]; only five have joined the Rome Convention for the Protection of Performers, Producers of Phonograms and Broadcasting Organizations (*Rome Convention*)[97]; and only six have joined the WCT and WPPT. The Arab countries that joined the WPPT and WCT include Bahrain, Jordan, Oman, Qatar, Morocco, and the UAE.[98] Economic and political goals heavily influenced their decisions to update their copyright laws and enter into these types of international copyright treaties.

It is important to stress that Arab countries are civil law countries, primarily influenced by the French legal system[99] and not the English common law system.[100] There is always confusion as to the role that Islamic law has to play in the Arab world. Islamic laws only play a major role in marital and family matters (particularly marriage, divorce, and inheritance).

Many of the other laws in the Arab region have been indirectly copied from French laws (such as the Napoleonic Code (Code Napoléon) and other secular legislation) and adopted into Egyptian law with some alterations. Many Egyptian scholars went to study law in France during the 1950s and 1970s and upon their return to Egypt were involved in drafting laws that, as a result, were very similar to the French legislation that they had been exposed to during their studies.

---

[91] *Copyright Law No. 22 of 1992*, as amended *(Copyright Law)*, Official Gazette No. 3821, 16 April 1992 (Jordan).

[92] *Protection of Copyright and Neighbouring Rights* (No. 22/2006) (Bahrain). See Bahrain, WIPO, <http://www.wipo.int/wipolex/en/details.jsp?id=7311>.

[93] *The Copyright and Related Rights Amending and Supplementing Law No. 2-00* (Law No. 34-05/2006) (Morocco). It came into force after the signature of the Morocco FTA with the US. See Moroco, WIPO <http://www.wipo.int/wipolex/en/text.jsp?file_id=181342>.

[94] *Promulgating the Law of Copyright (Royal Decree No. 65/2008)* (Oman). See Oman, WIPO, <http://www.wipo.int/wipolex/en/details.jsp?id=5832>.

[95] These include Jordan, the UAE, Bahrain, Djibouti, Kuwait, Morocco, Saudi Arabia, Tunisia, Egypt, Mauritania, Qatar, and Oman.

[96] These include Algeria, Bahrain, Egypt, Jordan, Lebanon, Oman, Qatar, Saudi Arabia, Sudan, Syria, Tunisia, the UAE, Morocco, Libya, Comoros, Yemen, and Djibouti.

[97] These include Algeria, Bahrain, Lebanon, Syrian Arab Republic, and the UAE.

[98] See WIPO, *WIPO-Administered Treaties* <http://www.wipo.int/treaties/en/>.

[99] See Eva Steiner, *French Law-A Comparative Approach*, part 1 (Oxford 2010).

[100] Except Sudan, which follows a legal system based on the English common law in addition to Islamic laws. Gaza also has some limited adoption of the common law but not the West Bank, which partially follows the civil law; this situation is due to historical reasons. See also Abdelsalam Hassan, *History of Law Reform in Sudan* (February 2008) Redress <http://www.redress.org/downloads/country-reports/HISTORY%20LAW%20REFORM%20FINALFeb08.pdf>. See, for more information on the legal systems in the Middle East, Chibli Mallat, *Introduction to Middle Eastern Law* (Oxford University, 2007) ch 1,7.

To date, there has been limited research on Arab copyright laws in Arabic[101] or English,[102] which examines the importance of those laws to future social and

[101] See, generally, the following research in Arabic: Faisel Al Kandry, 'Civil Protection of Computer Software in Kuwaiti Law' (a paper presented at the Computer and Law Conference, Emirates University, Dubai, 1-3 May 2000); Mustafa Arjawi, 'Civil Protection for Computer Software' (a paper presented at the Computer and Law Conference, Emirates University, Dubai, 1-3 May 2000); Nazeh AL Mahdi, 'Civil Protection of Computer Software according to Applicable Laws' (a paper presented at the Computer and Law Conference, Emirates University, Dubai, 1-3 May 2000); Ahmad Saman, 'Legal Protection of Computer Software – Applications in Comparative Laws and in the Gulf States' (a paper presented at Kuwaiti Conference on Law and Computers, Kuwait, 4-7 November 1989); Dala Essa Wasna, *Protection of Copyright on the Internet* (Sader, 2002); Nouri Hamad Khater, *Explanation of Intellectual Property Rules—Author's Rights and Neighbouring Rights* (Emirates University, 2008); Naeam Imgabgab, *Protection of Computer Software: A Comparative Study* (AL Halabi, 2006); Emad Salamah, *Legal Protection of Computer Software and Software Piracy Problem* (Dar Wael, 2005); Abd-Al Razaq al Sunhouri, *Explanation of the New Civil Code* 274-436 (AL Halabi, 3rd ed, 1998); Naeam Imgabgab, *Artistic Property and Neighbouring Rights—A Comparative Study* (AL Halabi, 2000); Mohamad Housam Loutfi, *Legal Protection of Computer Software* (Dar Althaqafa, Cairo, 1987); The Arab Organisation for Education, Culture and Science—Copyright in the Arab World in accordance with Arab and International Legislation (1999); Tourki Hamad Saqar, *The Protection of Copyright–Theory and Practice* (Arab Union Association, 1996); Mohamad Housam Loutfi, *Public Performance Right in Musical Work—A Comparative Study Between Egyptian and French law* (Egyptian Association for Books, 1987); Edward Eead, *Copyright and Neibouring Rights in the Lebanese, Arabic and Foreign Laws* (Sader, 2001); Abd al-Rasheed Mamoun and Mohamad Sami Abd Alsadak, *Copyright and Neighbouring Rights* (Dar Al Nahda, 2008).

[102] Among the limited research on the copyright law in Jordan and Arab countries in English, see generally, Fawzi Mulki, *Implementing National Copyright Law-a Jordanian Case Study* (proceedings of the 2nd international conference on Theory and practice of electronic governance, 2008) <http://dl.acm.org/citation.cfm?id=1509134&bnc=1> (one of the few articles that investigates the major challenges, including cultural and socio-economic, resulting from the implementation of a national copyright law in a country such as Jordan. The author argues that public education, awareness campaigns, and training programs are essential to the success of such law); Saleh Al-Sharieh, 'The Purpose of Copyright Protection in Jordan and Canada: A Brief Comparison' (2008) 2 (2), *Intellectual Property Management* 97-115 (comparing the copyright law in Jordan with the copyright law in Canada and arguing that the Jordanian law is not balanced and aligned toward the interests of copyright holders and not users; the author does not offer specific suggestions on how to improve the copyright law in the country); Fayad Al Qudah, 'Legal Protection of Databases; A Study of Jordanian Law' (2008) 22 *Arab Law Quarterly* 360-386 (explaining a descriptive study that deals with the legal protection of databases under the copyright law in Jordan and international conventions that Jordan has signed and arguing that the Jordanian protection of databases is in compliance with international standards in the TRIPS Agreement and that there is no further amendments needed to the law). See also David Price, 'Copyright Protection in Developing States and the Enforcements Dichotomy: The Case of the Arab Gulf States' (a paper presented at the 5th Asian Law Institute Conference, 22-23 May 2008, Singapore); Nowaf Kanan, *Jordanian Copyright Law* (Dar Al Thaqafa, 2004). See also Makeen F. Makeen, 'Moral Rights Protection under Egyptian Author's Rights Law' (2007) 83 (1) *International Review of Intellectual Property and Competition Law* 51; Makeen F Makeen, 'Authorship/Ownership of Copyright works under Egyptian Author's Rights' (2007) 35 (5) *International Review of Intellectual Property and Competition Law* 571; Ramzi Madi, 'Copyright Issues in Mobile Phone Ringtones in General and in the Light of the Jordanian Copyright Protection Law' (2012) 3 *Computer and Telecommunication Law Review* 76-83.

economic development and how such laws should be restructured in order to deal with digital technologies and the Internet.[103] The majority of literature on IP and the Arab world have focused on FTAs,[104] the pharmaceutical sector,[105] TRIPS,[106] and e-commerce and the Internet.[107] Another category of writing that addresses IP and

---

[103] See Housam Dean Al Sageir and Husam al Badrawi, *Copyright Law in the Egyptian Copyright Law–An Analytical Study from a Development Perspective* (in Arabic) (2008) Bibliotheca Alexandria <http://www.bibalex.org/a2k/attachments/references/reffileabuput55g4kzfh55mzm45 feh.pdf> (detailing one of the few studies in Arabic that discusses the importance of copyright from a development perspective and providing a good critique of the Egyptian Intellectual Property Law and suggestions for future improvement of the law).

[104] Mohammad Nasour, 'Fundamental Facts of the United States–Jordan Free Trade Agreement; Ecommerce, Dispute Resolution, and Beyond' 27 *Fordham International Law Journal* 742 <http://ir. lawnet.fordham.edu/cgi/viewcontent.cgi?article=1930&context=ilj> (a study that gives an overview of the JUSFTA without further analysis); Bashar H. Malkwai, 'The Intellectual Property Provisions of the United States—Jordan Free Trade Agreement: Template or not Template' (2006) 9 *Journal of World Intellectual Property* 213-229 (outlining the provisions of the JUSFTA in connection with IP and aruging that, in its current format, it does not serve as a good template for other Arab countries that want to also sign a FTA); David Price, 'The U.S. Bahrain Free Trade Agreement and Intellectual Property Protection in the Global IPRs Regime' (2004) 7 (6) *Journal of World Intellectual Property* 829 (the author argues that Bahrain's FTA will impact significantly on the other Gulf states by establishing the new regional benchmark for IP to which other states will be pressured to accede); Mohammed El Said, 'The European TRIPS-Plus Model and the Arab World: From Co-operation to Association- A New Era' (2007) 28 (1) *Liverpool Law Review* 143-174; Paul G. Johnson, 'Shoring U.S. National Security and Encouraging Economic Reform in the Middle East: Advocating Free Trade with Egypt' (2006) 15 *Minnesota Journal of International Journal* 457; Peter Drahos, 'Bits and Bibs: Bilateralism in Intellectual Property' (2001) 4 *Journal* of *World Intellectual Property* 791-808 (arguing that Jordan's FTA contains several TRIPS-Plus provisions that are 'more extensive protection' than is conferred by TRIPS); Ahmed Y. Zohny, 'The Egyptian Free Trade Agreement, Challenges and Prospects' (2001) 16 *Arab Law Quarterly* 106-132.

[105] Hamed EL Said and Mohammed El Said, 'TRIPS-Plus Implications for Access to Medicine in Developing Countries: Lessons from Jordan- United States Free Trade Agreement' (2007) 10 *Journal of World Intellectual Property* 438-475 (contending that, based on pure interviews, the USJFTA was not useful for the development of the Jordanian pharmaceutical sector).

[106] Mohammed El–Said, 'The Road from TRIPS-Minus, to TRIPS-Plus: Implications of IPRs for the Arab world' (2005) 8 *Journal of World Intellectual Property* 53-65 (examining how Jordan, Bahrain, and Morocco, in less that a decade, moved from TRIPS-Minus to TRIPS-Plus and how that might restrain their ability to implement their agreements and limit their negotiation power multilaterally); Mohammed El Said, *The Development of Intellectual Property Protection in the Arab World* (Edwin Mellen Pres, 2008); David Price, *The Development of Intellectual Property Regimes in the Arabian Gulf States:Infidels at the Gates* (Routledge, 2009).

[107] Valentina M. Donini, *Bridging The Gap: Privatization Policy, Internet and E-commerce in Jordan* (2006) European University Institute <http://cadmus.iue.it/dspace/bitstream/1814/6317/1/ RSCAS_2006_37.pdf<http://cadmus.iue.it/dspace/bitstream/1814/6317/1/RSCAS_2006_37. pdf> (stating the Jordanian e-transaction law and comparing it to other similar laws in the U.A.E and Tunisia; there is no mention of the importance of copyright laws to developments of Jordan and the Arab world); Soumitra Dutta and Mazen E. Coury, *ICT in the Arab World* (February 2003) *The World Economic Forum* <http://www.weforum.org/pdf/Global_Competitiveness_Reports/ Reports/GITR_2002_2003/Arab_World.pdf>; Virginia La Torre Jeker et al., 'E-Transaction Law and Online Dispute Resolution: A Necessity in the Middle East' (2006) 20 Arab *Law Quarterly* 43-67; Toni Essa, '*Legal Regulation of the Internet*' (Sader, 2001); Mahmoud

Arab countries[108] concentrate particularly on how Sharia and Islamic jurisprudence protect IP provisions.[109] There has also been research carried out by economists on copyright-based industries in the Arab countries,[110] the economic performance of

---

Al-Kandri, 'Infringements of Copyright and Trademarks in Electronic Commerce: A Kuwaiti and Comparative Approach' (2002) 17 *Arab Law Quarterly* 3 (2002) 3-27; Marwan Ibraheem & Hisaham Tahat, Paper, *21st BILETA Conference: Globalisation and Harmonization in Technology Law* at the University of Malta: 'Regulating Electronic Contracts in Jordan' (April 2006) SSRN <http://papers.ssrn.com/sol3/papers.cfm?abstract_id=1498320>; Rami Olwan, 'Contracting and Proving Contracts in Cyberspace' (2002) (in Arabic) 26 *Kuwait Law Journal* 229-288; Rami Olwan, 'Conflicts Over Domain Names' (in Arabic) (2005) 22 *Sharia and Law Journal* 239-327; Rami Olwan, *Critical Review of the Proposed Palestinian Electronic Commerce Law* (in Arabic) (Mas, 2006).

108 Essam Al Tamimi, 'Current U.A.E Copyright and how it Compares and Contrast with WTO's TRIPS Agreement and the Berne Convention' (1999) 2 *Journal of World Intellectual Property* 371-391; Eric Garduno and Frank J. Pietrucha, 'Intellectual Property in the Arab World', *Georgetown* (2003) 1 (1) *Journal of International Affairs,* 57-63 <http://www12.georgetown.edu/sfs/publications/journal/Issues/ws03/gardunolocked.pdf>; Nouri Khater, *Explanation of the Rules of Intellectual Property-Industrial Property—A Comparative Study between the Emarati, Jordanian and Frensh Laws* (Emirates University, 2005) (comparing, in Arabic, Emarati, Jordanian, and French laws).

109 Heba A. Raslan, 'Shari'a and the Protection of Intellectual Property Rights, the Example of Egypt' (2007) 47 *IDEA: Intellectual Property Law Review* 497; Muhammad Amanullah, 'Author's Copyright: An Islamic Perspective' (2006) 9 (3) *Journal of World Intellectual Property* 301-315 (analyzing how Muslims view copyright according to divergent Islamic jurisprudence schools) 301-315; Ali Khan, 'Islam as Intellectual Property-My Lord! Increase me in Knowledge' (2001) 31 *Cumberland Law Review* 361 <http://papers.ssrn.com/sol3/papers.cfm?abstract_id=936291>; Steven D. Jamar, 'The Protection of Intellectual Property under Islamic Law' (1992) 21 *Capital University Law Review* 1079 <http://papers.ssrn.com/sol3/papers.cfm?abstract_id=1148735>; Richard E. Vaughan, 'Defining Terms in the Intellectual Property Protection Debate: Are the North and South arguing past enough other when we say Property? A Property Lockean, Confusion, and Islamic Comparison' (1996) 2 *Journal of International and Comparative Law* 307; Amir H. Khoury, 'Ancient and Islamic Sources of Intellectual Property Protection in the Middle East: A Focus on Trademarks' (2003) 43 *IDEA: Intellectual Property Law Review* 151; Ida Madieha bt. Abdul Ghani Azmi, 'The Philosophy of Intellectual Property Rights over Ideas in Cyberspace: A Comparative Analysis between the Western Jurisprudence and the Shari'a' (2004) 19 *Arab Law Quarterly* 191-207; Jonathan A Claypod, 'Islamic Law and Modern Patent Law' (2007) 14 *CASRIP's Newsletter* <http://www.law.washington.edu/Casrip/Newsletter/default.aspx?year=2007&article=newsv14i2Claypool>; Sajjad Chowdhry, *Intellectual Property in Islam* (6 March 2006) Dinar Standard <http://dinarstandard.com/leadership/intellectual-property-rights-in-islam/>; Noera Ayaz, *Intellectual Property Gaining Protection in the Muslim World* 2 (March 2006) Science Development Network <http://www.sciencedev.net/fe/Article.aspx?Aid=592>; Naser M. Muhaisen, 'Intellectual Property: An Islamic Perspective' (2009) 56 (2-3) *Journal of the Copyright Society of the USA* 571-587.

110 Najib Harabi, *Copyright-based Industries in Arab Countries* (University of Applied Science, Paper No. 5181, 2004), <http://mpra.ub.uni-muenchen.de/5181/> (outlining empirically the economic performance of four key copyright-based industries in Morocco, Tunisia, Egypt and Jordan).

Arabic book translation industry,[111] the role of small and medium enterprises (SMEs) as copyright owners and copyright users,[112] software piracy,[113] and trademarks protection in the Arab countries.[114] It is also important to note that there is a great deal of research written on access to medicine in developing countries,[115] the expansion of IP,[116] and compulsory licensing.[117] In contrast, research that deals with digital copyright has focused only on the interests of developed countries, with limited particular consideration of the interests of developing countries.[118] Accordingly, the analysis and commentary concerning the

---

[111] Najib Harabi, *Performance of Arabic Book Translation: Industry in selected Arab Countries: Egypt, Lebanon, Morocco, Saudi Arabia and Syria* (University of Applied Science, Paper No. 4385, 2007) <http://mpra.ub.uni-muenchen.de/4385/1/MPRA_paper_4385.pdf>.

[112] Ahmead F. Ghoneim, *Intellectual Property in Arab Countries: SMEs as Copyright Owners and/or Copyright Users* (2003) WIPO <http://www.wipo.int/edocs/mdocs/sme/en/wipo_ip_mow_02/wipo_ip_mow_02_12.pdf>.

[113] Samir N Hamade, *The Legal and Political Aspects of Software Piracy in the Arab World* (2006) IEEE xplore <http://ieeexplore.ieee.org/stamp/stamp.jsp?arnumber=01611583> (a general study with no analysis of the situation of piracy in the Arab world. The author argues that there is a need for stronger copyright laws and enforcement based primarily on political preferences); Bassam Al Talhouni, 'New Tougher Copyright Legislation', (1996) 18 (10) *European Intellectual Property Law Review* 302-303.

[114] See Amir H. Khoury, 'The Development of Modern Trademark Legislation and Protection in Arab Countries of the Middle East' (2003) *16 Transnational Lawyer Review* 249; Fayad Alqudah, 'Protection of Well-Known Trademarks under Jordanian Law', *IP Forum* (2009) 76.

[115] See Rosa Castro Bernieri, 'Intellectual Property Rights in Bilateral Investment Treaties and Access to Medicines: The Case of Latin America' (2006) 9 (5) *Journal of World Intellectual Property* 548–572.

[116] David Lea, 'The Expansion and Restructuring of Intellectual Property and its Implication for the Developing World' (2008) 11 (1) *Ethical Theory and Moral Practice* 37-60.

[117] Tshimanga Kongolo, 'Compulsory License Issues in African Countries' (2004) 7 (2) *Journal of World Intellectual Property* 185–199; Sandra Bartelt, 'Compulsory Licensing Pursuant to TRIPS Article 31 in the Light of the Doha Deceleration on the TRIPS Agreement and Public Health' (2003) 6 (2) *Journal of World Intellectual Property* 283-310.

[118] Tana Pistorius, 'Developing Countries and Copyright in the Information Age—The Functional Equivalent Implementation of the WCT' (2006) 9 (2) Potchefstroom Electronic Law Journal/ Potchefstroomse Elektroniese Regsblad <http://www.saflii.org/za/journals/PER/2006/11.html>; Symposium Review: Locking up the Bridge on the Digital Divide—A Consideration of the Global Impact of the U.S Anti-Circumvention Measures for the Participation of Developing Countries in the Digital Economy, (2004) 20 *Santa Clara Computer and High Technology Law Review* 941 (arguing that technological measures may not be helpful for developing countries to realise the full potential of digital technologies and Internet networks); Peter Drahos, 'Developing Countries and International Intellectual Property Standard Setting' (2002) 5 (5) *Journal of World Intellectual Property* 765 (contending that IP standards settings have been dominated predominately by the West (US and EU), and hence developing countries can expect very few concessions on IP issues in either bilateral or multilateral agreements, and they should look for self-helps); Clemente Forero-Pineda, 'The Impact of Stronger Intellectual Property Rights on Science and Technology in Developing Countries' (2006) 35 (6) Research Policy 808-824 <http://www.sciencedirect.com/science/article/pii/S0048733306000631> (argues that stronger protection of IP has extended from developed countries, affecting pharmaceutics, biodiversity, and ethnic knowledge); John Feather,

Copyright Law in Jordan are of importance to many sectors of the economy and will help to provide a clear picture of the role that copyright law plays in the social and economic development of developing countries, particularly Arab countries.

5.2.5 Introduction to the Jordanian Copyright Law

The first *Copyright Law* in Jordan entered into force in 1992[119] and has since been revised on several occasions, the latest revision taking effect in 2005.[120] The *Copyright Law* in Jordan is primarily based on the 'author's rights' or 'droit d'auteur system',[121] as it has come to be applied in Continental Europe (particularly France), rather than the Anglo-Saxon 'copyright system'[122] present in common law jurisdictions, namely the US, Canada, and the UK.[123]

Amongst the differences that exist between the two systems is that the European 'copyright system' has been predominantly influenced by the natural law theory, while the common law 'copyright system' is influenced by the utilitarian theory.[124] The copyright law legislation in civil law countries is principle-based and more

'Copyright in Developing Countries: Necessity or Luxury?' (1993) 25 *International Information and Library Review* 15-25 (arguing that copyright is necessary for developing countries and is not regarded as luxury); Weerawit Weeraworawit, 'Why do Developing Countries Fail to Use IP as a Tool for Development?' (a paper presented at the 5th Annual Asian IP Law and Policy Day, New York, US, 26 March, 2008) ; E.S Nwauche, Intellectual Property Rights, Copyright and Development Policy in a Developing Country: Options for Sub Saharan African Countries (a paper presented at Copyright Workshop for Zimbabwe International Book Fair, Zimbabwe, 30 July, 2003); Peter Drahos, 'Bits and Bibs: Bilateralism in Intellectual Property' (2001) 4 (6) *Journal of World Intellectual Property* 803; Christophe Antons, 'Copyright Law Reform and Information Society in Indonesia' in Brian Fitzgerald (ed), *Digital Content and the Internet in Asia-Pacific* (Sydney University, 2008) <http://eprints.qut.edu.au/13632/1/13632.pdf>.

[119] Before the 1992 amendments to the copyright law in Jordan, the *Othman Copyright Law of 1906* (Turkey) was applicable in Arab countries, including Jordan.

[120] *Copyright Law No. 22 of 1992*, as amended (*Copyright Law*), Official Gazette No. 3821, 16 April 1992 (Jordan), see also *Amendments to the Copyright Law No. 14 of 1998*, Official Gazette No. 4304, 1 October 1998, *Amendments to the Copyright Law No. 29 of 1999*, Official Gazette No. 4383, 2 October 1999, *Amendments to the Copyright Law No. 78 of 2003*, Official Gazette No. 4606, 16 June 2003, *Amendments to the Copyright Law No. 88 of 2003*, Official Gazette No. 4634, 1 December 2003, *Amendment to the Copyright Law No. 8 of 2005*, Official Gazette No. 4702, 31 March 2005.

[121] See art 8 of the *Copyright Law* in Jordan.

[122] See art 9 of the *Copyright Law* in Jordan in relation to moral rights, which is based on the 'author's rights system' and not on the 'copyright system'.

[123] For further explanation of the difference between 'droit d'auteur system' and the Anglo-Saxon or Anglo-American 'copyright system', see Silke Von Lewinski, *International Copyright Law and Policy* (Oxford University, 2008) 33-63; SM Stewart, *International Copyright and Neighbouring Rights* (2nd ed, Butterworths, 1989) ch 14; Elizabeth Adeney, *The Moral Rights of Authors and Performers* (Oxford University, 2006) ch 8.

[124] Lewinski, above n 123, 38.

abstract; it is shorter and less detailed if compared to copyright status under the common law.[125] The main amendments to the *Copyright Law* in Jordan that has been to date include:

1) The protection of computer software[126];
2) The extension of the right of the copyright owners to include the right to control the online distribution of digital material[127];
3) The inclusion of civil and criminal provisions[128] for the removal or alteration of RMI[129];
4) The inclusion of civil and criminal provisions[130] on prohibiting the circumvention of TPMs[131];
5) The extension of the right of the performers to control the distribution of their work in any form, including electronic format[132]; and
6) The extension of the right of the producers of phonograms to control the distribution of their work in any form, including electronic format.[133]

---

[125] Ibid 43.

[126] Article 3 (B)(8) of the *Copyright Law No. 22 of 1992*, as amended.

[127] Article 9(A) of the *Copyright Law No. 22 of 1992*, as amended.

[128] Article 54 of the *Copyright Law No. 22 of 1992*, as amended.

[129] RMI is 'a technology such as digital watermarks that includes details about the copyright owners and terms and conditions of use of the copyright materials'. See Attorney General's Department, Australian Government, Fact Sheet: US Free Trade Agreement Implementation Act of 2004 (2005) <http://www.crimeprevention.gov.au/www/agd/agd.nsf/Page/Publications_Electronicrightsmanagement-Factsheet-March2005> (follow the link under 'Downloads').

[130] Article 55 of the *Copyright Law No. 22 of 1992*, as amended.

[131] TPMs are 'technical locks that copyright owners use to stop their copyright material from being copied or accessed' (*e.g.*, passwords, encryption software and access codes).' *Copyright Amendment (Technological Protection Measures) Bill 2006 and related Regulations—Exposure Drafts*, Australian Government <http://www.ag.gov.au/Publications/Pages/CopyrightAmendment(Technological-ProtectionMeasures)Bill2006andrelatedRegulationsExposureDrafts.aspx>. The EU Copyright Directive 2001/29/EC in chapter III defines TPMs as:

> [A]ny technology, device or component that, in the normal course of its operation, is designed to prevent or restrict acts, in respect of works or other subject- matter, which are not authorized by the right holder of any of any copyright or any right related to copyright as provided by law or the sui generis right.

See Council Directive 2001/29/EC of 22 May 2001 on the Harmonisation of Certain Aspects of Copyright and Related Rights in the Information Society ('Information Society Directive') [2001] OJ L167, 10. See also Ian Brown, 'The Evolution of Anti- Circumvention Law' (2006) (2) (3) *International Review of Law, Computers & Technology* 239-260 <http://eprints.ucl.ac.uk/3879/1/3879.pdf>.

[132] Article 23 A(2) of the *Copyright Law No. 22 of 1992*, as amended.

[133] Article 23 (C)(1) of the *Copyright Law No. 22 of 1992*, as amended.

Despite these developments, in its February 2008 submission to the US Trade Representative for the Special 301 Report,[134] the International Intellectual Property Alliance (IIPA) recommended Jordan for the IP-monitored watch list since piracy is still considered as a serious problem in the country and there are no proper enforcement measures.[135] Previously, in its 2007 submission for the Special 301 Report, the IIPA urged the US government to initiate immediate dispute settlement consultations under art 16 (consultation) and art 17 (dispute settlement) of the JUSFTA to bring Jordan into compliance with its international obligations.[136] The IIPA requested that Jordan amend its *Copyright Law* and to fully implement the FTA signed with the US in its 2009 Special 301 submission.[137] The 2010 and 2011 Special 301 submissions do not mention Jordan.[138]

5.3 Fundamentals of the Jordanian Copyright Law

This subsection will give an overview of the *Copyright Law* in Jordan for the purpose of understanding the law, prior to critiquing it in the next section.

5.3.1 Copyright Subject Matter

Copyright subject matter is defined in art 3(B) of the *Copyright Law* in Jordan in much the same way as in many other countries. Article 3(B) establishes the kinds of works that are copyright-protected mainly:[139]

---

[134] International Intellectual Property Alliance (IIPA), *Special 301 Report on Jordan* (2008) <http://www.iipa.com/2008_SPEC301_TOC.htm>.

[135] Ibid.

[136] Dispute Settlement: Jordan, International Intellectual Property Alliance (IIPA), *Special 301 Report on Jordan* (2007) <http://www.iipa.com/rbc/2007/2007SPEC301JORDAN.pdf>.

[137] *Jordan*, International Intellectual Property Alliance (IIPA), *Special 301 Report on Jordan* (2009) 385–88 <http://www.iipa.com/rbc/2009/2009SPEC301JORDAN.pdf>.

[138] International Intellectual Property Alliance (IIPA), *Special 301 Report* (2010) <http://www.ustr.gov/webfm_send/1906>; International Intellectual Property Alliance (IIPA), *Special 301 Report* (2011) <http://www.iipa.com/2011_SPEC301_TOC.htm>.

[139] The list of copyright subject matter is non-conclusive, and this evidenced by the wording of art 3(B), which provides that 'protection shall encompass works which are expressed in writing, sound, drawing, photography or movement and in particular'. *Copyright Law*, below n 141, art 3 (B) (Jordan) (as amended); see also Ibid, art 7(D) (expression of folklore); Ibid, art 3(D) (compilation of works); Ibid, art 3(D) (encyclopedias). See also art 7(D) (expression of folklore), art 3(D) (compilation of works) and art 3(D) (encyclopaedias) of the *Copyright Law* in Jordan.

- Books, booklets, or other written materials;
- Works that are recited orally, such as lectures, speeches, and sermons;
- Theoretical works, lyrical plays, musical plays, and mime;
- Musical works, whether digitised or not or accompanied with words or not;
- Motion picture works and audio and visual broadcast works;
- Works of paintings, photography, sculpture, engraving, architecture, and applied and ornamentation arts;
- Illustrative figures, maps, layouts, charts, and three-dimensional works related to geography and earth's level maps;
- Computer programs, whether in the source language or in the machine language.[140]

The *Copyright Law* in Jordan does not require any formality for copyright protection, including the registration of the work with any certain authority. One condition must be met to qualify for protection, and that is originality (art 3 (A)).

The *Copyright Law* allows reproduction of official documents without authorisation by the author or payment of any remuneration. There is no copyright in the official texts of legal, administrative, or judicial nature, according to the exclusion made by art 7(A).[141] Those documents fall immediately into the public domain.[142] Some copyright laws around the world have not protected government

[140] The *Copyright Law* also provides for the protection of rights related to performances (art 23 (A)), broadcasts and televisions (art 23(B)), and sound recordings (art 23(D)). These were some of the latest amendments that were made to the law. Ibid, art 23(A)–(B).

[141] Article 7(A) of the *Copyright Law* in Jordan provides as follows:

> Protection shall not include:
>
> 1. Official documents, whatever the source or target language thereto, including legal text, regulations, decisions, international agreements judicial rulings, arbitral awards, and judgments issued by administrative committees of judicial competence.

Copyright Law No. 22 of 1992, as amended *(Copyright Law*), Official Gazette No. 3821, 16 April 1992 (Jordan).

[142] See art 34 of the *Copyright Law* in Jordan, which contains a specific provision on public domain. See Ibid, art 34.

works and allow their use widely.[143] There are no clear rules under the *Copyright Law* in Jordan in connection with the status of government work therein.[144]

5.3.2 *Economic or Financial Rights*

The core exclusive economic or financial rights of the copyright owner are specified in art 9 of the *Copyright Law* in Jordan, which includes the following:

- The right to reproduce his work by any method or form, either temporarily or permanently, including photocopying or cinematography or digital recording (the reproduction right);

---

[143] The, *US Copyright Act of 1976*, as amended, defines government works as follows:

> A work of the United States government, as defined by United States copyright law, is 'a work prepared by an officer or employee of the U.S. government as part of that person's official duties.' The term only applies to the work of the federal government, not state or local governments. In general, under section 105 of the Copyright Act, such works are not entitled to domestic copyright protection under U.S. law, sometimes referred to as noncopyright. Section 105 of the *U.S. Copyright Act of 1976,* as amended provides that:
>
> > Copyright protection under this title is not available for any work of the United States Government, but the United States Government is not precluded from receiving and holding copyrights transferred to it by assignment, bequest, or otherwise.

Copyright Act of 1976, § 101, Pub. L. No. 94-553, 90 Stat. 2541 (1976) (codified at 17 U.S.C. § 101).

Copyright Act of 1976, 17 USC §101 (1976). The term only applies to the work of the federal government, not state or local governments. In general, under section 105 of the Copyright Act, such works are not entitled to domestic copyright protection under US law, sometimes referred to as non-copyright. Section 105 provides that:

> Copyright protection under this title is not available for any work of the United States Government, but the United States Government is not precluded from receiving and holding copyrights transferred to it by assignment, bequest, or otherwise

Ibid § 105; see also Anne Fitzgerald (ed), *Open Access Polices, Practices and Licensing: a Review of the Literature in Australia and Selected Jurisdictions, European Public Sector Information Platform Topic Report No. 13-State of Play: PSI Reuse in Australia* (2010) <http://eprints.qut.edu.au/33206/>.

[144] The Jordanian State Secrets and Documents Law authorises public officials to protect from public disclosure broad categories of information that they designate as state secrets and impose criminal liability on any person who violated its provision under the law. State secrets and documents are categorised as strictly confidential, confidential, and restricted. These official documents must be protected from tampering or any loss, and the contents of which may not be disclosed to anyone other than competent parties, unless otherwise authorised. See State Secrets and Documents *Law No. 150 of 1971*, Official Gazette of Jordan, No. 2315 (1 August 1971). See also Jordan Media, USAID, *An Introduction to News Media Law and Policy* 45–46 (Douglas Griffin & Libby Morgan (eds), 2009) <http://www.global.asc.upenn.edu/docs/jordanwebpage/JMSPprimer_eng.pdf>.

- The right to translate his work into another language, adapt it, orchestrate it, or make any alteration thereto (the right of translation and adaptation);
- The right to allow usage of one or more copies of his work by persons using it for rental, lending, or other actions related to displaying the work to the public (the right of rental and lending);
- The right of distribution and making copies either by selling or any other conduct of transfer of ownership (the right of distribution);
- The right of importing copies of a work in commercial quantities even if the copies were reproduced with an authorisation from the right owner (the right of importation); and
- The right to convey his work to the public through recital, display, acting, radio or television broadcasting, cinema, or through any other means (the right of communication to the public).[145]

5.3.3 Moral Rights

In many countries, copyright law also provides authors with moral rights. The *Copyright Law* in Jordan treats a protected work as an extension of the personality of the author. Article 8 encompasses the following as moral rights[146]:

- The right to attribute to himself his work and to have his name listed on all produced copies every time the work is put forward to the public unless the work is mentioned incidentally during a news representation of the current events (the right of respect or paternity);
- The right to make the decision regarding the publication of his work and the specification of the mode and date of publication (the right of divulgation);
- The right to make any amendments to his work, whether by change, revision, deletion, or addition (the right of consideration);
- The right to repel any attack on his work, to prohibit any distortion, misrepresentation, or any other amendments to the work that may harm his reputation and honour. However, if any deletion, change, addition, or other amendments took place during the translation of the work, the author shall not have the right to prevent it unless the translator neglected to refer to the places of this change or if the translation caused damage to the reputation of the author and his cultural or artistic standing or distorted the contents of the work (the right to object to derogatory treatment of the work); and

[145] Article 23 of the *Copyright Law* in Jordan outlines the economic or financial rights of copyright owners of related rights (performers, broadcast, television organisations, and producers of sound recordings). *Copyright Law*, above n 141, art 23.

[146] Compare the *Copyright Law* in Jordan with the French Code de la Propriété Intellectuelle [C.P.I] (French Intellectual Property Code No. 92-597 of 1 July 1992 as amended) L121-129 <http://www.legifrance.gouv.fr/html/codes_traduits/cpialtext.htm>.

- The right to withdraw his work from circulation in cases where serious and legitimate reasons existed for this withdrawal. In such cases, the author shall be obliged to fairly compensate the holder of the financial exploitation rights (the right of retraction).

In some countries like Australia, moral rights last for the duration of the copyright,[147] while in other countries such as China[148] and France,[149] moral rights are 'unlimited' or 'perpetual'; they last forever.[150] There is no express provision in the *Copyright Law* in Jordan that covers the duration of moral rights.[151] Under the law, moral rights 'are not liable for prescription or assignment'. The Jordanian position is similar to the *French Intellectual Property Code* in art L121 (1).[152] The scope of the moral rights, as discussed in art 8 of the *Copyright Law* in Jordan, is based on a literal adaptation of the *Berne Convention*.[153]

---

[147] Section 195AM of the *Australian Copyright Act*, 1968 provides that:

> (1) An author's right of integrity of authorship in respect of a cinematograph film continues in force until the author dies. (2) An author's right of integrity of authorship in respect of a work other than a cinematograph film continues in force until copyright ceases to subsist in the work. (3) An author's moral rights (other than the right of integrity of authorship) in respect of a work continue in force until copyright ceases to subsist in the work.

See the *Australian Copyright Act*, 1968, S. 195 AM, <http://www.austlii.edu.au/au/legis/cth/consol_act/ca1968133/>.

[148] Article 20 of the *Chinese Copyright Law*, as amended, provides that '[t]he rights of authorship, alteration and integrity of an author shall be unlimited in time'. (中华人民共和国著作权法) [Copyright Law of the People's Republic of China of 1990] (promulgated by the Standing Committee of the Seventh National People's Congress, 7 September 1990, art 20 (as amended) <http://www.chinaiprlaw.com/english/laws/laws10.htm>.

[149] See French Intellectual Property Code, below n 152.

[150] Brian Fitzgerald and Rami Olwan, 'Copyright in the UAE in the Digital Age' (2010) 32 (11) *European Intellectual Property Review* (EIPR) 565, 566.

[151] In Mahkamat al-Tamiex [Taimez] [Court of Cassation-Civil Division], case No. 2648/2003, 11 November 2001, the Court mentioned clearly that according to arts 3, 8, and 9 of the *Copyright Law* in Jordan, moral rights are personal rights protected after the death of the author. Transfer of economic rights will allow the author to object to any derogatory treatment or any other amendment on his work or abuse that causes damage to his honour and reputation. The latest draft of the copyright law of Jordan of 2010 provides clearly in art 7 that moral rights are unlimited and inalienable.

[152] Article L121-1 of the *French Intellectual Property Code* provides that an 'author shall enjoy the right to respect for his name, his authorship and his work' and that this right 'shall attach to his person', 'shall be perpetual, inalienable and imprescriptible', and 'may be transmitted to mortis causa to the heirs of the author'. French Intellectual Property Code, above n 146, L121-1.

[153] Article 6bis of the *Berne Convention* provides that:

> (1) Independently of the author's economic rights, and even after the transfer of the said rights, the author shall have the right to claim authorship of the work and to object to any distortion, mutilation or other modification of, or other derogatory action in relation to, the said work, which would be prejudicial to his honor or reputation.
>
> (2) The rights granted to the author in accordance with the preceding paragraph shall, after his death, be maintained, at least until the expiry of the economic rights, and shall be

5.3.4 Authors

Under art 4(A)(1) of the *Copyright Law* in Jordan, 'the person who publishes the work attributed as his own whether by indicating his name on the work or by any other way shall be considered the author unless there is proof to the contrary'. Under art 4(A)(2), persons publishing their name under a pseudonym or an anonym shall also be deemed as authors.[154] A corporate entity can also be recognised as the authors of collective work if it directed its creation (art 35(C)). Article 5 of the *Copyright Law*[155] in Jordan determines who is considered as

---

> exercisable by the persons or institutions authorized by the legislation of the country where protection is claimed. However, those countries whose legislation, at the moment of their ratification of or accession to this Act, does not provide for the protection after the death of the author of all the rights set out in the preceding paragraph may provide that some of these rights may, after his death, cease to be maintained.
> (3) The means of redress for safeguarding the rights granted by this Article shall be governed by the legislation of the country where protection is claimed.

Berne Convention for the Protection of Literary and Artistic Works, opened for signature 9 September 1886, S. Treaty Document No. 99-27 (1986) (as amended) (Berne Convention), art 4bis, art 9 <http://www.wipo.int/treaties/en/ip/berne/trtdocs_wo001.html>. Article 9 of the *Berne Convention* provides that:

> (1) Authors of literary and artistic works protected by this Convention shall have the exclusive right of authorizing the reproduction of these works, in any manner or form.
>
> (2) It shall be a matter for legislation in the countries of the Union to permit the reproduction of such works in certain special cases, provided that such reproduction does not conflict with a normal exploitation of the work and does not unreasonably prejudice the legitimate interests of the author.
> (3) Any sound or visual recording shall be considered as a reproduction for the purposes of this Convention.

Ibid art 9.

[154] *Copyright Law*, above n 141, art 4. See Amendments to the Copyright Law No. 8 of 2005, Official Gazette, No. 4702, 31 March 2005).

[155] According to art 5 of the *Copyright Law* in Jordan, as amended, the following persons shall also qualify as authors of works:

> A person who translates the work into another language, converts it from one form of the forms of literature, arts or sciences into another form, summarizes it, alters it, amends it, illustrates it, comments on it, catalogues it or performs any other action which makes the work appear appears in a new form;
>
> The performer which conveys to the public the work of others whether or not this performance was by singing, playing a musical instrument, rhythm, recital, photography, drawing, movement, steps or any other method; and
>
> Authors of encyclopaedias, collections, compiled data and compilations, which are granted protections by virtue of this law.

Copyright Law, above n 141, art 5(A)–(C).

authors,[156] including translators, performers, and creators of encyclopaedias and collections. Protection is given to authors with innovative literary, artistic, and scientific works, regardless of their kind, importance, or the purpose of their production (art 3).

5.3.5 Ownership and Duration/Term

Under the *Copyright Law* in Jordan, the author or his successors in title to the work may grant licenses and transfer some or all of his financial or economic rights either to a natural person or a corporate entity provided that the transfer is evidenced in writing. The transfer agreement must specify and detail every right being disposed of by indicating its 'extent, purpose, period and place of exploitation'.[157] The term or length of protection that copyright law provides will depend on the type of copyright subject matter that is in issue. For example, under the *Copyright Law* in Jordan, copyright in a book or software will last for the life of the author, plus 50 years after his death (art 30).[158]

---

[156] Joint authorship occurs under art 35(A) of the *Copyright Law* in Jordan when:

> More than one person contributed to making a single work such that the share contributed by each cannot be separated, they shall be considered as owners of the work with each having an equal share unless they agree to do something different. None of them shall, in this case, exercise the copyrights with respect to this work without the consent of all the authors.

Ibid art 35(A).

[157] Article 28 of the *Copyright Law* in Jordan provides that:

> The author may dispose of any of his rights with respect to the work on the basis of sharing with others in a percentage of the revenues or profits resulting from the financial exploitation of the work by the others. A precondition is that the author shall have the right to obtain an additional share of the said revenues or proceeds, if it is established that the agreement concerning the exploitation of his work was not fair to his interests, or became so for condition and circumstances which were not known at the date of the contracting or which took place afterwards.

Ibid art 28.

[158] For a performer or producer of phonograms, copyright will last for 50 years from the end of the year where the fixation was made or the performance took place (art 23(E)); for a broadcast organisation, copyright in a broadcast will last for 20 years from the end of the year when the broadcast took place (art 23(E)); and for applied works, copyright will last for 25 years starting from an arbitrary date for the archiving of the work (being the first of January in the calendar year in which the work was actually archived (art 32). Ibid arts 23(E), 32; see also *Berne Convention*, above n 153, art 7 (1); TRIPS, above n 25, art 9 (1).

5.3.6 Treatment of Foreign Copyright

Pursuant to a series of international conventions beginning with the *Berne Convention* and including the *Rome Convention*, the *TRIPS Agreement*, WCT, and WPPT, many countries protect the copyright of a foreigner under their law as if the foreigner were a citizen of their country. This is known as the 'national treatment' principle.[159] The *Copyright Law* in Jordan protects foreign works in art 56.[160] In art 56, 'reciprocity' is different from national treatment and fails to meet the standards of the *Berne Convention*, *Rome Convention*, TRIPS, WCT, and WPPT.[161] Article 56(C) suggests that Jordan has adopted national treatment in

---

[159] Edward J. Ellis, 'National Treatment under the Berne Convention and the Doctrine of Forum Non Convenient' (1996) 36 (1) *IDEA: Intellectual Property Law Review* 327-344.

Article 5 of the *Berne Convention* provides that:

> Authors shall enjoy, in respect of works for which they are protected under this convention, in countries of the union other than the country of origin, the rights which their respective laws do now or may hereafter grant to their nationals, as the rights especially granted by this Convention.

Berne Convention, above n 153, art 5.

[160] Article 56 of the *Copyright Law* in Jordan provides that:

> A. The provisions of this law shall apply to the works of Jordanians and foreigners which are published or not published and which are expressed by any of the means stipulated in paragraph (B) of article 3 inside the Kingdom as well as the works of Jordanians which are published or not published and which are expressed by any of the means stipulated in paragraph (B) of article 3 outside the Kingdom.
> B. Taking into consideration the provisions of the international agreements concerning copyright and in case of their non-applicability, the principle of reciprocity shall be applied. The provisions of this law shall apply to the works of foreign authors which are published or not published and which are expressed by any of the means stipulated in paragraph (B) of article 3 of this law outside the Kingdom.
> C. For the purposes of the application of this law, the authors who have regular residence in one of member countries in the international agreements dealing with copyright, which Jordan has acceded to, without being citizen of that country shall be treated as citizen of the Kingdom. This article shall also apply to the holders of the rights stipulated in article 23 of this law.

See *Copyright Law*, above n 141, art 56(A)–(C). Compare ibid with *United Arab Emirates Federal Law No. 7 of 2002 Pertaining to Copyright and Neighbouring Rights*, as amended, with art 44 ('Without prejudice to the provisions of International conventions applicable in the State; if disputes arise in respect of the laws, provisions of the law herein shall apply to the works, performances, phonograms and broadcasts made by foreigners, provided that the principle of reciprocity is applied.').

[161] On 'national treatment', see Adrian Sterling, *World Copyright Law* (Sweet and Maxwell, 2003) 151, 605. On the role of 'material reciprocity' under the Berne Convention, see Lewinski, above n 123, 100-101; 112-113; Fitzgerald and Olwan, above n 150, 567-568.

respect of foreign authors and that the principle of reciprocity in art 56(B) is being applied only where the relevant international conventions are not applicable.[162]

5.3.7 *Work for Hire*

Article 6 of the *Copyright Law*[163] in Jordan provides for the cases of the work created under a contract of employment. If the employee creates a work using the tools and experience of his employer, then the economic rights will be for the latter, unless otherwise agreed in writing.[164]

5.3.8 *Limitations to Author's Exclusive Rights*

Under copyright laws worldwide, the exclusive economic or financial rights of the copyright owner are normally subject to limitations and exceptions. These limitations and exceptions will usually permit various uses of copyright material for no cost and without the permission of the copyright owner in specified circumstances.[165] There are three categories of limitations and

---

[162] Fitzgerald and Olwan, above n 150.

[163] Amended by the latest amendments to the law.

[164] Article 6 of the *Copyright Law* in Jordan provides as follows:

> A. If the work was innovated for the account of another person, the copyright shall revert to the innovated author unless there is a written agreement stipulating otherwise.
> B. In spite of the inclusions of paragraph (A) of this article and in any other Law, if an employee created during his employment a work related to the activities or business of the employer, or uses the experiences, information, instruments or articles of the employer under the employee's own disposal in his attempt to create such work, the copyrights shall be to the benefit of the employer, unless otherwise agreed upon in writing.
> C. The Intellectual property rights shall be to the benefit of the employee, if the intellectual property right created by the same is not related to the business of the employer, and the employee does not use the experiences, information, instruments, or raw materials of the employer in his attempt to conduct such creation, unless otherwise agreed upon in writing.

Copyright Law, above n 141, art 6(A)–(C).

[165] See Teresa Hackett, *Exceptions and Limitations in Copyright Vital for South Countries*, (3 November 2008) Third World Network <http://www.twnside.org.sg/title2/intellectual_property/info.service/2008/twn.ipr.info.081102.htm>; Fernando dos Santos, Julieta Nhana and Filipe Sitoi, ACA2K, Country Report: Mozambique (2009) <http://www.aca2k.org/attachments/154_Mozambique_ACA2K_Country_Report.pdf>; Consumers International, *Copyright and Access to Knowledge, Policy Recommendations on Flexibilities in Copyright Laws* (2006) Soros Foundation <http://www.consumersinternational.org/media/303356/copyright%20and%20access%20to%20knowledge%20-%20full%20report%20(pdf).pdf>.

exceptions[166]: 1) those that safeguard fundamental user rights concerning the individual; 2) those concerning commercial interest, industry, practice, and competition; and 3) those concerning society at large and aimed towards the promotion and dissemination of knowledge and information.[167]

The *Copyright Law* in Jordan has its influences in the French and the European legal systems that do not use the terms 'fair use' or 'fair dealing' but instead make reference to 'limitations to an author's exclusive rights'. Jordan has followed, through its *Copyright Law*, the limitations and exceptions established by the *Berne Convention*: certain uses of public lectures for information purposes (art 2 bis(2)), reproduction in general (art 9(2)), quotation (art 10(1)), illustration for teaching (art 10 (2)), certain uses of works on certain events (art 10 bis (1)), and incidental uses of works when reporting on current event (art 10 bis (2)).[168] Any limitation and exceptions, as specified under the *Copyright Law* in Jordan, should comply with the so-called three-step test as follows:

1. The limitation or exception is set under specific cases.
2. There is no conflict with normal exploitation of the work.
3. The limitation and exception cannot prejudice the author's interest.[169]

5.3.9 Reproduction for Translation Purposes (Art 11(A))

Article 11(A) of the *Copyright Law* in Jordan gives any Jordanian who is working in a pre-college or a college, and for research purposes, the right to obtain a non-exclusive and non-assignable licence from the Minister of Culture (or whomever the Minster deputises) to translate any foreign work to Arabic and to publish that work in any form, provided that there has been the passage of 3 years since the first publication of the work and that there is no available Arabic translation of the work or, if there was a translation, it is out of stock. In the event of the granting of a

---

[166] Hackett, above n 165.

[167] Examples of the first kind include the reproduction of public speeches, the right to make quotations, reporting current events, parody, and reproduction for private non-commercial use. See Ibid. Examples of the second kind include press reviews, ephemeral recordings by broadcasting organisations, museum catalogues, and de-compilation/reverse engineering of computer programmes for interoperability. See Ibid. Examples of the third kind include provisions for libraries, educators for teaching and research, people with disabilities, reporting of parliamentary and judicial proceedings, and religious celebrations. See Ibid.

[168] See Lewinski above n 123, ch 23, 564; see also *TRIPS*, above n 25, art 9(1).

[169] Article 13 of the *TRIPS Agreement* provides that:

> Members shall confine limitations or exceptions to exclusive rights to certain special cases which do not conflict with a normal exploitation of the work and do not unreasonably prejudice the legitimate interests of the right holder.

TRIPS, above n 25, art 13.

non-exclusive licence for translation from the Minister of Culture, the author shall deserve fair compensation determined in accordance with the law.[170]

5.3.9.1 Reproduction of Published Works (Art 11(B))

Article 11(B) of the *Copyright Law* in Jordan also gives any Jordanian who is working in a pre-college or a college the right to obtain a non-exclusive and non-assignable licence from the Minister of Culture (or whomever the Minster deputises) to reproduce and publish any published work, provided that certain conditions are met.[171]

5.3.9.2 Reproduction for Private Purposes (Art 17(A) and (B))

The *Copyright* Law in Jordan allows the reproduction of a published work exclusively for the user's private purposes, without the need to obtain permission from the author or payment of any remuneration, provided that certain conditions are met.[172]

---

[170] *Copyright Law*, above n 141, art 11(D).

[171] These conditions according to art 11(B) of the *Copyright Law* in Jordan are as follows:

1. The passage of three years since the first publication date of any printed work related to technology, physical sciences, physics, or mathematics or the passage of 7 years since the first publication of poetry, theatrical or musical works, books of art and fiction or the passage of 5 years since the first publication of any other printed works.
2. The non-availability of enough copies that have been distributed of the works in the Kingdom as to fulfil the needs of the general public, pre-college education or college education by the holder of the reproduction right or through his authorization at a price commensurate with the prices in the Kingdom of similar works.
3. The copies published under this item are sold at a price which is equal or less than the price stipulated in item (2) of this paragraph.
4. Upon granting a non-exclusive and a non-assignable licence for reproduction from the Minister of Culture, the author of the work shall deserve a fair compensation determined in accordance with the law.

Ibid art 11(B).

[172] Article 17 of the *Copyright Law* in Jordan provides as follows:

The published works maybe used, without the consent of the author subject to the following conditions and in the following cases:

A. Presenting, displaying, reciting, acting or playing musically the work in a private family gathering or in an educational. Cultural or social institution by way of illustration for educational purposes. The musical bands of the State may play musical works provided that in all the foregoing no financial gain is achieved and the source and the name of the author, if available, are mentioned.
B. Employing the work for private personal usage by making a single copy by reproduction, recording, copyright, translation or musical orchestration, provided that all the

5.3.9.3 Reproduction for Teaching and Educational Purposes (Art 17(C))

Article 17(C) is one of the most important limitations related to A2K, and it provides that:

> The published works maybe used, without the consent of the author, subject to the following conditions, and in the following cases:
>
> C) Using the work for illustration in teaching, using publications or programs, audio recordings, and audio–video recordings for educational, cultural or religious purposes or for vocational training within the limits necessary to achieve these goals, provided that using this work does not result in any financial gain and that the name of the work and author are mentioned.

The law does not specify what is considered as a reasonable limit and leaves the matter to the judge, who might appoint an expert in cases where a dispute arises, to consider what is 'reasonable copying'. Copying should be, by all means, in accordance with the normal practice of research and should not exceed the main purpose of critiquing, discussing, explaining, educational, cultural, religious, and vocational training.[173]

5.3.9.4 Reproduction in the Form of Quotation (Art 17(D))

Reproduction in the form of quotation is allowed without the need of any permission by the author or payment of any remuneration, subject to the condition that the source and the author's name are mentioned.[174] The quotation as prescribed in art 17(D) above has to be in accordance with the normal custom and practice of research and must not exceed what is necessary to achieve its purpose.

> foregoing does not interfere with normal exploitation of the work and does not cause unjustified damage to the legitimate interests of the right holder...

Ibid art 17.

[173] According to article 17(C), teachers and vocational trainers should not reproduce publications, programs, audio recordings, and audio–video recordings for profit-making and in all cases must indicate clearly the name of the author and the title of his work. Ibid art 17(C).

[174] Article 17(D) provides that:

> The published works maybe used, without the consent of the author subject to the following conditions and in the following cases
>
> A) Quoting paragraphs of the work into another work for purposes of illustration, explanation, discussion, critique, cultivation, or examination within the limits justified by these purposes and provided that the names of the work and author are mentioned.

Ibid art 17 (D).

5.3.9.5 Reproduction for Information Purposes (Art 18 and Art 19)

To encourage freedom of expression, art 18 of the *Copyright Law* in Jordan allows the reproduction of an important public domain article on politics, economics, and religion published in a non-Jordanian newspaper without permission by the author or payment of any remuneration but subject to the obligation to mention the source where the article has been reproduced. Article 19 of the *Copyright Law* in Jordan also gives newspapers and media organisations the right to produce works for publication purposes, such as speeches, lectures, interviews, and other similar works that are presented openly or are directed to the public, without obtaining the consent of the right holder.[175]

5.3.9.6 Reproduction for Libraries, Non-Commercial Documentation Centres, Educational, Scientific, and Cultural Institutions (Art 20)

This generic limitation for libraries, non-commercial documentation centres, educational, scientific, and cultural institutions in art 20 of the *Copyright Law* in Jordan allows reproduction of part or entire works through photocopying or otherwise if the activities of those institutions are not directly profit-making.[176] Reproduction is allowed subject to three conditions:

- The number of photocopying and copies are limited to the needs of these institutions.
- The photocopying does not lead to damaging the copyright of the author.
- The photocopying does not interfere with the normal exploitation of the work.

It is worth noting that commercial and private libraries do not qualify for this particular limitation under art 20 of the *Copyright Law* in Jordan. The law does not mention commercial or private libraries. Indeed, the majority of the libraries in Jordan are either public libraries or connected to a university.[177] The photocopying quota for public libraries and educational institutions is not clear from the

---

[175] Article 7(B) of the *Copyright Law* in Jordan does not protect published, broadcasted, or publicly conveyed news unless they were distinguished by a personal effort involving innovation and arrangement. Ibid art 7 (B).

[176] Article 20 of the *Copyright Law* in Jordan provides as follows:

> Public libraries, non-commercial documentation centres, educational institutes and scientific and cultural institutions may reproduce any work by photocopying or otherwise and without the consent of the author provided that the number of photocopying and the number of the copies are limited to the needs of these institutions, provided that these actions do not lead to damaging the copyright of the author and do not interfere with the normal exploitation of the work.

Ibid art 20.

[177] There are also private libraries such as Abdul Hameed Shoman in Amman. Library, *Abdul Hameed Shoman* <http://www.shoman.org/en/content/about-library>.

Copyright Law in Jordan. This should be determined in accordance with accepted practices in research and the rules of each library.

5.3.10 Infringement and Remedies

Articles 46–55 of the *Copyright Law* in Jordan contain extensive provisions on infringement and remedies. Usually, judges appoint experts to determine whether a copyright infringement has taken place, but the final decision is left to the presiding judge, who should give proper justification for the decision. The *Copyright Law* provides the author or his successors with various remedies against infringers, including precautionary or provisional measures, enforcement measures at the border,[178] and civil and criminal penalties.

Article 51 of the *Copyright Law* in Jordan determines the acts that are considered as infringement of copyright.[179] Any infringement of arts (8), (9), (10), and 23 of

---

[178] Article 47 the *Copyright Law* provides also the following administrative measures: (1) the destruction of the reproductions of the work or the copies made of it that were illegally published, as well as the material used in its publication; (2) the change of the features of the reproductions, the copies, and materials or order that they be made unusable; and (3) the confirmation of the seizure for the settlement of the compensation adjudicated for the author if it is established that the copyright in the work will lapse after two years from the date the ruling become absolute. *Copyright Law*, above n 141, art 47.

The administrative measures, according to article 47, are not applicable on the following:

> (B) [T]he court shall not order the destruction of the reproductions of any work, the copies made thereof or the change of their features if the dispute is related to the translation of the work into Arabic. The ruling of the court should in this case be limited to confirming the seizure of the work, its reproductions, or the copies made thereof as may be required.
>
> (C) In no case shall buildings and what they have in or on them of engravings, drawings, ornamentations, or geometrical figures be subject to seizure. Furthermore, no ruling shall order their destruction, the change of their features, or their confiscation for the purpose of safeguarding the architect's rights whose designs were used in the buildings and whose drawings were put in them illegally. This shall not violate his right in obtaining a fair compensation regarding the foregoing.

Ibid.

[179] The infringing acts are in art 51 of the *Copyright Law* in Jordan as follows:

> 1. Any person who exercised without a legitimate reason any of the rights stipulated in the Articles (8), (9), (10) and (23) of this law.
> 2. Any person who offers for sale, circulation or rental any limited work, or reproduction thereof, disseminated it to the public in any way, or used it to obtain financial gain or imported it into the Hashemite Kingdom of Jordan or exported it outside the Kingdom while the knowledge or reasonable grounds to know that it was imitated work.

Ibid art 51(A).

the *Copyright Law* in Jordan shall be penalised according to art 51 by imprisonment for not less than three months and not exceeding 3 years and a fine of not less than 1,000 dinars (USD 1410) and not exceeding 6,000 dinars[180] (USD $8460) or any of these two sentences.[181] Article 52 punishes any person who violates the provisions of arts (38), (39), (41), and 42 of the *Copyright Law* in Jordan by a fine of not less than 500 dinars (USD 705) and not exceeding one thousands dinars (USD 1410).

5.3.11 Judicial and Administrative Decisions on Copyright in Jordanian Courts

The Jordanian legal system is based on civil law, and legislation is the primary source of law. Courts base their judgements primarily on legislation, and there is no binding precedent as understood in the common law system.[182] Therefore, Jordanian courts are not bound by the rulings of other courts, even if a higher court has issued them, nor are they bound by their own previous rulings. They are bound only by what is provided by the law.[183]

There are three types of courts in Jordan: civil,[184] religious,[185] and special courts.[186] Jordanian courts are divided into two main divisions: civil

[180] The amount was amended from JD 3,000 (USD 4,230) to JD 6,000 (USD 8,460) in accordance with the *Copyright Law* in Jordan.

[181] In case of repeat infringers with respect to any of the crimes stipulated, the person who commits it shall be sentenced to the maximum term of imprisonment and the maximum fine. The court may also issue a ruling for the closure of the establishment in which the crime was committed for a period not exceeding one year or the suspension of its license for a certain period of time or permanently (art 51(B)). Ibid art 51(B).

[182] Santos, Nhana and Sitoi, above n 165.

[183] Mohamed Olwan, *The Three Most Important Features of Jordan's Legal System* International Association of Law Schools <http://www.ialsnet.org/meetings/enriching/olwan.pdf>.

[184] See *Court Establishment Law* No. 17 of 2001 ('Court Establishment Law'), Official Gazette No. 4480, 18 March 2001 <http://www.lob.gov.jo/ui/laws/search_no.jsp?no=17&year=2001>.

[185] See *Sharia Court Establishment Law No. 19 of 1972*, Official Gazette No. 2357, 1 January 1972 <http://www.lob.gov.jo/ui/laws/search_no.jsp?no=19&year=1972>.

[186] See *Municipalities Court Establishment Law No. 35 of 2006*, Official Gazette No 4759; 16 May 2006 <http://www.lob.gov.jo/ui/laws/search_no.jsp?no=35&year=2006>; Militarily *Courts Establishment Law No. 23 of 2006*, Official Gazette No. 4751, 16 March 2006 <http://www.lob.gov.jo/ui/laws/search_no.jsp?no=23&year=2006>.

and criminal. The civil courts include Magistrates Courts,[187] Courts of First Instance,[188] Courts of Appeal,[189] High Administrative Court,[190] and the Court of Cassation (Supreme Court).[191] Magistrates Courts, the lowest in the civil system, hear minor criminal and civil cases. More important cases go to Courts of First Instance. Decisions of these courts are subject to review by the Courts of Appeal. The Supreme Court of Jordan presides over cases against the state, hears appeals, and interprets the law.[192] In practical terms, a number of copyright-related cases[193] have reached the courts in Jordan on various matters,

[187] Magistrate Courts hear civil actions where the amount involved does not exceed JD 750 (USD 1060) and criminal matters where the sentence is two years or less. See art 3 of the *Magistrate Courts Law No. 15 of 1952* which is still applicable. *Magistrate Courts Law No. 15 of 1952*, Official Gazette No. 1102, 1 January 1952. <http://www.lob.gov.jo/ui/laws/search_no.jsp?no=15&year=1952>.

[188] Court of First Instance hear criminal matters that fall outside the jurisdiction of the Magistrate's Court and all civil cases not heard in the Magistrate's Courts and where alleged damages exceed JD 750. See art 4(2) of the *Court Establishment Law* No. 17 of 2001. See also The Embassy of the United States in Jordan, *Jordanian Legal System* <http://jordan.usembassy.gov/acs_jordanian_legal_system.html>.

[189] Court of Appeals hears all appeal cases from judgments of the *Courts of First Instance* and all cases of appeal from the *Magistrate's Court* that are not heard by the *Court of First Instance*. The Court of Appeals may reconsider determinations of facts, as well as of law; they may therefore decide to rehear a case decided below. See also The Embassy of the United States in Jordan, above n 188.

[190] See the *High Court Administrative Court Law No. 12 of 1992*, Official Gazette No 3813, 25 March 1992 <http://www.lob.gov.jo/ui/laws/search_no.jsp?no=12&year=1992>. See also the *Court Establishment Law*, above n 186, art 8.

[191] The *Court of Cassation* considers appeals of felonies in criminal cases and all judgments exceeding JD 500 in civil cases. Other cases may be accepted for appeal by a special leave granted by the President of the Court.

[192] The *Court Establishment Law*, art 4(2), The Embassy of the United States in Jordan, above n 188.

[193] Before the issuance of the *Copyright Law No. 22 of 1992*, Jordanian courts have relied on the decisions issued by the Egyptian and Syrian courts in relation to copyright.

including publication contracts,[194] jurisdiction of local courts over copyright disputes,[195] review of judgements,[196] precautionary matters,[197] and others.[198]

---

[194] One case that was brought before the *Court of Cassation* (civil division) dealt with a publishing contract between a Jordanian author and a publisher. The dispute concerned the publisher's reproduction of some work of the author in another book, which did not reflect the actual work of the author. *The Court of Cassation* (civil division) held that the publisher had no authorisation to reuse the materials of the book that was the subject of the publishing contract without first obtaining necessary authorisation from the author, and this constituted an infringement action. The Court awarded the plaintiff a sum of JD 5000.00 (USD 7, 052) in damages, plus court and attorney's fees, in addition to ordering the destruction of all copies of the book that contained the infringing work. The *Court of Cassation* (Civil Division), Case No 2648/2003, 11 November 2003. See also the following cases:

Case No. 2648/2003, 11 November 2001; Case No 132/2001, 7 November 2001.

- In Case No 804/2005, the Court of First Instance decided that the defendant has infringed the economic and moral rights of the plaintiff when he wrote a book on information systems and copied 58%–60% of its content without the proper acknowledgement that is acceptable to scientific research. The court therefore applied the penalties in art 51 A(1). The Court of First Instance; Case No. 804/2005, 30 October 2005. See also Case No. 65/2006, 14 May 2006 and Case No. 120/96, 12 June 1969.

[195] The *High Court of Justice* decided that it has no jurisdiction in a copyright case as the case relates to a dispute over the ownership of a work registered at the National Library Department under the provisions of the *Copyright Law*. It was decided that the *Court of Cassation* has the jurisdiction to decide any copyright dispute as specified in art 2 of the *Copyright Law*; the case was therefore dismissed by the *High Court of Justice*. The *Court of Cassation* (civil division) further acknowledged that art 38 of the *Copyright Law* requires the filing of any work published or printed with the Jordanian national library before it is distributed in the country. Accordingly, any work that is sold or distributed before filing is not protected under the *Copyright Law*. Furthermore, the Court of Cassation decided that there is no order for damages in favour of the author, as prescribed in art 49 of the *Copyright Law*, and that art 256 of the *Civil Code* is not applicable as the private law (copyright law) should be applied in this situation and not the public law (civil law). See *Case No.* 78/1999, 10 November 1999; Case No. 2797/1999, 27 April 2000. See also for similar decisions, Case No. 47/1985, 15 May 1985; Case No. 1987/228, 26 July 1987 and case No. 47/1995, 25 February 1995.

[196] *The Court of Cassation* (Civil Division) also decided to return a copyright case to the *Court of Appeal* since that court did not issue a reasoned decision when it decided to dismiss a case without confirming the date of dismissal based on the issuance of a *General Pardon Law* and the application of art 272(B) of the *Civil Law* and art 339 of the *Criminal Procedure Law*, Case No. 3687/2006, 2 April 2007. See also Case No. 47/1995, 25 February 1995.

[197] The *Court of Cassation* (civil division) decided to revoke the decision of the *Court of Appeal*, which confirmed the decision of the Judge of expedited matters in refusing to allow a requester of a precautionary measure as all the conditions as prescribed in art 46 of the *Copyright Law* had been followed. The *Court of Cassation*, Case No. 2058/2004, 17 October 2004.

- The *Amman Court of Appeal* decided to return a request to appeal the decision of the *Court of First Instance* in issuing a precautionary measure as it did not have the authority to issue its decision. The Court revoked the decision of the *Court of First Instance* based on art 2 and art 46 of the *Copyright Law*, which does not allow the Judge of precautionary measures to issue a decision related to the subject matter of the case as this is left to the Judge presiding over the case. See the *Court of Appeal*, Case No. 1313/2000, 18 May 2000.

[198] The *Amman Court of Appeal* (Criminal division) held that the director of a company who used computer software without obtaining a licence was subject to a criminal liability and was sentenced to three months of imprisonment. *The Court of Appeal*, Case No. 2769/2005, 29

5.4 Critique of the Copyright Law in Jordan

This section examines the provisions of the *Copyright Law* in Jordan that deal with digital issues. It then analyses those provisions from a developmental perspective and provides recommendations for reform.

5.4.1 The Right of Reproduction

The right of reproduction is the most fundamental in the twenty-first century and, historically, the oldest among all the economic rights.[199] Its importance derives from how critically it affects the right of owners to control access to their work, combat piracy, and licence legitimate users. The right of reproduction has been dealt with in earlier copyright treaties such as the *Berne Convention*, but digital technologies raised new questions regarding its scope[200] and applicability over Internet networks.

Among the questions that any legislator must face is whether temporary transient copies made in the computer random access memory (RAM) can be considered as a reproduction and an infringement of the copyright law.

The appropriate application of the reproduction right in the case of temporary copies in RAM continues to be a subject of debate at both national and international levels.[201] Some argue that the temporary copying of a computer program into the RAM of the computer in which the program is being used is a reproduction of the program in a material form.[202] Many have criticised this principle in the context of Internet, arguing that it extends copyright protection for digital works too far.[203] Article 9(A) of the *Copyright Law*[204] provides as follows:

September 2005. Article 74(2)(3) of the Jordanian *Criminal Law No. 16 of 1960* (old law) makes corporation liable criminally through the acts of its managers and representatives. See also the recent Case No. 13783/2009, 19 March 2009, where the court acquitted the accuser of criminal copyright liability as she was not the manager of the corporation and was only responsible for registering the corporation under her name.

[199] Walter Arthur Copinger et al., *Copinger and Skone James on Copyright* (Sweet and Maxwell, 5th ed, 2005) 1870.

[200] Lewinski, above n 123.

[201] World Intellectual Property Organization, *Intellectual Property on the Internet: A Survey of Issues* (2002) (WIPO Survey) <http://www.wipo.int/export/sites/www/copyright/en/ecommerce/pdf/survey.pdf>.

[202] See in Australia Microsoft Corp v. Blanch (2002) 895 FCA; Microsoft Corp v Business Boost Pty Ltd (2000) 1651 FCA; Anne Fitzgerald and Brian Fitzgerald, *Intellectual Property in Principle* (Lawbook, 2005) 110; James Lahore and Warwick A Rothnie, *Copyright and Design* (3rd ed Butterworths, 2004) 1996; Digital Agenda- The Copyright Amendment (Digital Agenda) Act, 2000 <http://www.austlii.edu.au/au/legis/cth/consol_act/caaa2000294/>; Anne Fitzgerald and Dimitrios G. Eliades, *Intellectual Property* (Lawbook, 3rd ed, 2008) 70-73.

[203] Fitzgerald and Fitzgerald, above n 202, 110.

[204] Article 9(A) of the *Copyright Law* in Jordan was amended in the *Law No. 9 of 2005* after Jordan signed the WCT and the WPPT.

> The author shall have the right to financially exploit his work in any way he chooses. No other person may exercise this right without his written permission, or the permission of his successors. This right shall include:
>
> A. The right of reproduction of the work by any means or form whether it is temporary or permanent such as photocopying, cinematography or digital recording.

The *Copyright Law* in Jordan does not allow temporary copies to be made in RAM since art 9(A) gives the author the right to control all reproduction of his copies, whether it is temporary[205] or permanent. The result is that browsing of the Internet can be considered as an infringement of the reproduction right (if it is not subject to any limitation). The *Copyright Law* in Jordan currently does not provide any such limitation to transient or temporary copies. Article 9(A) differs from some copyright laws in Arab countries that allow temporary copying in the RAM and do not consider it an infringement of the reproduction right.[206] Article 9(A) gives extensive protection to the copyright owner. It has followed the position of art 4(10) JUSFTA[207] that does not allow any sort of temporary copying, even if it is not considered infringement.

Many argue that the inclusion of temporary copying within the scope of the reproduction right under art 9(A) of the *Copyright Law* in Jordan is overly restrictive from the perspective of consumers and Internet users because it would effectively make temporary reproductions occurring in the course of ordinary usage of electronic devices and digital networks illegal.[208] Furthermore, this provision is criticised for disturbing the flow of information over the Internet as the law needs to

---

[205] "Temporary" is not defined in the *Copyright Law* in Jordan and in the Berne Convention, WCT and the WPPT. It implies that a copy will be deleted, destroyed or otherwise disappear within some limited, although not necessarily short time. See also Copinger et al., above n 199, 479.

[206] The *Egyptian Intellectual Property Law*, in art 170(9), provides as follows:

> Without prejudice to the moral rights of the author, pursuant to the provisions of the law herein, the author may not prevent third parties, after the publication of his work, from undertaking any of the following acts:
>
> Temporarily reproducing work subsequent to or during the digital transmission of the work; or during exercising an act aiming at receiving a digitally stored work; and within the framework of normal operation of the device used by the right holder.

Law No. 82 of 2002 (Law on the Protection of Intellectual Property Rights), *Al-Jarida Al-Rasmiyya*, 3 June 2002, art. 171(9) (Egypt) <http://www.wipo.int/wipolex/en/text.jsp?file_id=126540>.

[207] Article 4(10) of the JUSFTA provides as follows:

> Each Party shall provide that all reproductions, whether temporary or permanent, shall be deemed reproductions and subject to the reproduction right as envisaged in the provisions embodied in WCT Article 1(4) and the Agreed Statement thereto, and WPPT Articles 7 and 11 and the Agreed Statement thereto.

JUSFTA, above n 20, art 4, 10.

[208] Suggested Revision to the Chairman's Basic Proposal for the Treaty Formerly Known as the Berne Protocol, Ad Hoc Alliance for a Digital Future (on file with the author).

be a facilitator, rather than an inhibitor, of knowledge distribution.[209] One Jordanian copyright scholar suggested that the *Copyright Law* in Jordan should find infringement occurring in the context of temporary copies when the work is distributed to the public.[210] This means that multiple copies that are done inside the machine and that are not distributed to the public are not considered as infringements.[211]

In the case of Infogag International *A/S v. Danske Dagblades Forening*,[212] a UK Court considered the nature and extent of 'transient copying' as follows:

> An act could be held to be 'transient'. . .. if its duration was limited to what was necessary for the proper completion of the technological process in question, it being understood that that process had to be automated so that it deleted that act automatically, without human intervention, once its function of enabling the completion of such a process had come to an end.[213]

It is suggested that art 9(A) of the *Copyright Law* in Jordan needs to be amended to make it clear that temporary acts of reproduction that constitute an integral and essential part of a technological process, and whose sole purpose is lawful and not infringing, shall be exempted from the application of the scope of the reproduction right.[214] The Electronic Information for Libraries (EIFL)—a non-profit organisation that advocates the wide availability of electronic resources for users in developing countries—recommended that the following provision be included in the copyright laws of developing countries:

Anyone is permitted to make temporary copies of a work:

1) That are transient or incidental;
2) That are an integral and essential part of a technical process;
3) The sole purpose of which is to enable a transmission of a work in a network between third parties by an intermediary or a lawful use of a work; and
4) That have no independent economic significance.[215]

It is suggested that this provision could be adopted into the *Copyright Law* in Jordan in order to consider transient copyright, which occurs when browsing the Internet, as a non-infringement of copyright law.

---

[209] See Brian Fitzgerald, 'Promoting Creativity and Innovation Through Law' in Leon Mann and Janet Chan, *Creativity and Innovation in Business and Beyond*' (Routledge, 2011) 117-131. (providing further explanation on how the law needs to be structured to promote the free 'flow of information').

[210] Professor Suhail Hadaden, Intellectual Property Law (2010) (class notes for LLB students at the University of Jordan) (on file with author).

[211] Ibid.

[212] Infopaq Int'l A/S v. Danske Dagblades Forening (C-5/08), 2009, FSR 20.

[213] Ibid.

[214] Copinger et al., above n 199, 478.

[215] Emanuella Giavarra and Teresa Hackett, Electronic Info for Libararies, *Draft Law on Copyright Including Model Exceptions and Limitations for Libraries and Consumers* (2009) eIFL-IP <http://www.eifl.net/system/files/201101/modellaw_v16.pdf>.

5.4.2 The Right of Communication to the Public

The right of communication to the public under the *Copyright Law* in Jordan is of special significance in the digital age. It was granted to authors under art 8 of the WCT[216] and to performers and phonograms under art 10 and art 14 of the WPPT, respectively.[217] Article 8 of the WCT[218] has been referred to as an 'umbrella solution' because it does not order member states to adopt a new right but rather

---

[216] The agreed statement concerning art 8 of the WCT mentions that:

> It is understood that the mere provision of physical facilities for enabling or making a communication does not in itself amount to communication within the meaning of this Treaty or the Berne Convention. It is further understood that nothing in Article 8 precludes a Contracting Party from applying Article 11bis(2).

WIPO Copyright Treaty (WCT), Geneva, 20 December 1996, entered into force on 6 March 2002. <http://www.wipo.int/treaties/en/ip/wct/trtdocs_wo033.html#P8_189>.

[217] Article 11 of the WPPT provides that:

> Performers shall enjoy the exclusive right of authorizing the making available to the public of their performances fixed in phonograms, by wire or wireless means, in such a way that members of the public may access them from a place and at a time individually chosen by them'. Art 14 of the WPPT provides that:
>
> Producers of phonograms shall enjoy the exclusive right of authorizing the making available to the public of their phonograms, by wire or wireless means, in such a way that members of the public may access them from a place and at a time individually chosen by them.

WIPO Performance and Phonograms Treaty (WPPT), Geneva, 20 December 1996, entered into force on 20 May 2002, art 11 <http://www.wipo.int/treaties/en/ip/wppt/trtdocs_wo034.html>.

Article 14 provides that:

> Producers of phonograms shall enjoy the exclusive right of authorizing the making available to the public of their phonograms, by wire or wireless means, in such a way that members of the public may access them from a place and at a time individually chosen by them.

Ibid art 14.

[218] Article 8 of the WCT provides as follows:

> Without prejudice to the provisions of Articles 11(1)(ii), 11*bis*(1)(i) and (ii), 11*ter*(1)(ii), 14(1)(ii) and 14*bis*(1) of the Berne Convention, authors of literary and artistic works shall enjoy the exclusive right of authorizing (any communication to the public) of their works, by wire or wireless means, including the making available to the public of their works in such a way that members of the public may access these works from a place and at a time individually chosen by them.

WIPO Copyright Treaty, above n 216, art 8.

gives member states the power to decide which exclusive right should be used to cover the act of making works available through the Internet.[219]

As a signatory to both the WCT and the WPPT, Jordan decided not to create the right of distribution but instead the right of communication to the public.[220] Article 9(F) of the *Copyright Law* in Jordan has been amended, based on art 8(1) of the WCT, to introduce a new communication to the public right.[221] It provides as follows:

> The author shall have the right to financially exploit his work in any way he chooses. No other person may exercise this right without his written permission, or the permission of his successors. This right shall include:
>
> E. Conveying his work to the public through recital, display, acting, radio or television broadcasting, cinema or through any other means.[222]

The *Copyright Law* in Jordan does not mention what constitutes communication to the public and when infringement occurs in the context of the Internet. It is suggested that the law should be amended to provide a precise definition of communication to the public in order to limit the scope of this right and its application.[223] This corresponds with Jordan's obligations under the WCT and the WPPT.

5.4.3 Protection of Technological Protection Measures (TPMs)

One controversial topic that has been the focus of much copyright research is the inclusion of TPMs and RMI provisions (anti-circumvention laws) to protect copyrighted materials transferred over Internet networks. Many copyright scholars argue that the copyright law is going too far in protecting anti-circumvention

---

[219] Mihaly Fiscor, *The Law of Copyright and the Internet* (Sweet and Maxwell, 2002) 496; Copinger et al., above n 199, 438; Press Release, International Federation of the Phonographic Industry, *The WIPO Treaties: Making Available Right* (March 2003) <http://www.ifpi.org/content/library/wipo-treaties-making-available-right.pdf>; Jane C. Ginsburg, 'The (New?) Right of Making Available to the Public' (2004) *Columbia Public Law & Legal Theory Working Papers* <http://lsr.nellco.org/cgi/viewcontent.cgi?article=1003&context=columbia_pllt>.

[220] See also Sterling, above n 161, 399.

[221] *Copyright Law*, above n 141, arts 23(A), 23(C)(5), 24 (introduced for the first time in the Jordanian law).

[222] Ibid art 9(F).

[223] The EIFL suggests the following definition of 'communication to the public':

> Any communication to the public of a work, sound recording, film or broadcast, by wire or wireless means, including the making available to the public of the work, sound recording, films or broadcasts in such a way that members of the public may access the work, sound recording, film or broadcast from a place and at a time individually chosen by them.

See Giavarra and Hackett, above n 215, 10.

measures,[224] and there must be serious consideration given to limiting those measures, especially in connection with developing countries.[225]

The WCT and the WPPT are the first international copyright treaties that request signatory countries to include anti-circumvention provisions in their domestic laws.[226] The WCT and the WPPT do not prescribe precise models for the protection

---

[224] Lawrence Lessig, *Free Culture: How Big Media Uses Technology and the Law to Lock Down Culture* (The Penguin, 2004); William W. Fisher, *Promises to Keep Technology, Law, and the Future of Entertainment* (Stanford University, 2004); Peter Biddle et al., *The Darkest and the Future of Content Distributions* (18 November 2002) Bearcave <http://www.bearcave.com/misl/misl_tech/msdrm/darknet.htm>. See also Niva Elkin-Koren and Neil Weinstock Netanel, *The Commodification of Information* (Kluwer, 2002) 79-106; Jessica Litman, *Digital Copyright* (Prometheus Books, 2001) 179; Urs Gasser and Silke Ernst, *From Shakespeare to Dj danger Mouse: A Quick Look at Copyright and User Creativity in the Digital Age* (2006) SSRN <http://papers.ssrn.com/sol3/papers.cfm?abstract_id=909223>; Pamela Samuelson, *Preliminary Thoughts in Copyright Reform* (2007) SSRN <http://papers.ssrn.com/sol3/papers.cfm?abstract_id=1002676>.

[225] Professor Peter Yu notes:

> It is important to remember that many of these countries institute or revamp their intellectual property systems in the first place mainly because of the TRIPs Agreement or external pressure from the developed world, such as what they currently experience in their bilateral and plurilateral trade negotiations. Oftentimes, they introduce reforms in the fear of losing trade benefits, export markets, and development If they had a choice to select the type of innovation systems they wanted to build, an anticircumvention regime would be very unlikely to be a top priority. After all, economists have shown empirically that countries with limited imitative capacity often do not benefit from a strong intellectual property regime.

Yu, above n 35, 53.

CIPR also criticised DRM provisions for developing countries as follows:

> For developing countries, where Internet connectivity is limited and subscriptions to online resources unaffordable, it may exclude access to these materials altogether and impose a heavy burden that will delay the participation of those countries in the global knowledge-based society.

Barton et al., above n 1, 106.

[226] Professor Ruth L. Okediji noted that:

> To date, fifty-two (52) countries are members of the WCT, of which forty-six percent (46%) are developing countries, ten percent (10%) are least-developed countries and thirty-eight percent (38%) are countries in transition. Only 6% of the members are developed countries. This is not simply a matter of the relative numbers of developing countries; the WCT is not in force in several notable countries such as Canada, Austria, and Germany. Many developing countries have already ratified, or made commitments to ratify, the treaties either as a result of bilateral/regional trade agreements, or by virtue of other economic pressures exerted on them. Nevertheless, it is remarkably ironic that a treaty dealing with digital copyright concerns has a membership comprising mainly of developing countries with limited Internet penetration rates and significant levels of illiteracy and poverty.

See Ruth L. Okediji, Limitations, *Exceptions and Public Interest Consideration for Developing Countries*, International Center for Trade and Sustainable Development Paper No. 15 (2006) UNCTAD <http://www.unctad.org/en/docs/iteipc200610_en.pdf at 32>. See also the following:

of TPMs and RMI. The treaties are limited to providing national and regional legislation with a general framework for such protection.[227] They also leave contracting parties influence over what types of remedies and sanctions they would apply.[228] The question is whether it is important for a developing country such as Jordan to have an anti-circumvention law in the first place. What are the elements necessary for effective and balanced anti-circumvention laws?

Article 4(13) of the JUSFTA provides as follows:

Nicola Lucchi, 'Intellectual Property Rights Digital Media: a Comparative Analysis of Legal Protection, Technological Measures and New Business Models under EU and US Laws' (2005) 53 (7) *Buffalo Law Review* 1111; Pamela Samuelson, 'Intellectual Property and the Digital Economy: Why the Anti Circumvention Regulations Need to be Revised' (1999) 14 *Berkeley Technology Law Journal* 519 <www.ischool.berkeley.edu/~pam/papers/dmcapaper.pdf>; Pamela Samuelson and John Browning, 'Confab Clips Copyright Cartel', (March 1997) Issue 5.03 *Wired Magazine* <http://www.wired.com/wired/archive/5.03/netizen.html>; *Frequently Asked Questions (and Answers) About Anti Circumvention (DMCA)*, Berkman Center for Interent and Society <http://www.chillingeffects.org/anticircumvention/faq.cgi#QID91>; *Rulemaking on Exemptions from Prohibition on Circumvention of Technological Measures that Control Access to Copyrighted Works,* US Copyright Office <http://www.copyright.gov/1201/>; Gwen Hinze, *Seven Lessons from a Comparison of the Technological Protection Measure Provisions, Electonic Frontier Foundation* <https://www.eff.org/pages/seven-lessons-comparison-technological-protection-measure-provisions>; Jane C. Ginsburg, 'Legal Protection of Technological Measures Protecting Work of Authorship: International Obligations and the US Experience' (2005) 29 *Columbia Journal of Law and Arts* SSRN <http://papers.ssrn.com/sol3/papers.cfm?abstract_id=785945>; Thomas A. Mitchell, 'Honouring David Shapiro: Note: Copyright, Congress and Constitutionality: How the Digital Millennium Copyright Act Goes Too far' (2004) 79 *Notre Dame Law Review* 2115; Laura N. Gasaway, *Anti-Circumvention: a View from Librarians and Educators (14 June 2001)* (unpublished manuscript) <www.alai-usa.org/2001_conference/pres_gasaway.doc>.

[227] Haochen Sun, 'Rethinking the Chinese Copyright Law in the Digital Age' (2003) 6 (6) *Journal of Intellectual Property* 912.

[228] Article 11 of the WCT provides that:

> Contracting parties shall provide adequate legal protection and effective legal remedies against the circumvention of effective technological measures that are used by authors in connection with the exercise of their rights under this Treaty or the Berne Convention and that restrict acts, in respect of their works, which are not authorized by the authors concerned or permitted by law.

WIPO Copyright Treaty, above n 216, art 11.

Article 18 of the WPPT also contains a similar article that states as follows:

> Contracting parties have to provide adequate legal protection and affective legal remedies against the circumvention of effective technological measures that are used by authors in connection with the exercise of their rights, and to restrict acts in respect of their performances or phonograms which are not authorized by the performers or the producers of phonograms concerned or permitted by law.

WIPO Performances and Phonograms Treaty, above n 217, art 18.

Each Party shall prohibit civilly and criminally the manufacture, importation or circulation of any technology, device, service or part thereof, that is designed, produced, performed or marketed for engaging in such prohibited conduct, or that has only a limited commercially significant purpose or use other than enabling or facilitating such conduct.

Article 54. of the *Copyright Law*[229] in Jordan provides that:

A) A person shall be considered in violating of the provisions of this law if same commits any of the following actions:

1. Deletes or changes any information set in an electronic form without the permission of the holder of the rights.
2. Distributes of imports for the purpose of distributions or announcement to the public without permission copies of the works or consolidated performances or audio recordings.

B) For the purposes of this Article the term (information that guarantees the administration of rights) shall mean any information provided by the holder of the rights that are defined with the following:

1. The work, audio recording or performance
2. The author or performers or producer of an audio recording
3. The holder of the right in the work or performance or while knowing or if the same has an adequate reason or evidence to know
4. The conditions that must be present to make use of any benefit from any work or performance or audio recording that purport to show this information
5. Any number or encoding that purport to show this information

C) The provisions of Article (46), (47), (50) and (51) of this law shall be applied if a violation of any of the rights stipulated in this Article occurs as the case may be.

Article 55. of the *Copyright Law*[230] in Jordan provide as follows:

A) A person shall be considered a violator of the provisions of this law if same commits any of the following actions:

1. Circumvents effective technological measure or counteracted them or disable any part thereof.
2. Produced or imported or sold or displayed for the purpose of selling or leasing or possessed for another commercial purpose or distributed or carried out marketing action for selling and leasing any piece or appliance or service or method that was designed or produced or used for the purposes of circumventions any effective technological measures or counteracting them or disabling any part thereof.

B) For the purpose of this Article the term (effective technological measures) shall mean any technology or measure or method used such as encoding or controlling the extraction of copies that are used to prohibit or limit carrying out any work unlicensed by the holder of the rights.

C) The provisions of Article (46), (47), (49) and 51 of this law shall be applied if a violation of any of the rights stipulated in this Article occurs.

[229] *Copyright Law*, above n 141, 54.

[230] *Copyright Law*, above n 141, 55.

Jordan added arts 54 and 55 to the *Copyright Law* to be in conformity with its treaty obligations under JUSFTA, WCT, and the WPPT. Article 4(13) of JUSFTA, in relation to TPMs, is overly restrictive and goes beyond Jordan's obligation under the WCT[231]and the WPPT.[232] Article 55(A) of the *Copyright Law* in Jordan prevents all kinds of uses, regardless of whether it is justified under art 17 (limitations). It does not require intention to infringe upon copyright for use to amount to circumvention; the activity is criminalised per se, regardless of the scientific importance or research value resulting from such use.[233] Article 55(B) of the *Copyright Law* in Jordan prohibits the manufacturing, importing, and distribution of any device or service that could be used to circumvent digital protection systems. It makes preparatory acts (such as obtaining the circumvention tools and devices) even before conducting the actual act of circumvention illegal. This language is broad and open-ended and threatens legitimate businesses working in the field of IT and software development.[234] In addition, art 55(C) of the *Copyright Law* in Jordan provides several remedies for the circumvention of TPMs. The remedies include all sorts of sanctions (temporary measures, administrative, civil, and criminal penalties), as explained earlier in art 51 and art 52. It does not provide any flexibility to exclude civil and criminal liability for innocent infringers such as non-profit libraries, archives, and educational institutions. It also includes a subjective standard for a circumvention of TPMs that would impose liability where a person accidentally circumvents.[235]

---

[231] *WIPO Copyright Treaty*, above n 216, art 11.

[232] Article 18 of the WPPT provides that:

> Contracting Parties shall provide adequate legal protection and effective legal remedies against the circumvention of effective technological measures that are used by performers or producers of phonograms in connection with the exercise of their rights under this Treaty and that restrict acts, in respect of their performances or phonograms, which are not authorized by the performers or the producers of phonograms concerned or permitted by law.

WPPT, above n 217, art 18.

[233] Al Sharieh, above n 102, 97-115.

[234] Ad Hoc Alliance for a Digital Future, above n 208.

[235] Compare with art 16.4(7) of the Singapore US Free Trade Agreement (SUSFTA), which provides that:

> In order to provide adequate legal protection and effective legal remedies against the circumvention of effective technological measures that authors, performers, producers of phonograms, and their successors in interest use in connection with the exercise of their rights and that restrict unauthorized acts in respect of their works, performances, and phonograms, each Party shall provide that any person who: (i) knowingly, or having reasonable grounds to know, circumvents without authority any effective technological measure that controls access to a protected work, performance, phonogram, or other subject matter.

See Singapore United States Free Trade Agreement (SUSFTA), signed on 6 May 2003 (entered into force 1 January 2004) <http://www.ustr.gov/sites/default/files/uploads/agreements/fta/singapore/asset_upload_file708_4036.pdf>. Compare the SUSFTA with the Chile United States

A general feature of art 55 of the *Copyright Law* in Jordan is that it does not contain any limitations that make it much more stringent than section 1201 of the DMCA.[236] The failure of the *Copyright Law* in Jordan to provide any limitations to TPMs demonstrates the extent to which Jordan aligned in favour of copyright owners and neglected users' rights. Despite the restrictive effect of art 55, the IIPA has requested that it be amended so that it specifically covers all forms of 'circulation' of circumvention devices, regardless of whether there is a financial benefit or not.[237] Furthermore, the IIPA wants Jordan to prohibit activities 'primarily designed, produced or used for the purpose of circumvention, deactivating or impairing'.[238]

It is argued that IIPA should discontinue its insistence that Jordan and other developing countries introduce specific wordings on TPMs where the content of such provisions is clearly covered by law.[239] Such amendments would result in decisional inconsistencies of the local system, leading to new problems[240] for local judges when this matter is brought before the courts. It is suggested that the current structure and wording of art 55 of the *Copyright Law* in Jordan is an insurmountable barrier to the freedom of Jordanians to use works for legitimate purposes and would create a formidable obstacle to A2K.[241] This obstacle exists because art 55 prohibits all forms of circumvention, even if it was done for legal purposes, including research, security, and other legitimate means that are provided for under various international copyright treaties. The *Copyright Law* in Jordan should include appropriate limitations and exceptions on TPMs in order to strike a necessary balance between the right of copyright owners and the general public. Furthermore, it is important to provide limitations and exceptions on criminal and civil liabilities for non-profit institutions such as libraries, archives, and educational institutions and flexible sanctions for innocent infringers.[242]

Free Trade Agreement (CUSFTA), art 17.7, signed on 6 June 2003 (entered into force 1 January 2004) <http://www.ustr.gov/trade-agreements/free-trade-agreements/chile-fta/final-text>.

[236] The DMCA contains specific narrow statutory exemptions that apply to the act of circumvention. See 17 U.S.C. § 1201. For an explanation of the exceptions under the DMCA that apply to the acts of circumvention and preparatory acts, *see* Urs Gasser, *Legal Framework and Technology Provisions of Digital Content: Moving Forward, Toward a Best Practise Model* (Berkman Center for Interent and Society, Paper No. 04, 2006) <http://papers.ssrn.com/sol3/papers.cfm?abstract_id=908998>. The US courts appear to have interpreted the DMCA in line with a narrow approach. Accordingly, TPMs will only be reinforced where they are preventing or inhibiting copyright infringement; see Brian Fitzgerald et al., *Internet and E-commerce Law-Technology Law and Policy* (Law Book, 2007) ch 4. See also Storage Tech Corp v. Custom Hardware Engineering and Consulting Inc., 421 F. 3d 1307 (fed. Cir. 2005).

[237] International Intellectual Property Alliance, above n 136. See also the European Union Council Directive 2001/31, on the Harmonisation of Certain Aspects of Copyright and Related Rights in the Information Society ('Directive on Copyright and Information Society'), 2001 O.J (L 167).

[238] International Intellectual Property Alliance, above n 136.

[239] Lewinski, above n 123, 42.

[240] Ibid.

[241] Xue, above n 37, 168, 176, 183.

[242] Gasser, above n 236.

5.4.4 *Limitations to Author's Exclusive Rights*

Unlike the US legal system's concept of open-ended fair use, the limitations and exceptions provided under the *Copyright Law* in Jordan are subject to rigid application and are determined on a case-by-case basis. This approach is too inflexible and stifles innovation[243] because it requires judges to apply strict rules that may not take into consideration the development of copyright law, digital technologies, and the Internet.

The limitations and exceptions are extremely important for developing countries as they are indispensable strategic and doctrinal tools used to facilitate social and economic development by providing citizens with the basic means to engage in intellectual endeavours and to participate in the global knowledge economy.[244] Appropriate limitations and exceptions will continue to safeguard public interest uses. The result will be a benefit to consumers, a benefit to rights holders, and a benefit to national cultures.[245]

The WCT and WPPT provide certain flexibilities to developing countries to develop what they can use in appropriate circumstances.[246] Any limitation and exception that were granted should abide by the three-step test under the *Berne Convention* and TRIPS. The three-step test was inserted into the *Berne Convention* only in relation to the reproduction right in art 9(2).[247] The *TRIPS Agreement* widened the application of the three-step test so that it applies to all exclusive rights granted by the *Berne Convention.*[248] Most commentators agree that the three-step test has a restrictive effect on limitations and exception, so that it should be regarded merely as a guiding principle rather than as a legal standard.[249] The Agreed Statement on art 10 of the WCT explicitly permits members to devise

[243] Knowledge Ecology, *KEI has Filed Comments on the EC's Green Paper on Copyright in the* <http://www.keionline.org/content/view/215/1>.

[244] Okediji, above n 226, 35.

[245] World Intellectual Properrty Organization, above n 201.

[246] Consumers International, *The statement on Provisional Committee on Proposals Related to A WIPO Development Agenda* (2006) <http://bit.ly/HOhBzv>.

[247] Article 9(2) of *Berne Convention* provides as follows:

> It shall be a matter for legislation in the countries of the Union to permit the reproduction of such works in certain special cases, provided that such reproduction does not conflict with a normal exploitation of the work and does not unreasonably prejudice the legitimate interests of the author.

Berne Convention, above n 153, art 9, 2.

[248] Wedage Danta Rodrigo 'Copyright Law in the Digital Era: A Comparative Study of Sri Lanka, Australia and the United States' (A PhD thesis, University of Queensland, 2007) 218.

[249] See Okediji, above n 226. A group of European and international IP scholars drafted a Declaration on the 'Three-Step-Test' in copyright law. The declaration proposes that 'an appropriately balanced interpretation of the Three-Step Test under which existing exceptions and limitations within domestic law are not unduly restricted and the introduction of appropriately balanced exception and limitation is not precluded'. Christophe Geiger (et al.), Max Planck

new limitations and exceptions appropriate for the digital environment. However, does the *Copyright Law* in Jordan have any specific limitation and exceptions related to the Internet?

5.4.5 Limitations for Teaching Purposes and Libraries

Jordan lacks the domestic institutional capacity to design appropriate limitations and exceptions to advance education and learning in the digital age. This is evidenced in art 17 of the *Copyright Law* in Jordan, which has been poorly drafted, is inadequate, and outmoded.[250] Articles 17(A), 17(C), and 20 contain specific limitations and exceptions for teaching institutions and libraries. Article 17(A) permits the performance or display of a work for educational purposes only within the classroom or educational institution. The requirement that the performance or display be confined to the classroom is an obstacle to remote students who can only view their lectures using the Internet as they live in rural areas.[251]

In addition, it is unclear under art 20 whether it is possible for libraries to make works that are in an electronic format, available online within the confines of the library premises. Article 17((A) and (C)) of the *Copyright Law* in Jordan does not support distance education.[252] The *Copyright Law* in Jordan should be designed so as to enable educational institutions to reproduce or to digitise copyright material where necessary for the benefit of remote students. This would be of immense value to students enrolled in distance education programs from remote and underdeveloped areas in Jordan as it would allow those students to pursue their studies from their hometowns and rural areas.[253]

Institute for Intellectual Property, *Decleration: A Balanced Interpretation of the 'Three- Step Test' in Copyright Law* <http://www.ip.mpg.de/shared/data/pdf/declaration_three_steps.pdf>.

[250] Pedro Nicoletti Mizukami el al, 'Limitations and Exceptions to Copyright in the Brazilian Law: A Need for Reform' in Lea Shaver (ed), *Access to Knowledge in Brazil* (Bloomburg, 2010) 67, 70-76.

[251] Margaret Ann Wilkinson, 'Filtering the Flow from the Fountains of Knowledge- Access and Copyright in Education and Libraries' in Michael Geist (ed), *In the Public Interest-The Future of Canadian Copyright Law* (Irwin, 2005) 331.

[252] With the advent and widespread use of digital technologies, distance education has now developed into a fully fledged system of education that is capable of even replacing traditional classroom education. The importance of distance education is that it affords unprecedented opportunities to extent teaching beyond the classroom and campuses. See Rodrigo, above n 248, 308, 309.

Ibid 309.

[253] See Wedage Danta Rodrigo, expressing similar views in connection with least developing countries (LDCs)). Rodrigo, above n 248, 332.

5.4.6 Limitations for Disabled Persons

According to the World Health Organization (WHO), more than 90% of visually impaired persons live in developing countries.[254] According to the UN Development Program (UNDP), 4%–5% of the Jordanian population[255] is disabled, 14.8% of males and 2.1% of females.[256]

There are currently no limitations for people with sensory disabilities or visually impaired people (whether blind, visually impaired, or deaf) in the *Copyright Law* in Jordan. This means that any use or adaptation of a work by a disabled person needs permission from the copyright owner as it constitutes copyright infringement. It is important for the *Copyright Law* in Jordan to permit copies of the work to be made in an accessible format for the benefit of people with disabilities, including the blind, visually impaired, and other reading-disabled people.[257] These limitations and exceptions would help those people to access copyrighted materials as the law does not permit this to happen without the copyright owner's authorisation.

Jordan and developing countries should also support the proposals that empower blind, visually impaired, and other disabled persons,[258] including the Treaty proposed by the World Blind Union (WBU) and WIPO's Standing Committee on Copyright and Related Rights (SCCR) Treaty for the Blind.[259]

5.4.7 Public Domain

The public domain includes any work that has never been under copyright or that is no longer within the term of copyright protection under the applicable copyright laws. It is crucial in preserving history, scientific knowledge, technology and inventions, and cultural heritage for present and future generations of developing countries.[260] Public access to the public domain fosters learning, innovation, and

---

[254] Giavarra and Hackett, above n 215.

[255] World Bank, *Jordan Country Brief* (2011) <http://siteresources.worldbank.org/JORDANEXTN/Resources/JordanCountryBrief.pdf>.

[256] UNDP JORDAN, *Towards Better Integration of Persons with Disabilities in Employment*, <http://www.undp-jordan.org/index.php?page_type=projects&project_id=81&cat=1>.

[257] Ibid.

[258] Knowledge Ecology International, above n 243.

[259] See WIPO, Proposal by Brazil, Ecuador and Paraguay, Relating to Limitations and Exceptions: Treaty Proposed by the World Blind Union (WBU) (2009) <http://www.wipo.int/edocs/mdocs/copyright/en/sccr_18/sccr_18_5.pdf>; Press Release, WIPO, SCCR Commits to Improving Access by Visually Impaired to Copyright-Protected Works (18 Dec 2009) <http://www.wipo.int/pressroom/en/articles/2009/article_0061.html>.

[260] Awad, El-Gheriani and Abou Zeid, above n 84, 15, 16.

creation of new works.[261] The purpose of copyright is to protect the public domain and leave an amount of works available in order to advance knowledge and develop human creativity.

The *Copyright Law* in Jordan recognises the public domain in art 34.[262] According to art 34(B) of the *Copyright Law* in Jordan, any person who is interested in printing, publishing, or translating a work that has not already been printed, published, or translated in Jordan first needs to apply to the Minister of Culture to obtain a licence to do so. Such a requirement acts as a barrier to A2K by imposing unnecessary cost and administrative delay on the ability of people to freely and easily use public domain works.[263] Whilst some countries have extended the term of copyright beyond the *Berne Convention*'s requirement for the life of the author, plus 50 years,[264] there is no compelling reason for Jordan—whether from an economic, a creative, or an innovative perspective—to extend the term of protection beyond what is currently available under the *Copyright Law* in Jordan.[265]

---

[261] IFLA et al., *The Public Domain, Why WIPO should Care, Provisional Committee on Proposals Related to a WIPO Development Agenda Third Session* 19-23 (2007), IFLA, <http://www.ifla.org/en/publications/the-public-domain-why-wipo-should-care>.

[262] Article 34 of the *Copyright Law* in Jordan, as amended, provides as follow:

> A) After the lapse of the protection period stipulated in this law of any work upon the nonexistence of heirs or upon the nonexistence of successors before the end of the protection period, the work shall revert to public domain such that any person shall have the right to print it, publish it or translate if it has already been printed, published or translated.
>
> B) If the work stipulated in paragraph (A) of this article was not printed, published or translated before reverting to public domain, none of its rights may be exploited including its printing, publication, or translation without a license from the minister. This licence shall be valid for 15 years. It shall be considered cancelled if not used within 1 year or if used then stopped afterwards for one whole year.

Copyright Law, above 141, art 34.

[263] See *Law No. 82 of 2002* (Law on the Protection of Intellectual Property Rights), Al-Jarida Al-Rasmiyya, 3 June 2002, art 183 (Egypt) <http://www.wipo.int/wipolex/en/text.jsp?file_id=126540> (expressing a similar position); Awad, El-Gheriani and Abou Zeid, above n 84.

[264] Article 26 of the *Omanian Copyright Law* provides that the 'term of protection for the economic copyrights, stipulated under this law, shall be the life of the author and seventy years starting from the beginning of the Gregorian calendar year following the year of his death'. Royal Decree No. 65/2008, above n 94, art 26.

[265] Michael Geist, *The Copyright Consultation: My Submission*, Michael Geist (11 Sept 2009) <http://www.michaelgeist.ca/content/view/4377/125/>.

5.4.8 *Liability of Online Service Providers (OSPs)*

The *Copyright Law* in Jordan has no specific provisions dealing with the liability of online service providers (OSPs).[266] It contains no provisions that expressly deal with secondary liability (also known in other jurisdictions as contributory, vicarious, inducement, or authorisation liability).[267] In the absence of a provision in the *Copyright Law*, secondary liability is dealt with under general tort law principles of joint liability under the Jordanian civil legal system.[268] The *Jordanian Civil Code*

---

[266] Bahrain, Morocco and Oman US-FTAs contain provisions and side letters on intermediary liability, safe harbours and notice and taken down. Art 14.10.29 of the BUSFTA provides that:

> For the purpose of providing enforcement procedures that permit effective action against any act of infringement of copyright covered under this Chapter, including expeditious remedies to prevent infringements and criminal and civil remedies, each Party shall provide, consistent with the framework set forth in this Article:
>
> (a) Legal incentives for service providers to cooperate with copyright owners in deterring the unauthorized storage and transmission of copyrighted materials; and
>
> (b) Limitations in its law regarding the scope of remedies available against service providers for copyright infringements that they do not control, initiate or direct, and that take place through systems or networks controlled or operated by them or on their behalf, as set forth in this subparagraph (b).
>
> (i) These limitations shall preclude monetary relief and provide reasonable restrictions on court-ordered relief to compel or restrain certain actions for the following functions and shall be confined to those functions:
>
> (A) Transmitting, routing, or providing connections for material without modification of its content, or the intermediate and transient storage of such material in the course thereof;
>
> (B) Caching carried out through an automatic process;
>
> (C) storage at the direction of a user of material residing on a system or network controlled or operated by or for the service provider; and
>
> (D) Referring or linking users to an online location by using information location tools, including hyperlinks and directories.
>
> (ii) These limitations shall apply only where the service provider does not initiate the chain of transmission of the material, and does not select the material or its recipients (except to the extent that a function described in clause (i)(D) in itself entails some form of selection).
>
> (iii) Qualification by a service provider for the limitations as to each function in clauses (i)(A) through (i)(D) shall be considered separately from qualification for the limitations as to each other function, in accordance with the conditions for qualification set forth in clauses (iv)–(vii).

BUSFTA, above n 31, art 14.10.29; see also OUSFTA, above 31, art 15.10.29; MUSFTA, above n 31, art 15.11.28.

[267] See, e.g.; MGM Studios Inc. v. Grokster Ltd., 545 U.S. 913 (2005); A & M Records Inc. v. Napster Inc., 239 F.3d 1004 (9th Cir. 2001); *Universal Music Austl. Pty. Ltd. v. Sharman License Holdings Ltd.* [2005] FCA 1242 (Australia) ('Kazaa').

[268] Nouri Khater and Adnan Serhan, *Explanation of the Jordanian Civil Code*, 359-367 (Dar al Thaqafa, 1997). See also Edward A. Tomlinson, 'Tort Liability in France for Act of Things:

No. 43 of 1976 (*Jordanian Civil Code*)[269] is the primary source of law, which should be consulted in cases where there is no specific provision in the *Copyright Law* in Jordan.[270] Article 256 of the *Jordanian Civil Code* provides that '[e]very injurious act shall render the person who commits it liable for damages even if he is a non-discerning person'. Three elements must be present for tort liability to arise under the *Jordanian Civil Code*: (i) a fault or error (which may be either an act or a failure to act), (ii) damage to another, and (iii) a causal connection between the fault and damage.

'Vicarious liability' is not strictly defined in the *Jordanian Civil Code* as in the case of French law.[271] The major provisions concerning liability for another person's act are to be found in art 288 of the *Jordanian Civil Code*,[272] which provides that:

1. No person shall be liable for the act of another and yet the court may on the application of the injured person and if it finds justifiable hold liable for the awarded damages.

A. Any person who is under a legal or a contractual obligation to supervise a person in need of supervision due to his minority or his mental or physical condition, unless he proves that he has fulfilled his duty of supervision or that damage was to be inflicted even

---

A Study of Judicial Lawmaking' (1988) 48 *Louisiana Law Review* 1299 (providing further explanation of tort law under the continental European systems, particularly France); Al Tamimi, *Law of Tort in the UAE* (on file with author).

[269] The *Jordanian Civil Code* was enacted in 1976 to replace the Ottoman Majallah of 1876, which was highly influenced by Sharia and Islamic Law. See Khater and Serhan, above n 268, 5-8.

The *Jordanian Civil Code* comprises rules derived from the *Egyptian Civil Code, Law No. 131 of 1948* (Civil Code), Al-Jarida Al-Rasmiya, 29 July 1948 (Egypt), which in turn was modeled on the French Napoleonic Code, *Civil Code No. 43 of 1976*, Offical Gazette, No. 2645 (1 Augst 1976); see also Mahkamat al-Tamiez [Taimez] [Court of Cassation], Case No. 228/1987, 26 July 1987.

[270] See *Commercial Law No. 12 of 1966*, art 2, Official Gazette, No. 1910 (30 Mar 1966). Article 71, paragraph 20 of the *Jordanian Civil Code* provides that the 'provisions of special laws shall be applicable to the right of the author, Inventor, trademarks and all other rights'. *Civil Code No. 43 of 1976*, art 71, 20 (Jordan).

[271] The major provisions concerning liability for another person's act are to be found in the *French Civil Code*. Article 1384 of the *French Civil Code* provides that a 'person is liable not only for the damages he causes by his own act, but also for that which is caused by the acts of persons for whom he is responsible, or by things which are in his custody'. *Code Civil* [C. CIV.], art 1384 (France) (as amended) <http://lexinter.net/ENGLISH/civil_code.htm>. Article 1384 contains a limited list of vicarious liability, but in a famous case in 1991, the Court of Cassation (cour de cassation) decided that the general statement in article 1384 allowed creating new heads of vicarious liability. See J. Spier, *Unification of Tort Law: Liability for Damage Caused by Others* (Kluwer, 2003) 85-88; Tomlinson, above n 268; Hannibal Travis, 'Opting Out of the Internet in the United Stated and the European Union: Copyright, Safe harbours, and the International Law' (2008) 84 331.

[272] Article 121, paragraph 7, of the *French Penal Code* provides that a 'person, who knowingly facilitates the preparation or the realisation of a crime or of a tort by providing her help or assistance, is an accomplice for this crime or tort'. *Code Penal* [C. Pén], art 121,7 (France); see also Travis, above n 271; Xavier Amadei, 'Standards of Liability for Internet Service Providers: A Comparative Study of France and the United States with Specific Focus on Copyright, Defamation, and Illicit Content' (2001) 35 *Cornell International Law Journal* 189. *Compare Code Penal* [C. PÉN] art 121, 7 (France), with *Criminal Law No. 16 of 1960*, arts 44-55, 76, Official Gazette, No. 1487 (1 Jan 1960).

The *Jordanian Civil Code*, above n 269, art 288(B).

though he fulfilled his duty of supervision or that the damage was to be inflicted even though he fulfilled his duty of exercising the necessary care.

B. Any person who had actual power to supervise and direct the person who had inflicted the damage even though he himself had no free choice if the injurious act was committed by the supervised person while or because of performing the duties of his position.

Article 288 of the *Jordanian Civil Code* is influenced by Islamic jurisprudence. It states a general rule on liability and then provides limitations to it. The judge has limited powers to determine those limitations, subject to the provisions of the law.[273] It is submitted that it would be difficult to apply art 288(B) to online service providers as OSPs might not have any authority, supervision, or direction over the person who is infringing copyright works online, especially with the use of the second generation of peer-to-peer networks.[274] To ensure continuous development of copyright law, legislators around the world have introduced 'safe harbour' provisions to shelter OSPs from copyright infringement actions. There are various legislations adopted in countries including Japan,[275] the US,[276] and France[277] addressing OSPs. It is vital to shelter OSPs from liability for copyright infringement suits that could be brought against them for the Internet services that they provide to the public. If this is not done, OSPs would impose practices and

---

[273] See Khater and Serhan, above n 268, 489-507.

[274] P2P technology is used widely over the Internet to share and distribute files and information between Internet users.

[275] On May 27, 2007, Japan has introduced the Provider Liability Limitation Law, which states under art 3(1) that a provider is liable only if:

i. It is technically possible to prevent transmission of the infringing material; and
ii. The provider knows of the existence of the material; and
iii. Knows that the transmission is infringing copyright; or
iv. Reasonably ought to know that the transmission infringes.

See WIPO, above n 201. A person whose rights have been infringed can ask a provider to disclose information about the person transmitting the material if the information is necessary for a legal claim or other legitimate reason (Art. 4(1)). Ibid.

[276] The US Congress has enacted 'safe harbor' provisions as part of the DMCA, the 'Online Copyright Infringement Liability Limitation Act,' in order to shelter OSPs from liability for copyright infringement in certain circumstances. *See* 17 U.S.C. § 512.

[277] In France, hosting service providers (technical intermediaries) are defined in the *Law on Confidence in the Digital Economy* (LCEN) of 21 June 2004 and are protected in certain circumstances from the infringing acts of online users. The Act brings France into compliance with the European Commission Directive 2000/31, on Certain Legal Aspects of Information Society ('Directive on Certain Aspects of Information Society'), 2001 O.J (L. 178). *See Loi N2004-575 du 21 Juin 2004 Pour la Confiance dans L'économie Numérique* [Law on Confidence in the Digital Economy of 21 June 2004, Journal Offcial De La Republique Française [J.O.] [Official Gazette of France], 22 June 2004, p 11168 <http://www.legifrance.gouv.fr/affichTexte.do?cidTexte=JORFTEXT000000801164&dateTexte>; Kylie Junik, *French Court Finds Daily Motion Liable for Copyright Infringement*, Citizen Media Law Project (18 July 2007) <http://www.citmedialaw.org/french-court-finds-dailymotion-liable-copyright-infringement>.

policies that would discourage people from using the Internet, and this would result in the undermining of innovation and creativity.[278] Jordan needs to consider legislating safe harbour provisions (including notice and takedown provisions) that will sensibly protect OSPs, especially if it wants to develop IT industries, which provide electronic information and Internet services.[279] The rules under which OSPs operate should be clear, fair, and simple to adhere to and should take into account the OSP laws applicable in other jurisdictions.[280] In the meantime, it is critically important to protect academic institutions from copyright infringements, which might take place through their networks when academics, staff, and students use the Internet.[281]

5.4.9 Software Protection

The software industry in Jordan was started in 1999, in accordance with King Abdullah II's vision to make Jordan a regional ICT centre and to develop Jordan as an internationally recognised exporter of ICT products and the world's leading producer of Arabic-language software. The question that remains is how Jordan can turn this ambitious plan into a reality.

Creating a successful software industry in Jordan requires different elements: necessary funding, supporting industries, infrastructure, and a supportive legal regime.[282] Article 3(8) of the *Copyright Law* in Jordan protects all forms of computer software, whether in the form of object or source code. It provides as follows:

---

[278] Fitzgerald and Olwan, above n 150, 570.

[279] China has also promulgated the Regulation on the Protection of the Right to Network Dissemination of Information. See (信息网络传播权保护条例) Regulation on the Protection of the Right to Network Dissemination of Information (promulgated by the Executive Meeting of the State Council, 18 May 2006, effective 1 July 2006) (China) <http://www.wipo.int/wipolex/en/text.jsp?file_id=182147>; see also Lin Xie, *Safe Harbors and Joint Liability of the OSPs in China—A Comparative Study Between the US and Australia and China* (unpublished manuscript) <http://papers.ssrn.com/sol3/papers.cfm?abstract_id=1358467>; Yiman Zhang, 'Establishing Secondary Liability with a Higher Degree of Culpability: Redefining Chinese Internet Copyright Law to Encourage Technology Development' (2007) 16 *Pacific Rim Law & Policy Journal* 257.

[280] Industry Canada and the Department of Canadian Heritage, A Framework for Copyright Reform (2001) <http://bca.archives.ca/docs/bca_comm_eng.pdf>; Industry Canada and the Department of Canadian Heritage, Consulting Paper on Digitial Copyright Issues (2001) <http://balancedcopyright.gc.ca/eic/site/crp-prda.nsf/vwapj/digital.pdf/$FILE/digital.pdf>.

[281] Ida Madieha bt. Abdul Ghani Azmi, 'Institutional Repositories in Malaysia: the Copyright Issues' (2009) 17(3) *International Journey of Law and Information Technology* 268, 272.

[282] Ramzi T. Abdel Jaber, 'Silicon Wadi: Can Jordan Develop an Internationally Respected and Competitive Software Industry?' Jordan Times (online) (8 April 1999) <http://www.jordanembassyus.org/040899009.htm>.

> Innovated literary, artistic and scientific works regardless of their kind, importance or the purpose of their production shall enjoy protection by virtue of this law:
>
> 8. Computer programs whether in the source or in machine language.

The *Copyright Law* in Jordan does not contain any limitations and exceptions that relate to the use of computer software, even if it was legally obtained. It should not be an infringement of copyright to incidentally reproduce a computer program merely as part of the technical process of running a copy of the program or for the purpose of studying the program, except where the reproduction is made from an infringing copy of the program or contrary to an express direction or licence of the copyright owner.[283] The *Copyright Law* in Jordan does not contain provisions that allow programmers to look at and examine other programs in order to enable compatible and competing software products to be produced.[284] This is known as 'interoperability of software'. IT developers in Jordan should be given a narrow limitation and exception to copyright infringement of software that allows reverse engineering.[285] This can result in the development of local IT expertise and the creation of new software programs.

It is noted that the *Copyright Law* in Jordan does not differentiate between the term of protection for a computer program and other works (including books) as it gives the same protection of 50 years after the author's death for all kinds of works. This approach is unrealistic and unjustified because the lifespan of most, if not all, software is shorter[286] and not more than 20 years. To this end, one scholar has argued that a suitable term for copyright is 20 years.[287] This would allow the software developer to recoup their investments and, at the same time, preserve the public interest by facilitating the growth of the public domain.[288] It is suggested that any future legislation in Jordan must take into consideration the real needs of the software industry in Jordan, including the small number of corporations currently developing Free and Open-Source Software (FOSS) and small medium enterprises (SMEs) working in the software industry.

---

[283] Fitzgerald and Fitzgerald, above n 202, at 111.

[284] See Copinger et al., above n 199, 540.

[285] John Abbott, 'Reverse Engineering of Software: Copyright and Interoperability' (2003) 14 *Journal of Law and Information Science* 7.

[286] Susanna H.S. Leong, 'Legal Protection of Factual Compilations and Databases-Rethinking the Copyright Protection Model in Singapore' (2007) 5 (2) *Journal of World Intellectual Property* 1047-1068.

[287] See Khater, above n 101, 301–03.

[288] ICTSD and UNCTAD, *Resource Book on TRIPS and Development* (Cambridge University, 2004), Chapter 11, 'Copyright: Term of Protection,' <http://www.iprsonline.org/unctadictsd/docs/RB_2.11_update.pdf>.

5.4.10 Database Protection

Economies are dominated by the creation, manipulation, and use of information and the time it takes to do so.[289] Many corporations are willing to pay huge sums of money to obtain databases that are useful to their work and business. This is because these databases contain important and copious amounts of information that significantly reduce the time needed to find and access information.[290]

Databases are protected under art 3(D) of the *Copyright Law* in Jordan as follows:

> Protection shall also encompass the collections of literary or artistic works such as encyclopaedias, selections and collected data whether or not collected in a machine readable form. Provided that such collections represent as to their selection or the arrangement of their contents innovated intellectual works, protection shall also encompass collections containing selective extracts of poetry, prose, music or other material, provided that the sources and authors of the extracts are specified in the said collections and without infringing the copyright of each work which represents a part of these collections.

Article 7 of the *Copyright Law* in Jordan provides as follows:

> The protection stipulated in this law shall not encompass the following works unless the collections of these works were distinguished by a personal effort involving innovation or arrangement.

Article 7 does not define what is considered as encyclopaedias, selections, and collected data and treats all works as being the same. In this regard, the position of the Jordan is similar to the position in other countries such as Singapore and Malaysia.[291] However, what level of originality, under art 3 of the *Copyright Law* in Jordan, is required to protect databases in Jordan?

There are two theories on the legal protection of databases, the 'sweat of the brow theory' and 'the labour/investment theory.' The first requires a low level of originality and minimum efforts to satisfy the law, whereas the second requires a higher level of originality and maximum efforts to gain protection under the law. There is no case law in Jordan on databases that tells to which theory the law refers. Although art 3 of the *Copyright Law* in Jordan is not explicit about the level of originality required under the law, it is inferred from the language of 'personal effort' used in the law that it requires only minimum effort (sweat of the brow theory) to satisfy the law. What is clear is that the copyright protection is limited only to the selection or arrangement of the data and not to the data itself since information per se is not protected.[292] This is consistent with art 2(5) of the *Berne Convention*.[293] More studies need to be conducted in Jordan to examine the

---

[289] Mark J. Davison, *The Legal Protection of Databases* (Cambridge University, 2003) 1.

[290] Ibid.

[291] See, for Singapore, Leong, above n 286, and for Malaysia, Azmi, above n 281, 271-272.

[292] This could be inferred from art 3(A)(D) of the *Copyright Law*. See *Copyright Law*, above n 141.

[293] Article 2(5) of the *Berne Convention* provides that:

> 5) Collections of literary or artistic works such as encyclopaedias and anthologies which, by reason of the selection and arrangement of their contents, constitute intellectual creations

businesses that are working on creating databases in the country and to examine their needs, so the law properly protects their rights and encourages creativity and innovation in the IT sector.

5.5 What Needs to Be Done?

It is clear that the *Copyright Law* in Jordan was not drafted with development goals in mind. To improve Jordan's IP regime, it will be important to take a developmental perspective when drafting the laws. This sect. provides some recommendations and suggestions that would improve the *Copyright Law* and the Jordanian IP system and render it pro-development.

5.5.1 Integrate the Development Dimension into Jordanian Intellectual Property Laws

It is important to move far beyond the view that only IP maximalist would benefit Jordan.[294] Jordan could gain from adopting a more balanced view of IP that not only favours copyright owners but also gives an equal importance to users and the public. Instead of drafting 'stronger IP laws,'[295] it is more important to have appropriate laws that correspond with the needs of Jordan and its citizens.[296] This could happen by studying the social and economic conditions of Jordan and by enacting laws that are in accord with its national development goals. Jordanian IP laws should also be drafted by experts in Jordan in a way that supports public policy objectives such as those relating to the transfer of technology, public health, education, and the environment.[297] These policies should not be forced

shall be protected as such, without prejudice to the copyright in each of the works forming part of such collections.

Berne Convention, above n 153, art 2.5.

[294] See Tabbaa and Partners, *Update on Compliance with Intellectual Property in Jordan* (2007) USAID <http://pdf.usaid.gov/pdf_docs/PNADM871.pdf>.

[295] Ibid.

[296] Mary Wai San Wong, *The Next Years in Copyright Law: An Asian Perspective* (16 February 2007) (unpublished manuscript) SSRN <http://papers.ssrn.com/sol3/papers.cfm?abstract_id=1017144#PaperDownload>. See also Mohammed El Said, 'Access to Knowledge, and Intellectual Property Protection, the Arab World: The Challenges of Development' in Hala Essalmawi, *Access to Knowledge Toolkit II (A2K), The Access to Knowledge Movement: Opportunities, Challenges and the Road Ahead* (2009) Bibliotheca Alexandria, 52-63 <http://www.bibalex.org/a2k/attachments/references/reffileu24bkg55ykqwgc55zysxzq45.pdf>.

[297] Abdel Latif, above n 30, 53.

from above but rather should be based on a real assessment of the local contexts.[298]

5.5.2 *Consider Seriously Alternative Approaches to IP*

Some observers think that IP laws are overly restrictive when applied in the Internet context. They argue that we should be looking for ways to reduce impediments to the use and reproduction of information over Internet networks.[299] This approach has not yet been fully explored by academics and researchers in Jordan. It is important to consider alternative approaches to IP, including FOSS and open content licensing. These alternatives could be helpful in assisting social and economic development in Jordan.

5.5.3 *Take Full Advantage of the Flexibilities of International Copyright Treaties*

There are certain flexibilities within the international copyright treaties (including *Berne* and TRIPS) that could be used to meet the unique needs of developing countries, including Jordan. These include 1) flexibilities in the scope of copyright protection, 2) flexibilities in relation to the duration of the copyright protection, and 3) flexibilities in relation to the limitations and exceptions.[300] Jordan has managed to include some of those flexibilities in the *Copyright Law* in Jordan (including the flexibilities in relation to the duration of the copyright term), but careful review of the provisions of the law reveal that not all of these flexibilities were introduced fully.

A study conducted by the organisation, Consumers International, has found that a number of developing countries and emerging economies, including Cambodia, China, Indonesia, Malaysia, Mongolia, and the Philippines have not benefited from the flexibilities available under international copyright conventions.[301] Jordan, in particular, has not taken advantage of the degrees of legislative flexibility offered to

---

[298] Meeting Report, *ICTSD-UNCTAD Dialogue, 2d Bellagio Series on Development and Intellectual Property*: 'Towards Development-Oriented Intellectual Property Policy: Advancing the Reform Agenda' (18–21 September 2003) <http://www.iprsonline.org/unctadictsd/bellagio/docs/Bellagio2_Report.pdf>.

[299] Jonathan Zittrain, *Alternatives to Intellectual Property* <http://cyber.law.harvard.edu/ilaw/mexico_2006_module_2_alttoip> (on file with author).

[300] See Consumers International, above n 246.

[301] Ibid.

countries under the *Berne Convention* and the *TRIPS Agreement*.[302] Accordingly, it is important to review the *Copyright Law* in Jordan and examine how Jordan could obtain maximum benefits from the flexibilities offered under the international copyright treaties. It is also important that Jordan and other developing countries closely monitor and become an active participant in the WIPO Development Agenda[303] since this Agenda could have an important impact upon future development of the international IP system.

5.5.4 Conduct a Review of the Copyright Law in Jordan

Despite the amendments that were made to the *Copyright Law* in Jordan in 2005, it still fails to meet the expectations of consumers and the general public.[304] This is because policymakers in Jordan have opted to increase the level of IP protection for copyright owners in exchange for foreign investment and economic assistance. This outlook is short-sighted because while it might encourage investments to pour into Jordan for a short period, it could have major implications for overall education and developmental goals. To ensure balanced IP laws, it is essential that consumers and the public at large are included in the legislative debates when amending any IP laws. The Jordanian government needs to be open about its development plans and should engage widely with its citizens, especially in relation to IP and development.

5.5.5 Popularise and Promote A2K

A2K is a concept put forward by those who believe that knowledge should be freely accessible to developing countries, with limited legal restrictions. The concept gained momentum with the ever-increasing amount of freely available content distributed through the Internet. Many IP scholars and international organisations support the concept of A2K, such as Consumers International[305] and the Library of Alexandria in Egypt[306] and other non-profit organisations.

The A2K movement tries to draw attention to another aspect of IP that has been long neglected: that a greater sharing of knowledge could be far more beneficial to

[302] On the flexibilities contained in the TRIPS Agreement, see generally Alhaj Tejan-Cole, Presentation, *Flexibilities in the TRIPS Agreement and its Impact on National Intellectual Property Policy*, Belize Intellectual Property Office <http://www.belipo.bz/wp-content/uploads/2011/12/TRIPS-FLEXIBILITIES.pdf>.

[303] WIPO, *Development Agenda for WIPO* <http://www.wipo.int/ip-development/en/agenda/>.

[304] There is a draft of a Jordanian Copyright Law in the process of being reviewed by the Parliament, and it is not clear when and whether it will be approved.

[305] Consumers International <http://www.consumersinternational.org/>.

[306] Library of Alexandria <http://www.bibalex.org/Home/Default_EN.aspx>.

overall human development and welfare rather than having knowledge restricted under the proprietary control of individuals. The A2K movement is not only against strong IP laws but also against any restriction on knowledge dissemination that will ultimately obstruct and oppose overall human welfare and social and economic development.

It is submitted that Jordan and developing countries should commit resources towards launching a public awareness campaign to educate people on how best they (particularly students, teachers, archivists, academics, and librarians) can access and capitalise on copyrighted materials, which they are legally entitled to access freely.[307] It is also important for Jordan and developing countries to observe the developments taking place with A2K and ensure that they are active participants in international organisations and NGOs that promote it, including Consumers International, Electronic Information for Libraries (EIL),[308] African Copyright & Access to Knowledge Project (ACA2K),[309] IFLA Committee for Copyright,[310] Knowledge Ecology International,[311] and others.

5.5.6 *Promote Open Access and Create Open Access Institutional Repositories*

Open access enables researchers to communicate their results to international researchers widely, quickly, and cheaply. This is important for researchers in Jordan and developing countries to help them to connect with global research communities.[312] Educational institutions in Jordan should adopt and support open access in order to benefit the local community and to spread knowledge among Jordanian citizens. The Jordanian government should look into the possibility of adopting an open policy across government institutions as this would bring immense value to researchers and government officials.

Repositories are rich sources of information, data, images, and valuable research.[313] It is not enough to adopt open policies that encourage open access; it is just as important to create repositories that would put these policies into practice. The Jordanian government should give its full support to any initiative, either local or international, that might develop the necessary repositories in its country.

---

307 Consumers International, above n 165.

308 EIFL <http://www.eifl.net/>.

309 The African Copyright and Access to Knowledge Project <http://www.aca2k.org/>.

310 Committee on Copyright and Other Legal Matters <http://www.ifla.org/clm>.

311 Knowledge Ecology International <http://keionline.org/>.

312 Julie M. Esanu and Paul F. Uhlir, 'Open Access and the Public Domain in the Digital Data and Information for Science' in Julie M. Esanu and Paul F. Uhlir (ed), *Open Access and Public Domain in Digital Data and Information For Scienc: A Processing of An International Symposium* (National Academies, 2004) <http://www.nap.edu/catalog.php?record_id=11030>.

313 Azmi, above n 281, 277.

5.5.7 *Expand the Range of Limitations and Exceptions for the Internet Environment*

Any copyright law in Jordan is criticised if it does not have proper limitations and exceptions in place, especially with regard to the Internet environment. Appropriate limitations and exceptions in the digital environment would give Internet users in Jordan the following:

- The right to reuse copyright materials in circumstances where there is no financial detriment to the copyright owner;
- The right to engage in transformative and 'fair use'; and
- The right to engage in format shifting, e.g., changing material from analogue to digital format or changing material from one digital format (CD) to another (mp3).[314]

The Jordanian legislature should adopt a maximalist approach when drafting limitations and exceptions in the *Copyright Law* in Jordan. This means adopting as many limitations and exceptions as possible for the Internet and digital technologies and making sure that new ones can be added in the future, as technology changes.[315] It is also important to permit proper limitations and exceptions for students, regardless of their physical location, and to clarify the library limitations and exceptions to cover any possible electronic use of a work in order to permit effective research, gathering, and organisation of information.[316] Adequate limitations and exceptions for libraries, archives, and museums (including provisions for accessing and providing information, digitisation, preservation, and digital creation (including migration to new technologies as they change)) must be included in the *Copyright Law* in Jordan. To the extent possible, Jordan should also consult with international organisations and NGOs, when drafting its limitations and exceptions, to help secure necessary legal advice.[317]

5.5.8 *Give Particular Consideration to Copyright Misuse*

In the context of copyright law, the balance in the copyright system has shifted dramatically toward copyright owners,[318] as shown in the *Copyright Law* of Jordan.

---

[314] Fitzgerald and Olwan, above n 150, 570.

[315] *TIPS for Developing Countries when Reviewing Copyright Laws* (9 September 2009) ACA2K <http://www.aca2k.org/index.php?option=com_content&view=article&id=229%3Atips-for-developing-countries-when-reviewing-copyright-laws&catid=69%3Adenise&lang=en>.

[316] Azmi, above n 281, 273-274.

[317] ACA2K, above n 315. See also Giavarra and Hackett, above n 215; WIPO, *Study for Limitations & Exceptions of Copyright & Related Rights in the Digital Environment* <http://www.wipo.int/meetings/en/doc_details.jsp?doc_id=16805>.

[318] John T. Cross and Peter K. Yu, 'Competition Law and Copyright Misuse' (2008) 56 *Drake Law Review* 427, 430 SSRN <http://papers.ssrn.com/sol3/papers.cfm?abstract_id=986891>.

Competition or unfair competition laws are particularly important from a developmental perspective[319] as they guarantee that the monopoly given to IP owners is not misused. These laws are important not only in relation to patent laws but also in the field of copyright. In Jordan, the *Unfair Competition and Trade Secret Law No. 15 for 2000*[320] protects licensees from unfair practices that might be committed by IP owners.[321] One Jordanian commentator has criticised the law for providing only very limited protection, which is not adequate to accommodate unfair competition cases.[322] Jordanian courts should make sure that its judges are capable of handling cases that relate to copyright abuses.[323]

---

[319] See Shiju Vaghese Mazhuvanchery, 'The Indian *Competition* Act: A Historical and Developmental Perspective' 2010 3 (2) *The Law and Development Review* 241.

[320] *Unfair Competition and Trade Secret Law No. 15 of 2000, Offcial Gazette*, No. 4423 (2 April 2000).

[321] Article 9 of the *Unfair Competition and Trade Secret Law* provides that:

> A. Every provision or condition restricting competition included in the license contract related to any of the intellectual property rights, which may have negative effect on commerce, or many hinder the transference or dissemination of the technology shall be void and null, and in particular:
>
> 1. To prohibit the licensee from transferring modifications done on the technology included in the license contract except for the licensor (Back transferring of technology).
> 2. Preventing the licensee from arising Juridical or Administrative disputes in respect of the licensed intellectual property right.
> 3. To compel the licensee to accept the license with number of rights instead of one right only.
>
> B. The intellectual property rights mentioned in paragraph (A) of this article particularly include:
>
> 1. Copyrights and neighbouring rights.
> 2. Trademarks.
> 3. Geographical indications.
> 4. Industrial drawings and Industrial designs.
> 5. Patents.
> 6. Layout designs of integrated circuits.
> 7. Trade secrets.
> 8. New varieties of plant.

Ibid art 9.

[322] Haitham A. Haloush, 'A Practitioner Guide to the Unfair Competition Law in Jordan' (2009) 2 *Open Law Journal* <http://bentham.org/open/tolawj/articles/V002/1TOLAWJ.pdf>; Haitham A. Haloush, 'Building a Trade Secrets System in Jordan: A Critique of the Current Legal Framework' (2009) 4 (6) *Journal of Intellectual Property Law & Practice* 425.

[323] Professor John Cross and Peter Yu define copyright abuse as 'the use of the rights of copyright owners in any improper way'. It is hoped that IP scholarship would give in depth analysis of the legal issues involved in relation to copyright abuse. See Cross and Yu, above n 318, 455.

5.6 Conclusion

There are few areas of law that touch so closely upon our everyday activities yet are as difficult for the average person to comprehend as copyright law.[324] It determines who may use and control the most important assets of the digital economy.[325] Despite this fundamental importance, copyright and its relationship to the social and economic conditions of developing countries remains poorly understood by policymakers in both Jordan and developing countries in general.[326]

Jordan has been a WTO member since 11 April 2000. As part of its membership obligations, it was required to become a signatory to the principal international copyright treaties (*Berne Convention,* WCT, and WPPT)—a move that necessitated major amendments to its IP systems and copyright law. More recently, Jordan became the third country and the first Arab state from the Middle East to sign an FTA with the US (the JUSFTA), which took effect on 17 December 2001. This in turn led to further amendments to its IP system, which were even more restrictive than those required by the WCT and WPPT. This experience is similar to that of other countries from the regions that have signed bilateral FTAs.

IP is not to be regarded as a magic formula that will solve the problems of any developing country but rather as 'a means to an end'. It is important for Jordan and other developing countries to move beyond the traditional view of IP towards a more development-oriented approach, which integrates IP into their broader development policies.[327] This chapter has suggested various means by which that goal may be achieved. It is important to engage in a detailed analysis of the provisions of the *Copyright Law* from a developmental perspective before introducing it into the laws of Jordan. This should be done in conformity with the international copyright treaties that Jordan has signed. Undertaking this process promises to not only satisfy the international obligation but also assist Jordan on its path to social and economic development.

[324] Lea Shaver (ed), *Access to Knowledge in Brazil* (Bloomburg, 2010) 7.

[325] Ibid.

[326] Ibid.

[327] Abdel Latif, above n 30.

Chapter 6
Voluntary Mechanisms, Copyright and Development

Of course information technology and open source in particular is not a silver bullet for longstanding development issues; nothing is. But the transformative potential of computing does create new opportunities to make progress on development problems that have been intransigent.[1]

Open source software has been called many things: a movement, a fad, a virus, a communist conspiracy, even the heart and soul of the Internet. Open source software is also a highly effective vehicle for the transfer of wealth from the industrialized world to developing countries.[2]

Video news footage is an essential part of modern journalism. Providing material under a Creative Commons license to allow commercial and amateur users to share, edit, subtitle and cite video news is an enormous contribution to the global dialog around important events. Al Jazeera has set the example and the standard that we hope others will follow.[3]

Abstract Having examined IP law, particularly copyright law, and how it needs to adopt a development perspective, it is important to consider innovative systems that can be used in combination with such laws for the benefit of developing countries. This chapter considers voluntary mechanisms, primarily Free and Open Source Software (FOSS) and Creative Commons (CC), and examines their relevance for developing countries. Voluntary mechanisms must be examined in the context of development as they are practical tools that can be localised for the benefit of developing countries. Most of the recent research on IP and development does not give proper attention to voluntary mechanisms or examine their relevance to the IP and development debate. This chapter calls on developing countries to seriously consider alternative approaches such as voluntary mechanisms and to use them in conjunction with traditional copyright laws. It examines the legal

[1] Steven Weber, *The Success of Open Source Software* (Harvard University, 2004) 254.

[2] *Andrew Leonard,* 'ALT/ An Alternative Voice: How the Tech-Poor Can Still Be Software-Rich', New York Times (online), 28 June 2001 <http://www.nytimes.com/2001/06/28/business/worldbusiness/28iht-btalt28.html?pagewanted=print>.

[3] Joi Ito <http://cc.aljazeera.net/content/about-repository>.

R.M. Olwan, *Intellectual Property and Development*,
DOI 10.1007/978-3-642-27907-2_6, © Springer-Verlag Berlin Heidelberg 2013

challenges and risks that those countries will face if they decide to adopt voluntary mechanisms. The chapter also looks at the civil legal system of Jordan as a case study for the adoption of FOSS and CC.

6.1 Overview

The Free and Open Source Software (FOSS) methodology has challenged traditional approaches to copyright management by using copyright to build 'openness' and reuse. In doing so, it not only has shown new ways for managing copyright but also has underpinned new methods for constructing and disseminating knowledge. To some extent, it has been seen to put the power to develop and share knowledge and technology in the hands of users rather than of an elite or cloistered group of experts. To this end, it has great significance for developing countries.

FOSS has been given great impetus by the rise of the Internet on two levels. Firstly, the Internet was built upon software infrastructure that consisted, in part, of FOSS. Secondly, the Internet epitomises the distributed and collaborative methodology of FOSS, as well as facilitates its actual development. If Richard Stallman, in 1984, could have envisaged a technology that would implement his vision in both the uptake of the software and in the development of the software, it would have been the Internet.

The special design features of the Internet[4] have assisted the development of many unique and novel inventions that were later distributed through this revolutionary, multinational, distribution channel. Creators and innovators from all over the world have placed their contributions online, which has led to the recognition of the Internet as a home for creativity and innovation. Within a short time of being popularised, the Internet became a place for the public to disseminate, express, and share ideas and build upon existing ones. The empowerment of people to publish their own opinions without restriction had a transformative effect on societies and economies. This is the very context, especially important to developing countries, in which new approaches to the production and dissemination of knowledge are being established in the network era.

The increasing uptake of FOSS and Creative Commons (CC) licensing schemes in business, government, and education sectors is one of the most interesting phenomena of the Internet, which has attracted the wide interest not only of IT experts but also of legal scholars and academics in various fields. There are

[4] The Internet is a huge project that was successful due to the numerous researchers, scientists, and innovators who made it real. Among these are Vincent Cerf (TCP/IP Protocol), Tim Berner Lee (Hyper Text Makeup Language (HTML)), and John Postel (Domain Name System (DNS)). See Naavi Na.Vijayashankar, *Cyber Laws For Every Netizen in India* (2004) <http://www.naavi.org/cl_editorial_07/bba_2004.pdf>.

now thousands of FOSS programs[5] that have been widely used and distributed over the Internet.[6] The FOSS philosophy has inspired hundreds of projects and initiatives that are using open licences or simply prefer the idea of 'openness'.[7] The same philosophy was adopted in numerous fields outside the IT sector, including music, media, encyclopaedia, science,[8] art, ethics, government, education, governance, and many others. Nevertheless, what makes FOSS sufficiently interesting for study by legal scholars and IP experts?

Many copyright systems, particularly those in common law jurisdictions, are based on the 'stimulus' or 'reward' or 'utilitarian' theories.[9] These legal systems justify giving limited property rights (copyright) to the author for the creative work that has been presented to the public. Without adequate compensation and protection of the work, the author[10] would not invest time and effort in producing creative work and society would suffer as a result.[11] FOSS challenges this long-established justification theory of copyright by proving that this is certainly not true for certain collaboration projects where the author produces software without being stimulated

---

[5] See, for example, the following websites that allow users to download FOSS: Red Hat <http://www.redhat.com>, Linux kernel <http://www.kernel.org>, Suse <http://www.suse.com>, Open Office <http://www.openoffice.org/>.

[6] Among the most famous ones are Linux (an operating system), Firefox (a popular Internet browser), BIND (the Domain Name System), Thunderbird (a free email and news clients), and Apache (a Hypertext Transfer Protocol (HTTP) Web server).

As of April 2012, Apache servers have a 65.5% of share in the servers market. See Aetcraft, *Web Server Survey* (April 2012) <http://news.netcraft.com/archives/category/web-server-survey/>.

[7] Among these projects and initiatives are MIT Open Courseware <http://ocw.mit.edu/index.htm>, Open Law <http://openlaw.wikia.com/wiki/Main_Page>, Open Wetware <http://openwetware.org/wiki/Main Page>, Open Source Mining <http://themineproject.org/>, Free Encyclopaedia <http://en.wikipedia.org/wiki/Main_Page>, Open Music <http://repmus.ircam.fr/openmusic/home>, Open Source Audio <http://www.archive.org/details/opensource_audio>, Open Hardware <http://www.openhardware.net/>, OpenBios <http://www.openfirmware.info/Welcome_to_OpenBIOS>, Open Access <http://www.oaklaw.qut.edu.au>.

[8] Lucie Guibault and Ot van Daalen, *Unravelling the Myth Around Open Source Licenses* (TMC Asser, 2006) 1.

[9] Axel Metxger and Till Jaeger, 'Open Source software and German Copyright Law' 32 (2001) *International Review of Intellectual Property and Competition Law* 57.

[10] Severine Dusollier, 'Open Source and Copyleft: Authorship Reconsidered?' (2002–2003) 26 *Columbia Journal of Law and Arts* 281, 293.

[11] In some cases, the free software developer may have a long-term vision to monetise reputation created through FOSS development, but this is not always the case. See Yochai Benkler, *Wealth of Networks* (Yale University, 2006).

by the 'reward theory', as known in copyright.[12] Furthermore, FOSS challenges the 'personal theory', which justifies giving protection to authors in continental European civil law system jurisdictions[13] by not considering their work to be a stamp of their singular personality but accepting that it might be altered by others for the purpose of contributing to a larger discourse and common goal.[14] The FOSS movement challenges the traditional notions of copyright by describing alternative approaches to software copyright protection and licensing as 'copyleft'.[15] This logic, which challenges the 'reward' and 'personal' theories of copyright, and the philosophy of encouraging authors to be more tolerant toward others in terms of sharing and building on their work, is an interesting subject of research in FOSS and IT.

Flickr,[16] the most famous online photo management website, hosts slightly over 150 million CC-licensed images in 2009.[17] CC-licensed works are numerous[18] and can be applied to a variety of works that include a website, a blog, a work of art, documentation, an interactive presentation, a government report, science-fiction movies, and other online and offline works.[19] The importance of the CC licensing schemes stems from the current debates that are taking place on their use in the government, business, and educational sectors not only in developed countries but

[12] Dusollier, above n 10, 287, 293. See also, José J. González de Alaiza Cardona, 'Open Source, Free Software, and Contractual Issues' (2007) 15 (2) *Texas Intellectual Property Law Journal*, 1; Metxger and Jaeger, above n 9, 74; Natasha T. Horne, 'Open Source Software Licensing: Using Copyright Law to Encourage Free Use' (2001) *17 Georgia State University Law Review*, 863, 872.

[13] See full explanation of the 'personal theory', William Fisher, 'Theories of Intellectual Property' in Stephen Munzer (ed), *New Essays in the Legal and Political Theory of Property* (Cambridge University, 2001) 168–199.

[14] Dusollier, above n 10, 293.

[15] Some commentators describe the FOSS movement as an end to copyright. See Patrick K. Bobko, 'Open Source Software and the Demise of Copyright' (2001) 27 *Rutgers Computer & Technology Law Journal* 51; Eben Moglen, 'Anarchism Triumphant: Free Software and the Death of Copyright' in Lucie Guibault (ed), *Copyright Limitations and Contracts: An Analysis of the Contractual Overidability of Limitations on Copyright* (Kluwer Law International, 2002).

[16] Flickr <http://www.flickr.com>.

[17] See the home page of Flickr <http://www.flickr.com/creativecommons>. See also Frederic Lardinois, *CC on Flicker: Users Prefer Restrictive Licenses* (26 March 2009) Read Write Web <http://www.readwriteweb.com/archives/creative_commons_on_flickr_users_choose_most_restr.php>.

[18] CC does not specify any number but acknowledged that since June 2007 there were at least 40–60 million CC-licensed materials. See Creative Commons, *Licensed Statistics* (2011) <http://wiki.creativecommons.org/License_statistics>; Terry Hancock, *Some Numbers on Creative Commons* (5 March 2007) Free Software Magazine <http://www.freesoftwaremagazine.com/columns/some_numbers_on_creative_commons>; Giorgos Cheliotis, *CC statistics* (2 July 2007) Hoikoinoi <http://hoikoinoi.wordpress.com/2007/07/02/cc-stats/>.

[19] Creative Commons <http://www.creativecommons.org>.

also in developing countries.[20] Unfortunately, voluntary mechanisms such as FOSS and CC have not been dealt with as they should be by legal scholars and experts in developing countries, and this is also applicable in the Arab world.[21] This is because most of the research that has been written so far in this part of the world examines traditional approaches to IP, including traditional approaches to software protection and management.[22]

This chapter will examine how voluntary mechanisms, mainly FOSS and CC, could act as paths for social and economic development in developing countries, but this could not be completed without studying the history, philosophy, and legal challenges that these two movements present for developing countries. This chapter studies the GNU GPL version 2, not version 3. This is because most of the international cases that discuss the validity of the GNU GPL are based on version 2, and it is important to analyse those particular cases in the chapter. There are many FOSS programmers and developers who are still using the GNU GPL version 2 instead of version 3. Version 3 of the GNU GPL has been criticised, and there

---

[20] This is evident by the many organisations in developing countries that have started their CC projects in their jurisdictions. See the International Creative Commons <http://creativecommons.org/international>.

[21] See, generally, the limited research in FOSS in Arabic: Kefah T. Issah, *Introduction to Free Software* (28 April 2005) <http://www.freesoft.jo/www/people/kefah/freesoftware_whitepaper_arabic.pdf>; Anas Tawileh, *Open Source, Options without Borders* (2004) <http://www.tawileh.net/anas//files/downloads/books/OpenSource.pdf?download>.

[22] See, generally, the following research in Arabic: Faisel Al Kandry, 'Civil Protection of Computer Software in Kuwaiti Law' (a paper presented at the Computer and Law Conference, Emirates University, Dubai, 1–3 May 2000); Mustafa Arjawi, 'Civil Protection for Computer Software' (a paper presented at the Computer and Law Conference, Emirates University, Dubai, 1–3 May 2000); Nazeh AL Mahdi, 'Civil Protection of Computer Software According to Applicable Laws' (a paper presented at the Computer and Law Conference, Emirates University, Dubai, 1–3 May 2000); Ahmad Saman, 'Legal Protection of Computer Software—Applications in Comparative Laws and in the Gulf States' (a paper presented at Kuwaiti Conference on Law and Computers, Kuwait, 4–7 November 1989); Dala Essa Wasna, *Protection of Copyright on the Internet* (Sader, 2002); Nouri Hamad Khater, *Explanation of Intellectual Property Rules—Author's Rights and Neighbouring Rights* (Emirates University, 2008); Naeam Imgabgab, *Protection of Computer Software: A Comparative Study* (AL Halabi, 2006); Emad Salamah, *Legal Protection of Computer Software and Software Piracy Problem* (Dar Wael, 2005); Abd-Al Razaq al Sunhouri, *Explanation of the New Civil Code* 274–436 (AL Halabi, 3rd ed, 1998); Naeam Imgabgab, *Artistic Property and Neighbouring Rights—A Comparative Study* (AL Halabi, 2000); Mohamad Housam Loutfi, *Legal Protection of Computer Software* (Dar Althaqafa, Cairo, 1987); The Arab Organisation for Education, Culture and Science—Copyright in the Arab World in Accordance with Arab and International Legislation (1999); Tourki Hamad Saqar, *The Protection of Copyright–Theory and Practice* (Arab Union Association, 1996); Mohamad Housam Loutfi, *Public Performance Right in Musical Work—A Comparative Study between Egyptian and French Law* (Egyptian Association for Books, 1987); Edward Eead, *Copyright and Neibouring Rights in the Lebanese, Arabic and Foreign Laws* (Sader, 2001); Abd al-Rasheed Mamoun and Mohamad Sami Abd Alsadak, *Copyright and Neighbouring Rights* (Dar Al Nahda, 2008).

are many, even within the legal scholarship community,[23] who prefer to discuss the GNU GPL version 2 instead of the GNU GPL version 3 because it is clearer and user friendly.[24]

6.2 Free and Open Source Software

Developing countries have looked with enthusiasm to FOSS to fill their urgent need for the use of software in government departments and institutions[25] and to bridge the digital divide in the use of ICT.[26] They have also seen FOSS as a unique opportunity to leverage their development goals[27] and help spur creativity and innovation. To understand this approach, this chapter is divided into three sections. Sects. 6.2.1 and 6.2.2 give an overview of the FOSS movement, focusing on its historical development and philosophy. Sect. 6.2.3 considers how FOSS can assist developing countries in their social and economic development. Sects. 6.2.4 and 6.2.5 consider the legal challenges and issues for the adoption of FOSS in developing countries.

---

[23] See Linus Torvalds, the initiator and developer of Linux Kernel who is still using the GNU GPL version 2. See Softpedia, *Linus Torvalds Says No to GPLv3* (9 January 2008) <http://news.softpedia.com/news/Linus-Torvalds-Says-No-To-GPLv3-75766.shtml>.

[24] Andrés Guadamuz González criticised the GPL v3 as follows:

> It is clear that the new version of the licence has lost clarity and gained length. This would not be a problem as such if this was followed by a strengthening of the existing provisions, but this does not seem to be the case at the moment. While there are some elegant and clever clauses in the new draft, others seem to be filled with explanatory paragraphs that seem to be out of place in a legal document. The draft could pick some drafting tips from the smaller and more elegant licences that solve some of its issues in a more efficient manner.

See Andrés Guadamuz González, 'GNU General Public License v3:A Legal Analysis' (2006) 3(2) *Scripted* 155. <http://www.law.ed.ac.uk/ahrc/script-ed/vol3-2/guadamuz.asp>.

[25] FOSS can be regarded as a viable alternative to 'proprietary software' such as Microsoft, which developing countries need to pay huge amounts to obtain. See Jonathan Zittrain, 'Normative Principles For Evaluation Free and Proprietary Software' (2004) 71 *Chicago Law Review* 274, 275.

[26] Richard Stallman believes that the 'digital divide comes from artificial obstacles to sharing of information. This includes licensing of proprietary software and harmfully restrictive copyright laws. See Richard Stallman, *World Summit on the Information Society*, GNU.org <http://www.gnu.org/philosophy/wsis.html>.

[27] Gilberto Camara and Frederico Fonseca, 'Information Policies and Open Source Software in Developing Countries' (2007) 58 (1) *Journal of the American Society for Information Science and Technology* 121–132.

6.2.1 *Brief History of the Free Software and Open Source Software Movements*

FOSS was given new life by Richard Stallman.[28] Richard Stallman, a software developer, while working at MIT encountered, along with his colleagues, a frustrating experience, where he wanted to fix a Xerox printer, but he could not do so as the source code (the human readable code) for the printer device driver was not provided. In other words, it was a closed software.[29] At that time, computer manufacturers had fundamentally changed their attitude toward software, stopped distributing source code, and began using copyright and restrictive software licences to limit or prohibit copying and redistribution.[30] Stallman had no other alternative but to accept such practices. He was challenged to work in an environment that he believed contradicted the fundamental values of freedom and the free exchange of ideas,[31] which were the essence of academic research and development in the rapidly changing field of computer science.[32] Stallman decided to stand up against traditional business models of software distribution and led a revolution in the way we should look at the development of computer engineering and software.

He left MIT in January 1984 and worked on a 'project to build a non-proprietary operating system' that he called 'GNU's Not Unix'.[33] The GNU project is explained in the GNU manifesto, which was published by Richard Stallman in 1984:

> GNU, which stands for Gnu's Not Unix, is the name for the complete Unix-compatible software system which I am writing so that I can give it away free to everyone who can use it... consider that the golden rule requires that if I like a program I must share it with other

---

[28] It was between 1969 and 1970 when UNIX was developed by a small number of developers at AT&T; see Andrés Guadamuz, 'Free and Open Source Software' in Lillian Edwards and Charlotte Waelde, *Law and the Internet* (Hart Publishing, 3rd ed, 2009) 360–393 (365); Maureen O'Sullivan, 'Making Copyright Ambidextrous: An Expose of Copyleft' 2002 (3) *The Journal of Information, Law and Technology* <http://www2.warwick.ac.uk/fac/soc/law/elj/jilt/2002_3/osullivan>; Eric S. Raymond, 'Brief History of Hackerdom' in Chris DiBona, Sam Ockman, and Mark Stone, *Open Sources: Voices from the Open Source Revolution* (O'Reilly Media; 1999).

[29] Software is a set of statements or instructions written in a programming language such as C, C++, Pascal, Fortran, Java, and Basic, which instruct the computer to do what the programmer wants it to achieve. See, for further explanation of the technicalities in software, Jane K. Winn and Benjamin Wright, *Law of Electronic Commerce* (Aspen *Law* & Business, 4th ed, 2001) 2–13; Lawrence Lessig, 'Open Source Baseline: Compared to What?' in Robert W. Hahn, *Government Policy Toward Open Source Software*, 52 <http://papers.ssrn.com/sol3/papers.cfm?abstract_id=1411617>; Horne, above n 12, 864–865.

[30] Gulbault and Daalen, above n 8, 8; Phoebe Ayers, Charles Matthews and Ben Yates, *How Wikipedia Works and How You Can be Part of It* (No Scratch, 2008) 38.

[31] Gulbault and Daalen, above n 8, 8.

[32] Dusollier, above n 10, 283. As L. Gulbault and O. Van Daalen rightly explained, Stallman 'was confronted by a "stark moral choice": Would he too follow the commercial road and create software that he would not be able to share with his fellow programmers, or would he end his career as a programmer?' See Gulbault and Daalen, above n 8, 10.

[33] Benkler, above n 11, ch 3, 64–65.

people who like it. Software sellers want to divide the users and conquer them, making each user agree not to share with others. I refuse to break solidarity with other users in this way. I cannot in good conscience sign a nondisclosure agreement or a software license agreement. For years I worked within the Artificial Intelligence Lab to resist such tendencies and other inhospitalities, but eventually they had gone too far: I could not remain in an institution where such things are done for me against my will. . .Copying all or parts of a program is as natural to a programmer as breathing, and as productive. It ought to be as free. . . GNU is not in the public domain. Everyone will be permitted to modify and redistribute GNU, but no distributor will be allowed to restrict its further redistribution. That is to say, proprietary modifications will not be allowed. I want to make sure that all versions of GNU remain free.[34]

Stallman also founded the Free Software Foundation (FSF) in 1985 to champion the ideas of sharing information, promote freedom of software principles,[35] and support the development of software with accessible source code known as 'Free Software'.[36] Professor Eben Moglen explains the role of FSF in supporting the free software movement:

The Free Software Foundation ("FSF") was founded in 1985 by Richard M. Stallman, who remains its President. The Foundation is a 501(c)(3) organization incorporated under the law of the Commonwealth of Massachusetts, with its primary place of business in Boston, Mass. The FSF's mission is to encourage the creation and distribution of computer programs, technical documentation, and other related materials that can be freely copied, modified and redistributed by their users. FSF refers to such computer programs as "free software," where the word "free" refers to freedom, not to price. FSF believes that by giving all users the right to copy, modify, and redistribute software, the ethical obligation to

[34] Richard Stallman, *The GNU Manifesto* GNU.org <http://www.gnu.org/gnu/manifesto.html>.

[35] Stefano Mazzocchi, *The Free and Open Source Software (FOSS) Movement, Betaversion.org* <http://www.betaversion.org/~stefano/papers/cms.pdf>.

[36] See also, for further explanation of the history of the FOSS movement, Benkler, above n 11, ch 3, 64–65; Mark Perry and Brian Fitzgerald, *FLOSS as Democratic Principle*, QUT eprint <http://eprints.qut.edu.au/4425/1/4425.pdf>; Dusollier, above n 10, 282–283, Metxger and Jaeger, above n 9, 53; Christopher May, 'The FLOSS Alternative: TRIPS, Non-Proprietary Software and Development' (2006) 18 (4) *Knowledge, Technology and Policy* 142, 149; Guadamuz, above n 28, 363, 365; Guibault and Daalen, above n 8, 7; Brian Fitzgerald and Rami Olwan, 'The Legality of Free and Open Source Software Licenses: the Case of Jacobsen v. Katzer', in Brian Fitzgerald (ed), *Knowledge Policy for the 21st Century*, (Irwin Law, 2011). Florian von Baum, *Open Source Regulations–Latest Update* (15 April 2008) <http://www.mlawgroup.de/team/florian-von-baum/index.php>; R. Van Wendel de Joode, J.A. de Brujin and M.J.G. Van Eeten, *Protecting the Virtual Commons Self-Organizing Open Source and Free Software Communities and Innovative Intellectual Property Regimes* (T.M.C. Asser, 2003) 7–12; Josh Lerner and Jean Tirole, 'Economic Perspectives on Open Source' in Joseph Feller et al., *Perspectives on Free and Open Source Software* (MIT, 2005) 50–52; Moreno Muffatto, *Open Source—A Multidisciplinary Approach* (Imperial College, 2006) 1–18; Brian Fitzgerald and Nic Suzor, 'Legal Issues for the Use of Free and Open Source Software in Government' (2005) 29 (2) *Melbourne University Law Review* 412, Andrew Stokes, 'Authorship, Collaboration and Copyright: A View from the United Kingdom' (2002) 13 (6) *Entertainment Law Review* 121–127; Paul B. Lambert, 'Copyleft, Copyright and Software IPRs: Is Contract Still King' (2001) 23 (4) *European Intellectual Property Law Review* 165–171.

> maintain freedom of thought is honoured.[37] FSF supports the development and distribution of free software in two basic ways: it writes and distributes free software of its own, and it helps others to write and distribute such software, primarily through the development and publication of the copyright licenses and associated legal materials that facilitate this hitherto-unusual means of software production.[38]

Keeping the software from being closed off and inaccessible 'out of reach' of programmers who might not be willing to share their modified code was a major concern to Stallman. To avoid a situation that could jeopardise his software freedom movement,[39] in 1989, he came up with what some would call his 'greatest hack'[40] or the 'genius of Stallman',[41] the GNU General Public Licence (GNU GPL).[42] This movement, referred to as the 'copyleft' movement,[43] has given the world a new way of thinking about how we use and practise copyright.[44]

Stallman's project of building a free operating system (GNU Kernel called Hurd) could not be completed[45] because it failed to attract enough interest from programmers and developers worldwide.[46] The lack of a widely adopted,

---

[37] Eben Moglen, Declaration of Eben Moglen in support of MySQL's motion for a preliminary injunction (Eben Moglen's Declaration) in Progress Software Corp et al. vs. Mysql AB, et al., <http://www.gnu.org/press/mysql-affidavit.pdf>.

[38] Ibid.

[39] See, for an explanation of Stallman's social movement, Zittrain, above n 25, 274–275.

[40] Laura Lambert et al. (eds), *The Internet—A Historical Encyclopaedia* (ABC-CLIO, 2005) Vol 1, 216; May, above n 36, 149.

[41] As Professor Lawrence Lessig noted, 'Stallman's real genius (from the perspective of a lawyer, and I apologize for that) was the GPL—a license that would use the power of copyright to guarantee that what was produced under GPL not be removed from the commons'. See Lawrence Lessig, 'Open Code and Open Societies: Values of Internet Governance' (1999) 41 *Chicago Kent Law Review* 101, 107 <http://cyber.law.harvard.edu/works/lessig/final.PDF>; Brian Fitzgerald, *A Short Overview of Creative Commons AustLII* <http://www.austlii.edu.au/au/journals/SydUPLawBk/2007/29.html>; Sam Williams, *Free as in Freedom, Richard Stallman's Crusade for Free Software* (O'Reilly, 2002), ch 3 <http://oreilly.com/openbook/freedom/ch09.html>; O'Sullivan, above n 28, 3.

[42] Stallman produced v2 of the GNU GPL in 1990, and the last draft v3 of the GNU GPL was released on 31 May 2007. See, on the history of the GPL, Freesoftorg, *The History of the GPL* <http://www.free-soft.org/gpl_history/>; Gulbault and Daalen, above n 8, 10; González, above n 24.

[43] José J. González de Alaiza Cardona noted:

> Richard Stallman and the copyleft advocates had been criticized for using copyright to achieve a system which is apparently contrary to copyright itself…The answer that Stallman gives to this critic is that the use of the copyleft clause "doesn't mean that we are in favour of copyright law as a general matter. We're not totally against copyright law, in a simple or blanket sense either, but we're not defending the global copyright system that has mostly been imposed on the world merely because we use it because it's there.

Cardona, above n 12, 40; Baum, above n 36; Dusollier, above n 10, 282

[44] Lambert et al., above n 40. Guibault and Daalen, above n 8, 89; Benkler, above n 11, ch 3, 64–65; Metxger and Jaeger, above n 9, 53–54; González, above n 24, 156.

[45] David A. Wheeler, *Secure Programming for Linux and Unix HOWTO* (2003) <http://www.dwheeler.com/secure-programs/Secure-Programs-HOWTO/index.html>.

[46] Matpal, *Origin and History of Linux* (30 Janyary 2011) <http://www.matpal.com/2011/01/origin-and-history-of-linux.html>.

free Kernel provided the impetus[47] for Linus Torvalds,[48] a Finnish programmer, to build his own version of the UNIX operating system and placed it online on August 1991.[49] Torvalds asked people from all over the world to develop and improve it.[50] As a result, Torvalds obtained the feedback from thousands of programmers and volunteers that led to the development and release, in September 1991,[51] of a newer operating system known widely as 'Linux',[52] but more accurately as 'GNU/ Linux'.[53]

Eric Raymond, the author of a highly influential 1997 paper (published later in a book in 1999), entitled Cathedral and Bazaar, compared two styles of software development: the traditional top-down and command-control approach (described as the 'Cathedral') and the bottom-up, decentralised, cooperative approach (described as the 'Bazzar'). An example of the first approach is the Microsoft's traditional mode of software development, while the second approach is epitomised by the methodology employed by Linux.[54] Raymond investigated the reasons for the success of the Bazzar mode of open software development and argued that it will eventually win over the traditional approach of software development. He explains:

> Perhaps in the end the open source culture will triumph not because cooperation is morally right or software "hoarding" is morally wrong...but simply because the closed-source world cannot win an evolutionary arms race with open source communities that can put orders of magnitude more skilled time into a problem.[55]

Eric Raymond established in February 1998, along with Bruce Perens,[56] the Open Source Initiative[57] (OSI) to 'educate and advocate for the benefits of open source'.[58]

---

[47] Ibid.

[48] Linus Torvalds has worked in Transmiteta in California from 1997 until 2003. He later joined Open Source Development Labs (OSDL) laboratories to develop the Linux Kernel that he wrote in the beginning of the 1990s. There is now a minor element of the Kernel of Linux that is written by Linus Torvalds still remaining, but he remains the ultimate decision-maker of what should be added to the Kernel. Linfo, *Linus Torvalds: A Very Brief and Completely Unauthorized Biography* <http://www.linfo.org/linus.html>.

[49] Linux Online, *Linus Torvalds Bio* <http://www.linux.org/info/linus.html>.

[50] Metxger and Jaeger, above n 9, 54.

[51] Linux Online, above n 49.

[52] Guadamuz, above n 28, 363.

[53] Moglen, above n 37.

[54] Steve Ireland, *The Cathedral and the Bazaar* (28 July 1998) CIO <http://www.cio.com.au/article/108703/cathedral_bazaar/>.

[55] Raymond, above n 28, 54. See also The Cooperation Commons, *Cathedral and the Bazaar* (1989) <http://www.cooperationcommons.com/node/396>.

[56] Bruce Perens <http://perens.com/>.

[57] Open source Initiative (OSI) <http://en.wikipedia.org/wiki/Open_Source_Initiative>.

[58] Open source <http://opensource.org/>.

The widespread expansion of the Internet in the late 1990s led to a dramatic acceleration[59] of FOSS later to establish it as a real alternative to 'proprietary software',[60] which until then was considered as the only route for creating and developing software.

6.2.2 *Philosophy of Free and Open Source Software*

The philosophical roots of the FOSS[61] movement can be found in the culture of a group of highly skilled programmers that originated at MIT in the 1960s–1980s. Steven Levy,[62] in *Hackers: Heroes of the Computer Revolution*,[63] written in 1984, described their culture (he calling it 'hacker ethics') as being based on fundamental principles of access, free information, and improvement to the quality of life.[64] As Bruce Byfield rightly explains, FSF and OSI have far more in common[65] than

---

[59] Lerner and Tirole, above n 36, 52.

[60] Jesus M Gonzalez-Barahona, *A Brief History of Open Source Software* (24 April 2004) Eu. conecta <http://eu.conecta.it/paper/brief_history_open_source.html>. See also for an excellent overview of the movement, Bruce Byfield, *FOSS: Free and Open Source Software* (30 May 2010) Datamation <http://itmanagement.earthweb.com/osrc/article.php/3885101/FOSS-Free-and-Open-Source-Software.htm>; Zittrain, above n 25.

[61] The Term free/libre open source software (FLOSS) is also used primarily in Europe. It was first coined in 2001 in a study prepared by the United Nations University of Maastricht (UNU MRT) by Rishab Ghosh. See Rishab Aiyar Ghosh <http://www.merit.unu.edu/>.

[62] Steven Levy <http://www.stevenlevy.com/>.

[63] Steven Levy, *Hackers: Heroes of the Computer Revolution* (November 1996) Penn Libraries <http://digital.library.upenn.edu/webbin/gutbook/lookup?num=729>.

[64] Guibault and Daalen, above n 8, 7.

[65] Both FSF and OSI give developers the right to charge for the software that they might wish to distribute. They are also not in any way against IP. On the contrary, they are both based on copyright principles. Yochai Benkler explains:

> Free software is, without a doubt, the most visible instance of peer production at the turn of the twenty-first century. It is by no means, however, the only instance. Ubiquitous computer communications networks are bringing about a dramatic change in the scope, scale, and efficacy of peer production throughout the information and cultural production system. As computers become cheaper and as network connections become faster, cheaper, and ubiquitous, we are seeing the phenomenon of peer production of information scale to much larger sizes, performing more complex tasks than were possible in the past for non-professional production.

Benkler, above n 11, 68.

they have differences.[66] This is because they share the same community,[67] similar licences,[68] and the same ideals,[69] which seek to maximise their use of software.[70] They are also both concerned about their long-term persistence and preservation in the software community and beyond.[71] Despite the philosophical differences[72] that

---

[66] Richard Stallman explains:

> While free software by any other name would give you the same freedom, it makes a big difference which name we use: different words *convey different ideas.* In 1998, some of the people in the free software community began using the term "open source software" instead of "free software" to describe what they do. The term "open source" quickly became associated with a different approach, a different philosophy, different values, and even a different criterion for which licenses are acceptable. The Free Software movement and the Open Source movement are today separate movements with different views and goals, although we can and do work together on some practical projects. The fundamental difference between the two movements is in their values, their ways of looking at the world. For the Open Source movement, the issue of whether software should be open source is a practical question, not an ethical one. As one person put it, "Open source is a development methodology; free software is a social movement." For the Open Source movement, non-free software is a suboptimal solution. For the Free Software movement, non-free software is a social problem and free software is the solution.

See Richard Stallman, *Why "Free Software" is better than "Open Source"* Gnu.org <http://www.gnu.org/philosophy/free-software-for-freedom.html>. See also Byfield, above n 60.

[67] Scholars identify different types of motivations to explain why programmers voluntarily give time to FOSS. See the extensive literature that explains the motivation for working on such projects: David A. Wheeler, *Why Open Source Software/ Free Software (OSS/FS, FLOSS or FOSS) Look at the Numbers!* <http://www.dwheeler.com/oss_fs_why.html>; UNCTAD, E-commerce and Development Report (2003), 106–108 <http://www.cnnic.net.cn/download/manual/international-report/edr03.pdf >; Ronald Mann, 'Commercializing Open Source Software: Do Property Rights Still Matter?' (2006) 20 (1) *Harvard Journal of Law and Technology*; Niranjan Rajani, Juha Rekola and Timo Mielonen, *Free as in Education: Significance of FLOSS for the Developing countries* (13 May 2003), International Telecommunication Union (ITU), 18 <http://www.itu.int/wsis/docs/background/themes/access/free_as_in_education_niranjan.pdf>; Eben Moglen, *Free Software Maters, When Code Isn't Law* (23 April 2000) Columbia University <http://emoglen.law.columbia.edu/my_pubs/lu-01.html>; Lambert, above n 36.

[68] FSF and OS both use the GNU GPL version 3.0 which can be found here <http://www.gnu.org/licenses/gpl-3.0.html>.

[69] Byfield, above n 60.

[70] Andrew Katz, Open Source Software (2010) 1 *Intellectual Property Magazine* 18, 19.

[71] Mazzocchi, above n 35.

[72] To be recognised by FSF as being "Free Software", the following four freedoms must be met:

Freedom 0; the freedom to run the program for any purpose, Freedom 1; the freedom to study how the program works and change it to make it do what you wish, Freedom 2; the freedom to redistribute copies so you can help your neighbour, Freedom 3; the freedom to improve the program and release your improvements (and modified versions in general) to the public, so that the whole community benefits.

To be recognised as "Open Source", according to the OSI definition, the following should be allowed; 1. no royalty or other fee imposed upon redistribution; 2. availability of the source code; 3. right to create modifications and derivative works; 4. may require modified versions to be distributed as the original version, plus patches; 5. no discrimination against persons or groups; 6. no discrimination against fields of endeavour; 7. all rights granted must flow through to/with

exist between FSF and OSI,[73] it is argued that they can be considered as one significant movement that contributes to a better understanding of what the Internet can offer and how humans across their disciplines can benefit from it. The wide dispersal of the 'commons-based peer production' models[74] (which imitate the GNU Linux mode of software development) does prove that new technologies are no longer solely in the hands of computer programmers[75] but rather within the hands of many people. It also shows the power of the Internet in harnessing the contributions of the participants (the power of us[76]) in those projects to a common goal that could prove beneficial to humans.

6.2.3 *Free and Open Source Software as a Path for Social and Economic Development*

FOSS is raising considerable interest in the private and the public sectors in developing countries and emerging countries such as India, China, Taiwan, South Korea, South Africa, Brazil, and others.[77] Several scholars argue that FOSS could

---

redistributed versions; 8. licence applies to the program as a whole and each of its components; 9. licence must not restrict other software, thus permitting the distribution of open source and closed-source software together, and 10. licence must be technology-neutral. See FSF, *the Free Software Definition* Gnu.org <http://www.gnu.org/philosophy/free-sw.html>; OSI, *OSI definition* Opensource.org <http://www.opensource.org/osd.html>.

[73] The FSF encourages people to use the term "Free Software" rather than "Open Source", as specified by OSI. Stallman critiques the use of the term "Open Source" and argues that it misrepresents the meaning that OSI founders have intended to achieve. On the other hand, OSI has criticised the approach of FSF (particularly Stallman) to software development, mainly for not taking into consideration the commercial nature of open projects that businesses might want to initiate. See the following on the different philosophies: Guadamuz, above n 28, 365); Zittrain, above n 25; Mazzocchi, above n 35; Stallman, above n 66; Perry and Fitzgerald, above n 36, 4; Sullivan, above n 28, 10; Richard Stallman, *Copyleft Idealism* Gnu.org <http://www.gnu.org/philosophy/pragmatic.html>; Eric Raymond, *Shut Up And Show Them the Code* (1999) Linux Today <http://www.linuxtoday.com/news_story.php3?ltsn=1999-06-28-023-10-NW-SM>; Eben Moglen, *Free Software Matters: Free Software or Open Source?* (12 August 2001) Columbia University <http://emoglen.law.columbia.edu/publications/lu-07.pdf>.

[74] Christian Siefkes, *Peer Production Everywhere, Thoughts About a Society Based on Common Peer Production—And How to Get There* (March 2009) Peerconomy.org <http://peerconomy.org/talks/ox4/>; Yochai Benkler and Helen Nissenbaum, 'Commons-Based Peer Production' (2006) 14 (4) *The Journal of Political Philosophy*, 394–419.

[75] See Walton Pantland, *Are Foss and Creative Commons Important for Unions* (2010) Cyberunions <http://cyberunions.org/2010/04/25/are-foss-and-creative-commons-important-for-unions/>.

[76] Robert D. Hof, *The Power of US*, Business Week (online), 20 June 2005 <http://www.businessweek.com/print/magazine/content/05_25/b3938601.htm?chan=gl>.

[77] UNCTAD, Free Software and Open Source Foundation for Africa, *The State of Free and Open Source Software in Africa & Proposed Action Plan* (June 2003), 3 <http://r0.unctad.org/ecommerce/event_docs/tunis03/fossfa.pdf>.

assist developing countries in their social and economic development. This section will examine the importance of FOSS for developing countries.

6.2.3.1 FOSS as a Path for Social Development

FOSS, when applied effectively, could bring several social advantages to developing countries, including openness and transparency, democratic accountability, competition, and collaboration (sharing ideas with peer organisations).[78]

Professor Mark Perry and Professor Brian Fitzgerald describe FOSS as a democratisation instrument, arguing that it allows citizens to better participate and improve on the process of democracy in their society.[79] To them, FOSS 'should be deployed in core democratic infrastructure because it will provide the level of transparency and openness that is required for the effective functioning of democratic processes'. FOSS can also enhance the independence[80] of developing countries by not relying on a particular corporation or technology imported from developed countries but instead developing local capabilities and talents.[81] This would boost innovation[82] and creativity in these countries.[83] As Professor Steven Weber has noted that:

> It is no surprise to industrial organization theorists that governments (like any customer) want to avoid locking themselves into a single private provider for crucial tools. And it is no surprise to international relations theorists that states want to avoid becoming dependent on software whose export is under U.S. legal jurisdiction and whose development is controlled by America's dominant software industry.[84]

---

[78] Paul Dravis, *Open Source Software—Perspectives for Development* (November 2003) The Dravis Group, 20 <http://www.infodev.org/en/Document.21.pdf>; Rishab Aiyer Ghosh, 'The European Politics of F/OSS Adoption' in Joe Karagains and Robert Latham (eds), *The Politics of Open Source Software Adoption* (May 2005) <http://joekaraganis.files.wordpress.com/2011/02/posa1-0.pdf>.

[79] Perry and Fitzgerald, above n 36, 2.

[80] Rajani, Rekola and Mielonen, above n 67, 79.

[81] Nagla Rizk and Lea *Shaver, Access to Knowledge in Egypt* (Bloomsbury Academic 2010) 141.

[82] Jennifer Papin Ramcharan and Frank Soodeen, 'Open Source Software: A Developing Country View' in Kirk St. Amant and Brian Still, *Handbook of Research on Open Source Software: Technological, Economic, and Social Perspectives* (IGI Global, 2007) 93, 97; UNCTAD, above n 77, 5, UNCTAD, above n 67, 110; Guadamuz, above n 28, 391.

[83] As Professor Eben Moglen noted that:

> Non-traditional means of production can be amazingly efficient. Large numbers of programmers can collaborate easily on enormous projects without having to be locked into a hierarchical organization. Everyone can participate in finding and fixing bugs and everyone can readily incorporate all the fixes, so the quality of free software can be much higher than that of programs produced by a limited number of developers and testers inside a commercial proprietary manufacturer.

Moglen, above n 67.

[84] Weber, above n 1, 253.

The *E-Commerce and Development Report* of the UN published in 2003 noted the importance of FOSS for developing countries, especially in promoting competition in the ICT sector, as it allows consumers not to be locked into one software provider[85] and gives them instead the opportunity to choose between various rivals in business that better suit their particular needs. This would ultimately put pressure on the providers of ICT to provide top-quality services to guarantee that their customers are satisfied with what they are offering. This has the potential, in the long run, to improve productivity and quality of life in developing countries.[86]

As the FOSS model is based on collaboration between thousands of developers, introducing it in developing countries would promote other collaborative projects between citizens and, at the same time, increase the amount of shared information between them. This is considered as an empowerment of self-expression.[87]

FOSS has a complementary and reciprocal relationship with education. It helps, enhances, and complements education by providing tools that promote it.[88] It is a knowledge liberalisation mechanism that neither 'commodifies' information nor imposes barriers to its acquisition.[89] It does so by extending computer usage to the poor people,[90] who cannot afford the payments of high royalties to the licensors of software, without which they would not be able to use computers and browse the Internet.[91] FOSS is described also as 'an alternative strategy for building, maintaining and changing the rules that govern information flows in the economy'.[92]

6.2.3.2 FOSS as a Path for Economic Development

The economic benefits that FOSS can bring to developing countries can vary from one country to another, but they include the potential reduction of financial revenues transfer from developing to developed countries, lowering of ICT investments and procurement costs,[93] development of local IT skills, and creation of new jobs and business opportunities.[94] Each of these will be explained.

---

85 Rizk and Shaver, above n 81, 141.

86 UNCTAD, above n 77, 5.

87 Rizk and Shaver, above n 81, 157.

88 Rajani, Rekola and Mielonen, above n 67, 78.

89 Rizk and Shaver, above n 81, 134.

90 Charles Leadbeater, *Brazil and Open Source* <http://www.charlesleadbeater.net/cms/xstandard/Brazil_Open_Source.pdf>.

91 May, above n 36, 152.

92 Sanjiva Weerawarana and Jivaka Weeratunga, *Open Source Software in Developing Countries* (January 2004), OpenIT@giz 33 <http://www.it-inwent.org/e2484/e3407/e3431/e3432/opensource_in_developing_countries_eng.pdf>.

93 Ibid; Fitzgerald and Suzor, above n 36; Ghosh, above n 78.

94 UNCTAD, above n 77, 5; Ramcharan and Soodeen, above n 82, 99; May, above n 36, 150; Rajani, Rekola and Mielonen, above n 67, 79; Ghosh, above n 78.

It is argued that governments in developing countries that choose the adoption of FOSS over proprietary software would be able to save public funds as they would no longer need to pay high royalties and IP licensing fees for MNCs.[95] This would mean that IT expenditure and investments would be minimised and would stay home to contribute to the national economy. As one open source enthusiast from an emerging economy, Brazil explains:

> [P]aying Microsoft fees was unsustainable economically when Linux offers a far cheaper IT solution. Switching to open source is an attempt to save public funds in a developing country with an indebted government and massive disparities in wealth within the population.[96]

This is also applicable to developing countries, including African countries, as they will be able to 'minimise risk through avoidance, where possible, of dollar-based software licence fees and through vigorous encouragement and support of local software development efforts'.[97] FOSS can break down the unique advantages that existing international software firms possess through control of products. Furthermore, it will provide a path for making profits for service-oriented, local, software firms that will be able to break into international product markets.[98]

Because governments' purchasing power can be relatively large in the ICT market, they need to adopt novel procurement practices that can stimulate innovation and creativity in developing countries.[99] Governments can mandate the use of FOSS in their departments and institutions or allow it to be used alongside proprietary software.[100]

The use of FOSS by governments could fulfil their responsibilities to provide public access to certain information and would also guarantee the secrecy of their public data.[101] Many experts believe that FOSS such as Linux provides a superior vehicle for making security vulnerabilities easier to spot and fix.[102] This is because open models force people to write clearer code and adhere to standards that facilitate security reviews.[103] Professor Peter Swire argues that the characteristic

---

[95] May, above n 36, 153, 159; Pablo Wegbrait, *Free and Open Source Software in Argentina Yaleisp.org* <http://yaleisp.org/publications/a2kresearch/>; Rizk and Shaver, above n 81, 156.

[96] Leadbeater, above n 90. See also Wegbrait, above n 95, 2.

[97] UNCTAD, above n 77, 4, 10.

[98] Ajay Shah, *What Open Source Software means to India* (16 December 1998) Mayin.org <http://www.mayin.org/ajayshah/MEDIA/1998/free-sw.html>.

[99] Cutler & Company, *Venturous Australia Report—Building Strength in Innovation, Building Strength in Innovation, Report for the Australian Government* (2008) Australian Government, Department of Industry, Innovation, Science and Tertiary Education <http://www.innovation.gov.au/Innovation/Policy/Documents/NISReport.pdf>.

[100] Dravis, above n 78, 7.

[101] UNCTAD, above n 67, ch 4, 113.

[102] Wheeler, above n 45.

[103] Linux Security, *Interview with Vincent Rijmen* <http://www.linuxsecurity.com/content/view/117552/49/>.

of open source being open does not mean that it is not secure.[104] He notes that open models are not 'self perpetuating', as commonly known, but companies that use open source software develop their own technical measures (such as password surveillance, non-standard configurations and settings, stealth firewall, and secure socket layers) to combine with FOSS and provide better security for open sources.[105] It is also noted that the use of FOSS brings further security because having the source code available would allow developing countries to inspect the software and develop it according to their particular needs.[106] A Peruvian congressman, defending a bill in Peru mandating the use of open source software, noted the danger of relying on closed models that would undermine national security as it would allow control of states' systems from a distance or the undesired transmission of information to third parties.[107]

Some developing countries have mandated the use of FOSS in governments by issuing laws[108] for that purpose.[109] Professor Lawrence Lessig is doubtful whether this approach is effective as he believes that governments should always be neutral in giving preference to any particular software over another, but he acknowledges that they would often arrive at the conclusion that 'open code' is preferable over 'proprietary code'.[110]

FOSS can act as a path for the economic development of developing countries because it gives their ICT businesses the flexibility they need in adapting the software to the local needs of the country.[111] Such localisation[112] would be beneficial in building local capacity and in establishing a knowledge base of software and IT developers for indigenous[113] and independent communities.[114] In the long term, this will enhance the skills and reputation of ICT[115] in developing countries.[116]

---

[104] Peter P. Swire, 'A Theory of Disclosure for Security and Competitive Reasons: Open Source, Proprietary Software, and Governments Systems' (2006) 42 (5) *Houston Law Review* 101–148.

[105] Ibid 120–122.

[106] Edgar David Villanueva Nunez, *Email to General Manager of Microsoft Peru, Lima* (8th of April, 2002) Gnuwin <http://www.theregister.co.uk/2002/05/19/ms_in_peruvian_opensource_nightmare/>.

[107] Ibid.

[108] Argentina was among the first countries that introduced a bill in Parliament that allows only the use of open source software in the government. See Marcelo Dragan, *Open Source Software Bill* Proposicion Project Website (proposal for the use of open technologies in the government) <http://proposicion.org.ar/proyecto/leyes/5613-D-00/index.html>.

[109] UNCTAD, above n 77, ch 4, 109.

[110] Lessig, above n 29, 67–68.

[111] Guadamuz, above n 28, 390.

[112] See also Rajani, Rekola, and Mielonen, above n 67, 59. In the Arab world, there are some initiatives such as ArabEyes dedicated to making FOSS Arabic; see <http://projects.arabeyes.org/index.php>.

[113] Rizk and Shaver, above n 81, 165.

[114] May, above n 36, 142.

[115] Weerawarana and Weeratunga, above n 92.

[116] Guadamuz, above n 28, 391.

According to Nagla Rizk and Lea Shaver, the 'real advantage of open source ends up being able to build up your own knowledge base. Such a base would provide a critical mass of intellectual capital, which would boost an infant industry in developing countries'.[117] Professor Steven Weber also agrees:

> In one sense the provision of a freely available technological infrastructure represents by itself a form of wealth transfer to poor countries, but it is a wealth transfer that developing countries can manoeuvre to their particular advantage. To provide real products and services on top of the infrastructure requires an investment of local labour. India, China, and many other developing countries have a surplus of inexpensive technical manpower. Combining this with free software tools creates the possibility of an interesting kind of competitive advantage that would certainly matter in local markets and in some cases might be important in global markets as well.[118]

Some local FOSS corporations would find the local market insufficient to fulfil their business development ambitions and decide to export software and services to international markets.[119] These corporations can be 'broadly classified into two categories: (a) those that distribute and retail various open source products; and (b) those that offer various FOSS- related services'.[120] There are several FOSS businesses in emerging economies (India and China) that have been engaged in such activities. Some of them have managed to do very well in terms of their economic revenues.[121]

6.2.3.3 FOSS and Social and Economic Development

It was noted earlier that FOSS is not a magic formula that can solve the social and economic development problems of developing countries, but along with other initiatives that may be taken, it can help in this regard. FOSS is relevant to the social and economic development efforts in developing countries only when there is a reasonable investment made in the ICT infrastructure of a particular country.[122] If a certain developing country has limited hardware, then software is not important and

[117] Rizk and Shaver, above n 81, 165.

[118] Weber, above n 1, 251.

[119] Weerawarana and Weeratunga, above n 92.

[120] Ibid 24.

[121] For example, the revenues of Red Flag Software Co, a Beijing-based distributor of Linux totalled US$8.1 million in 2003. See IDG, *China's Red Flag Linux to focus on Enterprise* (16 August 2004) IT World <http://www.itworld.com/040816chinaredflag>; Felix Oberholzer-Geee, Tarun Khanna and David Lane, *Red Flag Software Co* (26 October 2010).

[122] Rajani, Rekola and Mielonen, above n 67, 69.

would not be of very much relevance to the discussion above.[123] Education and experience are also critically important for FOSS to fulfil its full potential in developing countries.[124] There is a need for an educated and experienced population who can understand how to use FOSS and apply it accordingly, wherever needed. If there are not enough experienced and educated people, then FOSS would not be very beneficial to such a developing country.

Bibek Debroy and Julian Morris do not believe that FOSS can assist developing countries in achieving economic development. They criticise the arguments put forward by proponents of FOSS in developing countries, such as the argument that FOSS boosts local programming talents and ICT capabilities in developing countries. Bibek Debroy and Julian Morris state:

> With all of the source code available and the global feedback available on open source projects over the internet, novice programmers could gain valuable learning-by-doing experience. That said, it is difficult to see the next link in the chain of logic. It is unclear whether this kind of training opportunity would result in a sizable pool of programmer talent, or whether it would lead instead to a small cadre of programming leaders surrounded by a larger pool of minimal contributors. This has been the norm with many open source projects, including the typical Linux development.[125]

To the contrary, developing countries and emerging economies should not rely on a particular form of technology that comes from the developed world. Developing countries need to have their own programmers that pull technology development toward applications that fit specifically to the indigenous needs and demands of those countries.[126] As Rishab Ghosh puts it, 'the open source development community provides an environment of intensive interactive skills development at little explicit cost, which is particularly useful for local development of skills, especially in economically disadvantaged regions'.[127] The experience of some emerging economies, such as Brazil and India, in the field of FOSS is a good indication of the benefits that FOSS can bring in relation to the development of local talents. The boost for ICT local talent in developing countries can go a long way towards contributing to the economic development of individuals, which is necessary for the economic development of the society at large.

---

[123] Some suggest that developing countries that do not have the necessary hardware to run the software should think of using open hardware. See Mohamed A. Salem and Jamal I. Khatib, *An Introduction to Open Source Hardware Development* (2004) EE Times <http://www.eetimes.com/news/design/features/showArticle.jhtml?articleID=22103383>; Cameron Parkins, *OpenMoko CC Licenses CAD Files for Neo1973* (10 March 2008) Creative Commons <http://creativecommons.org/weblog/entry/8117>.

[124] Rajani, Rekola and Mielonen, above n 67, 78.

[125] Bibek Debroy and Julian Morris, *Open to Development: Open Source Software and Economic Development* (29 March 2004) International Policy Network, 15–16 <http://www.policynetwork.net/creativity-innovation/publication/open-development-open-source-software-and-economic-development-0>.

[126] Weber, above n 1, 253.

[127] Rishan Aiyer Ghosh, *Licence Fees and GDP Per Capita: The Case for Open Source in Developing Countries*, (2003) 8 (12) *First Monday* <http://firstmonday.org/htbin/cgiwrap/bin/ojs/index.php/fm/article/view/1103/1023>.

As for the argument that developing countries that use FOSS in governments would be able minimise ICT costs and investments, they note:

> Focusing on the costs of open source, though, distracts us from the real issue: relatively lower costs for software users do not imply that open source can lead to economic development. Growth requires sustainable profits with paid employment positions, and often involves exportable products or services.[128]

Clearly, initial costs can be lower for open source software as compared to proprietary software. Initial costs are not the full story, however. Several academic studies have investigated the total costs of ownership, or TCO, a concept that includes initial costs as well as set-up, training and support costs. ...for some applications, open source is likely to be the cheapest software option, but for others, the labour costs involved in personnel training and support dominate initial investments and tilt the advantage towards proprietary software.[129]

The problem with the argument provided by Debroy and Morris above is that it is too centered on the discussion that surrounds FOSS. It connects the success of FOSS with only economic growth in developing countries. The advantages of adopting FOSS in developing countries are not only economic. As Professor Steven Weber has noted:

> The potential leverage on development comes not from software itself, but from the broad organizational changes that the open source process, as a way of making software, will drive. FOSS should not be used to make up for lack of sufficient legal and economic infrastructure, or replace institutions by installing Internet connections. But there are interesting possibilities for building systems of distributed innovation within emerging developing countries and emerging economies that lead to autonomous innovation. This could have a significant impact on development prospects.[130]

It is true that choosing FOSS models over proprietary software by governments would not necessarily result in the economic development of developing countries and emerging economies, but it could, in the long term, save them huge amounts of money that they may use in other much-needed projects such as health and education. For example, the Brazilian government noted that, in October 2004 alone, it had saved over R$24 million (US$14 million) when it used FOSS instead of proprietary software.[131] In India, a study was conducted in September 2009 by Professor Rahul De from the Indian Institute of Management (IIM), Bangalore, on the use of FOSS in 20 various Indian organisations.[132] In terms of cost savings,

---

[128] Debroy and Morris, above n 125, 11.

[129] Ibid 10.

[130] Weber, above n 1, 254.

[131] Eugene Eric Kim, *F/OSS Adoption in Brazil: The Growth of a National Strategy* (31 March 2005) Blue Oxon Associates <http://blueoxen.com/paper/foss-adoption-in-brazil/#nid4ZC>.

[132] Rahul De, *Economic Impact of Free and Open Source Software—A Study in India* (September 2009), 4–5 <http://www.iimb.ernet.in/~rahulde/RD_FOSSRep2009.pdf>.

the study noted that several private companies had saved huge amounts of money when they adopted FOSS (for example, the Life Insurance Corporation (LIC), one of the largest insurers in India, was able to save an amount of Rs 420 million (US$8.75 million) by adopting FOSS).[133]

Another important point to make here is that when Debroy and Morris refer to Total Cost of Ownership (TCO) in relation to FOSS, they are not specifically referring to developing countries. This is a key issue because TCO such as labour costs, training, support, maintenance, and installation of FOSS can be less expensive in developing countries. This would result in the share of the licence fee in the total cost of ownership being much more significant in developed countries than in developing countries.[134]

It is noted that developing countries that are investigating the use of FOSS instead of proprietary software would be wise not to do so unless they conduct a systematic evaluation of all issues related to the use of software, including technical costs, competition, security, network effects, usability, and availability.[135] After considering all these issues, developing countries would be in a better position to determine whether it would be useful for them to switch to open software models from proprietary ones. The International Telecommunication Union (ITU), WTO, WIPO, UN Development Program (UNDP), and UNCTAD can help developing countries to prepare studies that guide them on the most appropriate ways to introduce FOSS in their countries.

6.2.4 Legal Challenges and Issues for Adoption of FOSS in Developing Countries

There are various challenges that can influence the decisions of developing countries to adopt FOSS. These could be technical challenges, especially the lack of affordable hardware to use.[136] There are also social and cultural challenges, especially

---

[133] See also Rishab Aiyer Ghosh, 'The Opportunities of Free/Libre/Open Source Software for Developing Countries' (A background paper to the UNCTAD-ICTSD Dialogue on *Moving the Pro-Development IP Agenda Forward: Preserving Public Goods in Health, Education and Learning*, Bellagio, 29 November – 3 December 2004) <http://www.iprsonline.org/unctadictsd/bellagio/docs/Gosh_Bellagio4.pdf>.

[134] Ibid.

[135] See, for an excellent explanation of these issues, Jyh-An Lee, 'New Perspectives on Public Goods Production: Policy Implications of Open Source Software' (2006) 9 (1) *Vanderbilt Journal of Entertainment and Technology Law* 45–112 <http://papers.ssrn.com/sol3/papers.cfm?abstract_id=963491>.

[136] For an explanation of the technical challenges that developing countries might face in the adoption of FOSS, see Katherine Noyes, *Why Doesn't Linux Dominate in the Developing World?* (2010) Linux Insider <http://www.linuxinsider.com/rsstory/69856.html?wlc=1277627734>.

the localisation of FOSS, as many computer users would not be able to use systems not in their local language.[137] In addition, there are also legal challenges.

The legal challenge that developing countries may face is the non-availability of adequate legal expertise, which is important to the effective implementation of open source projects. There are limited numbers of lawyers in the developing world knowledgeable in open source licensing, who could give proper advice to companies that are working in open source business. Many of these corporations would prefer to take the advice of foreign law firms, but this may prove costly. There is also the problem of not having qualified judges who can solve disputes that relate to open source software. These cases are technical in nature, and there is a need to have sufficient knowledge in the subject in order to give a proper analysis of the law and issue reasonable judgments in relation to FOSS. Governments in developing countries might find it difficult to find legal experts who could advise on the best way of adopting open source software in those countries. Legal advisors are needed in drafting internal regulations, policies, and agreements that are necessary for the adoption of FOSS. Open source software may also pose specific legal challenges in relation to its legality and enforceability.

6.2.5 The Legality and Enforceability of Open Source Licences

The use of open source licences[138] in business, government, and beyond can pose various legal issues that need to be addressed by scholars and IP experts.[139] These issues can be considered under various branches of law, including competition law, public procurement law, tax law, private international law, contract law, and copyright law.

---

[137] Richard Boateng and Silvia Aimasso, *Potential Benefits and Challenges of FOSS in Developing Countries*', 15 February 2011 <http://www.pctechmagazine.com/index.php?option=com_content&view=article&id=343:potential-benefits-and-challenges-of-foss-in-developing-countries&catid=50:research&Itemid=70>.

[138] For an explanation of open source licences, see May, above n 36, 149.

[139] See Brian Fitzgerald and Graham Bassett, *Legal Issues Relating to Free and Open Source Software*, 11–36 <http://www.law.qut.edu.au/files/open_source_book.pdf>; UNCTAD, above n 67, ch 4, 113–114; Dravis, above n 78, 30–31; Andrew Zangrilli, Interview on Open Source Software Licensing with Attorney Philip Albert <http://technology.findlaw.com/legal-software/interview-on-open-source-software-licensing-with-attorney-philip.html>; David McGowan, 'Legal Aspects of Free and Open Source Software' in Joseph Feller et al. (eds), *Perspectives on Free and Open Source Software* (2005, MIT) 382; Richard Fontana et al., *A Legal Issues Primer for Open Source and Free Software Projects* (3 March 2008) Software Freedom Law Center <http://www.softwarefreedom.org/resources/2008/foss-primer.html>; State Services Commission (New Zealand); *Guide to the Legal Issues in Using Open Source Software* (May 2006) United Nations Public Administration Network <http://unpan1.un.org/intradoc/groups/public/documents/APCITY/UNPAN024137.pdf>.

Open source licensing is an advanced topic in copyright law,[140] which is usually taught after gaining a basic knowledge of software copyright protection.[141] Open source licences can also be difficult to understand[142] as some licences are more complicated than others.[143] The section will concentrate primarily on copyright and contract laws as they are the most relevant to legal discussion around FOSS.[144] It will examine to what extent the GNU GPL can fit within the civil legal system adopted

[140] See Terry Carroll, *Frequently Asked Questions About Copyright* (11 September 2003) Copyright FAQ <http://www.tjc.com/copyright/FAQ/>; Lessig, above n 29, 52; Winn and Wright, above 29, 2–13; Andrew M. St. Laurent, *Understanding Open Source and Free Software Licensing* (O'Reilly, 2004), ch 1 <http://oreilly.com/catalog/osfreesoft/book/>; Horne, above n 12; Alan Story, *Intellectual Property and Computer Software* Commission on Intellectual Property Rights <http://www.iprcommission.org/papers/text/study_papers/sp5_story_study.txt>; Fitzgerald and Suzor, above n 36; Zangrilli, above n 139, Lambert, above n 36.

[141] It is now settled, according to international copyright treaties and national copyright laws, that computer software should be protected primarily through copyright and not by any other form of IP. Software is also protected through patent in some countries, including China; see, K.H. Pun and Tian Furong, 'Patent Protection for Computer Software: an Under-Explored Avenue in China' (1999) 5(6) *Computer and Telecommunication law Review* 172–178.

[142] Open-software licences are not all the same as they may vary in terms of having a strong or weak 'copyleft'. Professor Lawrence Lessig explains the two basic types of open source licences:

> [W]hile the variety of open source and free software licenses is broad, we can identify essentially two sorts: copylefted software and non-copylefted software. Copylefted software is software that is licensed under terms that require follow-on users to require others to adopt the same license terms for work derived from the copylefted code. The principle is "share and share alike." Non-copylefted open source software imposes no such condition on subsequent use. With copylefted software, the price of admission is that if you redistribute modified versions of the copylefted code, you must redistribute it under similar license terms; with non copylefted software, no such price is demanded. Non-copylefted open source software does not impose this condition on subsequent licensing. Not only is a user free to build upon it, but it also does not require that such building be released under similar licensing terms.

Lessig, above n 29, 52, 54. See also Story, above n 140, 7.

[143] There are roughly 70 FOSS Licences. These, for example, include the GNU GPL, the Mozilla Public License (MPL), the GNU Lesser General Public License LGPL (for libraries), the BSD Berkeley Software Distribution License, and the Apache Software License. See the following: GNU Project, *Categories of Free and Nonfree Software* <http://www.gnu.org/philosophy/categories.html>; GNU Project, *Various Licences and Comments about Them* <http://www.gnu.org/licenses/license-list.html>; González, above n 24; Baum, above n 36; Magnus Cedegren, 'Open Content and Value Creation' (2003) 8 (8) *First Monday* <http://firstmonday.org/htbin/cgiwrap/bin/ojs/index.php/fm/article/viewArticle/1071>.

[144] Open source licences are based on solid legal principles in copyright and contract law. See, for further explanation of the contractual issues, P. Bernt Hugenholtz, *Code as the Code or the End of Intellectual Property as we Know it* (Institute of Information Law, University of Amsterdam) <http://www.ivir.nl/publications/hugenholtz/maastricht.doc>; Laurent, above n 140, ch 1; Zangrilli, above n 139.

by many developing countries, particularly in Jordan. It is important to note that the *Jordanian Civil Code* is informed by Islamic Jurisprudence or Fiqh,[145] but to this point, there have been no detailed studies that analyse the validity of the GNU GPL from the perspective of Islamic Fiqh.

6.2.6 Legal Treatment of the GNU GPL under Jordanian Contract Law and Civil Code

The civil legal system distinguishes between two broad categories of law, private law and public law.[146] This section will examine private law issues in relation to the GNU GPL.

6.2.6.1 Consideration of the GNU GPL as a Bare Licence or a Contract

One of the important questions that are constantly asked is whether the GNU GPL should be considered as a bare licence or contract or even a hybrid of both.[147] The answer may differ from one jurisdiction and legal system to another, yet it has important practical implications that follow, including enforcement, jurisdiction, and applicable law. If the open source licence is treated as a contract, then it should be considered in accordance with the law of contract. If the open source licence is treated as a copyright licence, then it should be considered in accordance with the

[145] Article 2(2) of the *Jordanian Civil Code* provides:

> If the court shall find no provision in this code, it shall decide by the rules of Moslem Jurisprudence which are more adaptable to the provisions of this code, and if there none then by the principle of the Moslem sharia'a.

Jordanian *Civil Code No. 43 of 1976*, Official Gazette No 2645, 1 August 1976 (*Jordanian Civil Code*) (Arabic), art 2 (2) <http://www.lob.gov.jo/ui/laws/search_no.jsp?no=43&year=1976>.
Article 3 of the *Jordanian* Civil Code provides:

> The rules of Moslem Jurisprudence shall be referred to for the understanding of a provision, its interpretation and meaning.

Ibid art 3.

[146] Public law constitutes the body of laws that govern the relationship between states (international law) or between the state acting as sovereign power and individuals (criminal law). On the other hand, private law constitutes the body of laws that govern the relationship between individuals or between individuals and the state not acting as a sovereign power but as an ordinary person (civil law).

[147] See also Andrés Guadamuz-González, 'The License/Contract Dichotomy in Open Licenses: a Comparative Analysis' (2009) 30 (2) *European Intellectual Property Review* 101, 103; Cardona, above n 12, 42; Guadamuz, above n 28, 379; Stephan Meyer, *Nature and Validity of Licensing Relationships under the GPL* (an LLM paper, Columbia University, 2007) 52–53.

law of copyright.[148] If the open source licence is treated as a contract and a licence, then, at least in civil law system, it should be considered in accordance with contract and copyright laws.[149]

In the US, many would argue that the GNU GPL is treated as a bare licence and not as a contract.[150] The consideration of the GNU GPL as a licence has been widely studied by American legal scholars[151] and lawyers specialised in IP.[152] The

---

[148] This would have a practical consequence when choosing a law. For example, if the copyright law and not contract law is applicable, this means that remedies would be an injunctive relief in accordance with the copyright law and not compensatory damages available under contract law.

[149] See Harald Welte vs. D. Deutsshcland GmbH (2006) 2–6 0 224/06 (District Court of Frankfurt Am Main) ('Frankfurt Open Source Software Case') <http://www.jbb.de/judgment_dc_frankfurt_gpl.pdf>; S… Deutschland GmbH (2004) 21 O 6123/04 (District Court of Munich) ('Munich Open Source Software Case') <http://www.jbb.de/fileadmin/download/judgment_dc_munich_gpl.pdf>.

The Court noted in Robert Jacobsen v. Matthew Katzer and Kamind Associates, in particular:

> The heart of the argument on appeal concerns whether the terms of the Artistic License are conditions of, or merely covenants to, the copyright license. Generally, a "copyright owner who grants a nonexclusive license to use his copyrighted material waives his right to sue the licensee for copyright infringement" and can sue only for breach of contract. *Sun Microsystems, Inc., v. Microsoft Corp.*, 188 F.3d 1115, 1121 (9th Cir. 1999); *Graham v. James,* 144 F.3d 229, 236 (2d Cir. 1998). If, however, a license is limited in scope and the licensee acts outside the scope, the licensor can bring an action for copyright infringement. *See S.O.S., Inc. v. Payday, Inc.*, 886 F.2d 1081, 1087 (9th Cir.1989); Nimmer on Copyright, § 1015[A] (1999). Thus, if the terms of the Artistic License allegedly violated are both covenants and conditions, they may serve to limit the scope of the license and are governed by copyright law. If they are merely covenants, by contrast, they are governed by contract law. *See Graham,* 144 F.3d at 236–37 (whether breach of license is actionable as copyright infringement or breach of contract turns on whether provision breached is condition of the license, or mere covenant); *Sun Microsystems,* 188 F.3d at 1121(following *Graham;* independent covenant does not limit scope of copyright license). The District Court did not expressly state whether the limitations in the Artistic License are independent covenants or, rather, conditions to the scope; its analysis, however, clearly treated the license limitations as contractual covenants rather than conditions of the copyright license.

cf. Robert Jacobsen v. Matthew Katzer and Kamind Associates, Inc 2008 U.S. App. LEXIS 17161 (Fed. Cir. 2008).

[150] See MAI Systems Corp v Peak Computer 991 F.2d 511, 518 (9th Cir. 1993).

[151] Moglen, above n 73; Margaret Jane Radin, 'Humans, Computers and Binding Commitment' (2000) 75 *Indiana Law Journal* 1125.

[152] Lawrence Rosen suggests that contract law should be applied to the GNU GPL because it is richer and could provide proper answers to the legal issues raised by the use of open source licences. He argues:

> Contract law, unlike copyright and patent law, provides procedures and rules for license interpretation and enforcement. Contract law, in the published court decisions and in the statutes adopted by legislatures around the world, addresses almost every possible term or condition a lawyer could dream up for a contract. Contract law specifies how contracts are to be formed, how they are to be interpreted, how they are to be enforced, and the remedies

FSF argues that the GNU GPL is a licence and not a contract.[153] This is because it wants to base the legal validity of the GNU GPL on the national copyright laws that are based on harmonised international treaties[154] and not on national contract laws that differ greatly from one country to another.[155]

Professor José Cardona is of the opinion that we should not take an extreme approach to the matter and, instead, apply copyright law or contract law whenever necessary and possible.[156] Professor Abd AL Razaq Al Snhouri, a very prominent legal scholar from the Arab world, does not give much importance to the distinction between a licence and a contract[157] in civil legal systems.[158] It is submitted that determining whether to treat the GNU GPL as a contract or a licence in Jordan would not be that critically important. This is because judges in the civil legal

---

> for breach. In many situations, where a license is silent about a particular term or condition, contract law even provides default "fill-in" provisions.

See Lawrence E. Rosen, *Open Source Licensing: Software Freedom and Intellectual Property Law* (Prentice Hall, 2004) 53–57 <http://www.rosenlaw.com/oslbook.htm>: See also the following: Raymond T. Nimmer, *Legal Issues in Open Source and Free Software* <http://euro.ecom.cmu.edu/program/law/08-732/Transactions/LegalIssuesNimmer.pdf>; Douglas A. Hass, 'A Gentlemen's Agreement: Assessing the GNU General Public Licenses and its Adaptation to Linux' (2007) 6 *Chicago-Kent Journal of Intellectual Property* 213; Laurent, above n 140; Jeremy Malcolm, *Problems with Open Source Licensing* (ILaw Barristers and Consultants) <http://www.ilaw.com.au/public/licencearticle.html>.

[153] Cardona, above n 12, 44.

[154] Among these treaties are the *Berne Convention*, WCT, WPPT, and TRIPs.

[155] Cardona, above n 12, 44.

[156] José J. González de Alaiza Cardona noted:

> I consider that free software licenses are Janus-like. On the one hand, they are a non-contractual copyright license that allows end users private utilization of the program. On the other hand, they are a contractual license that allows redistributors to copy, distribute and/or modify the software, under the condition of recognizing to any sublicense the right to copy, distribute and/or modify the software. As a consequence of Janus-like nature of copyleft licenses, the relationship between author of the program and end user is exclusively governed by Copyright. In opposition, the agreement between author and redistributors must be examined not only under copyright, but also under contract law provisions.

Ibid 76.

[157] Professor Al Sanhouri differentiates between a contract and an agreement. 'An agreement is the joining and the consistence of two parties or more to create, transfer, and amend or to end an obligation. A contract on the other hand, is the joining and the consistence of two parties to create or to amend an obligation. A contract is more specific than an agreement and this means that every agreement can be a contract, but not every contract can be an agreement'. See Abd Al Razaq Al Sanhouri, *Al Waseet in the Explanation of the Civil Code* (Al Halabi, 3rd ed, 1998) vol 1, 117–118.

[158] See also for explanation of the civil legal system: John Bell and Sophie Boyron, *Principles of French Law* (Oxford University, 2nd ed, 2008) 294–416; Martin Vranken, *Fundamentals of European Civil Law* (Federation, 2nd ed, 2010) 101–122; P.D.V Marsh, *Comparative Contract Law England, France, Germany* (Gower, 1994); Maurice Sheldon Amos and Frederick Parker Walton, *Introduction to French Law* (Oxford, 3rd ed, 1967).

system are pragmatic in their approaches, and a licence and a contract have the same legal effects.

The legal nature of the GNU GPL has been widely debated in literature on open source licences. Courts,[159] scholars, judges, lawyers, and commentators from common law[160] and civil legal systems[161] have explored it at length in the legal literature.[162] In civil law countries, scholars and jurists divide contracts into various types. They can be divided, according to their subject, into nominated and non-nominated contracts.[163] The first is the most common contract, such as the contract of sale and insurance, which the law has regulated with special provisions in the Civil Code. The non-nominated contracts are un-common contracts, which the law has not regulated under special provisions and are therefore dealt with under the general principles of contract law.[164] As there is no specific provision in Jordan that deals with open source software licences, including the GNU GPL, it is important to refer to the *Jordanian Civil Code No. 43 of 1976 (Jordanian Civil Code)* as it is considered the 'basis' for all private laws,[165] including copyright law. Articles

---

[159] In the Munich Open Source Case, the Court noted that clause 4 of the GPL constitutes a *condition subsequent*. See Munich Open Source Case, above n 149. For an excellent analysis, see Guido Westkamp, 'The Limits of open Source: Lawful User Rights, Exhaustion and Co-existence with Copyright Law' (2008) 1 *Intellectual Property Quarterly* 14–57.

[160] See the following on the legality of open source software in common law systems: Moglen, above n 73, 3, 4; Radin, above n 151, Lawrence Rosen, 'OSL 3.0 A Better License for Open Source Software' (2007) <http://www.rosenlaw.com/OSL3.0-explained.pdf>, Malcolm, above n 152.

[161] See the following on the legality of open source software in civil legal system: Gulbault and Daalen, above n 8, 46–47; González, above n 147, 101–116; Cardona, above n 12, 44; Westkamp, above n 159.

[162] Some would classify open source licences as cohesion contracts. This is because the licensee can only accept the conditions available in the contract and cannot argue or ask for different conditions. Contracts are considered as a cohesion contract when two conditions are met. Firstly, the contract should be related to goods and public utilities that are regarded as essential for consumers or contractors. Secondly, the offeror should monopolise the goods or the utilities legally or, at the minimum, control the monopoly of such utility and good. It is noted that open source software licences are not adhesion contracts as the requirements of adhesion contracts are not present. See, for further explanation of cohesion contracts, Nouri Khater and Adnan Serhan, *Explanation of the Jordanian Civil Code—Personal Rights (Obligations)* (1997) 72–73. See *Jordanian Civil Code*, above n 145, art 104 and art 204.

[163] There are different kinds of contracts. Article 89 of the *Jordanian Civil Code* provides as follows:

1. The general rules in this chapter shall be applicable to contracts both specified or otherwise.
2. But the rules limited to certain civil contracts shall be subject the provisions of the chapter relating thereto and the rules of commerce shall determine the rules relating to commercial contracts.

Jordanian Civil Code, above n 145, art 89.

[164] Al Sanhouri, above n 157, 130-131

[165] For an excellent explanation of the Civil Code, particularly the Egyptian, see Ibid 130-131.

34–241 of the *Jordanian Civil Code* deal with all matters related to forming and concluding contracts.[166] However, what happens when there is a conflict between contract law and copyright law? What is the answer in the civil legal systems?

In the civil legal system, there is a basic legal principle that 'a specific law will overrule general law' (lex specials de rogat geneerali). This means that in case of conflict between specific law (in this situation, copyright law) and general law (in this situation, civil law); there is a need to apply first the specific law (copyright law) and then the general law (civil law).[167] This will only happen if there is a specific provision in the copyright law that deals with the matter; the civil law should be applied in the event that there is no provision available.[168]

In Case No 2797, the Court of Appeal (civil division) in Jordan rejected the argument provided by the appellant that art 256 of the *Jordanian Civil Code*[169] should be applied instead of art 49 of the *Copyright Law No 22 of 1992, as amended* (*Copyright Law*).[170] The Court noted that the *Copyright Law* is a specific law and the *Jordanian Civil Code* is a general law and that the law that should be applied in this situation is the copyright law and not the Civil Code.[171]

---

[166] The *Jordanian Civil Code* in arts 34-241 deal with all matters related to contracts. See *Jordanian Civil Code*, above n 145, art 34-221.

[167] See also, for explanations of the civil legal system, Bell and Boyron, above n 158; Vranken, above n 158; Marsh, above, 158; Amos and Walton, above n 158.

[168] Article 2 of the *Commercial Law No. 12 of 1966* in Jordan provides:

1. In case there is no provision in this law, the rules of the civil code shall be applied on commercial matters.
2. The rules of the civil law shall only be applied according when it is in agreement with the principles of commercial law.

Commercial Law No. 12 of 1966, Official Gazette No. 1910, 30 March 1966 (*Commercial Law*), art 2 (in Arabic) <http://www.lob.gov.jo/ui/laws/search_no.jsp?no=12&year=1966>.

[169] Article 256 of the *Jordanian Civil Code* provides that:

Every Injurious act shall render the person who commits it liable for damage even if he is anon discerning perron.

Jordanian Civil Code, above n 145, art 256.

[170] Article 49 of *Copyright Law No. 22 of 1992* before amendments provides:

The author who was infringed with respect to any of the rights he is entitled to regarding his work according to the provisions of this law, shall have the right to obtain a fair compensation in this regard. In deciding the compensation, the cultural standing of the author, the literary, scientific or artistic value of the work and the extent the infringer benefited by exploiting the work shall be taken into consideration. The adjudicated compensation for the author shall in this case be considered a privileged debt with respect to the net price of the sale of the objects which were used to infringe his rights and the sum of money seized in the lawsuit.

Copyright Law No. 22 of 1992, Official Gazette No. 3821, 16 April 1992 (*Copyright Law*), art 49. <http://www.lob.gov.jo/ui/laws/search_no.jsp?no=22&year=1992>.

[171] Mustafa Faraj, *Enforcement of Copyright* (in Arabic) <http://www.farrajlawyer.com/viewTopic.php?topicId=632>.

The GNU GPL and other open source licences are classified as non-nominated contracts as the law has not provided to deal with it. They can also be regarded as bilateral contracts,[172] which require each party to exchange a certain promise. It would fit well to classify the GNU GPL as a bilateral contract.[173] The developer is providing the source code to the user (without warranty), and the latter can use the source code, provided that the developer releases the changes that are made to the public and abides by the other conditions of the GNU GPL.

It is submitted that determining under which type of contract the GNU GPL should be classified may not have major practical implications or consequences, yet it will be of some importance to academics involved in the studying of contract law.[174] It would be interesting to see if the use of GNU GPL will ever be regulated in a specific law in the future, if it becomes regularly used and common between people. This has actually taken place in relation to certain contracts such as lease and sale, which the legislature has put under the regulation of civil law.

6.2.6.2 The Formation of the GNU GPL

Before examining the formation of the GNU GPL, it should be established whether the Jordanian civil legal system is applicable if a Jordanian programmer, based in Jordan, downloads and uses the GNU GPL and places his modified source code under this sort of licence. The answer for the choice of law is in art 20(1) of the *Jordanian Civil Code*. It provides as follows:

> Contractual obligations shall be governed by the law of the State of the common domicile of the two contracting parties if they are of the same domicile. But if they are different, the applicable law will be that of the State in which the contract was made, unless otherwise agreed by the contracting parties.[175]

---

[172] See, on bilateral contracts, the Jordanian *Civil Code*, above n 145, art 203.

[173] It can also be considered as unilateral contract. This could happen in the situation when one of the parties has not provided any sufficient promise to the other party. This may be particularly true in certain type of non-copy lefted licences that put minimum obligations on the user who is also free to use the source code in proprietary software.

[174] See Jordanian *Civil Code*, above n 145, arts 465-531 (sale contract), arts 685-722 (lease contract), and arts 582-610 (partnership contact).

[175] Article 21 of the *Jordanian* Civil *Code* provides:

> Contracts between livings persons shall in their form be governed by the law of the country in which they are made, they may also be governed by the law applicable to their substantive provisions, and they may be subject to the law of domicile of the two contracting parties or their commons national law.

Jordanian *Civil Code*, above n 145, art 21.

There are two circumstances here, each of which has a separate procedural rule of law. In the event that both licensor and licensee are Jordanian, then the Jordanian laws will be applicable. However, if one of the parties was not Jordanian (this is mostly the situation for open source projects that involve thousands of programmers coming from various jurisdictions), the applicable law shall be the law where the contract was made, unless there is an agreement between the parties to a particular law of jurisdiction.[176] The GNU GPL does not specify a particular law; therefore, the applicable law will be the law of the country where the contract is made.[177]

Most programmers who wish to obtain the source code will download it from the Internet. In some instances, the GNU GPL is located somewhere in the main directory of the downloaded software,[178] but in others, the licence is unavailable.[179] Questions that arise from this include: Is the GNU GPL legally binding? Does downloading the source code constitute a manifestation of intention to be bound by such a contract? Is the contract concluded from a distance legally formed? What is the position of the *Jordanian Civil Code*?

---

[176] See, for full explanation of the Jordanian conflicts of law rules, Hassan Al Hadawy—*Conflicts of Laws—General Principles and Solution in the Jordanian Law—A Comparative Study* (in Arabic) (1997).

[177] Article 101 of *Jordanian Civil Code* provides as follows:

> If the at the time of contracting the two contracting parties shall not be present the contract shall be deemed to have been made in the place and at the time of acceptance unless there is an agreement or legal provisions to a different effect.

Article 102 of the *Jordanian Civil Code* provides:

> Contracting by telephone or any similar method shall in respect of the place be considered as it has been completed between two contracting parties not present when the contract was made, but in respect of time it shall be considered as if it has been made between two present parties.

Jordanian *Civil Code*, above n 145, arts 101-102. See also In Mahkamat al-Tamiex [Taimez], *Court of Cassation*, 67/1988; Mahkamat al-Tamiex [Taimez], *Court of Cassation*, 697/1982, In Mahkamat al-Tamiex [Taimez], *Court of Cassation*, 539/1983.

[178] The General Counsel of *MontaVista Software, Inc.*, an open source software company noted that:

> [M]ost licensors get the GPL in one of two ways: they get a piece of paper with the GPL printed on it (but not normally "wrapped" around any box or piece of software) [physical delivery] or they get, along with the software, an electronic file containing the GPL (but normally without the file being designed as a clickwrap) [digital delivery].

Jason B. Wacha, '*Open Source, Free Software, and the General Public License*' (2003) 20 (3) *Computer and Internet Lawyer*, cited in Cardona, above n 12, 60.

[179] Gulbault and Daalen, above n 8, 57.

Sceptics of the open source movement contend that the GNU GPL does not qualify as a contract because it is made on a royalty-free basis and does not contain any consideration,[180] which is essential for the formation of a valid contract in common law jurisdictions but not in civil legal system jurisdictions. The licensee in the GNU GPL is not obliged to pay a fee in order to exploit the code. The *Jordanian Civil Code* recognises an ex gratia contract if it satisfies the formality requirement of gift contracts prescribed under the law.[181] As the GNU GPL is considered the 'legal heart of [the] Free Software Movement',[182] the FSF was among the first to argue that it is a properly formed,[183] legally binding licence.[184] Many legal scholars support such a conclusion based on the knowledge of the legal system they are mostly familiar with and their analysis of contract laws.[185]

---

[180] Ibid 46-47.

[181] See Jordanian *Civil Code*, above n 145, arts 557-581 on the requirements of gift contracts.

[182] Moglen, above n 37, 2

[183] Section 5 of the GPL is clear about acceptance and when it takes place. It provides:

> You are not required to accept this License, since you have not signed it. However, nothing else grants you permission to modify or distribute the Program or its derivative works. These actions are prohibited by law if you do not accept this License. Therefore, by modifying or distributing the Program (or any work based on the Program), you indicate your acceptance of this License to do so, and all its terms and conditions for copying, distributing or modifying the Program or works based on it.

The GNU GPL, version 2 <http://www.gnu.org/licenses/gpl-2.0.html>.

[184] Eben Moglen noted that:

> The license does not require anyone to accept it in order to acquire, install, use, inspect, or even experimentally modify GPL'd software. All of those activities are either forbidden or controlled by proprietary software firms, so they require you to accept a license, including contractual provisions outside the reach of copyright, before you can use their works. The free software movement thinks all those activities are rights, which all users ought to have; we don't even want to cover those activities by license. Almost everyone who uses GPL'd software from day to day needs no license, and accepts none. The GPL only obliges you if you distribute software made from GPL'd code, and only needs to be accepted when redistribution occurs. And because no one can ever redistribute without a license, we can safely presume that anyone redistributing GPL'd software intended to accept the GPL. After all, the GPL requires each copy of covered software to include the license text, so everyone is fully informed.

Eben Moglen, *Enforcing the GNU GPL* GNU.org <http://www.gnu.org/philosophy/enforcing-gpl.html>.

[185] González, above n 147, 106; Gulbault and Daalen, above n 8, 71; Cardona, above n 12, 51-52; Westkamp, above n 159,14-57.

A contract is concluded in Jordan when the offer from one of the contracting parties is joined with the acceptance[186] from the other party.[187] The availability of the offer and acceptance does not completely give the contract its legal validity.[188] In addition to having an offer and acceptance,[189] the parties should be legally capable of making contracts (legal capacity)[190]; the contract should have a valid subject matter[191] and a lawful purpose (cause) not contrary to public morals,[192] as specified under the law.[193]

The expression of will could be either express or implied. It is considered as express when the contracting parties assent in writing, verbally, through a customary

---

[186] Article 87 of the Jordanian *Civil Code* provides:

> The contract is the joining and consideration of the offer from one of the contracting parties with acceptance from the other in a manner which proves the effect thereof on the object of the contract and the obligation of each party by what he is bound with to the other.

Jordanian Civil Code, above n 145, art 87.

[187] Article 199 of the *Jordanian Civil Code* provides:

> 1. The effect of the contract shall on its formation attach to the contracted object and its consideration without being conditional on possession or any other thing unless the law otherwise provides.
> 2. But in respect of the rights of the contract each of the two parties perform his obligation prescribed by the contract.

Jordanian Civil Code, above n 145, art 199.

[188] Article 167 of the *Jordanian Civil Code* provides:

> The valid contract is the contract which is basically and descriptively lawful by being made by capable persons, relating to an object that can be subject to its provisions, having an existing valid and lawful purpose, having correct description and not subject to a vitiating condition.

Jordanian Civil Code, above n 145, art 167.

[189] Article 90 of the *Jordanian Civil Code* provides:

> The contract shall be made as soon as the offer is joined with the acceptance subject to the conditions which the law in additions prescribes.

Jordanian Civil Code, above n 145, art 90.

[190] See *Jordanian Civil Code*, above n 145, arts 116–134 that deal with the capacity to do contracts.

[191] See *Jordanian Civil Code*, above n 145, arts 157-164.

[192] See *Jordanian Civil Code*, above n 145, arts 165-166.

[193] In case that these conditions have not been fulfilled, the contract could be legally classified in the *Jordanian Civil Code* as void contract (arts 168-1), fasid contract (trained contract or voidable contract under French law) (arts 170-1), suspended (art 171), non-obligatory depending on which condition the contract is missing or incomplete (art 176).

sign, or by any other means of expression[194] that is common between people.[195] The expression is implied if any party to the contract has chosen to interpret certain behaviour to mean that they are willing to create a legal obligation.[196]

In Jordan, consideration is not important for a contract to be formed; only two conditions must be present to form a contract, and these are offer and acceptance.[197] This means that according to art 93 of the *Jordanian Civil Code*, the act of downloading the source code by a Jordanian programmer and placing his modified source under the licence would be considered as an 'implied acceptance' of the terms and conditions of the GNU GPL. This is, of course, provided that all other conditions related to the formation of the contract have been observed.

The *Jordanian Civil Code* recognises that contracts concluded from a distance[198] and online are fully regulated under the *Electronic Transaction Law No 85 of 2001*,[199] but unfortunately, shrink-wrap agreements[200] are not yet

---

[194] Article 93 of the *Jordanian Civil Code* provides that:

> The expression of the will shall be by word, writing, the customary sign, even from a person who is not dumb, the actual exchange denoting consent and by any other behaviour which in the circumstances leaves no doubt of its indication of consent.

Jordanian Civil Code, above n 145, art 93.

[195] Al Sanhouri, above n 157, 146.

[196] Ibid,147.

[197] Article 90 of the *Jordanian Civil Code* provides:

> The contract shall be made as soon as the offer is joined with acceptance subject to the conditions which the law in addition prescribes.

Jordanian Civil Code, above n 145, art 90.

[198] Article 102 of the *Jordanian Civil Code* provides that:

> Contracting by telephone or any similar method shall in respect of the place be considered as it has been made between two present parties.

Jordanian Civil Code, above n 145, art 102.

[199] Article 7 of *Electronic Transaction law No. of 85 of 2001* provides:

> A. The electronic records, contracts, messages, and signatures shall be considered to produce the same legal consequences resulting from the written documents and signatures in accordance with the provisions of the Laws in force in terms of being binding to the parties concerned or in terms of fitness thereof as an evidential weight.
> B. The legal consequence stated in Paragraph (A) of this Article shall not be excluded for reasons of conducting the transaction by electronic means so long as it complies with the provisions of this Law.

Article 13 of the *Electronic Transaction law No. of 85 of 2001* provides:

> The electronic message shall be considered as a means of expressing the will legally admissible for offer or acceptance for contractual intent.

Electronic Transaction Law No. 85 of 2001, Official Gazette No 4524, 31 February 2001 (Electronic Transaction Law), art 7, art 13 <http://www.lob.gov.jo/ui/laws/search_no.jsp?no=85&year=2001>.

[200] See, on shrink-wrap agreements, Cardona, above n 12, 53.

recognised under the law or known in Jordanian courts.[201] The decisions discussed below from German and French courts show that the GNU GPL is legally valid in a civil legal system.

The German courts considered for the first time the validity of the GNU GPL in the case of *Herald Welte v S Deutschland*, which was brought before the Court of Munich in 2004. It was decided that the GNU GPL is a legally valid agreement that satisfies the *German Civil Code (BGB)*. The Court noted in particular:

> The Panel considers the license conditions to be general business conditions which are to be examined under application of German Civil Code Sections 305 et seqq. ......To begin with, the Panel has no doubt whatsoever that the general business conditions have been effectively incorporated into a possible contractual relationship between the defendant and the plaintiff pursuant to German Civil Code Section 305 Para. 2. On the Internet page, reference is made to the general business conditions. Furthermore, the general business conditions are universally available. Even though the German translation may not be an official one, there are no concerns whatsoever as to the fact that the official conditions are only available in English language, since English is a prevalent foreign language in the computer industry. This applies at least where a contractual relationship between the authors and a commercial software business is concerned.[202]

---

[201] Professor Nouri Khater argues that click-wrap agreements constitute valid contracts. The contract is concluded when the user either opens the product online or offline, which constitutes an implied acceptance to the offer that has been put forward by the seller. The user has to respect all his obligations as a buyer when he accepts the agreements, and in the case that there is no fulfilment of the obligation under the contract, there could be a breach of the contract law under the law. See, Nouri Khater, *The Licence Contract on Shrink Wrap and Click Wrap—A study of Art 12 of the UAE Federal Law No 6 of 2002 Concerning Copyrights and Neighbouring Rights* (in Arabic) 7 (on file with author).

Article 12 of the *UAE Federal Copyright Law No. 7 of 2002* as amended provides:

> Without prejudice to the provisions of article 9 of the Law herein; the transfer of financial rights, in respect of the works of computer software and applications thereof or data basis shall be subject to contractual license included or affixed on the product, either appearing on the medium that carry the program or on the computer screen, upon downloading or storing the program. The purchaser or user of such program shall observe the terms included in such license.

The *UAE Federal Copyright Law No. 7 of 2002* as amended, art 12 <http://www.wipo.int/wipolex/en/text.jsp?file_id=124612>.

[202] Munich Open Source Software Case, above n 149. Section 305 (1) of the *Civil Code* in Germany defines standard business terms as follows:

> (1) Standard business terms are all contract terms pre-formulated for more than two contracts which one party to the contract (the user) presents to the other party upon the entering into of the contract. It is irrelevant whether the provisions take the form of a physically separate part of a contract or are made part of the contractual document itself, what their volume is, what typeface or font is used for them and what form the contract takes. Contract terms do not become standard business terms to the extent that they have been negotiated in detail between the parties.

See *Civil Code* in Germany, as amended (latest amendment 28 September 2009) <http://www.gesetze-im-internet.de/englisch_bgb/englisch_bgb.html#BGBengl_000P305>.

In another case, the Frankfurt Court, in the case of *Harald Welte v D Deutschland GmpH*, decided in 2006 that the GNU GPL constituted a formal, binding agreement between the parties. In particular, the Court found in relation to the formation of the GNU GPL:

> In the case of free software it is to be assumed that the copyright holder by putting the program under the GPL makes an offer to a determinable or definite circle of people and that this offer is accepted by users [of the software] through an act that requires consent under copyright law; in this respect, it can be assumed that the copyright holder enters into this legal relationship without receiving an actual declaration of acceptance [from the users] (Section 151 of the German Civil Code (BGB)).[203]

The Paris Court of Appeals, in the case of *EDU 4 v AFPA*, on 16 September 2009 (discussing the GNU GPL as a side question)[204] held that it was a breach of an IT contract not to deliver the GNU GPL software in fulfilment of the contractual obligations.[205] The Court noted:

> [The court] considers that it follows from all of these elements that the entity EDU 4 had not fulfilled its contractual obligations with its delivery in December 2001, the date on which the performance of EDU 4 was to be assessed, that on the one hand posed privacy risks to the users of EOF and on the other hand did not satisfy the terms of the GNU GPL license, since the entity EDU 4 had removed the original copyright notices of VNC from two files, replacing them with its own copyright notices, and since it had deleted the text of the license.[206]

It is not surprising to find that the contractual basis of the GNU GPL can be fitted relatively smoothly within the *Jordanian Civil Code*. Table 6.1 in page 300 compares the common law system and the civil legal system in relation to the legal validity of the GNU GPL.

It will now be important to examine other legal issues that are related to contract law.

---

[203] Frankfurt Open Source Software Case, above n 149.

[204] Martin Von Willbrand commented that:

> One can conclude that the above paragraph does not concern enforcement of the GPL, but rather appreciation of fulfilment of the contract between EDU 4 and AFPA. To the extent that the decision relates to the terms of the GPL, it is very limited in reach. It may be noted that the removal of copyright and similar notices could be considered violations of law, and not merely violation of GPL license requirements.

Martin von Willebrand, 'A Look at EDU4 v. AFPA, also Known as the "Paris GPL Case"' (2009) 1 (2) *International Free and Open Source Software Law Review* 124 <http://www.ifosslr.org/ifosslr/article/download/17/42>. See also Fabrice Perbost and Alan Walter, 'Open Source Software in France' in Ywein Van den Brande, Shane Coughlan and Till Jaeger (ed), *The International Free and Open Source Software Law Book* <http://ifosslawbook.org>.

[205] Till Jaeger, Enforcement of the GNU GPL in Germany and Europe (2010) 1 (1) *International Free and Open Source Software Law Review* <http://www.jipitec.eu/issues/jipitec-1-1-2010/2419/dippadm1268746871.43.pdf> 37. See also Willbrand, above n 204.

[206] Willbrand, above n 204.

Table 6.1 The legal validity of the GNU GPL under the Common law system and the Civil law system

Common law system	Civil legal system
It is held to be a licence (no final decision on its status as a contract)	Whether or not the GNU GPL is considered to be a licence or a contract is not the significant issue under the civil law system because the licence has substantively the same legal effect whether considered to be a contract or a licence
Consideration is required to form a contract (in addition to offer and acceptance)	Consideration is not required to form a contract (offer and acceptance are necessary)
The remedies available under copyright law apply	Remedies available in copyright law apply and not the remedies available generally under the civil law in accordance with the principle that 'a specific law will overrule a general law'

6.2.6.3 Miscellaneous Contract Law Issues

There are four important legal matters that are often discussed when dealing with the contractual issues of the GNU GPL. These are the lack of privity of contract; remedies, the validity of the warranty/disclaimer clause; and finally, the termination of the GNU GPL based on non-observance of its terms and conditions.

Privity of Contract

The doctrine of privity, as understood in Anglo-American common law (known in French law as the 'relative effect of contracts'), is a fundamental principle in contract law. It means that parties who agreed to be bound by a contract can only confer rights and obligation on themselves and not on others (third parties) who are not party to the contract.[207] The GNU GPL has been questioned by legal scholars who argue that there is an absence of the privity requirement. Article 208 of the *Jordanian Civil Code* states clearly that a contract shall not prescribe an obligation on third parties, but it might earn them a right.[208] The law provides some exceptions to that rule in art 210 of the *Jordanian Civil Code*, which states

1. A person may contact in his own name on rights he stipulated for the benefit of a third party if he has an interest in their fulfilment whether material or moral.
2. The said stipulation shall result in the earning by the third party of a direct right against the undertaker in the fulfilment of the stipulation by the latter from whom he can claim fulfilment unless it is otherwise agreed and that undertaker may avail himself of the defences resulting from the contract against the beneficiary

[207] See also William Reynell Anson, *Anson's Law of Contract* (Oxford University, 1998).

[208] *Jordanian Civil Code*, above n 145, art 208.

3. And the person who made the stipulation may claim the fulfilment of what he stipulated for the benefit of the beneficiary unless it is ascertained from the contract that the beneficiary is the sole owner of the right therein.[209]

Some scholars have suggested that these exceptions, along with the decreasing importance of privity, mean that privity of contract is not an important issue in relation to the GNU GPL. Others may argue that any talk of privity misunderstands Section 6 of the GNU GPL,[210] which creates a direct licence model rather than a sub-license model. A direct licensing model arguably raises no issues of privity. As the commentator Rod Dixon explains:

> Section 6 of the GNU GPL overcomes the privity-of-contract-issue, to the extent that privity is still relevant in contract law, by providing that the original licensor, regardless of who actually provides the software to the end-user licenses each distribution of an open source program. Even so, with one notable exception, there [are] little reasons to challenge an open source licence on grounds of lack of privity, since the open sauce licence grants freedoms to end-users that, absent the licence, would violate copyright law if end-users are shown to have engaged in those activities.[211]

Professors Anne Fitzgerald and Brian Fitzgerald support such conclusion in Fig. 6.1, arguing that in open licensing models each downstream recipient of the copyright work (B, C, D, and E) obtains a direct licence from the original licensor.[212]

---

[209] Article 210 of the *Jordanian Civil Code* provides as follows:

1. A person may contact in his own name on rights he stipulated for the benefit of a third party if he has an interest in their fulfilment whether material or moral.
2. The said stipulation shall result in the earning by the third party of a direct right against the undertaker in the fulfilment of the stipulation by the latter from whom he can claim fulfilment unless it is otherwise agreed and that undertaker may avail himself of the defences resulting from the contract against the beneficiary
3. And the person who made the stipulation may claim the fulfilment of what he stipulated for the benefit of the beneficiary unless it is ascertained from the contract that the beneficiary is the sole owner of the right therein.

Jordanian Civil Code, above n 145, art 210.

[210] Section 6 of the GNU GPL provides as follows:

> Each time you redistribute the Program (or any work based on the Program), the recipient automatically receives a license from the original licensor to copy, distribute or modify the Program subject to these terms and conditions. You may not impose any further restrictions on the recipients' exercise of the rights granted herein. You are not responsible for enforcing compliance by third parties to this License.

The GNU GPL version 2 <http://www.gnu.org/licenses/gpl-2.0.html>.

[211] Rod Dixon, *Open Source Software Law* (Artech Home, 2004) 24.

[212] Anne Fitzgerald, Neale Hooper and Brian Fitzgerald, 'Enabling Open Access to Public Sector Information With Creative Commons Licences: The Australian Experience' in Brian Fitzgerald (ed), *Access to Public Sector Information: Law, Technology and Policy* (2010, Sydney University) Vol 1, 71, 93.

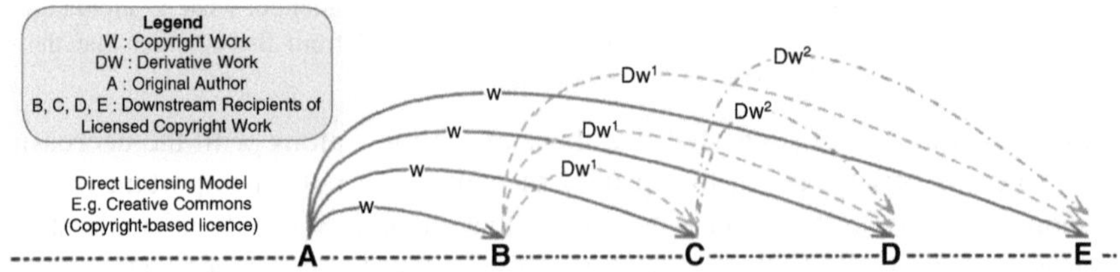

Fig. 6.1 Direct and indirect licensing models

On this basis, it is plausible to suggest that the Jordanian courts would hold that Section 6 of the GNU GPL creates a contractual bond directly between the licensee and all recipients removing any issue relating to privity. At a more pragmatic level, Professor José J. González de Alaiza suggests that the doctrine of privity will not be such a problem for the GNU GPL in a civil legal system. This is because if a 'third party does not respect the terms of the licence, then there will be no contract at all and the original author will have a cause of action against any infringer based on his exclusive rights of copyright'.[213] The Court of Frankfurt in the case of *Harald Welte v D Deutshland GmbH* did not find that the privity of contract would constitute a problem in the context of the GNU GPL. It also agreed with the analysis provided by Professor González de Alaiza. It noted in particular that:

> [I]n addition, if the GPL were not sufficient to form a legal relationship with Plaintiff, Defendant would not have any right to copy, distribute or modify the three programs, such that a copyright infringement by the Defendant would have taken place. In particular, the conditions of the GPL can in no case be interpreted to contain a waiver of legal positions afforded by copyright law. The GPL precisely stipulates that the freedom to use, modify and distribute the corresponding software initially afforded by way of a grant of a non-exclusive license to everyone is automatically terminated upon a violation of the GPL (cf. Dreier/Schulze, § 69a, Rz.11).... The regulations of the GPL must be understood to provide that the grant of the non-exclusive right of use under the GPL is subject to the condition subsequent (Section 158 of the German Civil Code (BGB)) that the licensee must not fail to comply with the terms of the agreement. Upon occurrence of the condition the license [granted under the GPL] is terminated.[214]

[213] Cardona, above n 12, 66. See also Yang Xia, 'Introduction to Software Protection Under Chinese Law' in Brande, Coughlan and Jaeger, above n 204, 6.

[214] Frankfurt Open Source Software Case. The District Court of Munich also noted:

> If the open development of the software is endangered by the invalidity of the clause and a fundamental concept of open source software is affected, there is – in the opinion of the Panel – considerable ground for the argument that in such cases there has been no agreement *in rem* at all with the consequence that any use of the software is illegal.

Munich Case, above n 149.

Remedies

There are various remedies available under the *Jordanian Civil Code* and the *Copyright Law* in Jordan. In the *Jordanian Civil Code*, the remedies that a judge can give include execution of the promised obligation, resolution (termination) of the agreement, and damages. In the *Copyright Law*, there are precautionary measures (injunctions and confiscation of the work), civil penalties, and criminal penalties.[215] The remedies available in the *Copyright Law* will be applied first and not the remedies available in the *Jordanian Civil Code* as they should be given preference based on the principle that 'a specific law overrules private law'.

Warranties

Most, if not all, open source licences contain a section that disclaims any warranty for the program.[216] This is usually found to eliminate the economic risk of those persons who provide this kind of software without any licence charges.[217] The warranty disclaimer is provided in sections 11 and 12 of the GNU GPL.[218] There are two main types of liability under Jordanian civil law: a) liability resulting from a breach of contract[219] and b) liability resulting from a tort.[220] The principle of freedom of contract allows the parties to determine any limitations that they might find appropriate to their contractual relationship.[221] The *Jordanian Civil Code* has not clearly accepted the total exemption of liability, although this can be inferred from the law.[222] The law does not uphold contractual limitation of liability clauses to protect public interest or to protect a particular party when the limitation of

[215] *Copyright Law*, above n 170, arts 46-55. See also Fabrice Perbost and Alan Walter, 'Open Source Software in France' in Brande, Coughlan and Jaeger, above n 204, 8-9.

[216] Gulbault and Daalen, above n 8, 78; Louis Carbonneau, Open Source: *The Good, the Bad and the Ugly* (17 March 2011) <http://www.fizzlaw.com/article/open-source-the-good-the-bad-and-the-ugly>.

[217] Metxger and Jaeger, above n 9, 69.

[218] See Sections 11 and 12 GNU GPL <http://www.gnu.org/licenses/gpl.html>.

[219] The *Jordanian Civil Code* does not specify specific rules for contractual liability under one section. *Jordanian Civil Code*, above n 145, arts 199(2), 202, 213, 241. For further explanation, see Nouri Khater and Adnan Serhan, above n 162, 312-338.

[220] See *Jordanian Civil Code*, above n 145, arts 256-287. Khater and Serhan, above n 162, 368-470; Gulbault and Daalen, above n 8, 81.

[221] *Jordanian Civil Code*, above n 145, arts 88, 93, 214 and 199. See also Khater and Serhan, above n 162, 28-33.

[222] See *Jordanian Civil Code*, above n 145, art 213 and art 514.

liability is against public order and morals.[223] In addition, the law does not allow limitation of liability in cases of cheating[224] and grave mistakes.[225]

Sect. 6.2.6 discussed the legal validity of the GNU GPL under the Jordanian legal system. It was found that the contractual formation of the GNU GPL can fit relatively smoothly within the *Jordanian Civil Code*. More generally, contractual issues under the *Jordanian Civil Code* do not seem insurmountable, and with common sense and good judgement, they can be accommodated under the civil law system. It is now important to examine the legal issues related to the GNU GPL in relation to copyright law.

6.2.7 The Legal Treatment of the GNU GPL under Copyright Law

The FSF argues that GNU GPL is a copyright licence and not a contract because they want to make sure that consistent international legal rules are applied to it when it is brought before any competent court across the world. This section will examine the legal validity of the GNU GPL under the *Copyright Law* in Jordan. It will examine first authorship and then moral rights.

6.2.7.1 Authorship in Collaborative Open Source and Free Software Projects

The authorship of open source projects[226] raises many thorny legal issues that IP experts and scholars are continuing to examine. The aim of these projects is to harness the creativity of thousands of programmers worldwide to the progress of the Internet and many other computing projects.[227] This section examines how the

---

[223] Khater and Serhan, above n 162, 333.

[224] Article 270 of the *Jordanian Civil Code* provides:

> Any condition for exemption from the liability resulting from the injurious act shall be void.

Jordanian Civil Code, above n 145, art 270.

[225] Article 358 of the *Jordanian* Civil Code provides:

> 1. If the obligation of the debtor is the preservation of a thing or its administration or the exercise of care in the performance of his obligation if he has exercised in its performance all that is exercised by an ordinarily person even if he has excursive in its performance all that is exercised by an ordinarily person even if the intended purpose us not achieved, unless the law or the contract otherwise provide
> 2. And in any case the debtor shall remain liable for his deceit or gross default.

Jordanian Civil Code, above n 145, art 358. See also Khater and Serhan, above n 162, 335-336.

[226] Sourceforge <http://sourceforge.net/>.

[227] Gregory B. Newby, Jane Greenberg and Paul Jones, 'Open Source Development and Law Bolometric Patterns in Programming' (2003) 54 (2) *Journal of the American Society for Information Science and Technology* 169–178 <http://portal.acm.org/citation.cfm?id=767383>.

Copyright Law of Jordan treats the contribution in those projects and whether they are considered as a 'joint authorship' or 'collective work'.

The *Copyright Law* is applicable, according to art 53, to Jordanian authors and foreigners who are residing in any of the signatory countries to the international copyright treaties (mainly Berne, WPPT, and 1961 Rome Convention for the Protection of Performers, Producers of Phonograms and Broadcasting Organisations (Rome Convention)). This means that the copyright law will be applied in the situation where a case is brought by a Jordanian contributing to the development of an open source project in Jordan. In the event that the Jordanian courts are the proper forum to examine the issue, then the Jordanian law will be applicable to all the issues in relation to authorship and copyright protection under the *Copyright Law*.[228]

There are various modes of software production that exist on the Internet, but they are all similar in one way or another as they use the power of the Internet to bring all people together to contribute to a common goal. Usually, one developer or a group of developers will initiate an open source project and place their source code on the Internet and encourage other developers to help them improve and fix its errors. To make this development model process as efficient as possible, one person or a group of persons will be appointed to oversee the development of such a project. A good example of an open source project is the development of the Linux Kernel. Linus Torvalds and some others[229] are appointed to control the development of the project, and their main job is to approve the patches and their incorporation into the original software that Trovalds published in 1991.[230]

The *Copyright Law* in Jordan does not contain special provisions related to software development, and therefore, we need to refer to the general rules of the law. Any contributor to an open source project will be regarded as the author[231] if his contribution meets the originality[232] requirement that is needed for any work to be given protection under the law. With respect to the works that are created by more than one author, the *Copyright Law* in Jordan differentiates between two categories. The first is referred to as 'joint authorship', and the second is referred to

[228] See also Andreas Weibe, 'Validity of Open Source Licence' (2004) 1 *Computer Law Review International* 156, 157-158.

[229] Along with others, including, Marcelo Tosatti, Alan Cox, and Andrew Morton.

[230] The Linux-Kernel Mailing List FAQ <http://www.tux.org/lkml/>.

[231] An author under art 4(A)(1) of the *Copyright Law* in Jordan is deemed to be 'the person who publishes the work attributed to his own whether by indicating his name on the work or by any other way shall be considered the author unless there is proof to the contrary'.

Copyright Law, above n 170, art 4(A)(1).

[232] Article 3 of the *Copyright Law* in Jordan states that:

> Protection is given to authors with innovative literary, artistic and scientific works regardless of their kind, importance or the purpose of their production.

(C) The right to translate his work into another language, adapt it, orchestrate it, or make any alteration thereto.

See *Copyright Law*, above n 170, art 3(C).

as 'collective work' or 'works created under the supervision of another person'. Article 35(A) and art 35(B) of the *Copyright Law* in Jordan explain when the work is categorised as 'joint authorship',[233] and art 35(C) of the *Copyright Law* in Jordan explains when the work is categorised as 'collective work'.[234]

The difference between the two categories of work is that in the first, there is no single contributor who is organising and guiding the contributions of others, but instead, every contributor is sharing almost the same as the other. In the second category of work, the individual contributions are not clearly identifiable and cannot be separated from each other.

What follows is that in a 'collective work', 'the person who directed and arranged the innovation of the work shall be considered the author and shall have exclusively the right to exercise its copyrights'. By contrast, in the case of the 'joint authorship', all authors enjoy the rights over the work in joint ownership, which must be exercised with the consent of every author.[235] Table 6.2 in page 307 explains the various types of authorship under the *Copyright Law* in Jordan.

According to art 35(C) of the *Copyright Law*, the Linux Kernel development project could be considered as a 'collective work'. This is because Linus Torvalds is the main author of the project (called 'benevolent dictator') as he guides, supervises, compiles, and finally approves the various contributions that are made on his original source code and program. Torvalds would own the whole copyright in the program as he provided the first version of his source code and contributed more than any programmer to the project, but he has to publish the program under his sole name.

The Linux Kernel development project could also be regarded in accordance with art 35(A) as joint authorship work (merged joint work)[236] in the situation

---

[233] Article 35(A) of the *Copyright Law* in Jordan provides that:

> If more than one person contributed to making a single work such that the share contributed by each cannot be separated, they shall be considered as owners of the work with each having an equal share unless they agree to do something different. None of them shall, in this case, exercise the copyrights with respect to this work without the consent of all the authors.

See *Copyright Law*, above n 170, art 35(A).

[234] Article 35(C) of the *Copyright Law* in Jordan provides that:

> If a group participated in innovating a work under the direction of a natural or juridical person (called a collective work) and that person committed himself to publish the said work under his name and his control such that the contributions of the participants merged into the general purpose intended by that person for the work or the idea which he innovated for it such that the contribution of each of the contributors in the work cannot separated and distinguished apart, then the person who directed and arranged the innovation of the work shall be considered the author and shall have exclusively the right to exercise its copyrights.

See *Copyright Law*, above n 170, art 35(C).

[235] Gulbault and Daalen, above n 8, 91-95.

[236] Peter W. Hansen, *Intellectual Property and Practice of the United Arab Emirates* (Oxford University, 2009) 177-178.

Table 6.2 Authorship of FOSS projects under the *Copyright Law* in Jordan

Copyright Law No. 22 of 1992, as amended	Type of work	Conditions	Impact/significance
Article 35(C)	Collective work	1. Legal or natural person under whose direction the work is created and published 2. Two authors or more; and 3. The contribution of each author merges with others[237]	Only one author
Article 35 (A)	Joint authorship (merged joint work)	1. Does not fall within collective work; and 2. Individual contribution cannot be separated	Equal share in authorship unless agreed otherwise
Article 35 (B)[238]	Joint authorship (assembled work)	1. Does not fall within collective work; and 2. Individual contribution can be separated/distinguished	Every author owns copyright in their piece of work

where the individual contribution of each programmer cannot be separated from the other. In this kind of work, all programmers, including Linus Torvalds, would own equal shares in the copyright of the project. The Linux development project could also be regarded in accordance with art 35(B) as joint authorship work (assembled work)[239] in the situation where the individual contribution of each programmer can be separated from the other. In this kind of work, Linus Torvalds retains copyright

[237] Professor Makeen Makeen has noted that:

> The special category of 'collective works' was developed initially in France to cover dictionaries. It was designed to regulate the exploitation of works made by several contributors, in which it is impossible to identify the part contributed by each author.

See Makeen F. Makeen, 'Authorship/Ownership of Copyright works under Egyptian Author's Rights' (2007) 35 (5) *International Review of Intellectual Property and Competition Law* 571, 582-585.

[238] Article 35(B) of the *Copyright Law* in Jordan provides that:

> However if it is possible to separate the share of each of the contributors to the work apart from the shares of the other contributors, then each of them shall have the right to exploit the copyright in the part he contributed to the work provided that this exploitation causes no damage to the exploitation of the work itself and does not infringe the rights of all the partners in the work, unless they agreed to something different.

Copyright Law, above n 170, art 35(B).

[239] Ibid.

in his original code, but at the same time, every contributor or programmer would be deemed as author[240] of his own original contribution.[241]

It is submitted that considering the Linux development project as a joint authorship work (assembled work) on the basis that each individual contribution is regarded as separate work protected under the copyright law would accord to the common practice of FOSS projects to assign the copyright to a central person or an entity/organisation[242] and provide the best result for FOSS programmers and contributors who are also acknowledged for their contributions. Finally, it is important to note that not all FOSS and 'peer productions' projects would be regarded under the *Copyright Law* in Jordan as being of 'joint authorship' (assembled work), but this matter should be left to the courts to determine the category of work on a case-by-case basis.

6.2.7.2 The Validity of Exploitation of Economic Rights under the GNU GPL

One of the most interesting provisions of open content licences, particularly the GNU GPL, is its 'copyleft' or 'share-alike' clause. 'Copyleft' can be defined as a 'play on the word copyright'[243] and a novel use 'of the existing copyright law to ensure work remains freely available'.[244] It intends to forbid any closing of software by indirect means such as requiring the signature of a non-disclosure agreement that is required in the context of proprietary software.[245]

---

[240] Section 2 of the GNU GPL provides that:

> These requirements apply to the modified work as a whole. If identifiable sections of that work are not derived from the Program, and can be reasonably considered independent and separate works in themselves, then this License, and its terms, do not apply to those sections when you distribute them as separate works. In addition, mere aggregation of another work not based on the Program with the Program (or with a work based on the Program) on a volume of a storage or distribution medium does not bring the other work under the scope of this License.

The GNU GPL version 2 <http://www.gnu.org/licenses/gpl-2.0.html>.

[241] Gulbault and Daalen, above n 8, 91-95.

[242] See also Eben Moglen, *Why FSF Gets Copyright Assignment From Contributors* Gnu.org <http://www.gnu.org/licenses/why-assign.html>.; Omar Johnny, Marc Miller and Mark Webbink, 'Copyright in Open Source Software Understanding The Boundaries' (2010) 2 (1) *International Free and Open Source Software Law Review* <http://www.ifosslr.org/ifosslr/article/view/30>; Andrew Stokes, 'Authorship, Collaboration and Copyright: A view from the United Kingdom' (2002) 13 (6) *Entertainment Law Review* 121-127.

[243] Fontana et al., above n 139. See also Aaron Krowne and Raymond Puzio, *The Fog of Copyleft* (2006) 11 (7) *First Monday* <http://firstmonday.org/htbin/cgiwrap/bin/ojs/index.php/fm/article/viewArticle/1368>.

[244] Katz, above n 70, 19.

[245] Gulbault and Daalen, above n 8, 112; Lambert, above n 36.

To the FSF, it is an 'obligation on the part of the programmer or the user of the open source software to distribute modified versions of the software, subject to the same conditions that it is used under'.[246] Richard Stallman defines 'copyleft' as 'a general method for making programs or other work free, and requiring all modified work and extended versions of the [work] to [be] free as well'.[247] Section 2 of the GNU GPL implements the FSF idea of 'copyleft'.[248] The 'copyleft' requirement can be enforced as Section 6 of the GNU GPL creates a direct licence with each new recipient of the code.[249] The failure to respect the 'copyleft' provision will result in automatic termination of the GNU GPL, but this would not affect the rights of third parties.[250]

The GNU GPL requires the licensor to give extended freedom to use, reproduce, modify, and (re)distribute the software.[251] The copyright law gives the author various economic rights, including the reproduction right, the distribution right,

[246] FSF, *What is Copyleft* Gnu.org <http://www.gnu.org/copyleft/>.

[247] Richard Stallman, *What is Copyleft?* Gnu.org <http://www.gnu.org/copyleft/copyleft.html>.

[248] Section 2(B) of the GNU GPL states:

> You must cause any work that you distribute or publish, that in whole or in part contains or is derived from the Program or any part thereof, to be licensed as a whole at no charge to all third parties under the terms of this License, whose permissions for other licensees extend to the entire whole, and thus to each and every part regardless of who wrote it.

The GNU GPL version 2, <http://www.gnu.org/licenses/gpl-2.0.html>. See also Laurent, above n 140.

[249] It provides as follows:

> Each time you redistribute the Program (or any work based on the Program), the recipient automatically receives a license from the original licensor to copy, distribute or modify the Program subject to these terms and conditions. You may not impose any further restrictions on the recipients' exercise of the rights granted herein. You are not responsible for enforcing compliance by third parties to this License.

The GNU GPL version 2 <http://www.gnu.org/licenses/gpl-2.0.html>.

[250] Section 4 of the GNU GPL provides as follows:

> You may not copy, modify, sublicense, or distribute the Program except as expressly provided under this License. Any attempt otherwise to copy, modify, sublicense or distribute the Program is void, and will automatically terminate your rights under this License. However, parties who have received copies, or rights, from you under this License will not have their licenses terminated so long as such parties remain in full compliance.

The GNU GPL version 2 <http://www.gnu.org/licenses/gpl-2.0.html> See also Metxger and Jaeger, above n 9, 63 <http://www.campussource.de/org/opensource/docs/art10.pdf>.

[251] Gulbault and Daalen, above n 8, 99

and the communication to the public right.[252] The author may exploit some or all of his financial or economic rights.[253]

The exploitation of the economic rights should be made in accordance with art 13 of the *Copyright Law* in Jordan. It provides as follows:

> The author is free to dispose of his financial rights of his work, provided that the disposition is made *in writing* and specifies therein and in detail every right being disposed of by indicating its *range*, *purpose*, *period* and *place of exploitation*.[254]

The *Copyright Law* in Jordan does not differentiate clearly between a licence and assignment,[255] and there is no specific provision that deals with licences.[256] If art 13 only relates to assignment or transfer of rights, then the GNU GPL being a licence is not affected by art 13. If art 13 covers assignment or transfer of rights and licences, then the GNU GPL will have to satisfy art 13 of the *Copyright Law* in Jordan.

The GNU GPL does not mention the geographic extent and the duration for which the licence is granted. This may be considered to not be in accordance with a mandatory rule of copyright that is available to protect authors and may result in a court holding the GNU GPL as null and void under the Jordanian law.[257] It is

---

[252] Article 9 of the *Copyright Law* in Jordan provides:

> The author shall have the right to financially exploit his work in any way he chooses. No other person may exercise this right without his written permission, or the permission of his successors. This right shall include:
>
> A. The right to print broadcast and produce his work.
>
> B. The right to reproduce his work through all physical means such as photography, cinematography or recording.
>
> C. The right to translate his work into another language, adapt it, orchestrate it, or make any alteration thereto.
>
> D. The right to allow usage of one or more copies of his work by persons using them for rental, lending or other actions related to displaying the work to the public.
>
> E. The right to convey his work to the public through recital, display, acting, radio or television broadcasting, cinema or through any other means.
>
> F. The right to convey his work to the public through recital, display, acting, radio or television broadcasting, cinema or through any other means.

Copyright Law, above n 170, art 9.

[253] If any person exploits these rights without the author's permission, this will be considered as an infringement; see *Copyright Law*, above n 170, arts 49-55.

[254] *Copyright Law*, above n 170, art 28.

[255] Assignment encompasses the transfer of rights held by one party—the assignor—to another party—the assignee. See also Upex, R. V. et al., *Davies on Contracts* (Sweet & Maxwell, 2008) 209–222.

[256] *Copyright Law*, above n 170, art 11 and 34.

[257] The Civil law system differentiates between two kinds of rules, *default and mandatory rules*. Whereas the *default rules* can be modified by agreement of the parties, *mandatory rules* cannot be modified by the parties, and in case of the parties agreeing to do so, the contract shall be considered

useful in this context to compare the situation in Jordan with other countries that apply the same Continental European legal system of 'author's rights' and have similar provisions in relation to the exploitation of economic rights.

Article 149 of the *Intellectual Property Code No 82 of 2002* in Egypt[258] provides as follows:

> The author shall have the right to transfer to a third party all or some of his economic rights stated in this Law. Such a transfer shall be certified in writing and contain an explicit and detailed indication of each right to be transferred with the extent and purpose of transfer and the duration and place of exploitation.[259]

Professor Makeen Makeen commented on art 149 as follows:

> [A]rticle] 149(3) of the IP Code employs the term "authorisation to exploit", i.e. licence, in a provision that deals with assignment, it could be inferred that the legislature decided to use "assignment" and "licence" interchangeably. Accordingly, all the principles which govern assignments are applicable *mutatis mutandis* to licensing.[260]

---

null and void. Article 163 of the *Jordanian Civil Code* gives a non-conclusive list of matters that are considered as public order that parties entering into a contract cannot be in contrast with. Article 163 of the *Jordanian Civil Code* provides:

> 1. The subject matter shall be a matter to which the provisions of the contract can be applied
> 2. And if the legislator prohibits dealings in a thing or if it shall be contrary to public orders or morals the contract shall be void.
> 3. The provisions relating to personal status like capacity and succession and the provisions relating to transfer, the procedures prescribed for disposition of the property of al waqaf and immovable property, the disposition of property of an interdicted person, al-waqaf property and the property of the State, the legislation relation the obligatory fixing or prices and all legislation enacted to cope with the needs of consumers in exceptional circumstances, shall be considered matters of public order.

Jordanian Civil Code, above n 145, art 163. Unfortunately, the copyright law in Jordan does not clearly delineate between mandatory and default rules. Courts should look to the language of the relevant provisions in determining what rules are mandatory. See Makeen, above n 237; Cem Kaner, *Law of Software Contracting: New Rules Coming* (July 2007) <http://www.kaner.com/pdfs/Law%20of%20Software%20Contracting.pdf>; Cardona, above n 12, 73.

[258] See also art 37 of the repealed *Copyright Law No. 354 of 1954* in Egypt (in Arabic) <http://upload.wikimedia.org/wikipedia/commons/e/e8/Egyptian_Copyright_Law_354_of_1954.pdf>.

[259] Article 149 of *Intellectual Property Law* No. 82 of 2002 in Egypt. Article 150 of the same law provides:

> The author shall be entitled to such remuneration, in cash or in kind, as he considers fair for the transfer of one or more of the economic rights of his work to a third party, on the basis of a percentage of the revenue made as a result of exploitation, a lump sum or a combination of both.

See *Law No. 82 of 2002* (*Law on the Protection of Intellectual Property Rights*), Al-Jarida Al-Rasmiyya, 3 June 2002, (Egypt) <http://www.wipo.int/wipolex/en/text.jsp?file_id=126540>; see also *Egypt*, WIPO <http://www.wipo.int/wipolex/en/details.jsp?id=7296>.

[260] Makeen, above n 237, 577.

Article 9 of the *Federal Law No 7 of the Year 2002 Concerning Copyright and Neighbouring Rights* as amened in the United Arab Emirates (*UAE Copyright Law*) provides as follows:

> The author or his successors can transfer to a natural or legal third party, all or part of his economic rights stipulated in this law provided that such action be in writing specifying the object of the right to be exploited along with the purpose, the duration and place of exploitation. The author is the owner of all the rights except what he disposes openly.

The commentator Peter Hansen was of the opinion that art 9 of the *UAE Copyright Law* is applicable to both assignments and licences. He criticised the approach of the *UAE Copyright Law* for not clearly differentiating between the two:

> Putting assignment and licences together as if they were the same has the potential for mischief. What is required to regulate one does not necessarily apply to the other and vice versa... Assignments are once-and-for-all disposals of rights. Licences are generally, but not always, limited by time and can be given to many different persons at the same time (non-exclusivity). They may be so limited in what they grant that they are little more than a contractual permission to do something that the licensee could not do otherwise. Other licences give the licensees such extensive rights that it is as if it were an assignment.... In any case, assignments and licences are different creatures and the language and concepts used to speak about them are distinct. Whether it is more correct to speak of the *grant* of rights or the *transfer* of rights in relation to licenses may be only a matter of terminology, but in this context, a linguistic distinction needs to be maintained between the rights that are contractually granted and expire in time and rights that are transferred and disposed of once-and-for-all.[261]

Professor Nouri Khater argues that using the term ‘transfer of rights’ in art 9 of the *UAE Copyright Law* is inaccurate and that it is more accurate to use assignment (‘cession’ in French). He defines an assignment as a waiver of one of the economic rights of the author to reproduce, perform, or make derivative works or any other kind of exploitation that is appropriate to the kind of work.[262]

Article L131-3 of the *French Intellectual Property Code* states that:

> Assignments of copyright are subject to the condition that each of the rights transferred is clearly detailed in the assignment contract and that the scope for exploiting the assigned rights is determined in terms of its extent, destination and duration.[263]

---

[261] Hansen, above n 236, 229.

[262] Nouri Khater, *Explanation of Intellectual Property Rules—Copyright and Neighbouring Rights* (Emirates University, 2008) 307. See Al Sanhouri, above n 157, vol 8, 383-390.

[263] *The French Intellectual Property Code* (Code de la propriété intellectuelle) (France), art 131-3. In another translation provided by Legi France, art 131-3 of the Intellectual Property Law provides:

> Transfer of authors’ rights shall be subject to each of the assigned rights being separately mentioned in the instrument of assignment and the field of exploitation of the assigned rights being defined as to its scope and purpose, as to place and as to duration.

See Code de la Propriété Intellectuelle [C.P.I.] L131-3 (France) http://www.legifrance.gouv.fr/html/codes_traduits/cpialtext.htm (*French Intellectual Property Code* No. 92-597 of 1 July 1992 as amended).

On 13 December 2006, the Paris Court of Appeal held in a case concerning computer software that any assignment of copyright is subject to the requirements in art L131-3 of the *French Intellectual Property Code*, which will apply to all assignments of copyright, and parties must state clearly the terms and scope of the assignment—particularly in relation to duration and territorial limitations.[264] In reading the English translation of the case, there does not seem to be a confusion as to whether a software licence (authorisation) or an assignment of licence is involved.

In the case of *Herald Welte v D Detshland GmbH*, the Munich Court did not find that the GNU GPL contravened art 31 of the *German Copyright Law* (referred to as 'Urhebergesetz or Urheberrechtsgesetz').[265] The Court also did not find that GNU GPL constitutes a waiver of the *German Copyright Law*.[266] It noted that:

> [T]o begin with, the Panel shares the view that one cannot perceive the conditions of the GPL (General Public License) as containing a waiver of copyright and related legal positions. On the contrary, the users avail themselves of the conditions of copyright law in order to secure and carry into effect their concept of the further development and dissemination of software.[267]

It is submitted that the aim of art 13 of the *Copyright Law* in Jordan is to protect authors who want to conclude agreements to exploit their economic rights. Any agreement to transfer economic rights should observe various requirements (written, purpose, range and period). The GNU GPL should be treated as a licence

---

[264] Julie Ruelle, *French Court Holds that any Assignment of Copyright Must be Clearly Set Out its Scope and Terms* (17 December 2007) Bird & Bird <http://www.twobirds.com/English/News/Articles/Pages/2007/French_court_assignment_copyright_set_terms.aspx>.

[265] Article 31(1) of the *Copyright Law* as amended in Germany provides:

> The author may grant a right to another to use the work in a particular manner or in any manner (exploitation right). An exploitation right may be granted as a non-exclusive right or as an exclusive right and maybe limited geographically, temporarily or with regard to content.

The German Author's Rights as amended (amendments dated 27 October 2009), art 31 (1) <http://www.transpatent.com/gesetze/urhg.html>. See also the Munich Open Source Software Case, above n 149; Tim Engelhardt, 'Free and Open Software—Under German Law' in Brande, Coughlan and Jaeger, above n 204.

[266] In the Frankfurt Open Source Software Case, the Court found the GNU GPL does not constitute a waiver of the *Copyright Law* in Germany. The court noted that:

> In particular, the conditions of the GPL can in no case be interpreted to contain a waiver of legal positions afforded by copyright law. The GPL precisely stipulates that the freedom to use, modify and distribute the corresponding software initially afforded by way of a grant of a non-exclusive license to everyone is automatically terminated upon a violation of the GPL (cf. Dreier/Schulze, § 69a, Rz.11).

Frankfurt Case, above n 149.

[267] Munich Case, above n 149.

Table 6.3 The conformity of the GNU GPL to the assignment requirements under the *Copyright Law* in Jordan

Assignment requirements under art 13 of the *Copyright Law* in Jordan	How the GNU GPL satisfies the assignment requirements under the *Copyright Law* in Jordan
Written requirement	The GNU GPL is written and requires programmers to attach a copyright notice whenever they copy and distribute new programs
Range (scope of rights)	The kinds of rights that are given by the author are explicitly stated in the GNU GPL
Purpose (cause)	The purpose of the GNU GPL is to guarantee that the licensed source code remains open for other programmers to access, use, and modify the source code and that the modified source code is made available to other programmers under the GNU GPL. This is a lawful purpose and is not contrary to public order or moral in accordance with art 165 and 166 of the *Jordanian Civil Code*[268]
Period (duration of rights)	The licence is 'perpetual', that is, for the full duration of the copyright protection (i.e., 50 years in the Jordanian law). This is so even though the licence itself does not explicitly mention any duration[269]. The licence is to be considered to be perpetual in order to give maximum implementation to the purpose of the GNU GPL (i.e., the period is to be the maximum duration possible under the *Copyright Law* in Jordan)
Place (geographical scope)	Because of the borderless nature of the Internet, the scope of the licence is global. This means that the licence operates in all countries around the world wherever the open source software may be used by programmers

under the *Copyright Law* in Jordan and not as an assignment. This is because the GNU GPL does not require authors to relinquish their copyright, and there is no danger that they will lose their rights, as would be in the case of an assignment. If art

[268] Article 165 of the *Jordanian Civil Code* provides that:

1. The cause is the direct purpose intended in the contract.
2. And it shall be existent, valid, permissible and not contrary to public orders and morals.

Article 166 provides that

1. The contract shall not be valid unless it entails a lawful benefit for its parties.
2. And in contracts that lawful benefit shall be deemed to exist unless there is evidence to the contrary.

Jordanian Civil Code, above n 145, arts 165-166.

[269] Section 3 of the GNU GPL, version 3 provides that:

All rights granted under this License are granted for the term of copyright on the Program, and are irrevocable provided the stated conditions are met. This License explicitly affirms your unlimited permission to run the unmodified Program. The output from running a covered work is covered by this License only if the output, given its content, constitutes a covered work. This License acknowledges your rights of fair use or other equivalent, as provided by copyright law.

The GNU GPL version 3 <http://www.gnu.org/licenses/gpl.html>

13 applies to licences, then the GNU GPL can still satisfy art 13 of the *Copyright Law* in Jordan.

Table 6.3 explains in page 314 how the GNU GPL satisfies the assignment requirements for copyright under the *Copyright Law* in Jordan.

6.2.7.3 Moral Rights under the GNU GPL

In addition to economic rights, copyright law also gives authors moral rights. Moral rights are given very high importance, especially in civil law countries such as Spain,[270] France,[271] the Netherlands,[272] and Germany[273] since authorship work is considered an extension of the author's personality.[274] According to art 8 of the *Copyright Law* in Jordan, authors are entitled to several moral rights, and these include the right of respect or paternity, the right of divulgation, the right of consideration, the right to object to derogatory treatment of work, and the right of retraction or withdrawal. Article 8 of the *Copyright Law* in Jordan provides as follows:

> A - The right to attribute to himself his work and to have his name listed on all produced copies every time the work is put forward to the public, unless the work is mentioned incidentally during a news representation of the current events.
> B- The right to make the decision regarding the publication of his work and the specification of the mode and date of publication;
> C-The right to make any amendments to his work whether by change, revision, deletion or addition;
> D- The right to repel any attack on his work, to prohibit any distortion, misrepresentation, or any other amendments to the work which may harm his reputation and honour. However, if any deletion, change, addition or other amendments took place in the translation of the work, the author shall not have the right to prevent it unless the translator neglected to refer to the places of this change, or if the translation caused damage to the reputation of the author and his cultural or artistic standing or distorted the contents of the work; and
> E-The right to withdraw his work from circulation in case serious and legitimate reasons existed for this withdrawal. In such case the author shall be obliged to fairly compensate the holder of the financial exploitation rights.[275]

The perpetuity and inalienability of moral rights is unclear under the *Copyright Law*, although this is settled in other laws, including the *French Intellectual*

[270] Ruben Iglesias Posse, 'The Legal Status of Copyleft Before the Spanish Courts' (2009) 4 (11) *Journal of Intellectual Property and Practice* 815, 824.

[271] See the situation in France, Julien Dufay and Xavier Pican, 'The Erosion of the Moral Right: Comparison France-United States' (2004) 4 *International Business Law Journal* 461-488.

[272] Gulbault and Daalen, above n 8, 122-128.

[273] Metxger and Jaeger, above n 9, 64.

[274] Silke Von Lewinski, *International Copyright Law and Policy* (Oxford University, 2008) 47-48.

[275] *Copyright Law*, above n 170, art 8.

Property Code.[276] The GNU GPL is based on an Anglo-American approach to copyright and licensing that does not give very much importance to moral rights[277] and only grants them in limited situations.[278] The question here is to what extent the GNU GPL satisfies the mandatory rules of moral rights in civil legal system.

The limited mention of moral rights in the GNU GPL[279] has not been a major concern to several scholars and commentators from European countries who argue

---

[276] Article L121-1 of the *French Intellectual Property Code* provides that:

> An author shall enjoy the right to respect for his name, his authorship and his work. This right shall attach to his person. *It shall be perpetual, inalienable and imprescriptible*. It may be transmitted to mortis causa to the heirs of the author.

French Intellectual Property Code, above n 263, L121-1. See also Dufay and Pican, above n 271, 464. See also Posse, above n 270, 824.

In Mahkamat al-Tamiex [Taimez], *Court of Cassation*, Civil Division) No. 2648/2003, 11 November 2001, it was mentioned that according to arts 3, 8, and 9 of the *Copyright Law* in Jordan, moral rights are personal rights protected even after the death of the author. The new draft of the Copyright Law of 2010 in Jordan provides clearly in art 7 that moral rights are perpetual and inalienable.

[277] See also section 3 and 4 of the GNU GPL, version 3, provides that:

> 3. You may convey a work based on the Program, or the modifications to produce it from the Program, in the form of source code under the terms of section 4, provided that you also meet all of these conditions: a) The work must carry prominent notices stating that you modified it, and giving a relevant date.
>
> 4. Conveying Verbatim Copies. You may convey verbatim copies of the Program's source code as you receive it, in any medium, provided that you conspicuously and appropriately publish on each copy an appropriate copyright notice; keep intact all notices stating that this License and any non-permissive terms added in accord with section 7 apply to the code; keep intact all notices of the absence of any warranty; and give all recipients a copy of this License along with the Program.

The GNU GPL version 3 <http://www.gnu.org/licenses/gpl.html>. See also González, above n 24, 155.

[278] *The Visual Artists Rights Act of 1990* (VARA) in the US recognises moral rights only in visual art. <http://www.law.cornell.edu/uscode/17/usc_sec_17_00000106—A000-.html>.

[279] The Preamble of the GPL states:

> Also, for each author's protection and ours, we want to make certain that everyone understands that there is no warranty for this free software. If the software is modified by someone else and passed on, we want its recipients to know that what they have is not the original, so that any problems introduced by others will not reflect on the original authors' reputations.

See section 2 of the GPL that provides:

> 2. You may modify your copy or copies of the Program or any portion of it, thus forming a work based on the Program, and copy and distribute such modifications or work under the terms of Section 1 above, provided that you also meet all of these conditions:
>
> c) If the modified program normally reads commands interactively when run, you must cause it, when started running for such interactive use in the most ordinary way, to print or display an announcement including an appropriate copyright notice and a notice

that software developers should be given limited moral rights. This is because 'computer programs are considered as minor works of art that are primarily serving utility purposes and not artistic works that should be given full moral rights under the law'.[280] To this extent, *French Intellectual Property Code Law*, in art L121-7, provides that the right to control moral rights in relation to adaptation (within the limit of the rights that has been granted), reconsideration, and withdrawal are not available unless there is a stipulation to say otherwise.[281] In the UK, authors have no moral rights in respect of the computer programs that they create,[282] while in

---

> that there is no warranty (or else, saying that you provide a warranty) and that users may redistribute the program under these conditions, and telling the user how to view a copy of this License. ... Thus, it is not the intent of this section to claim rights or contest your rights to work written entirely by you; rather, the intent is to exercise the right to control the distribution of derivative or collective works based on the Program.

The GNU GPL version 2 <http://www.gnu.org/licenses/gpl-2.0.html> See also, Gulbault and Daalen, above n 8, 91-95, 125; Laurent, above n 140, ch 3, 38; Metxger and Jaeger, above n 9, 64.

[280] Metxger and Jaeger, above n 9, 64; Gulbault and Daalen, above n 8, 123.

[281] Article L121-7 of the *French Intellectual Property Code* provides:

> Except for any stipulation more favourable to the author, such author may not:
>
> 1. Oppose modification of the software by the assignee of the rights referred to in item 2 of Article L122-6 where such modification does not prejudice either his honour or his reputation;
> 2. Exercise his right to reconsider or of withdrawal.

Article L122-6 of the *French Intellectual Property Code* provides:

> Subject to the provisions of Article L122-6-1, the exploitation right belonging to the author of the software shall include the right to do or to authorize:
>
> 1. The permanent or temporary reproduction of software by any means and in any form, in part or in whole. Insofar as loading, displaying, running, transmission or storage of the software necessitate such reproduction, such acts shall be possible only with the authorization of the author;
> 2. The translation, adaptation, arrangement or any other alteration of software and the reproduction of the results thereof;
> 3. The placing on the market for consideration or gratuitously, including rental, of the software or of copies thereof by any process. However, the first sale of a copy of software on the territory of a Member State of the European Community or of a State party to the agreement on the European Economic Area by the author or with his consent shall exhaust the right of placing on the market of that copy in all Member States, with the exception of the right to authorize further rental of a copy.

French Intellectual Property Code, above n 263, L121-7, L122-6.

[282] Article 71 of the *Copyright, Design and Patent Act of 1988*, as amended, in the UK provides:

> (1) The right conferred by section 77 (right to be identified as author or director) is subject to the following exceptions. ...
>
> (2) The right does not apply in relation to the following descriptions of work
>
> (a) a computer program;
> (b) the design of a typeface;
> (c) any computer-generated work.

Germany, authors enjoy the full complement of moral rights in relation to computer programs.[283] In considering the relationship between the GNU GPL and moral rights, it can be said that at a general level the moral rights of diviguation, paternity, and integrity are not an issue. The author in the GNU GPL situation

1) Is always required to be attributed;
2) Has released his code to the public, removing any issue relating to divulgation; and
3) Anticipates reuse and modifications of the code by entering into the FOSS project, thereby significantly reducing the power to control reuse of their code (as noted, this is expressly covered in French law in relation to computer programs).

On this last point, it is important to note that lawyer Jill Applebaum argues that 'while French courts continue to reaffirm the notion that authors cannot explicitly waive their moral rights, they have shown that they are not hostile to the idea of implicit waiver'.[284] Professors Paul Goldstein and Bernt Hugenholtz agree, along with other scholars, with this analysis.[285] Professor Goldstein and Bernt Hugenholtz note:

Article 81 of the *Copyright, Design and Patent Act of 1988*, as amended, in the UK provides:

> (1) The right conferred by section 80 (right to object to derogatory treatment of work) is subject to the following exceptions. . . .
>
> (2) The right does not apply to a computer program or to any computer-generated work..

The *Copyright, Design and Patent Act of 1988* as amended (UK), art 71-81. <http://www.legislation.gov.uk/ukpga/1988/48/contents>

[283] J.A.L Sterling, *World Copyright Law* (Sweet and Maxwell, 2003) 350, 351.

[284] Jill Appelbaum gives the following example '.. if an author of a book authorizes a third party to adapt his work into a play, courts may find that he implicitly waived his integrity rights (such as a change in medium)'. See Jill R. Applebaum, 'The Visual Artists Rights Act of 1990: An Analysis Based on the French Droit Moral' (1992) 8 *American University Journal of International Law and Policy* 183, 189.

[285] Professor James M. Treece from the University of Texas notes:

> [T]he notion that the moral right is inalienable is riddled with exceptions: the courts consistently permit reasonable changes without the author's consent in collective works and in adaptations-where changes are necessary-and courts enforce express as opposed to tacit waivers of the moral right.

James M. Treece, 'American Law Analogues of the Author's "Moral Right" (1968) 16 (4) *The American Journal of Comparative Law* 487, 506. See also Russel J. DaSilva, 'Droit Moral and Amoral Copyright: A Comparsion of Artits' Rights in France and the United States' (1980) 28 *Bulletin of the Copyright Society* 1.

> Reviewing legislative exceptions to moral rights in the civil law countries, Adolf Dietz has concluded that they "only exemplify the concept that moral rights questions have always to be judged in their individual context and that correspondingly different solutions have to be found in different categories of works and manners of work uses." For example, while moral rights are in civil law deemed unwaivable and [non-transferable], it is generally accepted that a licence granted to adapt a work implies a degree of freedom to the adapter. Motion picture provide[s] a prominent example of how civil law countries extensively accommodate moral rights to the exigencies of the marketplace. These countries have carved out similarly broad exceptions for works, such as computer programs and architecture that occupy the borderland between literary or artistic property and industrial property.[286]

As the GNU GPL is silent on the right of withdrawal of the source code from circulation, it could be argued that it does not satisfy this particular moral right provided for in art 8(D) of the *Copyright Law* in Jordan. Professor Makeen Makken explains how this right works in practice in author's right systems (in this case the *Intellectual Property Law No. 82 of 2002* in Egypt):

> Although there is no case law relating to the right of withdrawal from circulation, the legislation is clear that the author cannot exercise the right without restraint. In order for this right to be exercised by the author, four requirements have to be satisfied. First, this right may only be used by the author if serious reasons dictate the withdrawal of the work. Secondly, the author must request that the competent court order such a withdrawal. Thirdly, the author must indemnify the assignee of any economic right beforehand for any harm such an order may cause. Fourthly, the indemnity, which must be in the form of financial compensation, must be payable within the period specified in the order; otherwise the order becomes void.[287]

At first impression, the exercise of this right requires both court approval and compensation, and on this basis one would not expect that it would create a major obstacle for the operation of the GNU GPL (and in French law, this is expressly stated to not apply to computer programs).[288] In relation to the right of reconsideration, it either has a temporal limitation expiring on publication[289] or is subject to the same limitations as the right of withdrawal and should not be a present problem in relation to the GNU GPL.[290] It is interesting to note that the German courts (in a jurisdiction where moral rights are strictly applied to computer programs)[291] have had no difficulty in upholding the legal validity of the GNU GPL in relation to moral rights.[292] Table 6.4 explains in pages 320 and 321 how the GNU GPL operates in the context of the moral rights requirements under the *Copyright Law* in Jordan.

---

[286] Paul Goldstein and Bernt Hugenholtz, *International Copyright: Principles, Law and Practice* (Oxford University, 2010) 356-357 (quoting "le Petit Prince," Court of Cassation, 12 June, 2001, 191 R.I.D.A 266 (2002), noting that a contract allowing animated film adaptation of Saint-Exupery work, the Little Prince, implies "a degree of freedom afforded to the adapter", moral right notwithstanding)).

[287] See Makeen F. Makeen, 'Moral Rights Protection under Egyptian Author's Rights Law' (2007) 83 (1) *International Review of Intellectual Property and Competition Law* 51, 63.

[288] *French Intellectual Property Code*, above n 263, art L121-7; art L122-6.

[289] Nowaf Kanan, *Copyright Law* (in Arabic) (2004) 110.

[290] Sterling, above n 283, 351.

[291] Ibid.

[292] Munich Case, above n 149; Frankfurt Case, above n 149.

Table 6.4 The conformity of the GNU GPL to the moral requirements under the *Copyright Law* in Jordan

Moral Rights Requirements under Art 8 of the *Copyright Law* in Jordan	How the GNU GPL Operates in the Context of the Moral Rights Requirements under the *Copyright Law* in Jordan
The right of respect and paternity	The author must always be attributed. The GNU GPL requires every licensor and contributor to FOSS projects to provide their name and give details about their program[293]
The right of divulgation	The software developers agree to publish their work and make it available to other developers and have exercised their right of divulgation
The right of integrity	Firstly, the licence does not purport to override the right of integrity and could be read in such a way that it operates subjects to the right of integrity.[294] However, as the authors voluntarily agree to allow their code to be reused and modified by others, it could be argued that the right of integrity must be interpreted in the context of the licence. This is expressly provided for in art 121–7 of the *French Intellectual Property Code*, which makes the right of integrity inapplicable in cases where the author has allowed modifications of the software[295]
The right of reconsideration and the right of withdrawal	The right of withdrawal most likely includes the right of amendment to the work. The GNU GPL does not purport to override this moral right. Authors cannot exercise their right of withdrawal without having serious reasons that dictate the withdrawal of their work. The authors also

(continued)

6.2.8 The Enforceability of the GNU GPL in International and Local Courts

The legal validity and enforceability of open content licences in courts are important for software developers who are using such licences on a daily basis and want

[293] The GNU GPL provides in the end of its terms that:

If you develop a new program, and you want it to be of the greatest possible use to the public, the best way to achieve this is to make it free software which everyone can redistribute and change under these terms.

To do so, attach the following notices to the program. It is safest to attach them to the start of each source file to most effectively convey the exclusion of warranty; and each file should have at least the 'copyright' line and a pointer to where the full notice is found.

one line to give the program's name and an idea of what it does.

Copyright (C) *yyyy* name *of author.*

The GNU GPL version 2 <http://www.gnu.org/licenses/gpl-2.0.html>.

[294] It should be noted that not every reuse and modification of code will amount to a breach of the right of integrity.

[295] *French Intellectual Property Code*, above n 263, art L121-7, art L122-6. See also Goldstein and Hugenholtz, above n 286; Appelbaum, above n 284; Treece, above n 285; Sterling, above n 283.

Table 6.4 (continued)

Moral Rights Requirements under Art 8 of the *Copyright Law* in Jordan	How the GNU GPL Operates in the Context of the Moral Rights Requirements under the *Copyright Law* in Jordan
	need to request the competent court to order the withdrawal of their work, and they need to compensate the affected third parties. This should not be an obstacle for FOSS projects because in the Internet context, the court would be unlikely to act except in extreme circumstances, and if they did, there is a requirement that affected third parties be compensated. This is also expressly confirmed in French Law in art 121–7 of the *French Intellectual Property Code*, which makes these rights inapplicable in relation to software[296]

to be assured of their operation in practice. The failure to comply with the source code distribution and abide by terms and conditions of the GNU GPL may result in a dispute before the competent court that ultimately has to determine the legality and enforceability of the licence under the law. The numbers of disputes that reach the court are considered relatively low compared to private, out-of-court settlements that take place quite regularly.[297] In most cases, there is no need to resort to judicial proceedings as it will be enough to request the licensee to comply with the obligations of the GNU GPL.[298] This certainly does not happen on all occasions, and they may be required to take legal action against certain violators of

[296] *French Intellectual Property Code*, above n 263, art L121-7, art L122-6.

[297] The Software Freedom Law Centre (SFLC) in the US and the GPLviolations.org Organisation in Europe both developed their own procedures to deal with violations of the GNU GPL that are brought to their attention. Usually, they would contact the licensee and request him to come 'into compliance with the GNU GPL terms and conditions or alternatively, cease copying, modifying or distributing the GNU GPL software'. See SFLC <http://www.softwarefreedom.org/>; Gpl-violations.org, *Project Prevails in Court Case on GPL Violation by D-Link* <http://gpl-violations.org/news/20060922-dlink-judgement_frankfurt.html>; Till Jaeger, 'Enforcement of the GNU GPL in Germany and Europe' (2010) 1 *Journal of Intellectual Property, Information Technology and E-Commerce Law* 34, 37; James G. Gatto, 'Doubts Wane over GPL Enforceability' (2007) *Managing Intellectual Property* <http://www.pillsburylaw.com/siteFiles/Publications/A9A22185D029BBE6EAA4332F1A7249E2.pdf>; Bradely M. Kuhn, Aeron Williamson and Karen M. Sandler, *A Practical Guide to GPL Compliance* (2008) <http://www.softwarefreedom.org/resources/2008/compliance-guide.html>.

[298] Moglen, above n 73, 7; O'Sullivan, above n 28; Eben Moglen, *Enforcing the GPL* (2001) Linux for Devices <http://www.linuxfordevices.com/c/a/Linux-For-Devices-Articles/Guest-editorial-Enforcing-the-GNU-GPL/>; Katz, above n 70, 19.

the terms and conditions of the licence. This section examines the enforcement of the GNU GPL in international courts, and then in Jordanian courts.

6.2.8.1 The Enforcement of the GNU GPL in International Courts

Europe has witnessed several judicial decisions on open content licences and particularly the GNU GPL.[299] The German courts were the first in issuing judgements that discuss the legal validity and the enforceability of such licences,[300] the non-compliance with the terms of the licence,[301] and the payment of damages for violation.[302] There are also a number of other cases that were heard in Germany[303] and France.[304]

Unlike the situation in Europe, most of the cases that have been filed in the US on the GNU GPL are between private companies and rival business competitors

---

[299] Posse, above n 270, 816.

[300] On 19 May 2004, a Munich District Court granted a preliminarily injunction against the defendant, Sitecom Deutschland GMbH, for using an open source software in one of its wireless products without complying with certain notice requirements of the GNU GPL. The Court of Appeals agreed with the findings of the Court of First Instance and ruled that the defendant was in violation of the GNU GPL conditions and that this constituted a copyright infringement. See the Munich Case, above n 149; Gatto, above n 297.

[301] Another case was brought before the Munich District Court in 2005. The plaintiff, Welte, filed a case against Forntient, alleging that the defendant 'was using Linux in its own code without releasing modification under the GPL'. The case was settled out of court when Forntient complied with its obligations under the licence. See Guadamuz, above n 28, 386.

[302] In September 2006, the Frankfurt District Court ordered the defendant, D-link, to pay damages (out-of-court enforcement expenses and legal fees) to Welte's GPL-violations.org project, which they incurred for bringing the defendant into compliance with the terms and conditions of the GNU GPL. The Court confirmed that the GNU GPL is valid under German law and, for the first time, ordered the payment of damages in such a dispute. See the Frankfurt Case, above n 149; Gatto, above n 297.

[303] Harald Welte also brought another case before the First Regional Court in Munich against Luxembourg-based Skype Technologies, alleging that they failed to provide the source code royalty-free and attach the text of the GNU GPL licence. The Court issued its decision on July 2007 in favour of the plaintiff and ordered the defendant to comply with its obligations under the licence. See Groklaw, *GPL Upheld in Germany Again—Translation* <http://www.groklaw.net/articlebasic.php?story=2007072513105421>.

[304] In France, the Association pour la Formation Professionnelle des Adultes (AFPA) filed a suit against Edu4 in 2002 for violation of the 'copyleft' clause. The Paris Court of Appeals examined the GNU GPL as a preliminary question and decided in September 2009 that the defendant violated the terms and conditions of the GNU GPL when he denied users access to its corresponding source code. The French legal system allowed a user of the GNU GPL to file this case as he was granted rights from the author who allowed him to do so. See, Opendot Blogspot, *Big Win for GNU GPL in France* (2009) <http://opendotdotdot.blogspot.com/2009/09/big-win-for-gnu-gpl-in-france.html>; Ryan Paul, *Big GPL Copyright Enforcement win in Paris Court of Appeals* (24 September 2009) Ars Technica <http://arstechnica.com/open-source/news/2009/09/big-gpl-copyright-enforcement-win-in-paris-court-of-appeals.ars>; Jaeger, above n 297, 37, para.1.

working in open source software.[305] There are also limited numbers of cases that have been filed by the FSF as compared to the number of cases that were brought by the GPL violations organisation in Europe.[306] One of the first most important cases in the US was considered on 13 August 2008. Robert Jacobsen filed against Matthew Katzer and Kamind Associates Inc[307] for not abiding by the terms and conditions of the Artistic Licence (an open source software licence). *The Court of Appeals for the Federal Circuit*, for the first time, examined the enforceability of the artistic licence and found that it is legally valid under the law.[308] The court also considered, by analogy, the nature and scope of CC licences.[309]

[305] In 2002, MYSQL brought a suit before the United Stated District Court against Progress Nusphere for not distributing a database linked to their product, which was under the GNU GPL. In that case, the Court treated the GNU GPL as an enforceable and binding licence but refused to issue the injunction requested by the plaintiff. The case was eventually settled out of court. In 2005, the US District Court for Indiana considered the legality of the GNU GPL in *Wallace v Free Software Foundation Inc*. It decided that 'the GPL is a vertical agreement (meaning it is an agreement among different levels of users within the same chain of distribution) and, as such, cannot alone form the basis of a per se violation of U.S antitrust laws'. See Gatto, above n 297. See also, Planetary Motion, Inc. V. Techsplosion, Inc, where the court decided that "the GNU GPL is not necessarily ceded to the public domain and the licensor purports to retain ownership rights ...' 261 F 3d 1188, 1198 (11th circuit). See also Guadamuz, above n 28, 385; Jonathan Zittrain, Isaac Lidsky, Dotan Oliar and Bekhzod Abdurazzakov, *Alternatives to Intellectual Property* (2006) <http://cyber.law.harvard.edu/ilaw/mexico_2006_module_2_alttoip> (on file with author).

[306] On 11 December 2008, FSF filed a case against Cisco Systems Inc. for copyright infringement because it distributed programs under the GPL and LGPL without respecting the obligations of those licences. FSF later withdrew the case as both parties reached a settlement agreement under which Cisco Systems would establish a compliance department that would work closely with the FSF to achieve full compliance with the terms and conditions of the GNU GPL. See Wegbrait, above n 95, 22-23; Guadamuz, above n 28, 387.

[307] 2008 U.S. App. LEXIS 17161 (Fed. Cir. 2008).

[308] Fitzgerald and Olwan, above n 36.

[309] The Appeals Court noted that:

> Public licenses, often referred to as open source licenses, are used by artists, authors, educators, software developers, and scientists who wish to create collaborative projects and to dedicate certain works to the public. Several types of public licenses have been designed to provide creators of copyrighted materials a means to protect and control their copyrights. Creative Commons, one of the amicicuriae, provides free copyright licenses to allow parties to dedicate their works to the public or to license certain uses of their works while keeping some rights reserved.

See *Jacobsen v. Katzer* 2008 U.S. App. LEXIS 17161 (Fed. Cir. 2008) 3.

6.2.8.2 The Enforcement of the GNU GPL in Local Jordanian Courts

After this brief overview of the cases that have been brought internationally, it is important to ask whether these decisions could have any particular significance outside the jurisdictions where they were issued, particularly in Jordanian courts.

The legal discussion over the legality of the GNU GPL that has taken place in international courts would not necessarily take place in the same manner in local Jordanian courts.[310] Copyright laws are considered territorial in their nature. This means that they are regulated under local laws and only in limited situations on a regional basis.[311] There is no obligation on any Jordanian court to enforce a foreign judgement, unless there is a bilateral or multilateral treaty[312] between Jordan and another country to that effect. In civil law countries, precedents are not important as judges are not guided principally by the decisions, even from a higher court, but by the law itself. The Jordanian courts will not enforce a precedent from another country, even those from a civil law country. It may rely on similar precedents from a Jordanian court for guidance only but does not have to follow them in its decisions.[313]

The American lawyer James G. Gattos argues that 'doubts about the GPL enforcement ability will continue to wane'.[314] He believes this is happening especially because of the increase in the number of international lawsuits involving the GNU GPL that are gradually obviating the questions about its validity and enforceability.[315] It is noted that even with the increase in the number of foreign decisions that validate and enforce open content licences, these are not applicable outside the countries in which they were made. Jordan is one of those civil law countries that are yet to explore the legality and enforceability of open source software licences.

Until a specific decision is issued in the country on the legality of open source software licences, Jordanian scholars should be familiar with the legal issues associated with the use of open content licences and the international cases that have been decided on the subject. They should write frequently on those issues in

---

310 For example, the discussion as to whether to treat the GNU GPL as a contract or as a bare licence would not play a major role under the civil legal system in Jordan. This is because the law in Jordan does not recognise bare licences but only contracts, which should be in accordance with arts 34-241 of the *Jordanian Civil Code*.

311 WIPO, *WIPO Forum on Private International Law and Standard Policy* (29 January 2001) <http://www.wipo.int/edocs/mdocs/mdocs/en/wipo_pil_01/wipo_pil_01_9.pdf>.

312 The Jordanian Constitution does not have a specific provision that deals with the relationship between an international treaty and domestic law, but Jordanian courts have ruled in some cases that treaties should be given more weight in case a conflict arises between an international treaty and domestic law. See, for further explanation, Fayad Al Qudah, 'The Legal Protection of Databases: A Study of the Jordanian Law' (2008) 22 *Arab Law Quarterly* 359, 365.

313 Opendot Blogspot, above n 304.

314 Gatto, above n 297.

315 Ibid.

prominent Arabic and international legal journals to raise the importance of the subject and provide judges with sufficient jurisprudence that they could rely on to make proper judgements in the future.

From the perspective of the *Copyright Law* in Jordan, Sect. 6.2.7 considered several important copyright issues, mainly authorship in collaborative projects, validity of exploitation rights, and moral rights. Several European courts have found that the GNU GPL is enforceable, even under a civil legal system. This might provide some kind of minimal guidance to other international courts that are yet to decide on the legality of open content licences, including the GNU GPL.

6.2.9 Final Remarks on FOSS and Developing Countries

FOSS is open for anyone to study, change, and improve in accordance with the certain conditions stipulated by its licensors. FOSS is known in many developing countries[316] and emerging economies as it represents a real opportunity to develop an innovation-oriented, home-grown IT technology[317] that suits local and developmental needs.

The role of governments is critically important for the flourishing of FOSS in developing countries.[318] This is because they constitute the largest ICT users and set the economic and regulatory boundaries that allow FOSS businesses to flourish.[319] Governments spend millions of dollars using ICT, and they can be a test bed for innovation. In the Internet era and web 2.0, governments in developing countries need to do all in their power to cultivate innovation.[320]

Developing countries should develop and implement concrete FOSS policies, with clearly defined objectives[321] to spread the adoption of FOSS and spur the interest of people. Particularly, they should have appropriate competition laws, offer incentives and tax exemptions for local corporations providing FOSS services, and finally, ensure that the educational curriculum in universities includes FOSS alongside proprietary software.[322] The implementation of these policies, with others, would increase the popularity and adoption of FOSS in developing countries, which is needed to spur innovation and development.

---

[316] For example, in Jordan there is currently a small but growing group of Linux and open source software users. See Robin 'Roblimo' Mille, *Advocating Linux and Open Source in Amman, Jordan* (24 December 2002) Linux <http://archive09.linux.com/feature/27045>.

[317] Ibid.

[318] Rizk and Shaver, above n 81, 168

[319] CIBESA, *FOSS Incorporation in African ICT Development: Should it be a Government Initiative or Simply Market-Driven?* <http://www.cipesa.org/african_voices/155>.

[320] Cutler & Company, above n 99.

[321] Ibid.

[322] Rizk and Shaver, above n 81, 168.

6.3 Creative Commons

CC is a relatively new movement that has gained wide international attention and acclaim in the last few years. This is evidenced by the large number of digital works that are licensed under its copyright licensing systems and the use of its licences by large businesses and various organisations, including Flickr,[323] Google,[324] Massachusetts Institute of Technology Open Courseware (MIT Open Courseware),[325] Public Library of Science,[326] Wikipedia,[327] Aljazeera,[328] and the Obama administration in the White House.[329]

This section is divided into three parts. Sects. 6.3.1 and 6.3.2 give an overview of the CC movement, discussing its history, its philosophy, and the criticism addressed to it. Sect. 6.3.3 considers how CC can act as a path for social and economic development in developing countries, and Sect. 6.3.4 examines the importance of CC for research and education in developing countries. Sects. 6.3.5 and 6.3.6 examine the adoption of CC in Arab countries, and Sect. 6.3.7 considers some of the challenges and the legal issues for the adoption of CC in developing countries. Finally, Sect. 6.3.8 provides final remarks on CC and developing countries.

6.3.1 The History and Philosophy of Creative Commons

In 2001, after the passage of the *Digital Millennium Copy Right Act* (DMCA), a group of American cyber law and IP experts established a Massachusetts non-profit organisation named CC,[330] headquartered in San Francisco.[331] They developed a set

---

[323] See Flickr <http://www.flickr.com/>.

[324] See Google <http://www.google.com.au/ig?hl=en>.

[325] See MIT <http://ocw.mit.edu/index.htm>.

[326] See Public Library of Science <http://www.plos.org/>.

[327] See Wikipedia <http://www.wikipedia.org/>.

[328] See Aljazeera <http://cc.aljazeera.net/>.

[329] See the White House <http://www.whitehouse.gov/>.

[330] They believed that the DMCA had gone too far in protecting the commercial interests of copyright owners on the account of the public interests. See Terry Flew, 'Creative Commons and Creative Industries' 2005 *Media and Arts Law Review 10* (4), 257-264 <http://eprints.qut.edu.au/39367/>; Maureen O'Sullivan, 'Creative Commons and Contemporary Copyright: A Fitting Shoe or "a load of old Cobblers?' (2008) *First Monday* 13 (1) <http://firstmonday.org/htbin/cgiwrap/bin/ojs/index.php/fm/article/viewArticle/2087/1919>.

[331] See Flew, above n 330, 10; Bas Bloemsaat and Pieter Kleve, 'Creative Commons: A Business Model for Products Nobody Wants to Buy' (2009) 23 (3) *International Review of Law, Computers and Technology* 237-249; Severine Dusollier, 'The Master's Tolls v. The Master's House: Creative Commons vs. Copyright' (2006) 29 (3) *Columbia Journal of Law and Arts* 271-293; Arianna Enjung Cha, *Creative Commons is Rewriting Rules of Copyright*, Washington Post

of 'some rights reserved' copyright licences to be used over the Internet to increase the amount of creative materials available over the Internet[332] and reduce the restrictions and costs associated with copyright licensing.[333] Although Professor Lawrence Lessig envisaged that CC would offer practical solutions[334] to combat the international trend toward restrictive copyright laws,[335] he was clear in acknowledging that CC would not create the necessary change immediately but would eventually lead to more general reform in the copyright field.[336] How exactly will this take place and when this will take place are not specified by CC.

The licences were developed by CC to be used for all kinds of works, but they are particularly useful in the digital environment (websites, music, film, photographs, etc.) where technologies made it easy for anyone to digitise materials and publish online speedily. These licences are constituted of the legal code, the human code, and the digital code.[337] The first set of CC licences was

---

(online), 15 March 2005 <http://www.washingtonpost.com/wp-dyn/articles/A35297-2005Mar14.html>; Adrenne K. Goss, 'Codifying A Commons: Copyright, Copyleft, and the Creative Commons Project' (2007) 82 (2) *Chicago Kent Law Review* <http://www.cklawreview.com/wp-content/uploads/vol82no2/Goss.pdf>; Noric Dilanchian, *Creative Commons Licences are Useful but Oversold* (2 January 2008) Dlanchain Lawyers and Consultants <http://www.dilanchian.com.au/index.php?option=com_content&view=article&id=233:creative-commons-licences-are-useful-but-oversold&catid=5:ip-tech-a-e-biz&Itemid=144>; David Mathison, *Be the Media, How to Create and Accelerate Your Message, Your Way* (Natural E Creative, 2009) 427-441.

[332] The offering of CC of various licences for the public for free was inspired by earlier initiatives such as FSF's Foundation's GNU GPL developed by Richard Stallman. See Creative Commons, *History of Creative Commons* <http://creativecommons.org/about/history/>.

[333] Flew, above n 330.

[334] By establishing CC, he was aiming 'to build a layer of reasonable, flexible copyright in the face of increasingly restrictive default rules'. This was to support 'a rich public domain' by offering creators and other holders of copyright free and easy-to-use legal and technical tools that would help them publish and distribute their works over the Internet. See, for explanation of Creative Commons, Lawrence Lessig, *The Future of Ideas, the Fate of Commons in a Connected World* (Random House; 2001); Lawrence Lessig, *Free Culture: How Big Media Uses Technology to Lock Down Culture and Control Creativity* (Penguin, 2004) See also Ben Adidda, *Creative Commons Announced* (16 May 2002) <http://creativecommons.org/press-releases/entry/3421>.

[335] Professor Lawrence Lessig, the founder of CC, was of the opinion, in a number of influential books he published, that the Internet should remain open and innovative, and to do that, we should not place laws, particularly IP laws (copyright), that restrict the freedom of Internet users to access and use creative works. See Lessig (2004), above n 334.

[336] Stephanie Woods, *Creative Commons –A Useful Development in the New Zealand Copyright Sphere?* (2008) 14 (1) *Canterbury Law Review* 31, 52.

[337] The first is a legal document that is mostly useful for lawyers as it contains detailed legal provisions explaining the rights and obligations of the original creators of the work and users. The human readable version is a simple document that is written for non-lawyers (laymen) who cannot understand the complex legal provisions that are involved in contract and copyright licensing. Finally, there is also the digital code (metadata), which allows the machine to search for CC-licensed works over the Internet. See Lessig (2004), above n 334. See also Catharina Maracke, 'Creative Commons International: The International License Porting Project–Origins, Experiences and Challenges' 1 (2010) *Journal of Intellectual Property, Information Technology and*

released in December 2002[338] and based primarily on the Anglo-American legal system[339] as many lawyers drafted it.[340] In 2007, CC published version 03 of its licences, which were more internationally oriented as they were drafted in accordance with international copyright treaties, mainly the WCT and the WPPT.[341] On 2 April 2012, CC announced the release of the draft of CC version 04 for public discussions and comments.[342]

As a result, CC licences were adopted in more than 60 jurisdictions around the world, and the list of countries that have recently joined the project is constantly increasing.[343] CC has also made other initiatives outside the legal arena to help in its scientific and educational discovery, use, and reuse,[344] including the Science Commons and Resource Commons (OER Commons).[345]

E-Commerce Law (JIPITEC) 4, 5; CC, *Creative Commons Licences* <http://creativecommons.org/about/licenses/>.

[338] There are six licenses that users can choose from, and these include Attribution (BY), Attribution ShareAlike (BY-SA), Attribution No Derivatives (BY-ND), Attribution Non-commercial (BY-NC), Attribution Non-commercial Share Alike (BY-NC-SA), and Attribution Non-commercial No Derivatives (BY-NC-ND). There are also specialised Creative Commons' licences including the Public Domain Dedication (PD), CC GNU GPL and CC GNU GPL. See Creative Commons, *Meet the Licences* <http://creativecommons.org/about/licenses/meet-the-licenses>.

[339] To make the CC movement more internationally appealing, its founders wanted it to be different from the Free Software movement, which is why they created iCommons, asking intellectual law experts from around the world to translate the licences into their languages and local legal systems. See Severine Dusollier, 'Sharing Access to Intellectual Property through Private Ordering' (2007) 82 (3) *Kent* Chicago *Kent Law Review* 1391, 1431; Mia Garlick, *Creative Hamburg? Bah the Humbug, Let's get Creative!* (27 July 2005) Indicare <http://www.indicare.org/tiki-read_article.php?articleId=124>. See also CC, *Overview of Porting* <http://wiki.creativecommons.org/International_Overview>.

[340] Herkko Hietanen, 'The Pursuit of Efficient Copyright Licensing — How Some Rights Reserved Attempts to Solve the Problems of All Rights Reserved' (A PhD thesis, Lappeenranta University of Technology, 2008) 218.

[341] Ibid 44.

[342] Diane Peters, *Version 4.0—License Draft Ready for Public Comment!* (2 April 2012) Creative Commons <http://creativecommons.org/weblog/entry/32157?utm_campaign=newsletter_1204&utm_medium=email&utm_source=newsletter>.

[343] See Creative Commons <http://www.creativecommons.org>.

[344] Sharee L. Broussard, *The Copyleft Movement: Creative Commons Licensing* (September 2007) CBC Interactive <http://findarticles.com/p/articles/mi_7081/is_3_26/ai_n28457434/?tag=content;col1>.

[345] See Science Commons <http://sciencecommons.org/> and OER <http://www.oercommons.org/>.

6.3.2 Criticism of CC

Among the criticisms that are often addressed to CC[346] is that it lacks clarity on its objectives.[347] This is different from many non-profit organisations such as the FSF, which has clear, specific, defined goals of promoting software freedom principles and supporting the development of 'Free Software'. Critics have posed many questions about CC, including the following: Does CC want to change international copyright law and copyright licensing practices? Does it want to change traditional mindsets toward copyright? Does it want to increase the amount of creative content available online? Does it want to raise the awareness of copyright issues and how they affect individual artists, creators, and users? Does it want to increase knowledge and culture? What exactly does it intend to achieve? This last question is yet to be answered by CC and its founders, who cannot agree on specific goals that the organisation aims to achieve.

CC licences were also criticised for 'adding another layer of bureaucracy'[348] on top of the existing legal environment of copyright law and practice.[349] By doing this, it made copyright more complex to understand, especially for non-lawyers

[346] For criticism to Creative Commons, see the following: Niva Elkin-Koren, 'Creative Commons: A Sceptical View of a Worthy Pursuit' in P. Bernt Hugenholtz and Lucie Guibault (eds), *The Future of the Public Domain*, (Kluwer Law International, 2006) <http://papers.ssrn.com/sol3/papers.cfm?abstract_id=885466>; Bloemsaat and Kleve, above n 331; Dusollier, above n 331; David Berry and Giles Moss, *On the "Creative Commons": A Critique of the Commons without Commonalty is the Creative Commons Missing Something*? <http://www.fabricemous.nl/wordpress/wp-content/uploads/2007/01/berry.pdf>; Dilanchian, above n 331; Péter Benjamin Tóth, 'Creative Humbug' (2005) *Indicare Monitor* 2 (4) <http://www.indicare.org/tiki-read_article.php?articleId=118>; Lawrence Liang, *Free/ Open Source Software Open Content* (2007) United Nations Development Programme –Asia-Pacific Development Information Programme (UNDP-APDIP) <http://www.apdip.net/publications/fosseprimers/foss-opencontent-nocover.pdf>; Andrew Orloowski, *The Tragedy of Creative Commons* (16 July 2009) <http://andreworlowski.com/tag/creative-commons/>; John C. Dvorak, *Creative Commons Humbug* (18 July 2005) PC Magazine <http://www.pcmag.com/article2/0,2817,1838244,00.asp>; Zachary Zatz, 'Pitfalls of Open Licensing: An Analysis of Creative Commons Licences' (2006) IDEA—The Intellectual Property Law Review, 46 (3) 391-413; Mikko Valimaki, *The Rise of Open Source Licensing* (Turre Publishing, 2005) 159-160 <http://lib.tkk.fi/Diss/2005/isbn9529187793/isbn9529187793.pdf>.

[347] Creative Commons says the following:

> Creative Commons is a non-profit corporation dedicated to making it easier for people to share and build upon the work of others, consistent with the rules of copyright. We provide free licenses and other legal tools to mark creative work with the freedom the creator wants it to carry, so others can share, remix, use commercially, or any combination thereof.

Zatz, above 346. See also Creative Commons <http://www.creativecommons.org>.

[348] Woods, above n 336, 57.

[349] Dilanchian, above n 331.

who have to struggle with the various licences[350] written in different languages and based on different legal systems.[351] Another criticism was addressed to CC for not explaining the meaning of non-commercial, an essential element in its three licences.[352] For this reason, CC has prepared a study on the meaning of 'commercial use' and 'non-commercial use'. The study did not come up with any major findings on the meanings and acknowledged that this study only constitutes a starting point for future research in this area.[353]

Others are doubtful whether CC can truly increase creative content online, arguing that it might encourage people to put more work online, but there is no guarantee that such work would ultimately lead to high quality uses[354] and increased creativity on the Internet. As for benefiting developing countries, the Copysouth[355] has argued that there is only a small percentage of works that are available under CC each year, compared to the majority of published works or music that are still under restrictive copyright regimes.[356] The non-availability of such works would be of limited value to developing countries in meeting the expansive access needs to copyrighted materials that their citizens want to be able to use.[357]

6.3.3 Creative Commons as a Path for Social and Economic Development

CC allows people to share and reuse a variety of materials published and distributed by researchers, amateurs, professionals, governments, and scientists. This

---

[350] As two commentators have explained:

> Lessing's attempt to make it easier to understand which creative works can, or cannot, be used for modification (due to copyright) has spawned a monster of a thousands heads. This would ultimately make creators of original work unsure of what rights they hold under the law and what they can actually license under the CC licensing scheme.

See Dusollier, above n 339, 1431; Garlick, above 339. See also, Creative Commons, *Overview of Porting* <http://wiki.creativecommons.org/International_Overview>; Berry and Moss; above n 346, Woods, above n 336.

[351] Valimaki, above n 346, 160; Koren, above n 346.

[352] Those licences are Attribution Non-Commercial (BY-NC), Attribution Non-Commercial Share Alike (BY-NC-SA) and Attribution Non-Commercial No Derivatives (BY-NC-ND) licences. See Creative Commons <http://creativecommons.org/about/licenses/meet-the-licenses>. See also Zatz, above n 346.

[353] CC, *Defining Creative Commons*, 14-15 <http://mirrors.creativecommons.org/defining-noncommercial/Defining_Noncommercial_fullreport.pdf>; Jessica Coates, *Not Primarily Intended for Commercial Advantage or Profit: The Logic and Meaning of "non-commercial" in the Creative Commons Licences*, (An LLM thesis, Melbourne University, 2009).

[354] Woods, above n 336, 28.

[355] See Copysouth <http://www.copysouth.org/>.

[356] Liang, above n 346.

[357] Ibid.

subsection will examine how CC could act as a path for social and economic development in developing countries.

6.3.3.1 Creative Commons as a Path for Social Development

The social benefits of using the CC licensing system in developing countries include educating the public about copyright issues, empowering individual creators, and increasing the pool of creative works that the public can use for their benefit. Mia Garlick, the former Legal Counsel to CC International, has noted:

> One of Creative Commons objectives is to raise awareness of copyright issues, and in particular, how they affect individual artists and creators, as well as users...[358] The point of Creative Commons' three different expressions of its licenses is to facilitate greater use of copyrighted works, educate people about respect for copyright and how to comply with copyright laws...[359]

According to Rodro Mizukami and Ronaldo Lemos, CC teaches people the importance of open content licences, which 'are considered as the most important political documents of communities built around the production of information over the Internet'.[360] The open content licences function as social contracts and establish the ground rules for collaborative projects.[361] This is particularly useful for citizens of developing countries who are unsure about the basic principles of copyright that touch upon their daily activities, especially in the Internet era. Discussing and debating copyright legal and policy issues are important to formulating public opinions on how IP (particularly copyright) should be structured in developing countries for the benefit of the society.[362] One such practical example of how CC can assist in that regard is the CC Arab world list, which includes more than 250 members working in various fields (including law, art, media, journalism, and information technology), discussing many topics around IP and other emerging issues.[363]

The CC model supports a variety of creators, including amateurs, hobbyists, creators, artists, researchers, scientists, teachers, and non-profit organisations. Most of them are more interested in sharing their work than in having financial returns. This kind of model would facilitate the social dialogue between creators and the

[358] Garlick, above n 339.

[359] Ibid.

[360] Rodro Nicoletti Mizukami and Ronaldo Lemos, 'From Free Software to Free Culture: The Emergence of Open Business' in Lea Shaver (ed), *Access to Knowledge in Brazil* (Bloomsbury, 2010) 53.

[361] Ibid.

[362] Dusollier, above n 331, 281.

[363] Anyone can apply to join, see CC Arab world group <http://groups.google.com/group/cc-arab-world>.

public[364] by allowing the latter to express their opinion clearly on the quality of the work that they have received.

The most important social benefits that CC gives to individual creators is that it empowers them to exercise their rights and control their creative works without the need to obtain the approval of content providers[365] or any other authority. As a result of giving creators the power they need to control their work and its distribution, this would result in the growth of the 'Internet commons', which is available for anyone to use, share, and re-mix.[366] As of June 2006, there were approximately 140 million CC-licensed works freely available to be used and reused by the public, in accordance with the permissions granted by the licensors.[367]

As for developing countries, Ronald Lemos has noted that copyright-based industries are failing to promote local content and dissemination of culture and knowledge in developing countries and emerging economies (Brazil).[368] In these countries, the CC licensing model would come into play where there is a thriving culture that needs to be disseminated to the public.[369] CC-licensed works can also be used to educate the masses in developing countries. One of the most important initiatives that can be used in that way is MIT Open Course Ware (OCW),[370] which provides free undergraduate and postgraduate courses licensed under a CC licensing system, to be used by anyone who has the required technology that allows him to do so.[371]

Science Commons[372] is a CC project launched in 2006 that can also be used for the social advantage of developing countries. Among the projects that are particularly useful in this regard are the Biological Materials Transfer (BMTP),[373] the Health Commons (HC),[374] and Neurocommons.[375] The first would help research institutions in developing countries that want to employ standard,

[364] Dusollier, above n 331, 279, 281.

[365] Woods, above n 336, 55.

[366] Maracke, above n 337, 6; Hietanen, above n 340, 109.

[367] Ronald Lemos, *From Legal Commons to Social Commons: Brazil and the Culture Industry in the 21 Century*, Center for Brazilian Studies, Oxford University, Working Paper Number CBS-80-07, 43 <http://virtualbib.fgv.br/dspace/bitstream/handle/10438/2677/Ronaldo%20Lemos%20-%20From%20legal%20commons%20to%20social%20commons.pdf?sequence=1>.

[368] Ibid 52.

[369] Ibid.

[370] MIT OCW <http://ocw.mit.edu/index.htm>.

[371] Bloemsaat and Kleve, above n 331, 245.

[372] Science CC <http://sciencecommons.org/>.

[373] Science CC <http://sciencecommons.org/projects/licensing/>.

[374] Health Commons <http://www.healthcommons.net/>.

[375] Science CC <http://sciencecommons.org/projects/data/>

modular contracts to lower the costs of transferring biological materials (such as DNA, cell lines, model animals, and more)[376] The Health Commons and Neurocommons could help to advance biological and health research in developing countries.

CC licences are considered as standard tools for open content distribution.[377] Developing countries should use the same tools that are being recognised by various international organisations, including the UN, which is currently publishing many of its reports under CC licences.

Recently, there has been a trend by certain governments in developed countries (e.g. Australia,[378] New Zealand[379]) to publish works that are produced by government departments and institutions under a CC licensing system. There is also increasing debate between international organisations, including the UN, that developing countries should participate in freeing-up government materials that need to be distributed and shared for the benefit of citizens.[380] The CC licensing system should be seriously considered in developing countries to foster creativity and innovation in the government sector.

6.3.3.2 Creative Commons as a Path for Economic Development

Can CC help businesses that are using its licences to make money? How could businesses located in developing countries benefit from such a licensing system?

Businesses that license their work under a CC licensing scheme are motivated to do so for various reasons. These include marketing advantages, reducing legal costs, building their reputation,[381] and possibly, concluding commercial agreements with interested corporations.

---

[376] Wikipedia, *Science Commons* <http://en.wikipedia.org/wiki/Science_Commons>.

[377] Hietanen, above n 340, 53. See also Dilanchian, above n 331.

[378] See, for example, the Queensland Government Information Licensing Framework (GILF) project in Australia. The GILF project noted:

> [O]wing to Creative Commons' status as an international movement, and its recognition as a standard for flexible copyright licensing, the government can gain significant leverage from adopting Creative Commons. No point in needlessly re-inventing the wheel.

See Creative Commons, *Case Studies* <http://wiki.creativecommons.org/Case_Studies/Government_Information_Licensing_Framework>.

[379] See the New Zealand Government Open Access and Licensing framework (NZGOAL), which was approved by NZ Cabinet on 5 July 2010 as a government guidance for state services that are releasing copyrighted work for the use by the public in New Zealand. NZ Government, *New Zealand Government Open Access and Licensing (NZGOAL) Framework* <http://www.e.govt.nz/policy/nzgoal>.

[380] See also Anne Fitzgerald (ed), *Open Access Polices, Practices and Licensing: a Review of the Literature in Australia and Selected Jurisdictions, European Public Sector Information Platform Topic Report No. 13—State of Play: PSI Reuse in Australia* (2010) <http://eprints.qut.edu.au/33206/>.

[381] Hietanen, above n 340, 175, 215.

Bjorn Hartmann, an accomplished musician, supports CC as he believes that it would allow artists to be free from the economic pressure of big companies releasing their work, even if it was of limited commercial value. Hartmann believes that the CC licensing model is helpful for artists in promoting their work and allowing them to reach a larger audience that they could not previously reach. Furthermore, it develops the relationship between the artist and his music fans,[382] leading to producing music that is more suitable to their tastes and needs.

One of the first issues faced by businesses involved in content distribution is to determine an appropriate legal model that is suitable to their needs. Legal consultation might be highly costly for start-up creators and companies that cannot afford such payments. CC gives these companies some leverage in that regard as it allows them to use its web-based licence chooser application,[383] that is freely available online. This would lower the legal costs (advice, negotiations, and drafting of contracts) that these creators and businesses might otherwise incur.

For creators and businesses who want their work to be popularised, CC can assist a great deal in advertising their talents[384] and work over the Internet. The various search engines (Yahoo and Google) that can now facilitate locating CC-licensed works over the Internet. This kind of advertising is not an end in itself but can lead to concluding commercial agreements with the businesses that are interested in doing so.[385] This has happened for a number of creators and artists. One such example is a Slovakian artist who licensed his music under CC and later managed to conclude two commercial contracts with American companies that wanted to use his music in their projects.[386]

Among the new business strategies that are currently been practised by publishers is to publish a book in a hard copy format and, at the same time, license it under a CC licence in a digital format. The online version of the book would encourage sales of the work in the hard copy format.[387] One of the most successful examples of this is Professor Lawrence Lessig, who published over the Internet his book, *Free Culture: How Big Media Uses Technology and Law to Lock Down Culture and Control Creativity*, under a CC licence, and this increased the sales of the printed version of his book.

Cory Doctorow is another example. He released his science fiction book under a CC licensing scheme. As a result, he became well known, and over sixty thousand copies of his printed book have been sold.[388] There are many other examples of businesses

---

[382] Bjorn Hartmann, 'Netlabels and The Adoption of Creative Commons in the Online Electronic Music Community' in Daniele Bourcier, Pompeu Casanovas and Melaine Dulong, *Intelligent Multimedia-Managing Creative Works in a digital World* (Romilat, 2004), 149-153.

[383] Hietanen, above 340, 59.

[384] Garlick, above n 339.

[385] Hietanen, above 340, 73

[386] Garlick, above n 339.

[387] Ibid.

[388] Hietanen, above n 340, 199.

that are using the CC licensing system in the online world, and these include Flickr, Revver,[389] Scoopt, Magnature and MusicBrianz,[390] and Trent Renzor.[391]

Professor Severine Dusollier, however, is doubtful that a CC model could actually help businesses to make money. She notes that:

> [O]ne should not be naïve: the existing circulation of the work for free under a Creative Commons scheme reduces the commercial interest in the work. By using a "non-commercial" Creative Commons license, the author can retain the possibility of offering her creation to a commercial publisher or producer. But the latter might doubt the ability to make money off a work that is available for free on the Internet or anywhere else.[392]

The examples cited by proponents for the use of CC licensing system in business are few in number. There is also an issue of bargaining power that is likely to arise. On one hand, if someone is already famous and successful in his career, he may be able to dictate his own terms of business to the other party. On the other hand, if someone is talented but unknown, he will be unable to implement his own terms of business when contracting with another party. We live in a demanding world, and businesses will not change their rules and simply follow different ones because they appear to be helping creators and society. The CC model is not a stand-alone solution for all issues, situations, and players.[393] Mostly, amateurs, up-and-coming creators, and small businesses will be able to benefit from the CC licensing model, but this is not the same for big corporations that want to acquire the highest revenues as this is not possible with such a model. However, can this model assist economically creators in developing countries?

It is noted that such a model could assist creative people and small businesses in developing countries to become more internationally well known and provide them with the legal and technical tools to be more professionally developed. It will remain to be seen to what extent the CC can align itself more with the interests of businesses in the future.

6.3.4 Creative Commons and Research and Education in Developing Countries

CC is helpful for enabling developing countries to increase access to educational materials and research. It allows researchers in developing countries to legitimately access scientific and educational materials through CC-licensed materials from researchers and public institutions in the developed world. This does not solve all

389 Revver <http://revver.com/>.

390 Dilanchian, above n 331.

391 Trent Renzor <http://www.nin.com/>.

392 Dusollier, above n 331, 281.

393 Dilanchian, above n 331.

A2K problems in developing countries but can help these countries to access works available under permissive licences.[394]

The Department of Labor and Education in the US announced on 20 January 2011 that the Obama administration had granted $2 billion to create Open Education Resource (OER) materials to provide community colleges and other eligible institutions of higher education with funds to expand and improve their ability to deliver education and career training programs. All the resources created using these funds must be released under the CC Attribution 3.0 licence (CC BY). This particular licence will allow subsequent users to copy, distribute, transmit, and adapt the copyrighted work, provided that attribution is given to the author.[395]

Developing countries can use the CC licensing scheme in 'licensing in' and 'licensing out'. In the first situation, researchers, educators, and government officials in developing countries need to use and benefit from CC-licensed works that are available in developed countries. Examples of important research initiatives that are using CC include the following:

1) Public Library of Science in the US (PLoS)[396];
2) The PubMed Central in the US (PMC) and the Europe PubMed Central (EUROPEPMG)[397];
3) Polar Information Commons—a global portal for research data in Antarctica[398]; and
4) World Bank.[399]

---

[394] On 26 April 2010, CC submitted the following statement to WIPO Committee on Development and Intellectual Property (CDIP 5) in Geneva:

> We also strongly believe that Creative Commons offers developing countries opportunities to legitimately access scientific and educational materials released under a Creative Commons licence by researchers and public institutions in the developed world, something that is already taking place. We are aware that this does not solve digital divide access issues, but we believe that making the works available under permissive licences is a step in the right direction.

Andres, *CC Statement at WIPO CDIP* (26 April 2010) Tecnoliama <http://www.technollama.co.uk/creative-commons-statement-at-wipo-cdip>.

[395] Timothy Vollmer, *New federal education fund makes available $2 billion to create OER resources in community Colleges,* (20 January 2011) Creative Commons <https://creativecommons.org/weblog/entry/26100>.

[396] PLoS <http://www.plos.org/journals/>.

[397] PubMed Central (PMC) <http://www.ncbi.nlm.nih.gov/pmc/>; Europe PubMed Central PubMed Central (EUROPEPMC) <http://europepmc.org/ >.

[398] Polar Information Commons <http://www.polarcommons.org/>.

[399] World Bank <www.worldbank.org>. See also World Bank, *What the World Bank's Open Access Policy Means for Development* (21 May 2012) <http://live.worldbank.org/bank-open-access-policy-development-liveblog>; Timothy Vollmer, World Bank Live Event Report: Open Access Policy and Development (24 May 2012) Creative Commons <http://creativecommons.org/weblog/entry/32839>.

Scholars, researchers, and government officials in developing countries should also be encouraged to explore the use of CC in 'licensing out' their work to the general public. This would allow others to access their work and build on it. This would be helpful in popularising creative works and other knowledge that are available in developing countries and share it with like countries and the rest of the world.

The African Copyright Access to Knowledge (ACA2K) Report noted the importance of using flexible licensing regimes such as CC in developing countries. It stated that:

> A valuable access-building practice for Africa is the promotion and utilisation of flexible approaches to the licensing and distribution of locally produced works. The Publishing and Alternative Licensing Model of Africa (PALM Africa) Project has successfully supported publishing of three open access books, under Creative Commons (CC) open licences, by Fountain Publishers, a traditional publisher in Uganda. In Egypt, the CC flexible copyright licences are also starting to gain exposure. In South Africa, the use of these licences has been ongoing since they were 'ported' into that country in 2005. Also, South Africa is home to the pioneering Free High School Science...The ACA2K English-language book is published by one of Africa's leading publishers, UCT Press, under a Creative Commons licence agreement...[400]

CC licensing system is suited to the cultural needs of producers in developing countries. This is because it allows them to choose between the different CC licences according to their particular needs and circumstances. For example, in relation to Rai Music (popular in the Maghreb or western Arab world), musicians can choose the maximum freedom CC license (attribution only) to allow others to use and build upon their work.

Developing countries should also explore 'the importance of better access and reuse of Public Sector Information (PSI)'.[401] Professor Brian Fitzgerald has noted that PSI should be made available through technical formats that promote access and reuse of data.[402] CC licensing regimes can be used, where appropriate, by governments in developing countries as simple and effective mechanisms to support the reuse of their copyright-protected PSI, particularly where materials are made available in digital form online.[403]

6.3.5 *The Adoption of CC in Developing Countries: The Case of the Arab World*

Jordan was the first country in the Arab world to start a CC project. Since March 2004,[404] CC Jordan has been working with CC to translate and port the CC licenses

[400] Chris Armstrong et al., *ACA2K Comparative Review of Research Findings* (August 2010) ACA2K <http://idl-bnc.idrc.ca/dspace/bitstream/10625/48978/1/IDL-48978.pdf>.

[401] Fitzgerald (ed), above n 212, vii.

[402] Ibid.

[403] Ibid 72.

[404] Creative Commons <http://creativecommons.org>.

into the Jordanian legal system. The first regional CC meeting of CC Arab world took place on 14 March 2009, with the support of Al Jazeera.[405] The meeting discussed various initiatives to be taken by supporters of the movement to develop further CC in the Arab world. CC Jordan was launched on 15 November 2009 in Amman, and a CC salon event also took place on 16 November 2009 in Amman in order to encourage Arab artists to canvass their work, released under CC, to a global audience.

The second regional CC meeting was held on 23 October 2010 in Qatar and was hosted by ICT Qatar. It continued the discussion of the development of the CC movement in the Arab world.[406] The third regional CC meeting was held in Tunisia on 29 June–2 July 2012, and it was attended by various supporters of CC in the region.[407]

Other Arab countries are expected shortly to instigate CC in their countries, including Egypt, Syria, Lebanon and Tunisia, Qatar, and other countries.

6.3.6 Examples of the Use of CC in the Arab World

The section provides some practical examples of the use of CC licenses in the Arab world. Although these projects are only beginning to emerge in the Arab world, they clearly show that CC licenses can be advantageous to creators and users of copyright materials and can foster innovation and development amongst Internet users, researchers, politicians, musician, artists, and the general public.

(a) Al Jazeera Repository

On 13 January 2010, the Al Jazeera Network released the world's first repository of broadcast-quality, video footage of the War on Gaza, under the CC 3.0 Attribution licence. The reason for starting such an initiative was to allow news agencies, filmmakers, and bloggers to easily share, remix, and reuse footage[408] for encouraging wider debate and a richer understanding[409] amongst all those interested in the development of politics in the Middle East.

---

[405] See AL Jazeera English <http://english.aljazeera.net/>, see also Brian Fitzgerald and Rami Olwan, 'Copyright in the UAE in the Digital Age' (2010) 32 (11) *European Intellectual Property Review* (EIPR) 565, 566.

[406] See Rami Olwan, *Report Digitally Open: Innovation and Open Access Forum* (23 Oct 2010) <http://www.olwan.org>.

[407] Brian, *Creative Commons Arab World Meeting Starts Tomorrow in Tunis* (28 June 2011) Creative Commons Qatar *<http://www.creativecommons.qa/tunis>*.

[408] CC Aljazeera <http://cc.aljazeera.net/>.

[409] Al Jazeera, *Al Jazeera Announces Launch of Free Footage under Creative Commons License* (13 January 2009) <http://cc.aljazeera.net/content/launch-press-release>; Noam Cohen, 'Al Jazeera Provides an Inside Look at Gaza Conflict' New York Times (online), 1 January 2009 <http://www.nytimes.com/2009/01/11/technology/11iht-jazeera.4.19256575.html>; Creative

(b) Hindawi Publishing Corporation
Hindawi Publishing Corporation is an Egyptian, commercial, peer-reviewed journal covering all major areas of science, technology, and medicine. It was founded in 1997 and currently employs more than 300 people and publishes more than 300 open access and peer-reviewed journals.[410] Hindawi publishes its open access journals under a CC Attribution licence.[411]

(c) Samandal
Launched in 2007, Samandal is a non-governmental organisation dedicated to the proliferation of comic art production in the Arab world. Samandal is published quarterly worldwide but mainly in the UAE, Lebanon, the UK, Germany, and the US. It makes its comics works online[412] under a CC Attribution Noncommercial-ShareAlike licence.[413]

(d) 7iber.com
7iber was founded in Amman, Jordan, on 25 May 2007.[414] It is a commercial media platform that allows young Jordanians to actively engage in new media and online content. 7iber is licensed under a CC Attribution-NonCommercial-NoDerivative 3.0 unported licence.[415]

(e) Naeema Zarif
Naeema Zarif is a visual artist based in Beirut, Lebanon.[416] Her visual arts deal with a variety of matters, including heritage, behaviours, and the social and cultural development of humans. She publishes her visual arts in a blog licensed under a CC Attribution-NonCommercial-ShareAlike 3.0 US licence.[417]

(f) Maya Zankoul
Maya Zankoul is a graphic and web designer who writes about her daily experiences and the problems she encounters in her daily life in Lebanon. Her blog (mayzankoul.com) writings are licensed under a CC Attribution-NonCommercial 3.0 unported licence.[418]

Commos, *Al Jazeera Launches Creative Commons Repository* <http://creativecommons.org/weblog/entry/12049>.

410 Handawi <http://www.hindawi.com/>.

411 Ibid.

412 Samandal <http://samandal.org/eng-trans.html>.

413 CC, *Samandal: Publishing Comics Online in Three Languages under CC Licenses* <http://wiki.creativecommons.org/Grants/Samandal_:_Publishing_Comics_Online_in_Three_Languages_Under_CC_Licenses>.

414 7iber <http://www.7iber.com/about/about-7iber/>.

415 Ibid.

416 NeemaZarif <http://naeemazarif.com/>.

417 Ibid.

418 Mayazankoul <http://mayazankoul.com/about-2/>.

(g) Meen
Meen is an Arabic band that promotes Arabic rock. They aim to promote rock music and increase their business revenues. They have published some of their albums under a CC Attribution-NonDirective-NonCommercial licence.

6.3.7 *The Legal Challenges and Issues for the Adoption of CC in Developing Countries*

Developing countries might face a variety of legal challenges when they adopt CC licences either in business or in government. In addition to the legal issues previously discussed in Sects. 6.2.6 and 6.2.7, this section will examine moral rights and the enforcement of CC licences.

6.3.7.1 The Treatment of Moral Rights under Creative Commons Licences

As explained in Sect. 6.2.7.3, several moral rights are given to the author in accordance with art 8 of the *Copyright Law* in Jordan, and these include the right of paternity, the right of divulgation, the right of integrity, the right of reconsideration, and the right of withdrawal.[419]

The right of paternity (attribution) does not constitute a major problem as all CC licences contain the 'BY' or the attribution requirement that satisfies art 8(A) of the *Copyright Law* in Jordan in that regard. Whenever a work is copied or redistributed under a CC licence, the original creator (and any other nominated parties) must be credited and a link should be made to the Internet address where the source can be found.[420] The right of divulgation is also satisfied as authors agree voluntarily to publish their work and allow others to use and remix it.

---

[419] *Copyright Law*, above n 170, art 8. See also art 5.

[420] For example, Section 4(d) of the Attribution-NonCommercial-ShareAlike 3.0 Unported licence provides as follows:

> d) If You Distribute, or Publicly Perform the Work or any Adaptations or Collections, You must, unless a request has been made pursuant to Section 4(a), keep intact all copyright notices for the Work and provide, reasonable to the medium or means You are utilizing: (i) the name of the Original Author (or pseudonym, if applicable) if supplied, and/or if the Original Author and/or Licensor designate another party or parties (e.g., a sponsor institute, publishing entity, journal) for attribution ("Attribution Parties") in Licensor's copyright notice, terms of service or by other reasonable means, the name of such party or parties; (ii) the title of the Work if supplied; (iii) to the extent reasonably practicable, the URI, if any, that Licensor specifies to be associated with the Work, unless such URI does not refer to the copyright notice or licensing information for the Work; and, (iv) consistent with Section 3(b), in the case of an Adaptation, a credit identifying the use of the Work in the Adaptation (e.g., "French translation of the Work by Original Author," or "Screenplay based on original Work by Original Author"). The credit required by this Section 4(d) may

As for the right of integrity, it has been suggested that it is not clear how CC licences operate in the context of this particular moral right. This has provoked legal concerns, particularly from lawyers who come from jurisdictions that have strong 'droit d'auteur' legal systems', such as France and Germany.[421] Those lawyers argue that the unclear position of CC licences in relation to the right of integrity might be an obstacle to recognising their legal validity in civil law countries that give particular attention to this kind of moral right.

CC tried to address this problem by requiring each CC jurisdiction to implement in its localised licence a clause stating that '[m]oral rights remain unaffected to the extent they are recognized and not waivable by applicable law'.[422] Catharina Marake, the former CC International Director explained why it was necessary for CC to introduce such a clause in its licences. She noted:

> To provide clarity regarding the treatment of moral rights, it was agreed to explicitly retain the moral right of integrity in those jurisdiction licenses that have to deal with a strong level of protection for the moral right of integrity, considering the risk that local courts could take a dim view of a license that does not expressly include moral rights.[423]

On their face, CC licences do not purport to override the moral rights of integrity and the right of withdrawal (which arguably include the moral right of reconsideration). Furthermore, under civil law system, most clearly in France, when authors licence their work to be adapted, they give licensors some degree of freedom to adapt the work for the purpose it is lawfully licensed (see Sect. 6.2.7.3).

As for the moral right of withdrawal, which arguably also includes the right of consideration, it is suggested that the right of withdrawal will not be applied in a strict sense because the competent court needs to approve this right, and this can only be done in extreme circumstances where any affected party or parties are to be compensated. The competent court may find that it is impractical to withdraw the

---

> be implemented in any reasonable manner; provided, however, that in the case of a Adaptation or Collection, at a minimum such credit will appear, if a credit for all contributing authors of the Adaptation or Collection appears, then as part of these credits and in a manner at least as prominent as the credits for the other contributing authors. For the avoidance of doubt, You may only use the credit required by this Section for the purpose of attribution in the manner set out above and, by exercising Your rights under this License, You may not implicitly or explicitly assert or imply any connection with, sponsorship or endorsement by the Original Author, Licensor and/or Attribution Parties, as appropriate, of You or Your use of the Work, without the separate, express prior written permission of the Original Author, Licensor and/or Attribution Parties.

Creative Commons, Attribution-NonCommercial-ShareAlike 3.0 Unported licence <http://creativecommons.org/licenses/by-nc-sa/3.0/legalcode>.

This applies to every Creative Commons work. Whenever a work is copied or redistributed under a Creative Commons licence, the original creator (and any other nominated parties) must be credited and the source linked to. See CC Australia, *About the Licences* <http://creativecommons.org.au/>.

[421] Maracke, above n 337, 7.

[422] Ibid 9.

[423] Ibid 8.

Table 6.5 The conformity of CC licenses to the moral requirements of the *Copyright Law* in Jordan

Moral rights requirements under art 8 of the *Copyright Law* in Jordan	How CC licences operates in the context of the moral rights requirements under the *Copyright Law* in Jordan
The right of respect and paternity	Authors must always be attributed. All 6 CC licences contain the attribution requirements[424]
The right of divulgation	The content owners agree to publish their work and make it available to others to use and remix
The right of integrity	CC licences contain a clause that states that '[m]oral rights remain unaffected to the extent they are recognized and not waivable by applicable law'.[425] Under some civil law systems, most clearly in France, it may be the case that licensors have a degree of freedom to adapt a work that has been lawfully licensed to them for this purpose[426]
The right of reconsideration and the right of withdrawal	The right of withdrawal most likely includes the right of amendment to the work. Authors cannot exercise their right of withdrawal without having serious reasons that dictate the withdrawal of their work. The authors also need to request the competent court to order the withdrawal of their work and they need to compensate the affected third parties

work of the author who agreed to publish it online under a CC licence and may order the withdrawal to take affect for the future only as it is difficult to enforce the moral right against all unknown Internet users. Table 6.5 explains how CC licences operate in the context of the moral rights requirements under the *Copyright Law* in Jordan.

6.3.7.2 The Enforceability of the Creative Commons Licences

A number of cases have been brought in various international courts that discuss the legality and enforceability of CC licences. In March 2006, the Dutch court was the first court to test the validity of CC licences.[427] A copyright infringement case was brought by Adam Curry, a media celebrity, against Weekend, a Dutch boulevard magazine, for using one of his pictures from his Flickr account under CC (Attribution Non-Commercial Share Alike (BY-NC-SA)) without respecting the terms of the licence, mainly the non-commercial requirement. While the court rejected the

[424] See Creative Commons, above n 420.

[425] It should be noted that not every remix and modification of content will amount to a breach of the right of integrity.

[426] See also Goldstein and Hugenholtz, above n 286; Appelbaum, above n 284; Treece, above n 285; Sterling, above n 283.

[427] Curry v. Audax, *Rechtbank Amsterdam, No. 334492/ KG 06-176 SR, 3/9/06 (Cury v Audax)* <http://mirrors.creativecommons.org/judgements/Curry-Audax-English.pdf>.

request of the plaintiff to award him compensation, it acknowledged that CC licences are enforceable copyright contracts that are valid under the civil legal system in the Netherlands.[428]

The second case was brought in Dallas before a Texas court. The plaintiff (the Chang family) filed against Virgin Mobile USA, Virgin Mobile Australia, and CC.[429] They alleged that the use of their daughter's amateur photo, posted online into a Flickr account, under a CC licence for an expensive advertising campaign for Virgin Mobile Australia, violated her privacy rights and, furthermore, constituted defamation and breach of contract. The family was particularly furious that the use of their daughter's photograph was demeaning to her as she became known as the 'dump-your-pen-friend girl'.[430] The plaintiff alleged that CC was negligent for failing 'to adequately educate and warn [them] of the meaning of commercial use and the ramifications and effects of entering into a license allowing such use'.[431] The plaintiffs later dropped the case as they found that the laws of Texas and the US do not give them a cause of action to sue CC.[432]

The Spanish courts have also considered the legal validity of CC licences in a number of cases. In the first case on CC, the Spanish court, in the case of *Sociedad General de Autores Y Editores (SGAE) (the major collecting society in Spain) v Luis*, did not regard CC licences as legally valid, as they lacked any kind of signature.[433] In another case, *SGAE v Ricardo Andrés Utrera Fernández*, the lower court number 6 of Badajoz, in the city of Extremadura in Spain, considered whether SGAE was entitled to collect royalties from a local bar in Badajoz; SGAE alleged that the bar owner had publicly performed the music they were managing from November 2002

---

[428] Groklaw, *Creative Commons License Upheld by Dutch Court* <http://www.groklaw.net/article.php?story=20060316052623594>; Mia Garlick, *Creative Commons Upheld in Dutch Court* (16 March 2006) Creative Commons <http://creativecommons.org/press-releases/entry/5822>; Hietanen, above n 340, 81; Bloemsaat and Kleve, above n 331, 237-249.

[429] Susan Chang vs. Virgin Mobile USA, Virgin Mobile Australia and CC (The Complaint) <http://lessig.org/blog/complaint.pdf>.

[430] Andrew Srlowski, *Creative Commons Sued for Deception* (24 September 2007) <http://andreworlowski.com/tag/creative-commons/>.

[431] Hietanen, above n 340, 62; Lawrence Lessig, On the Texas Suit against Virgin and Creative Commons (2007) <http://lessig.org/blog/2007/09/on_the_texas_suit_against_virg.html>; Mike Linksvayer, *Lawsuit against Virgin Mobile and Creative Commons –FAQ* (27 September 2007) Creative Commons <http://creativecommons.org/weblog/entry/7680>.

[432] Lawrence Lessig, *From the Why-a-GC-from-Cravath-is-Great Department: The Lawsuit is Over* (2007) <http://lessig.org/blog/2007/11/from_the_whyagcfromcravathisgr.html>.

[433] The Court noted that:

> The document presented by the defendant-appellant as license of free musical use is nothing but a mere informatory leaflet about the contents of the license and is lacking any signature; therefore it cannot be asserted any value.

See Posse, above n 270, 815.

to August 2005 but failed to pay them any royalties for doing so.[434] The court rejected SGAE's claims because the owner proved to the court that he was not performing the music managed by SGAE, but instead, the music was licensed under a royalty-free CC licence.[435]

As for developing countries, CC licences have never been tested in local courts. As a result, some would argue that they are not legally enforceable because they are not compatible with the legal system of those countries. It is hoped that courts in developing countries will give people clear answers to the legal validity of CC licences in the near future.

6.3.8 *Final Remarks on CC and Developing Countries*

Many developing countries have not yet fully explored the importance of CC in encouraging innovation and development in those countries.

CC is an innovative tool that uses copyright intelligently rather than relying on the current default position of users having, or not having, rights to use works. It allows people to share and remix works legally across a wide spectrum of areas, including science, government, health, education, and business. The importance of CC is that it creates a 'free culture', where people are at no legal risk in using works to build legitimate business models.[436]

It is submitted that there is a tremendous volume of material available in developing countries that could be shared under the CC licence system. CC could assist developing countries in popularising their works and expanding the range of creative works made available not only to other developing countries but also to the

[434] Mia Garlick, *Spanish Court Recognizes CC-Music* (23 March 2003) Creative Commons <http://creativecommons.org/weblog/entry/5830>; Posse, above n 270, 824.

[435] On February 17th, 2006, the judge in the Lower Court number six of Badajoz, Extremadura, Spain said:

> The author possesses some moral and economic rights on his creation. And the owner of these rights, he can manage them as he considers appropriate, being able to yield the free use, or hand it over partially. "Creative Commons" licenses are different classes of authorizations that the holder of his work gives for a more or less free or no cost use of it. They exist as different classes of licenses of this type they allow third parties to be able to use music freely and without cost with greater or minor extension; and in some of these licenses, specific uses require the payment of royalties. The defendant proves that he makes use of music that is handled by their authors through these Creative Commons licenses.

Garlick, above n 434. See also, Hietanen, above n 340. 112; Thomas Margnoi, *English translation of Spanish CC decision* (2007) Creative Commons <http://mirrors.creativecommons.org/wp-content/uploads/2007/02/luis-cc-spanish-decision-final.pdf>; Posse, above n 270, 815.

[436] Brian Fitzgerald, *Open Content Licensing (OCL) for Open Educational Resources*, Paper commissioned by the OECD's Centre for Educational Research and Innovation (CERI) for the project on Open Educational Resources (2007) 10 <http://www.oecd.org/dataoecd/33/10/38645489.pdf>.

rest of the world. This would also foster greater understanding between developing and developed countries.

6.4 Conclusion

Voluntary mechanisms such as FOSS and CC could act as paths for social and economic development. They can also be used as knowledge-exchanging tools for their users in developing countries.

FOSS can support economic development, at least on an individual level, if not the national level, as this model can be profitable for certain businesses working in ICT, in addition to providing FOSS services. It can also be socially advantageous to citizens in developing countries if they use it as a democratisation instrument and knowledge liberalisation tool. It can also help people in developing countries to use IT in innovative ways and develop their local skills in that regard.

As for the CC licensing system, it can provide economic benefits for rising creators in developing countries, but it would not be appealing to big corporations that would not be interested economically in such a system. Creators who use CC in the beginning of their career would leave such a system and adopt commercial licences when they become more successful and famous.[437] On the other hand, CC would be socially beneficial for people in developing countries in empowering local creators and increasing the pool of creative work that the public can use, build upon, and benefit from. It is important for researchers and educators in developing countries to utilise CC-licensed materials such as the Obama government's initiative to improve research and education in their respective countries. They need also to utilise research materials available in the global research repositories that use CC for their advantage.

There is much to explore in developing countries, and both FOSS and CC could show the pool of talents available in those countries in various fields, including ICT, research, science, art, music, and many others. They could help them to popularise their work and make it available to a wider audience to use and build upon. In the long term, this would expand the range of the developing countries' creative input available to the world and humanity.

[437] Bloemsaat and Kleve, above n 331, 248.

Chapter 7
Policy Road Map for Intellectual Property and Development

7.1 Overview

The theory of IP and social and economic development needs to be translated into implementation strategies if it is to be effectively applied in developing countries. This chapter seeks to convert into practice the ideas presented in the previous chapters and recommends measures that can be implemented by developing countries to ensure that their IP strategies are aligned with, and serve, their social and economic development objectives. This chapter first examines (Sect. 7.2) the policies that developing countries need to consider in the context of IP and development. It then suggests (Sects. 7.3 and 7.4) some practical measures that can be adopted by developing countries.

7.2 IP and Development Policies for Developing Countries

Developing countries seeking to benefit from the introduction of IP systems should consider the following policies in their IP strategies.[1]

Policy 1: Tailor the IP Regime to Social and Economic Circumstances Developed countries and international organisations concerned with IP should acknowledge that little is to be gained from imposing a predetermined agenda (or template) on developing countries. Many of the IP models that have been promoted to developing countries have not been successfully implemented because they failed to fully take into account the countries' social and economic circumstances. The history of the introduction of IP systems into developing countries does not evidence a correlation between the strength of IP protection

[1] See also Hirouki Odagiri et al (eds), *Intellectual Property Rights, Development and Catch UP* (Oxford, 2010) 417-430.

R.M. Olwan, *Intellectual Property and Development*,
DOI 10.1007/978-3-642-27907-2_7, © Springer-Verlag Berlin Heidelberg 2013

and social and economic development. It is also important to recognise that economic development will not necessarily occur merely as a result of the introduction of a system of IP laws. Developing countries must understand that development is a complicated process, often achieved over many years. In pursuing economic development, developing countries must address a range of policies and issues, including efficient and effective government, coherent economic policies, political stability, human capital, technical infrastructure, and the rule of law.

Policy 2: Rethink Traditional Views of IP in Developing Countries

The traditional view in developing countries is that IP is an essential tool for promoting economic development. According to this view, the availability of IP protection and enforcement is a key factor in encouraging FDI and technology transfer from developed countries.

Developing countries must critically reassess their attitude toward IP and ensure that they adopt appropriately structured models of IP that are designed to promote their cultural, as well their economic development. IP is not merely a matter of interest for legal professionals but also essential to the development of local industry. As well as understanding the legal implications of IP, developing countries need to understand its economic dimension and its relevance to their particular economic circumstances.

Developing countries must reconsider the purpose for adopting IP systems. The rationale for introducing IP laws is much more ambitious than merely attracting foreign investment. Such laws should also underpin social and economic development. However, if IP laws are to serve this objective, they must not be simply copied from statutes in force in other jurisdictions but must be crafted to suit localised social and economic conditions.

Policy 3: Understand the Economic and Cultural Dimensions of IP

IP should not be looked upon as an end in itself but as one of a range of possible tools that developing countries can use to promote innovation, creativity, education, technological capacity, and development.[2] It is also important to recognise IP not only from an economic perspective but also from a cultural perspective. This requires developing countries to design IP systems that promote not only economic development but also local culture and boost local innovation.

Developing countries must adopt legal models—whether through copyright or sui generis laws—that will best promote their culture and their indigenous knowledge. Such measures must be based on an examination and understanding of the relationship between IP, culture, and social development in their jurisdictions. Those studies would then form the basis for developing national and international policies that promote and protect their culture, traditional cultural expressions (TKEs), and traditional knowledge (TK).

---

[2] UNCTAD ICTSD, *Towards Development–Oriented Intellectual Property Policy: Advancing the Reform Agenda*, 2nd Bellagio Series on Development and Intellectual Property, 18-21 September 2003, IPRonline <http://www.iprsonline.org/unctadictsd/bellagio/docs/Bellagio2_Report.pdf>.

Policy 4: Engage Government Actively in Developing IP Strategies

The Internet offers many opportunities for developing countries in terms of accessing up-to-date information related to health, education, science, environment, government, law, and many other topics. It is important for developing countries to understand the power of the Internet and use it to their advantage.

Every developing country, each with its particular cultural outlook and its own distinctive history, can benefit from the usage and exploitation of the Internet and digital technologies. The role of governments is highly important in that regard. Governments should design appropriate policies that maximise the benefits of the Internet for the country's social and economic development. These policies include appropriate regulation and macro-economic strategies in areas such as human capital and social and economic development.[3] Drafting proper policies requires coordinated planning across several large policy areas such as telecommunications, copyright, patents, education, and culture.[4] Developing countries should give urgent attention to encouraging investment in human capital, particularly through channelling investment into health and education. In addition, these countries should think creatively about models of governance for the production of knowledge, which maximises their participation in the processes of innovation.[5]

Developing countries should also commit resources towards launching an awareness campaign to educate the public, particularly students, teachers, archivists, academics, and librarians, about how they can best access and capitalise

---

[3] Ruth L. Okediji, *Development in the Information Age*, UNCTAD- ICTSD Project on IPRs and Sustinable Development, Issue Paper Number 9, (May 2004), IPRonline 31 <http://www.iprsonline.org/unctadictsd/docs/CS_Okediji.pdf>.

The commentator Sisule Musungu proposes the following:

> Instead of the extreme positions-one-size-fits-all and outright rejection of Western-style IP law—there are many shades of gray allowed under the current international agreements. The proposed solution to this current schism is threefold: 1) implementation, in phases, of IP laws that are tailored to a country's needs; 2) greater guidance an involvement by international organizations to help a country build on its strengths and pre-existing industries; and 3) a mandatory level of investment or involvement by developed countries in the creation and development of these IP law regimes and industries in the developing countries.

See Sisule F Musungu, *Rethinking Innovation, Development and Intellectual Property in the UN: WIPO and Beyond TRIPS*, Quaker International Affairs Programme, Issue Paper 5, (2005), The Quaker United Nations Office (QUNO) <http://www.quno.org/geneva/pdf/economic/Issues/TRIPS53.pdf>.

[4] Dalindyebo Shabalala, *Towards A Digital Agenda for Developing Countries, Research Papers 13* (August 2007) South Center <http://www.southcentre.org/index.php?option=com_content&task=view&id=65&Itemid=1>.

[5] Peter Drahos, *An Alternative Framework for the Global Regulation of Intellectual Property Rights* Centre for Governance of Knowledge and Development Working Paper (October 2005) <https://www.anu.edu.au/fellows/pdrahos/articles/pdfs/2005analternativeframework.pdf>.

on the free materials that are available online.[6] Developing countries should consider adopting related national education policies and working toward raising literacy rates, building knowledge capacity, and infrastructure.[7] All such policies need to work in harmony with developing countries' IP policies.

Policy 5: Develop an IP and Development Strategy to Deal with FTAs
It is important for any developing country that is considering entering into an FTA with the US, EU, or any developed country to prepare its own strategy to deal with the consequences of signing that FTA. Any developing country that is considering entering an FTA should ask itself a number of questions. What are the social, economic, and cultural implications of signing the FTA? Does signing the FTA serve or impede social and economic development? Which type of FTA best suits the country's national interests? Will any IP provisions included in the FTA have a major impact upon the social and economic development of the country?

IP provisions should be considered to be an important part of any FTA that is signed by any developing country because those provisions can have a major effect on the law and practice of law in that developing country. It is important to study carefully the legal, health, educational, social, and cultural implications of the IP provisions that are to be introduced in the FTA. If the FTA puts more IP obligations on the developing country than are required in the international IP treaties that it has actually signed, it should seriously consider not introducing such provisions or at least negotiate softer provisions that do not go beyond its international obligations.

For example, if a particular developing country has signed the *Berne Convention*, which obliges the country to protect copyright for 50 years after an author's death, the country should not approve a provision that requires them to extend copyright protection to 70 years without careful consideration. An extension of protection to 70 years affects the opportunity of people to benefit from works that would otherwise enter into the public domain. It is also important to give particular attention to digital rights management (DRM) provisions. If the FTA requires a developing country to introduce provisions that prohibit the circumvention of technological protection measures (TPMs), it is important to make sure that these provisions are balanced. This means that such provisions should not only protect owners but also give the public appropriate limitations and exceptions for the circumvention of TPMs. These limitations and exceptions should include interoperability of computer software, national security, enforcement agencies, encryption research, and certain educational purposes. Developing countries that have signed FTAs need to ensure that they are given enough flexibility in implementing the IP provisions into their local laws to meet their specific needs.

Developing countries that have signed an FTA with the US, such as Mexico, Jordan, Chile, and others need to be encouraged to share their experiences with

---

[6] Consumers International, *Copyright and Access to Knowledge, Policy Recommendations on Flexibilities in Copyright Laws* (2006) Soros Foundation <http://www.consumersinternational.org/media/303356/copyright%20and%20access%20to%20knowledge%20-%20full%20report%20(pdf).pdf>.

[7] Margaret Chon, 'Intellectual Property and the Development Divide' (2006) 27 *Codozo Law Review* 2813 <http://papers.ssrn.com/sol3/papers.cfm?abstract_id=894162>.

other developing countries as to the impact of their implementation of the FTAs in their economy and their society.

Policy 6: Encourage WIPO to Adopt a Pragmatic Approach to Developing IP Capabilities
Although WIPO adopted the Development Agenda in 2007, there is little evidence of the results of its adoption. The Development Agenda is an ongoing process, and it remains to be seen how it will help the social and economic development of developing countries. The Development Agenda Group (DAG) suggested that a successful implementation of the WIPO Development Agenda requires

> a multifaceted approach to the range of issues related to IP; proactive leadership; continuous commitment; cooperation; engagements and oversight by member states; an enduring development cultural transformation with the WIPO secretariat; a member-state-driven organisation; and engagement with other international organisations and civil societies.[8]

It is also important for WIPO to develop a new generation of IP experts who are capable of helping developing countries to understand and implement IP from the perspective of development. These experts should advise developing countries on how best to draft and implement laws that suit their social and economic needs. WIPO technical assistance should be directed towards building the capacities of developing countries in the field of IP. This involves giving developing countries advice not only on what kind of laws they should have but also on how to use these laws to their benefit. WIPO should prepare an IP and development handbook that could help developing countries to draft and to implement IP laws that suit their individual social and economic conditions and identify the matters they need to consider in drafting their laws. There are also many other initiatives that WIPO could adopt, many of which have been outlined for future adaptation by the Provisional Committee on Proposals Related to a WIPO Development Agenda (PCDA).

7.3 Practical Measures for Developing Countries for IP and Development

It is important to think of IP as being "outside the box". This means that developing countries have to take practical measures towards IP protection. There is no single action or practical measure that could be utilised, and developing countries will need to adopt a combination of measures.

1) Educated Policymakers in Developing Countries on IP and Development Issues
It is critically important to educate policymakers and those involved in the drafting of IP laws in developing countries on IP and its relationship to development theory. IP is no longer seen as a tool that is used for the sole benefit of inventors and

---

[8] Statement By Egypt on Behalf of the Development Agenda Group (DAG), IP Watch <http://www.ip-watch.org/weblog/wp-content/uploads/2009/11/compilation-of-proposals.pdf>.

intellectual creators. IP is now seen as important for many people in developing countries as it impacts their lives on a wide range of issues, including education, innovation, creativity, and health.

Policymakers and legislatures in developing countries need to familiarise themselves with the subject of IP and development. The following is a primary reading list:

- Amartya Sen, *Development as Freedom* (Oxford: Oxford University Press, 1999)
- Ha Joon Chang, *Kicking Away the Ladder—Development Strategy in Historical Perspective* (Anthem, 2003); and
- Hirouki Odagiri, Akira Goto, Atsushi Sunami (eds), *Intellectual Property Rights, Development and Catch UP* (Oxford, 2010).

It is also important to teach people in developing countries about IP from the perspective of development. This means that IP scholars in those countries should teach IP to students in a balanced way that takes into consideration the needs of businesses, as well as consumers and the general public. IP scholars in developing countries should also make sure that appropriate educational materials reflecting this approach are made available for the benefit of the students.

2) Revise IP Laws

It is important to recognise that developing countries cannot refuse to adopt IP. Developing countries need to work with IP and to adapt it to suit their individual interests. This means that every provision that is introduced into the law should be studied and examined from a development perspective before it is implemented. IP laws will also need to be amended from time to time to adapt to the changing needs of each developing country as it grows. Some developing countries have strengthened their domestic IP laws to reflect the highest standards of protection under the treaties they have joined. This can impose an unduly restrictive regime where one is not required to appropriate. Developing countries should only adopt domestic IP laws to the extent required under such treaties to which they are signatories.

Law reform for the adoption of IP in developing countries should be an open process. Such a process would give citizens, interested groups, and organisations who are affected by IP laws the opportunity to make submissions about the law to the government. This would require legal experts involved in the drafting of the law to engage with the public at large and to solicit their opinions when needed. For its effective implementation, the law should be simple and understood by a wide audience, and not just the lawyers.

3) Encourage the Adoption and Use of Voluntary Mechanisms

It is imperative for developing countries to understand and use open code and content licensing systems (voluntary mechanisms) such as FOSS and CC. FOSS is an important tool that can help developing countries in their social and economic development, especially when it has been localised for the benefit of the people working in the government, business, and education sectors. CC is also a useful tool that can be used by Internet users, bloggers, and others for encouraging wider debates and spurring innovation, remixing culture and development through the Internet.

However, an open code and open content licensing system could be used alongside traditional models of copyright licensing when needed. The international copyright system suffers from many problems, and such licensing models could be used until reform of the copyright system occurs at a global level. A global system may not be that far away, as many international organisations such as WIPO are interested in playing an active role in that reform.[9] Finally, developing countries must be open to adopt other voluntary mechanisms for open content licensing that may be developed in the future and to use them, as appropriate to their circumstances.

4) Engage with Civil Society

Developing countries need to be open about their development plans, express their views, and engage widely with their citizens, especially in relation to IP and development. It is important for developing countries to work closely with international organisations and NGOs operating in the field of IP and development. These include Consumers International,[10] in the field of access to knowledge; Knowledge Ecology International,[11] in the field of IP and public health; CopySouth,[12] in the field of copyright; South Centre,[13] in global trade for development and innovation and access to knowledge; Electronic Information for Libraries (EIFL), working for public access and libraries;[14] COMMUNIA, working to preserve the digital public domain;[15] and the International Centre for Trade and Sustainable Development (ICTSD) in the field of innovation, trade and IP.[16] Developing countries will benefit from closely following the work of these international organisations and NGOs, soliciting their opinions in relation to IP in their jurisdictions and participating in the events, forums, and conferences they convene.

5) Form Effective IP Government Organisations That Understand Development Needs

Many of the IP government organisations (such as copyright and patent offices) in developing countries need to be restructured to meet the needs of those countries and to help in their development. These government organisations should not only work (or be seen to be working) to promote the IP rights of foreign corporations or to

[9] Francis Gurry, 'Blue Sky Conference: Future Directions in Copyright Law' (A speech by the Director General of WIPO to the Future of Copyright Conference, Queensland University of Technology, Sydney, 25 February 2011) <http://www.wipo.int/about-wipo/en/dgo/speeches/dg_blueskyconf_11.html>.

[10] Consumers International <http://www.consumersinternational.org/>.

[11] Knowledge Ecology International <http://keionline.org/>.

[12] CopySouth <http://www.copysouth.org/portal/>.

[13] South Centre <http://www.southcentre.org>.

[14] EIFL <http://www.eifl.net/>.

[15] COMMUNIA <http://communia-project.eu/>.

[16] ICTSD <http://ictsd.org/>.

increase their portfolio of IP registrations. They should also work closely with local inventors and creators, especially those who are keen to protect local culture and indigenous knowledge. This will require them to educate the public on how to use IP for the benefit of the domestic economy. These organisations should also advise governments on the proper policies that need to be implemented in order to gain maximum benefits under the international IP systems.

IP government institutions in the various developing countries should work together much more closely, especially in terms of sharing their experiences on how best to run their offices. Developing countries that are proximate to each other could develop mechanisms that allow them to achieve that coordination. For example, in relation to TK, a number of developing countries could work together to establish a TK database that would allow them to share their registration information. Developing countries also need to work with international organisations and even with developed countries that offer various programs that could enhance the experience of their IP offices.

6) Prepare Empirical Studies on the Importance of IP to Various Sectors

Empirical studies that relate to the importance of IP to various sectors of the economy are not very common in developing countries. It is important to undertake studies to evaluate the economic and cultural impacts of industries that rely on IP, in developing countries. Such studies should help understand the needs of various sectors of the economy and how they can be encouraged by the IP system. These studies would aid the drafting of appropriate IP laws that correspond with the economic and cultural needs of developing countries.

If a developing country does not have strong inventive capabilities but has strong industries based on TK, then IP laws should be particularly focussed on the protection and cultivation of TK. Basic protection for inventions would still exist, but this refocusing on industries important to developing economies would ensure that the IP system is geared towards protecting and promoting domestic IP instead of being seemingly geared towards solely protecting the patents of foreign corporations.

7) Give Particular Consideration to IP Exceptions and Limitations

It is critical to acknowledge the importance of having liberal and generous limitations and exceptions in the IP laws of developing countries as they are an essential part of achieving a balance between private and public rights.[17] There are many provisions

[17] See Lea Shaver (ed), *Access to Knowledge in Brazil* (Bloomsbury, 2010) 68. The Gowers Review of Intellectual Property was concerned that "the limitations in developing countries are too narrow and this may result in stunning new creators from generating and producing new works". The Gowers Review of Intellectual Property (November 2006) HM Treasury United Kingdom <http://www.hm-treasury.gov.uk/d/pbr06_gowers_report_755.pdf>.

Professor Margret Chon argues also that:

> There is a lot of "room for manoeuvre" both for intellectual property protection in the form of copyright, on the one hand, and for limitations and exceptions to copyright in order to access knowledge goods for essential education, on the other.

Chon, above n 7.

that create flexibility throughout the international IP agreements, including the *TRIPS Agreement*, which could be used to the advantage of developing countries.[18]

The copyright laws in developing countries should be flexible enough to allow creativity to flourish. This could be achieved by ensuring that appropriate limitations and exceptions are drafted in a way that promotes education, innovation, and development. It is also critically important for developing countries to include proper limitations and exceptions for blind and visually impaired people. These limitations and exceptions are critically needed to help those people to access copyrighted materials as, generally, copyright law in developing countries does not permit this degree of access without the copyright owner's authorisation.

8) Coordinate among Developing Countries on IP and Development Issues
Developing countries have worked together in international forums to bring IP and development issues that are important to them to the discussion table. They have managed to achieve limited success on a number of occasions. This happened in 1971, in Paris, when members of the *Berne Convention* adopted the *Berne Appendix on Special Provisions regarding Developing Countries*. It has also happened in 2001, in the Doha WTO Fourth Ministerial Conference, when developing countries were provided with the widest flexibilities in the *TRIPS Agreement* for public health purposes such as AIDS. Brazil, Argentina, and others were also successful in 2007 in making WIPO approve the Development Agenda for developing countries. This latest success was built on the continued work of developing countries to push for recognition of IP systems that take into consideration their development needs.

It is important to continue the efforts of developing countries in that regard and recognise that they have a great opportunity to make the changes they need to the international IP system. There is strong agreement between IP scholars and international organisations working in the field of IP that there is a need to change the current international IP system for the benefit of developing countries. WIPO's support is very important as it can play a leading role in that regard. WIPO is going through a restructuring of its main objectives and mission, and its new director, Francis Gurry, has stated on a number of occasions that WIPO should rethink its attitude towards IP. This will prove to be a critical time for developing countries, which need to coordinate their efforts in that regard, both nationally and internationally.

It is important for developing countries to have the best legal experts, with sufficient knowledge in IP and development, at the WIPO Development Agenda meetings. This would guarantee that those experts could express their views clearly and bring their concerns in relation to the IP system, to WIPO. Those experts should work together for one purpose, and that is to make sure that the Development Agenda is operationally effective for their benefit.

Locally, it is important to spread awareness among IP officers, IP scholars, international organisations, and others in developing countries of the importance

[18] See ch 5, 228–229 and 258–260.

of the Development Agenda and the implications that it might have on the practice of IP in those countries and beyond.

Finally, developing countries should understand the power of the Internet and use it for their advantage. This could be achieved by legal experts and IP scholars using the Internet to discuss the appropriate ways of structuring IP systems that suit the developmental needs of developing countries. The Internet can also be used to solicit the opinions of the public on IP laws that can touch their lives in important areas, including access to knowledge, education, environment, and health.

9) Structure Strong Competition Laws That Do Not Allow IP Misuse

To guarantee against the misuse of the IP system by any powerful corporation or owner and to make sure it is used for the benefit of the citizens and the economy, it is important for developing countries to put in place strong competition laws that support the proper use of the IP system. History has shown, in countries such as Japan, the importance of drafting proper competition laws that support the development of the country in its early stage of development. The competition laws should be carefully drafted to ensure that they are aligned with the country's economic circumstances and the requirements of local industry.

IP laws should not be simply transposed from laws introduced in another country, even where that other country is also a developing country. The legislation should be drafted specifically for the particular developing country and should take into account the country's stage of economic development, including the extent of knowledge of IP law and its application. The laws should also be reviewed on a regular basis and revised as necessary to ensure that they meet the country's changing economic and industrial needs. A committee of legal experts and economists should be established to meet regularly to discuss the effects of competition and IP laws on the development of the economy and to make sure that the laws are amended when required.

10) Develop Strategies That Enforce IP Rights Internationally

This has proven to be very important in a number of cases related to registration of IP rights owned by developing and emerging economies. In the case of India, in September 1997, a Texas-based corporation registered a patent with the US Patent Trademark Office (USPTO), which allowed it to sell basmati rice to the US market.[19] India was outraged by the action of the foreign corporations and threatened to take the matter to the WTO as a violation of the *TRIPS Agreement*. The case was later resolved when the USPTO decided to cancel the patent after a review.

In another case, in 2006 Starbucks denied Ethiopian farmers the right to register their famous branded coffee as trademarks with the USPTO.[20] In June 2007,

[19] Anurag Jadli, 'Rice Companies in Court: Searching for A Grain of Truth' Midday (Delhi) (online), 23 February 2011 <http://www.mid-day.com/news/2011/feb/230211-news-delhi-Two-major-exporters-Rice-companies-copyright-issues.htm#>; BBC, *'South Asia King of Rice in Court'*, BBC (online), 17 July 1998 <http://news.bbc.co.uk/2/hi/south_asia/134609.stm>.

[20] Ibid.

Starbucks agreed, under pressure from activists and consumer groups, to sign a trademark licensing agreement for the names owned by the Ethiopian farmers. These two cases, and others, have shown the importance of developing countries and emerging economies preparing action plans that they can implement in the event that foreign corporations seek to register their IP rights in developed countries.

The action plan should have clear, practical measures that local farmers, or any IP owners, from developing countries can follow in the event that their IP rights have been infringed internationally. Developing countries should also work with international organisations and NGOs that could help them protect their IP rights in developed countries, such as Oxfam International, which helped the Ethiopian government in its case against Starbucks.

11) Utilise Fully Resources Available Under WIPO Development Agenda

Developing countries need to study closely the 45 recommendations adopted by the WIPO member states that were made by the Provisional Committee on Proposals Related to a WIPO Development Agenda (PCDA). The recommendations provide an opportunity for developing countries to further develop policy and outcomes. The strategies outlined in the recommendations have the potential to provide guidance and resources to developing countries in seeking to achieve much of what has been recommended in this chapter. However, an unimaginative implementation of the recommendations will lead to little, whereas utilising the recommendations in a way that truly furthers the needs of developing countries has the potential to achieve much more. This book can be used as a primary tool in helping developing countries to understand and utilise these recommendations to their best advantage. For example, if developing countries could take the insights developed in the book and use them to conform to the recommendations of WIPO's PCDA, such as recommendations 35 and 37[21] (IP evaluation studies) and recommendations 14 and 17[22] (flexibilities), that would greatly assist those countries in their path to social and economic development.

---

[21] Recommendations 35 and 37 of the PCDA provides that:

35) To request WIPO to undertake, upon request of Member States, new studies to assess the economic, social and cultural impact of the use of intellectual property systems in these States.

37) Upon request and as directed by Member States, WIPO may conduct studies on the protection of intellectual property, to identify the possible links and impacts between intellectual property and development.

See WIPO, *The 45 Adopted Recommendations under the WIPO Development Agenda* (2007) <http://www.wipo.int/ip-development/en/agenda/recommendations.html>.

[22] Recommendations 14 and 17 of the PCDA provides as follows:

14) Within the framework of the agreement between WIPO and the WTO, WIPO shall make available advice to developing countries and LDCs, on the implementation and operation of the rights and obligations and the understanding and use of flexibilities contained in the TRIPS Agreement.

17) In its activities, including norm-setting, WIPO should take into account the flexibilities in international intellectual property agreements, especially those which are of interest to developing countries and LDCs. Ibid.

7.4 Other Suggested Practical Measures for Developing Countries for IP and Development

In addition to the above measures, there are additional measures that developing countries can implement.

1) Establish a Centre for IP and Development for Developing Countries
The knowledge economy is a key driver in the global economy and a robust and sophisticated approach to the development of the law, and policy relating to the knowledge economy is vital. Developing countries lack fully informed guidance in this area. It is important to establish a leading international centre for IP and development in developing countries. The centre would provide assistance and leadership for developing countries on IP and development and could assist them in harnessing the social, cultural, and economic benefits of Internet and digital technologies.

The Centre could be established in one of the emerging economies such as India, China, or Brazil or any other developing country that wants to play an important role in that field and that has the financial capabilities to implement such an initiative. The centre should encourage IP experts from developing countries and beyond to discuss issues related to IP and development. This should be done through the use of the Internet and digital technologies that will allow the centre to distribute knowledge and to engage with the public. The main objective of the centre would be to distribute knowledge to the public and to engage in debates regarding the future development of IP systems in developing countries.

2) Conduct an International Conference for IP and Development
WIPO and other international organisations involved in IP and trade could help developing countries by organising a yearly conference on IP and development. The conference would aim to invite senior policymakers (judges, government officials, ministers, and academics) and industry leaders to discuss IP and its relevance to developing countries. The conference could also invite legal scholars and IP experts to assess the extent to which voluntary mechanisms such as FOSS and CC can operate with the legal systems of developing countries. Such a conference would raise public awareness of the importance of IP and how it could assist developing countries in their social and economic development. It could be an important event that could enable government officials, leaders of educational institutions, and business people to discuss how the Internet and digital technologies are impacting on their activities. It would also allow legal scholars to examine how legal rules facilitate or hinder such activities.

3) Implement an International Course on IP and Development
In 1998, the WIPO Academy was established to advance the knowledge of IP and research worldwide.[23] The Academy has a number of IP courses that are offered through distance education to professionals and researchers from developing countries. Moreover, most of the courses that are taught only focus on increasing

[23] See WIPO Academy <http://www.wipo.int/academy/en/>.

the knowledge of participants about IP systems and treaties.[24] There is currently no course offered that is specifically directed towards IP in developing countries. When teaching IP, it is important to shift developing countries from the perspective that 'more IP laws are better' by explaining how IP laws should be structured to assist developing countries in their social and economic development.

WIPO should present practical workshops that bring together policymakers and legal experts involved in drafting IP laws in developing countries. Representatives should come together in Geneva to discuss how best they can structure IP laws that support their social and economic development.

7.5 Conclusion

IP systems can indeed assist developing countries in their social and economic development. However, this is something that cannot happen instantly. Developing countries must have the patience and persistence to work to achieve this outcome. IP laws and systems will not help developing countries if they are introduced without proper consideration of the social and economic conditions for each country.

Developing countries have to ensure that their IP system is interlinked with their other policies and development plans. They have to structure IP laws that suit their interests and local conditions and guard against the wholesale transplanting of IP systems from abroad (even if those systems were successful in the countries where they have been implemented). It is important to understand the needs of the culture and economy of developing countries before introducing any IP law. IP systems will not bring social and economic development to developing countries without having other policies in place that encourage development. These policies should be considered as part of the foundation for the visions of a developing country in relation to IP. Such policies should be based on an understanding of the historical lessons of the development of the international IP system and also on the experiences of those countries that have used IP systems to further their development.

There are a number of practical measures that can be utilised by developing countries to ensure that they can use IP systems to their benefit. These policies can change from time to time, depending on the changing circumstances of each developing country. It may be true that these strategies will require a substantial amount of time and financial investment for their implementation. However, it has been proven that current IP systems are not working in developing countries as their social and economic development are not yet accelerating. Therefore, developing countries must invest whatever resources they can to work with international organisations, NGOs, and other developing countries to create IP systems that truly benefit those countries.

---

[24] The courses offered by the WIPO Academy are available here: <http://www.wipo.int/academy/en/courses/distance_learning/catalog/c_index.html>.

Chapter 8
Conclusions

Prior to the adoption of the Development Agenda by WIPO in 2007, there was little research and information to guide developing countries on how IP systems may be structured in a way that assists them at their particular stages of social and economic development. Much of the research on IP and development was outdated and uncritically favoured the adoption of IP systems in developing countries on the ground that doing so would automatically be conducive to their economic development. Such research has predominantly been produced by English-speaking commentators and approached the subject of IP and development from a theoretical perspective or an empirical viewpoint without adequately addressing historical and cultural factors. While focusing on the benefits that IP can bring to developing countries, the research neither addressed nor provided any effective guidance as to how developing countries can appropriately adapt IP laws to gain the greatest benefits having regard to their local circumstances.

It is clear that merely adopting IP laws, irrespective of their form, will not in itself bring about economic development in developing countries. It is imperative to go beyond the 'traditional argument' urged on developing countries that if they adopt IP laws, economic development will follow. Rather, to advance economically, developing countries must first ensure that they have effective governments, good economic policies, sound infrastructure, educated human capital, and the rule of law. Those responsible for drafting IP laws for developing countries must better understand how IP can impact on economies and how IP laws must be appropriate to each country's economic realities. While IP may bring foreign direct investment (FDI), technology transfer, domestic innovation, and research and development activity (R&D) to developing countries, the enactment of IP laws is no gurantee that economic development will automatically follow.

IP scholars express divergent opinions on what kind of IP systems promote economic development in developing countries. While they may support the proposition that IP laws can promote economic development, for the most part they do not provide practical, detailed information to developing countries on which IP regimes they should adopt or how the process can be managed. It is important for IP scholars to be more specific and practical when addressing the situation of

R.M. Olwan, *Intellectual Property and Development*,
DOI 10.1007/978-3-642-27907-2_8, © Springer-Verlag Berlin Heidelberg 2013

developing countries. Before advocating that developing countries should adopt IP systems to promote their economic development, they need a sound understanding of theories of development. The introduction of IP in developing countries will only truly be of benefit if it assists in both their economic *and* their social development.

IP and development must be studied against the background of the historical evolution of the international IP system. From this perspective, it can be seen that, from an early stage, developing countries attempted to change and reform the international IP system, so that their interests and local conditions were recognised. While reforms proposed by developing countries were opposed by developed countries, developing countries nevertheless occasionally achieved a degree of success, through revisions to the Berne and the UCC conventions and the Doha WTO Fourth Ministerial Conference. The recognition by WIPO of the Development Agenda followed persistent calls by developing countries for reform of the international IP system so that it takes their interests into account. IP scholars must study IP and development from this historical prespective and provide developing countries with practical guidance to maximise the benefits that may be leveraged from the WIPO Development Agenda.

Culture has an important effect on how people perceive and enforce IP laws. It is inappropriate for developing countries to uncritically adopt foreign IP laws and impose them on their citizens and businesses without having proper regard to whether or not these laws will complement or suit their national culture. Developing countries must ensure that IP laws are culturally sensitive. Further, their local and international cultural policies should ensure that IP laws respect traditional knowledge (TK) and are geared towards promoting—not stifling—culture. It is imperative that IP scholars pay due regard to the cultural aspects of IP, instead of viewing IP from an exclusively economic perspective.

The Internet is a powerful tool and a source of opportunities that should be harnessed by developing countries to further their development. Accordingly, it is important that IP laws in developing countries do not unreasonably interfere with their citizens' usage of the Internet and ensure that such usage contributes to the country's social and economic development. IP laws in developing countries should faciliate online access to knowledge and allow citizens to develop their educational capabilties through the Internet. Voluntary mechanisms such as Free and Open-Source Software (FOSS) and Creative Commons (CC) licences have not been fully considered in the scholarship on IP and development. FOSS is an important tool for fostering the growth of localised software industries, and CC can help scholars, researchers, government officials find, use, and share information and knowledge. IP and legal experts in developing countries need to understand these developments so they can advise their governments on how they can be used to their advantage.

It is necessary for each developing country to develop its own policies and roadmaps for IP and development. Developing countries need to reexamine their IP laws to ensure that they are in fact conducive to their social and economic development. IP laws should be designed to be 'pro-development', based on an understanding of the circumstances in the particular country, its local needs, and its international obligations. This book considers how a development-oriented approach may be implemented in the copyright laws of Jordan. A similar approach could be adapted by other developing countries and could be applicable to other forms of IP such as trademark, patent, and design laws. WIPO has an important role to play in facilitating the implementation of IP systems in developing countries. One way in which WIPO could contribute to this process would be by producing an authoritative handbook on IP and development, containing practical advice and guidance for developing countries on how to structure their IP laws to best serve their social and economic development objectives. Under the auspices of WIPO, developing countries need to work together to ensure that their IP and development needs and concerns are appropriately addressed.

Appendix A
Universal Copyright Convention as Revised at Paris on 24 July 1971, with Appendix Declaration Relating to Article XVII and Resolution Concerning Article XI 1971

The Contracting States,

Moved by the desire to ensure in all countries copyright protection of literary, scientific and artistic works,

Convinced that a system of copyright protection appropriate to all nations of the world and expressed in a universal convention, additional to, and without impairing international systems already in force, will ensure respect for the rights of the individual and encourage the development of literature, the sciences and the arts,

Persuaded that such a universal copyright system will facilitate a wider dissemination of works of the human mind and increase international understanding,

Have resolved to revise the Universal Copyright Convention as signed at Geneva on 6 September 1952 (hereinafter called 'the 1952 Convention'), and consequently,

Have agreed as follows:

Article I

Each Contracting State undertakes to provide for the adequate and effective protection of the rights of authors and other copyright proprietors in literary, scientific and artistic works, including writings, musical, dramatic and cinematographic works, and paintings, engravings and sculpture.

Article II

1. Published works of nationals of any Contracting State and works first published in that State shall enjoy in each other Contracting State the same protection as that other State accords to works of its nationals first published in its own territory, as well as the protection specially granted by this Convention.

R.M. Olwan, *Intellectual Property and Development*,
DOI 10.1007/978-3-642-27907-2, © Springer-Verlag Berlin Heidelberg 2013

2. Unpublished works of nationals of each Contracting State shall enjoy in each other Contracting State the same protection as that other State accords to unpublished works of its own nationals, as well as the protection specially granted by this Convention.
3. For the purpose of this Convention any Contracting State may, by domestic legislation, assimilate to its own nationals any person domiciled in that State.

Article III

1. Any Contracting State which, under its domestic law, requires as a condition of copyright, compliance with formalities such as deposit, registration, notice, notarial certificates, payment of fees or manufacture or publication in that Contracting State, shall regard these requirements as satisfied with respect to all works protected in accordance with this Convention and first published outside its territory and the author of which is not one of its nationals, if from the time of the first publication all the copies of the work published with the authority of the author or other copyright proprietor bear the symbol © accompanied by the name of the copyright proprietor and the year of first publication placed in such manner and location as to give reasonable notice of claim of copyright.
2. The provisions of paragraph 1 shall not preclude any Contracting State from requiring formalities or other conditions for the acquisition and enjoyment of copyright in respect of works first published in its territory or works of its nationals wherever published.
3. The provisions of paragraph 1 shall not preclude any Contracting State from providing that a person seeking judicial relief must, in bringing the action, comply with procedural requirements, such as that the complainant must appear through domestic counsel or that the complainant must deposit with the court or an administrative office, or both, a copy of the work involved in the litigation; provided that failure to comply with such requirements shall not affect the validity of the copyright, nor shall any such requirement be imposed upon a national of another Contracting State if such requirement is not imposed on nationals of the State in which protection is claimed.
4. In each Contracting State there shall be legal means of protecting without formalities the unpublished works of nationals of other Contracting States.
5. If a Contracting State grants protection for more than one term of copyright and the first term is for a period longer than one of the minimum periods prescribed in Article IV, such State shall not be required to comply with the provisions of paragraph 1 of this Article in respect of the second or any subsequent term of copyright.

Article IV

1. The duration of protection of a work shall be governed, in accordance with the provisions of article II and this article, by the law of the Contracting State in which protection is claimed.
2. (a) The term of protection for works protected under this Convention shall not be less than the life of the author and 25 years after his death. However, any Contracting State which, on the effective date of this Convention in that State, has limited this term for certain classes of works to a period computed from the first publication of the work, shall be entitled to maintain these exceptions and to extend them to other classes of works. For all these classes the term of protection shall not be less than 25 years from the date of first publication.
   (b) Any Contracting State which, upon the effective date of this Convention in that State, does not compute the term of protection upon the basis of the life of the author, shall be entitled to compute the term of protection from the date of the first publication of the work or from its registration prior to publication, as the case may be, provided the term of protection shall not be less than 25 years from the date of first publication or from its registration prior to publication, as the case may be.
   (c) If the legislation of a Contracting State grants two or more successive terms of protection, the duration of the first term shall not be less than one of the minimum periods specified in sub-paragraphs (a) and (b).
3. The provisions of paragraph 2 shall not apply to photographic works or to works of applied art; provided, however, that the term of protection in those Contracting States which protect photographic works, or works of applied art in so far as they are protected as artistic works, shall not be less than 10 years for each of said classes of works.
4. (a) No Contracting State shall be obliged to grant protection to a work for a period longer than that fixed for the class of works to which the work in question belongs, in the case of unpublished works by the law of the Contracting State of which the author is a national, and in the case of published works by the law of the Contracting State in which the work has been first published.
   (b) For the purposes of the application of sub-paragraph (a), if the law of any Contracting State grants two or more successive terms of protection, the period of protection of that State shall be considered to be the aggregate of those terms. However, if a specified work is not protected by such State during the second or any subsequent term for any reason, the other Contracting States shall not be obliged to protect it during the second or any subsequent term.

5. For the purposes of the application of paragraph 4, the work of a national of a Contracting State, first published in a non-Contracting State, shall be treated as though first published in the Contracting State of which the author is a national.
6. For the purposes of the application of paragraph 4, in case of simultaneous publication in two or more Contracting States, the work shall be treated as though first published in the State which affords the shortest term, any work published in two or more Contracting States within 30 days of its first publication shall be considered as having been published simultaneously in said Contracting States.

Article IV bis

1. The rights referred to in article I shall include the basic rights ensuring the author's economic interests, including the exclusive right to authorize reproduction by any means, public performance and broadcasting. The provisions of this article shall extend to works protected under this Convention either in their original form or in any form recognizably derived from the original.
2. However, any Contracting State may, by its domestic legislation, make exceptions that do not conflict with the spirit and provisions of this Convention, to the rights mentioned in paragraph 1 of this article. Any State whose legislation so provides, shall nevertheless accord a reasonable degree of effective protection to each of the rights to which exception has been made.

Article V

1. The rights referred to in article I shall include the exclusive right of the author to make, publish and authorize the making and publication of translations of works protected under this Convention.
2. However, any Contracting State may, by its domestic legislation, restrict the right of translation of writings, but only subject to the following provisions:

   (a) If, after the expiration of a period of 7 years from the date of the first publication of a writing, a translation of such writing has not been published in a language in general use of the Contracting State, by the owner of the right of translation or with his authorization, any national of such Contracting State may obtain a non-exclusive licence from the competent authority thereof to translate the work into that language and publish the work so translated.

   (b) Such national shall in accordance with the procedure of the State concerned, establish either that he has requested, and been denied, authorization by the proprietor of the right to make and publish the translation, or that, after due diligence on his part, he was unable to find the owner of the right. A licence may also be granted on the same conditions if all previous editions of a translation in a language in general use in the Contracting State are out of print.

(c) If the owner of the right of translation cannot be found, then the applicant for a licence shall send copies of his application to the publisher whose name appears on the work and, if the nationality of the owner of the right of translation is known, to the diplomatic or consular representative of the State of which such owner is a national, or to the organization which may have been designated by the government of that State. The licence shall not be granted before the expiration of a period of 2 months from the date of the dispatch of the copies of the application.

(d) Due provision shall be made by domestic legislation to ensure to the owner of the right of translation a compensation which is just and conforms to international standards, to ensure payment and transmittal of such compensation, and to ensure a correct translation of the work.

(e) The original title and the name of the author of the work shall be printed on all copies of the published translation. The licence shall be valid only for publication of the translation in the territory of the Contracting State where it has been applied for. Copies so published may be imported and sold in another Contracting State if a language in general use in such other State is the same language as that into which the work has been so translated, and if the domestic law in such other State makes provision for such licences and does not prohibit such importation and sale. Where the foregoing conditions do not exist, the importation and sale of such copies in a Contracting State shall be governed by its domestic law and its agreements. The licence shall not be transferred by the licensee.

(f) The licence shall not be granted when the author has withdrawn from circulation all copies of the work.

Article V bis

1. Any Contracting State regarded as a developing country in conformity with the established practice of the General Assembly of the United Nations may, by a notification deposited with the Director-General of the United Nations Educational, Scientific and Cultural Organization (hereinafter called 'the Director-General') at the time of its ratification, acceptance or accession or thereafter, avail itself of any or all of the exceptions provided for in articles V ter and V quater.
2. Any such notification shall be effective for 10 years from the date of coming into force of this Convention, or for such part of that ten-year period as remains at the date of deposit of the notification, and may be renewed in whole or in part for further periods of 10 years each if, not more than 15 or less than 3 months before

the expiration of the relevant ten-year period, the Contracting State deposits a further notification with the Director-General. Initial notifications may also be made during these further periods of 10 years in accordance with the provisions of this article.

3. Notwithstanding the provisions of paragraph 2, a Contracting State that has ceased to be regarded as a developing country as referred to in paragraph 1 shall no longer be entitled to renew its notification made under the provisions of paragraph 1 or 2, and whether or not it formally withdraws the notification such State shall be precluded from availing itself of the exceptions provided for in articles V ter and V quater at the end of the current ten-year period, or at the end of 3 years after it has ceased to be regarded as a developing country, whichever period expires later.
4. Any copies of a work already made under the exceptions provided for in articles V ter and V quater may continue to be distributed after the expiration of the period for which notifications under this article were effective until their stock is exhausted.
5. Any Contracting State that has deposited a notification in accordance with article XIII with respect to the application of this Convention to a particular country or territory, the situation of which can be regarded as analogous to that of the States referred to in paragraph 1 of this article, may also deposit notifications and renew them in accordance with the provisions of this article with respect to any such country or territory. During the effective period of such notifications, the provisions of articles V ter and V quater may be applied with respect to such country or territory. The sending of copies from the country or territory to the Contracting State shall be considered as export within the meaning of articles V ter and V quater.

Article V ter

1. (a) Any Contracting State to which article V bis (1) applies may substitute for the period of 7 years provided for in article V (2) a period of 3 years or any longer period prescribed by its legislation. However, in the case of a translation into a language not in general use in one or more developed countries that are party to this Convention or only the 1952 Convention, the period shall be 1 year instead of 3.

   (b) A Contracting State to which article V bis (1) applies may, with the unanimous agreement of the developed countries party to this Convention or only the 1952 Convention and in which the same language is in general use, substitute, in the case of translation into that language, for the period of 3 years provided for in sub-paragraph (a) another period as determined by such agreement but not shorter than 1 year. However, this sub-paragraph shall not apply where the language in question is English, French or Spanish. Notification of any such agreement shall be made to the Director-General.

(c) The licence may only be granted if the applicant, in accordance with the procedure of the State concerned, establishes either that he has requested, and been denied, authorization by the owner of the right of translation, or that, after due diligence on his part, he was unable to find the owner of the right. At the same time as he makes his request he shall inform either the International Copyright Centre established by the United Nations Educational, Scientific and Cultural Organization or any national or regional information centre which may have been designated in a notification to that effect deposited with the Director-General by the government of the State in which the publisher is believed to have his principal place of business.

(d) If the owner of the right of translation cannot be found, the applicant for a licence shall send, by registered airmail, copies of his application to the publisher whose name appears on the work and to any national or regional information centre as mentioned in sub-paragraph (c). If no such centre is notified he shall also send a copy to the international copyright information centre established by the United Nations Educational, Scientific and Cultural Organization.

2. (a) Licences obtainable after 3 years shall not be granted under this article until a further period of 6 months has elapsed and licences obtainable after 1 year until a further period of 9 months has elapsed. The further period shall begin either from the date of the request for permission to translate mentioned in paragraph 1 (c) or, if the identity or address of the owner of the right of translation is not known, from the date of dispatch of the copies of the application for a licence mentioned in paragraph 1 (d).

(b) Licences shall not be granted if a translation has been published by the owner of the right of translation or with his authorization during the said period of 6 or 9 months.

3. Any licence under this article shall be granted only for the purpose of teaching, scholarship or research.

4. (a) Any licence granted under this article shall not extend to the export of copies and shall be valid only for publication in the territory of the Contracting State where it has been applied for.

(b) Any copy published in accordance with a licence granted under this article shall bear a notice in the appropriate language stating that the copy is available for distribution only in the Contracting State granting the licence. If the writing bears the notice specified in article III (1) the copies shall bear the same notice.

(c) The prohibition of export provided for in sub-paragraph (a) shall not apply where a governmental or other public entity of a State which has granted a licence under this article to translate a work into a language other than English, French or Spanish sends copies of a translation prepared under such licence to another country if: (i) the recipients are individuals who are nationals of the Contracting State granting the licence, or organizations grouping such individuals; (ii) the copies are to be used only for the purpose of teaching, scholarship or research; (iii) the sending of the copies and their subsequent distribution to recipients is without the object of commercial purpose; and (iv) the country to which the copies have been sent has agreed with the Contracting State to allow the receipt, distribution or both and the Director-General has been notified of such agreement by any one of the governments which have concluded it.

5. Due provision shall be made at the national level to ensure:
   (a) that the licence provides for just compensation that is consistent with standards of royalties normally operating in the case of licences freely negotiated between persons in the two countries concerned; and
   (b) payment and transmittal of the compensation; however, should national currency regulations intervene, the competent authority shall make all efforts, by the use of international machinery, to ensure transmittal in internationally convertible currency or its equivalent.
6. Any licence granted by a Contracting State under this article shall terminate if a translation of the work in the same language with substantially the same content as the edition in respect of which the licence was granted is published in the said State by the owner of the right of translation or with his authorization, at a price reasonably related to that normally charged in the same State for comparable works. Any copies already made before the licence is terminated may continue to be distributed until their stock is exhausted.
7. For works which are composed mainly of illustrations a licence to translate the text and to reproduce the illustrations may be granted only if the conditions of Article V quater are also fulfilled.
8. (a) A licence to translate a work protected under this Convention, published in printed or analogous forms of reproduction, may also be granted to a broadcasting organization having its headquarters in a Contracting State to which Article V bis (1) applies, upon an application made in that State by the said organization under the following conditions:

   (i) the translation is made from a copy made and acquired in accordance with the laws of the Contracting State; (ii) the translation is for use only in broadcasts intended exclusively for teaching or for the dissemination of the results of specialized technical or scientific research to experts in a particular profession; (iii) the translation is used exclusively for the purposes set out in condition (ii), through broadcasts lawfully made which are intended for recipients on the territory of the Contracting State, including broadcasts made through the medium of sound or visual recordings lawfully and exclusively made for the purpose of such broadcasts; (iv) sound or visual recordings of the translation may be exchanged only between broadcasting organizations having their headquarters in the Contracting State granting the licence; and (v) all uses made of the translation are without any commercial purpose.

(b) Provided all of the criteria and conditions set out in sub-paragraph (a) are met, a licence may also be granted to a broadcasting organization to translate any text incorporated in an audio-visual fixation which was itself prepared and published for the sole purpose of being used in connexion with systematic instructional activities.
(c) Subject to sub-paragraphs (a) and (b), the other provisions of this Article shall apply to the grant and exercise of the licence.

9. Subject to the provisions of this Article, any licence granted under this Article shall be governed by the provisions of Article V, and shall continue to be governed by the provisions of Article V and of this Article, even after the seven-year period provided for in Article V (2) has expired. However, after the said period has expired, the licensee shall be free to request that the said licence be replaced by a new licence governed exclusively by the provisions of Article V.

Article V quater

1. Any Contracting State to which article V bis (1) applies may adopt the following provisions:

(a) If, after the expiration of (i) the relevant period specified in sub-paragraph (c) commencing from the date of first publication of a particular edition of a literary, scientific or artistic work referred to in paragraph 3, or (ii) any longer period determined by national legislation of the State, copies of such edition have not been distributed in that State to the general public or in connexion with systematic instructional activities at a price reasonably related to that normally charged in the State for comparable works, by the owner of the right of reproduction or with his authorization, any national of such State may obtain a non-exclusive licence from the competent authority to publish such edition at that or a lower price for use in connexion with systematic instructional activities. The licence may only be granted if such national, in accordance with the procedure of the State concerned, establishes either that he has requested, and been denied, authorization by the proprietor of the right to publish such work, or that, after due diligence on his part, he was unable to find the owner of the right. At the same time as he makes his request he shall inform either the international copyright information centre established by the United Nations Educational, Scientific and Cultural Organization or any national or regional information centre referred to in subparagraph (d).
(b) A licence may also be granted on the same conditions if, for a period of 6 months, no authorized copies of the edition in question have been on sale in the State concerned to the general public or in connexion with systematic

instructional activities at a price reasonably related to that normally charged in the State for comparable works.

(c) The period referred to in sub-paragraph (a) shall be 5 years except that: (i) for works of the natural and physical sciences, including mathematics, and of technology, the period shall be 3 years; (ii) for works of fiction, poetry, drama and music, and for art books, the period shall be 7 years.

(d) If the owner of the right of reproduction cannot be found, the applicant for a licence shall send, by registered air mail, copies of his application to the publisher whose name appears on the work and to any national or regional information centre identified as such in a notification deposited with the Director-General by the State in which the publisher is believed to have his principal place of business. In the absence of any such notification, he shall also send a copy to the international copyright information centre established by the United Nations Educational, Scientific and Cultural Organization. The licence shall not be granted before the expiration of a period of 3 months from the date of dispatch of the copies of the application.

(e) Licences obtainable after 3 years shall not be granted under this article: (i) until a period of 6 months has elapsed from the date of the request for permission referred to in sub-paragraph (a) or, if the identity or address of the owner of the right of reproduction is unknown, from the date of the dispatch of the copies of the application for a licence referred to in sub-paragraph (d); (ii) if any such distribution of copies of the edition as is mentioned in sub-paragraph (a) has taken place during that period.

(f) The name of the author and the title of the particular edition of the work shall be printed on all copies of the published reproduction. The licence shall not extend to the export of copies and shall be valid only for publication in the territory of the Contracting State where it has been applied for. The licence shall not be transferable by the licensee.

(g) Due provision shall be made by domestic legislation to ensure an accurate reproduction of the particular edition in question.

(h) A licence to reproduce and publish a translation of a work shall not be granted under this article in the following cases: (i) where the translation was not published by the owner of the right of translation or with his authorization; (ii) where the translation is not in a language in general use in the State with power to grant the licence.

2. The exceptions provided for in paragraph 1 are subject to the following additional provisions:

(a) Any copy published in accordance with a licence granted under this article shall bear a notice in the appropriate language stating that the copy is available for distribution only in the Contracting State to which the said licence applies. If the edition bears the notice specified in article III (1), the copies shall bear the same notice.

(b) Due provision shall be made at the national level to ensure: (i) that the licence provides for just compensation that is consistent with standards of royalties normally operating in the case of licences freely negotiated between persons in the two countries concerned; and (ii) payment and transmittal of the compensation; however. should national currency regulations intervene, the competent authority shall make all efforts, by the use of international machinery, to ensure transmittal in internationally convertible currency or its equivalent.

(c) Whenever copies of an edition of a work are distributed in the Contracting State to the general public or in connexion with systematic instructional activities, by the owner of the right of reproduction or with his authorization, at a price reasonably related to that normally charged in the State for comparable works, any licence granted under this article shall terminate if such edition is in the same language and is substantially the same in content as the edition published under the licence. Any copies already made before the licence is terminated may continue to be distributed until their stock is exhausted.

(d) No licence shall be granted when the author has withdrawn from circulation all copies of the edition in question.

3. (a) Subject to sub-paragraph (b), the literary, scientific or artistic works to which this article applies shall be limited to works published in printed or analogous forms of reproduction.

(b) The provisions of this article shall also apply to reproduction in audiovisual form of lawfully made audio-visual fixations including any protected works incorporated therein and to the translation of any incorporated text into a language in general use in the State with power to grant the licence; always provided that the audio-visual fixations in question were prepared and published for the sole purpose of being used in connexion with systematic instructional activities.

Article VI

'Publication', as used in this Convention, means the reproduction in tangible form and the general distribution to the public of copies of a work from which it can be read or otherwise visually perceived.

Article VII

This Convention shall not apply to works or rights in works which, at the effective date of this Convention in a Contracting State where protection is claimed, are permanently in the public domain in the said Contracting State.

Article VIII

1. This Convention, which shall bear the date of 24 July 1971, shall be deposited with the Director-General and shall remain open for signature by all States party to the 1952 Convention for a period of 120 days after the date of this Convention. It shall be subject to ratification or acceptance by the signatory States.
2. Any State which has not signed this Convention may accede thereto.
3. Ratification, acceptance or accession shall be effected by the deposit of an instrument to that effect with the Director-General.

Article IX

1. This Convention shall come into force 3 months after the deposit of twelve instruments of ratification, acceptance or accession.
2. Subsequently, this Convention shall come into force in respect of each State 3 months after that State has deposited its instrument of ratification, acceptance or accession.
3. Accession to this Convention by a State not party to the 1952 Convention shall also constitute accession to that Convention; however, if its instrument of accession is deposited before this Convention comes into force, such State may make its accession to the 1952 Convention conditional upon the coming into force of this Convention. After the coming into force of this Convention, no State may accede solely to the 1952 Convention.
4. Relations between States party to this Convention and States that are party only to the 1952 Convention, shall be governed by the 1952 Convention. However, any State party only to the 1952 Convention may, by a notification deposited with the Director-General, declare that it will admit the application of the 1971 Convention to works of its nationals or works first published in its territory by all States party to this Convention.

Article X

1. Each Contracting State undertakes to adopt, in accordance with its Constitution, such measures as are necessary to ensure the application of this Convention.
2. It is understood that at the date this Convention comes into force in respect of any State, that State must be in a position under its domestic law to give effect to the terms of this Convention.

Article XI

1. An Intergovernmental Committee is hereby established with the following duties:
   (a) to study the problems concerning the application and operation of the Universal Copyright Convention; (b) to make preparation for periodic revisions of this Convention; (c) to study any other problems concerning the international protection of copyright, in co-operation with the various interested international organizations, such as the United Nations Educational, Scientific and Cultural Organization, the International Union for the Protection of Literary and Artistic Works and the Organization of American States; (d) to inform States party to the Universal Copyright Convention as to its activities.
2. The Committee shall consist of the representatives of eighteen States party to this Convention or only to the 1952 Convention.
3. The Committee shall be selected with due consideration to a fair balance of national interests on the basis of geographical location, population, languages and stage of development.
4. The Director-General of the United Nations Educational, Scientific and Cultural Organization, the Director-General of the World Intellectual Property Organization and the Secretary-General of the Organization of American States, or their representatives, may attend meetings of the Committee in an advisory capacity.

Article XII

The Intergovernmental Committee shall convene a conference for revision whenever it deems necessary, or at the request of at least ten States party to this Convention.

Article XIII

1. Any Contracting State may, at the time of deposit of its instrument of ratification, acceptance or accession, or at any time thereafter, declare by notification addressed to the Director-General that this Convention shall apply to all or any of the countries or territories for the international relations of which it is responsible and this Convention shall thereupon apply to the countries or territories named in such notification after the expiration of the term of 3 months provided for in article IX. In the absence of such notification, this Convention shall not apply to any such country or territory.
2. However, nothing in this article shall be understood as implying the recognition or tacit acceptance by a Contracting State of the factual situation concerning a country or territory to which this Convention is made applicable by another Contracting State in accordance with the provisions of this article.

Article XIV

1. Any Contracting State may denounce this Convention in its own name or on behalf of all or any of the countries or territories with respect to which a notification has been given under article XIII. The denunciation shall be made by notification addressed to the Director-General. Such denunciation shall also constitute denunciation of the 1952 Convention.
2. Such denunciation shall operate only in respect of the State or of the country or territory on whose behalf it was made and shall not take effect until 12 months after the date of receipt of the notification.

Article XV

A dispute between two or more Contracting States concerning the interpretation or application of this Convention, not settled by negotiation, shall, unless the States concerned agree on some other method of settlement, be brought before the International Court of Justice for determination by it.

Article XVI

1. This Convention shall be established in English, French and Spanish. The three texts shall be signed and shall be equally authoritative.
2. Official texts of this Convention shall be established by the Director- General, after consultation with the governments concerned, in Arabic, German, Italian and Portuguese.
3. Any Contracting State or group of Contracting States shall be entitled to have established by the Director-General other texts in the language of its choice by arrangement with the Director-General.
4. All such texts shall be annexed to the signed texts of this Convention.

Article XVII

1. This Convention shall not in any way affect the provisions of the Berne Convention for the Protection of Literary and Artistic Works or membership in the Union created by that Convention.
2. In application of the foregoing paragraph, a declaration has been annexed to the present article. This declaration is an integral part of this Convention for the States bound by the Berne Convention on I January 1951, or which have or may

become bound to it at a later date. The signature of this Convention by such States shall also constitute signature of the said declaration, and ratification, acceptance or accession by such States shall include the declaration, as well as this Convention

Article XVIII

This Convention shall not abrogate multilateral or bilateral copyright conventions or arrangements that are or may be in effect exclusively between two or more American Republics. In the event of any difference either between the provisions of such existing conventions or arrangements and the provisions of this Convention, or between the provisions of this Convention and those of any new convention or arrangement which may be formulated between two or more American Republics after this Convention comes into force, the convention or arrangement most recently formulated shall prevail between the parties thereto. Rights in works acquired in any Contracting State under existing conventions or arrangements before the date this Convention comes into force in such State shall not be affected.

Article XIX

This Convention shall not abrogate multilateral or bilateral conventions or arrangements in effect between two or more Contracting States. In the event of any difference between the provisions of such existing conventions or arrangements and the provisions of this Convention, the provisions of this Convention shall prevail. Rights in works acquired in any Contracting State under existing conventions or arrangements before the date on which this Convention comes into force in such State shall not be affected. Nothing in this article shall affect the provisions of articles XVII and XVIII.

Article XX

Reservations to this Convention shall not be permitted.

Article XXI

1. The Director-General shall send duly certified copies of this Convention to the States interested and to the Secretary-General of the United Nations for registration by him.

2. He shall also inform all interested States of the ratifications, acceptances and accessions which have been deposited, the date on which this Convention comes into force, the notifications under this Convention and denunciations under article XIV.

APPENDIX DECLARATION RELATING TO ARTICLE XVII

The States which are members of the International Union for the Protection of Literary and Artistic Works (hereinafter called 'the Berne Union') and which are signatories to this Convention,

Desiring to reinforce their mutual relations on the basis of the said Union and to avoid any conflict which might result from the co-existence of the Berne Convention and the Universal Copyright Convention.

Recognizing the temporary need of some States to adjust their level of copyright protection in accordance with their stage of' cultural, social and economic development,

Have, by common agreement, accepted the terms of the following declaration:

(a) Except as provided by paragraph (b), works which, according to the Berne Convention, have as their country of origin a country which has withdrawn from the Berne Union after 1 January 1951 shall not be protected by the Universal Copyright Convention in the countries of the Berne Union;
(b) Where a Contracting State is regarded as a developing country in conformity with the established practice of the General Assembly of the United Nations, and has deposited with the Director-General of the United Nations Educational, Scientific and Cultural Organization, at the time of its withdrawal from the Berne Union, a notification to the effect that it regards itself as a developing country, the provisions of paragraph (a) shall not be applicable as long as such State may avail itself of the exceptions provided for by this Convention in accordance with article V bis.
(c) The Universal Copyright Convention shall not be applicable to the relationships among countries of the Berne Union in so far as it relates to the protection of works having as their country of origin, within the meaning of the Berne Convention, a country of the Berne Union.

RESOLUTION CONCERNING ARTICLE XI

The Conference for Revision of the Universal Copyright Convention.

Having considered the problems relating to the Intergovernmental Committee provided for in article XI of this Convention, to which this resolution is annexed,

Resolves that:

1. At its inception, the Committee shall include representatives of the twelve States members of the Intergovernmental Committee established under article XI of the 1952 Convention and the resolution annexed to it, and, in addition. representatives of the following States: Algeria, Australia, Japan, Mexico, Senegal and Yugoslavia.
2. Any States that are not party to the 1952 Convention and have not acceded to this Convention before the first ordinary session of the Committee following the entry into force of this Convention shall be replaced by other States to be selected by the Committee at its first ordinary session in conformity with the provisions of article XI (2) and (3).
3. As soon as this Convention comes into force the Committee as provided for in paragraph I shall be deemed to be constituted in accordance with article XI of this Convention.
4. A session of the Committee shall take place within 1 year after the coming into force of this Convention; thereafter the Committee shall meet in ordinary session at intervals of not more than 2 years.
5. The Committee shall elect its Chairman and two Vice-Chairmen. It shall establish its Rules of Procedure having regard to the following principles:

   (a) The normal duration of the term of office of the members represented on the Committee shall be 6 years with one-third retiring every 2 years, it being however understood that, of the original terms of office, one-third shall expire at the end of the Committee's second ordinary session which will follow the entry into force of this Convention, a further third at the end of its third ordinary session, and the remaining third at the end of its fourth ordinary session.
   (b) The rules governing the procedure whereby the Committee shall fill vacancies, the order in which terms of membership expire, eligibility for re-election, and election procedures, shall be based upon a balancing of the needs for continuity of membership and rotation of representation, as well as the considerations set out in article XI (3).

Expresses the wish that the United Nations Educational, Scientific and Cultural Organization provide its Secretariat.

IN FAITH WHEREOF the undersigned, having deposited their respective full powers, have signed this Convention.

DONE at Paris, this 24 day of July 1971, in a single copy.

Appendix B
1971 Appendix to the Berne Convention, Special Provisions Regarding Developing Countries

Article I

Faculties Open to Developing Countries:

1. Availability of certain faculties; declaration;
2. Duration of effect of declaration;
3. Cessation of developing country status;
4. Existing stocks of copies;
5. Declarations concerning certain territories;
6. Limits of reciprocity

(1) Any country regarded as a developing country in conformity with the established practice of the General Assembly of the United Nations which ratifies or accedes to this Act, of which this Appendix forms an integral part, and which, having regard to its economic situation and its social or cultural needs, does not consider itself immediately in a position to make provision for the protection of all the rights as provided for in this Act, may, by a notification deposited with the Director General at the time of depositing its instrument of ratification or accession or, subject to Article V(1)(c), at any time thereafter, declare that it will avail itself of the faculty provided for in Article II, or of the faculty provided for in Article III, or of both of those faculties. It may, instead of availing itself of the faculty provided for in Article II, make a declaration according to Article V (1)(a).

(2) (a) Any declaration under paragraph (1) notified before the expiration of the period of 10 years from the entry into force of Articles 1 to 21 and this Appendix according to Article 28(2) shall be effective until the expiration of the said period. Any such declaration may be renewed in whole or in part for periods of 10 years each by a notification deposited with the Director General not more than 15 months and not less than 3 months before the expiration of the ten-year period then running.

R.M. Olwan, *Intellectual Property and Development*,
DOI 10.1007/978-3-642-27907-2, © Springer-Verlag Berlin Heidelberg 2013

(b) Any declaration under paragraph (1) notified after the expiration of the period of 10 years from the entry into force of Articles 1 to 21 and this Appendix according to Article 28(2) shall be effective until the expiration of the ten-year period then running. Any such declaration may be renewed as provided for in the second sentence of subparagraph (a).

(3) Any country of the Union which has ceased to be regarded as a developing country as referred to in paragraph (1) shall no longer be entitled to renew its declaration as provided in paragraph (2), and, whether or not it formally withdraws its declaration, such country shall be precluded from availing itself of the faculties referred to in paragraph (1) from the expiration of the ten-year period then running or from the expiration of a period of 3 years after it has ceased to be regarded as a developing country, whichever period expires later.

(4) Where, at the time when the declaration made under paragraph (1) or (2) ceases to be effective, there are copies in stock which were made under a license granted by virtue of this Appendix, such copies may continue to be distributed until their stock is exhausted.

(5) Any country which is bound by the provisions of this Act and which has deposited a declaration or a notification in accordance with Article 31(1) with respect to the application of this Act to a particular territory, the situation of which can be regarded as analogous to that of the countries referred to in paragraph (1), may, in respect of such territory, make the declaration referred to in paragraph (1) and the notification of renewal referred to in paragraph (2). As long as such declaration or notification remains in effect, the provisions of this Appendix shall be applicable to the territory in respect of which it was made.

(6) (a) The fact that a country avails itself of any of the faculties referred to in paragraph (1) does not permit another country to give less protection to works of which the country of origin is the former country than it is obliged to grant under Articles 1 to 20.

(b) The right to apply reciprocal treatment provided for in Article 30(2)(b), second sentence, shall not, until the date on which the period applicable under Article I (3) expires, be exercised in respect of works the country of origin of which is a country which has made a declaration according to Article V(1)(a).

Article II

Limitations on the Right of Translation:

1. Licenses grantable by competent authority;
2. to 4. Conditions allowing the grant of such licenses;
5. Purposes for which licenses may be granted;
6. Termination of licenses;

7. Works composed mainly of illustrations;
8. Works withdrawn from circulation;
9. Licenses for broadcasting organizations

(1) Any country which has declared that it will avail itself of the faculty provided for in this Article shall be entitled, so far as works published in printed or analogous forms of reproduction are concerned, to substitute for the exclusive right of translation provided for in Article 8 a system of non-exclusive and non-transferable licenses, granted by the competent authority under the following conditions and subject to Article IV.

(2) (a) Subject to paragraph (3), if, after the expiration of a period of 3 years, or of any longer period determined by the national legislation of the said country, commencing on the date of the first publication of the work, a translation of such work has not been published in a language in general use in that country by the owner of the right of translation, or with his authorization, any national of such country may obtain a license to make a translation of the work in the said language and publish the translation in printed or analogous forms of reproduction.

(b) A license under the conditions provided for in this Article may also be granted if all the editions of the translation published in the language concerned are out of print.

(3) (a) In the case of translations into a language which is not in general use in one or more developed countries which are members of the Union, a period of 1 year shall be substituted for the period of 3 years referred to in paragraph (2)(a).

(b) Any country referred to in paragraph (1) may, with the unanimous agreement of the developed countries which are members of the Union and in which the same language is in general use, substitute, in the case of translations into that language, for the period of 3 years referred to in paragraph (2)(a) a shorter period as determined by such agreement but not less than 1 year. However, the provisions of the foregoing sentence shall not apply where the language in question is English, French or Spanish. The Director General shall be notified of any such agreement by the Governments which have concluded it.

(4) (a) No license obtainable after 3 years shall be granted under this Article until a further period of 6 months has elapsed, and no license obtainable after 1 year shall be granted under this Article until a further period of 9 months has elapsed

(i) from the date on which the applicant complies with the requirements mentioned in Article IV(1), or

(ii) where the identity or the address of the owner of the right of translation is unknown, from the date on which the applicant sends, as provided for in Article IV(2), copies of his application submitted to the authority competent to grant the license.

(b) If, during the said period of 6 or 9 months, a translation in the language in respect of which the application was made is published by the owner of the right of translation or with his authorization, no license under this Article shall be granted.

(5) Any license under this Article shall be granted only for the purpose of teaching, scholarship or research.

(6) If a translation of a work is published by the owner of the right of translation or with his authorization at a price reasonably related to that normally charged in the country for comparable works, any license granted under this Article shall terminate if such translation is in the same language and with substantially the same content as the translation published under the license. Any copies already made before the license terminates may continue to be distributed until their stock is exhausted.

(7) For works which are composed mainly of illustrations, a license to make and publish a translation of the text and to reproduce and publish the illustrations may be granted only if the conditions of Article III are also fulfilled.

(8) No license shall be granted under this Article when the author has withdrawn from circulation all copies of his work.

(9) (a) A license to make a translation of a work which has been published in printed or analogous forms of reproduction may also be granted to any broadcasting organization having its headquarters in a country referred to in paragraph (1), upon an application made to the competent authority of that country by the said organization, provided that all of the following conditions are met:

(i) the translation is made from a copy made and acquired in accordance with the laws of the said country;

(ii) the translation is only for use in broadcasts intended exclusively for teaching or for the dissemination of the results of specialized technical or scientific research to experts in a particular profession;

(iii) the translation is used exclusively for the purposes referred to in condition (ii) through broadcasts made lawfully and intended for recipients on the territory of the said country, including broadcasts made through the medium of sound or visual recordings lawfully and exclusively made for the purpose of such broadcasts;

(iv) all uses made of the translation are without any commercial purpose.

(b) Sound or visual recordings of a translation which was made by a broadcasting organization under a license granted by virtue of this paragraph may, for the purposes and subject to the conditions referred to in subparagraph (a) and with the agreement of that organization, also be used by any other broadcasting organization having its headquarters in the country whose competent authority granted the license in question.

(c) Provided that all of the criteria and conditions set out in subparagraph (a) are met, a license may also be granted to a broadcasting organization to translate any text incorporated in an audio-visual fixation where such fixation was itself prepared and published for the sole purpose of being used in connection with systematic instructional activities.
(d) Subject to subparagraphs (a) to (c), the provisions of the preceding paragraphs shall apply to the grant and exercise of any license granted under this paragraph.

Article III

Limitation on the Right of Reproduction:

1. Licenses grantable by competent authority;
2. to 5. Conditions allowing the grant of such licenses;
6. Termination of licenses;
7. Works to which this Article applies

(1) Any country which has declared that it will avail itself of the faculty provided for in this Article shall be entitled to substitute for the exclusive right of reproduction provided for in Article 9 a system of non-exclusive and non-transferable licenses, granted by the competent authority under the following conditions and subject to Article IV.
(2) (a) If, in relation to a work to which this Article applies by virtue of paragraph (7), after the expiration of

(i) the relevant period specified in paragraph (3), commencing on the date of first publication of a particular edition of the work, or
(ii) any longer period determined by national legislation of the country referred to in paragraph (1), commencing on the same date, copies of such edition have not been distributed in that country to the general public or in connection with systematic instructional activities, by the owner of the right of reproduction or with his authorization, at a price reasonably related to that normally charged in the country for comparable works, any national of such country may obtain a license to reproduce and publish such edition at that or a lower price for use in connection with systematic instructional activities.

(b) A license to reproduce and publish an edition which has been distributed as described in subparagraph (a) may also be granted under the conditions provided for in this Article if, after the expiration of the applicable period, no authorized copies of that edition have been on sale for a period of 6 months in the country concerned to the general public or in connection with systematic instructional activities at a price reasonably related to that normally charged in the country for comparable works.

(3) The period referred to in paragraph (2)(a)(i) shall be 5 years, except that

(i) for works of the natural and physical sciences, including mathematics, and of technology, the period shall be 3 years;
(ii) for works of fiction, poetry, drama and music, and for art books, the period shall be 7 years.

(4) (a) No license obtainable after 3 years shall be granted under this Article until a period of 6 months has elapsed

(i) from the date on which the applicant complies with the requirements mentioned in Article IV(1), or
(ii) where the identity or the address of the owner of the right of reproduction is unknown, from the date on which the applicant sends, as provided for in Article IV(2), copies of his application submitted to the authority competent to grant the license.

(b) Where licenses are obtainable after other periods and Article IV(2) is applicable, no license shall be granted until a period of 3 months has elapsed from the date of the dispatch of the copies of the application.
(c) If, during the period of 6 or 3 months referred to in subparagraphs (a) and (b), a distribution as described in paragraph (2)(a) has taken place, no license shall be granted under this Article.
(d) No license shall be granted if the author has withdrawn from circulation all copies of the edition for the reproduction and publication of which the license has been applied for.

(5) A license to reproduce and publish a translation of a work shall not be granted under this Article in the following cases:

(i) where the translation was not published by the owner of the right of translation or with his authorization, or
(ii) where the translation is not in a language in general use in the country in which the license is applied for.

(6) If copies of an edition of a work are distributed in the country referred to in paragraph (1) to the general public or in connection with systematic instructional activities, by the owner of the right of reproduction or with his authorization, at a price reasonably related to that normally charged in the country for comparable works, any license granted under this Article shall terminate if such edition is in the same language and with substantially the same content as the edition which was published under the said license. Any copies already made before the license terminates may continue to be distributed until their stock is exhausted.
(7) (a) Subject to subparagraph (b), the works to which this Article applies shall be limited to works published in printed or analogous forms of reproduction.

(b) This Article shall also apply to the reproduction in audio-visual form of lawfully made audio-visual fixations including any protected works incorporated therein and to the translation of any incorporated text into a language in general use in the country in which the license is applied for, always provided that the audio-visual fixations in question were prepared and published for the sole purpose of being used in connection with systematic instructional activities.

Article IV

Provisions Common to Licenses Under Articles II and III:

1. and 2. Procedure;
3. Indication of author and title of work;
4. Exportation of copies;
5. Notice;
6. Compensation

(1) A license under Article II or Article III may be granted only if the applicant, in accordance with the procedure of the country concerned, establishes either that he has requested, and has been denied, authorization by the owner of the right to make and publish the translation or to reproduce and publish the edition, as the case may be, or that, after due diligence on his part, he was unable to find the owner of the right. At the same time as making the request, the applicant shall inform any national or international information center referred to in paragraph (2).

(2) If the owner of the right cannot be found, the applicant for a license shall send, by registered airmail, copies of his application, submitted to the authority competent to grant the license, to the publisher whose name appears on the work and to any national or international information center which may have been designated, in a notification to that effect deposited with the Director General, by the Government of the country in which the publisher is believed to have his principal place of business.

(3) The name of the author shall be indicated on all copies of the translation or reproduction published under a license granted under Article II or Article III. The title of the work shall appear on all such copies. In the case of a translation, the original title of the work shall appear in any case on all the said copies.

(4) (a) No license granted under Article II or Article III shall extend to the export of copies, and any such license shall be valid only for publication of the translation or of the reproduction, as the case may be, in the territory of the country in which it has been applied for.

(b) For the purposes of subparagraph (a), the notion of export shall include the sending of copies from any territory to the country which, in respect of that territory, has made a declaration under Article I(5).

(c) Where a governmental or other public entity of a country which has granted a license to make a translation under Article II into a language other than English, French or Spanish sends copies of a translation published under such license to another country, such sending of copies shall not, for the purposes of subparagraph (a), be considered to constitute export if all of the following conditions are met:

(i) the recipients are individuals who are nationals of the country whose competent authority has granted the license, or organizations grouping such individuals;

(ii) the copies are to be used only for the purpose of teaching, scholarship or research;

(iii) the sending of the copies and their subsequent distribution to recipients is without any commercial purpose; and

(iv) the country to which the copies have been sent has agreed with the country whose competent authority has granted the license to allow the receipt, or distribution, or both, and the Director General has been notified of the agreement by the Government of the country in which the license has been granted.

(5) All copies published under a license granted by virtue of Article II or Article III shall bear a notice in the appropriate language stating that the copies are available for distribution only in the country or territory to which the said license applies.

(6) (a) Due provision shall be made at the national level to ensure

(i) that the license provides, in favour of the owner of the right of translation or of reproduction, as the case may be, for just compensation that is consistent with standards of royalties normally operating on licenses freely negotiated between persons in the two countries concerned, and

(ii) payment and transmittal of the compensation: should national currency regulations intervene, the competent authority shall make all efforts, by the use of international machinery, to ensure transmittal in internationally convertible currency or its equivalent.

(b) Due provision shall be made by national legislation to ensure a correct translation of the work, or an accurate reproduction of the particular edition, as the case may be.

Article V

Alternative Possibility for Limitation of the Right of Translation:

1. Regime provided for under the 1886 and 1896 Acts;
2. No possibility of change to regime under Article II;
3. Time limit for choosing the alternative possibility

(1) (a) Any country entitled to make a declaration that it will avail itself of the faculty provided for in Article II may, instead, at the time of ratifying or acceding to this Act:

(i) if it is a country to which Article 30(2)(a) applies, make a declaration under that provision as far as the right of translation is concerned;

(ii) if it is a country to which Article 30(2)(a) does not apply, and even if it is not a country outside the Union, make a declaration as provided for in Article 30(2)(b), first sentence.

(b) In the case of a country which ceases to be regarded as a developing country as referred to in Article I(1), a declaration made according to this paragraph shall be effective until the date on which the period applicable under Article I(3) expires.

(c) Any country which has made a declaration according to this paragraph may not subsequently avail itself of the faculty provided for in Article II even if it withdraws the said declaration.

(2) Subject to paragraph (3), any country which has availed itself of the faculty provided for in Article II may not subsequently make a declaration according to paragraph (1).

(3) Any country which has ceased to be regarded as a developing country as referred to in Article I(1) may, not later than 2 years prior to the expiration of the period applicable under Article I(3), make a declaration to the effect provided for in Article 30(2)(b), first sentence, notwithstanding the fact that it is not a country outside the Union. Such declaration shall take effect at the date on which the period applicable under Article I(3) expires.

Article VI

Possibilities of applying, or admitting the application of, certain provisions of the Appendix before becoming bound by it:

1. Declaration; 2. Depository and effective date of declaration

(1) Any country of the Union may declare, as from the date of this Act, and at any time before becoming bound by Articles 1 to 21 and this Appendix:

(i) if it is a country which, were it bound by Articles 1 to 21 and this Appendix, would be entitled to avail itself of the faculties referred to in Article I(1), that it will apply the provisions of Article II or of Article III or of both to works whose country of origin is a country which, pursuant to (ii) below, admits the application of those Articles to such works, or which is bound by Articles 1 to 21 and this Appendix; such declaration may, instead of referring to Article II, refer to Article V;

(ii) that it admits the application of this Appendix to works of which it is the country of origin by countries which have made a declaration under (i) above or a notification under Article I.

(2) Any declaration made under paragraph (1) shall be in writing and shall be deposited with the Director General. The declaration shall become effective from the date of its deposit.

1. *Entry into force:* Refer to Articles 26, 28, and 29. *Source:* International Bureau of WIPO.
2. This Table of Contents is added for the convenience of the reader. It does not appear in the original (English) text of the Convention.
3. Each Article and the Appendix have been given titles to facilitate their identification. There are no titles in the signed (English) text.
4. The Governing Bodies of WIPO and the Unions administered by WIPO adopted, with effect from 1 January 1994, a new contribution system that replaces the contribution system set forth in Article 25(4)(a), (b), and (c) of the Berne Convention. Details concerning that system may be obtained from the International Bureau of WIPO.

MIX
Papier aus verantwortungsvollen Quellen
Paper from responsible sources
FSC® C105338

If you have any concerns about our products,
you can contact us on
ProductSafety@springernature.com

In case Publisher is established outside the EU,
the EU authorized representative is:
Springer Nature Customer Service Center GmbH
Europaplatz 3, 69115 Heidelberg, Germany

Printed by Libri Plureos GmbH
in Hamburg, Germany